# Drawing And Design of Residential & Commercial Buildings


**S. K. A. ZAIDI**

*D.E.C., B.E. Civil,*
*Msc.E. Civil (Building Engg.)*

&

**S. SIDDIQUI**

*D. Arch, B.E. Civil,*
*M-Tech Civil (Hydraulics Structure)*





**STANDARD PUBLISHERS DISTRIBUTORS**

1705-B NAI SARAK, POST BOX No. 1066, DELHI-110 006

www.standardpublishers.com Email: stpub@vsnl.com

*Published by :*
**A.K. Jain**
For Standard Publishers Distributors
1705-B, Nai Sarak, Delhi-110006.
Ph.: 23262700, 23285798 Fax : 23243180

First Edition, 2004
Second Revised & Enlarged Edition, 2008
**Reprint:- 2010 2012 2013 2015**



**Price : ₹ 300.00**

**ISBN** : 81-8014-114-4

***Laser Typesetting by :***
Bhargave Laser Printers, Delhi.
***Printed by :***
Lomus Offset Press, Delhi.

# PREFACE

*The book Drawing and Design of Residential & Commercial Buildings has been written strictly in accordance with the latest syllabi prescribed by all India Council for the Technical Education. In this book, language of the text has been kept very simple, lucid and concise. We have written this book in such a simple style that even the students of weaker academic background will be able to understand drawing very easily. We are sure that after going through this book the student will develop a special interest and they would like to study the basics of drawing in the class as well as in the design office. We think that the real judges of a book are the teachers concerned and the students for whom it is written. We there for request to teachers, friends as well as the students to bring mistakes and errors to our notice and send their comments and suggestion for the further improvement of this book.*

*The authors wish to express their sincere thanks to Principal and all teachers of University Polytechnic and Department of Civil Engg, A.M.U. Aligarh for constant help and their keen interest in the publication of this book.*

New Year Day
1st January, 2008

**S. K. A. ZAIDI**
**S. SIDDIQUI**

# CONTENTS

# 1
# *Foundation*

Foundation is the lowest part of structure, ultimately transfers its loads to the underlying earth crust *i.e.* soil or rock with in its safe bearing capacity and permissible settlement of the soil below.

## 1.1. PURPOSE OF FOUNDATION

1. These are provided to distribute the load uniformly over a large area thus avoiding the unequal settlement
2. Foundations are provided below the ground level to increase the stability of a structure in such a manner that no damage occurs to the structure.
3. To provide the uniform plain surface for super structure.

## 1.2. OBJECT OF PROVIDING LEAN CONCRETE BELOW THE FOOTING

It is an intermediate layer of concrete between soil and masonry known as lean concrete used in shallow foundation consisting of a mixture of ordinary Portland cement, sand, and aggregates (stone or brick ballast) for the following purposes.

1. It increases the bearing capacity of soil.
2. The defects in the form of small holes or pockets in the bed of trench are rectified by filling the concrete.
3. The lean concrete provides the bed of foundation and balance the upward reaction from soil.

Foundation may either in the forms of footing or raft or pile or wells (caissons). Footing may support a single column or number of columns.

## 1.3. TYPES OF FOUNDATION

1. **Shallow Foundation.** The depth of footing is lesser or equal to width of the footing is known as shallow foundation. The vertical distance between the base of the footing and the ground level is called depth of footing.
2. **Deep Foundation.** If depth of footing is greater than 1.5 times width of the footing than it is called deep foundation.

### Types of Shallow Foundation

1. **Spread Foundation.** In spread foundation the super structure load at the base of footing is spread over a large area *i.e.* width of foundation is considerably more than the wall thickness. In this foundation sufficient width is covered under the walls by providing steps in masonry and concrete layer. A footing that supports a wall is called a strip footing or a continuous footing. (Fig. 1.1, 1.1A, 1.1B).
2. **Isolated Foundation.** If a footing support a single column it is called an isolated footing. Isolated footing is provided under a column to transfer the load safely to the soil. The column footing may have a slab, stepped, or slopy one. (Fig. 1.2, 1.2 A)

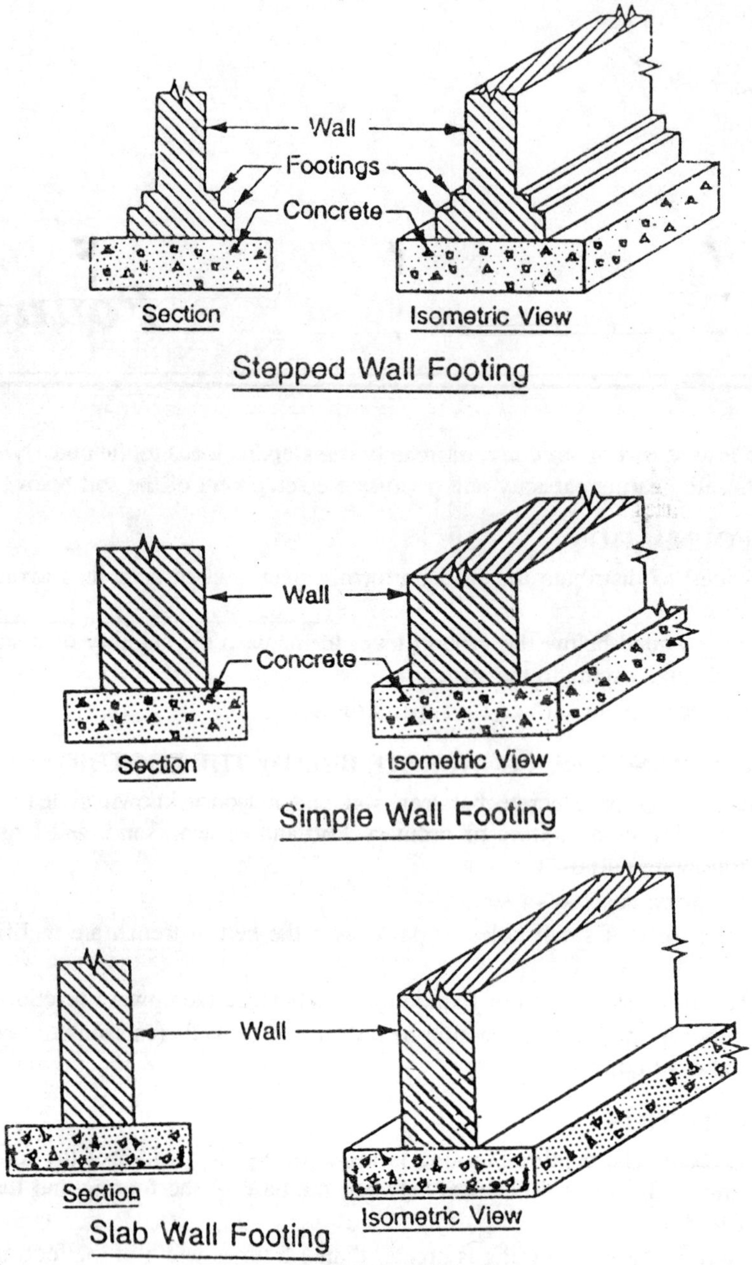


**Fig. 1.1.** Spread footing

3. **Inverted arch Foundation.** Inverted arch are constructed between the two walls at the base. The load is distributed over a large area and hence even week soil can resist the pressure safely. This type of foundation is provided where the bearing capacity is low and depth of foundation is to keep at low level. (Fig. 1.3)
4. **Grillage Foundation.** This type of foundation is generally used to transfer the heavy load from steel column known as stanchions to a soil of low bearing capacity. It is economical to avoid deep excavations and provides the large base area, to reduce the intensity of pressure. Grillage foundations are constructed using rolled steel joist that are placed in single or double tier. (Fig. 1.4)
5. **Moderns Foundation**

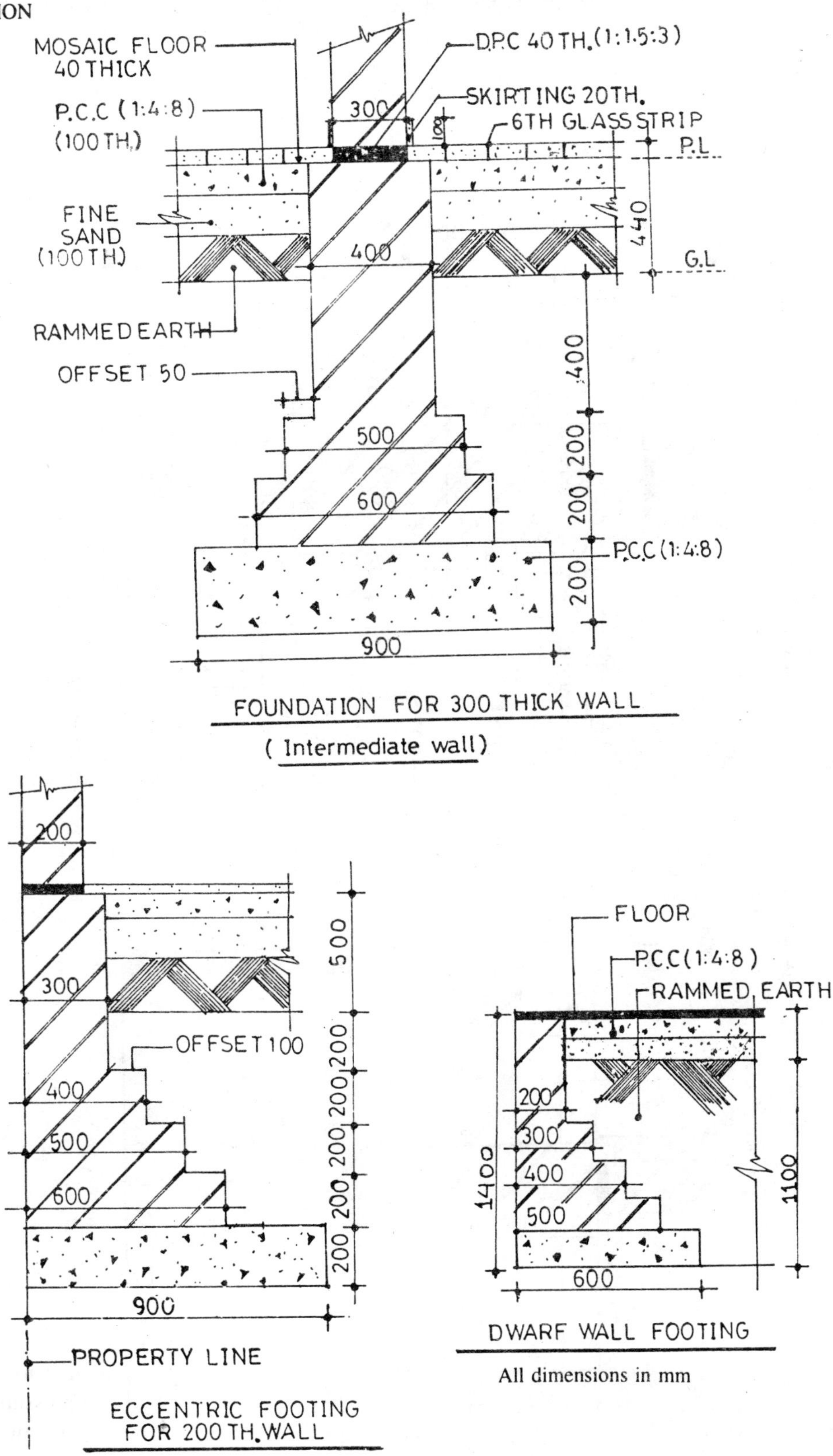


**Fig. 1.1. A.** Spread Footing

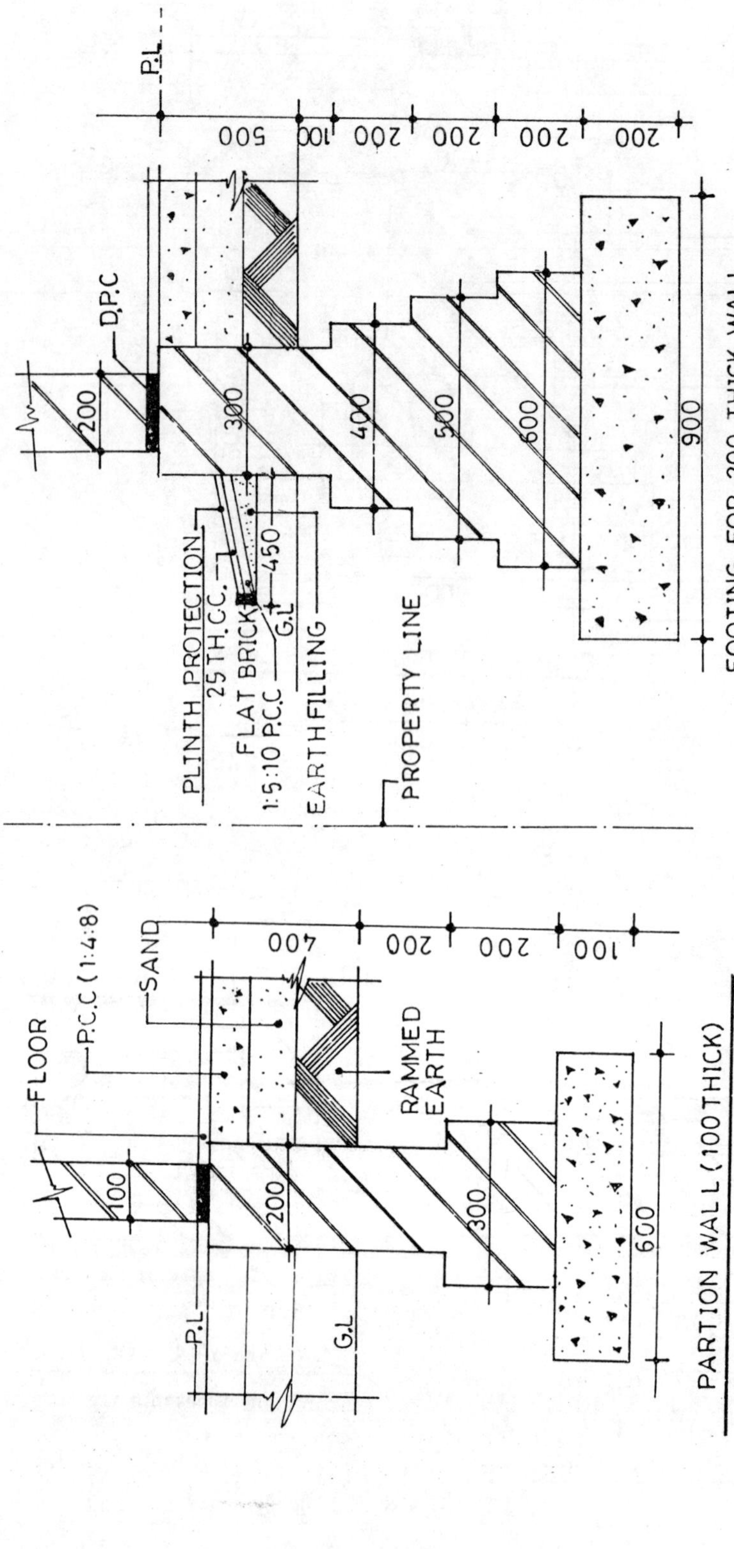


Fig. 1.1. B. Spread Footing

All dimensions in mm

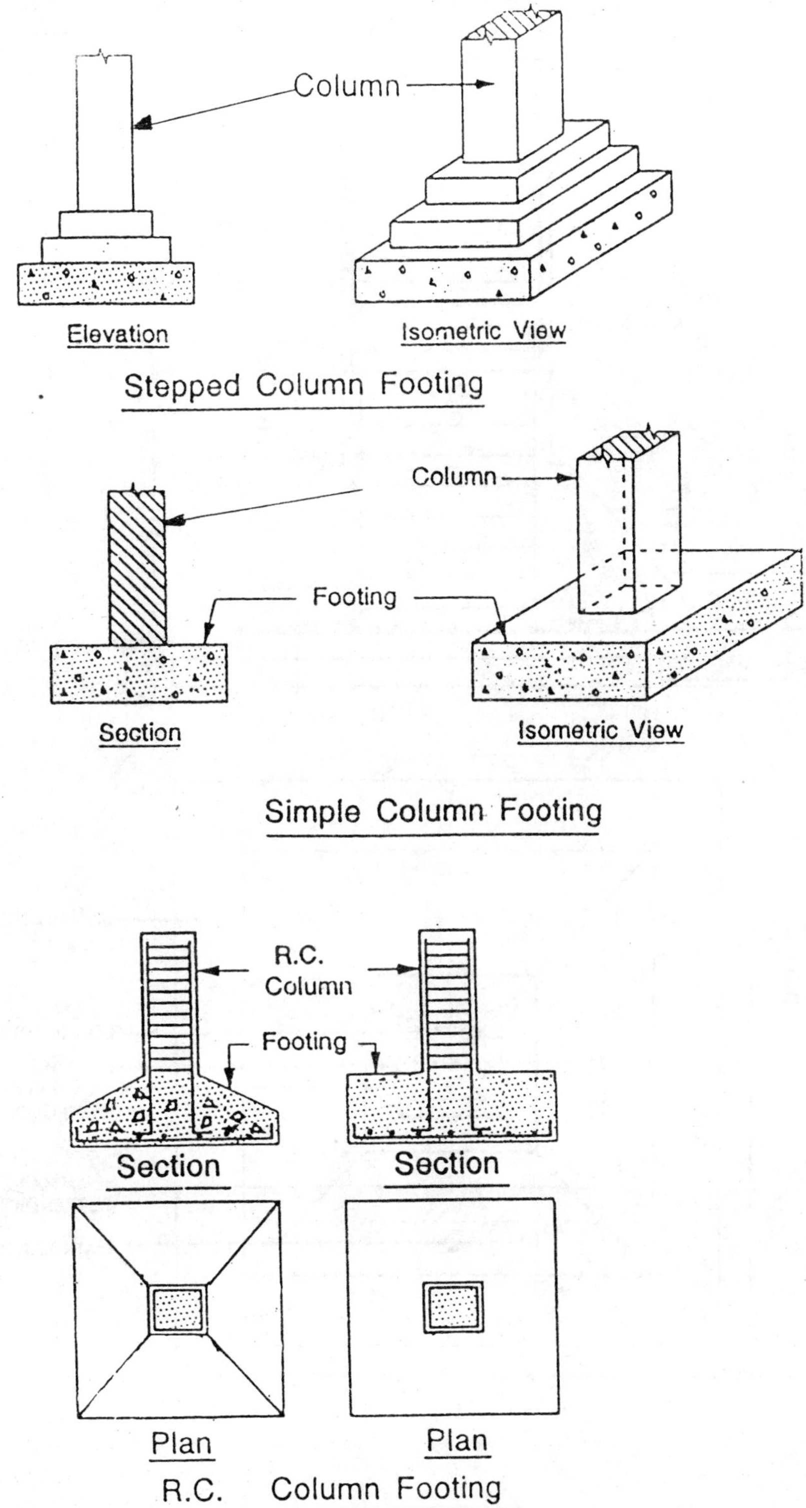


**Fig. 1.2.** Isolated Foundation

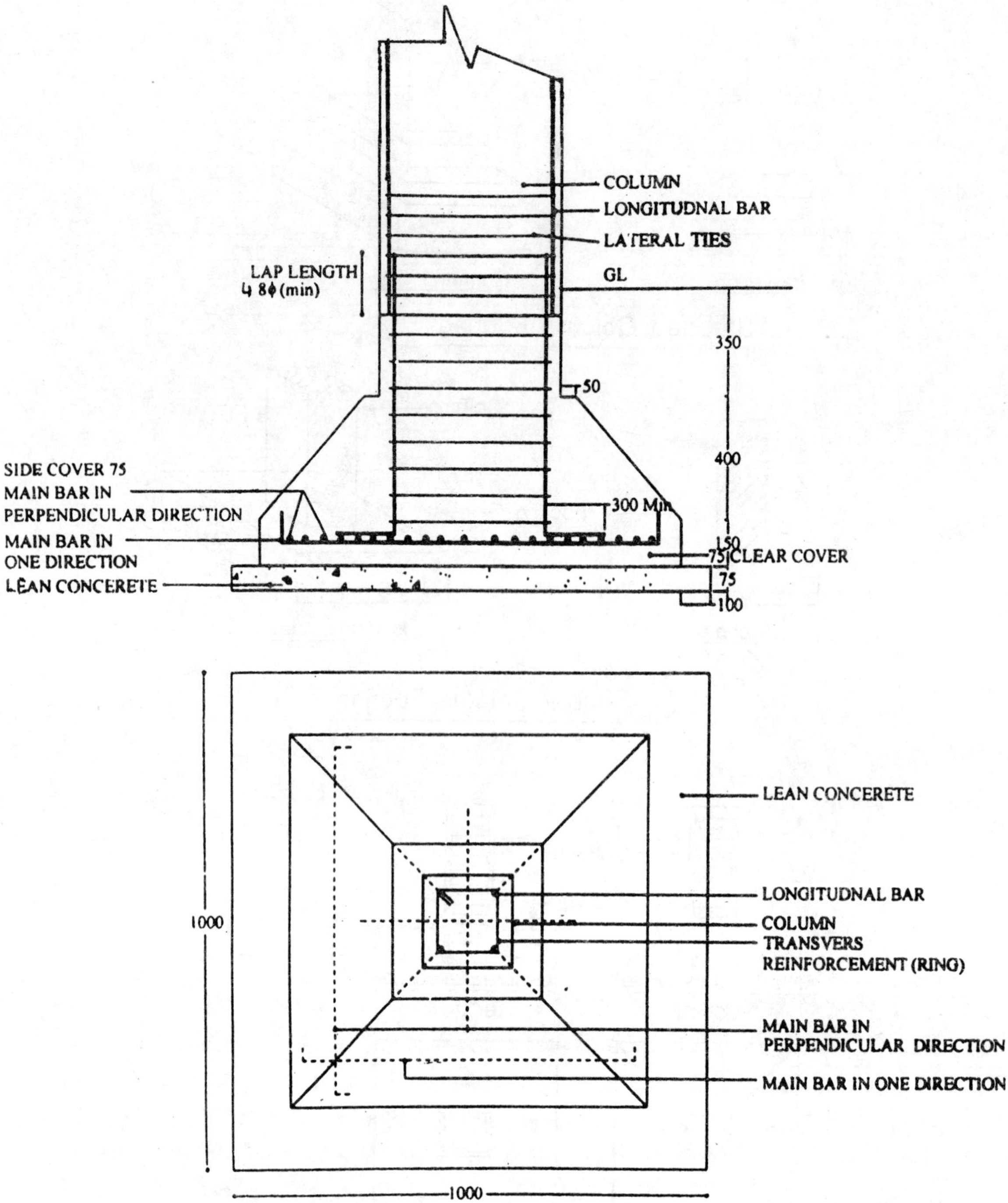


Fig. 1.2. A. Plan Square Footing

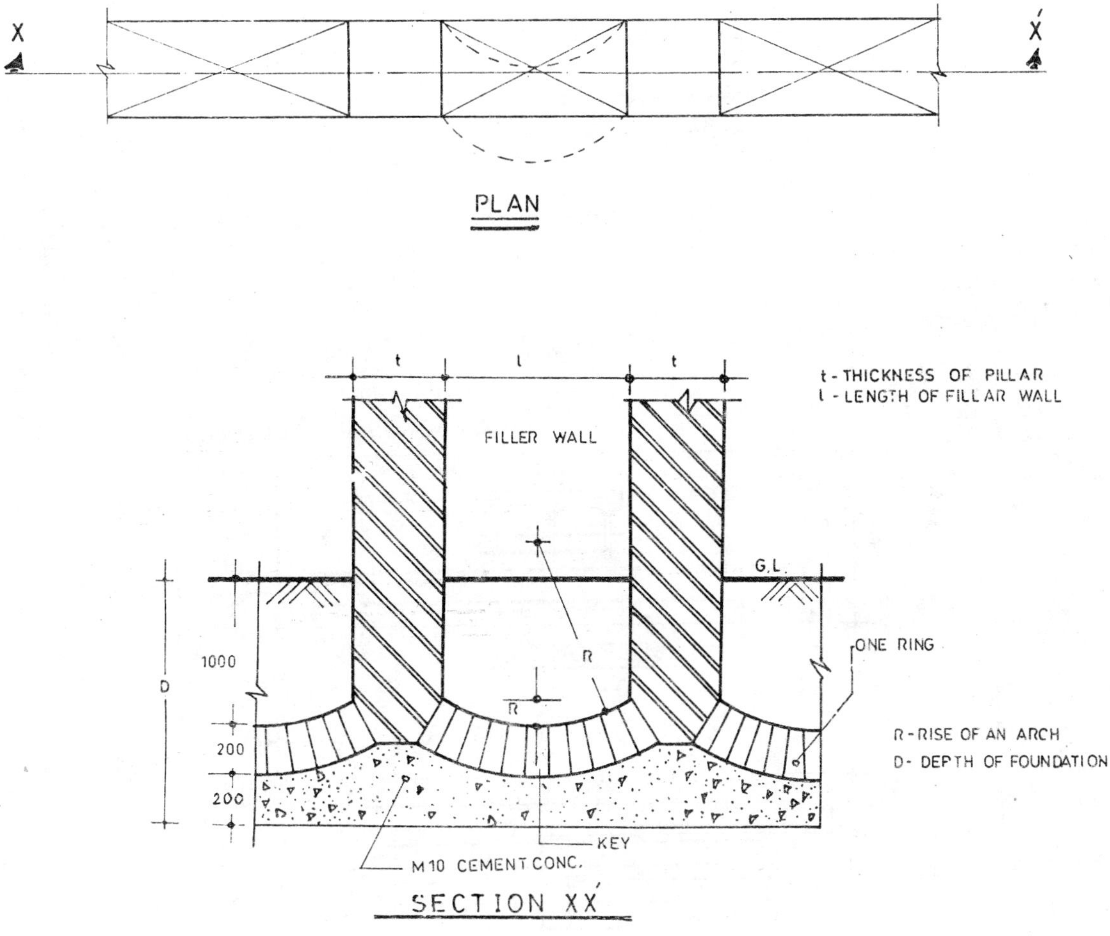


**Fig. 1.3.** Inverted Arch Foundation

**6. Conical shell foundation.** A larger dimension cone serves as foundation for a single column. (Fig. 1.5)

**7. Folded plate foundation.** A pyramidal shape combination of four inclined trapezoidal plate support a column at the center. (Fig. 1.6)

**8. Parabolic foundation.** Its shape resembles to an inverted umbrella roof resting on central column. (Fig. 1.7)

**9. Combined Foundation.** A footing supporting two or more columns in combination is called combined footing. A two-column footing in which there is a property line, restricting the extension of the footing on one side. In this case the non-availability of space near the exterior column make it impossible to project the footing symmetrically on both sides of the column. The plan of the

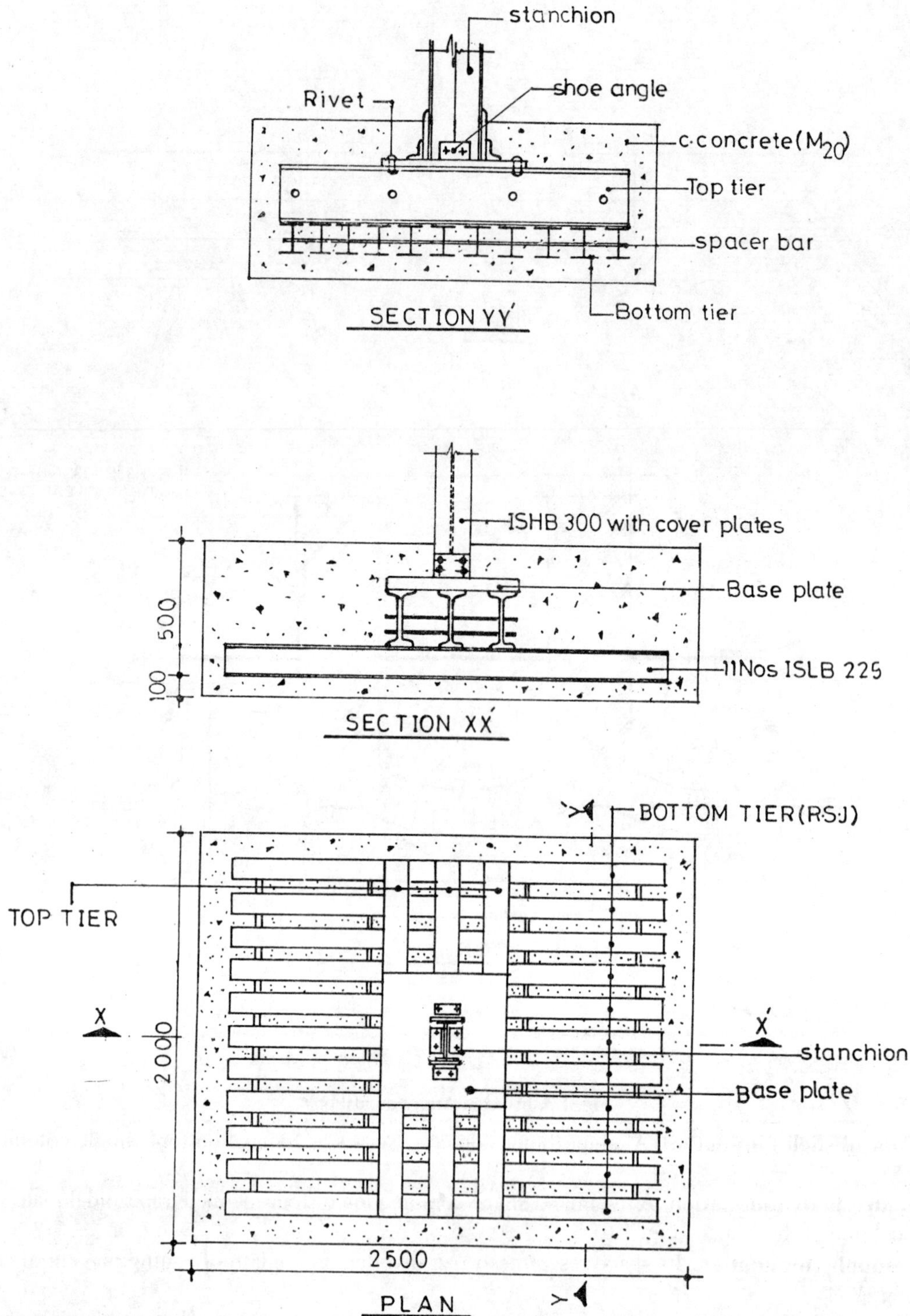


**Fig. 1.4.** Steel Grillage Foundation

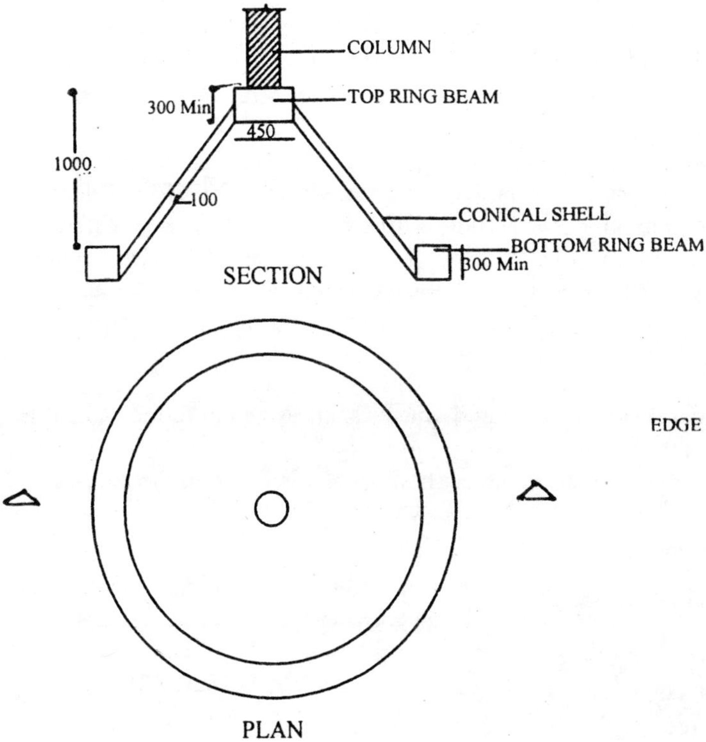


Fig. 1.5. Conical Shell Footing

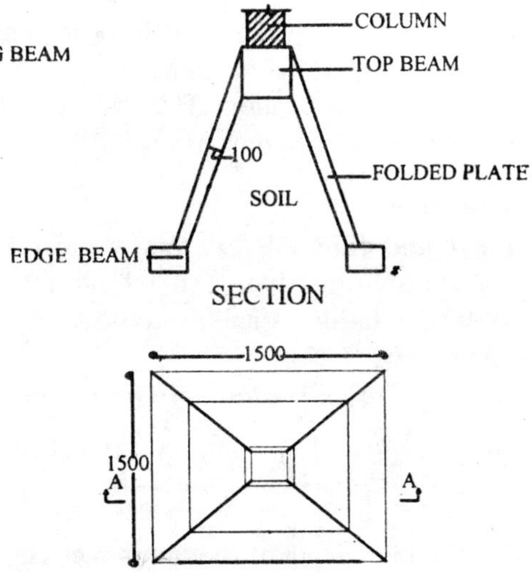


Fig. 1.6. Folded Plate Foundation

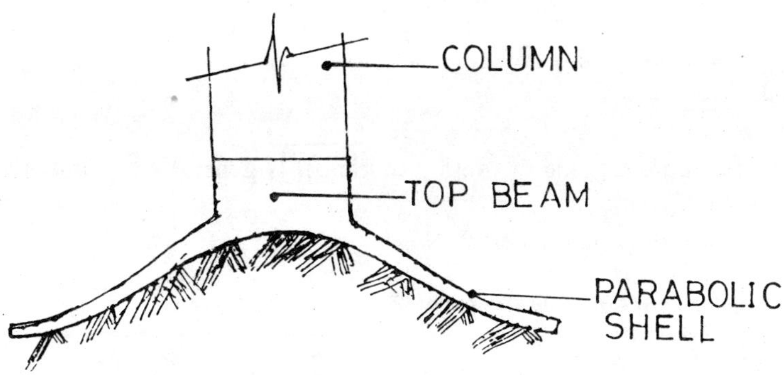


Fig. 1.7. Parabolic Foundation

footing may be kept uniform or tapered. Some times it is economical to provide a central (T) shaped beam interconnecting the column base. (Fig. 1.8)

10. **Cantilever footing or strap footing.** It is also a combined footing in which the columns are supported essentially on isolated footing and interconnected with a beam.
11. **Continuous strip footin.** This foundation is used when the columns are three or more in number are aligned in one direction only.
12. **Raft Foundation or mat Foundation.** Some times it's called as floating foundation. Raft is provided were there is a grid of multiple columns. A raft is a large single slab of uniform thickness, or with locally thicker panels near column base, or with stiffening beams interconnecting the columns supporting the entire structure as a whole. (Fig. 1.9, 1.9 A). Annular raft is also a modern type of raft foundation .This type of foundation is used for overhead water tanks to support a circular row of columns. (Fig. 1.10).

**Deep Foundation**

1. **Pile foundation.** Pile is a long vertical relatively a small diameter shaft driven in to the ground for load transferring. (Fig. 1.11, 1.11 A, 1.11 B)
2. **Well foundation.** A hallow vertical large circular diameter shaft usually sunk up to the hard bed of ground (Fig. 1.12).
3. **Design of brick wall or column footing**

The required depth of footing by Rankin 's formula $D = \frac{P}{W} \cdot \frac{(1 - \sin \phi)}{(1 + \sin \phi)^2}$

*Where,*

$D$ = Minimum depth of footing in meters.

$\phi$ = Angle of repose of the soil in degree

$P$ = Safe bearing capacity in KN/m$^2$

$W$ = Density of soil in KN/m$^3$

Width of footing $B = \frac{W_1}{P}$

or $B$ = 2 (width of wall + Offset of concrete bed) $= 2\,(t + j)$

Which ever is greater.

Where $W_1$ = Total load per meter length of wall in KN

Depth of concrete bed $d = \left(\frac{1}{58000}\right) \sqrt{Pj^2 / m}$

or $d = 0.775\,j$

Greater value of d shall be used.

*Where,*

$j$ = Offset of concrete bed on each side of footing in mm. It is generally taking between 100 mm to 200 mm on each side of footing.

$m$ = Safe modulus of rupture of concrete bed in N/mm$^2$

**Values of modulus of rapture of various concrete mixes**

| *S. No.* | *Types of concrete* | *m in N/mm$^2$* |
|---|---|---|
| 1. | $M_{7.5}$ Lean cement concrete (1:4:8) | $2.46 \times 10^{-3}$ |
| 2. | $M_{10}$ Lean cement concrete (1:3:6) | $3.52 \times 10^{-3}$ |
| 3. | $M_{15}$ Lean cement concrete (1:2:4) | $5.27 \times 10^{-3}$ |

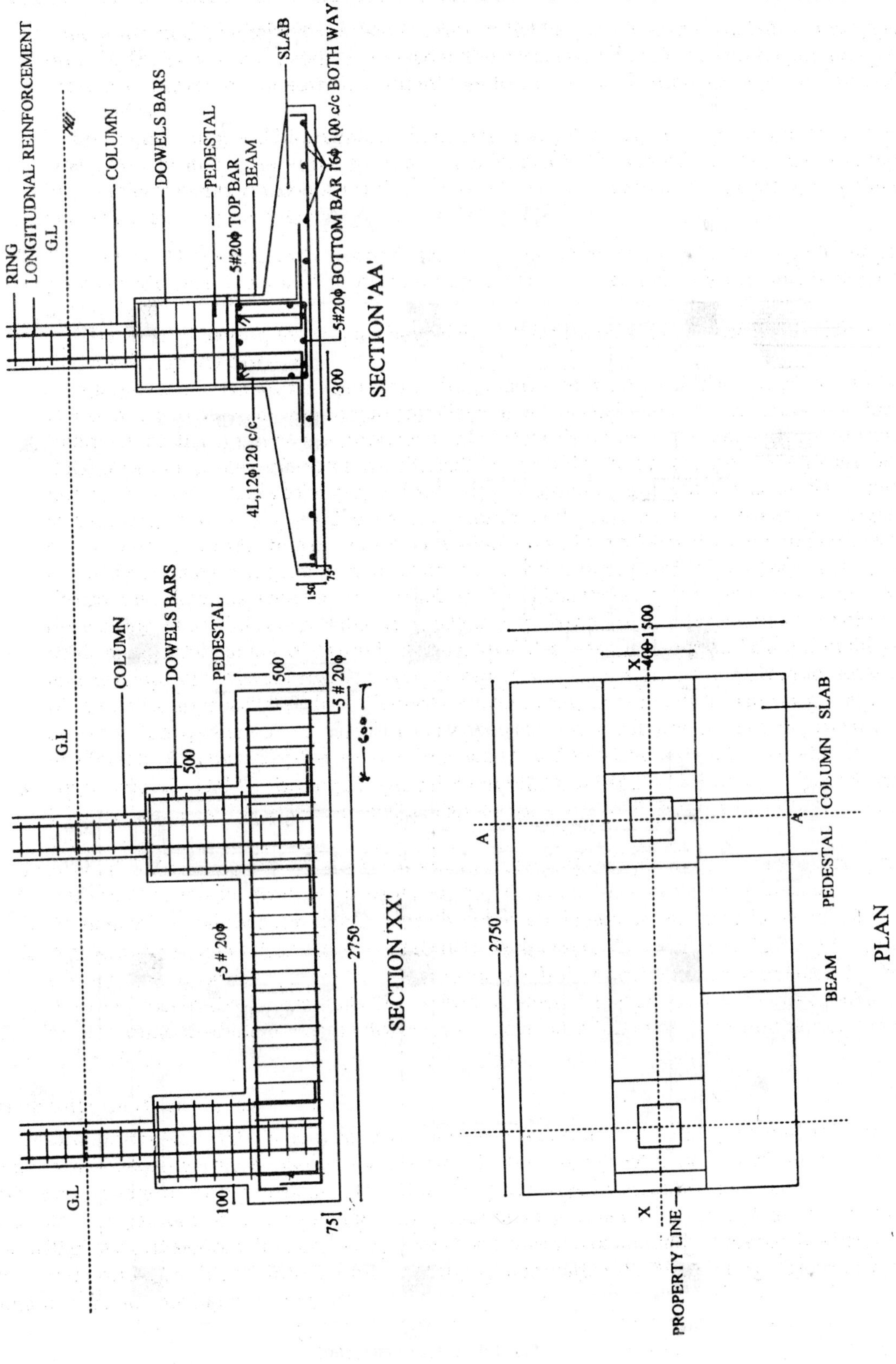


**Fig. 1.8.** Beam-Slab Combined Footing

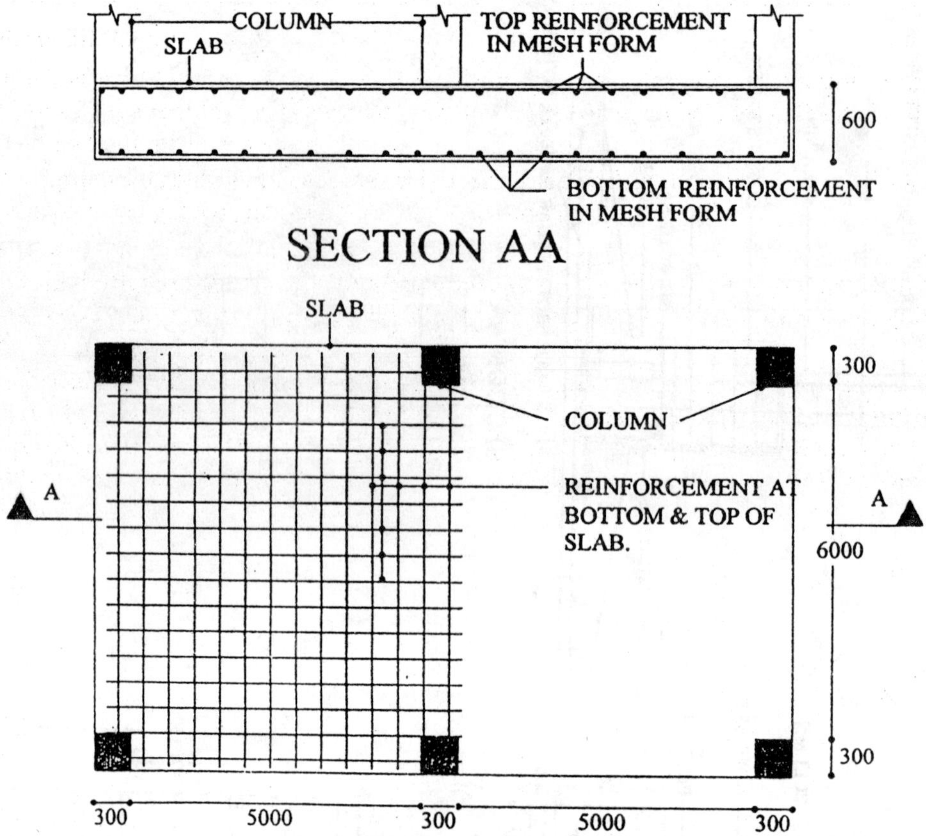


**Fig. 1.9.** Raft Foundation

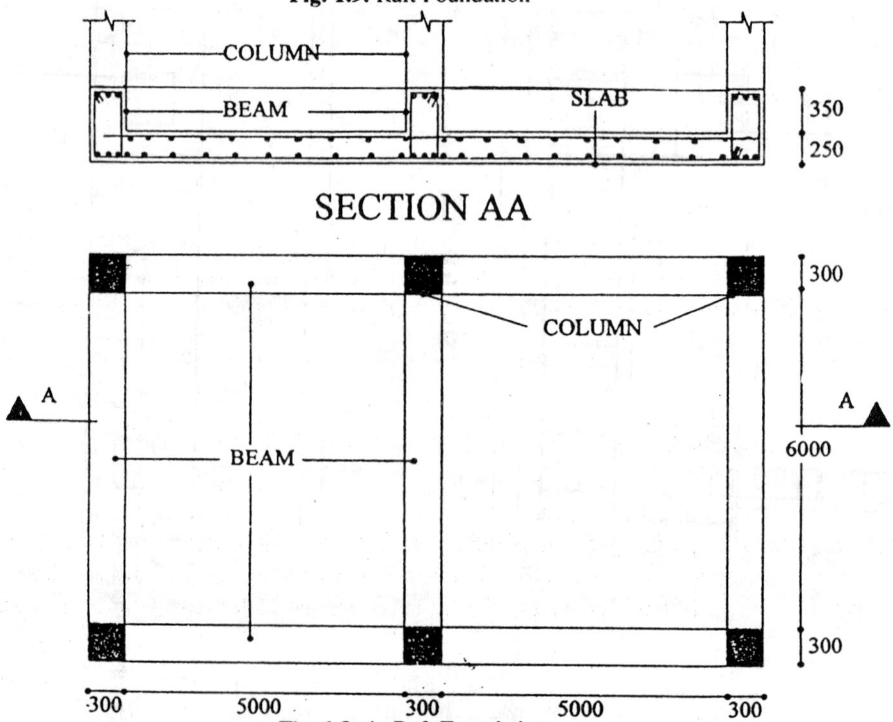


**Fig. 1.9. A. Raft Foundation**

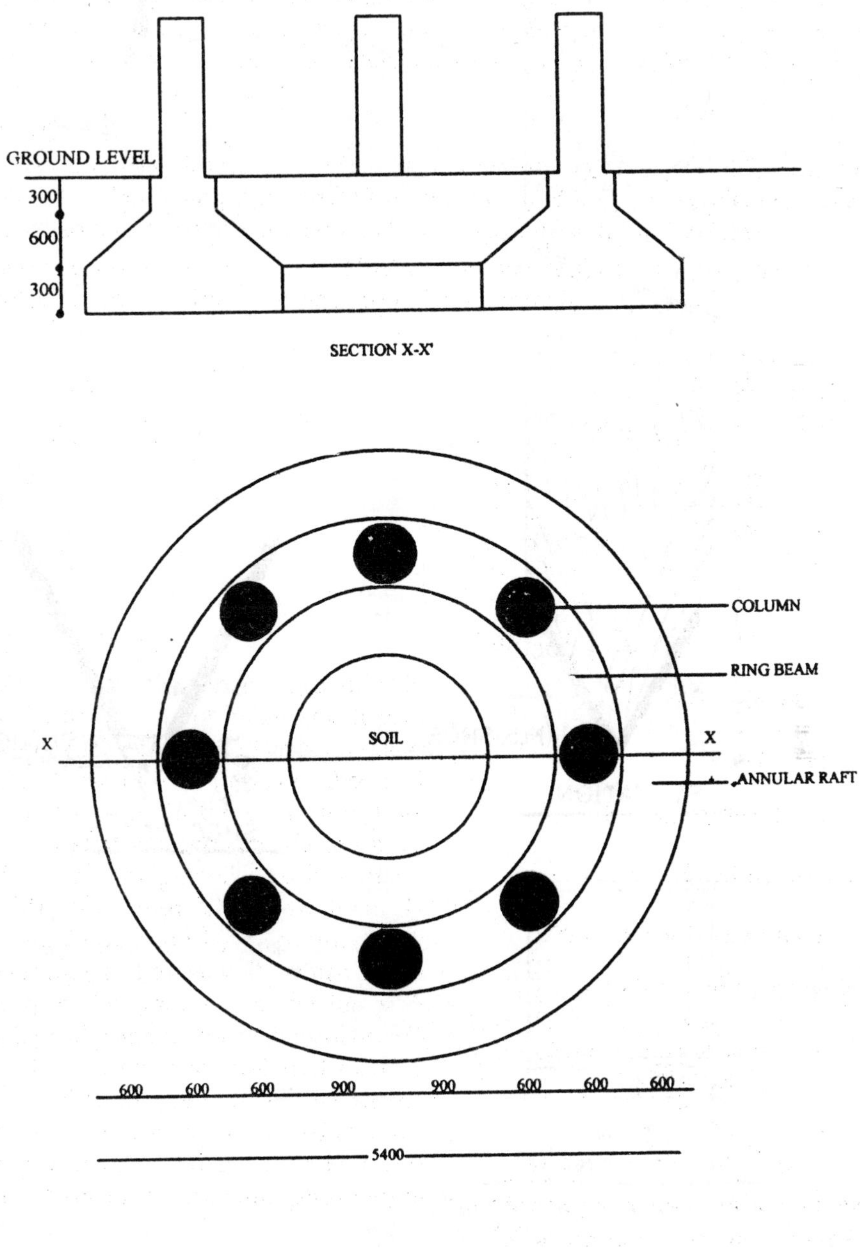


**Fig. 1.10.** Annular Raft

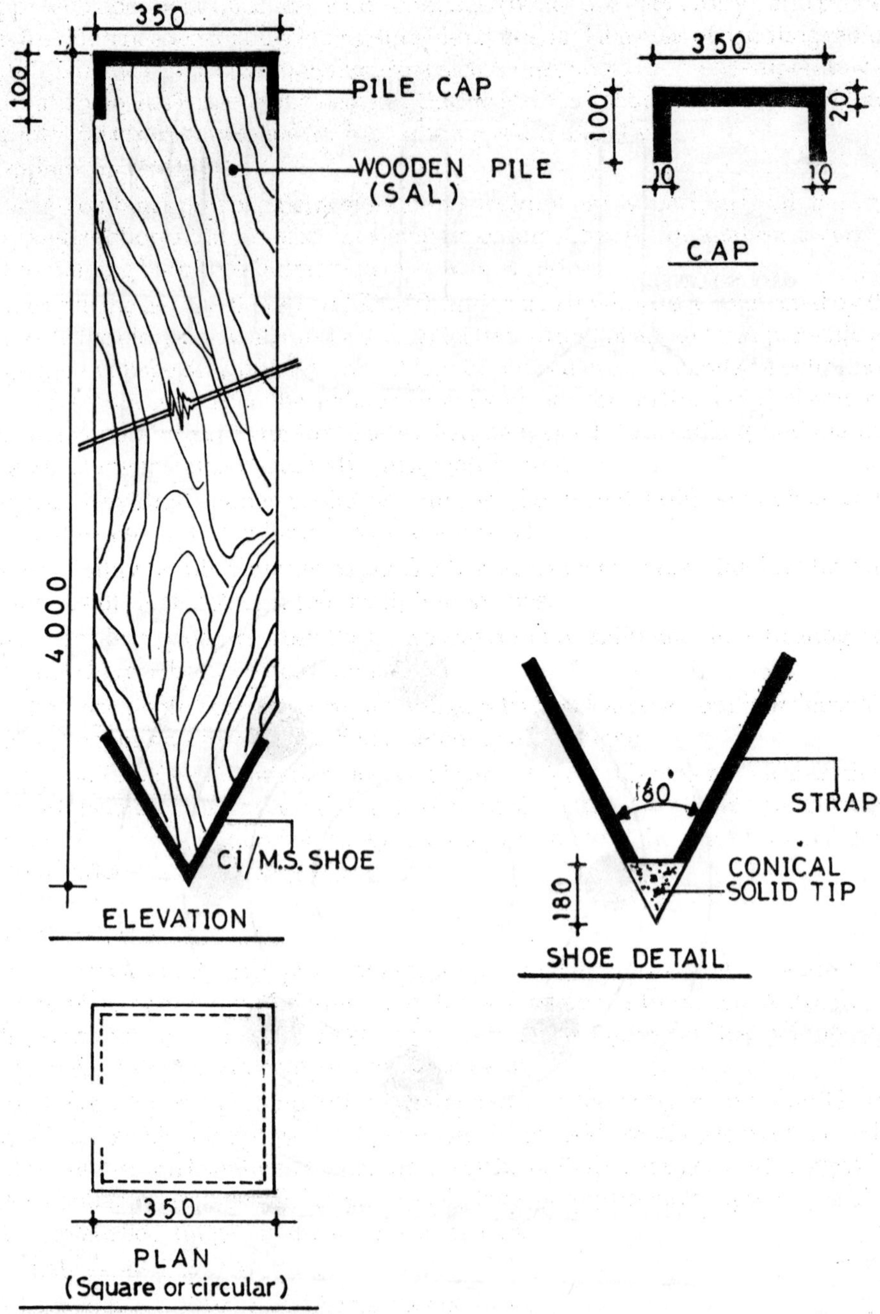


Fig. 1.11. Wooden Pile

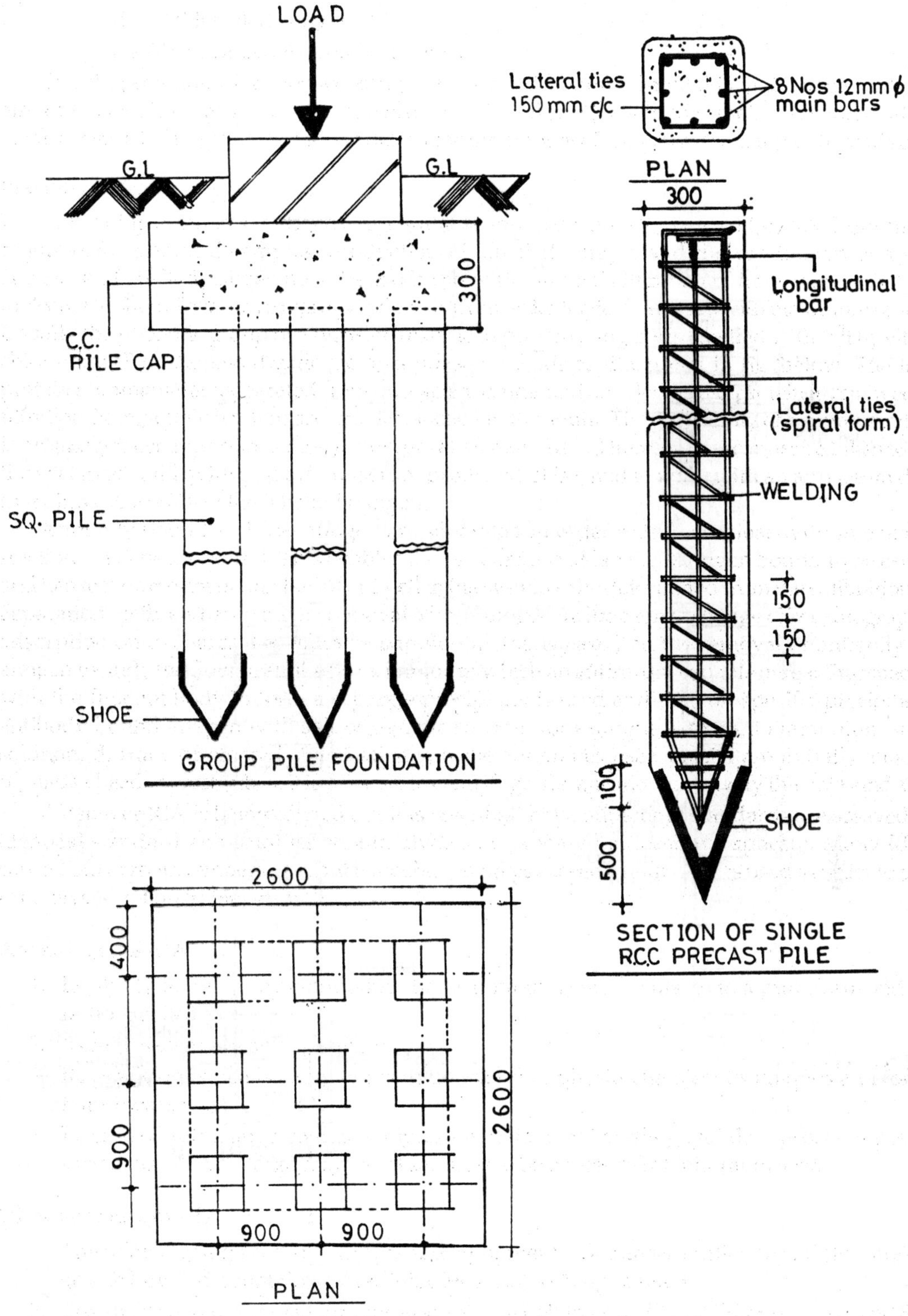


**Fig. 1.11. A.** Pile Foundation in group

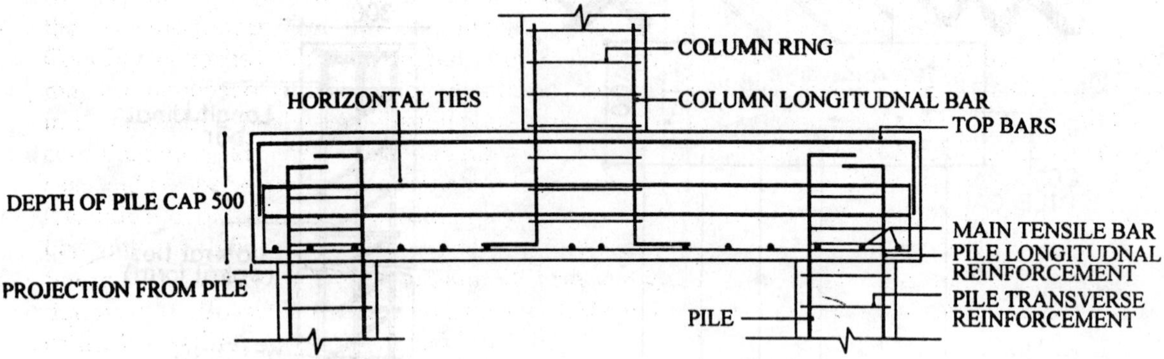


SECTION FOR PILE CAP

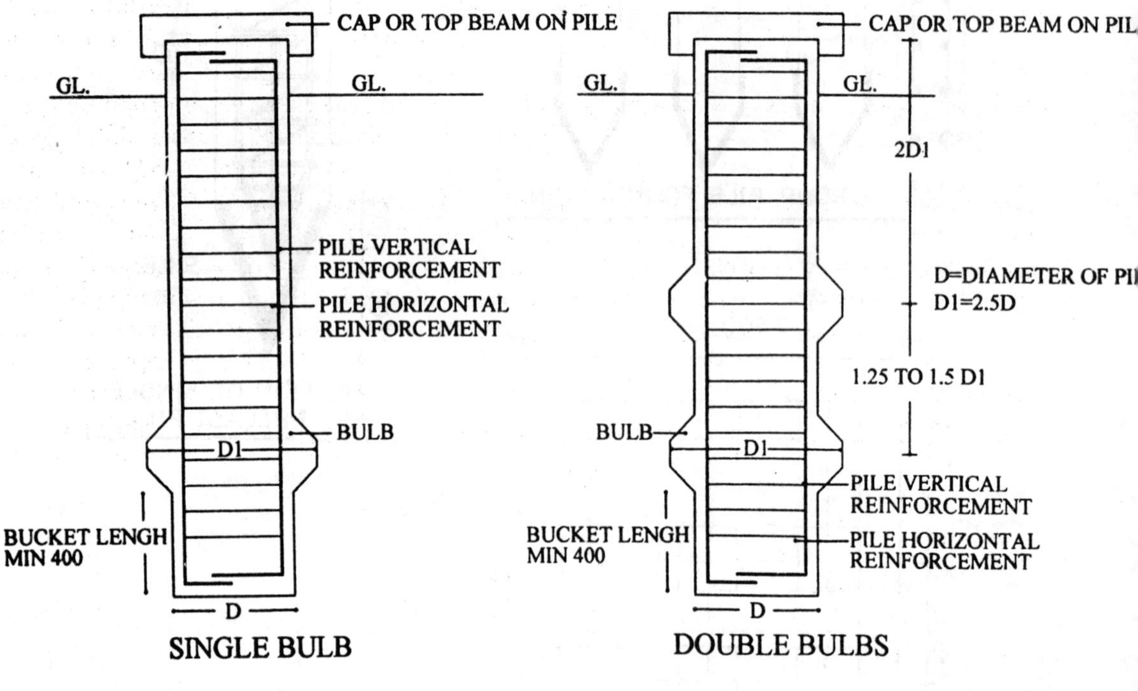


**Fig. 1.11. B.** Under Reamed Piles

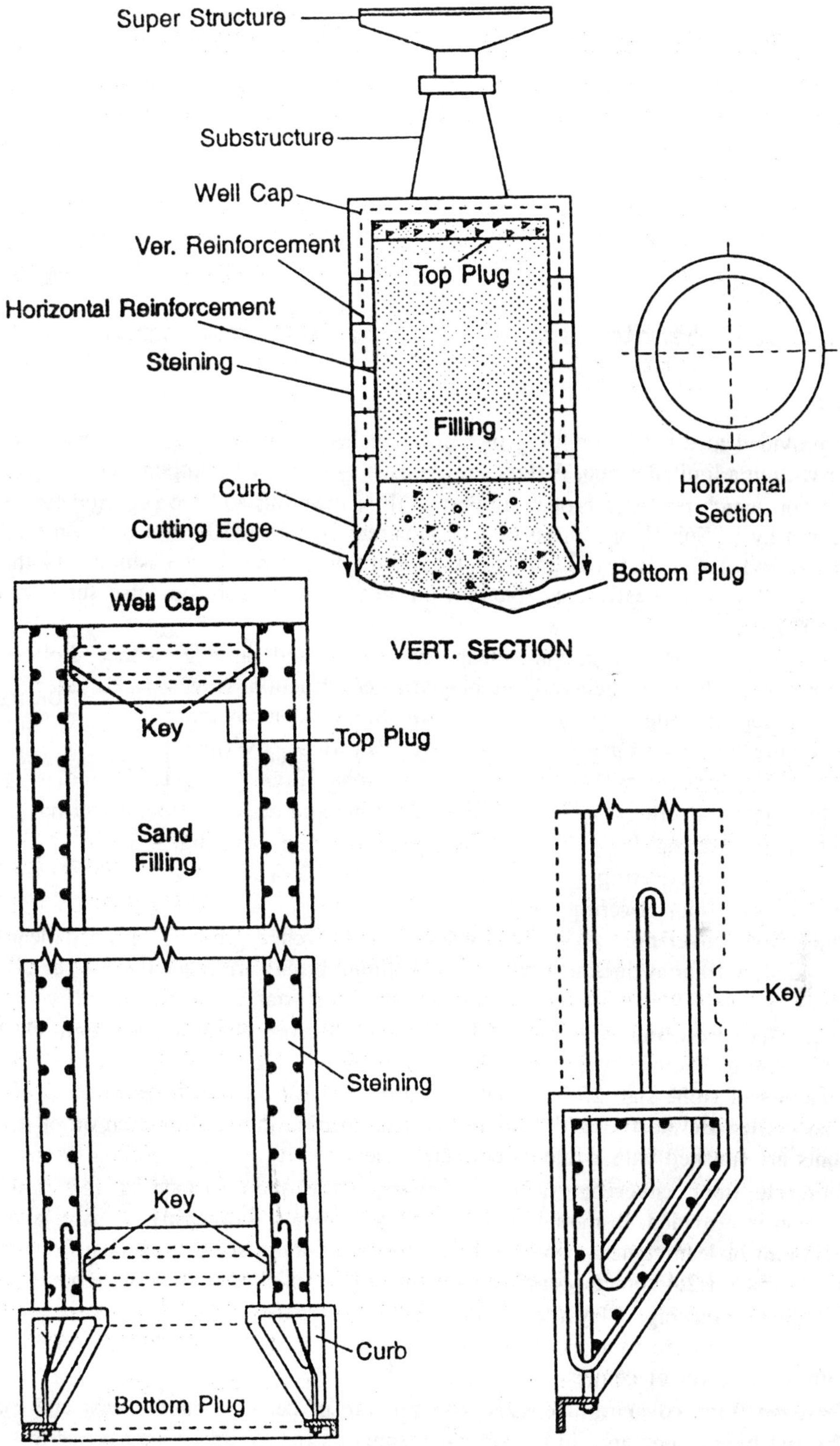


**Fig. 1.12.** Well Foundation

# 2
# Floors

## 2.1. FLOORS

Floors are provided to divide a building into different levels for creating more accommodation one above the other with in a limited space. A floor may consist of two main components.

1. A sub floor, which provides proper support to floor covering and the superimposed loads which are carried by it. Sub floor consist of lean concrete 75 mm to100 mm thick in the ratio (1:4:8 or 1:5:10) and 100 mm to150 mm thick layer of fine sand as a cushion and the remaining portion is filled with locally available soil on ground floor. The roof also serve as a sub floor for upper floor.
2. Floor covering provides a smooth, clean, impervious and durable surface. Following are the floor coverings which are generally employed in construction. (Fig. 2.1, 2.1 A)

   (*a*) Brick floor covering
   (*b*) Stone floor covering
   (*c*) Concrete floor covering
   (*d*) Tile floor covering
   (*e*) Terrazzo floor covering
   (*f*) Asphalt floor covering
   (*g*) Rubber floor covering
   (*h*) Linoleum or vinyl floor covering
   (*i*) Cork floor covering
   (*j*) Glass floor covering
   (*k*) Magnetite floor covering
   (*l*) Plastic floor covering
   (*m*) Wood block floor covering

   (***a***) **Brick floor covering:** Over well-compacted and levelled ground, a layer of lean concrete is provided in 100mm thickness. Over this, bedding bricks are placed in proper bonds on their edges or flats. Their joints are filled with cement mortar.

   (***b***) **Stone floor covering:** The earthen base is leveled, compacted and watered. On this surface a 100 mm to 150mm thick layer of plain cement concrete is laid and properly rammed. The thickness of stone slab 25 mm to50 mm are fixed with a thin layer of 1:1.5 cement coarse sand mortar. Before fixing the stones slabs in position they are dressed on all edges and the joints are finished with white or colored cement.

   (***c***) **Concrete floor covering:** Over the compacted earthen surface, a 150 mm thick sand cushion is provided. It should be watered and rammed thoroughly. A base layer of 75 mm to100mm of lean cement concrete is laid on the cushion sand. lastly, c.c floor consisting of 40mm thick 1:2:4 cement concrete as a topping is finished with neat cement.

   (***d***) **Tile floor covering:** Clay tiles of different sizes, shapes, thickness, colors are available in the market and are used as floor covering. They are placed in position on a concrete base with a thin layer of cement mortar.

   (***e***) **Terrazzo floor covering:** Terrazzo is a mixture of cement, marble dust and marble chips. The sub base is prepared in the similar manner as in case of cement concrete flooring. The top layer consist of 40 mm thick flooring in which 31mm cement concrete and a layer of

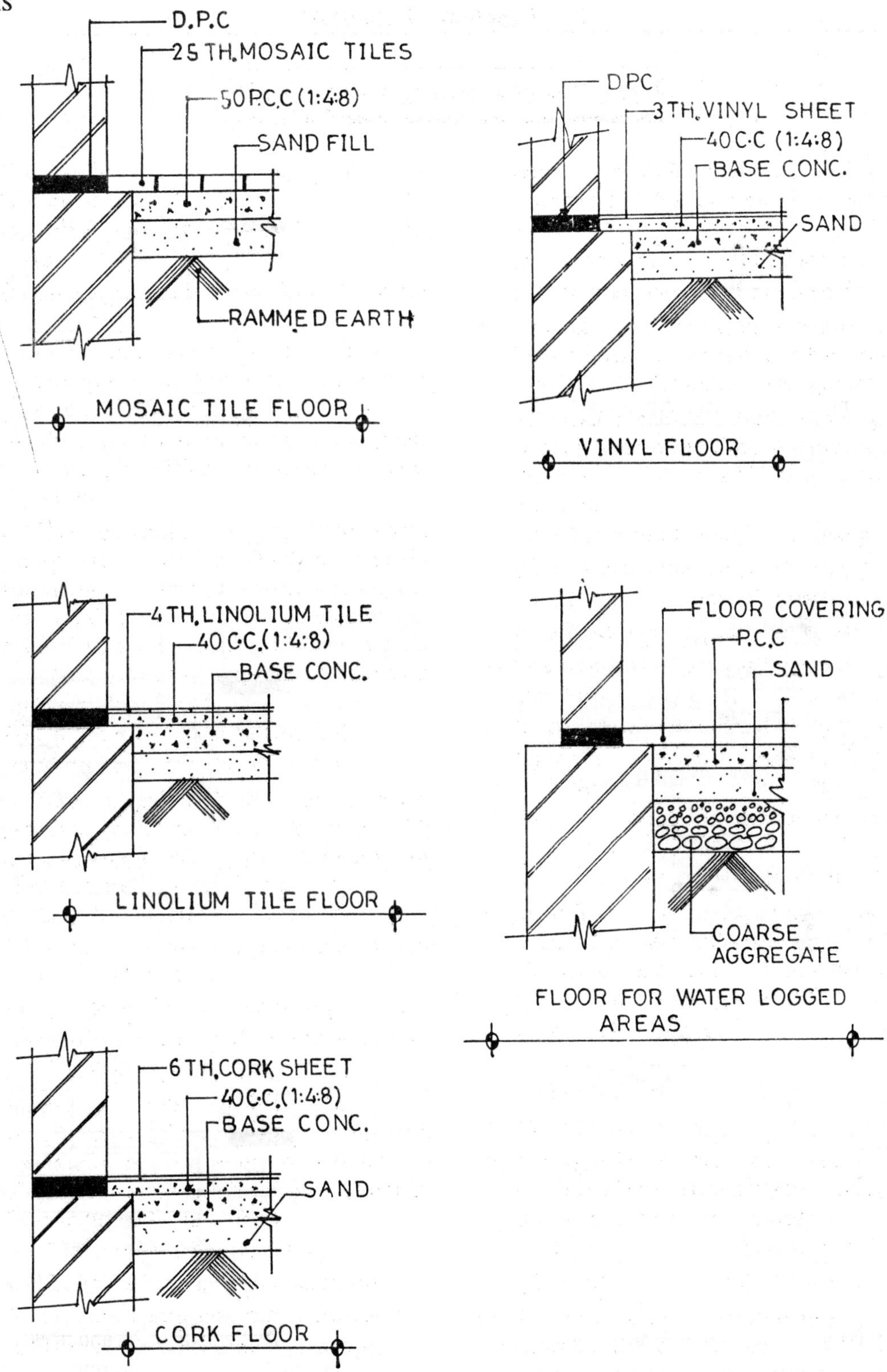


**Fig. 2.1.** Types of Floor Coverings

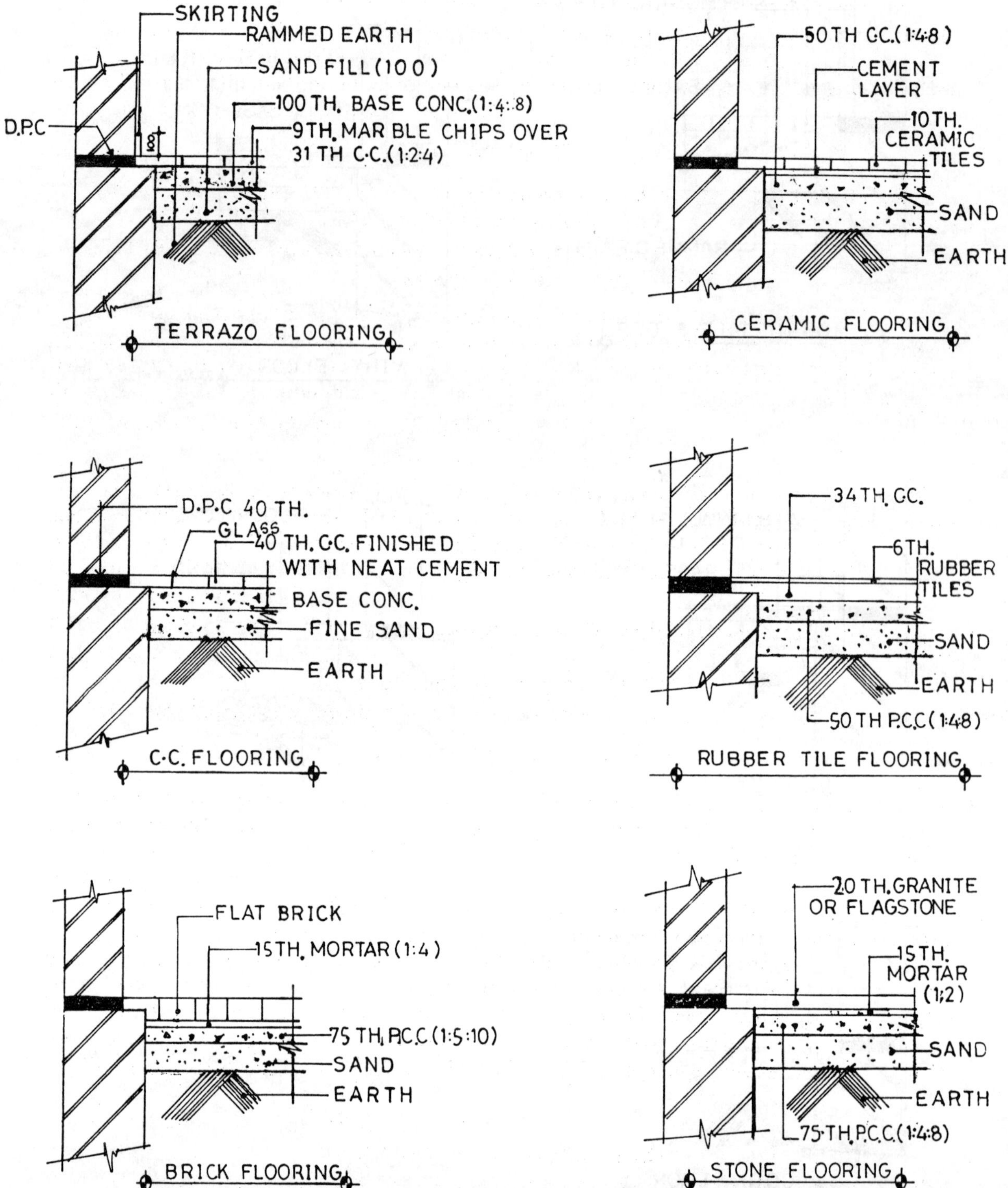


**Fig. 2.1. A.** Types of Floor Coverings

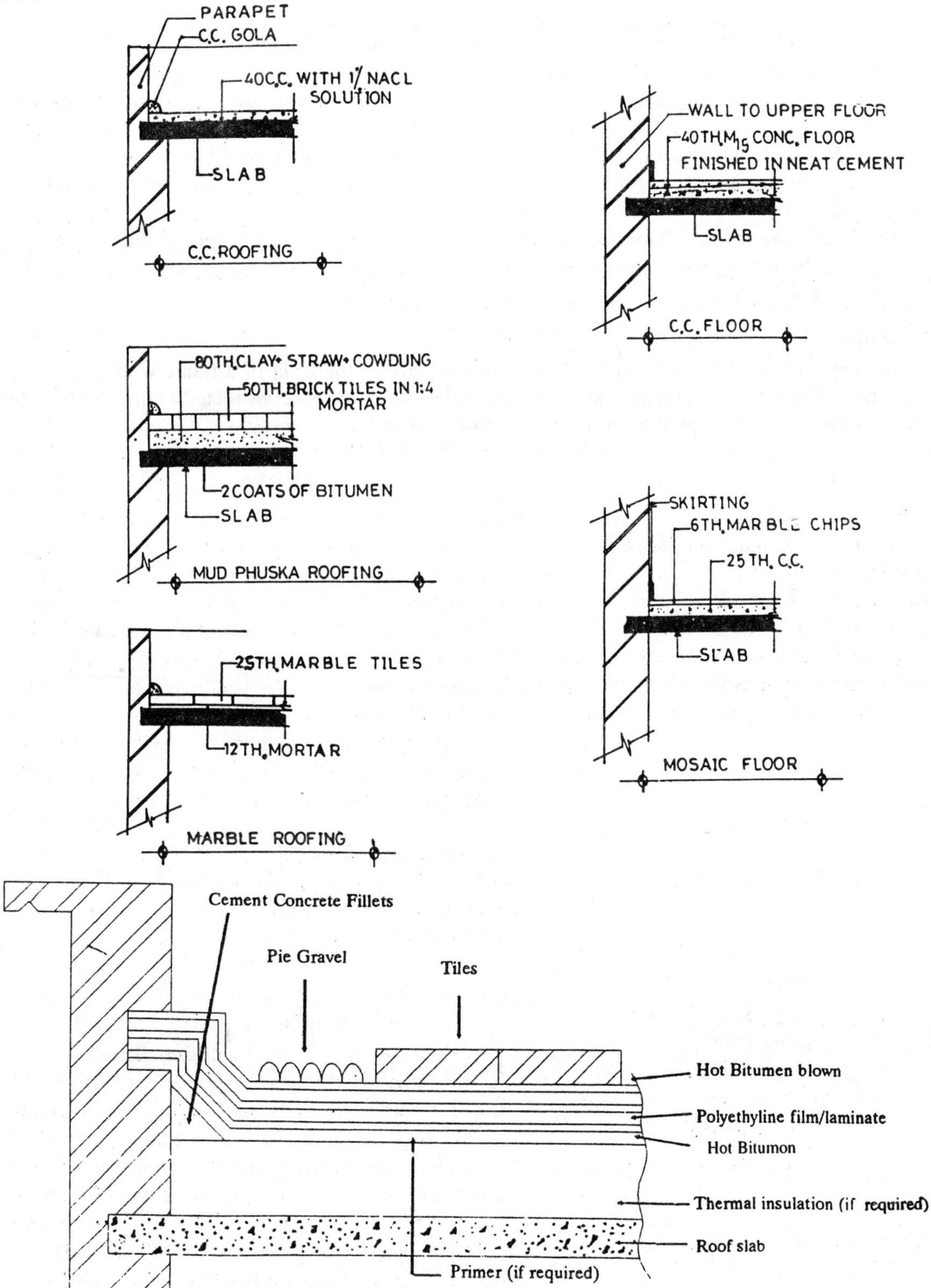


Polyethylene Film.

**Fig. 2.2. Various Floors at Upper Levels**

9 mm thick marble chips (2 parts) mixed with white or colored cement (1part) and marble dust (1 part) in proportion of 4:7.

(*f*) **Asphalt floor covering:** Asphalt tiles of desired shapes and sizes are available in market. The asphalt terrazzo is provided over the c.c floors.

(*g*) **Rubber floor covering:** Its thickness varies from 3 to 10 mm in many design and patterns. It is available in the form of tiles or sheet and can be directly laid by using a special adhesive over the sub floor.

(*h*) **Linoleum or vinyl floor covering:** It is available in the market in rolls width of 2 m to 4m and thickness varies from 2 to 6 mm. Vinyl is covering laid over concrete floor with help of an adhesive.

**Roof and upper floor**

It's the upper most part of a building which is constructed in the form of a frame work to give protection to the building against rain, heat, snow, wind etc. The Roof may be constructed as flat, sloping, shell or domes etc.The roof is also used as floor for upper story. (Fig 2.2)

# 3

# *Doors and Windows*

## 3.1. DOOR

Doors are meant to provide access to the rooms and good ventilation within the building. They are located in such a way that there is an easy movement of the user and privacy of the room is maintained. While deciding the location of the door, the purpose and utility of the rooms need proper consideration. Doors should not be provided at the corners of the wall in a room because corners are very week to resist lateral forces. If single shutter is used for fitting the door then it is known as single leaf, while double shutter is known as double leaf door.

## 3.2. SIZES OF DOORS

The size of the door depends upon the size of room and the largest size of object likely to be used, the doors is allows free access in the room. Following are the generally sizes of doors for a residential building.

| | |
|---|---|
| Main door | 1200 mm × 2100 mm |
| Side door | 1000 mm × 2100 mm |
| Kitchen door | 900 mm × 2100 mm |
| Toilet door | 750 mm × 2100 mm |
| Garage door | 2500 mm × 2300 mm |

## 3.3. TECHNICAL TERMS USED IN DOORS AND WINDOWS

**Frame.** It is a combination of several wooden, or steel, members to support a door or a window. Doorframes consisting of two vertical members (vertical post) and one horizontal member (head) but window frame consist of two vertical members (vertical post) and two horizontal member (head) (Fig 3.1).

**Jamb.** It is a vertical face of a door or windows opening which supports the frame.

**Sill.** It is the bottom most horizontal member forming the frame.

**Transom or intermediate rail.** It is a horizontal member, which divides the door or window frame in to several panels.

**Style.** Style is an external vertical member of the shutter.

**Top rail.** It is the topmost horizontal member of the shutter.

**Lock rail.** It is the central horizontal member of the shutter where locking attachment is fixed.

**Bottom rail.** It is the lowest most horizontal member of the shutter.

**Frieze rail.** It is the horizontal member between top rail and lock rail of the shutter.

**Mullion.** It is the vertical member used to increase the panels running through a shutter.

**Louver.** Louver is a timber piece, which is attached in inclined position with in frame.

**Horn.** It is a horizontal projection of head member or sill beyond the face of the door or window frame.

**Holdfast.** These are made of steel and provided on both side of the vertical door or window frames to keep the frame in its position.

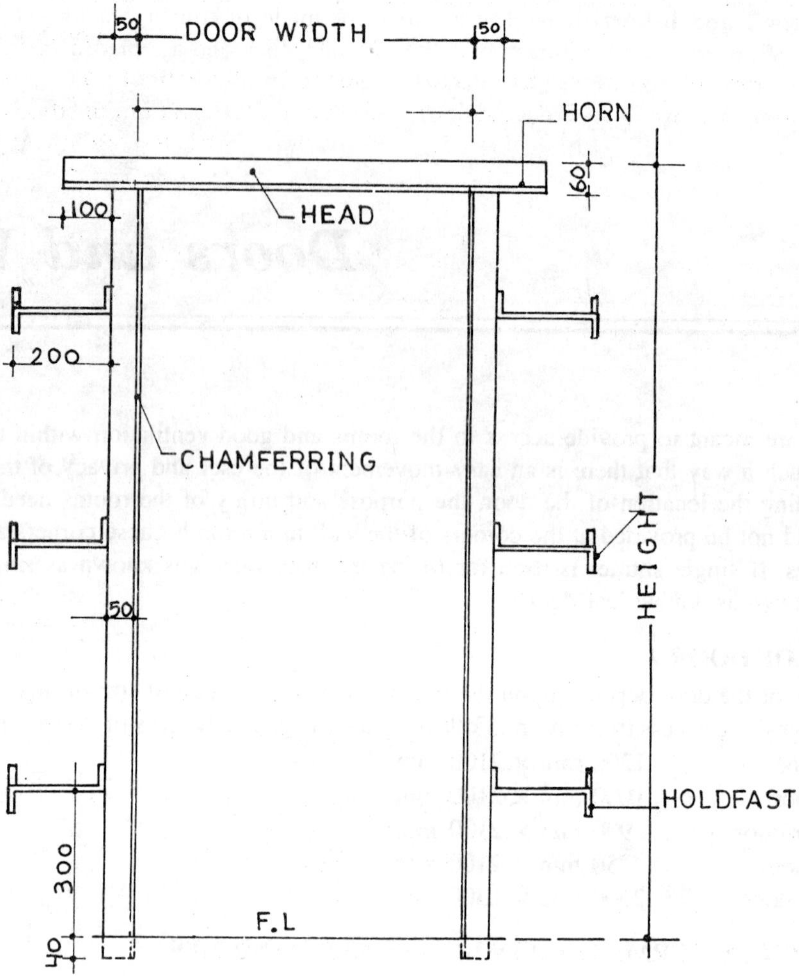


**Fig. 3.1.** Door Frame and Holdfasts

**Rebate.** It is a depression cut in the frame or shutter to accommodate the door or shutter.

**Sash.** It is a frame made of light section and used for fixing the glass in the panels. It consists of two horizontal and two vertical members.

**Moulding.** The space between the two vertical and two horizontal members are filled with wooden pieces generally 10 mm to 20 mm.

**Beading.** These are the thick wooden members used at the joints of panels, horizontal, and vertical members for decoration purpose.

## 3.4. TYPES OF DOOR

1. Battened and ledged door
2. Battened ledged &braced door
3. Framed, Battened &braced door
4. Framed, and panelled door
5. Glazed and panelled door
6. Flush door
7. Wire gauged door
8. Collapsible door
9. Rolling shutters
10. Sliding door
11. Revolving door
12. Louvered doors

1. **Battened and ledged door.** These doors are made of timber planks known as battens whose dimensions are 150 to 300 mm wide and 25 mm thick and are placed vertically side-by-side and are fixed in position by horizontal member known as ledges. Ledges are 100 mm to150 mm wide and 40 mm in thickness. These doors are very simple and provided in narrow openings such as toilets etc.

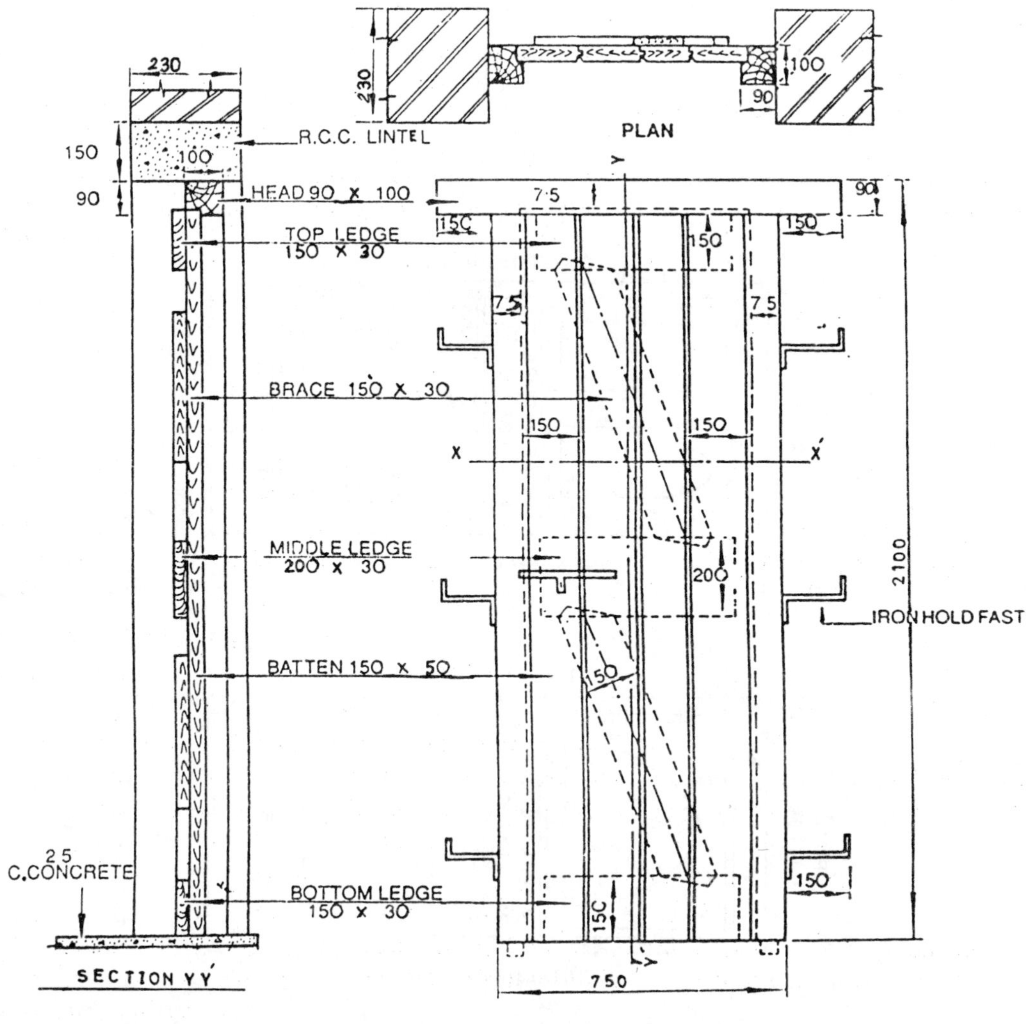


All dimensions in mm

**Fig. 3.2.** Batenned Ledged and Braced Door

2. **Battened ledged &braced door.** They are similar to battened and ledged doors except two additional inclined timbre member known as braces are provided between the ledges. Such types of doors are much stronger than the previous one hence can be used for wider opening. (Fig 3.2)
3. **Framed, Battened &braced door.** These types of doors are much stronger than the Battened ledged &braced door. The frame works for shutters is made by two vertical style and three horizontal rails and planks are fixed between them.
4. **Framed, and panelled door.** It consist of a frame work in which panels are fitted. The styles

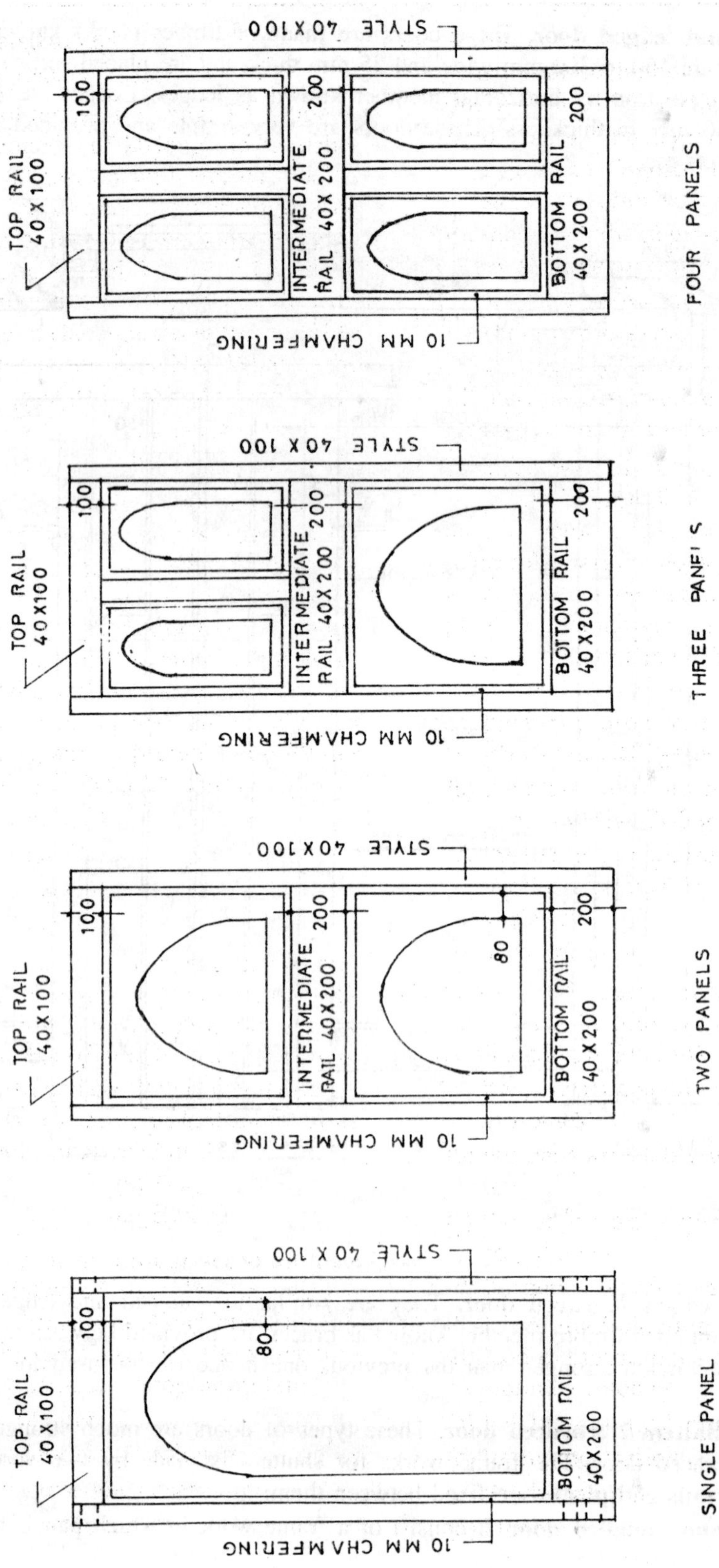


**Fig. 3.3.** Panelled Doors

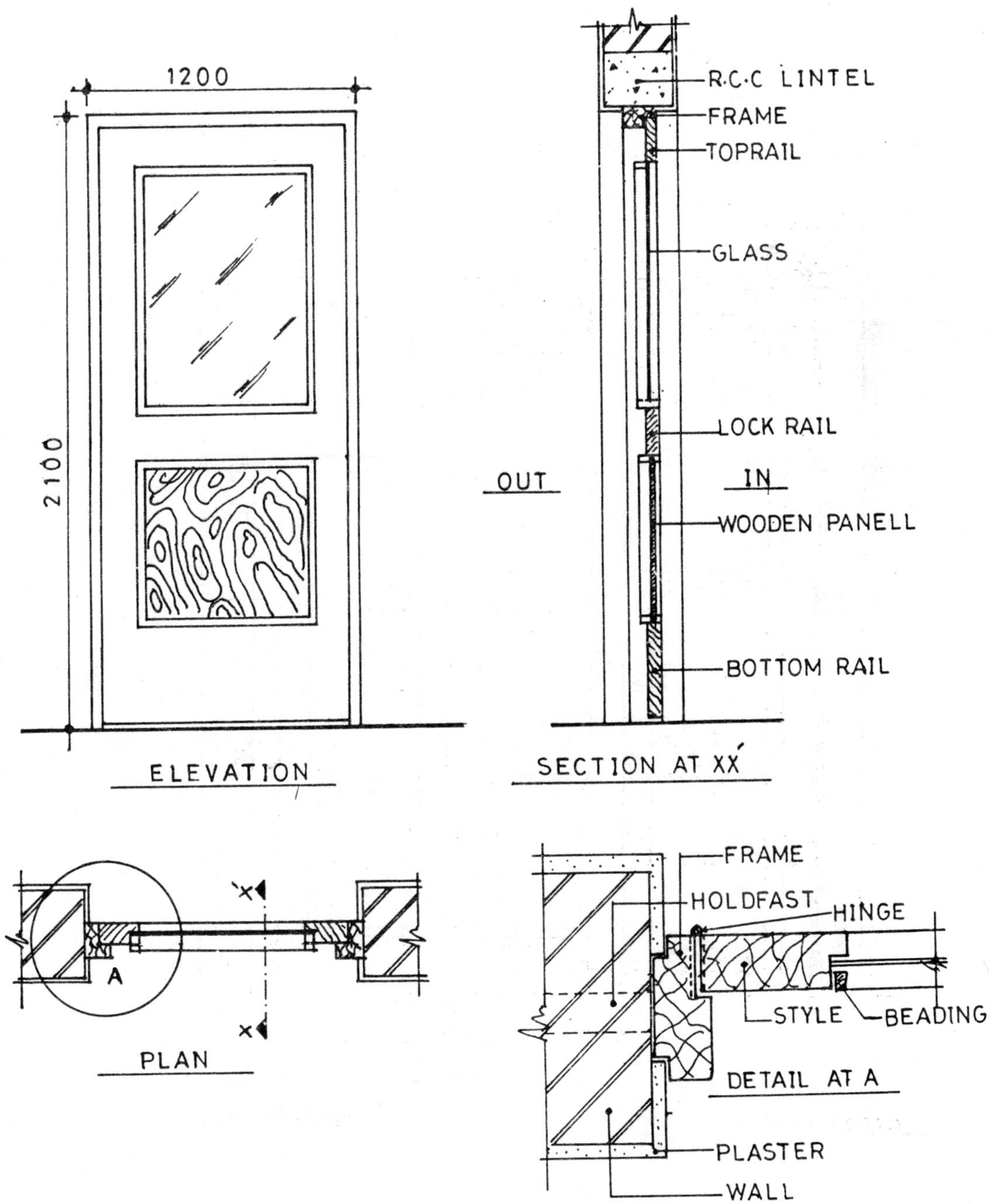


**Fig. 3.4.** Glazed and Panelled Door

are continuous from top to bottom. The top, middle and bottom rails are joined to the style. Mullions are also provided to reduce the size of panels. These doors are very common and are provided in any buildings. Further they enhance the appearance of door. Beadings are also provided on the joints of the panels for face lifting. (Fig. 3.3, 3.4, 3.4B).

5. **Glazed and panelled door.** When it is desired to admit more light beside that coming from the windows, such type of doors are provided. The glass is fixed into the rebates made in the

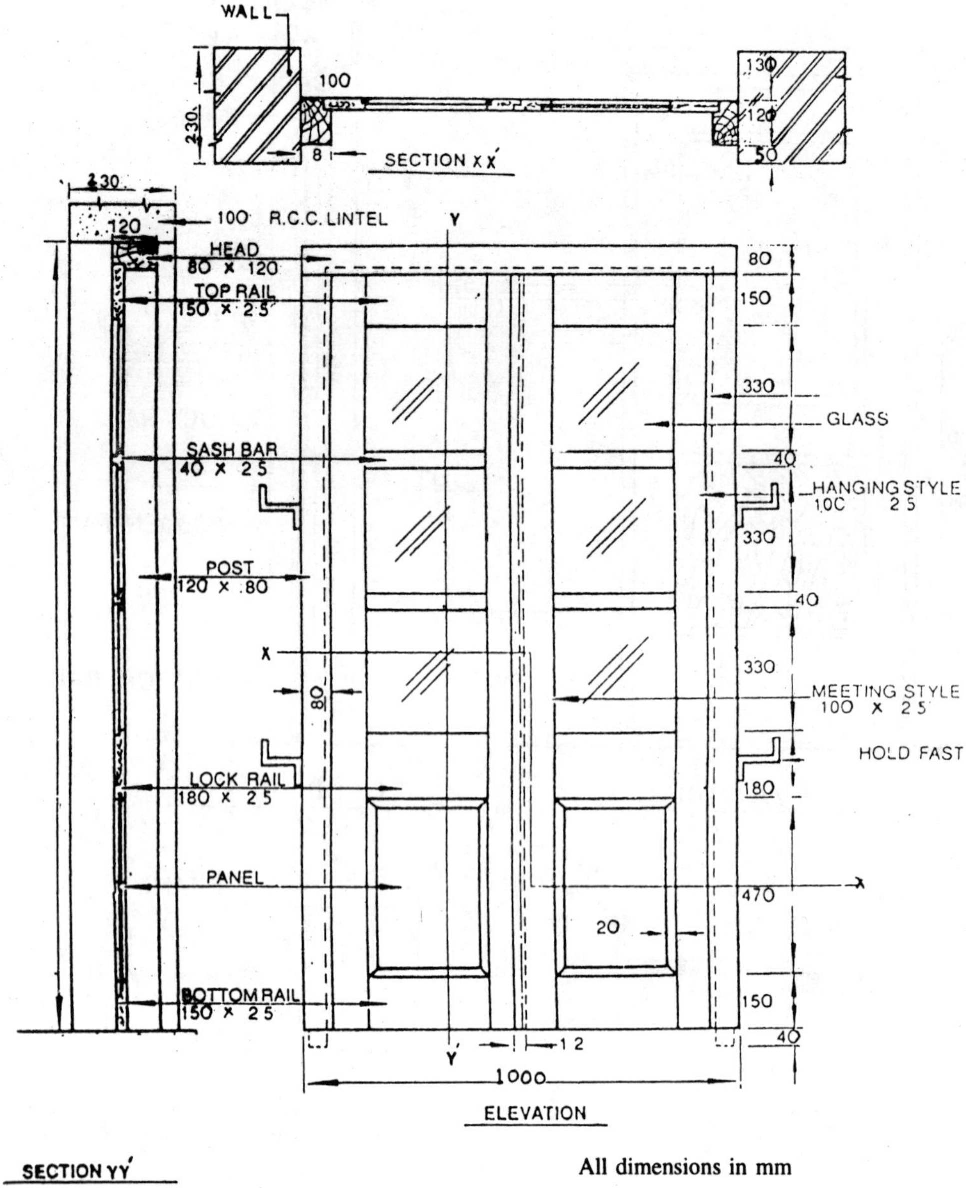


All dimensions in mm

**Fig. 3.4. A.** Glazed and Panelled Door

wooden sash bars with the help of small nails and putty. These doors are generally provided in offices, classrooms and hospitals building, etc. (Fig. 3.4A).

6. **Flush Door.** These types of doors are provided for smooth and clean surface. They are very strong and durable. It consists of a frame work of timber styles and rails and Plywood's cover both the faces of the framework. Flush door may be framed flush door, hollow core flush door and laminated flush door. (Fig. 3.5).

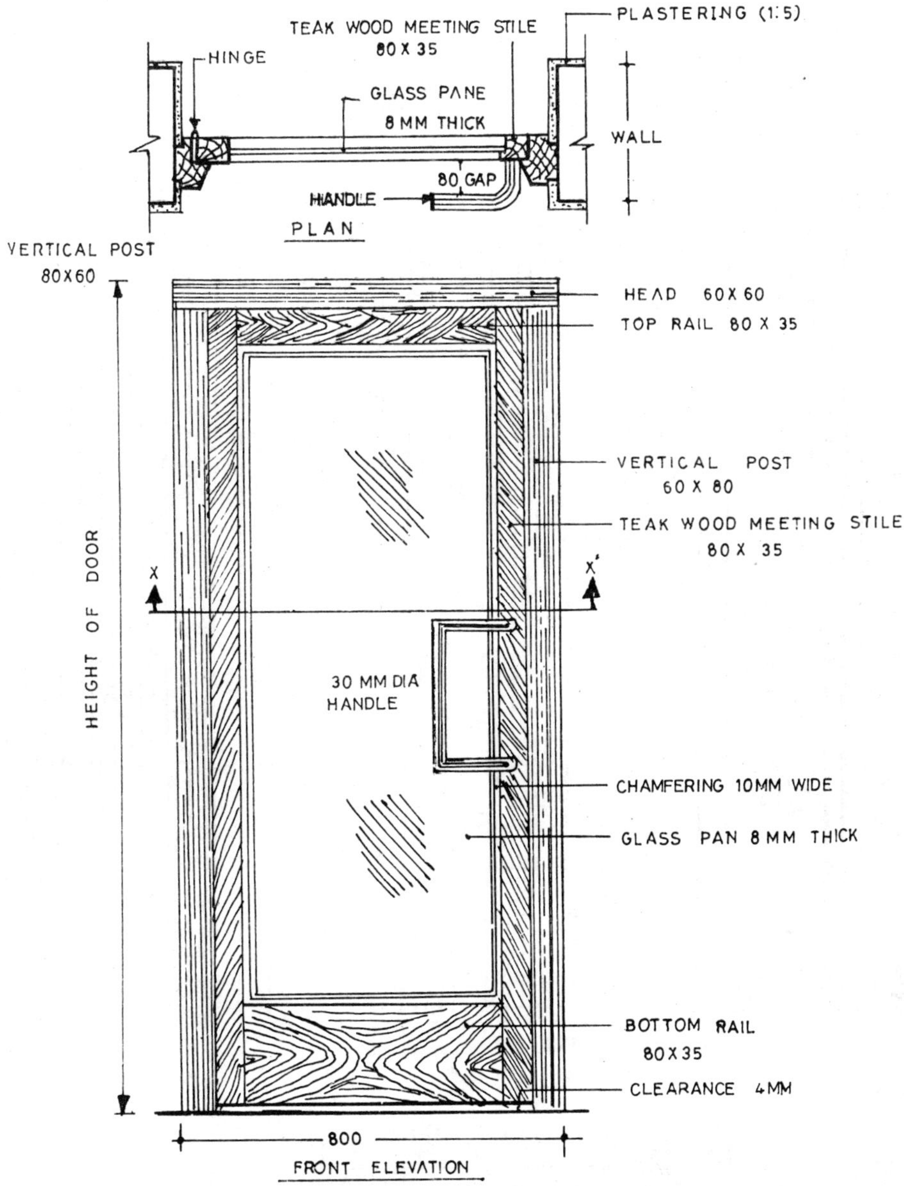


**Fig. 3.4. B.** Fully Glazed Shutter

7. **Wire gauged door.** This door is fixed on the external face of the doors located in external walls of the building. The function of the door is to prevent entrance of fly's and mosquitoes inside the building. The construction of the door is same as the panelled door but wire gauge is fixed instead of wooden or glass panels. (Fig. 3.6)
8. **Collapsible door.** The door is fabricated from thin mild steel frame. It consists of vertically placed double channels each of 15 to 20 mm in width at a spacing of 100 to150 mm. These channels are braced with 15 to 20 mm wide mild steel flats, which permit the doors to open or fold. The whole assembly is mounted on two rails in the form of T- section fixed on the floor and lintel. This framework can be opened or closed by a slight pull or push.

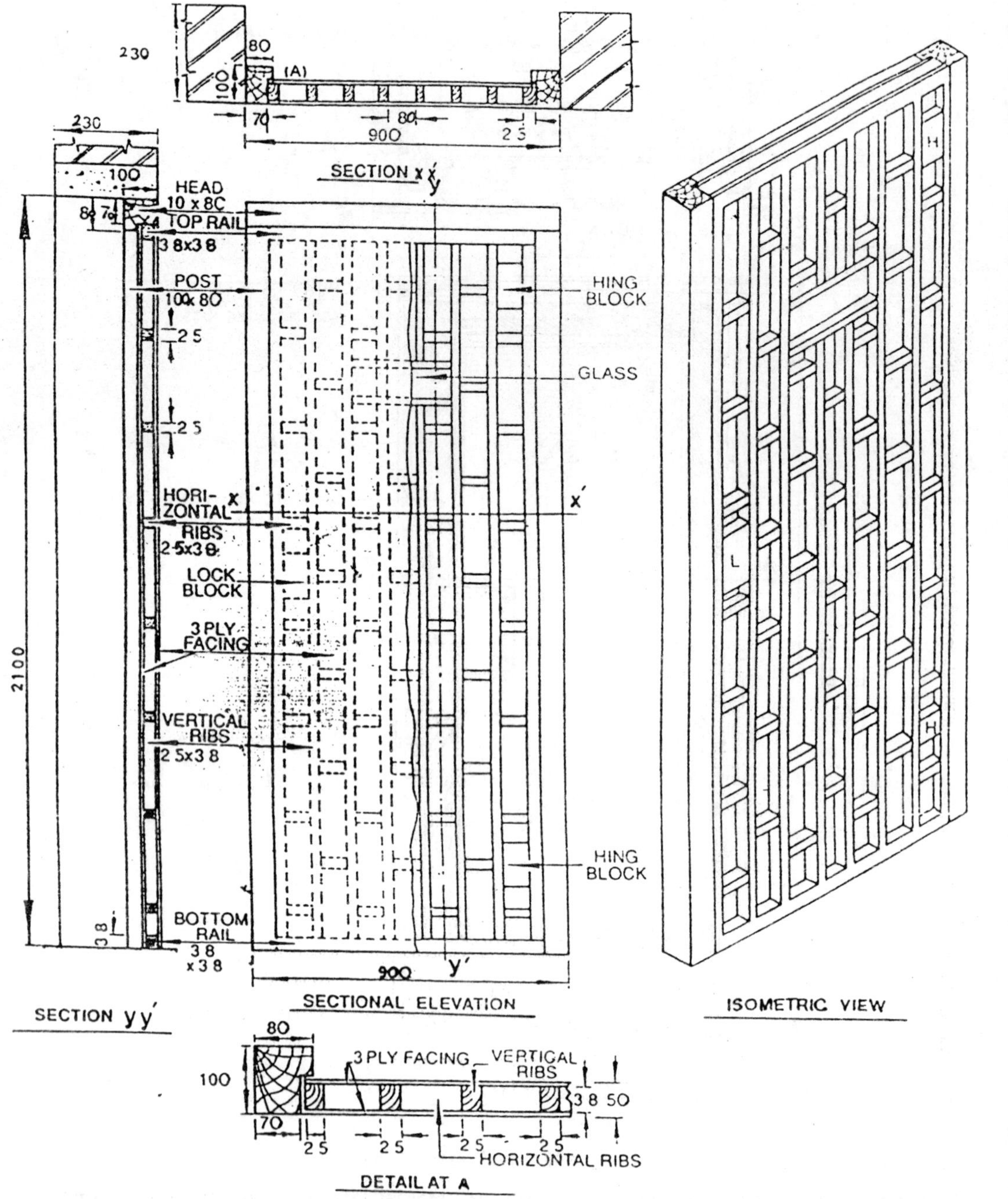


**Fig. 3.5.** Flush Door

9. **Rolling shutters.** These are commonly used for garages, show rooms, shops etc. It consists of a frame, a drum, and a shutter of thin steel plates or iron sheet. The door has interlocked steel slabs coiled upon a drum at the top of the opening. The door shutter moves up and down in steel guides mounted at the sides of the door opening. The weight of the door is countered-balanced by the helical spring provided in the drum and a steel cover is provided to protect the drum from weathering action. (Fig 3.7)

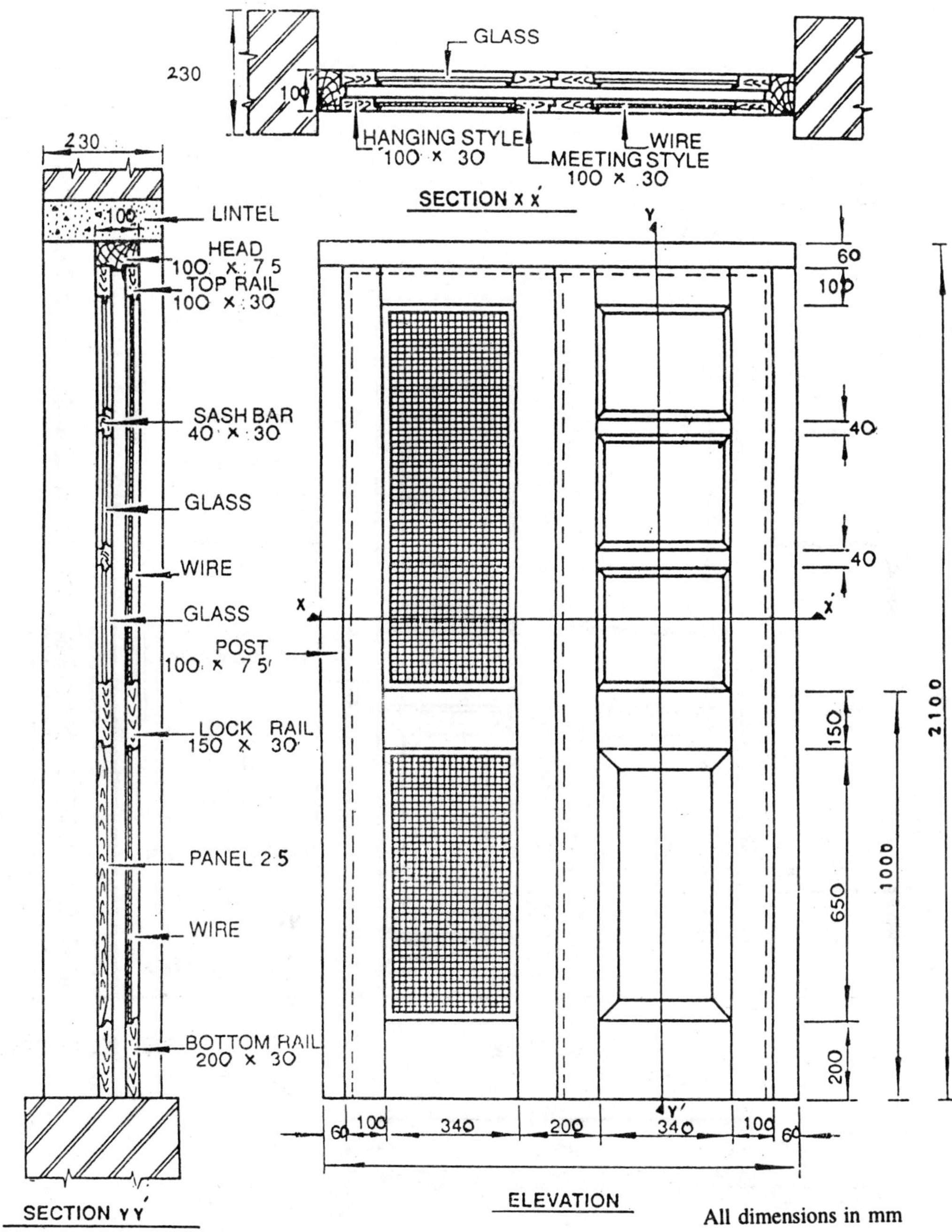


**Fig. 3.6. A.** Panelled and Glazed wire Gauge Door

10. **Sliding door.** The shutter of the door slides on the side rather than opening out side or inside. Cavities are provided in the wall to receive the door shutters in open position. This is commonly used where the obstruction in the movement of users.
11. **Revolving door.** It consist a central supporting shaft and four radiating shutters are attached with the central shaft. The shutters may be fully or partly glazed. Rubber pads are fixed to the

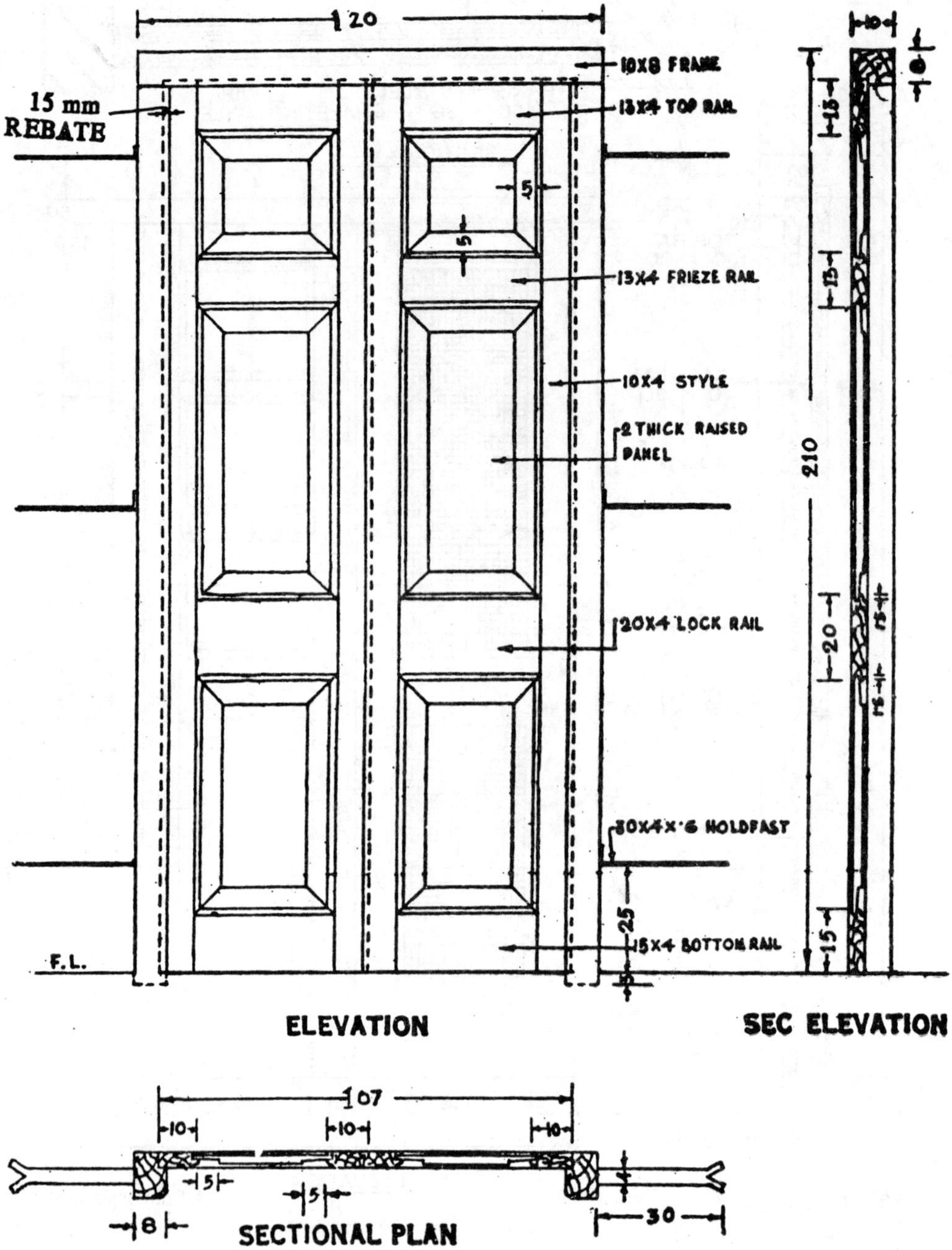


**PANELLED DOOR SHUTTER WITH FRAME**

ALL DIMENSIONS ARE IN CM

Fig. 3.6. B. Panelled Door Shutter with Frame

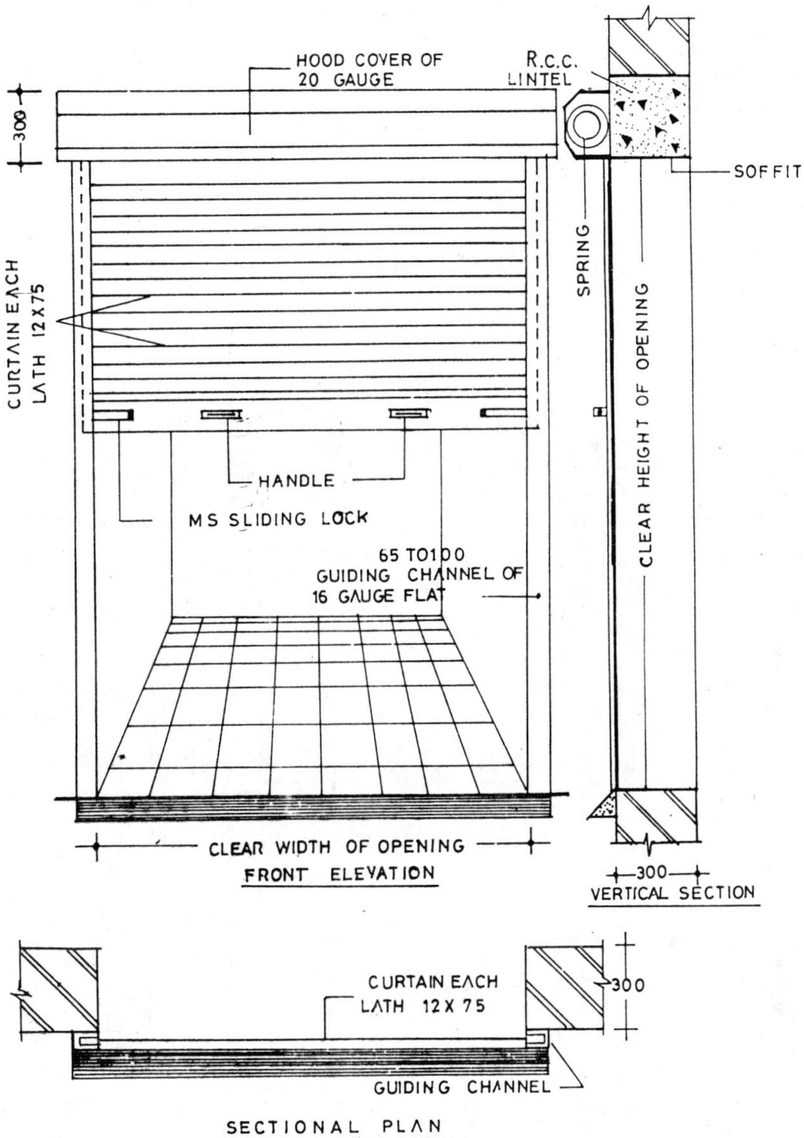


**Fig. 3.7.** Steel Shutter

bottom of the shutters. They are used to regulate the entrance of the persons in bank, theater etc (Fig. 3.14).

12. **Louvered doors.** The shutter of this door is provided with fixed louvers or movable louvers, they are provided partly or fully up to the height of door. Louvers are arranged at such an inclination that horizontal vision is obstructed. It allow sufficient amount of ventilation and at the same time it maintains privacy.

## 3.5. WINDOW

Windows are provided in the building to allow natural light and fresh air into it. The area of the window should not be less than 1/10 of floor area in residential building, and for public building it may be taken as 1/5 of floor area. Ventilator is also a small window provided above the lintel of door or window for disposal of hot gasses.

1. **Types of window.** Windows are provided in the building to allow natural light and fresh air into it. The area of the window should not be less than 1/10 of floor area in residential building, and for public building it may be taken as 1/5 of floor area. Ventilator is also a small window provided above the lintel of door or window for disposal of hot gasses.
2. **Panelled window.** The construction of panelled window is same as the panelled door. The size of style and horizontal rails are 45 to 100 mm wide and 25 mm thick in section. The shutter of windows made of by wooden panels or ply wood panels. (Fig. 3.8)

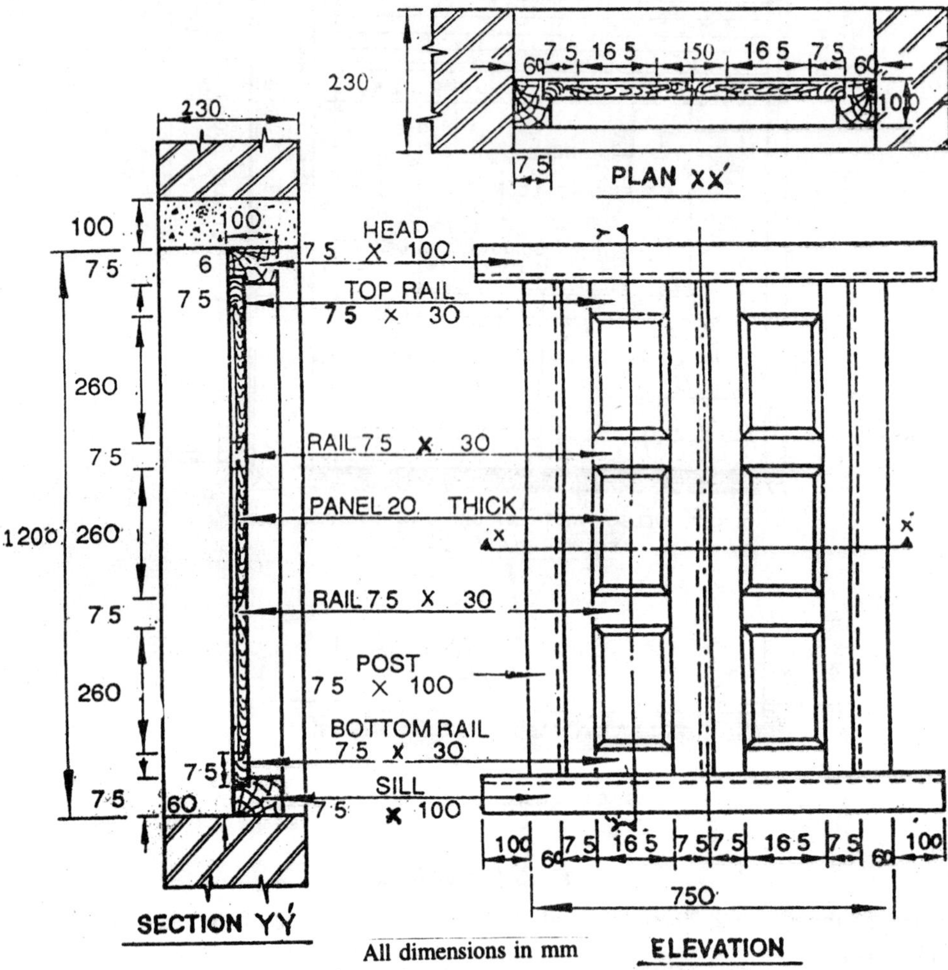


**Fig. 3.8.** Panelled Window

3. **Casement window.** Casement window consist of a square or rectangular window frame of metal or wood, with a casement hinges at one side of the frame to open out. The side hinged opening part of the window is known as casement and it consist of glass surrounded and supported by steel or wooden strip. (Fig. 3.9)
4. **Sash or glazed window.** It is similar to panelled window except that Glass panels are fixed in sash bar with the help of putty or nails. (Fig. 3.10)

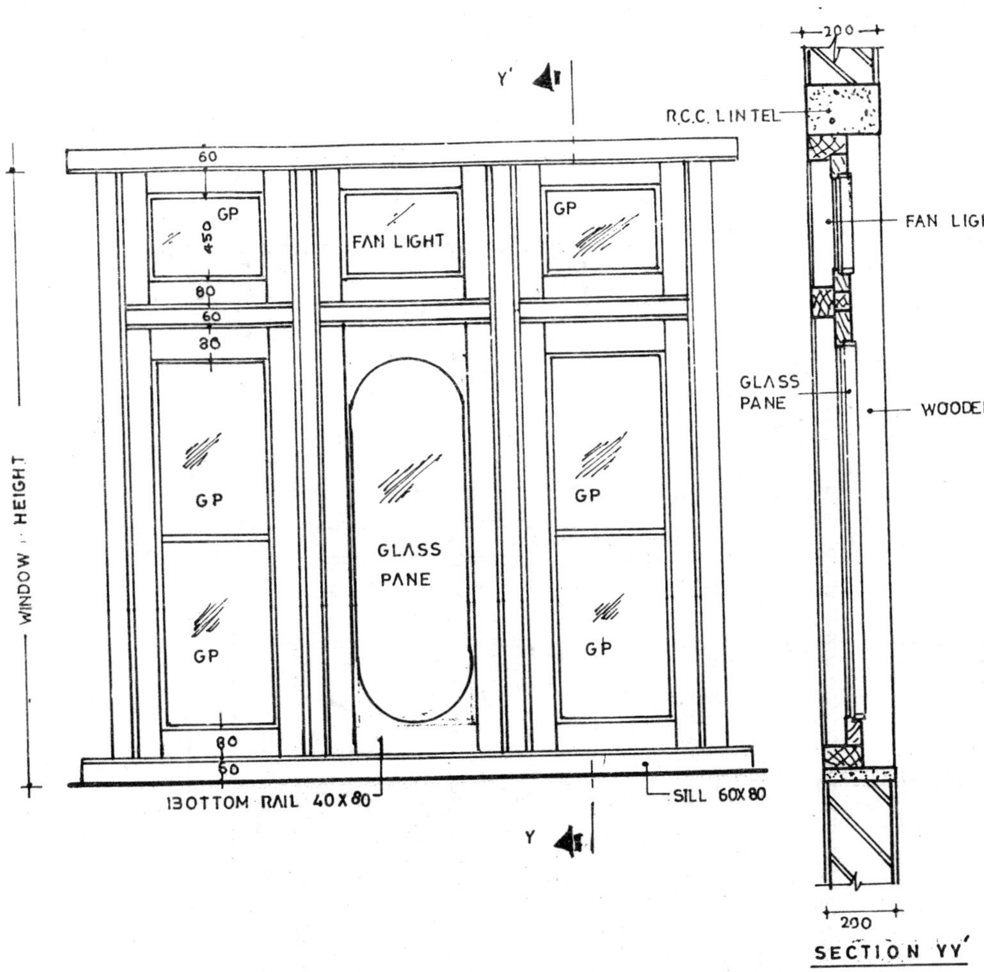


Fig. 3.9. Casement Window

5. **Double hung window**
6. **Pivoted window.** The shutter of the window swing in round pivots. It may be horizontally or vertically pivoted.
7. **Louvered window.** It is also similar to louvered door. It is employed when privacy and enough ventilation is required. This window is used in toilets.
8. **Corner window.** This is provided at the corners of a room to increase the ventilation and improve the elevation of the building. (Fig. 3.12).
9. **Bay window.** This type of window is generally provided in the external wall of living room. It improves the architectural elevation; provide more light and ventilation with in the building. (Fig. 3.13).
10. **Gable window.** This window is provided at the gable ends of an inclined roof building *i.e.* in god owns. (Fig. 3.15)
11. **Dormer window.** It is provided in the slopy roof (inclined roof) for providing air and light in side the building (Fig. 3.15).
12. **Lantern window** such type of widow is provided in flat roof to admit light and air through the roof.

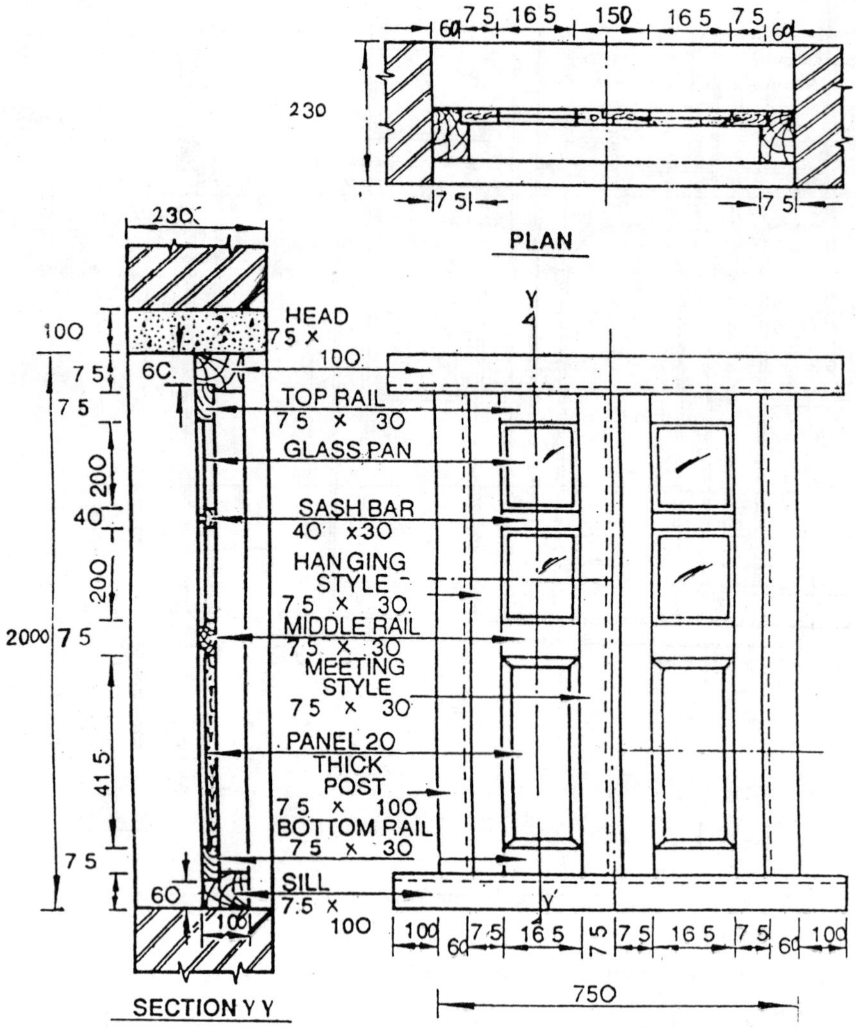


All dimensions in mm

**Fig. 3.10.** Panelled and Glazed Window

**13. Clerestory window.** such type of widow is provided near the roof in the wall to admit light and air. (Fig. 3.11)

## QUESTION FOR PRACTICE

1. Draw the elevation, sectional plan and side sectional elevation of a panelled door of size 1200mm × 2100 mm.
2. Draw the front elevation, sectional plan and side sectional elevation of a fully glazed window of size 1500 × 1200 mm. Assume all data suitably.

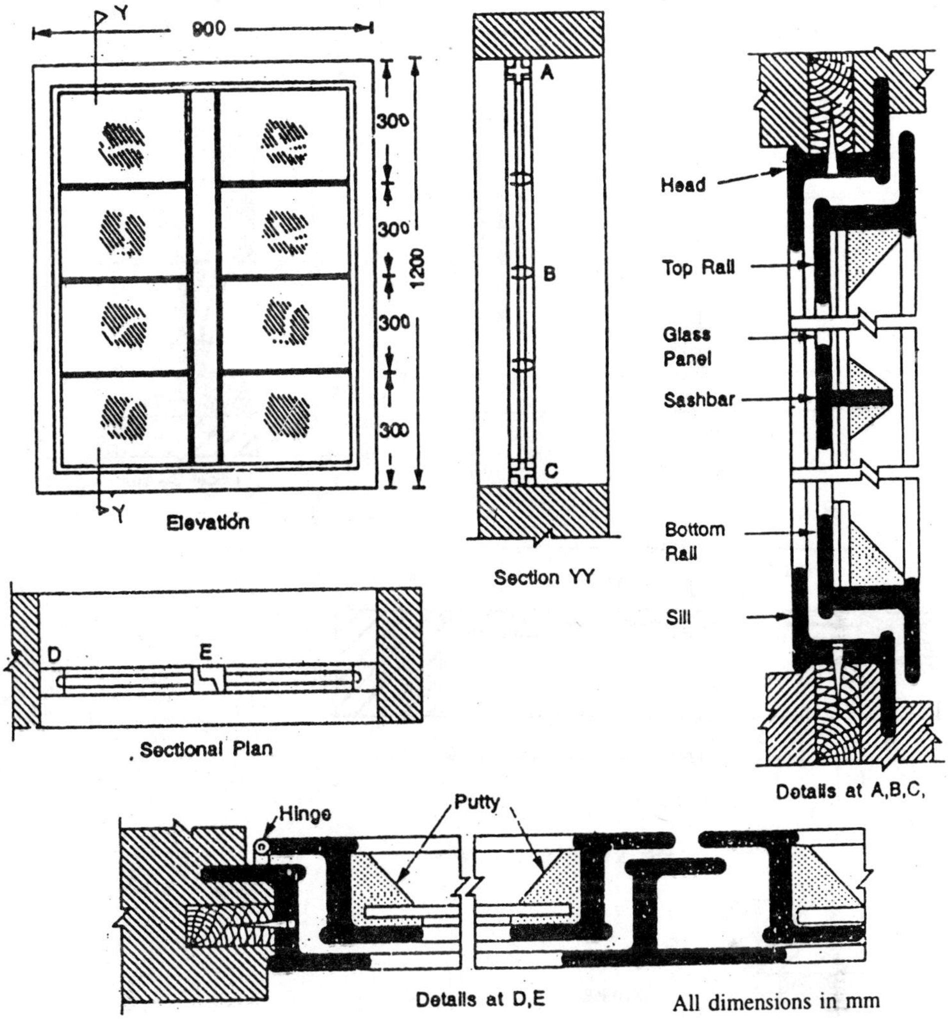


**Fig. 3.10. A.** Steel Window

3. Draw the front elevation, sectional plan and sectional side elevation of a fully panelled door with the following specifications

| | |
|---|---|
| Size of door | 1200 × 2100 mm |
| Door frame | 100 × 80 |
| Top and intermediate rail | 125 × 40 mm |
| Bottom rail | 200 × 40 mm |
| Thickness of door | 40 mm |
| Thickness of panel | 25 mm |
| Style- | 100 × 40 mm, the door should be double leaf shutter having three panels in each leaf. |

4. Draw the front elevation, sectional plan and sectional side elevation of a lower 2/3 paneled and upper1/3 glazed door with the following specifications

| | |
|---|---|
| Size of door | 1000 × 2100 mm |
| Door frame | 100 × 65 |
| Top and intermediate rail | 125 × 35 mm |
| Bottom rail | 200 × 35 mm |

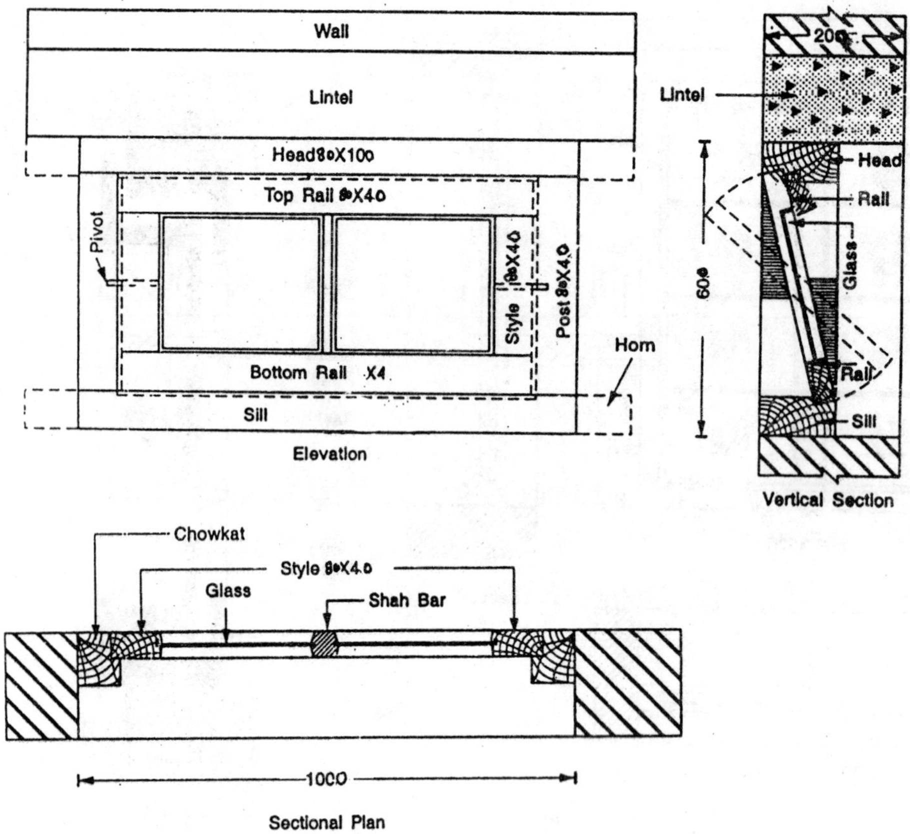


**Fig. 3.11.** Clerestory Window

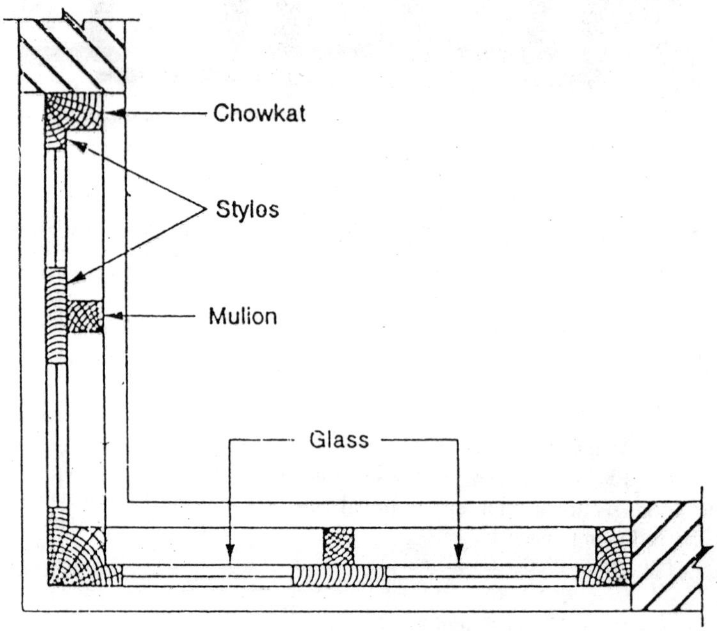


**Fig. 3.12.** Corner Window

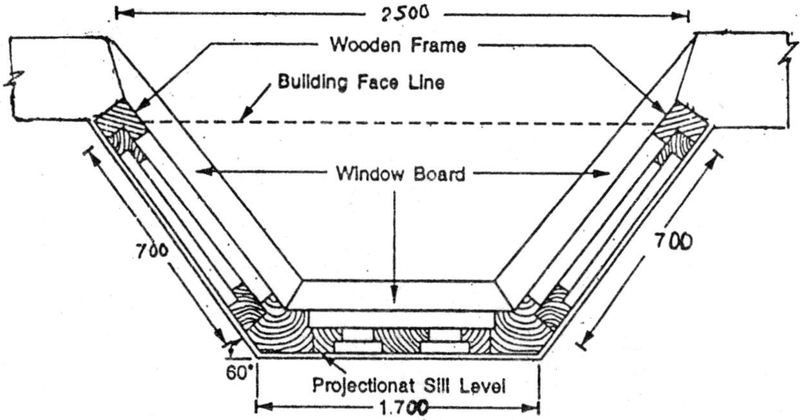


**Fig. 3.13.** Bay Window

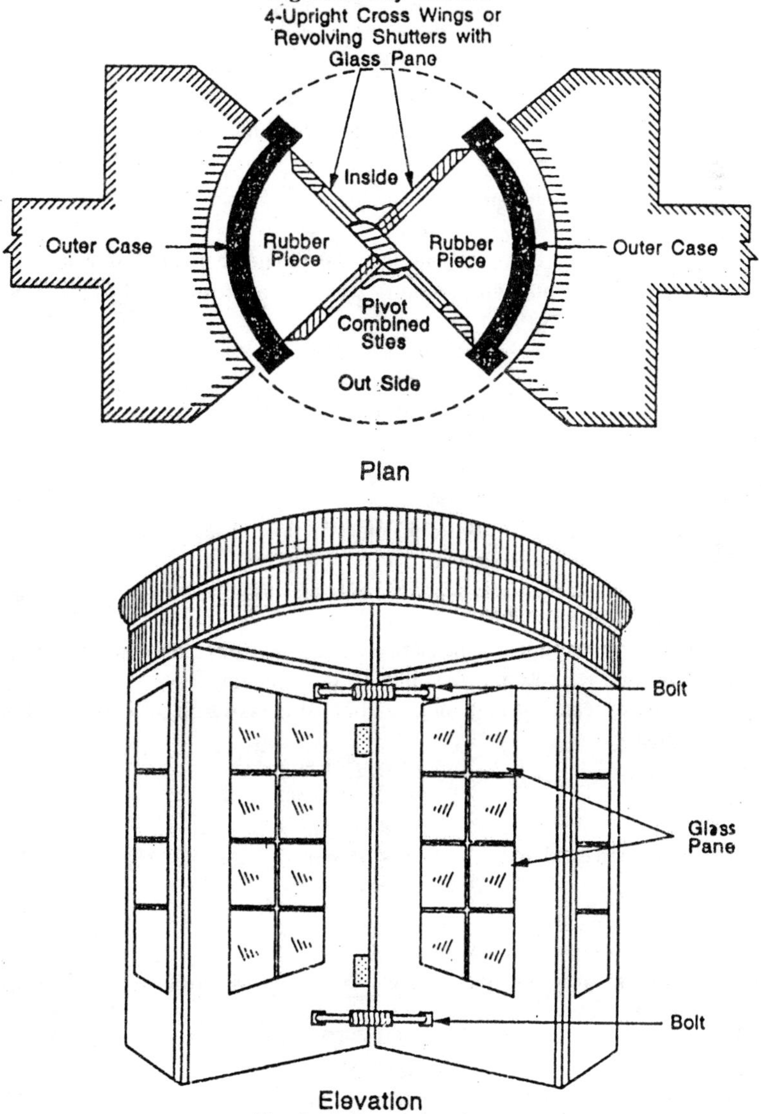


**Fig. 3.14.** Revolving door

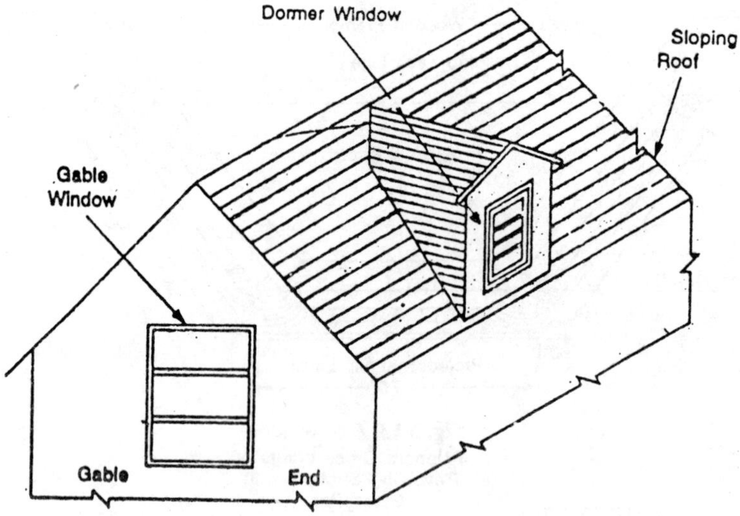


**Fig. 3.15.** Dormer Window

| | |
|---|---|
| Thickness of door | 35 mm |
| Thickness of panel | 20 mm |
| Thickness of glass | 6mm |
| Style- | 100 × 35 mm, the door should be single leaf shutter. |

5. Draw the elevation, sectional plan and sectional side elevation of a fully glazed door with the following specifications

| | |
|---|---|
| Size of door | 1200 × 2100 mm |
| Door frame | 100 × 80 |
| Top and intermediate rail | 125 × 40 mm |
| Bottom rail | 200 × 40 mm |
| Thickness of door | 40 mm |
| Thickness of panel | 25 mm |
| Style | 100 × 40 mm, the door shutter should be double leaf. |
| Thick ness of glass | 6 mm |

6. Draw the elevation, sectional plan and sectional side elevation of a fully glazed window of size 1200 mm × 1500 mm. Assume all data suitably.
7. Draw the elevation, sectional plan and sectional side elevation of a partly glazed and partly paneled window of size 1200 mm × 1500 mm. Assume all data suitably.
8. Draw the front elevation, sectional plan and sectional side elevation of a single shutter flush door with the following specifications

| | |
|---|---|
| Size of door | 1200 × 2100 mm |
| Door frame | 100 × 75 mm |
| Size of horizontal; ribs | 30 × 20 mm |
| Size of top and Bottom rails and style | 50 × 28 mm |
| Thickness of door | 40 mm |
| Thickness of vertical ribs 80mm@ | 125 mm |

Thickness of plywood cover on both side of shutter 6 mm each.

9. Draw the front elevation, sectional plan and sectional side elevation of a fully paneled window with the following specifications

| | |
|---|---|
| Size of window | 1500 × 1500 mm |
| Window frame | 100 × 80 |
| Top and intermediate rail | 100 × 30 mm |

| | |
|---|---|
| Bottom and top rail | 200 × 30 mm |
| Thickness of door | 30 mm |
| Thickness of plywood panel | 12 mm |
| Width of groove | 15 mm |

Style-100 × 30 mm, the window should be double leaf shutter having two panels in each leaf.

10. Draw the front elevation, sectional plan and sectional side elevation of a fully paneled aluminum door with the following specifications

| | |
|---|---|
| Size of door | 1500 × 2500 mm |
| Door frame | 125 × 50 |
| Top, Bottom and intermediate rail | 125 × 50 mm |
| Thickness of glass panel | 10 mm |
| Scale | 1:50 |

Assume any data if required.

# 4

# Stairs

## 4.1. STAIRS

A stair is a series of steps provided to afford the means of ascent or descent between the floors or landings of a building. The room or apartment of a building in which the stair is located is known as a stair case or stair hall. The stair should be located at such a place where it can serve the purpose for which it has been provided. They should be placed near the main entrance in the public building and in case of residential building, it should be provided centrally for easy access to all the dwellers and also maintain privacy simultaneously.

## 4.2. TECHNICAL TERMS

1. **Baluster.** It is an intermediate vertical member provided between string and hand- rail. It may be constructed of wood, steel and concrete.
2. **Balustrade.** The combined framework of handrail and balusters is called balustrade.
3. **Flight.** A continuous series of steps between two landings or between landing and floor.
4. **Going.** It's the horizontal projection plan of an inclined flight of steps between the first and last riser in a staircase.
5. **Hand Rail.** It is the grasp to hand during communications& may be made of wood, steel, concrete and synthetic material in the form of sheet.
6. **Headroom.** It is the vertical height between treads of steps and ceiling just above it.
7. **Landing.** The horizontal platform at the ends of steps or between two flights of a stair is known as landing. It is provided to change the direction and take rest while using the stair.
8. **Newel post.** It is the heavy vertical member provided at the ends of a handrail in one flight. This may be of wood, steel, concrete.
9. **Nosing** .The projected part of a tread beyond the face of riser.
10. **Pitch.** Inclination of a stair with the floor is known as a pitch.
11. **Rise.** It is the vertical height between two consecutive treads.
12. **Riser.** The vertical or front portion of a step is known as riser. It connects the treads of two successive steps.
13. **Run.** The total length of a stair including landing in a horizontal plane.
14. **Scotia.** It is an additional finish provided to the nosing or tread.
15. **Soffit.** It's the under surface of a stair is known as soffit.
16. **Step.** It's a Combination of a tread and a riser.
17. **Stringer.** These are inclined members of a stair which support the ends of steps.
18. **Tread.** The horizontal upper surface of a step on which foot is kept is called tread.
19. **Waist.** It's the thickness of slab which supports the steps.

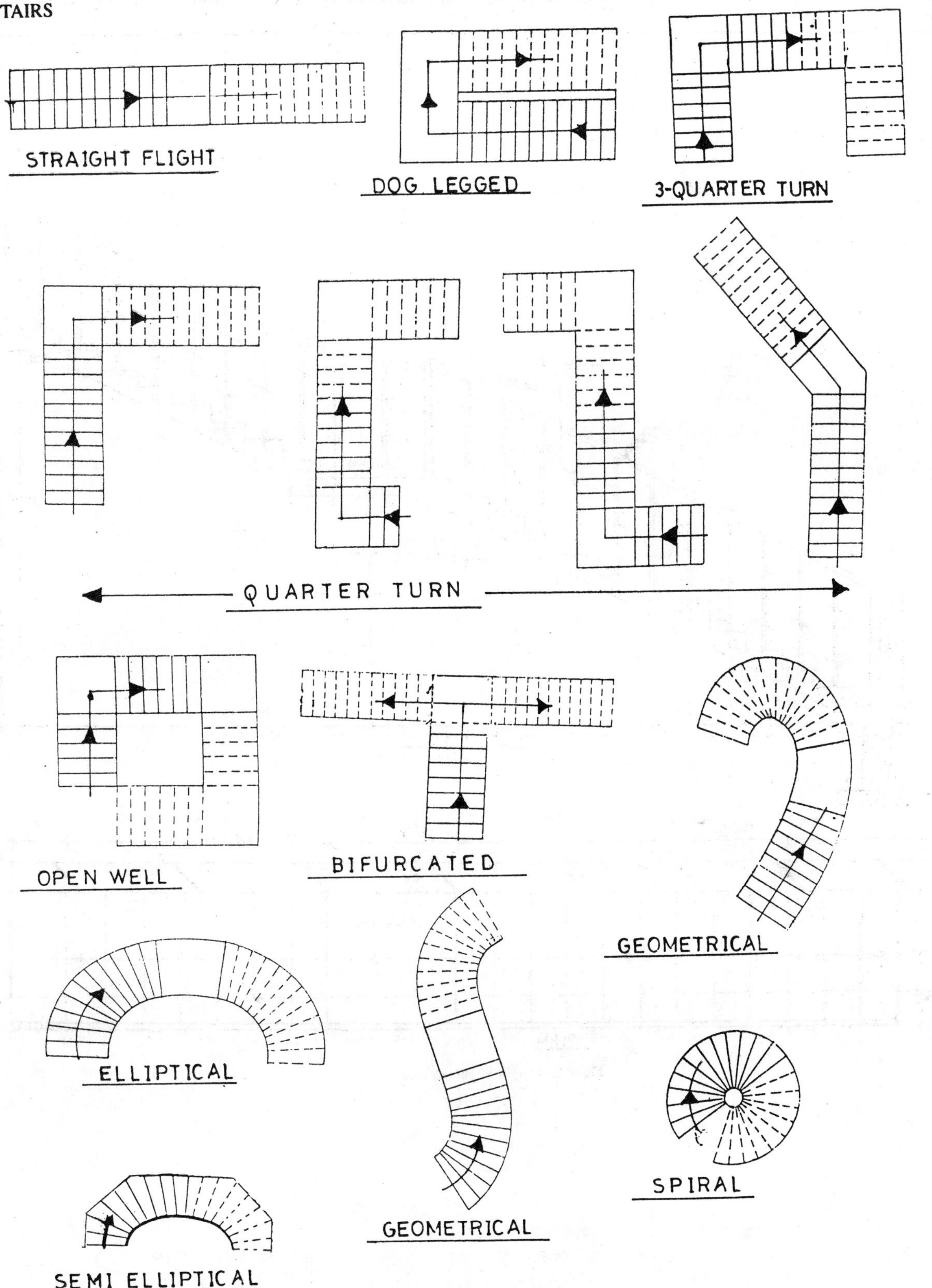


**Fig. 4.1.** Types of Stairs

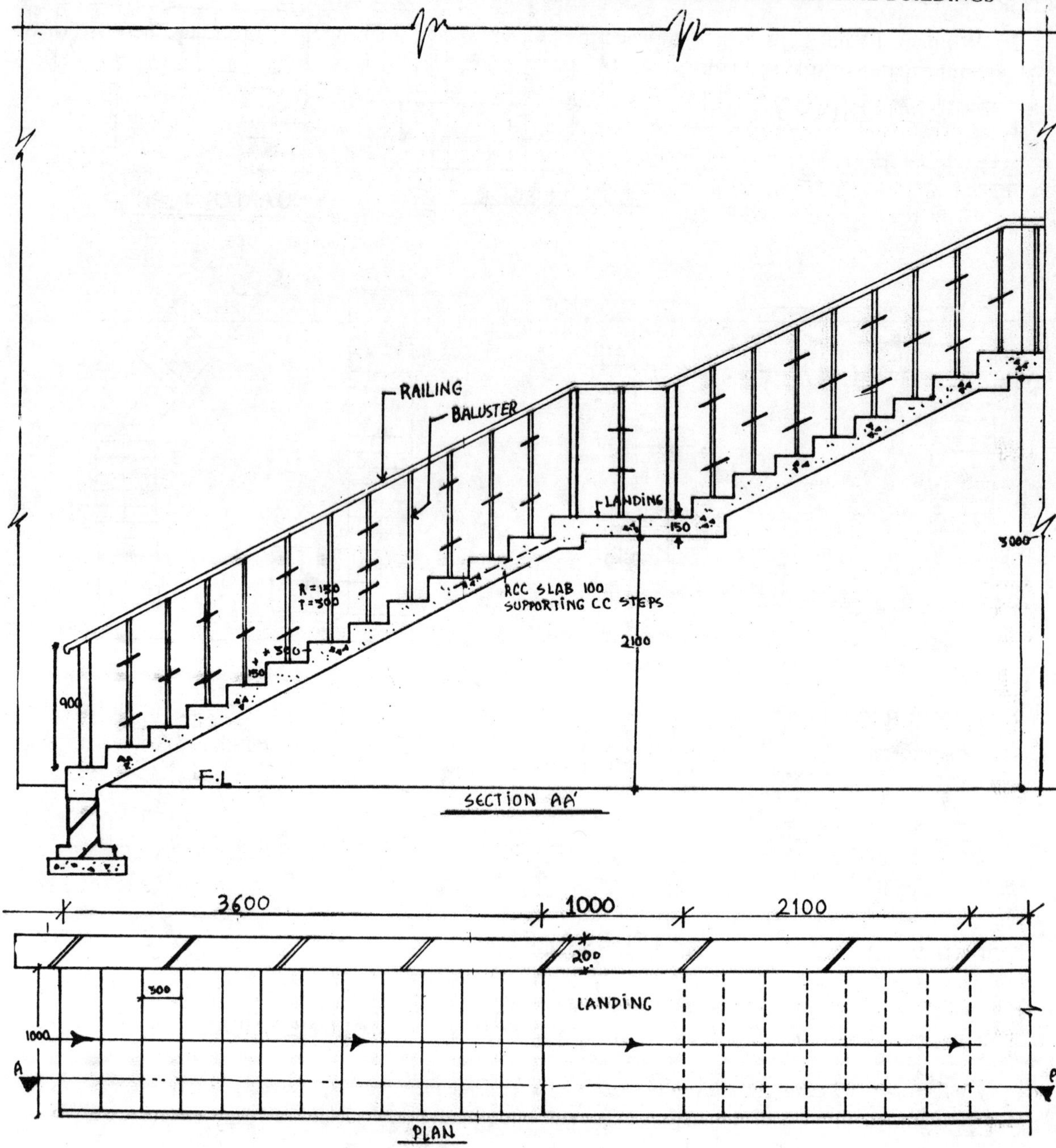


Fig. 4.2. Straight Flight Sta.rcase

**20. Winders.** Radial steps, which are used in place of landing to change the direction. These are wider on the external, side and tapered inside.

### 4.3. TYPES OF STAIRS (Fig. 4.1)

### 4.4. GEOMETRICAL CLASSIFICATION

They are classified as below:

1. Straight flight stair. [With or without intermediate landing]
2. Quarter turn stair
3. Half turn stair:
   - 3.1. Doglegged stair
   - 3.2. Open well stair
4. Three Quarter turn stair
5. Bifurcated stair
6. Geometrical stair
7. Circular stairs
8. Spiral stair
9. Rise and tread stair

### 4.5. STRAIGHT FLIGHT STAIR

This type of stair consist of one or more long and narrow flight in one direction only. Landing should be provided to break the continuity of flight (Fig. 4.2)

### 4.6. DOGLEGGED STAIR

Flight runs in opposite direction and there is no space between flights in plan. This type of stair is generally recommended for residential buildings. (Fig. 4.3)

### 4.7. QUARTER TURN STAIR

This stair turns through 90 degree or one right angle. Landing or winders are provided at quarter space junctions. (Fig. 4.4)

### 4.8. OPEN WELL STAIRS

Flight runs in opposite direction and there is a space (well) between the flights in plan. This stair is generally used in public buildings. (Fig. 4.5)

### 4.9. GEOMETRICAL STAIR

It is similar to the open well stair but only difference is that the open well between the forward and backward flights is curved. Winders are used to change the direction. (Fig. 4.6)

### 4.10. CIRCULAR OR SPIRAL STAIRS

In this type of stairs, all steps radiates from a newel post at the center and in the forms of winders. This stair is generally provided at the back side of the building, for rendering access to its various floors for service purposes.

### 4.11. BIFURCATED STAIR

In this stair, flights are so arranged that there is a wide flight at the start which splits in to two narrow flights at the landing. The two narrow flights start from either side of the mid landing. It is generally used in public building and bungalows. (Fig. 4.7)

### 4.12. RISE AND TREAD STAIR

This type of stair is called as a slab less stair because the riser and one half of each tread on either side is supposed to be a independently a beam having Z shape cross section. (Fig. 4.8)

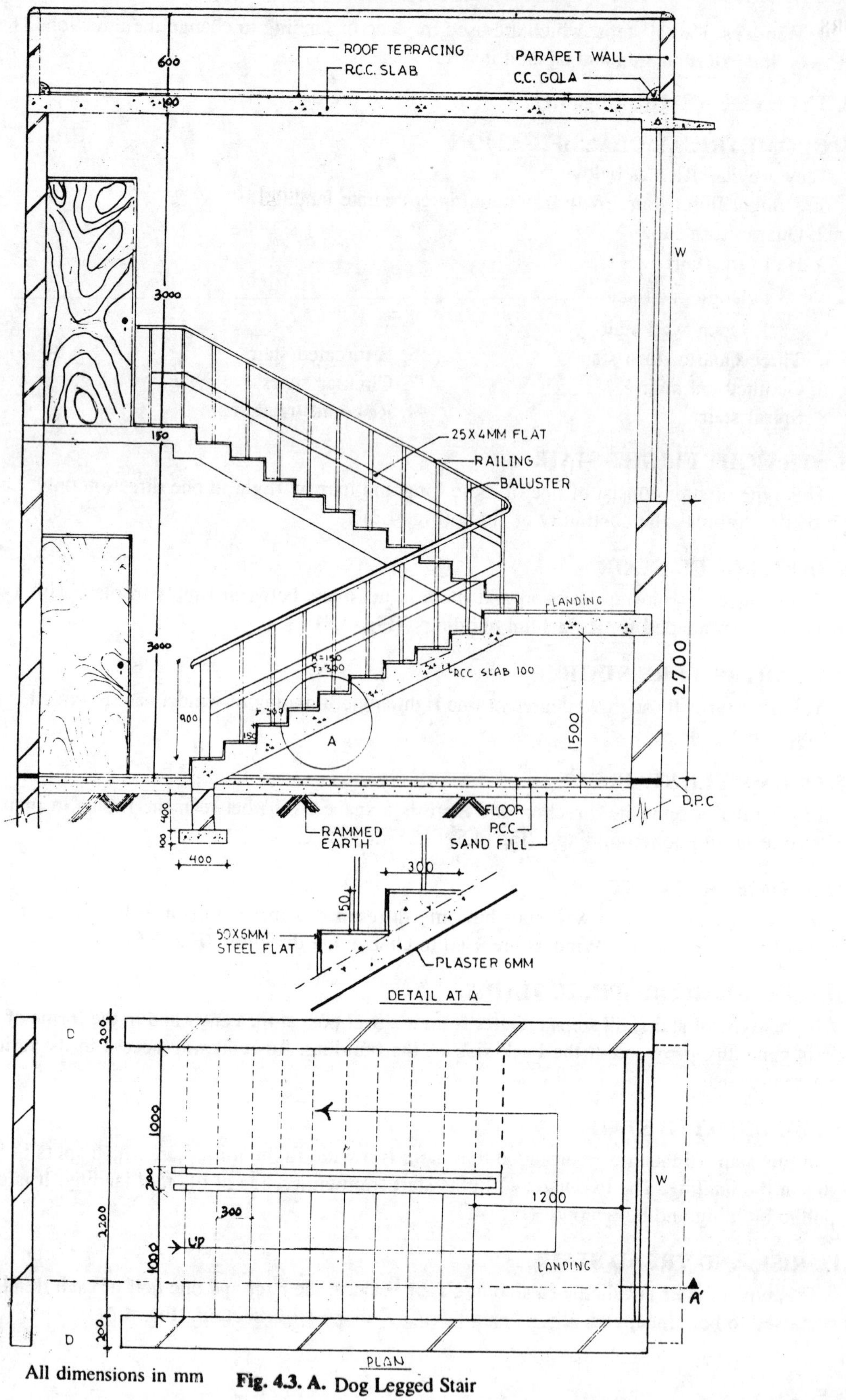


All dimensions in mm

**Fig. 4.3. A.** Dog Legged Stair

# DETAILS OF STAIRCASE

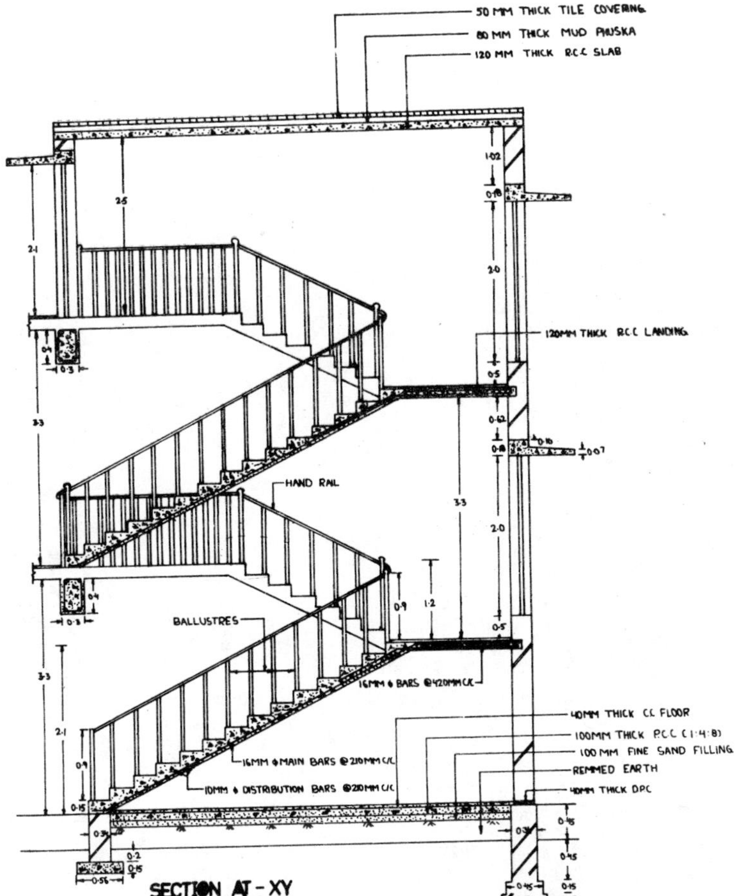


SECTION AT - XY

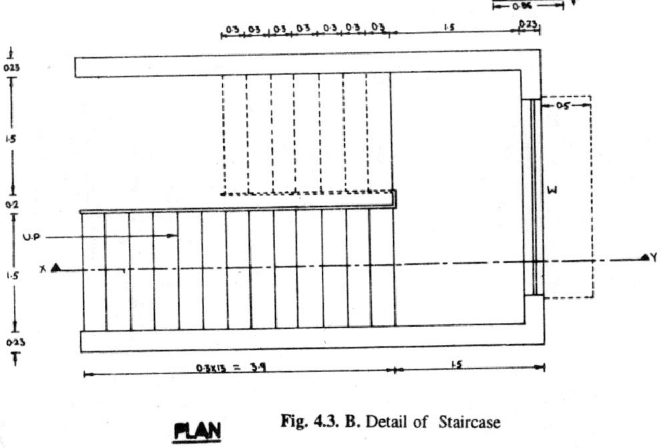


PLAN

**Fig. 4.3. B.** Detail of Staircase

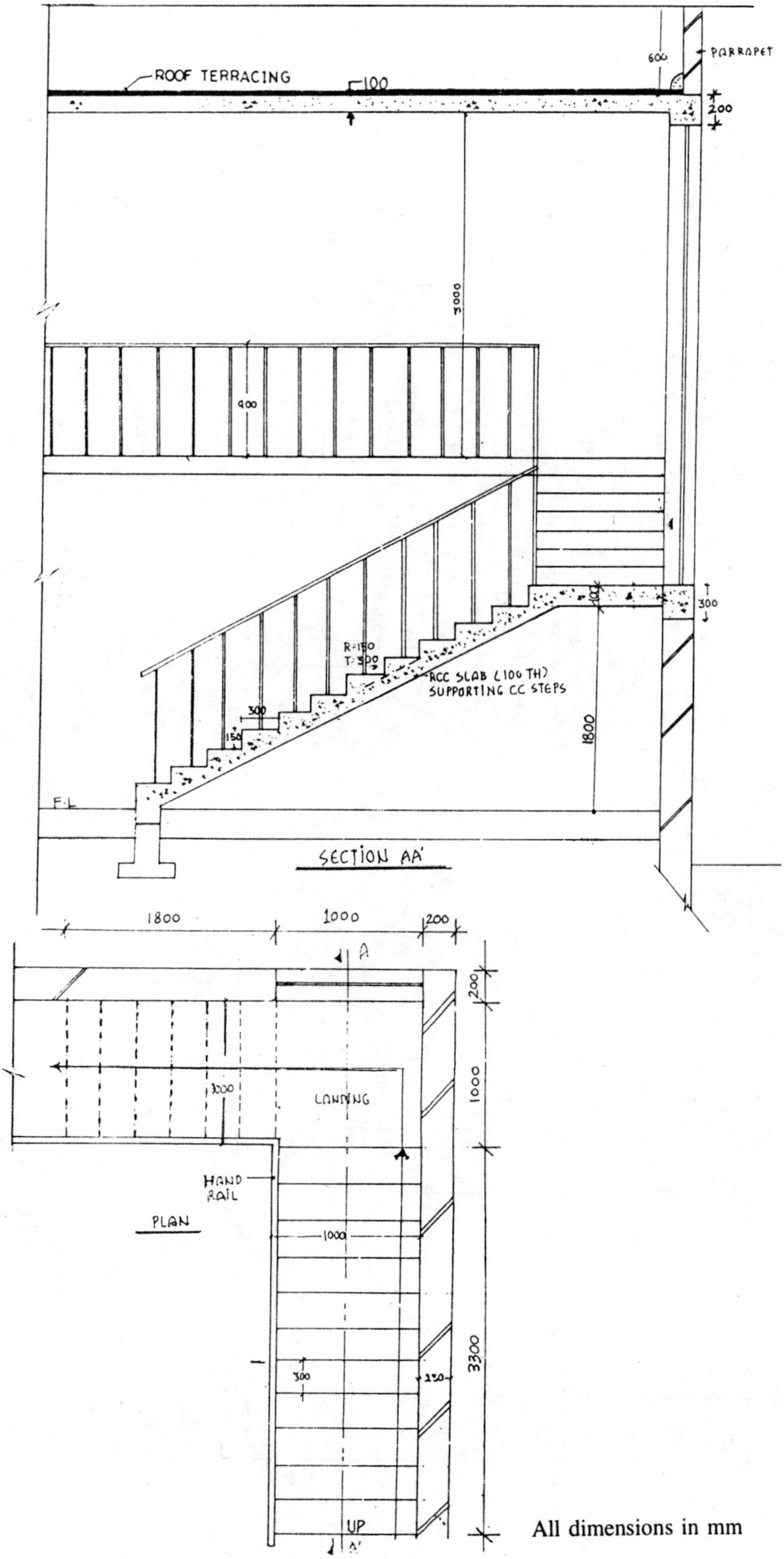


All dimensions in mm

**Fig. 4.4.** Quarier Turn Stairs

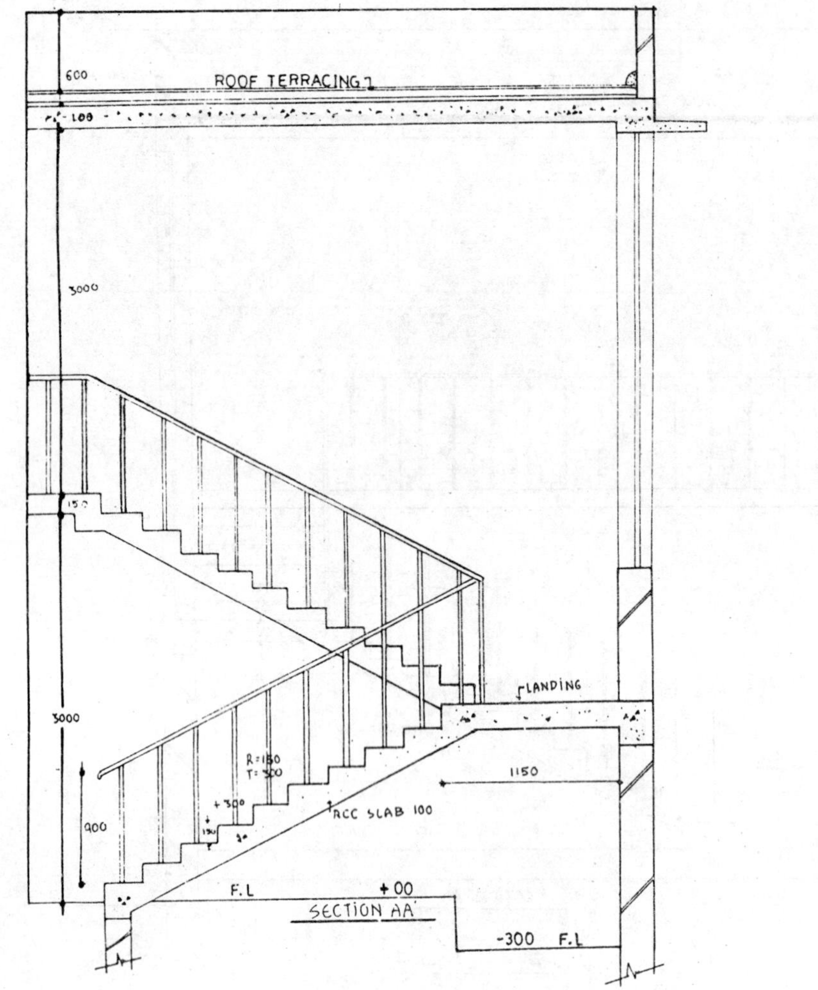


All dimensions in mm

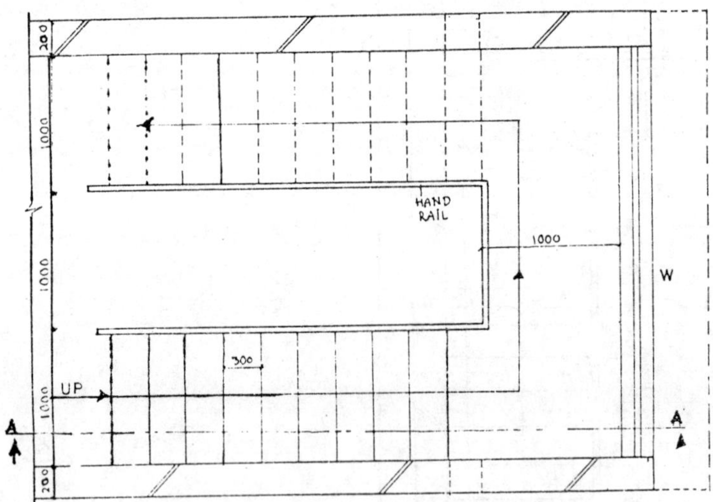


**Fig. 4.5.** Open well stair case (Plan)

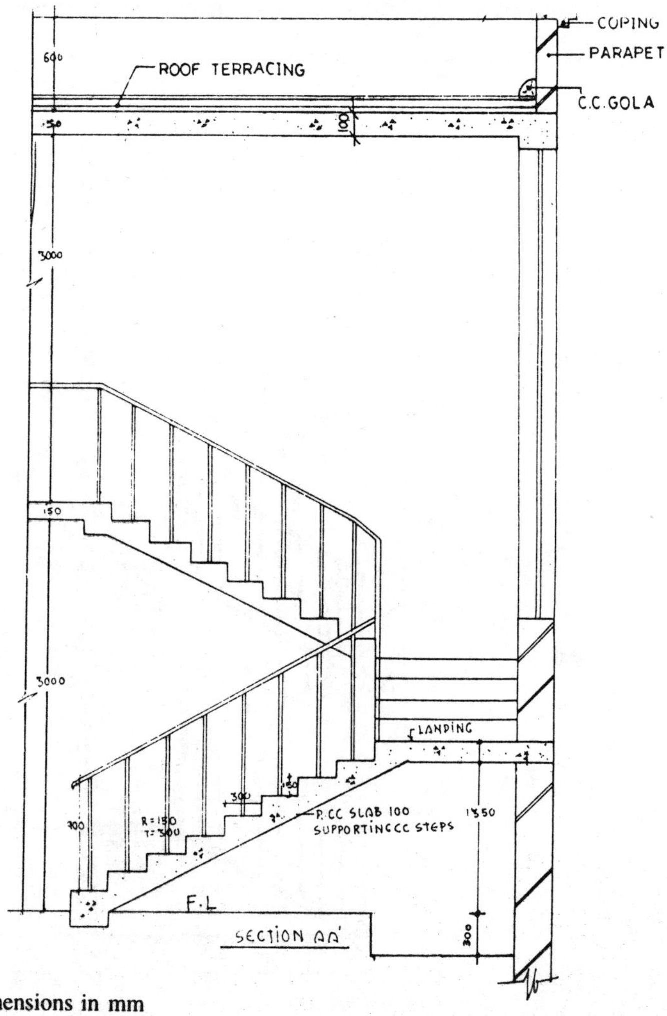


All dimensions in mm

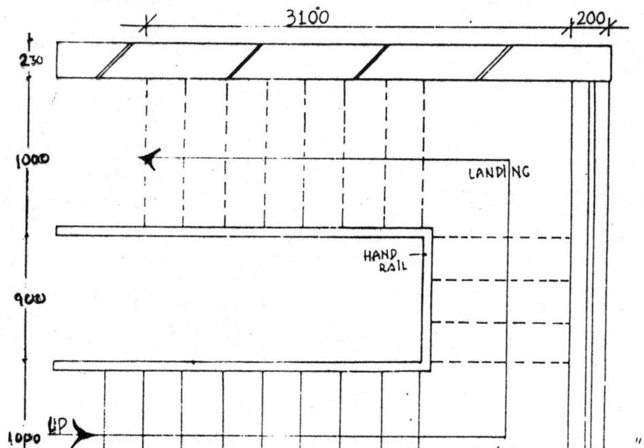


**Fig. 4.6. A.** Geometrical stairs

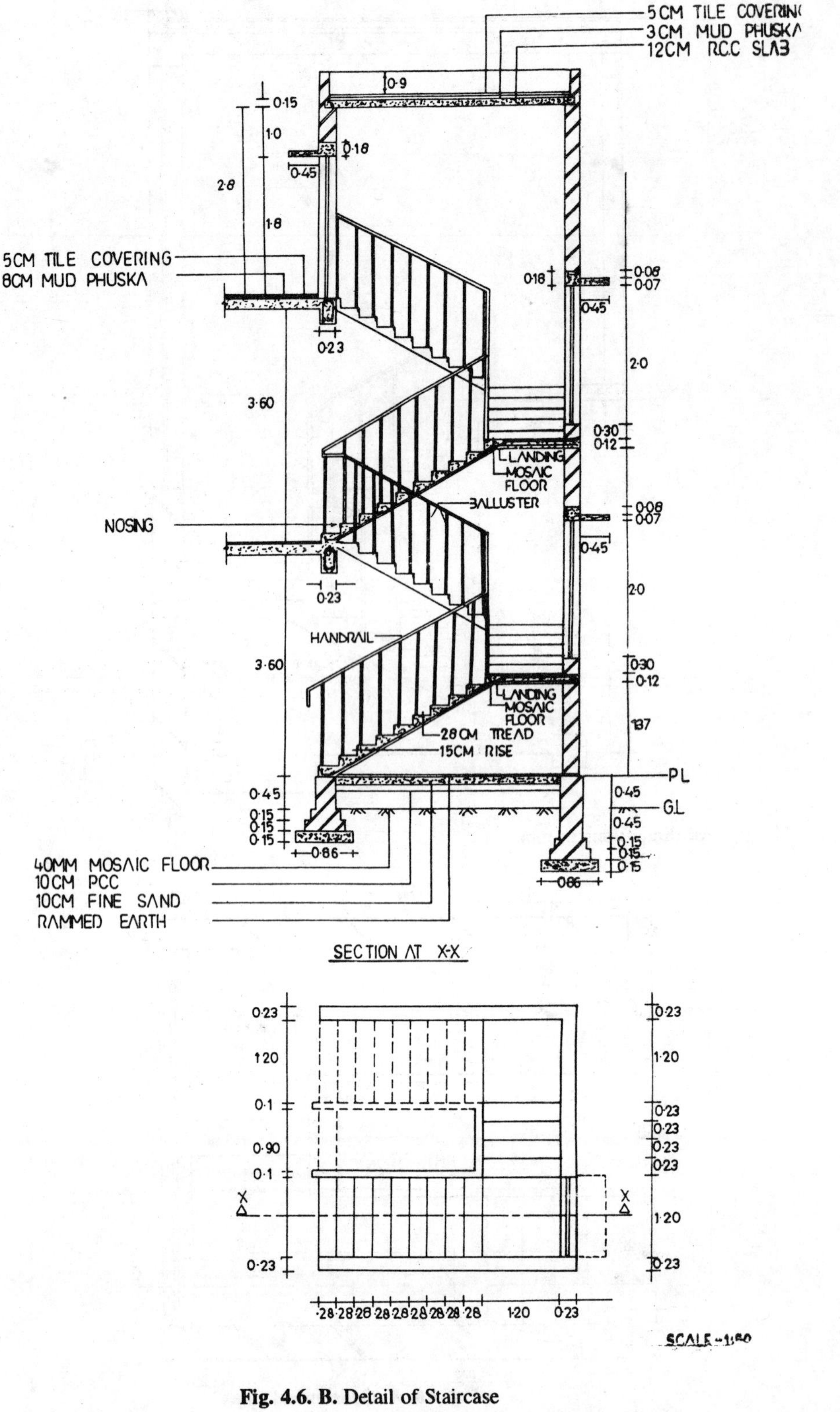


**Fig. 4.6. B.** Detail of Staircase

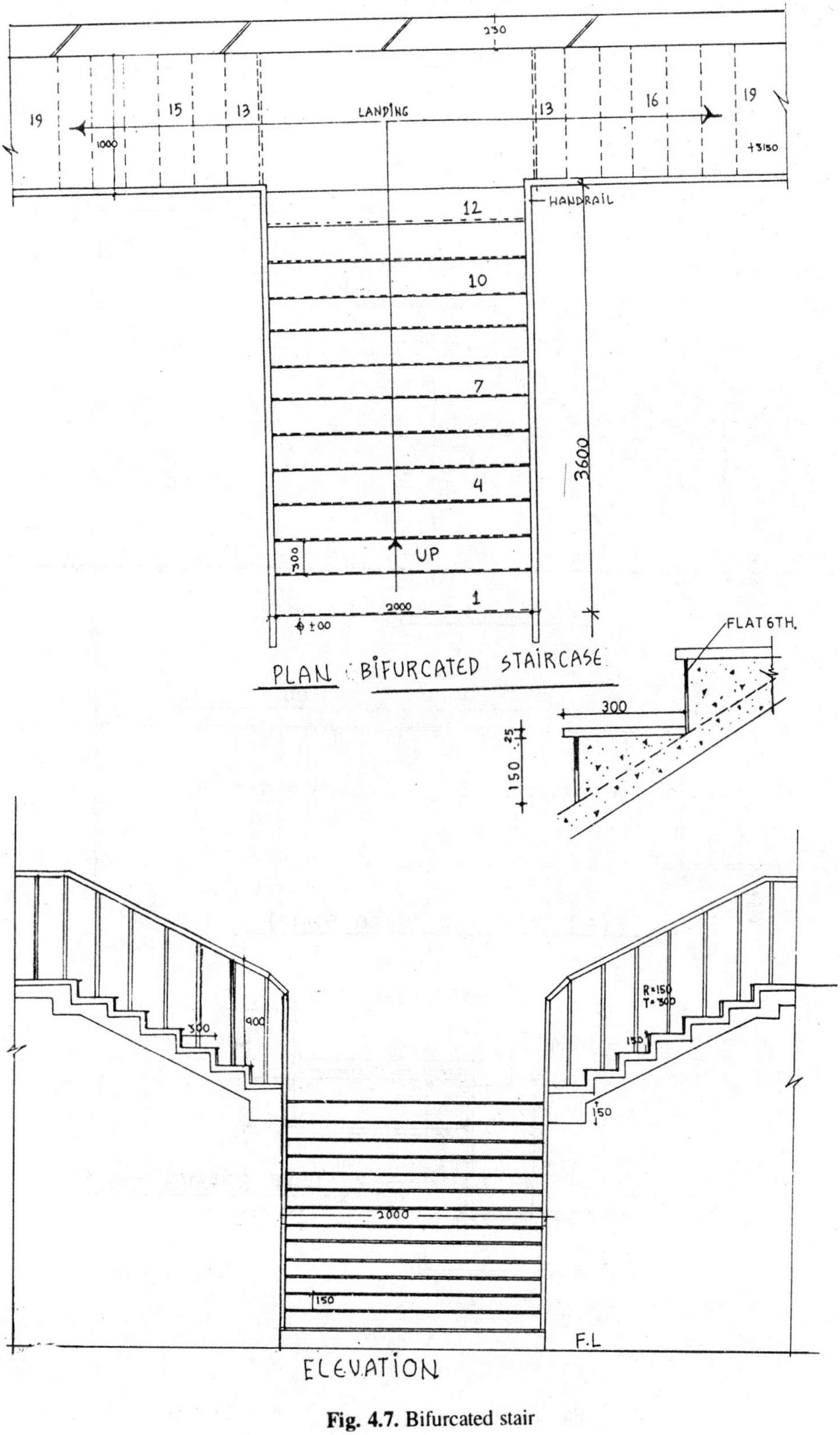


**Fig. 4.7.** Bifurcated stair

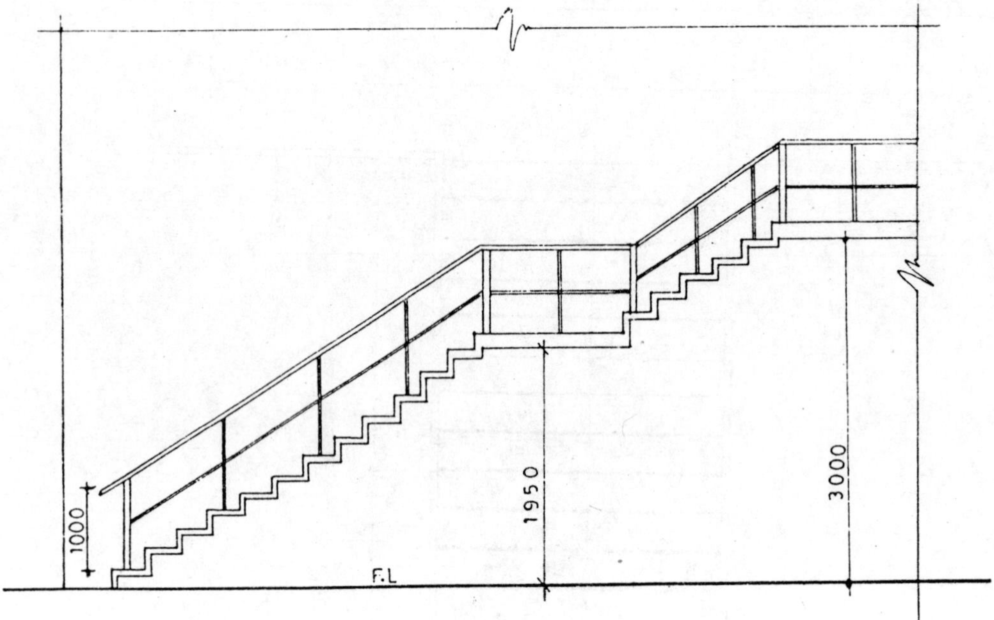


ELEVATION

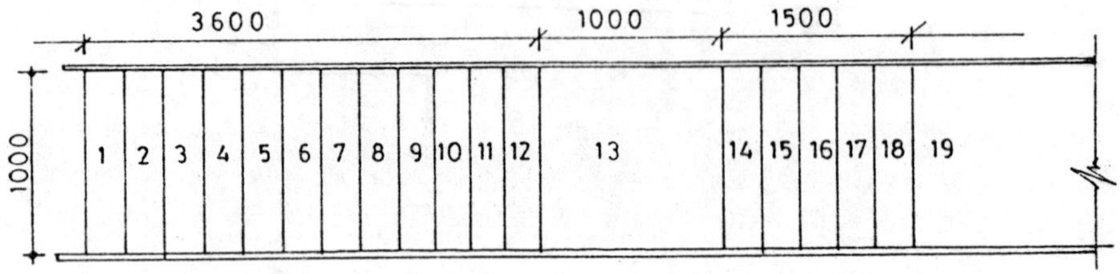


PLAN (RISE AND TREAD STAIR)

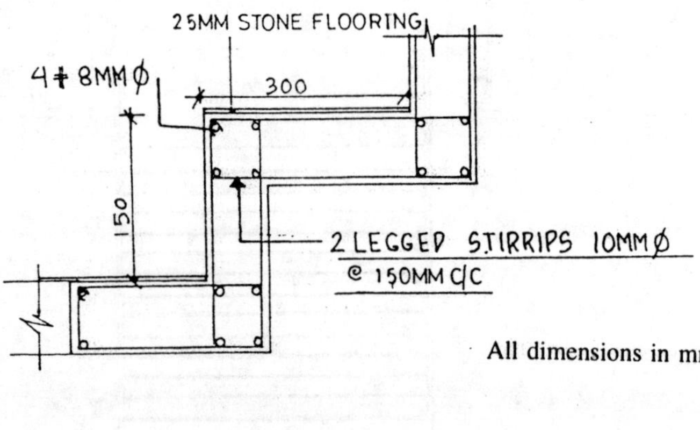


All dimensions in mm

**Fig. 4.8.** Reinforcement Detail

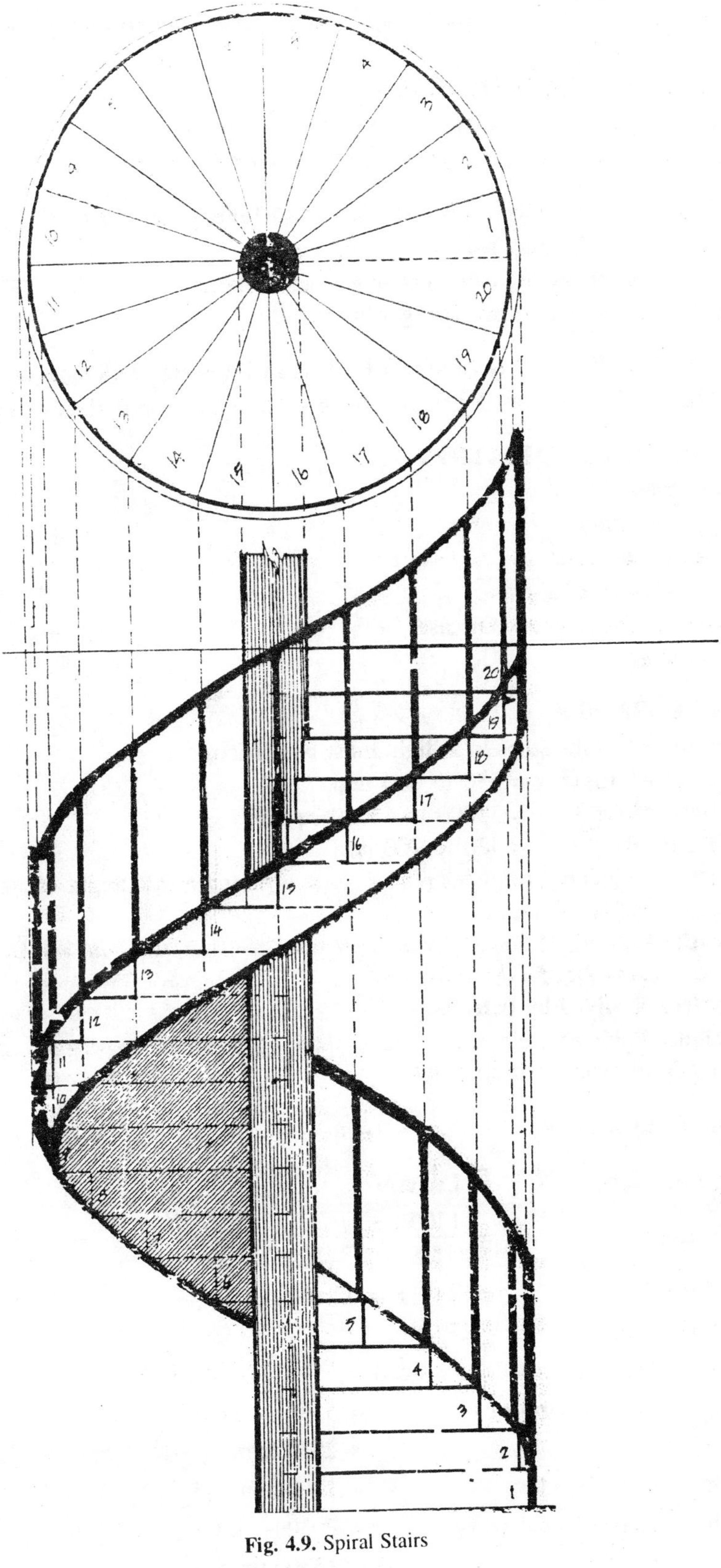

**Fig. 4.9.** Spiral Stairs

## 4.13. STRUCTURAL CLASSIFICATION

A. Waist slab spanning transversely [along the width of flight]

B. Waist slab spanning longitudinally [along the length of flight]

## 4.14. WAIST SLAB SPANNING TRANSVERSELY [along the width of flight]

1. Cantilever slab projecting from a spandrel beam
2. Cantilever slab projecting from a central spandrel beam
3. Waist slab supporting on two-stringer beam

## 4.15. WAIST SLAB SPANNING LONGITUDINALLY [along the length of flight]

All stairs such as quarter-turn, doglegged, open well, circular, and bifurcated comes under this category.

## 4.16. MATERIAL CLASSIFICATION

Wooden staircase

Stone masonry staircase

Brick masonry staircase

Reinforced brickwork staircase

Reinforced cement concrete staircase

Steel stair case

## 4.17. DESIGN FORMULA

Tread and rise of all the steps in a flight must be constant.

I. Tread +2*Rise = 550 to 600 mm

II. Tread *Rise = 38000 to 42000 sq mm

III. Tread *Rise = 420 to 700 mm

No of riser = [ceiling height+depth of floor + floor finish]/Height of riser

No of tread = No of riser-1

**Example 4.1.** *A room of 5.5 m × 2.4 m is provided for staircase. The height of building including slab and floor finish is 3.4m. Design the staircase.*

**This problem is solved by three way.**

**Ist Solution.** Width of stair hall is more than 1.2m hence dog-legged stair be suitably arranged (Number of treads are equal in each flight)

Height of each flight $= \frac{3.4}{2} = 1.7$ m

Height of riser = 150 mm

No of riser $= \frac{1700}{150} = 12$

No of tread = 12 − 1 = 11

Width of tread = 270 mm

Space required for provided 11 tread = 11 × 270 = 2970

Space left for two landing = 5500 − 2970

= 2530 mm

Width of bottom landing = 1200 mm

Width of intermediate landing = 2530 − 1200

= 1330 mm

**IInd Solution.** Taking Width of each flight = 1.1 m and provided open well stair.

Height of each flight $= \dfrac{3.4}{2} = 1.7$ m

Height of riser = 150 mm

No of riser $= \dfrac{1700}{150} = 12$

No of tread = 12 – 1 = 11

Width of tread = 270 mm

Space left between flight = 2400 – (2 × 1100) = 200 mm

Space required for provided 11 tread = 11 × 270 = 2970

Space left for two landing = 5500 – 2970 = 2530 mm

Width of bottom landing = 1200 mm

Width of intermediate landing= 2530 – 1200 = 1330 mm

**III rd Solution.** Provided doglegged stair of 1.2 m wide flight and number of treads are not equal in each flight.

Height of first flight = 2100 mm

Height of riser = 150 mm

No of riser $= \dfrac{2100}{165} = 13$

No of tread = 13 – 1 = 12

Height of second flight = 3400 – 2100 = 1300 mm

No of riser $= \dfrac{1300}{165} = 8$

No of tread = 8 – 1 = 7

Width of tread = 270 mm

Space required for provided 12 tread = 12 × 270 = 3240 mm

Space required for provided 7tread = 7 × 270 = 1890 mm

Space left for two landing = 5500 – 3240 = 2260 mm

Width of bottom landing = 1000 mm

Width of intermediate landing = 2260 – 1000 = 1260 mm

## QUESTION FOR PRACTICE

1. Two floors of a building are to be connected by a open well stair with a difference in the height of 3.5 m between floors. The stair should be 1 m wide. Design and draw the dimensional sketches in detail.
2. Design a R.C.C spiral staircase of 2000 mm diameter to reach the mezzanine floor of a building. The floor-to-floor height is 3000 mm. Draw the plan and sectional elevation of the staircase.
3. Draw the plan and sectional elevation through first flight of a dog legged stair case. The size of the stair hall = 6000 mm × 2600 mm (clear dimension). Floor to floor height = 3600 mm. Width of one flight = 1200 mm landing width 1200 mm. Assume size of tread and rise at your ends.
4. Draw the plan and sectional elevation through first flight of an open well stair. The size of stair hall = 6000 mm × 2600 mm (inside dimensions). Floor to floor height = 3600 mm, width of stair-flight = 1200 mm, landing width = 1200 mm, width of tread = 300 mm and height of rise = 150 (Scale 1:50).

# 5

# Planning of Buildings

## 5.1. INTRODUCTION

Since the evolution of human being, the basic need has been a shelter. During the early ages the shelters were in the form of caves but as the time passed on, the need of human being kept on increasing and so the types of buildings to fulfill the various purpose. The building, which are in existence today such as residential, cultural, monumental, educational, commercial, etc are out come of architectural planning. Any building comes into existence through an idea, which is later given shape on paper through the art of building drawing. All the merits and demerits are considered very carefully before actual construction work starts.

Different areas of activities are functionally laid by making circulation diagram, than the building is planned in such a way that it fulfills the purpose for which it has been designed. This early stage of planning is in the form of single line plans. It is than change into detail working drawing, which explains it location, shape, size, and materials to be used. Lastly a model based on working drawing is made or a perspective view is drawn to clarify the shape of the building to a layman.

## 5.2. ARCHITECTURE

Architecture is a combination of art and science which transforms an idea in to a form, a design and a functional structure. It involves a combined effort of an architect, civil engineer, town planner, service consultant, contractor, project manager etc. Architecture concerns not only with external outlook of the building but also with the functional planning inside the building through the best utilization of space

## 5.3. ROLE OF AN ARCHITECT

The architect is the person who transfers an idea into a design according to the requirements of the owner. He is the man with imagination who prepares the preliminary designs and estimates. After the approval from the owner, the submission and working drawings are prepared. At this stage architect becomes the representative of the owner. Now the execution of the works starts with the help of a civil engineer and contractor. Various stages of a construction project are shown in flow diagram. (Fig. 5.1)

## 5.4. PRINCIPLES OF ARCHITECTURE

A building should be designed in such a way that it must satisfy the day-to-day needs of its users. It should be comfortable and provide protection from weather and seasons. The following principles of architecture are followed while designing any building.

## 5.5. FUNCTIONAL PLANNING

While planning any building, the aim is to utilize the spaces according to need of its users .It is very important that the purpose for which the building has been designed is fulfilled. Normally the form follows function principles is used but in certain cases where appearance of the building is the main consideration like exhibition gates, shop fronts, recreational spots, picnic spots etc function follows form principle is used.

## 5.6. DURABILITY

This principle aims is providing strength to the building. The building should be strong and durable to

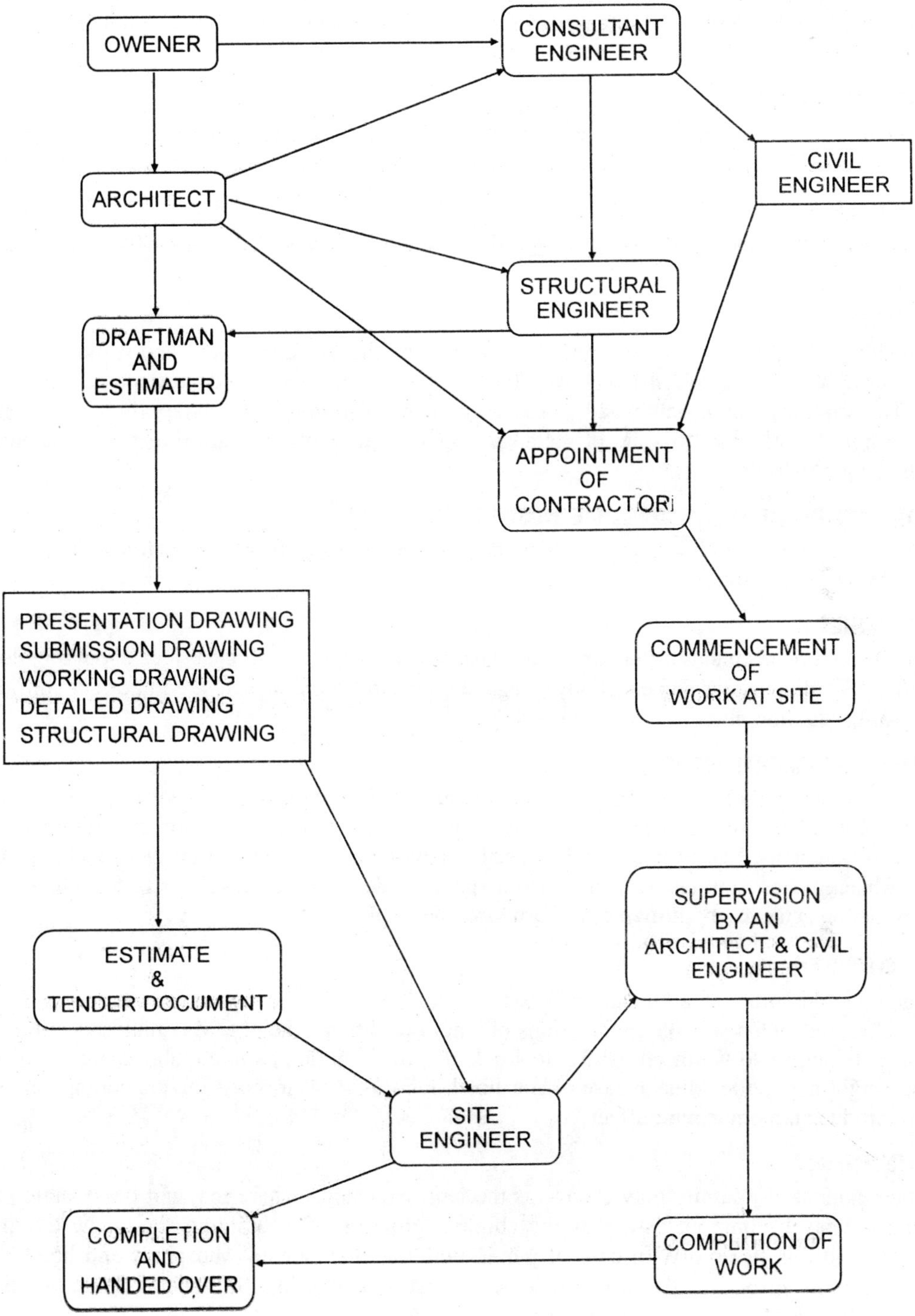
OWENER
CONSULTANT ENGINEER
CIVIL ENGINEER
ARCHITECT
STRUCTURAL ENGINEER
DRAFTMAN AND ESTIMATER
APPOINTMENT OF CONTRACTOR
PRESENTATION DRAWING
SUBMISSION DRAWING
WORKING DRAWING
DETAILED DRAWING
STRUCTURAL DRAWING
COMMENCEMENT OF WORK AT SITE
SUPERVISION BY AN ARCHITECT & CIVIL ENGINEER
ESTIMATE & TENDER DOCUMENT
SITE ENGINEER
COMPLETION AND HANDED OVER
COMPLITION OF WORK

Fig. 5.1

sustain the various loads like dead load (self weight), live load (moving load) wind loads, earth quake acceleration etc. This can be achieved by the proper structural designing of various components such as slab, beams, stair case, lintel, column, and its foundation.

## 5.7. ESSENTIAL SERVICE

This includes the sanitary fittings, water supply, electricity, air conditioning, sound insulation etc. These services should be provided with out causing any hindrance to the functional utility of the building.

## 5.8. AESTHETICS

The external appearance, outlook of the building should be beautiful and attractive and must suit the surrounding.

## 5.9. ECONOMY

The building should always be designed by considering the available funds and resources. A detailed estimates means calculation of different quantity of items to be used and abstract of cost should be prepared. The economy can be achieved by providing rooms of minimum necessary dimensions, minimum openings, simple finishes etc. In spite of rectangular plan, square plan should offers most economy as it reduces the length of walls.

## 5.10. PRINCIPLES OF PLANNING OF BUILDING

Before planning any building like a residential, commercial, educational, recreational etc the following principle taken in to account.

## 5.11. SITE VISIT

Before the commencement of planning a site visit is necessary to get a clear idea about the plot and its surroundings. The dimensions slopes (if any), vegetation, nearer buildings etc are important considerations before preparing the line plan.

## 5.12. SPACE REQUIREMENT

Every room in a building has different function and so it requires spaces. Hence the next stage is to think about the functions of the various rooms along with the space necessary. For example in case a class room the no of students, size of chair, and respective tables, no of column and rows, teaching plateform, visibility of black board from last row, movement space etc decides the capacity, size and shape of a class room. This can be achieved by drawing the furniture layout plans.

## 5.13. ROOMINESS

In planning a building, an architect deals with space. The feeling for space *i.e.* whether it is sufficient less or more depends upon suitable preparations of length, width, and height. Maximum benefit is obtained by preparing the length to width ratio 1.3:1 to 1.5:1. In case of buildings like clubs, canteens, restaurants, the ceiling height may be low but in case of star hotel, lobby, courts, airports etc the ceiling height should be more to produce a monumental effect.

## 5.14. FLEXIBILITY

The requirement of a family may change as the family expands. There may not be separate rooms for children but it may become necessary as the children grow up. The building should be designed with special regards to this flexibility. In case of public buildings like schools, hospitals and hotels etc there should be flexibility in planning to accommodate any future expansions In general flexibility allows the same space to be used for some other purposes.

## 5.15. SANITATION

This deals with the proper drainage of sewage and rainwater. The level of the building is kept a little higher with respect to the roads and streets for the good drainage. Proper lighting and ventilation is very important in all the rooms. To achieve this, the doors, windows and ventilators should be placed suitably.

## 5.16. LIGHTING

This is very important from the view of illumination and hygiene. Lighting is of two types.

**Natural lighting:** Sun is the source of natural lighting which illuminates as well as destroys germs. In case of hot climates, the area of windows should be one-seventh of the floor area of room.

**Artificial lighting:** It is required to replace natural lighting. Proper lighting in an office or factory may increase the efficiency of the workers. Lighting should not be of very high illumination as it may effects the eyes. The illumination is measured in lux, which is lumen per square meter.

## 5.17. CLEANLINESS

Smoke and dust is not desirable in a building as it allows the growth causing microorganisms. The corners, cornices, skirting are the places of dust accumulation.

## 5.18. VENTILATION

The system of supplying or removing air by natural or mechanical means to or from any enclosed room to maintain comfortable condition is called as ventilation.

1. **Natural ventilation.** It is suitable for residential units and can be achieved by placing windows and ventilators opposite to each other. The window area should not be less then 25% of the wall area on which the window is to be provided.
2. **Artificial ventilation.** This becomes necessary when more then 45 persons occupy the room. Exhaust and extract system is the widely used artificial ventilation

## 5.19. ORIENTATION

It is the placement of building in such a way that it derives maximum benefits from the natural elements such as sun, wind, rain and topography. Different units in a building have different functions. For example in case of residential building following points should be taken into consideration.

1. The bedroom should face eastward so that morning sunshine enters into the room.
2. The living room should face east or north
3. Windows should be located in a such a way that remain visual control on the main entrance orientation help in creating a comfortable conditions in a building and there fore should always be kept in mind while planning.

## 5.20. PRIVACY: PRIVACY IS OF TWO TYPES

1. Privacy in different units of a building. This can be achieved by correct position of doors and shutters. The shutter when opened should give a minimum view of the other room. Single shutter may be preferred.
2. Privacy of the whole building from the surrounding buildings, road and street. This can be achieved by screening, planting of creepers and plants.

## 5.21. ELEGANCE

Elegance is related to the effect produced by the external look (elevation) of the building. The elevation of a building mostly depends upon the blocking, color scheme, finishing material and vegetation.

## 5.22. ECONOMY

In most of the cases, financial resources inhabit the freedom of an architect, Design should be based on the available resources but scope for future expansion should always be taken into design. Economical design can be achieved by providing rooms of minimum necessary dimensions, minimum openings, simple finishing etc.

# 6
# Residential Buildings

## 6.1. RESIDENTIAL BUILDINGS

Civil and architectural views are normally drawn in third angle projection. Before designing and drawing the building following definitions should be understood clearly.

## 6.2. DEFINITIONS

**PLAN.** The views projected to horizontal plane and observed from the above are called Plans. The building is imagined to be cut by a horizontal plane at a chest level of man of a normal height, which is taken as1.5 m from floor level.

**ELEVATION.** The views projected to vertical plane and observed from any side of the building are called Elevation. This view gives information about the height and width/ length, external finishes of the building. It can be observed as front, back, and sides Elevation.

**SECTION.** It is the projected view of the building cut by a vertical plane showing various details of the building components such as width of wall and footing, depth of slab, beam and lintel, thickness of concrete in floor and foundation, DPC, height of parapet, depth of foundation etc and their respective levels.

**AXONOMETRIC VIEWS.** It is an orthographic projection drawn by tilting the plan at 30, 45 and 60 degree by considering the height of the building up to chest level. In another words axonometric view is a three dimensional projection of a plan.

## 6.3. PRINCIPLES OF PLANNING FOR A RESIDENTIAL BUILDINGS

A Residential Buildings such as detached house, Bungalow or an apartment can be divided in to four major areas *i.e.*, Living, Sleeping, Service and circulation.

## 6.4. LIVING AREA

This includes living room and drawing room. Following considerations should be taken in to account while planning living area.

Living\drawing room should be near to the entrance.

Dining room should be attached to living area.

It should offer a pleasant view of lawn& garden

It should be located on a south face.

## 6.5. SLEEPING AREA

This includes bedrooms with or without attached toilets. The bedroom should be located on north or east face. While designing sleeping area privacy should be kept in mind and position of bed should be in the direction of air movement.

## 6.6. SERVICE AREA

This includes kitchen dining and toilets.

## 6.7. KITCHEN

Generally it is provided in front of main gate and is attached to dinning room having approachable from out side. Kitchen should face on eastern direction. Window should be provided for well ventilation and proper dispose off smoke and heat. Kitchen should be design in such a way that refrigerator, Owen, sink, and a number of shelves can be easily adjusted.

## 6.8. DINING ROOM

It is the area where the meals are served there for it should be close to kitchen, so that catering of food should be easy. A service window may also be provided between kitchen and dining room. One cub board for keeping utensils and a washbasin for washing hand must be adjusted in it.

## 6.9. TOILETS

They may be attached to bedrooms but also be approachable from other rooms. There should be proper ventilation, good drainage and availability of water supply round the clock. Separate w.c and bathroom should also be provided. Walls may be finished with ceramic tiles.

## 6.10. CIRCULATION AREA

Passages, corridors, lobbies and lounges come under horizontal Circulation while stairs ramps elevators and lifts are provided for vertical circulation.

**Passage.** It is an open area out side the building for easy movement and proper ventilation.

## 6.11. CORRIDORS

It is a covered passage inside a house for independent entrance to connect other components of the building.

## 6.12. LOBBY

Well-ventilated and centrally located hall provided for connecting to the other parts of the building.

## 6.13. PORCH AND PORTICO

Impart beauty to a building in addition to safety and security in front of building for parking of vehicles etc. The slab of porch is rested on cantilever beams while portico slab on simply supported beams.

## 6.14. STAIRCASE

It should be located at such a place in a building that it remains an easy access from all components of the building. Staircase should be well ventilated with adequate lighting arrangement. A staircase should have minimum two flights in between landings equal to minimum width of flights for comfortable to climb.

## 6.15. MINIMUM DIMENSIONS AND AREAS

| *S. No.* | *Description* | *Floor Area* | *Width* | *Height* |
|---|---|---|---|---|
| 1. | Living/drawing | 12 – 15 sqm | 2.4 | 2.75 |
| 2. | Bed room | 10 – 12 | 2.4 | 2.75 |
| 3. | Kitchen | 4.5 – 6.0 | 1.8 | 2.75 |
| 4. | Kitchen cum store | 5.0 – 6.5 | 1.8 | 2.75 |
| 5. | Toilet | 2.8 | 1.2 | 2.2 |
| 6. | Bath room | 1.5 | 1.2 | 2.2 |
| 7. | Water closet | 1.0 | 0.9 | 2.2 |
| 8. | Verandah | — | 1.8 m | 2.5 |
| 9. | Dressing | 6.0 – 7.5 | 1.5 | 2.2 |

| S. No. | Description | Floor Area | Width | Height |
|---|---|---|---|---|
| 10. | Box room | 6.0 – 10 | 1.5 | 2.2 |
| 11. | Garage | 10.0 | 2.05 | 2.40 |
| 12. | Stair hall | 6.0 – 7.5 | 2.0 | |
| 13. | Head room | — | — | 2.1 |
| 14. | Pitch of flight | 25 – 40 degree | — | — |
| 15. | Width of flight | — | 0.9 m with landing of 1.2 m wide | — |

## 6.16. MINIMUM DEPTH

| S. No. | Description | Height (mm) |
|---|---|---|
| 1. | Plinth level | 450 to 600 from G.L. |
| 2. | Window sill level | 900 from floor level |
| 3. | Lintel level | 2100 from floor level |
| 4. | Slab level | 3000 to 3500 from floor level |
| 5. | Parapet | 600 to 900 from roof top |
| 6. | Court yard and garage | 150 from G.L. |
| 7. | Foundation for single storey | 750 to 1000 below G.L. |
| 8. | Foundation for double storey | 900 to 1200 below G.L. |
| 9. | Railight height | 850 from Tread |
| 10. | Raiser | 150 to 190 |

Minimum number of riser in one flight 12 (for residential building)
Minimum number of riser in one flight 15 (for public building)
Width of treads 200 mm to 300 mm

## 6.17. LIGHTING AND VENTILATION

| S. No. | Description | Requirement |
|---|---|---|
| 1. | Living/drawing room | 200 – 250 LUX |
| 2. | Bed room | 100 – 150 LUX |
| 3. | Kitchen | 175 – 200 LUX |
| 4. | Stair hall | 100 LUX |
| 5. | Window area | 1/10 of floor area for hot and dry climate |
| 6. | Window area | 1/7 of floor area for hot and humit climate |

**Lux:** Unit of illumination

## 6.18. OPEN SPACE (SET BACK) FOR RESIDENTIAL BUILDING

| S. No. | Size of plots (sqm) | Front (m) | Back (m) | Left side (m) | Right side (m) |
|---|---|---|---|---|---|
| 1. | Up to 40 | 1.0 | — | — | — |
| 2. | 41 to 80 | 1.5 | 2.0 | — | — |
| 3. | 81 to 120 | 2.4 | 3.0 | — | — |
| 4. | 121 to 200 | 3.0 | 3.0 | — | — |
| 5. | 201 to 350 | 3.0 | 3.0 | 1.8 | — |
| 6. | 351 to 450 | 4.5 | 4.5 | 3.0 | — |
| 7. | 451 to 600 | 4.5 | 4.5 | 3.0 | 1.8 |
| 8. | More than 600 | 6.0 | 6.0 | 3.0 | 3.0 |

## 6.19. SIZE OF SHAFT OPEN TO SKY (O.T.S)

| *S. No.* | *Storey* | *Area (sqm)* | *Min Width (m)* |
|---|---|---|---|
| 1. | 2 | 1.2 | 0.9 |
| 2. | 4 | 2.0 | 1.2 |
| 3. | 6 | 4.0 | 1.5 |
| 4. | 9 | 5.4 | 1.9 |
| 5. | 10 or more | 6.0 | 2.4 |

Open to sky or shaft generally provided for cross ventilation.

## 6.20. PLANNING AND DRAWING OF BUILDING

Before starting the construction of any project, drawing should be prepared according to functional planning and design. The drawing is completed in following stage.

1. By taking measurements
2. By single line plan
3. By standards specifications

## 6.21. BY TAKING MEASUREMENTS

In this type of drawing the measurements are taken of an existing building including thickness of walls, internal sizes of rooms, positions of doors, windows etc. and their respective heights. These measurements are plotted on drawing paper and further extension or alterations may be adjusted and drawn for the completing the drawing.

## 6.22. BY SINGLE LINE PLAN

In this type of drawing building are so adjusted on a plot that the requirements of planning are achieved including thickness of walls, internal sizes of rooms, positions of doors and windows etc. The single line plans are drawn in different combination dependent on the requirementsof the owner and best being finalized

## 6.23. BY STANDARDS SPECIFICATIONS

The settings of various rooms are designed as per the requirement. It is also decided whether proposed building is a single story or multiple one for deciding the type and size of foundation.

**Submission drawing**

Consisting of the following views:

1. Double line ground and first floors plans
2. Front elevation
3. Sectional Elevation passing through staircase
4. Terrace plan
5. Key plan
6. Site plan
7. Details of foundation
8. References

**Working drawing**

Consisting of the following views:

1. Detail Double line ground and first floors plans
2. Front elevation
3. Sectional Elevation passing through staircase
4. Detail section of building components
5. Terrace plan
6. Key plan
7. Site plan
8. Detail of foundation
9. References

## 6.24. CIRCULATION DIAGRAM

The arrangement of various components of a building in functional order can be achieved by preparing

**a circulation diagram. While preparing circulation diagram it is imagined that the designer is moving through the various spaces of the building. (Fig. 6.1)**

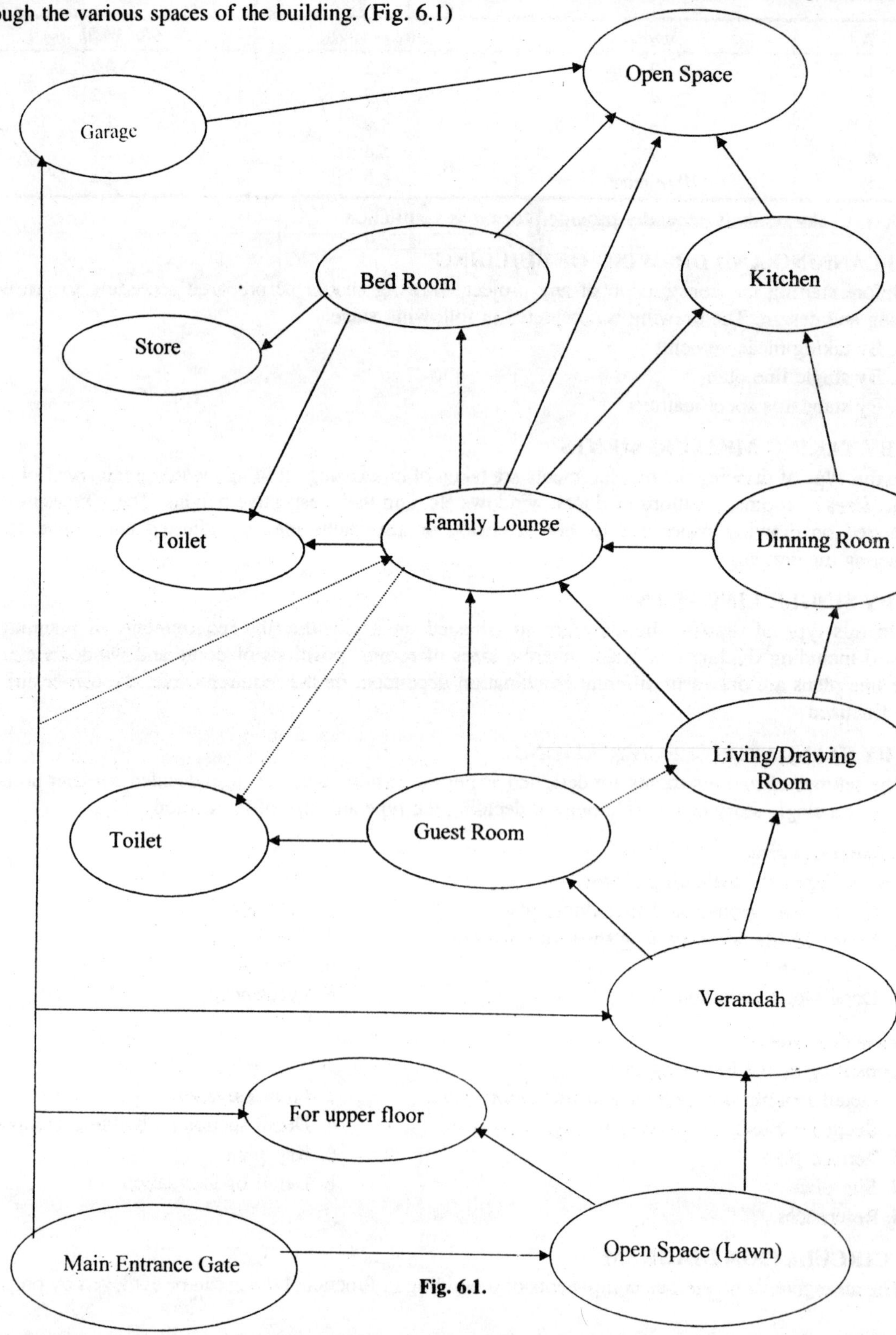


**Fig. 6.1.**

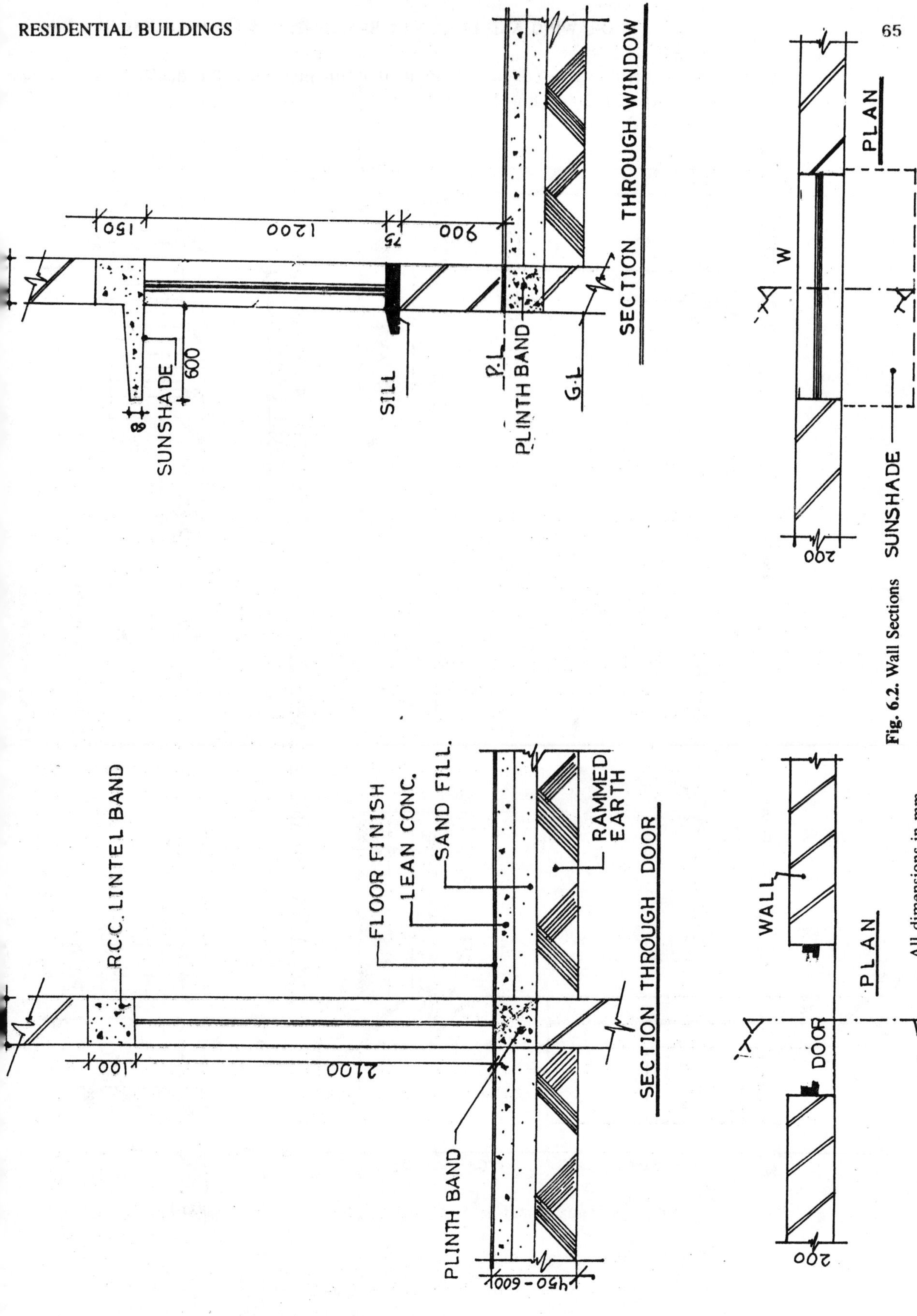


**Fig. 6.2.** Wall Sections

All dimensions in mm

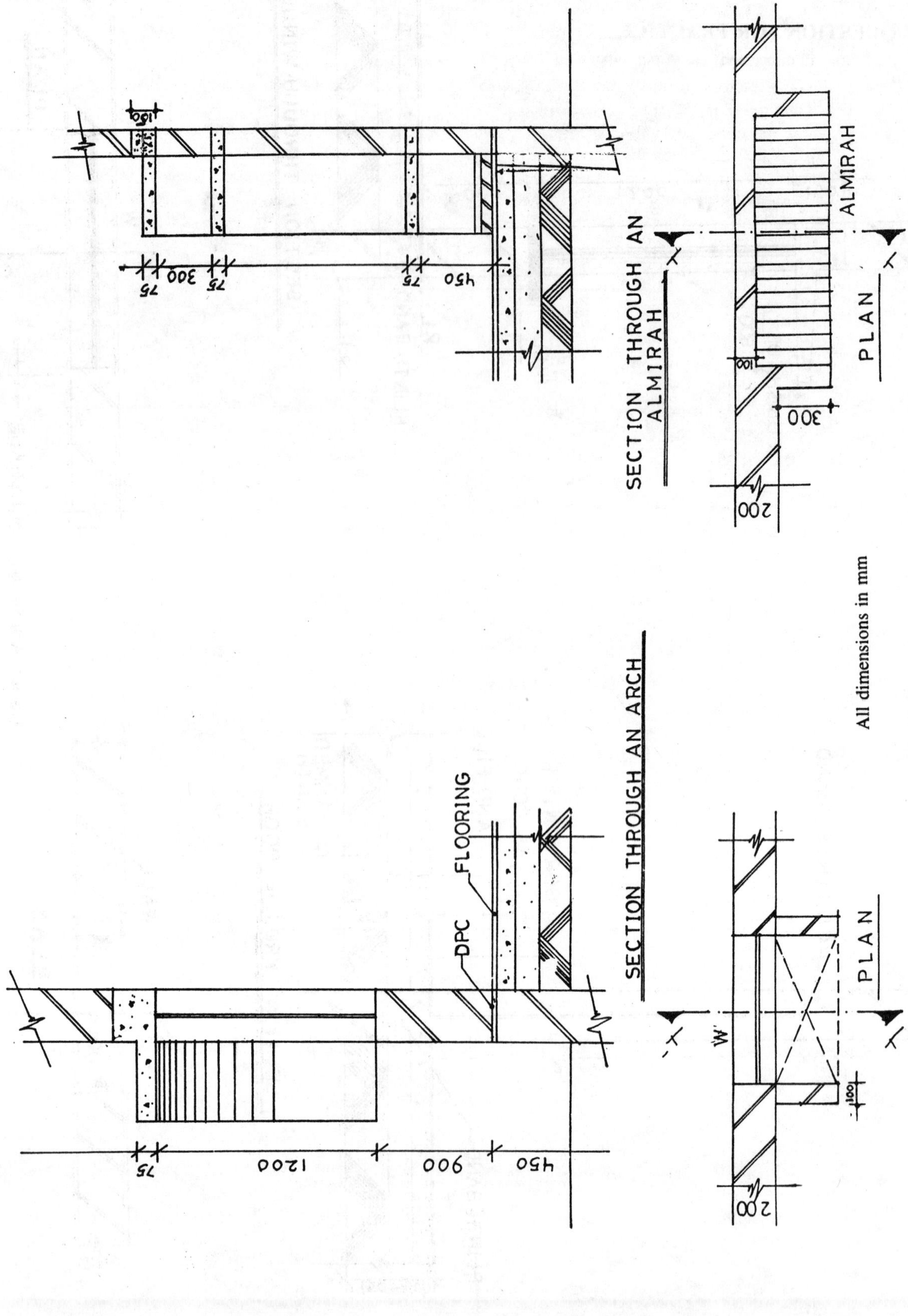


All dimensions in mm

**Fig. 6.3. Wall Sections**

## QUESTION FOR PRACTICE

Note all dimensions are in mm other wise specified

1. Draw the cross-sectional elevation of a 230 mm thick brick wall of a building taken across the door. Assuming all dimensions at your end.
2. Draw the cross-sectional elevation of a wall through a window (1.5 m × 1.5 m) in size, the thickness of wall is 200 mm. Assuming suitable data yours self.
3. Draw 230 mm thick brick wall section at a suitable scale, for double storey building showing details of all components of wall from bottom of foundation up to the parapet passing through door on the ground floor and window on first floor. Assume all data at yours end. Show the necessary sunshade and step.

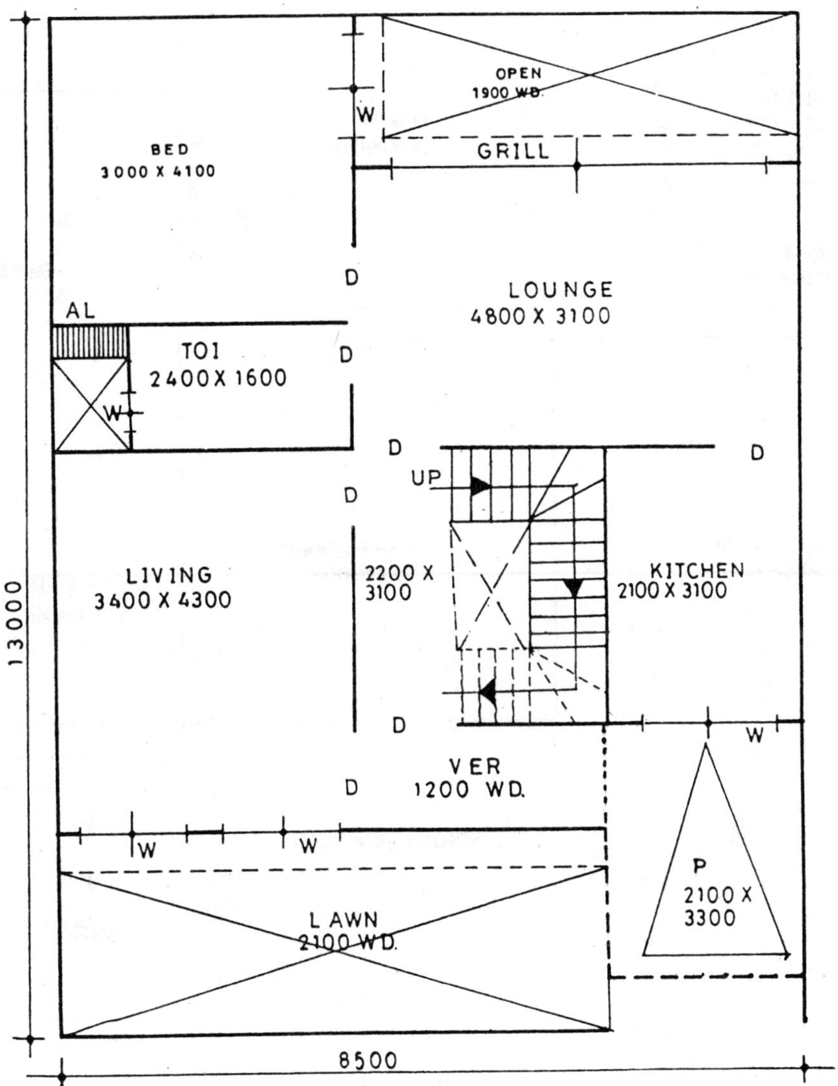


Scale-1:100 All dimensions in mm

Fig. 6.4. A.

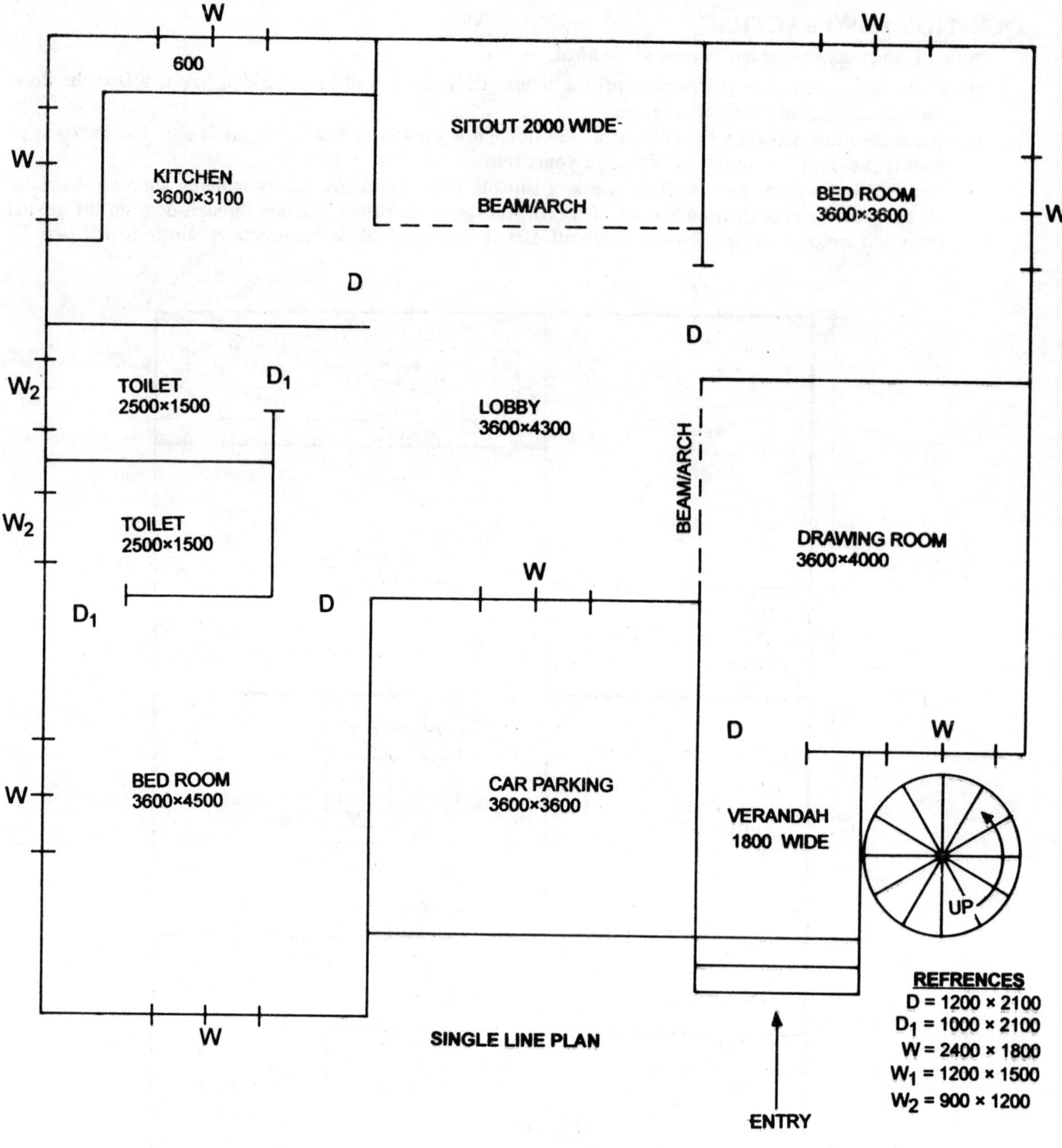


**Fig. 6.4. B.** Single Line Plan

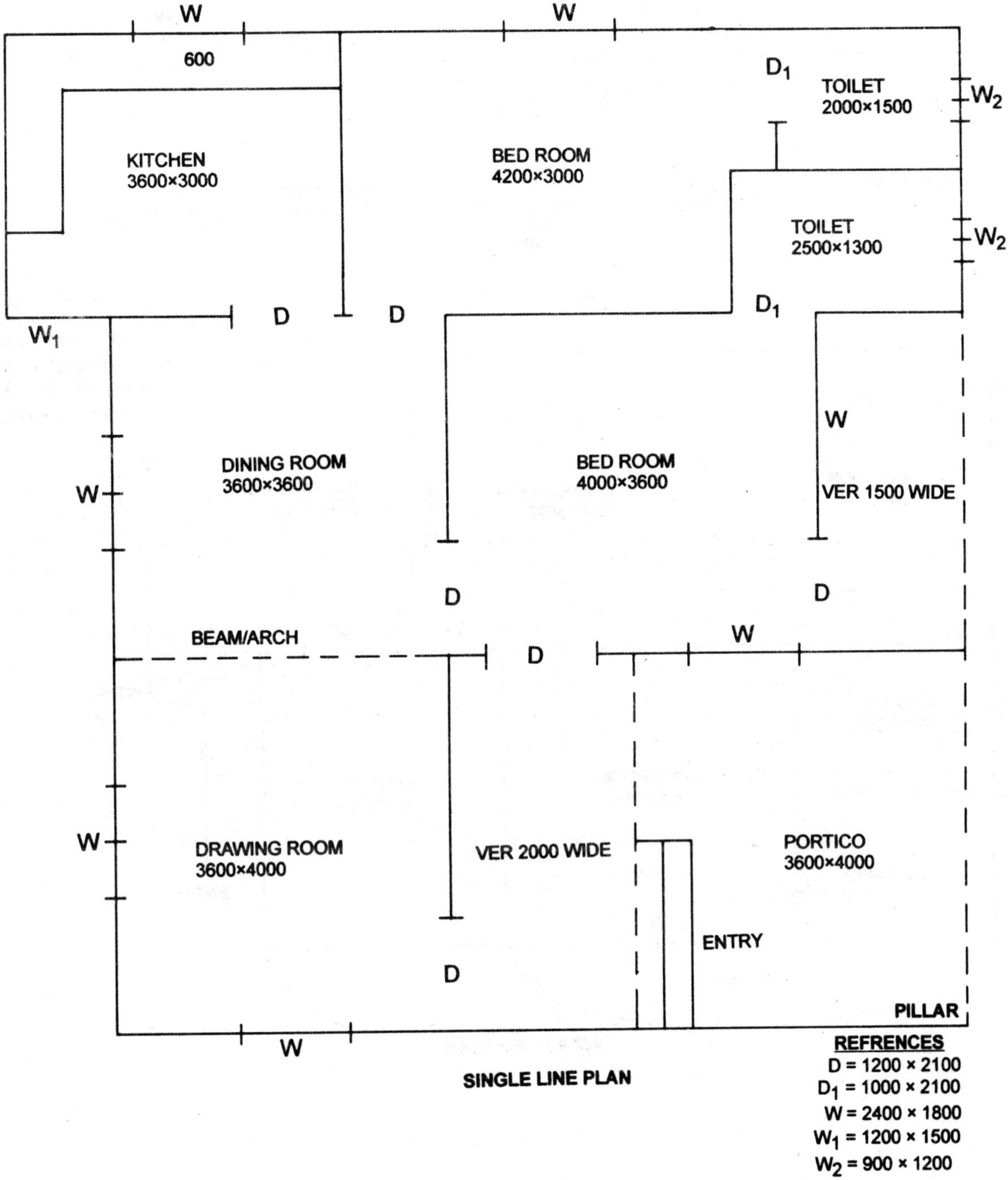


**Fig. 6.4. C.** Single Line Plan

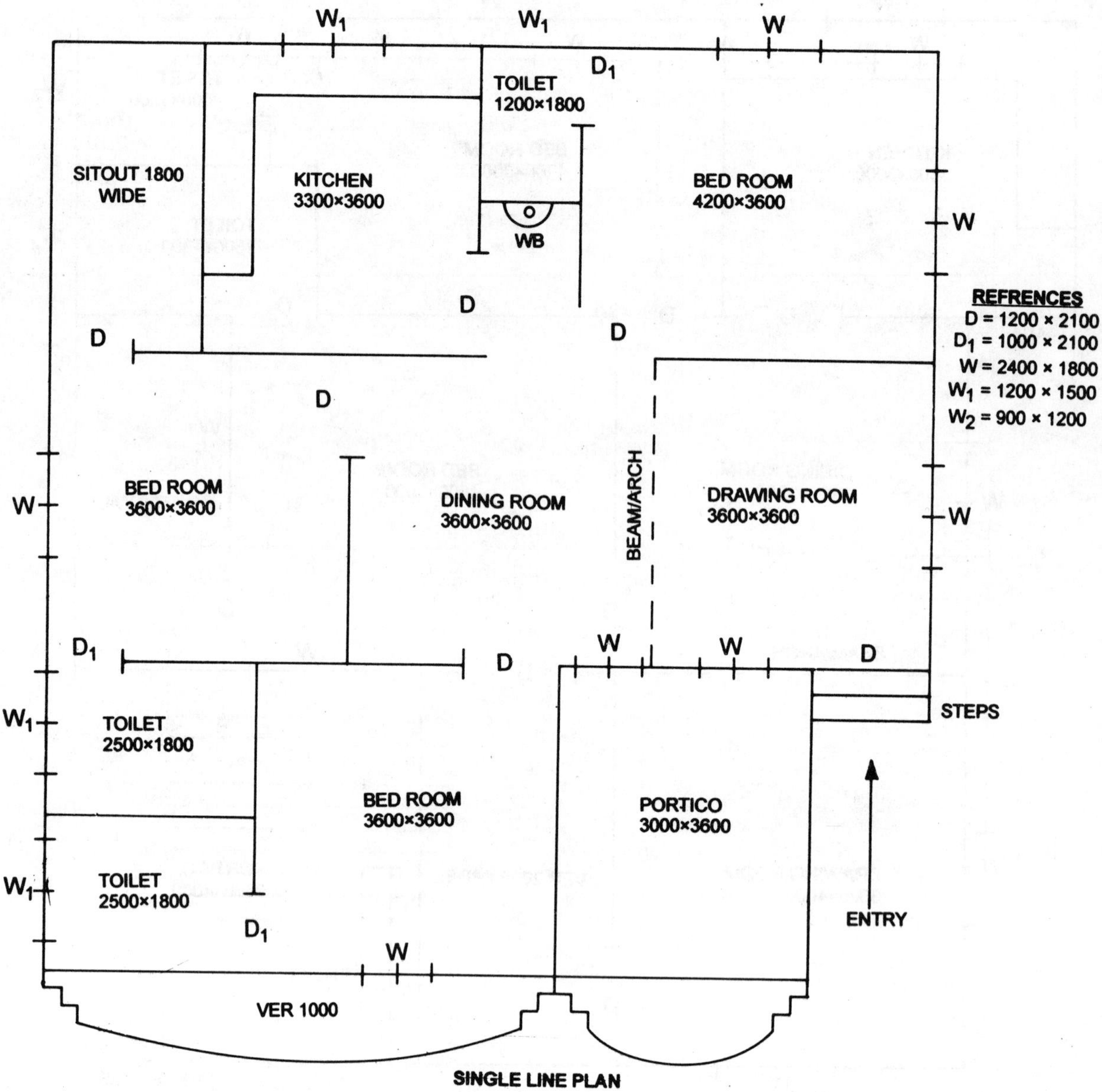


**Fig. 6.4. D.** Single Line Plan

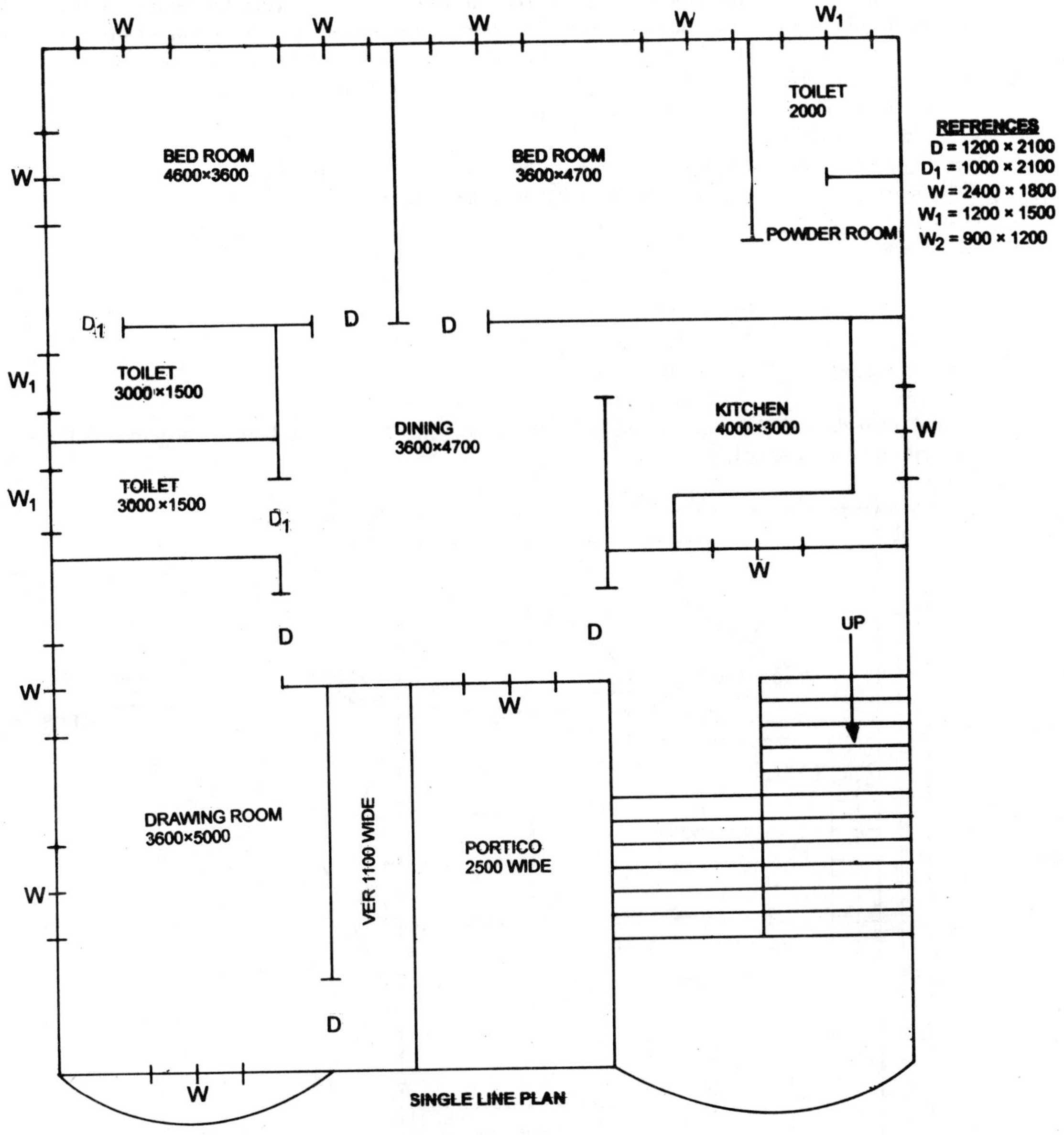


**Fig. 6.4. E.** Single Line Plan

4. Draw intermediate 230 mm thick brickwall section with a suitable scale for double storey building, showing details of all components of wall from bottom of foundation upto the ceiling of first floor passing across window on ground floor and door on first floor. Assume all other data at your end.
5. From single line plan of a building draw the following views with suitable scale:
   (*a*) Double line Plan (*b*) Front Elevation
   (*c*) Sectional elevation through AB
6. The single line plan of a residential house is shown with some specification are as under. (Fig. 6.4.A)
   Wall thickness = 200mm, other wise specified
   Level of plinth above ground = 400mm
   Size of doors:
   $D$ = 1200 × 2100
   $D_1$ = 1000 × 2100
   $D_2$ = 750 × 2100
   Size of window $w$ = 1200 × 1500
   Ventilator = 800 × 600
   Assume other data as you required and draw the double line Plan of the building at windowsill level and Front elevation to a scale1:100.

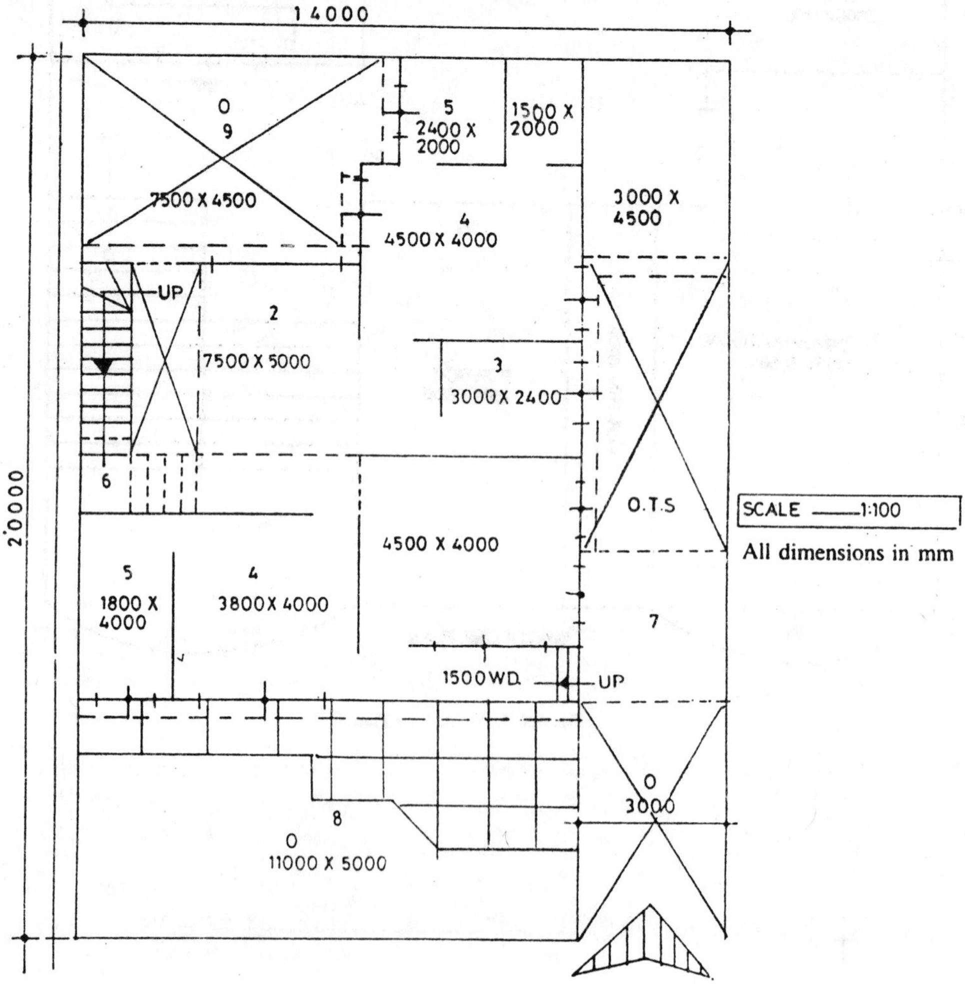


Fig. 6.5.

7. From given single line plan of a building, draw the following views with suitable scale: (Figs. 6.5 to 6.16)
   (*a*) Plan (*b*) Front Elevation
   (*c*) Section on AB

   Following are the specifications:
   (*i*) All load-bearing walls are of 200 mm thick
   (*ii*) All partition walls are of 100 mm thick
   (*iii*) Floor to ceiling height of rooms, verandah, & kitchen = 3200 mm
   (*iv*) Floor to ceiling height of w.c and bathroom = 2800 mm
   (*v*) Height of parapet = 700 mm
   (*vi*) Height of plinth above G.L = 500 mm
   (*vii*) Foundation will be 900mm deep and 1000 mm wide

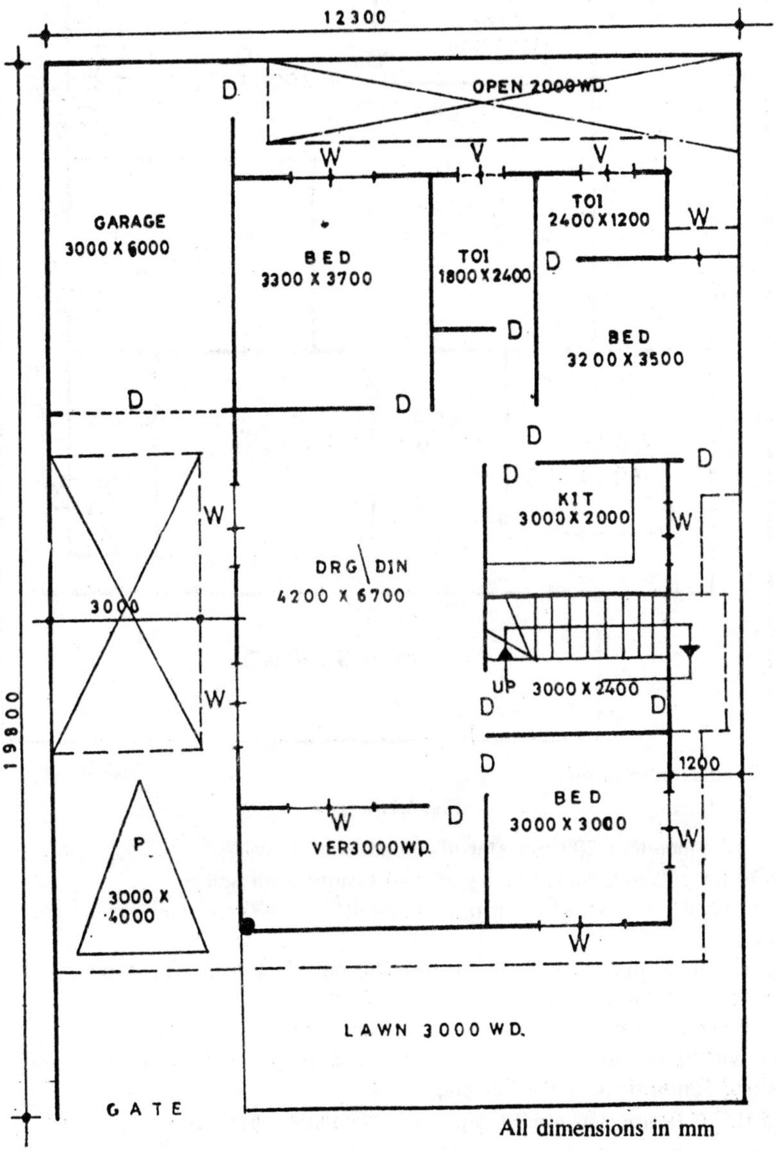


All dimensions in mm

Scale-1:100

Fig. 6.6.

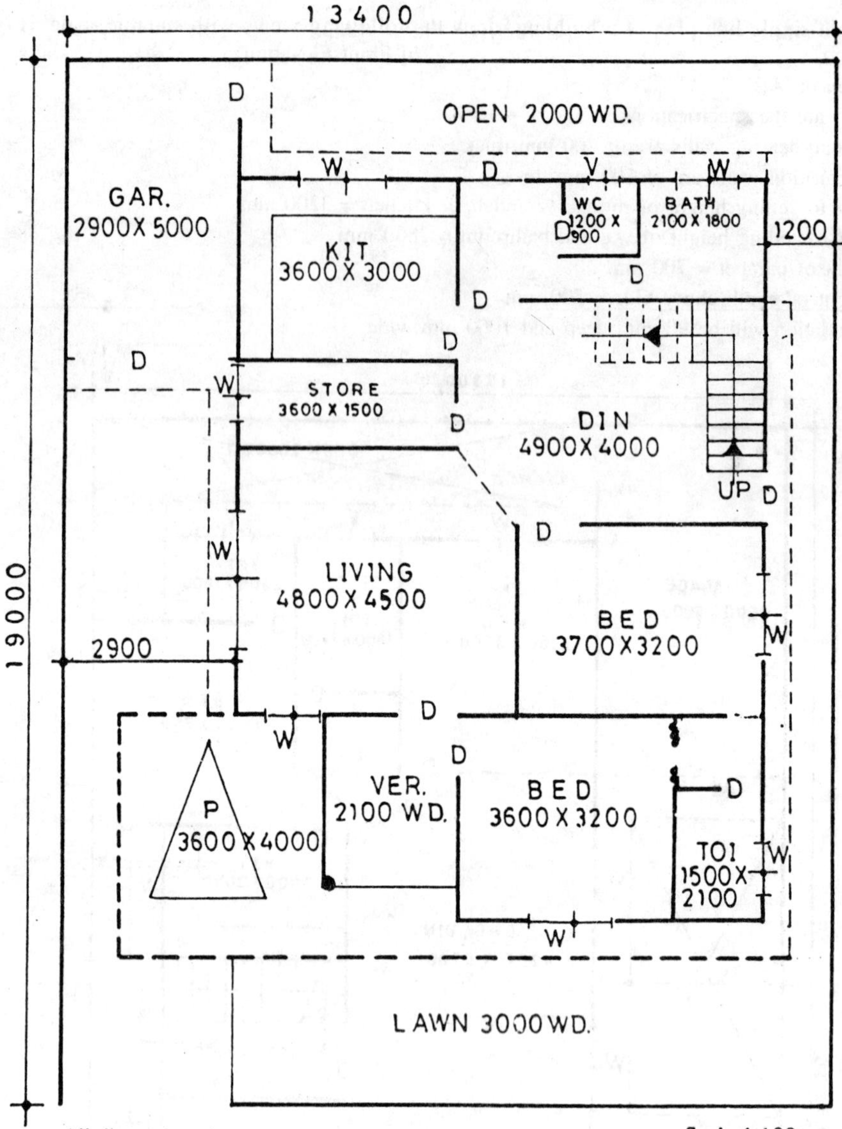


Fig. 6.7.A.

(*viii*) Thickness of concrete = 200 mm (for all foundation of wall)

(*ix*) Foundation for 100 mm walls and dwarf wall assume your self

(*x*) Roofing to be R.C.C slab 120 mm thick covered with 100mm mud phuska and tiles of 200 × 100 × 50 mm.

(*xi*) Flooring will be 40 mm thick c.c 1:2:4 over 100 mm thick lean cement concrete1: 4:8 over 100 mm thick sand over rammed earth.

(*xii*) Provided200mmthich R.C.C lintels over doors and windows opening.

(*xiii*) Sunshade will be provided in R.C.C 600 mm wide projected from the walls, 80 mm thick at fixed supports and 50mm thick at the free end.

(*xiv*) Provided R.C.C beams 350 mm in depth over verandah opening.

(*xv*) Thickness of damp proofing course = 40 mm

(*xvi*) Doors, Windows and shelf are as below:

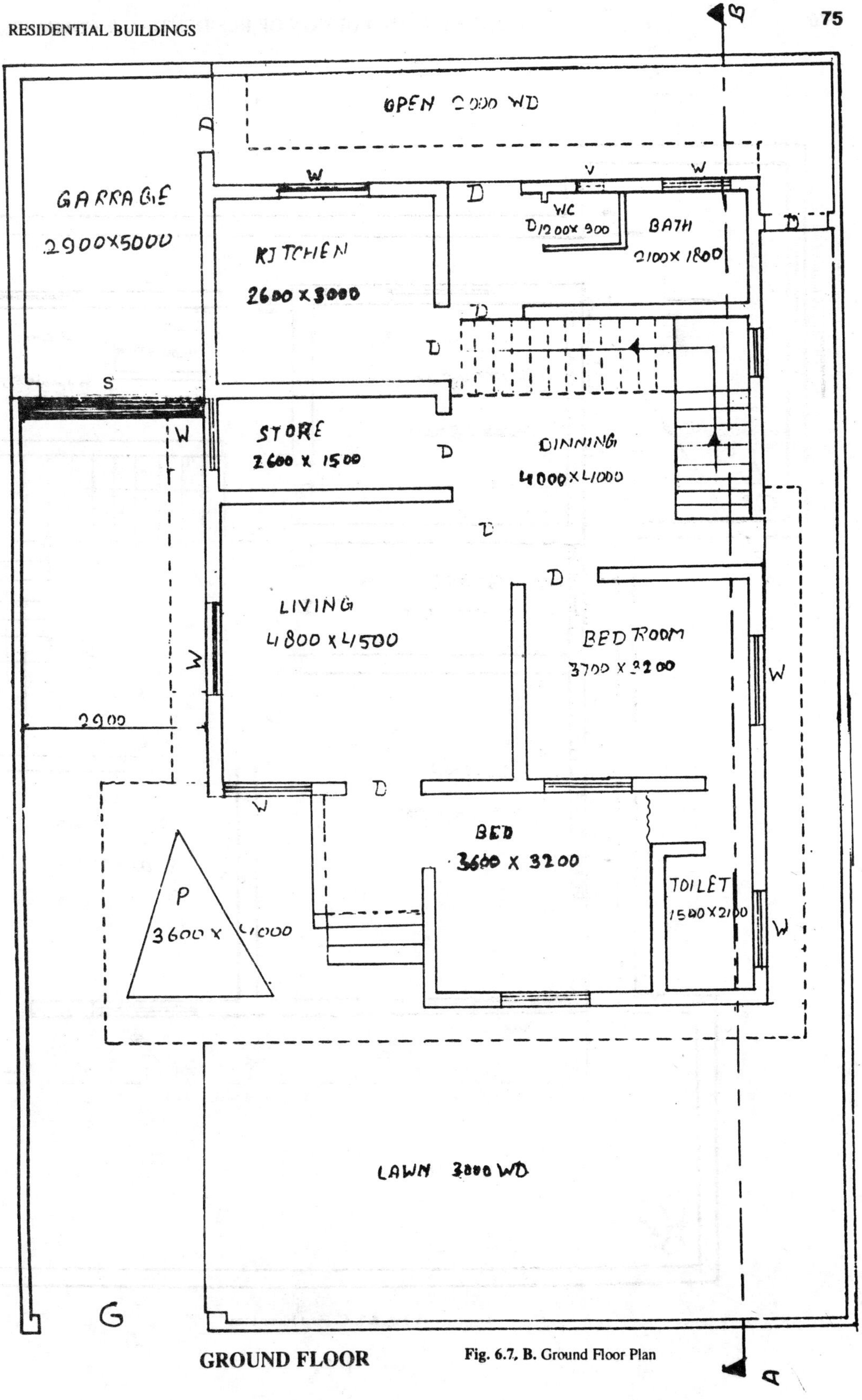


GROUND FLOOR

Fig. 6.7. B. Ground Floor Plan

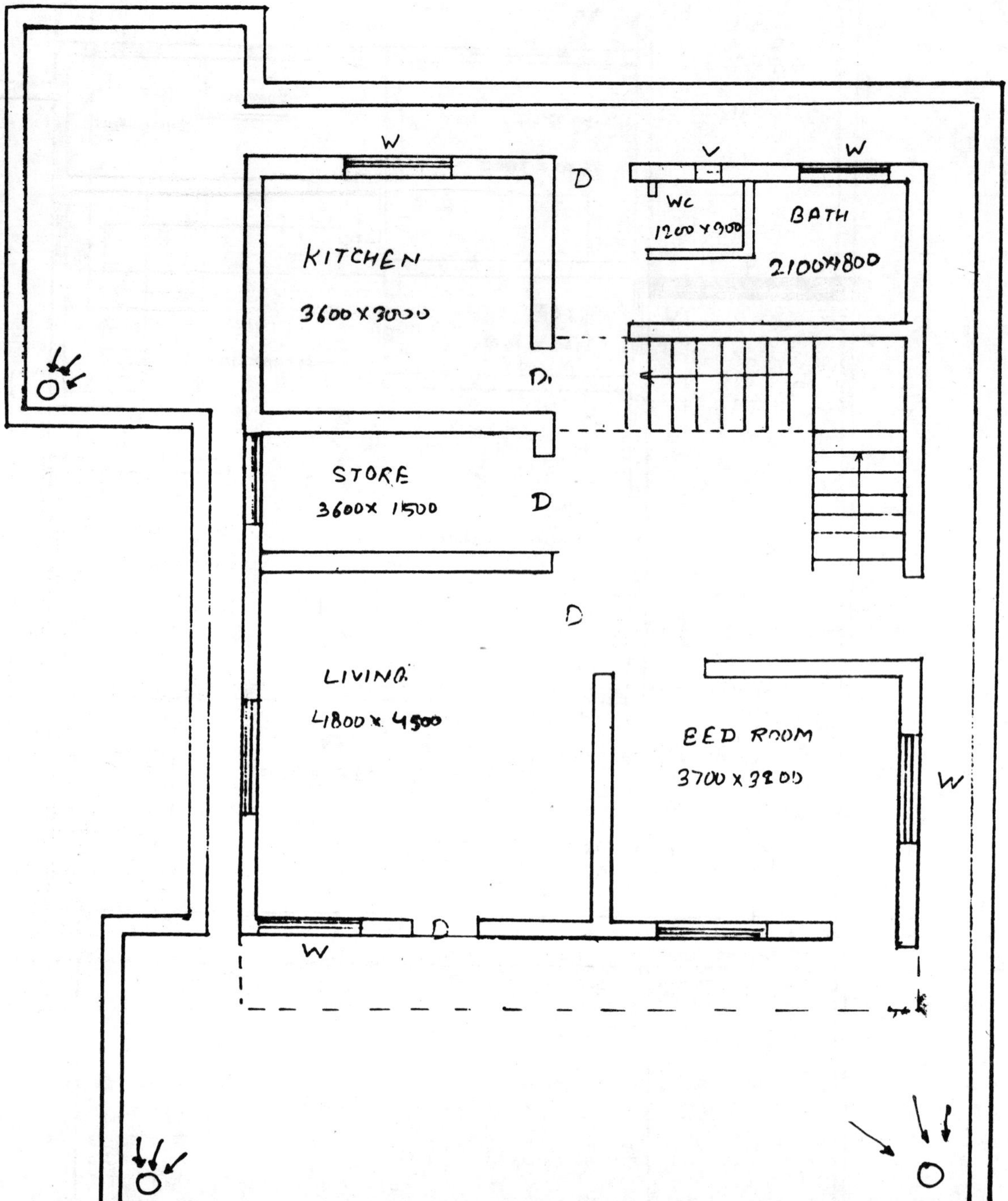


Fig. 6.7. C. First Floor Plan

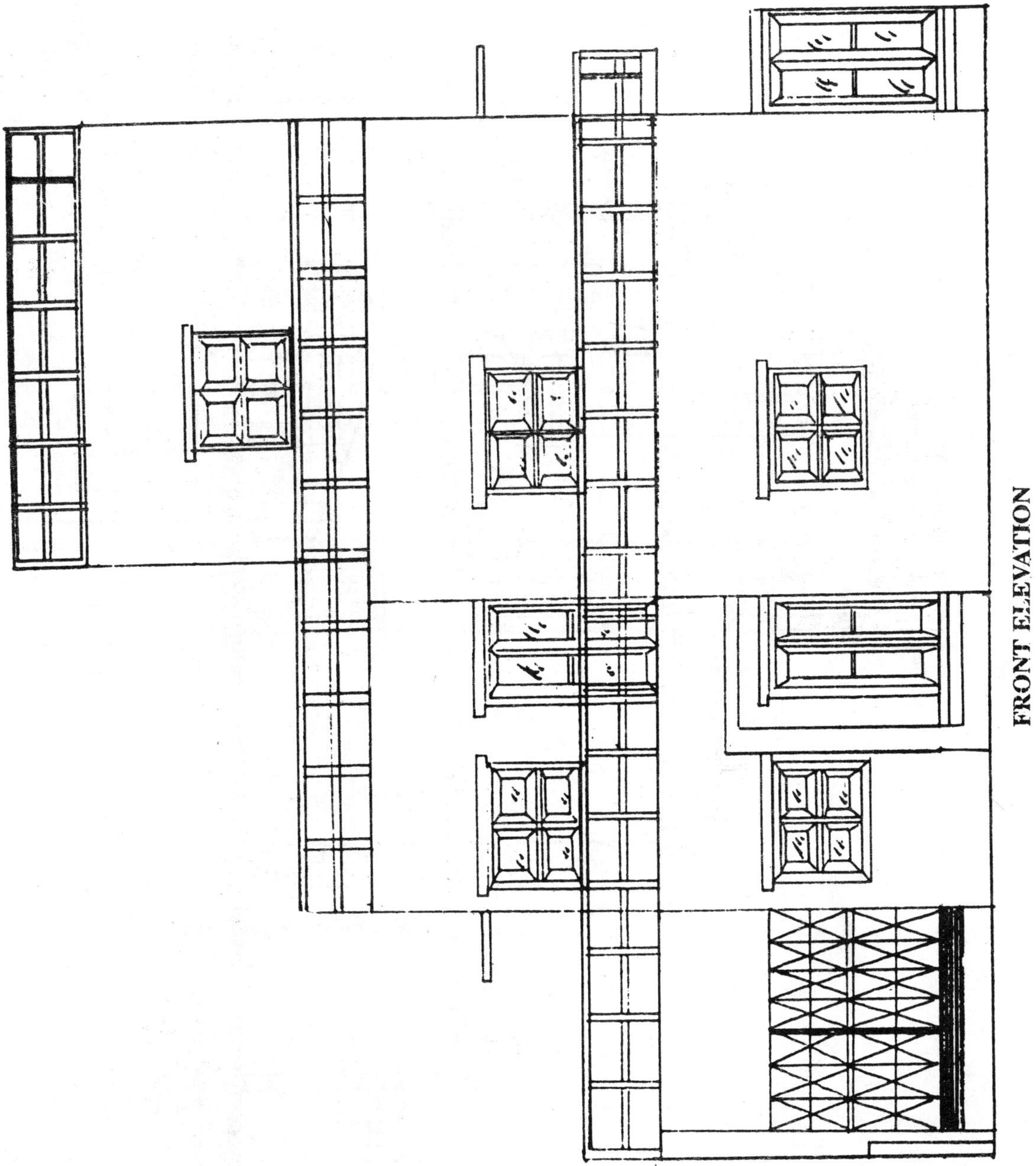


Fig. 6.7. D. Front Elevation

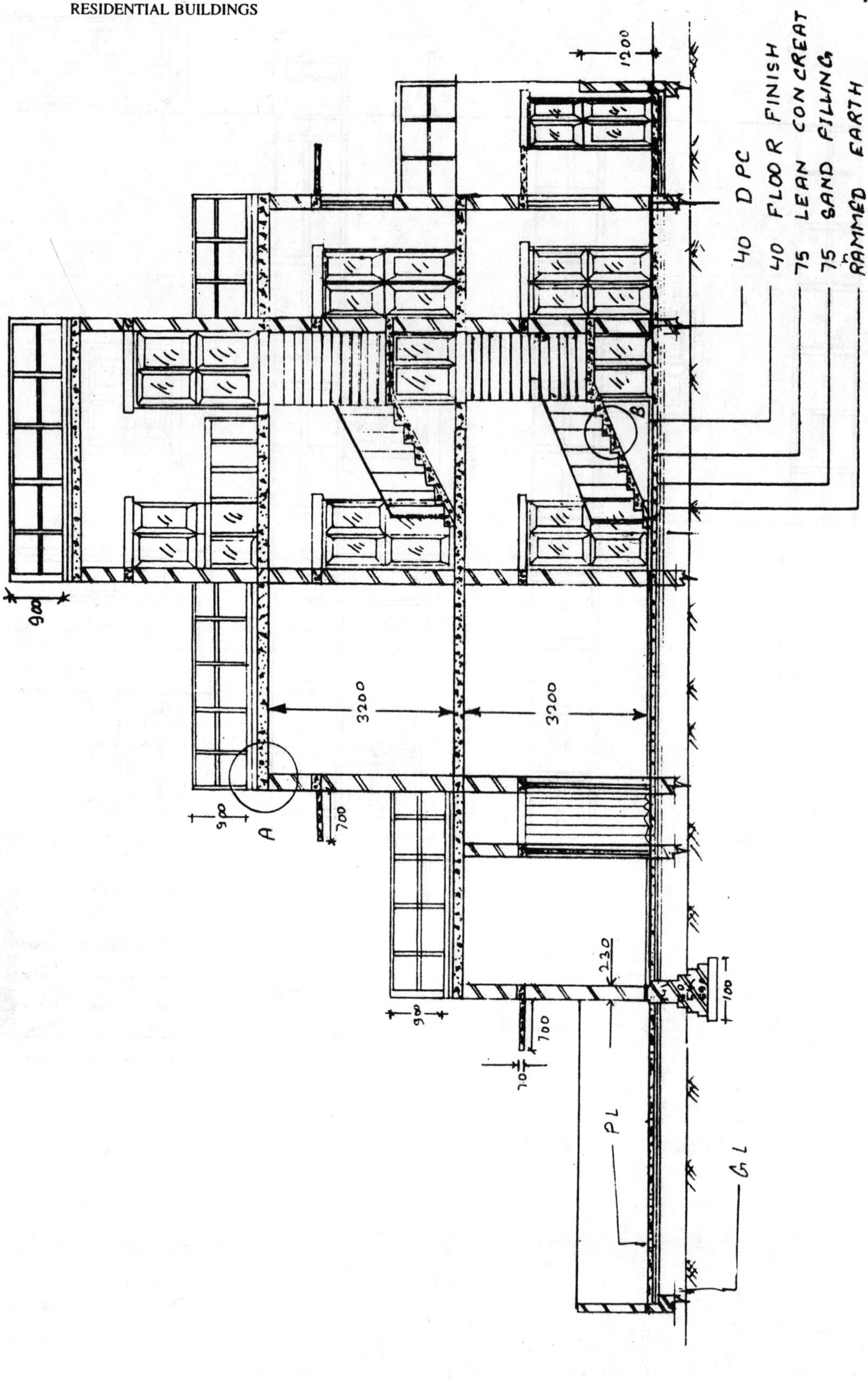


Fig. 6.7. E. Section Through "AB"

$D = 1200 \times 2100$
$D_1 = 1000 \times 2100$
$D_2 = 900 \times 2100$
$W = 1500 \times 1200$
$W_1 = 1200 \times 1200$
$S = 1200 \times 1400$

Assume any data if required.

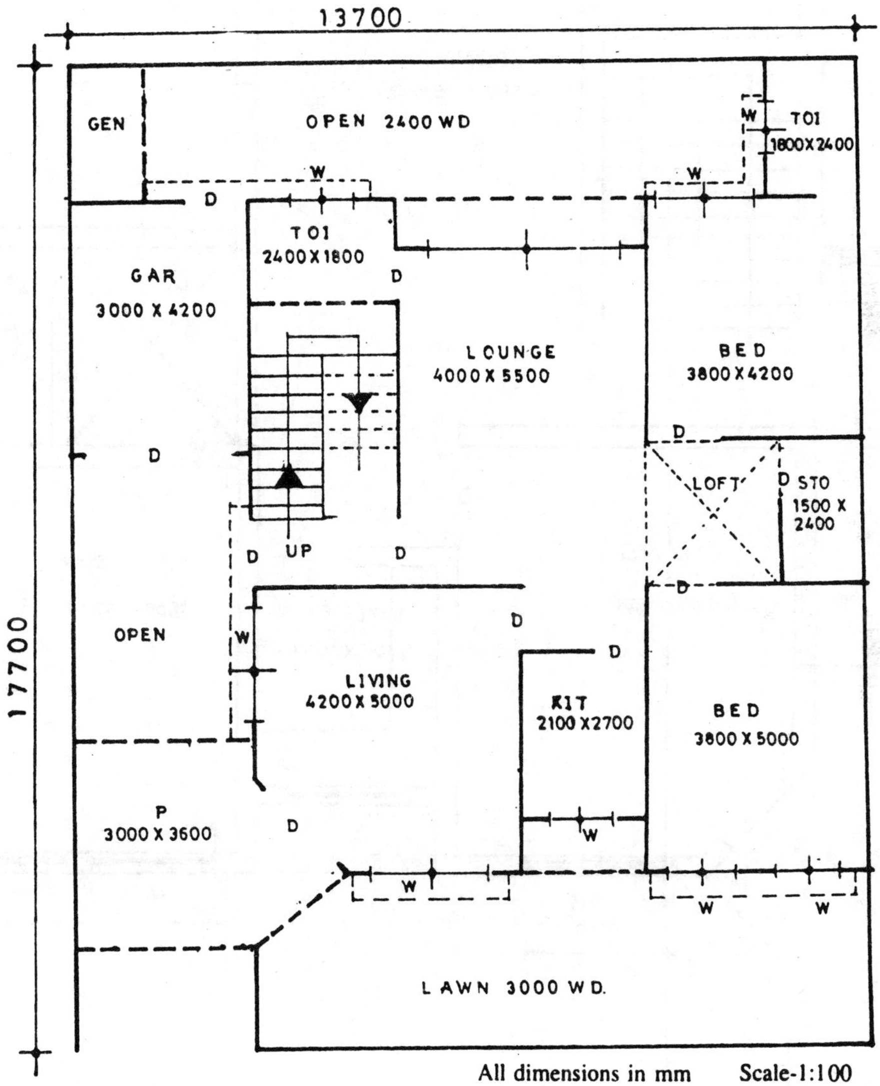


All dimensions in mm Scale-1:100

Fig. 6.8. A.

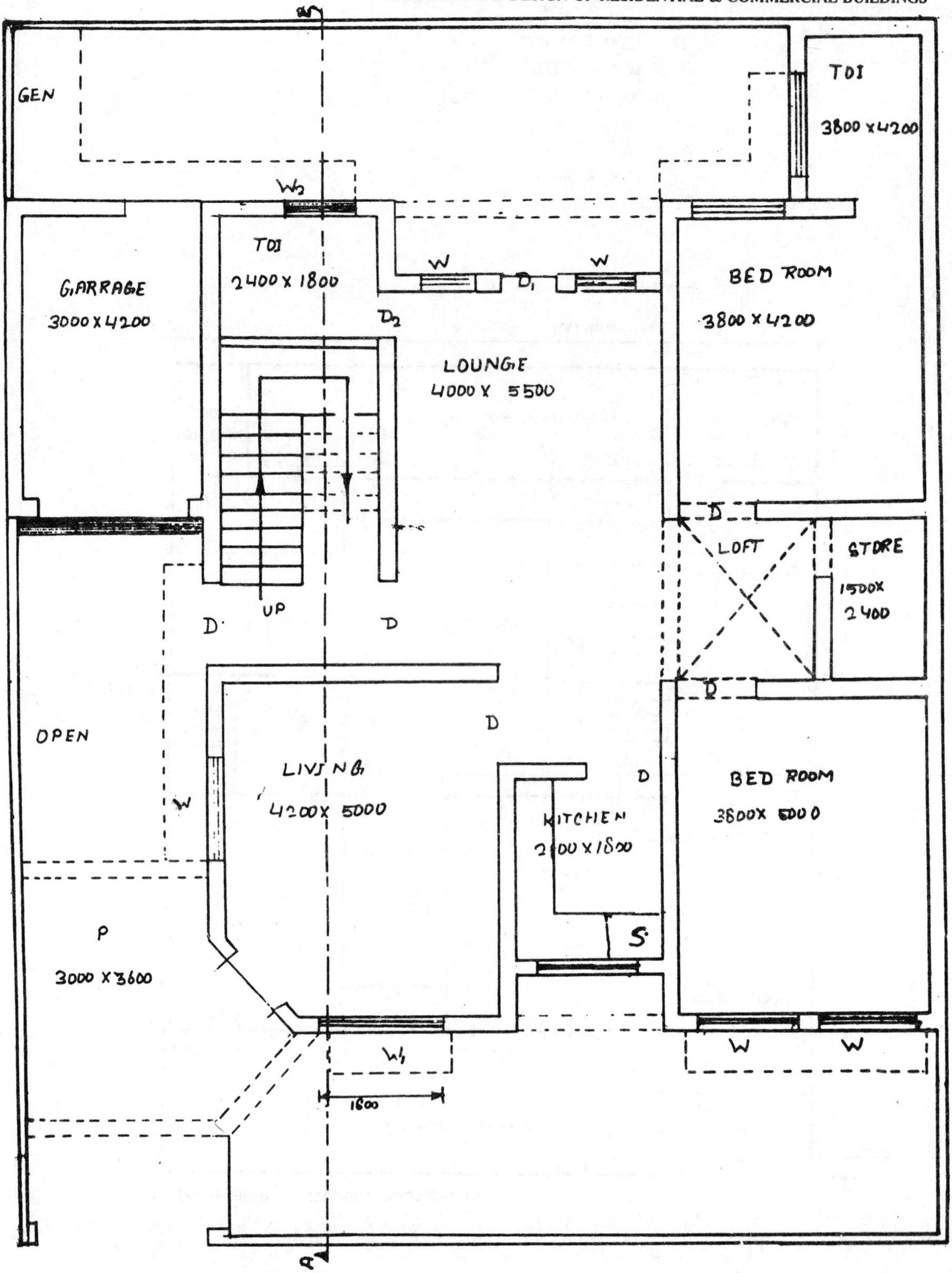


**GROUND FLOOR**

**Fig. 6.8. B.** Ground Floor Plan

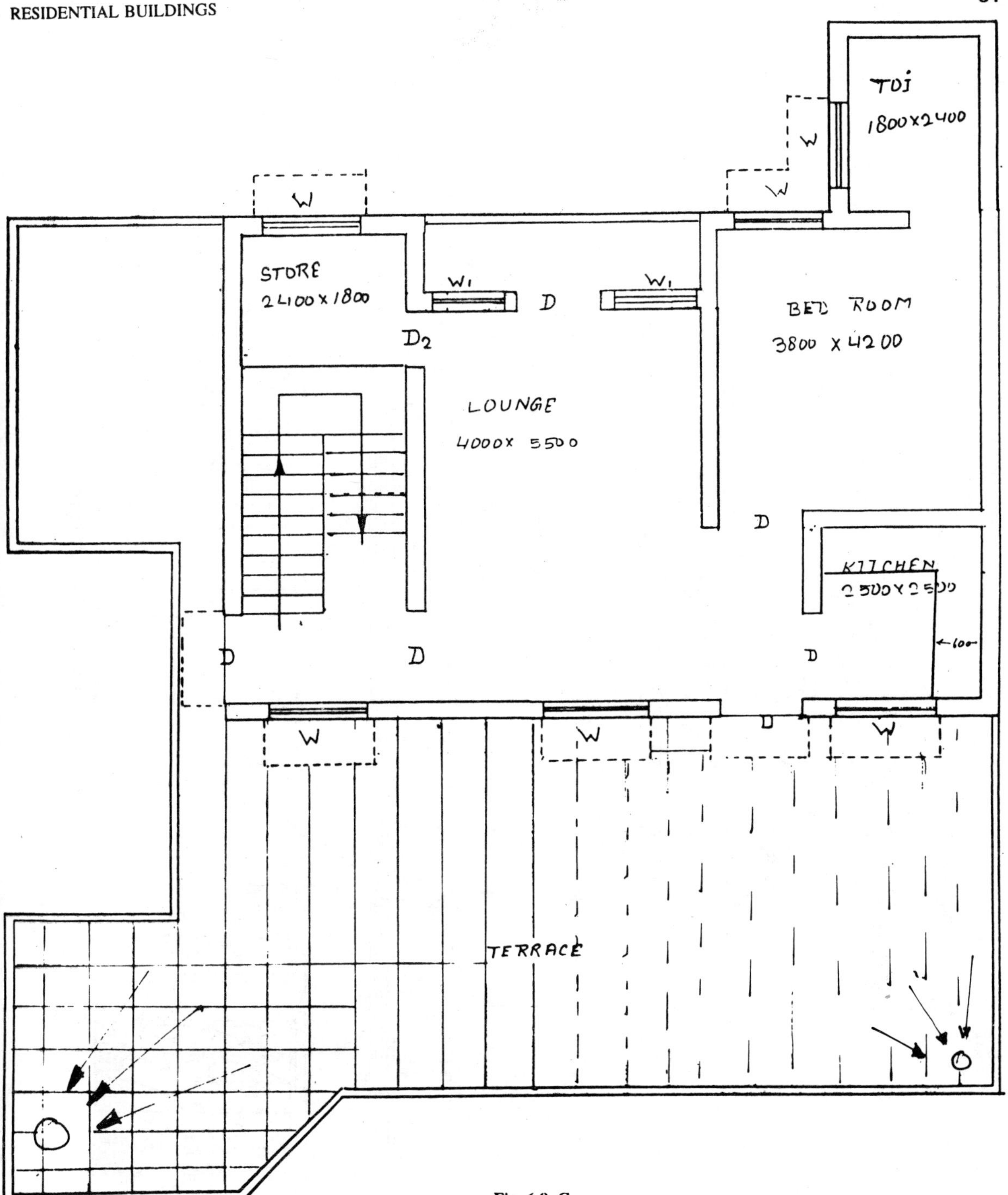
TOI
1800x2400
W
W
W
STORE
2400x1800
W1
D
W1
BED ROOM
3800 X 4200
D2
LOUNGE
4000x 5500
D
KITCHEN
2500x2500
←100
D
D
D
W
W
D
W
TERRACE

Fig. 6.8. C.

**Fig. 6.8. D.** Front Elevation

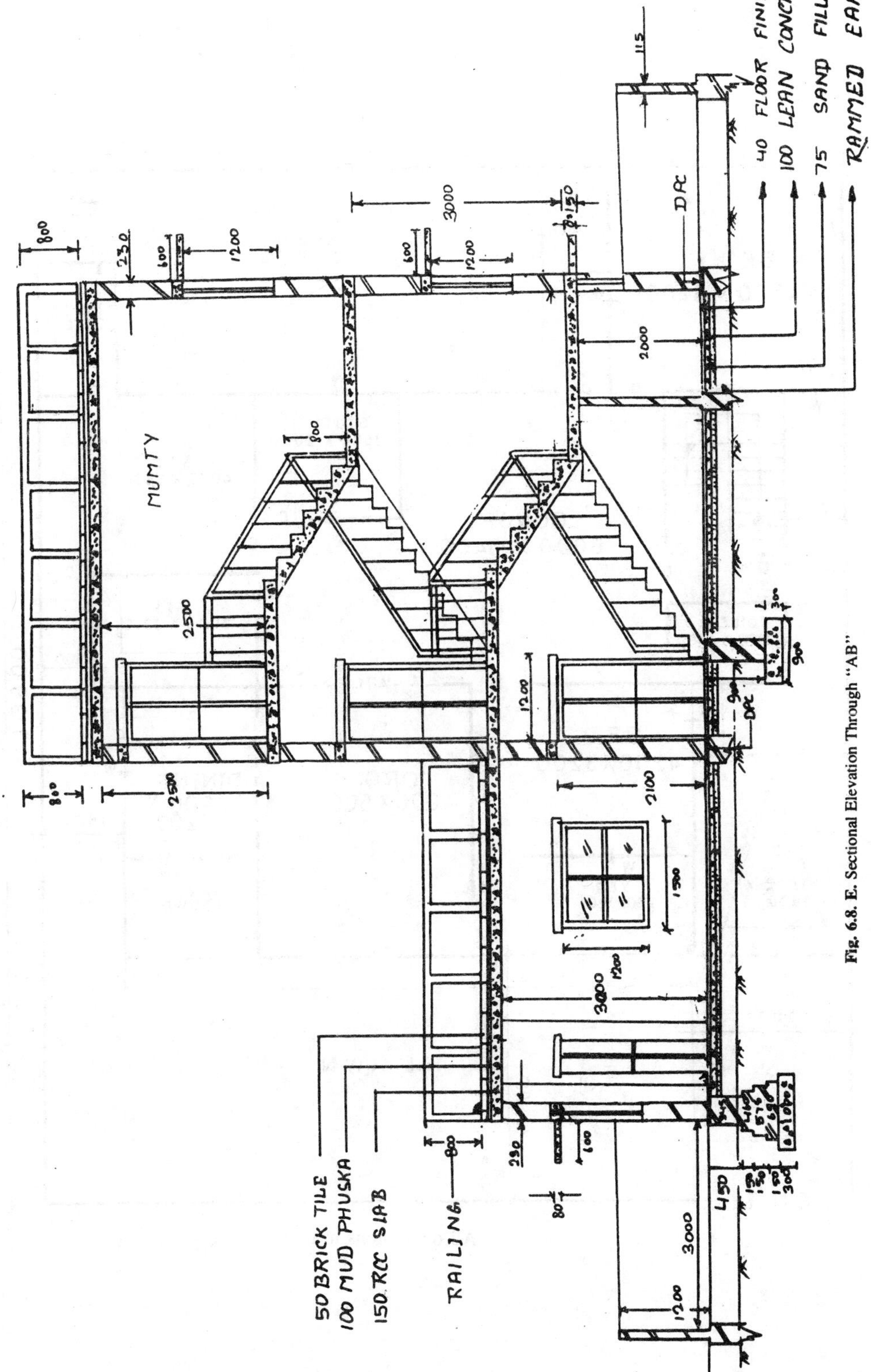


Fig. 6.8. E. Sectional Elevation Through "AB"

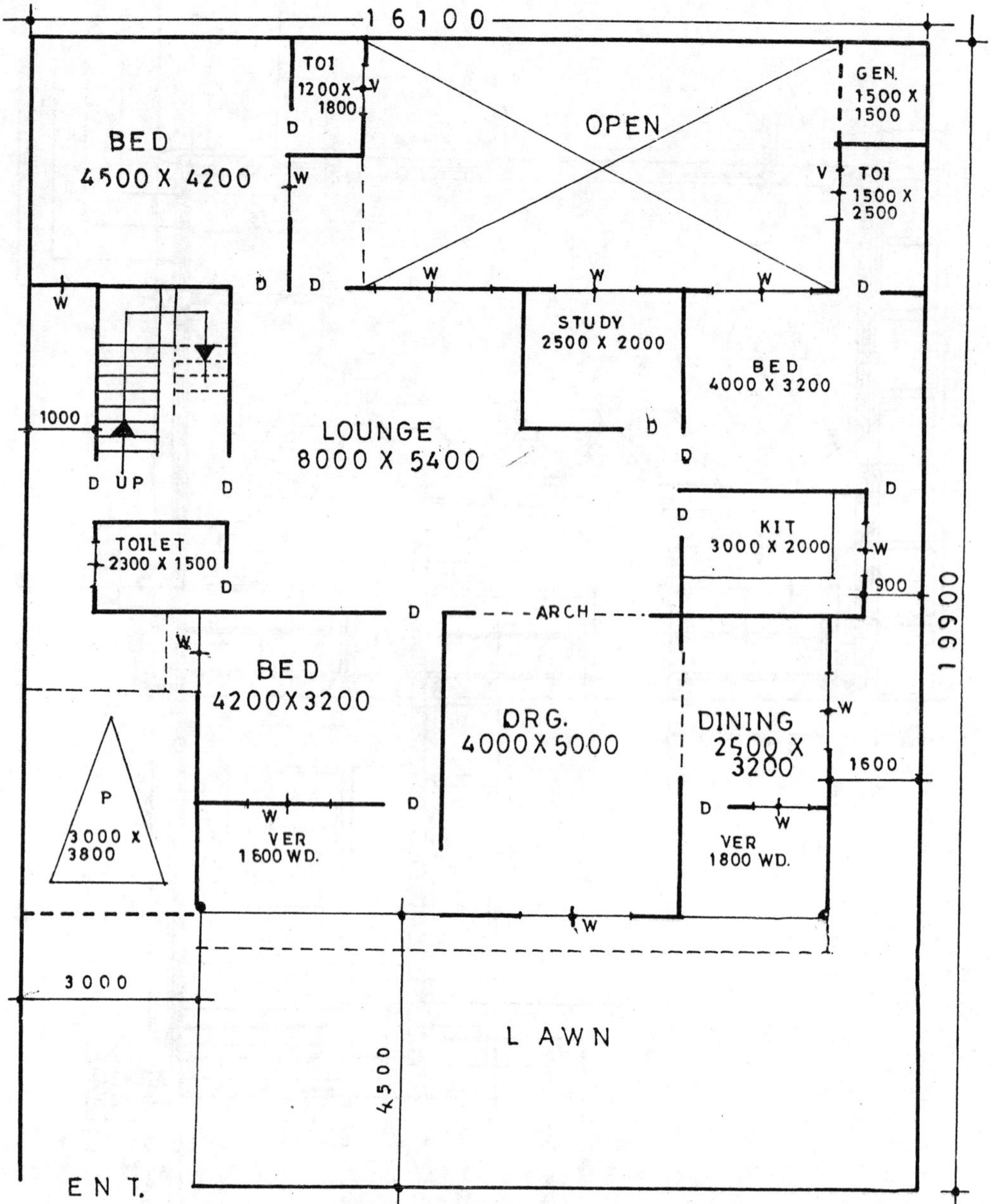


All dimensions in mm Scale-1:100

Fig. 6.9.

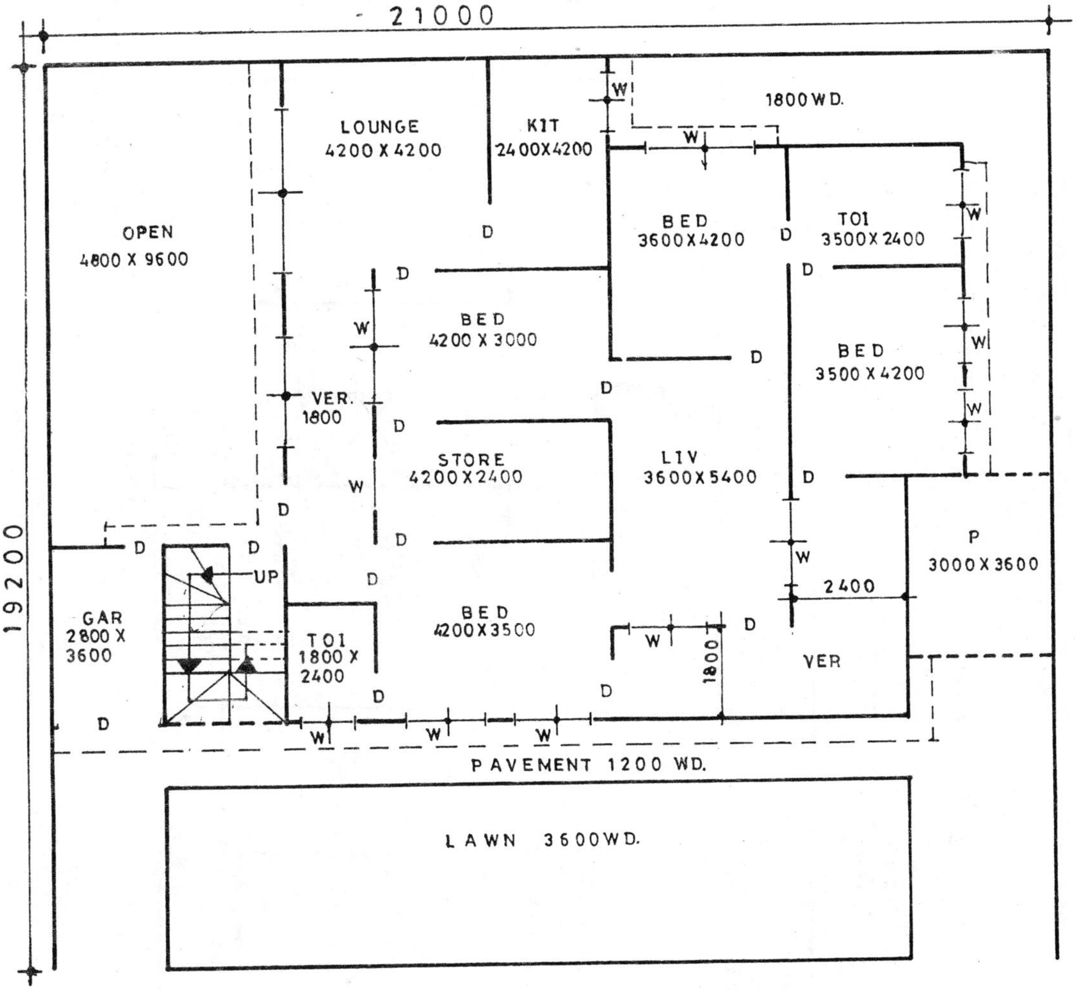


All dimensions in mm Scale-1:100

Fig. 6.10.

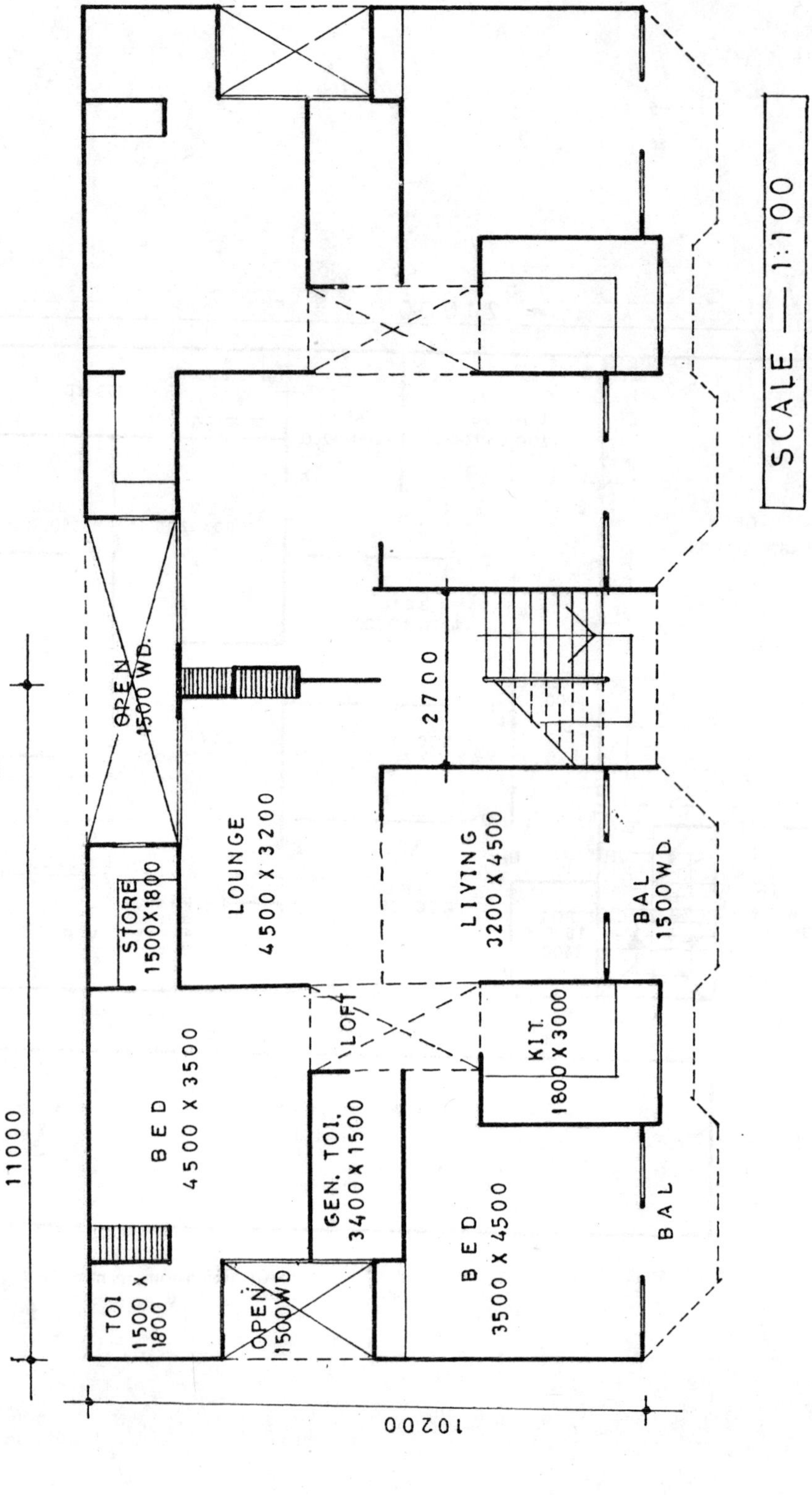


All dimensions in mm

**Fig. 6.11.** Typical Floor Plan

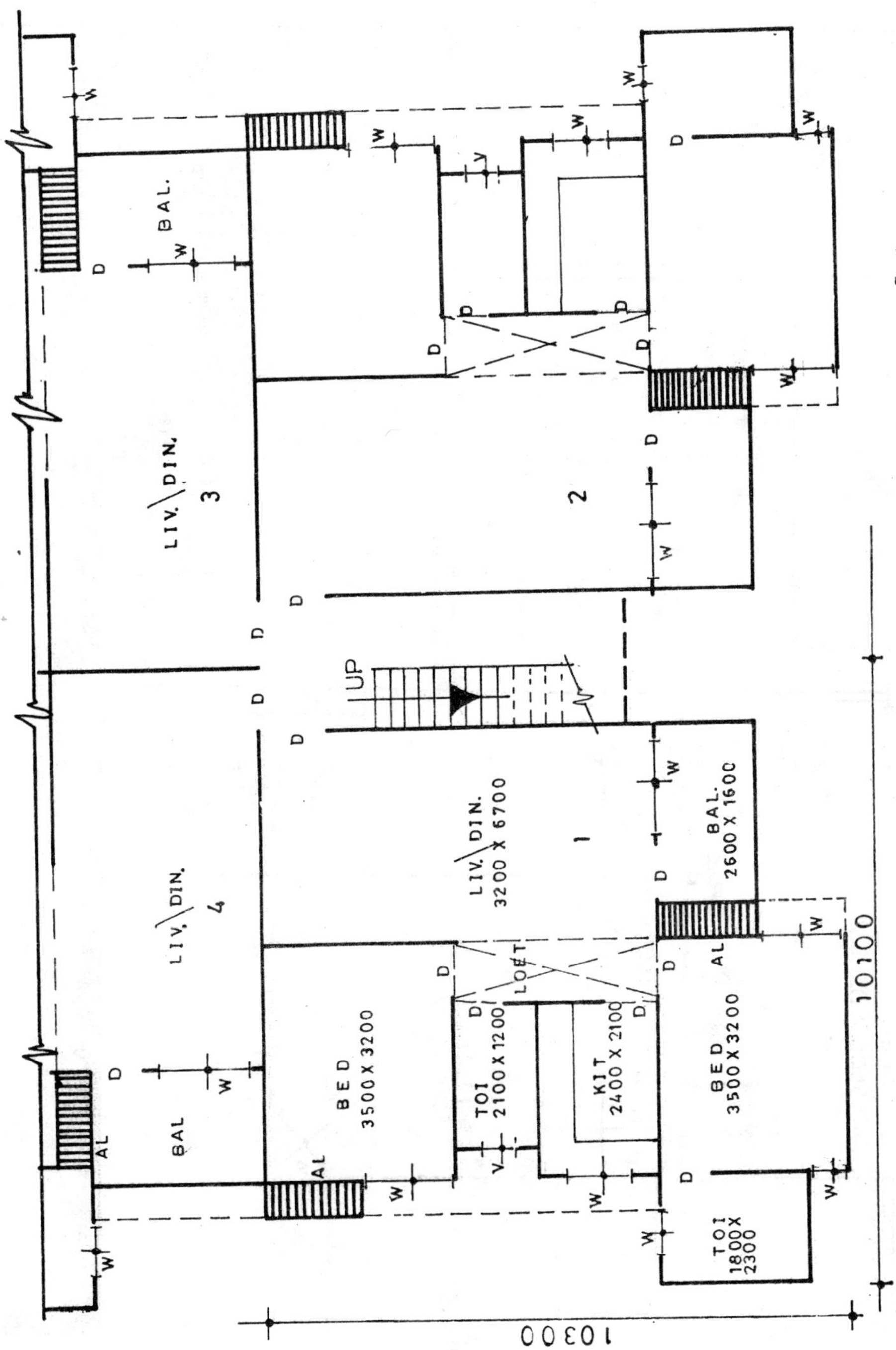


All dimensions in mm Scale-1:100

**Fig. 6.12.** Typical Floor Plan of 3-rooms apartments

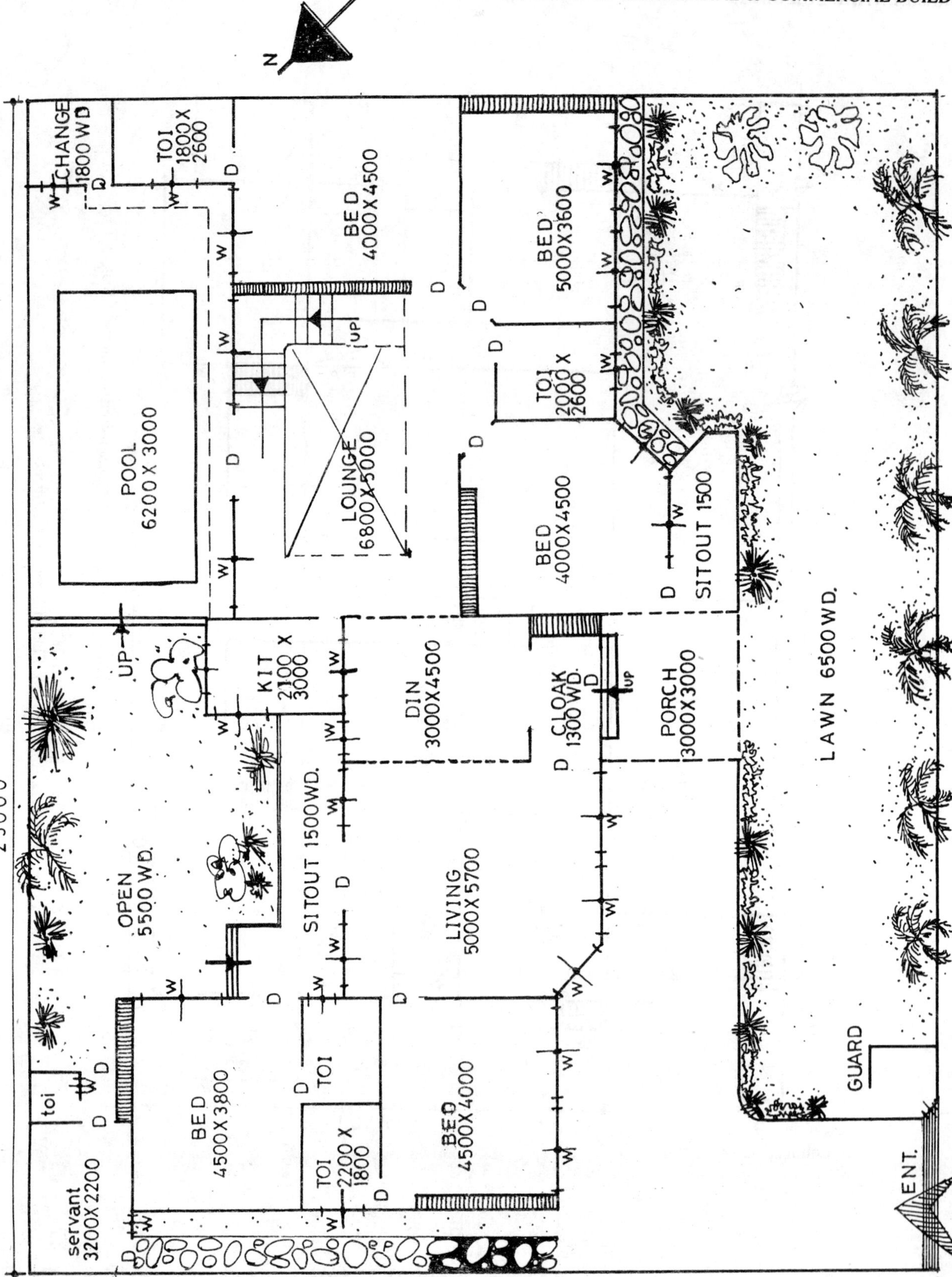


Scale-1:100 All dimensions in mm

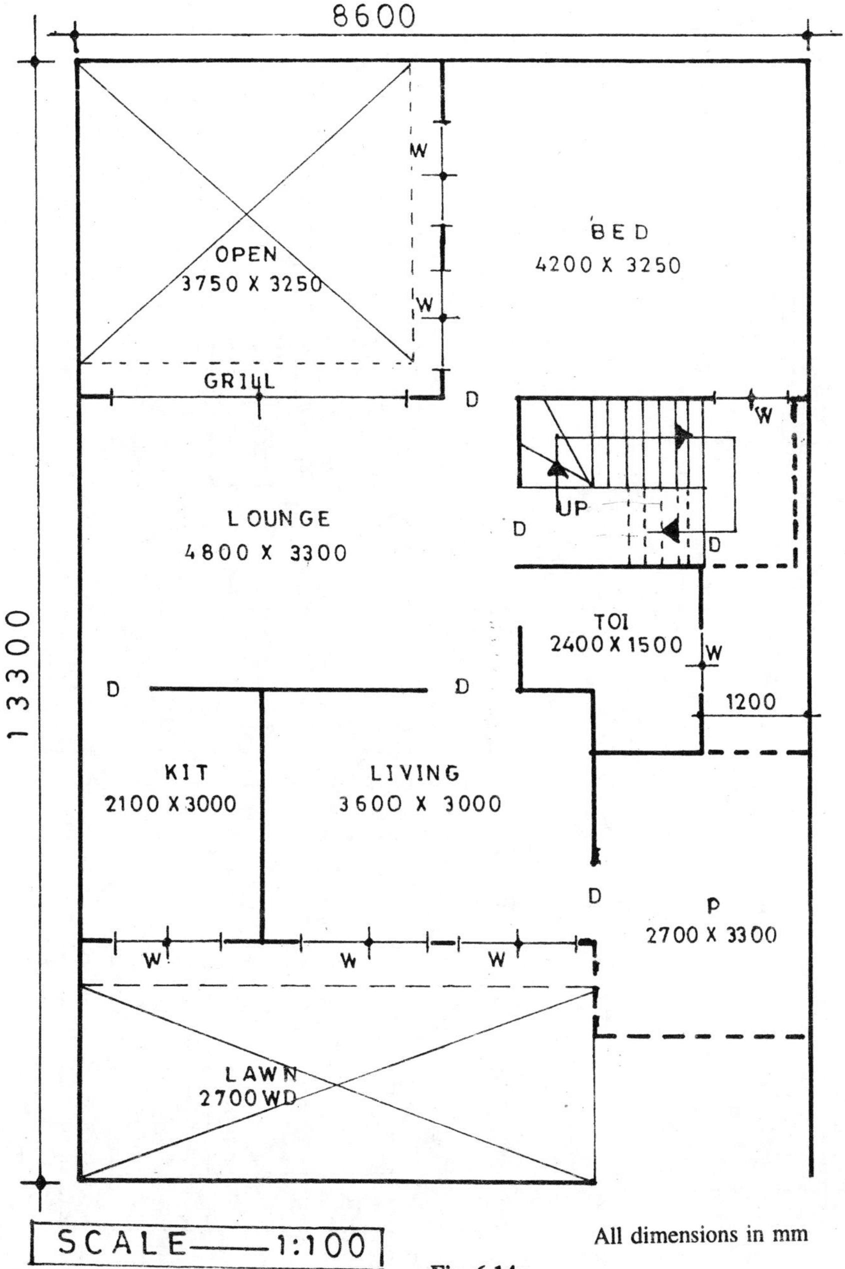


All dimensions in mm

**Fig. 6.14**

8. Plan a residential house over a plot size of 20 m × 31.5 m. The 31.5 m side of the plot-faces east and10m wide road runs parallel to 20 m side of the plot. Apply the local building bye-laws provide, Drawing cum dinning room, Kitchen, Two bed rooms with attached toilets, Guest room with attached toilet study room, Store, Lounge, passage, staircase 1.2 m wide, porch, garage, and courtyard etc, may suitable be provided. Draw the following, showing necessary details:
   (*i*) Ground floor plan and Istfloor plans
   (*ii*) Half sectional elevation through staircase showing full width of building.
   (*iii*) Architectural elevation

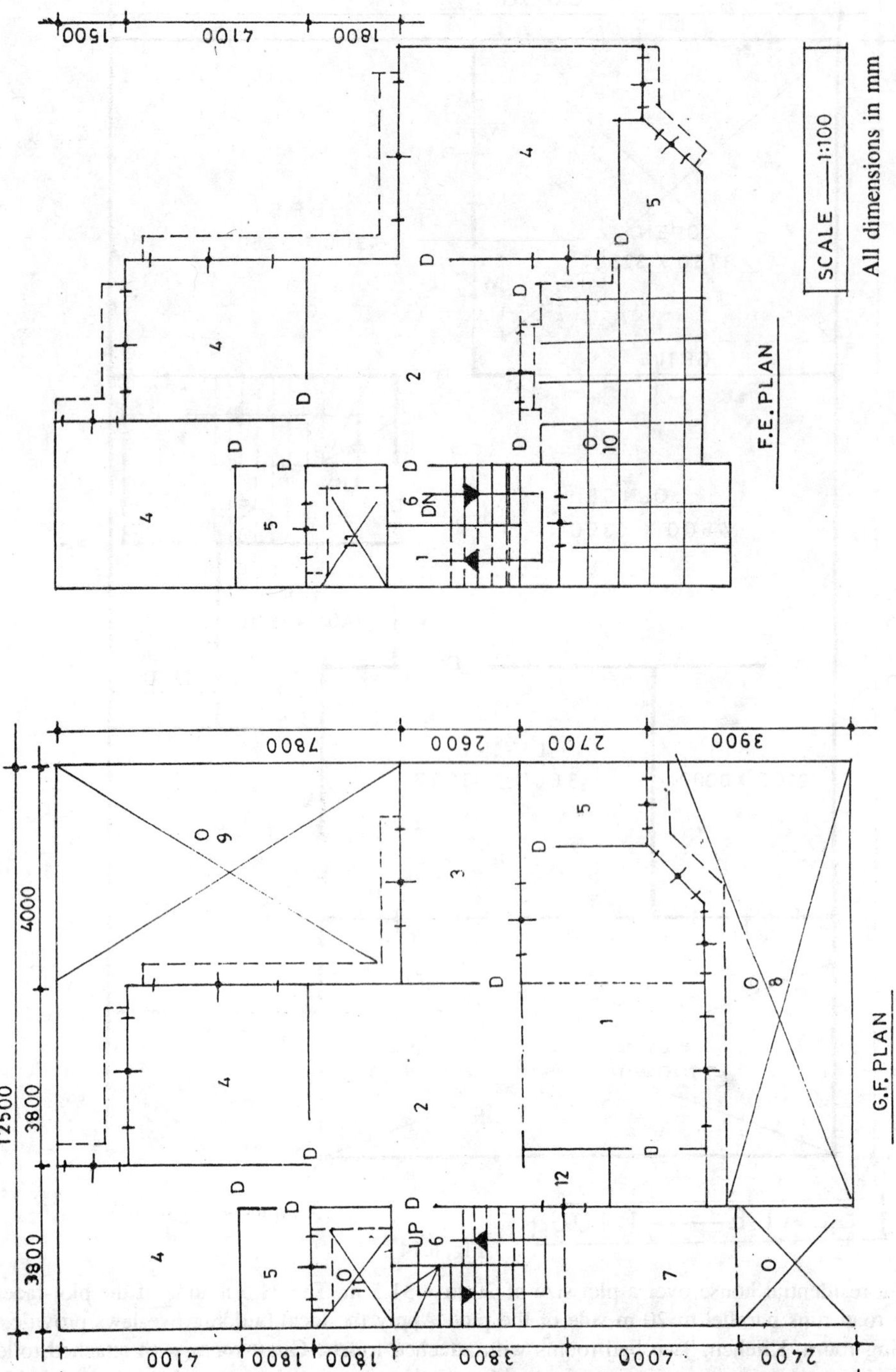


Fig. 6.15.

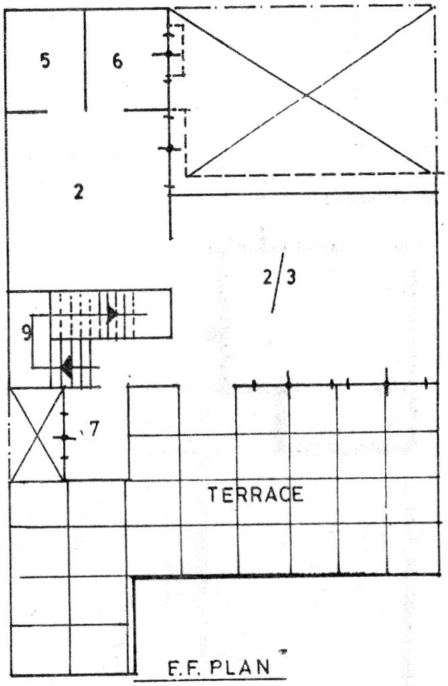


| LEGEND | | |
|---|---|---|
| 1 | LIVING | 3400X3850 |
| 2 | BEDROOM | 3400X4000 |
| 3 | LOUNGE | 4800X4000 |
| 4 | KITCHEN | 2000X3000 |
| 5 | STORE | 1600X2300. |
| 6 | TOILET | 1600X2300 |
| 7 | TOILET | 1200X2000 |
| 8 | C·YARD | 5000X4000 |
| 9 | STAIRCASE | 3500X2000 |
| 10 | LAWN | 6000X3600 |
| P | PARKING | 2600X4000 |
| O | O.T.S | |
| L | LOFT | |
| PLOT AREA—154·80 SQ MTS. | | |
| SCALE ——1:100 | | |
| NORTH | | |

All dimensions in mm

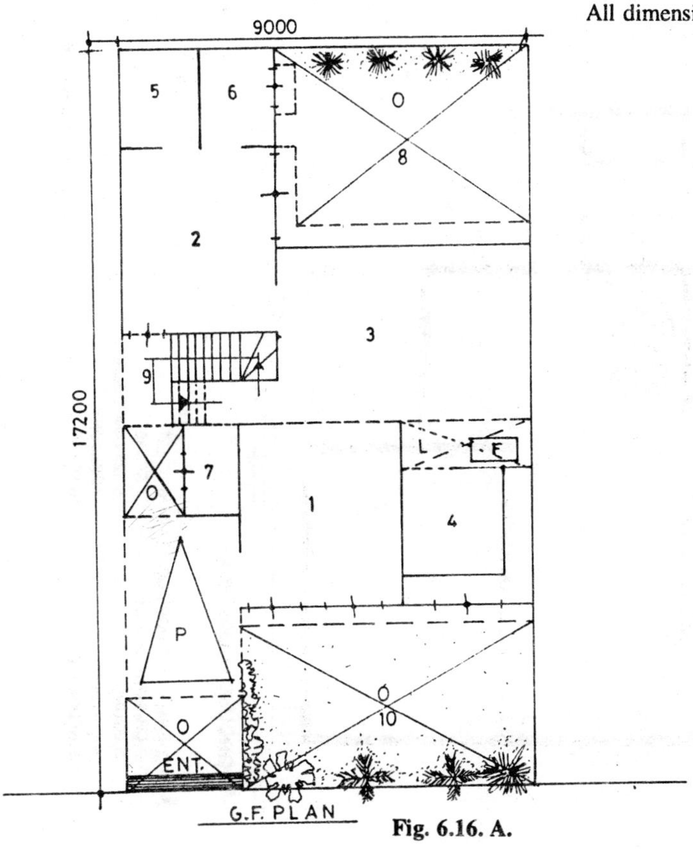


Fig. 6.16. A.

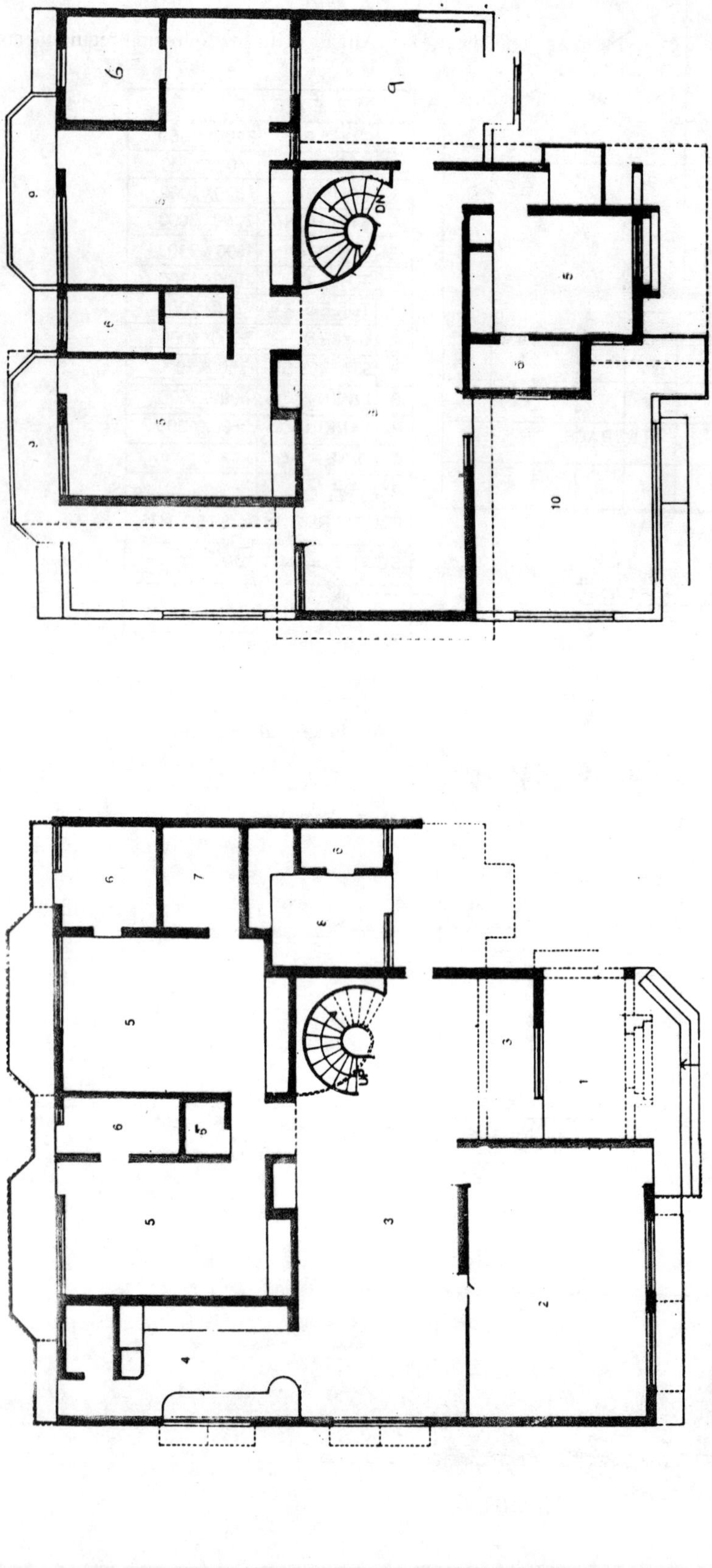

FIRST FLOOR PLAN

GROUND FLOOR PLAN

1 ENTRANCE PORTICO
2 DRAWING ROOM
3 LOUNGE
4 KITCHEN
5 BEDROOM
6 TOILET
7 STORE
8 SERVANT'S ROOM
9 BALCONY
10 TERRACE

Fig. 6.16. B.

9. It is proposed to construct a residential building at medical road, Aligarh with the following requirements;
   Size of plot = 25 × 35 m
   A 25 m wide side of the plot is facing north and parallel with the 12 m wide roads.
   Drawing hall24 sqm, Kitchen about 10 sqm, Dinning room 15 sqm, Two bed rooms 15 sqm each with attached toilet, Guest room with attached toilets 12 sqm, Store, Lounges, passage, staircase minimum 1.2 m wide, porch, garage, and courtyard etc, may suitable be provided. Draw the following, giving detailed dimension:
   (*i*) Ground floor plan
   (*ii*) Half sectional elevation through staircase showing full width of building (half width in elevation rest half showing staircase in sectional elevation).
10. Design a residential building for the university employees on a plot size 16 m × 25 m.The requirement of the building with sizes of rooms are given below

| Accommodation required | Sizes desired |
|---|---|
| Drawing, and dinning room | 4.5 m × 7.0 m |
| Three bed rooms ie one for guest, one master bed& one bed room | 4.5 m × 3.5 m |
| Three toilets (one attached to master bed) | 1.2 m × 2.5 m |
| Dress attached with master bed | 1.2 m × 2.5 m |
| Kitchen with Store | 2.5 m × 3.5 m |
| A good staircase has to be provided | 1.2 m wide |

   You can include other requirements to design, but excluding the front set back as 4.5 m, rear set back as 6.0m and side set back as 2.5 m
   Draw the following, giving detailed dimension:
   (*i*) Ground floor plan
   (*ii*) Sectional elevation.
   (*iii*) Elevations (front& sides)
   (*iv*) Area chart and circulation diagram.
   (*v*) Site plan showing entrance, exits, security check etc.
11. A residential building is to be planned over a plot of 300 sqm.The built up area should not exceed 45% of the plot area. Apply local building bylaws assuming suitable dimensions of the plot and draw the following.
   (*i*) Plans
   (*ii*) Sectional elevation
12. Design and draw the working drawings of a frame structure residential building (flats) on a plot size of 18.5 m × 26.75 m. The requirements of a flat is as fallows
   One drawing/dinning room
   Two bed room
   One kitchen
   One general and one attached Toilet
   Staircase common
   A small lobby
   Note cross ventilation is very important while designing a flat.
13. Draw the working drawings of the following plans (Fig. 6.24 to 6.29).
14. Draw the layout plan (Foundation Plan) for the single line plan shown in Fig. Take detail of foundation from Q. No. 15.
15. Draw the plan and vertical sectional elevation of a R.C. footing upto top of column with the following data:
   Size of column = 400 mm × 400 mm
   Base of column footing = 1500 mm × 1500 mm
   Depth of foundation = 1200 mm
   Reinforcement 10 mm $\phi$ @ 100 mm c/c both way in footing
   Thickness of footing at end = 200 mm
   Thickness of footing at face of column = 500 mm
   Height of column = 3600 mm
   Reinforcement: longitudinal bars 8 # 16 mm $\phi$
   lateral ties = 8 $\phi$ @ 150 mm c/c

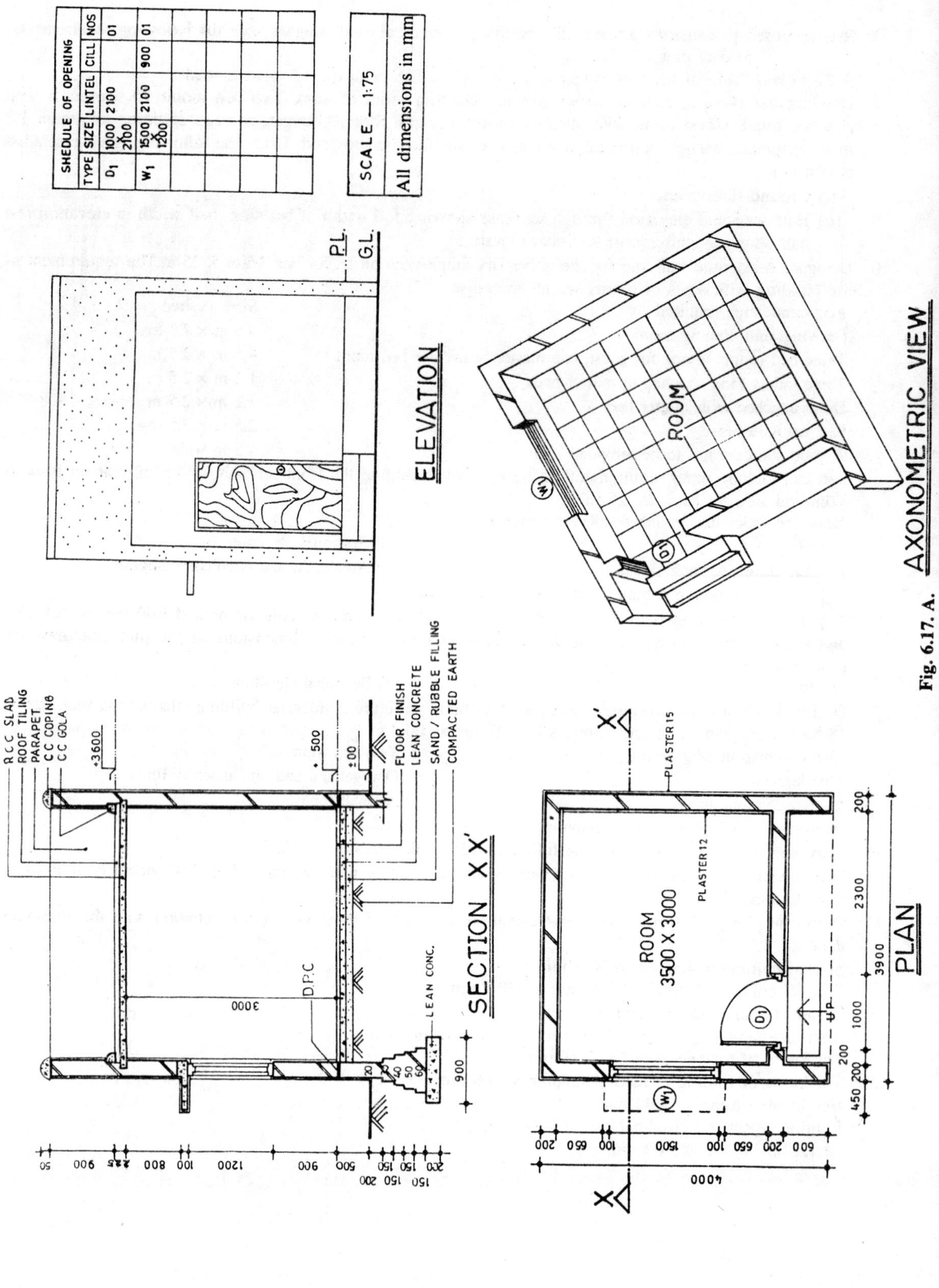


| TYPE | SIZE | LINTEL | CILL | NOS |
|---|---|---|---|---|
| $D_1$ | 1000 X 2100 | 2100 | | 01 |
| $W_1$ | 1500 X 1200 | 2100 | 900 | 01 |
| | | | | |
| | | | | |
| | | | | |
| | | | | |
| | | | | |

Fig. 6.17. A.

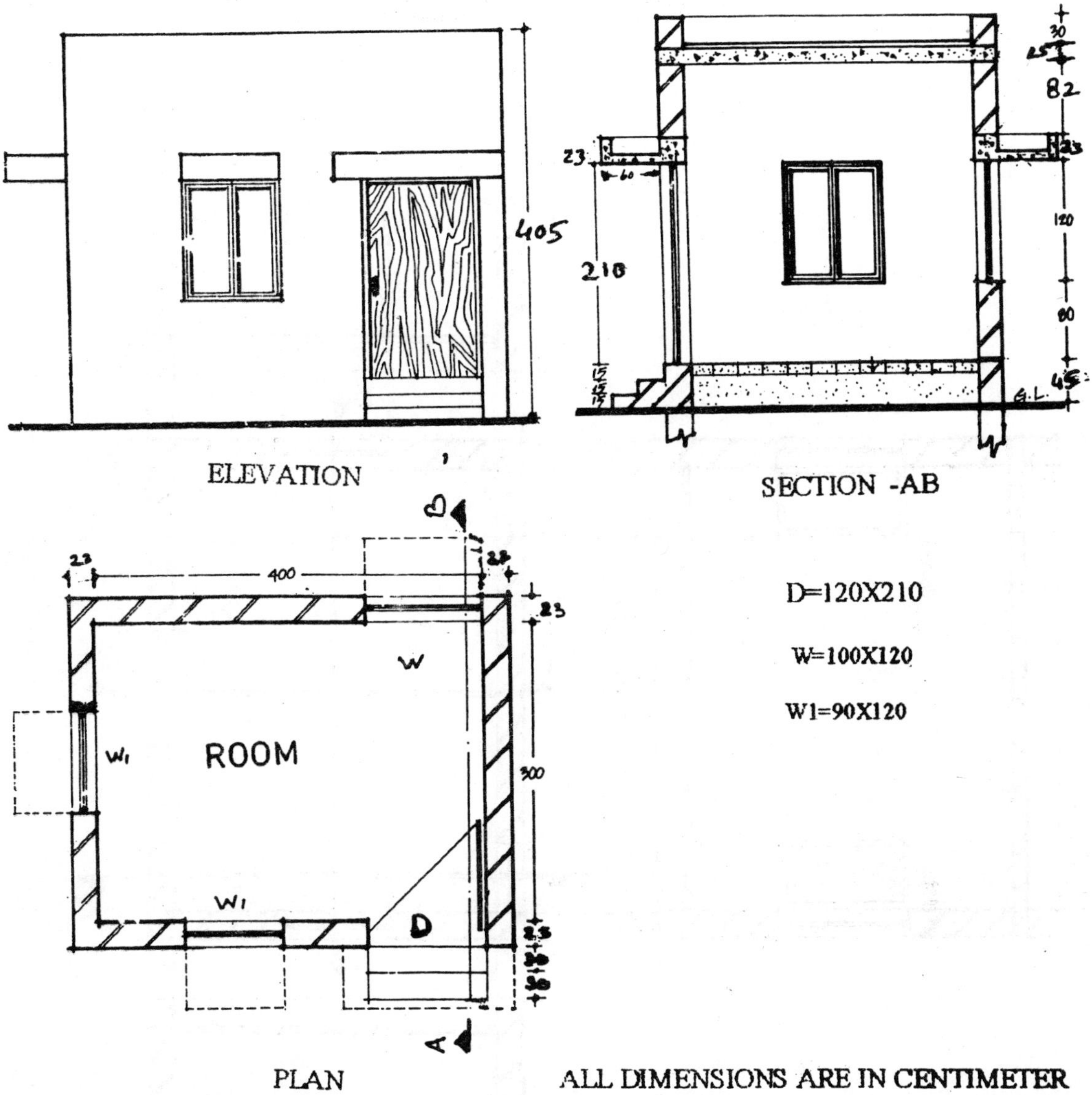
405
ELEVATION
23
60
210
82
120
80
45
G.L.
SECTION -AB
23
400
23
W
W1
ROOM
300
W1
D
A
B
D=120X210
W=100X120
W1=90X120
PLAN
ALL DIMENSIONS ARE IN CENTIMETER

Fig. 6.17. B.

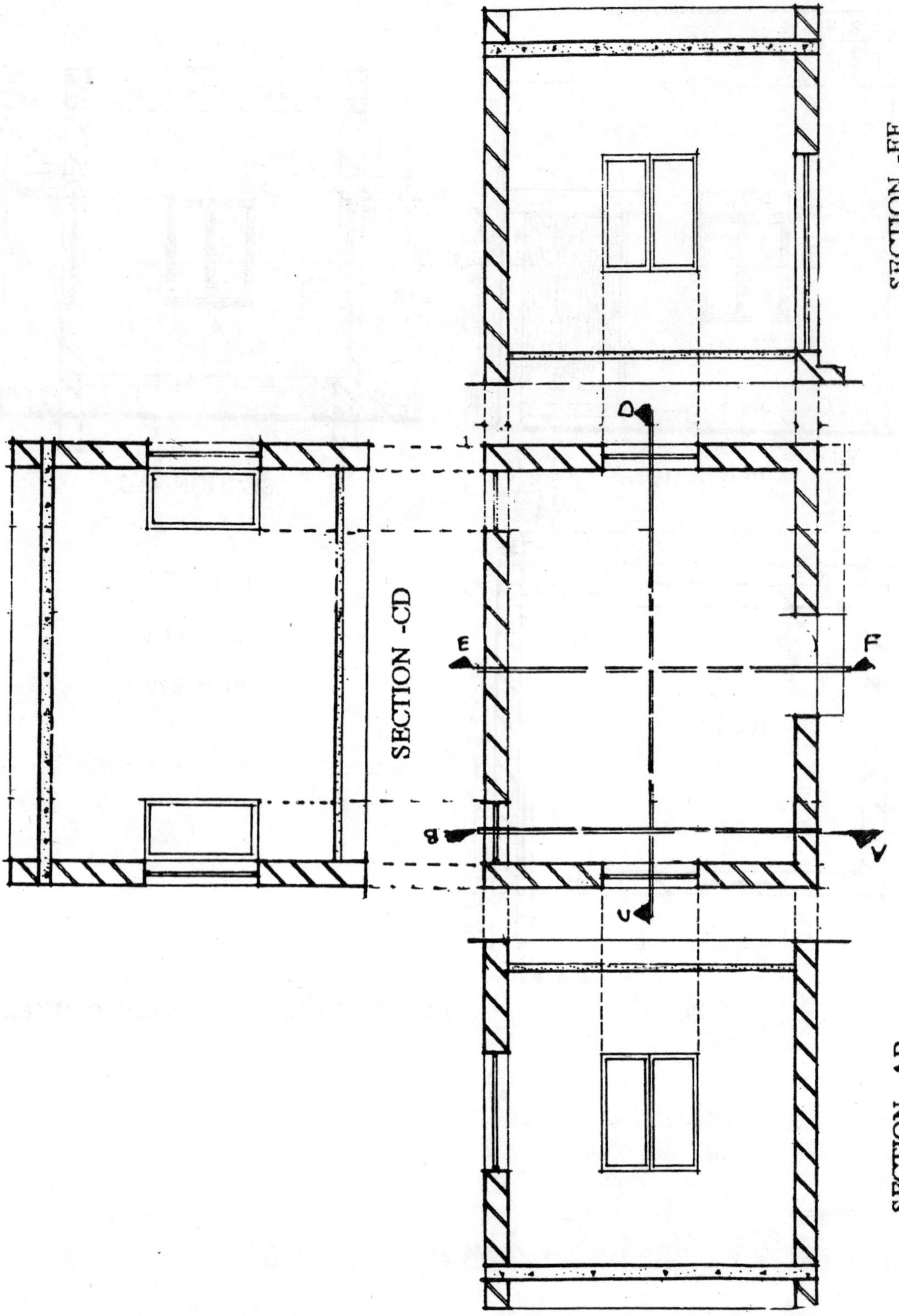


Fig. 6.17. C.

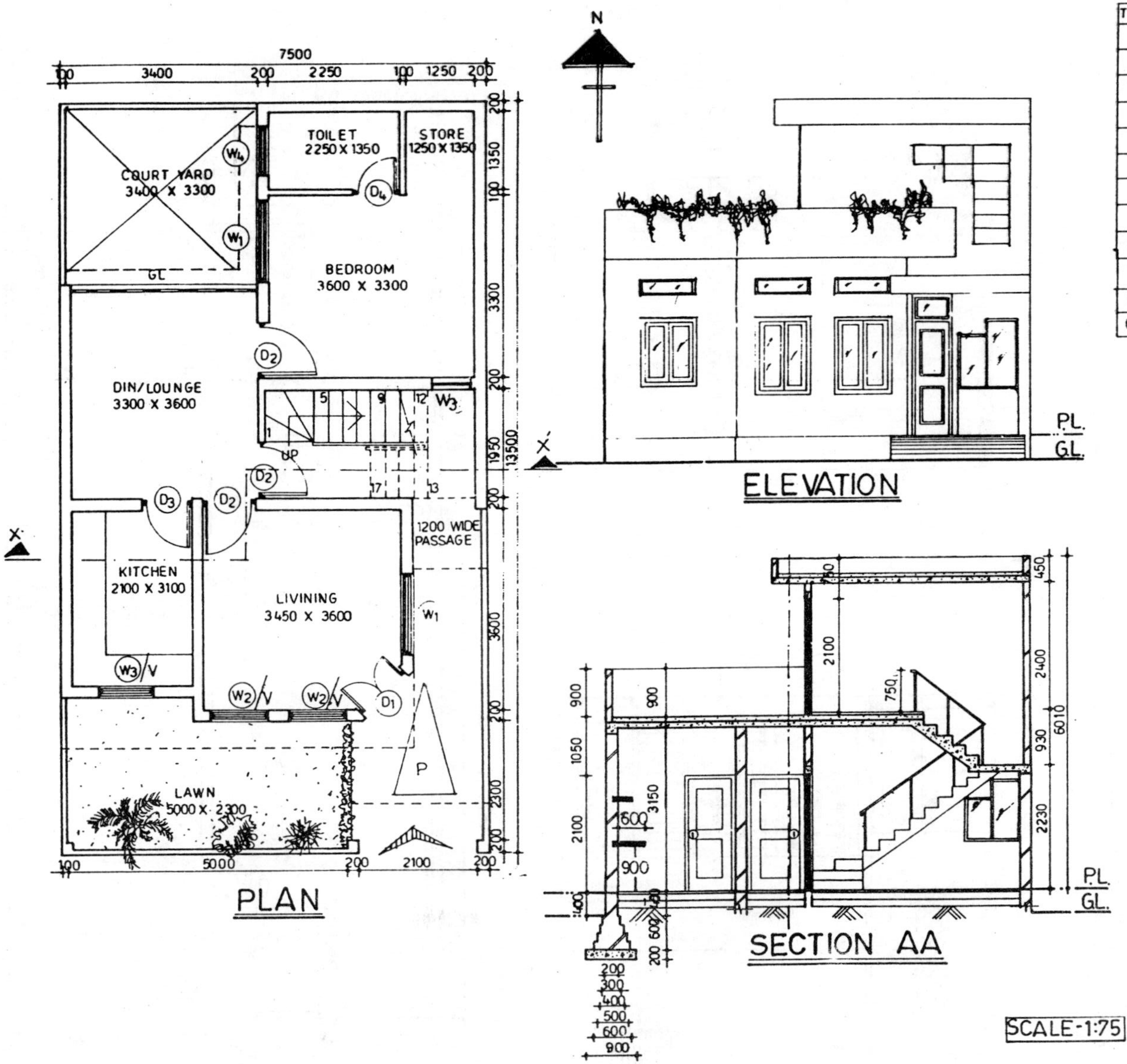


| TYPE | SIZE | CILL | LINTEL | NOS |
|---|---|---|---|---|
| $D_1$ | 1000 X 2550 | — | 2550 | 01 |
| $D_2$ | 1000 X 2100 | — | 2100 | 03 |
| $D_3$ | 900 X 2100 | — | 2100 | 01 |
| $D_4$ | 750 X 2100 | — | 2100 | 01 |
| $W_1$ | 1500 X 1800 | 750 | 2550 | 02 |
| $W_2$ | 1000 X 1800 | 750 | 2550 | 02 |
| $W_3$ | 1000 X 1650 | 900 | 2550 | 01 |
| $W_4$ | 900 X 1200 | 1350 | 2550 | 01 |
| GL | 3300 X 2550 | — | 2550 | 01 |
| V | 1000 X 300 | 2700 | 3000 | 03 |
| PLOT AREA - 110.0 $M^2$ | | | | |
| COVD. AREA - 78.0 $M^2$ | | | | |

All dimensions in mm

Fig. 6.18.

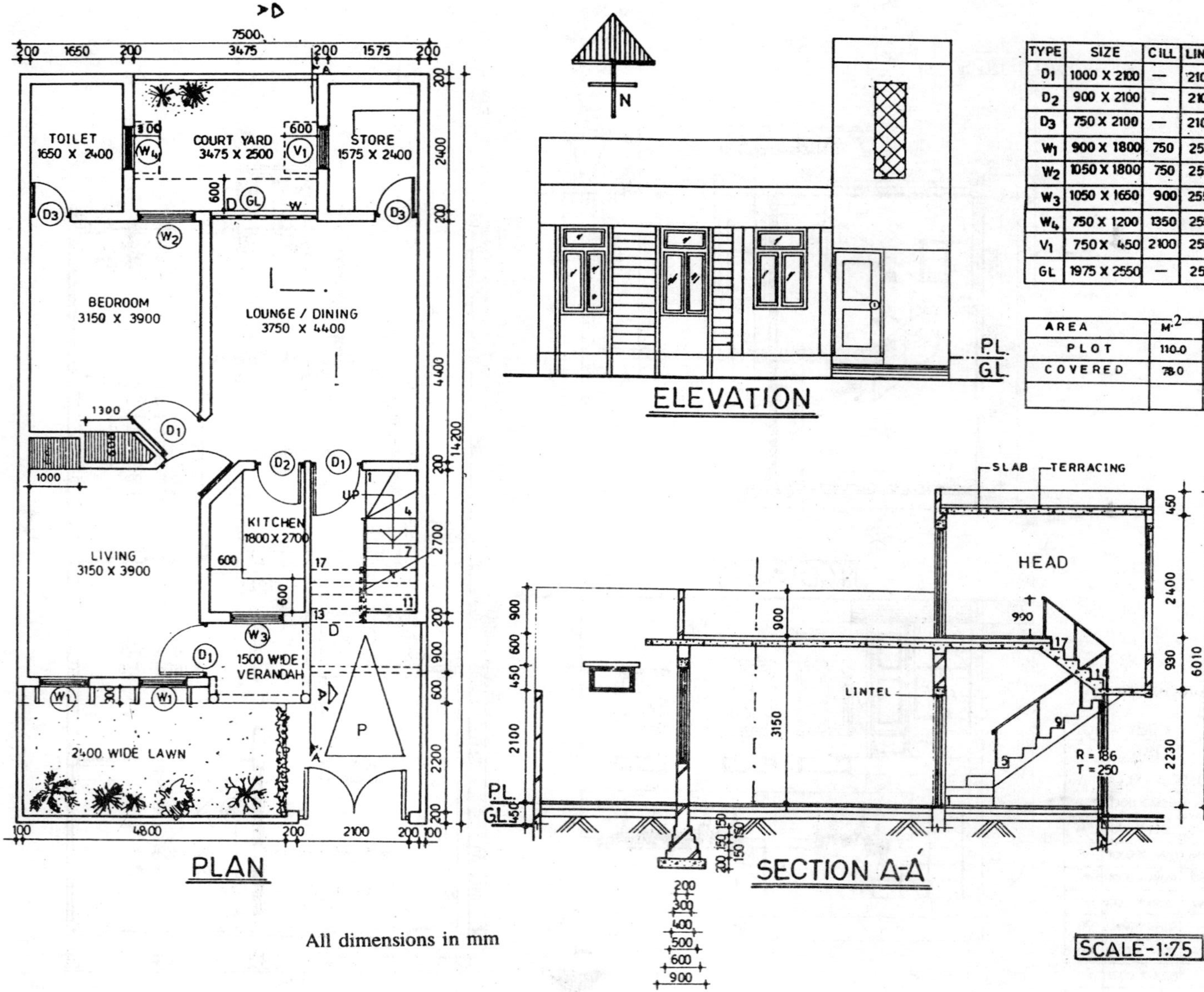


| TYPE | SIZE | CILL | LINTEL | NOS |
|---|---|---|---|---|
| $D_1$ | 1000 X 2100 | — | 2100 | 03 |
| $D_2$ | 900 X 2100 | — | 2100 | 01 |
| $D_3$ | 750 X 2100 | — | 2100 | 02 |
| $W_1$ | 900 X 1800 | 750 | 2550 | 02 |
| $W_2$ | 1050 X 1800 | 750 | 2550 | 01 |
| $W_3$ | 1050 X 1650 | 900 | 2550 | 01 |
| $W_4$ | 750 X 1200 | 1350 | 2550 | 01 |
| $V_1$ | 750 X 450 | 2100 | 2550 | 01 |
| GL | 1975 X 2550 | — | 2550 | 01 |

| AREA | $M^2$ | |
|---|---|---|
| PLOT | 110.0 | |
| COVERED | 78.0 | |
| | | |

All dimensions in mm

SCALE-1:75

Fig. 6.19.

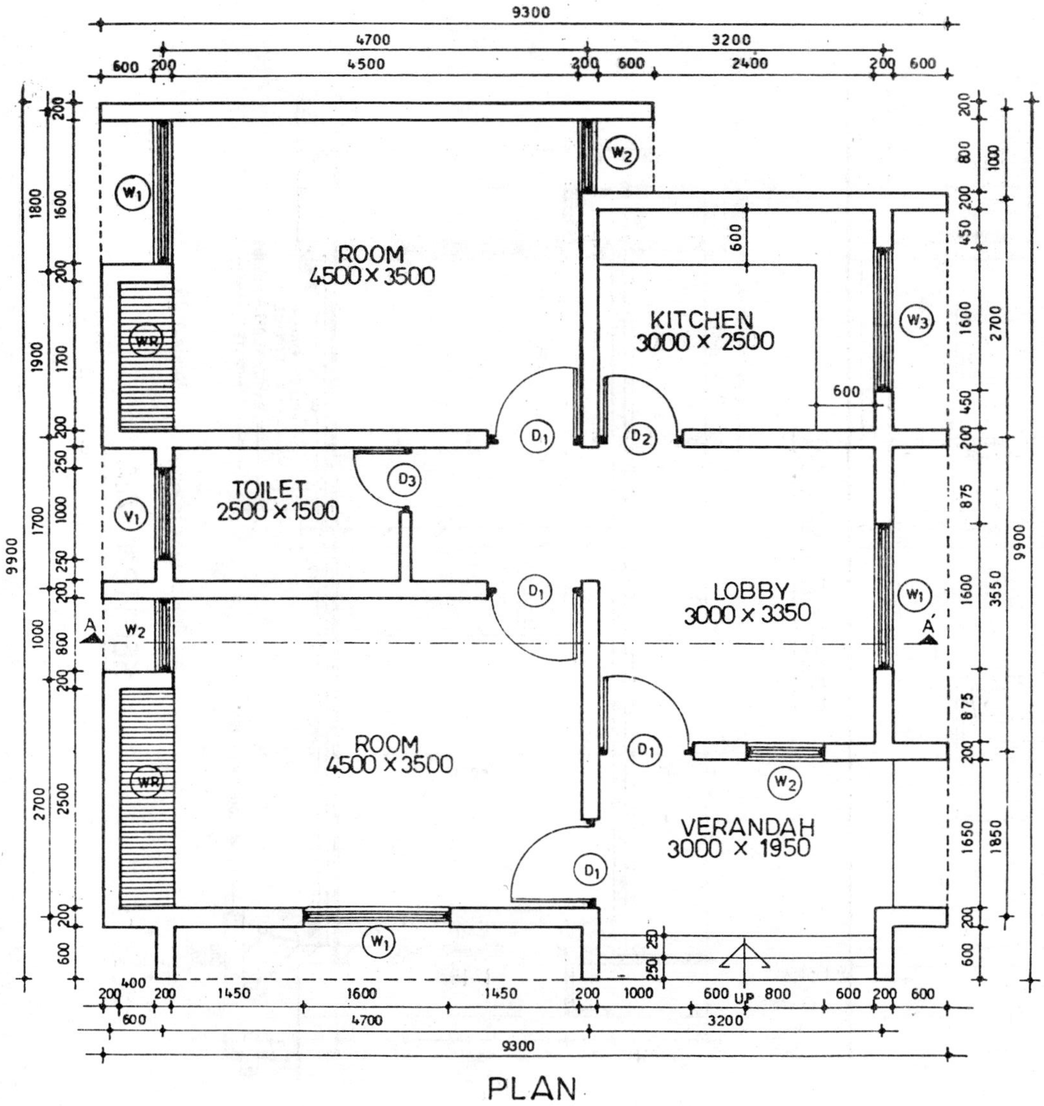


| SCHEDULE OF OPENING | | | | |
|---|---|---|---|---|
| TYPE | SIZE | LINTEL | CILL | NOS. |
| $D_1$ | 1000 × 2500 | 2500 | — | 04 |
| $D_2$ | 900 × 2500 | 2500 | — | 01 |
| $D_3$ | 750 × 2500 | 2500 | — | 01 |
| $W_1$ | 1600 × 1750 | 2500 | 750 | 03 |
| $W_2$ | 800 × 1750 | 2500 | 750 | 03 |
| $W_3$ | 1600 1600 | 2500 | 900 | 01 |
| $V_1$ | 1000 500 | 2500 | 2000 | 01 |

SCALE —— 1:75

STAFF QUARTERS

All dimensions in mm

**Fig. 6.20.**

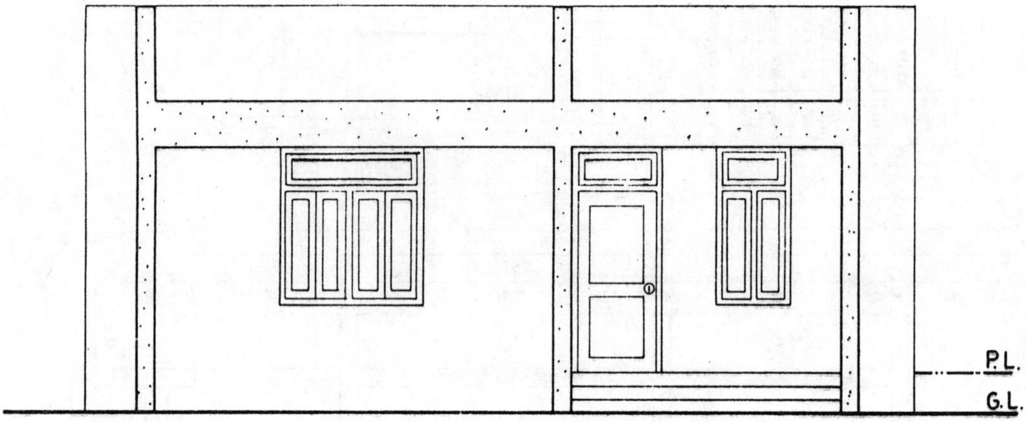


FRONT ELEVATION

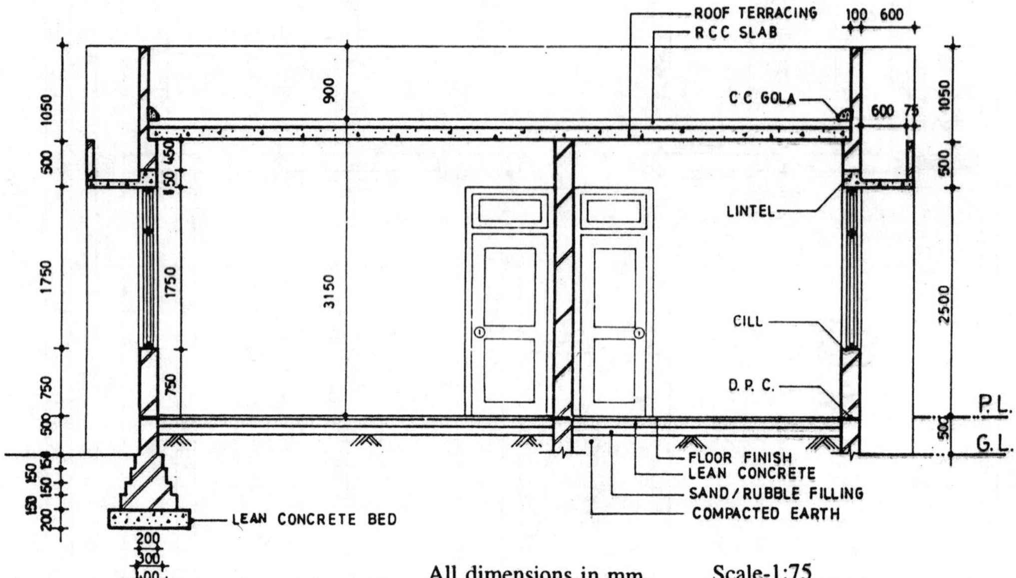


All dimensions in mm Scale-1:75

SECTION A-A

Fig. 6.20 A.

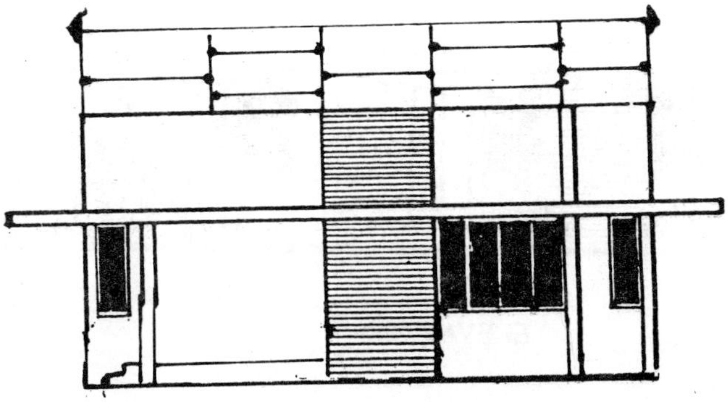

ELEVATION

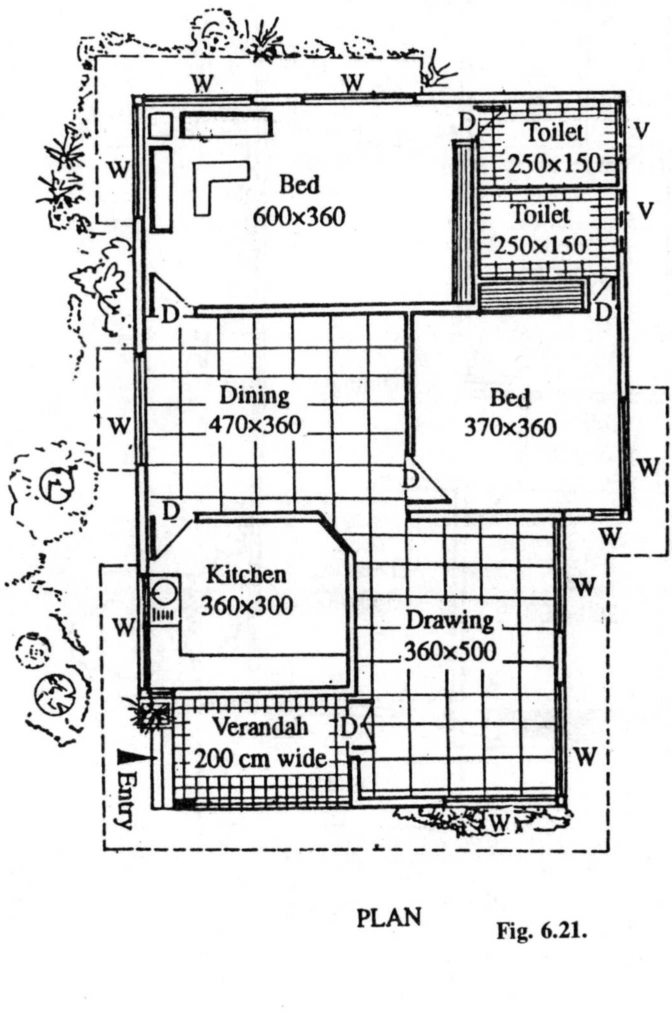


PLAN

Fig. 6.21.

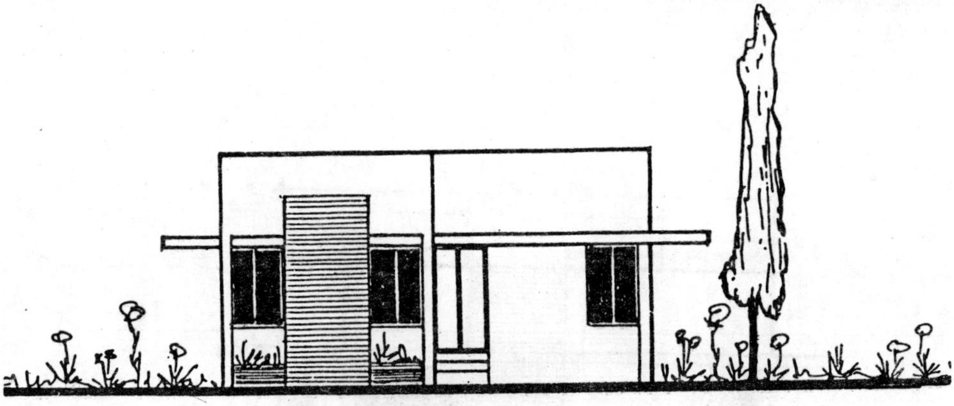

ELEVATION

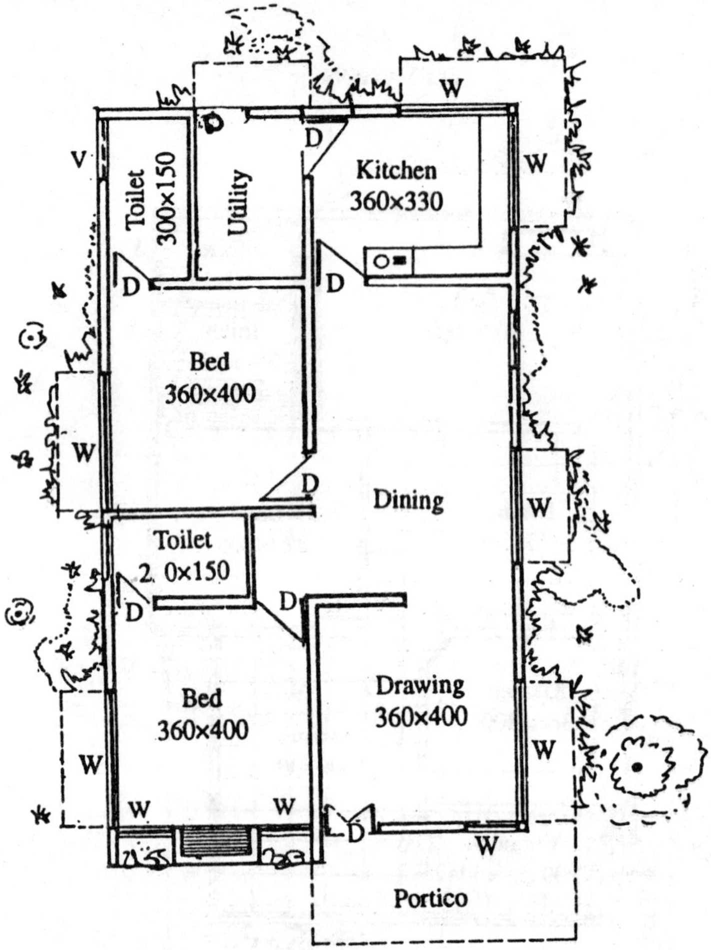


PLAN Fig. 6.22.

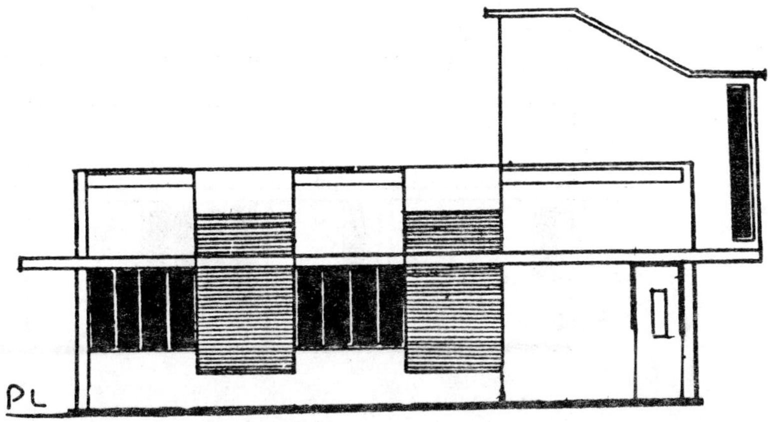


ELEVATION

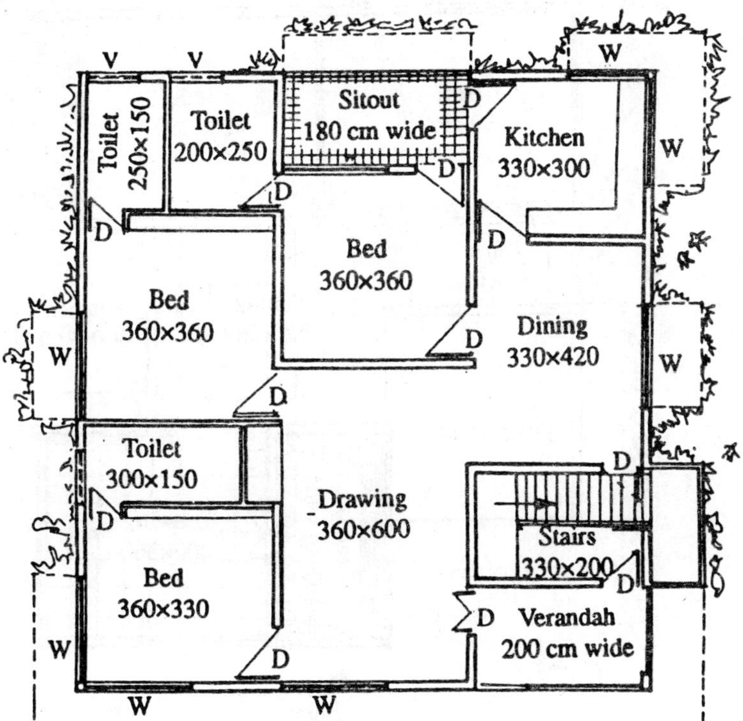


PLAN

Fig. 6.23.

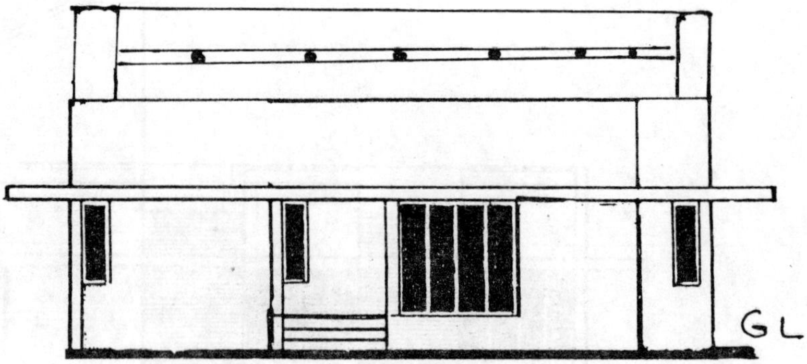


ELEVATION

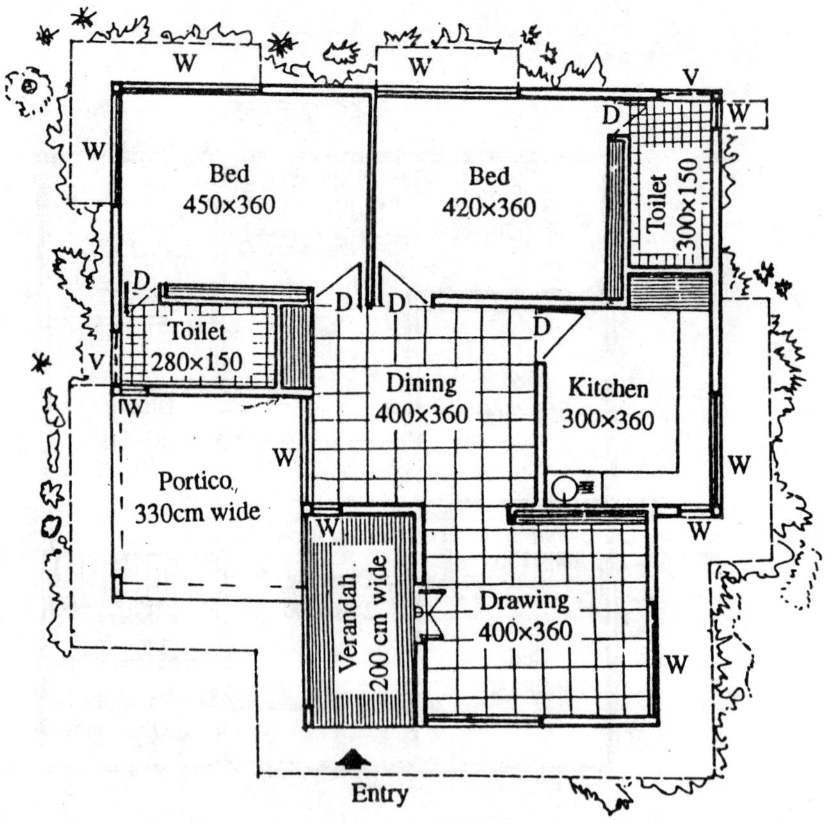


PLAN

Fig. 6.24.

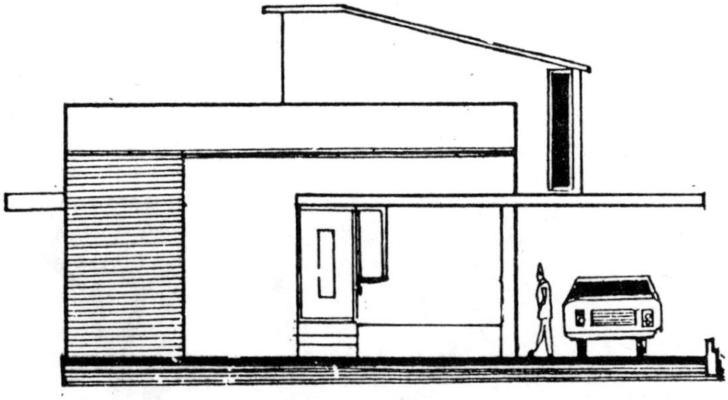

ELEVATION

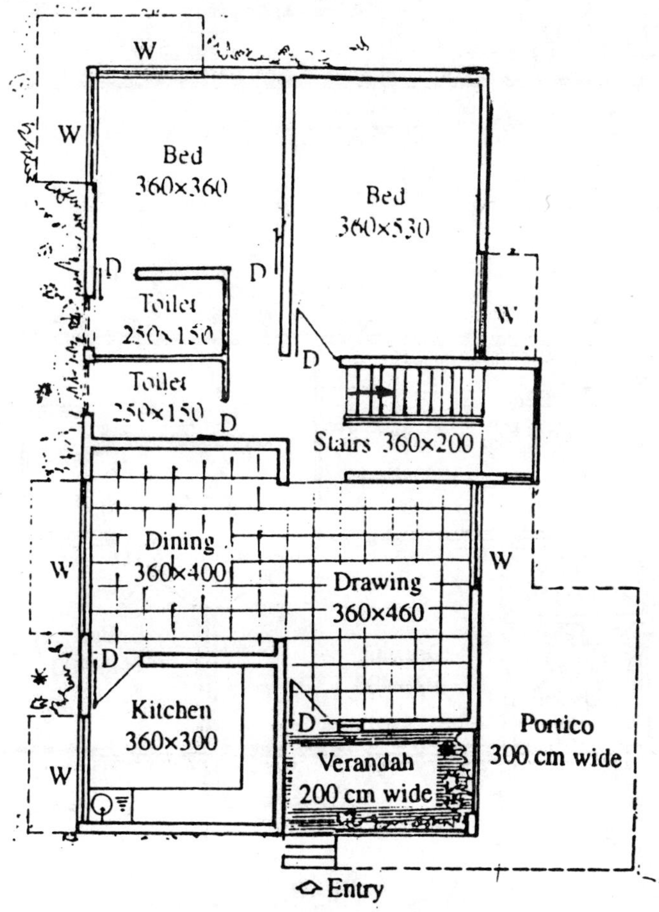


PLAN Fig. 6.25.

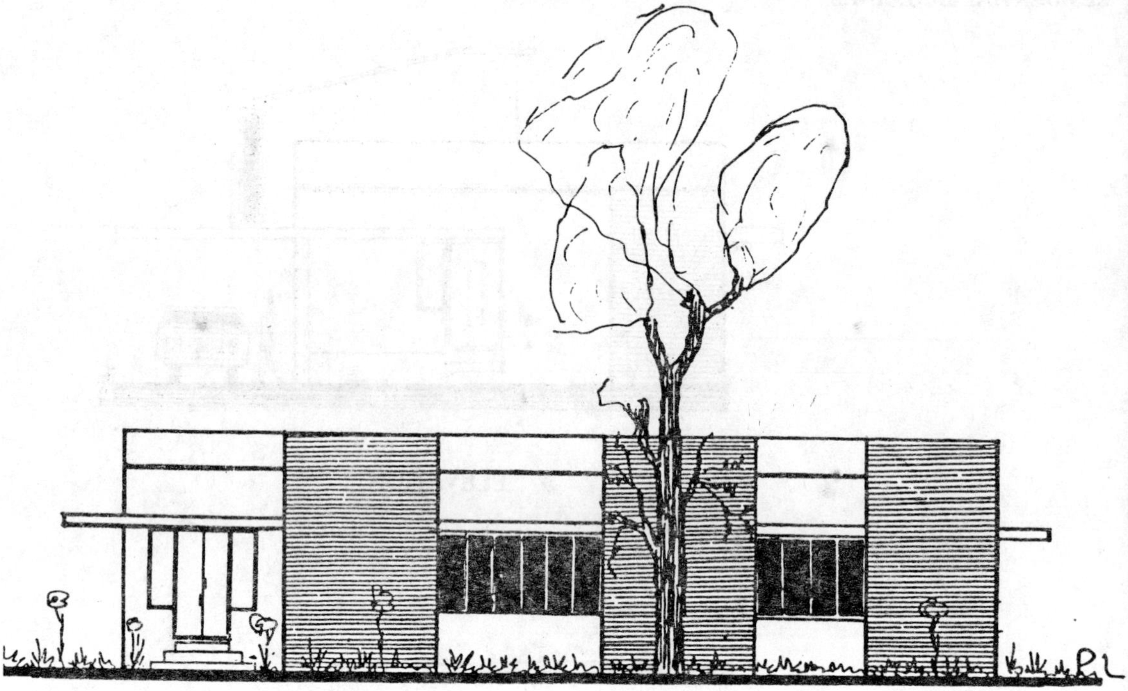

ELEVATION

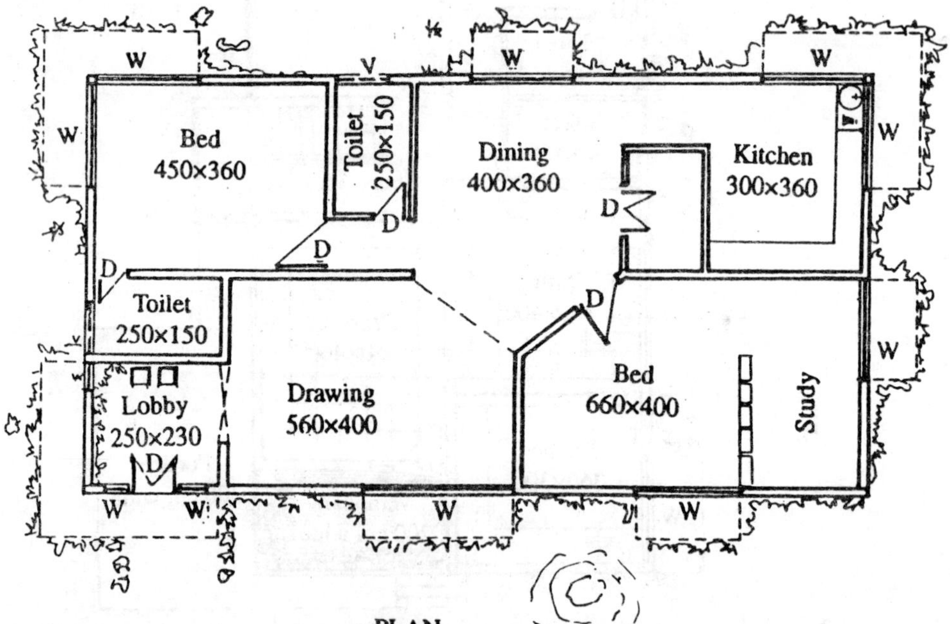


PLAN

Fig. 6.26.

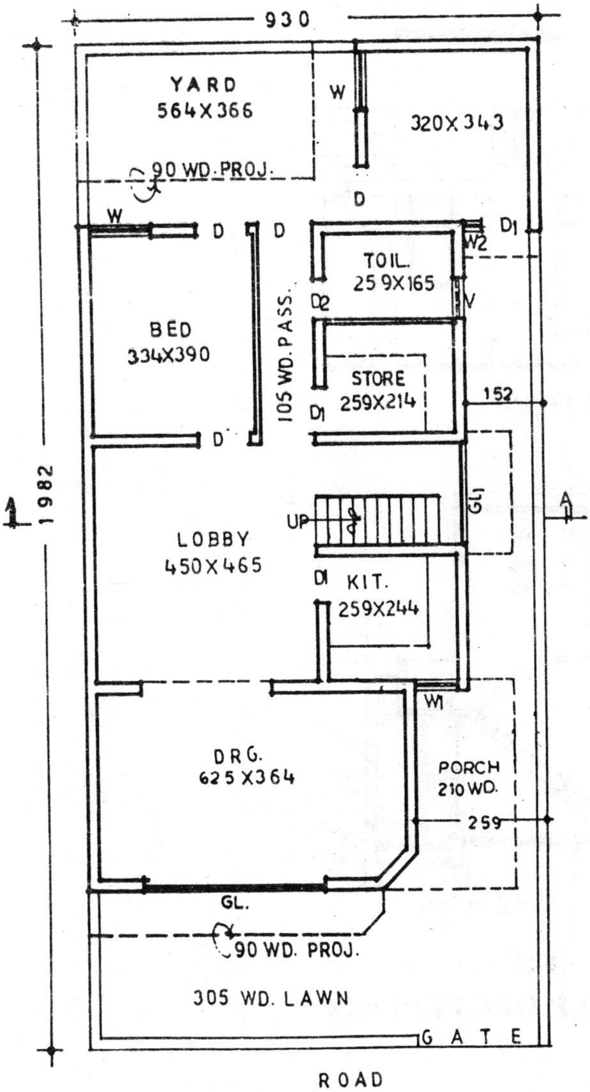


**GROUND FLOOR**

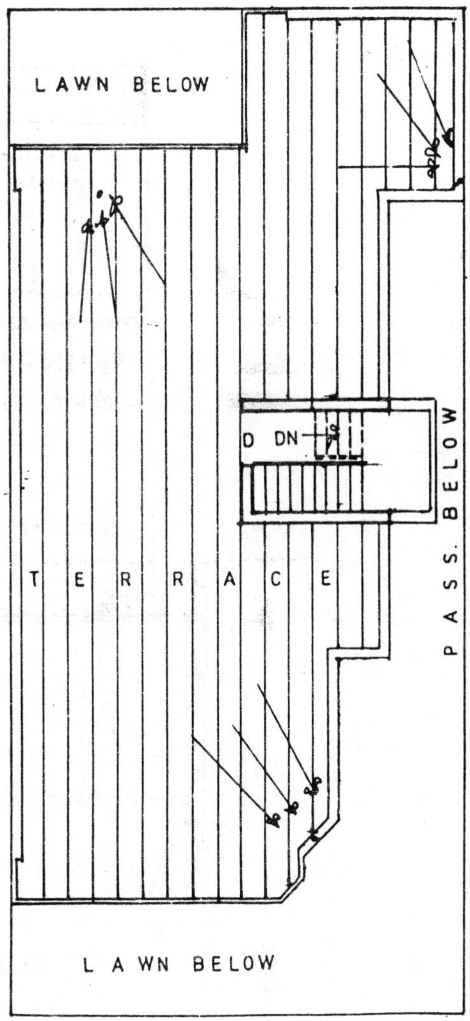


**TERRACE PLAN**

Fig. 6.27. A.

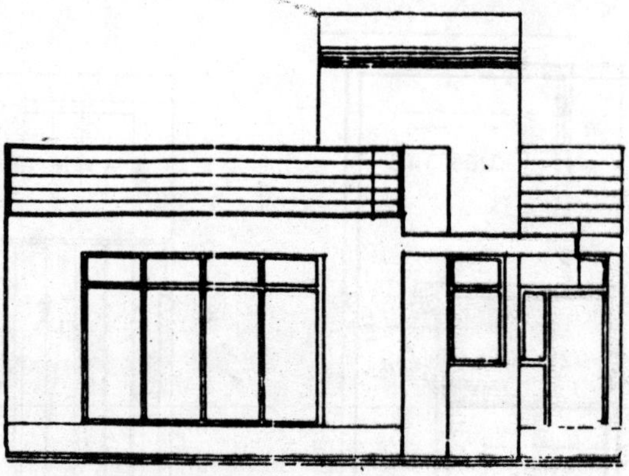

**FRONT ELEVATION**

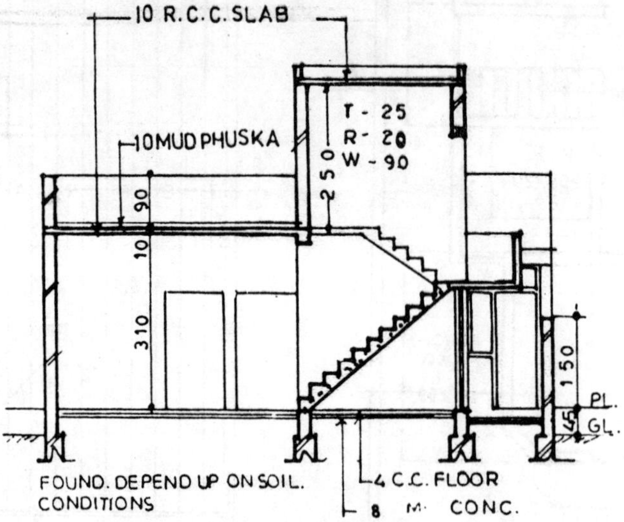


**SEC-A-A**

## SCHEDULE OF OPENINGS

| | | |
|---|---|---|
| D | DOOR | 105 X 210 |
| D1 | " | 90 X 210 |
| D2 | " | 75 X 210 |
| W | WINDOW | 120 X 120 |
| W1 | " | 84 X 120 |
| W2 | " | 39 X 120 |
| V | VENT | 75 X 45 |
| GL. | GLAZING | 366 X 210 |
| GL1 | " | 198 X 210 |

## AREA STATEMENT

| | SQ.M |
|---|---|
| PLOT AREA | 184.3 |
| COV. AREA AT. G.F. | 111.6 |
| OPEN AREA AT G.F. | 72.7 |

**Fig. 6.27. B.** ALL DIMENSIONS IN CM.

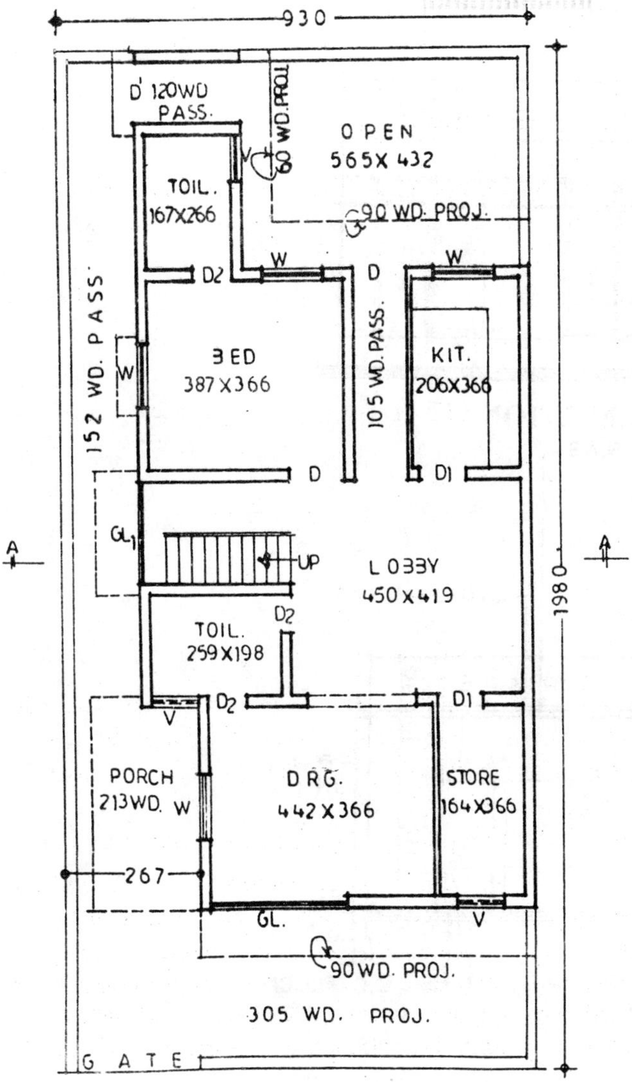


GROUND FLOOR

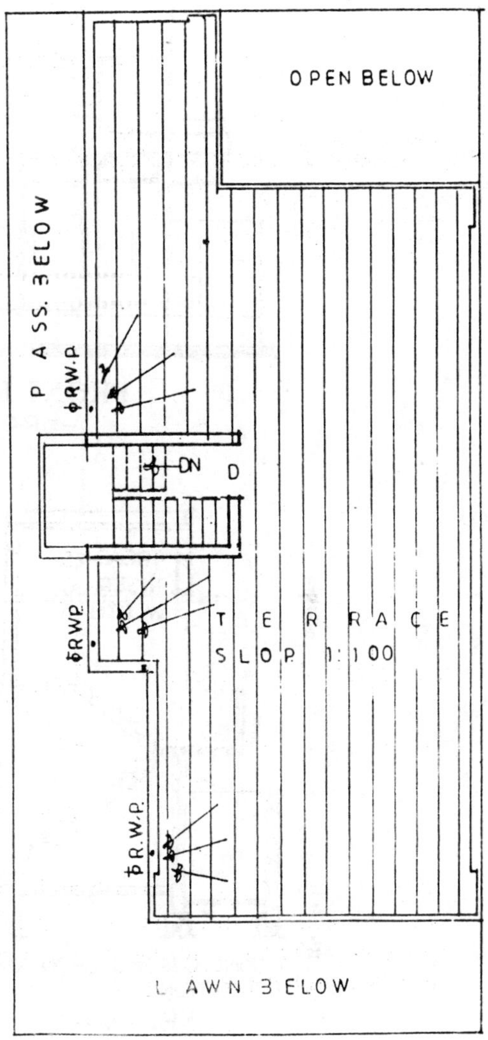


TERRACE PLAN

Fig. 6.28. A.

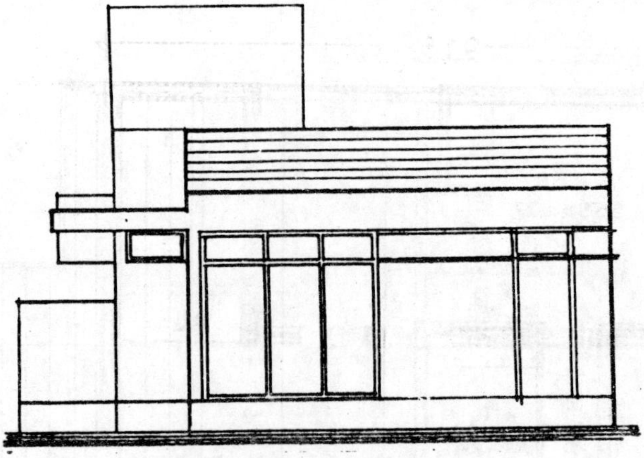

**FRONT ELEVATION**

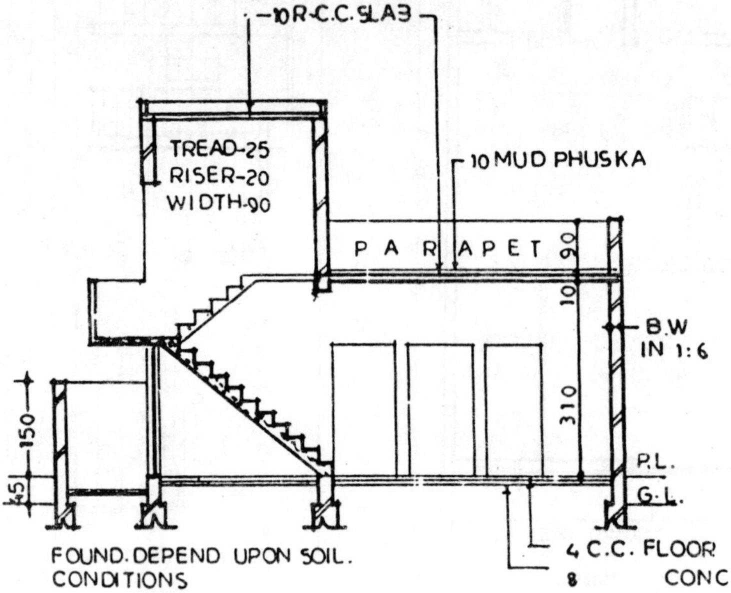


**SEC-A—A**

**SCHEDULE OF OPENINGS**

ALL DIMENSIONS IN CM

| | | |
|---|---|---|
| D' | DOOR | 120 X 210 |
| D | " | 105 X 210 |
| D1 | " | 90 X 210 |
| D2 | " | 75 X 210 |
| W | WINDOW | 120 X 120 |
| V | " | 90 X 45 |
| GL | GLAZING | 270 X 210 |
| GL1 | " | 198 X 210 |

**AREA STATEMENT**

| | SQ·M |
|---|---|
| PLOT AREA | 179·50 |
| COV. AREA AT G.F. | 101·40 |
| OPEN AREA AT G.F. | 78·10 |

**Fig. 6.28. B.**

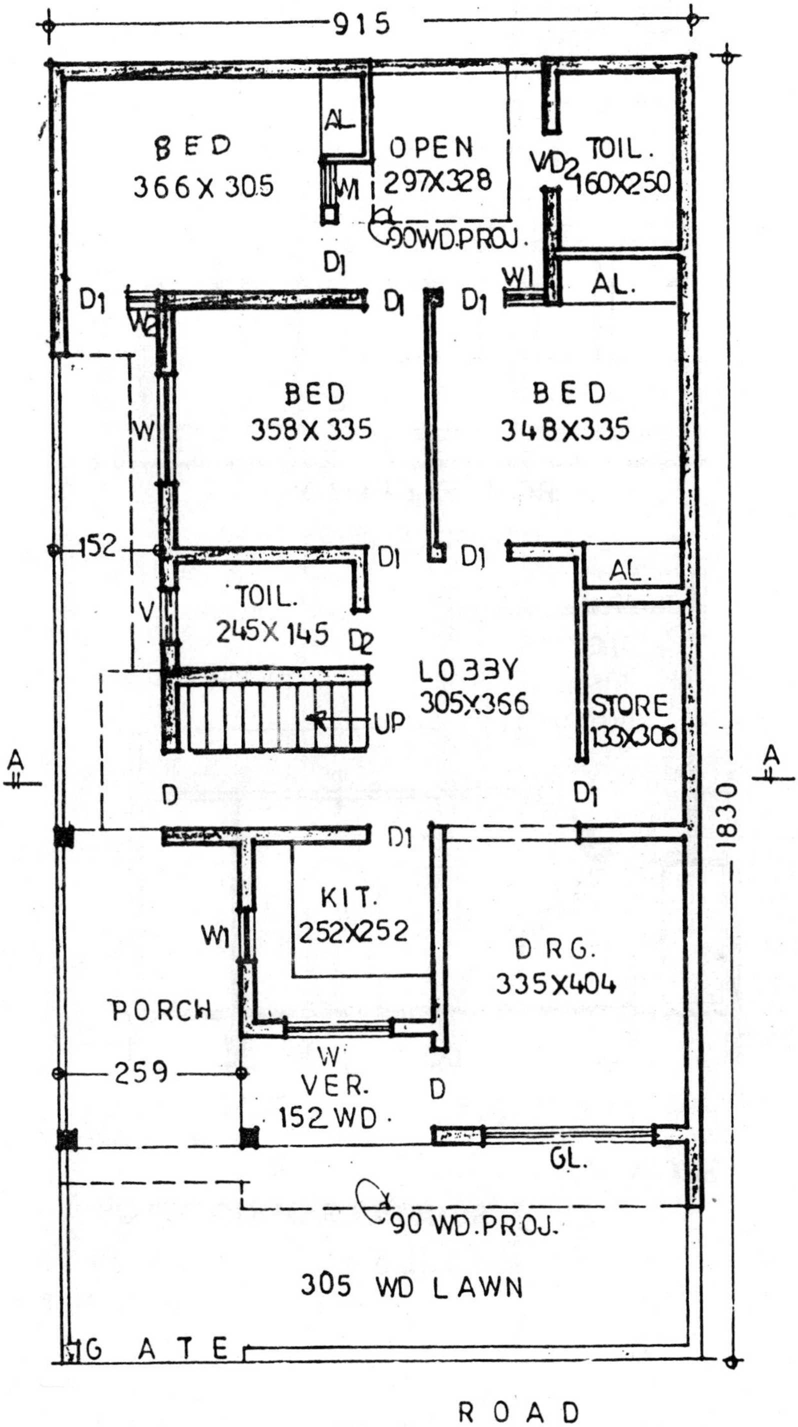


## GROUND FLOOR

**Fig. 6.29. A.**

All dimensions in cm

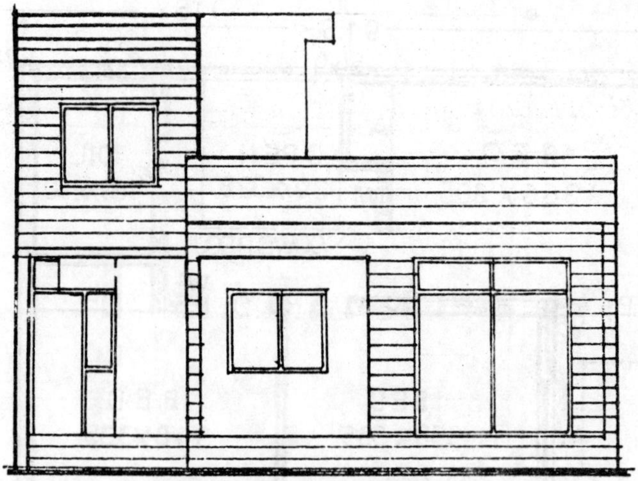

**FRONT ELEVATION**

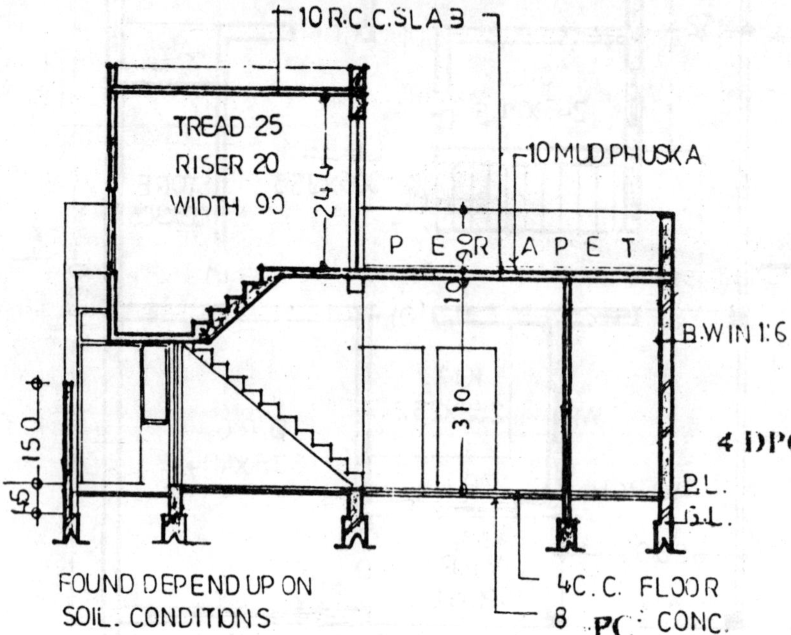


**SEC-A—A**

## SCHEDULE OF OPENINGS

| | | |
|---|---|---|
| D | DOOR | 105 X 210 |
| D1 | " | 90 X 210 |
| D2 | " | 75 X 210 |
| V/D2 | " | 75 X 255 |
| W | WINDOW | 150 X 120 |
| W1 | " | 55 X 120 |
| W2 | " | 39 X 120 |
| GL | GLAZING. | 240 X 210 |

Fig. 6.29. B.

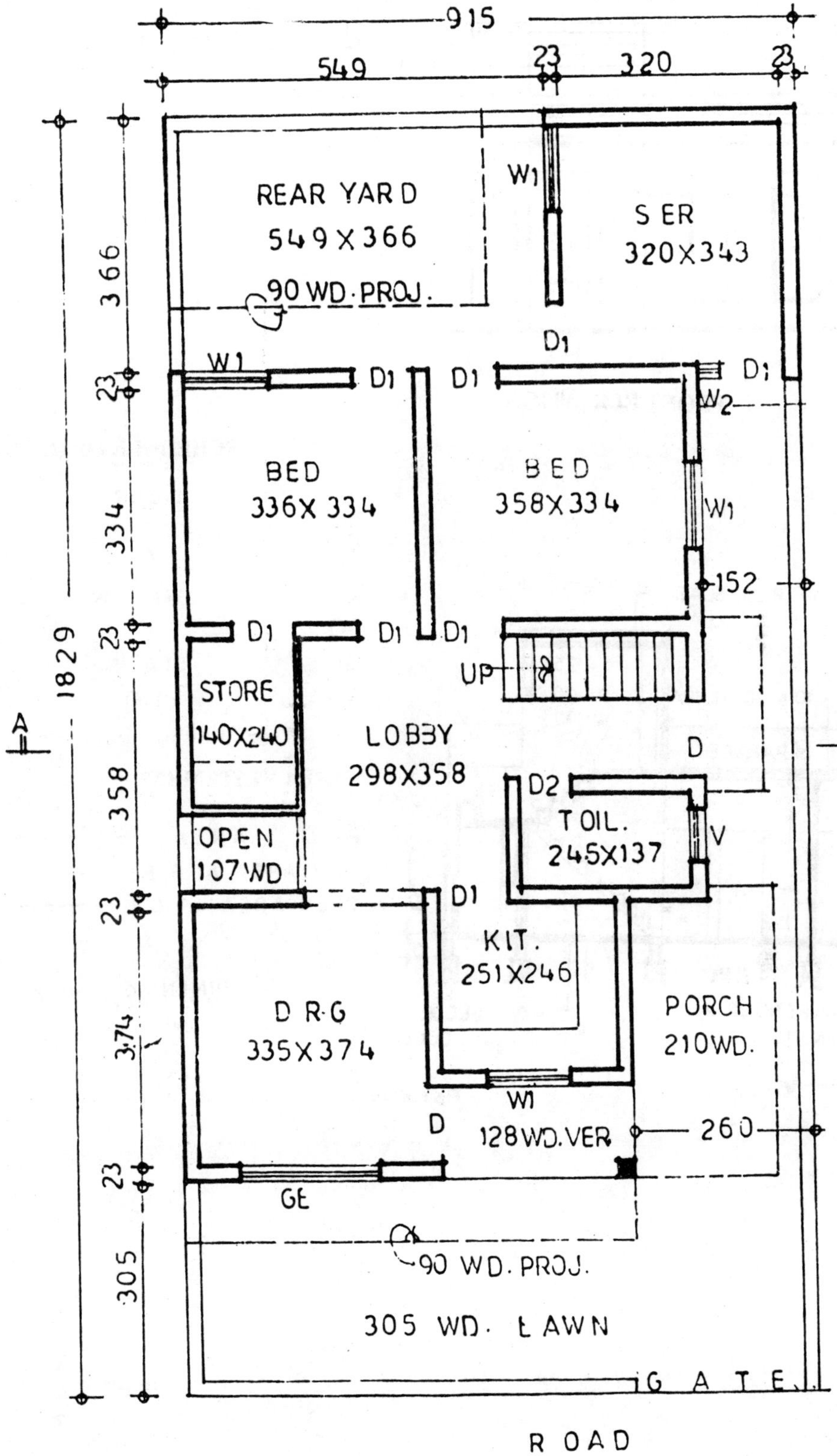


Fig. 6.30. A. **GROUND FLOOR**

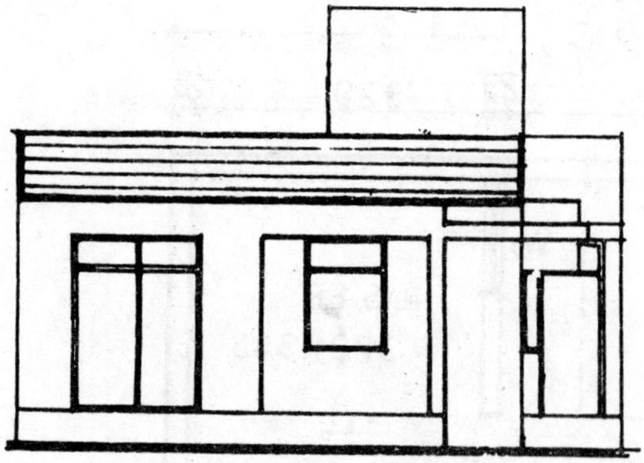

**FRONT ELEVATION**

### SCHEDULE OF OPENINGS

| | | |
|---|---|---|
| D | DOOR | 105 X 2 |
| D1 | " | 90 X 2 |
| D2 | " | 90 X 2 |
| W1 | WINDOW | 120 X 1 |
| W2 | " | 39 X 1 |
| GL | GLAZING | 210 X 2 |
| V | VENT | 75 X |

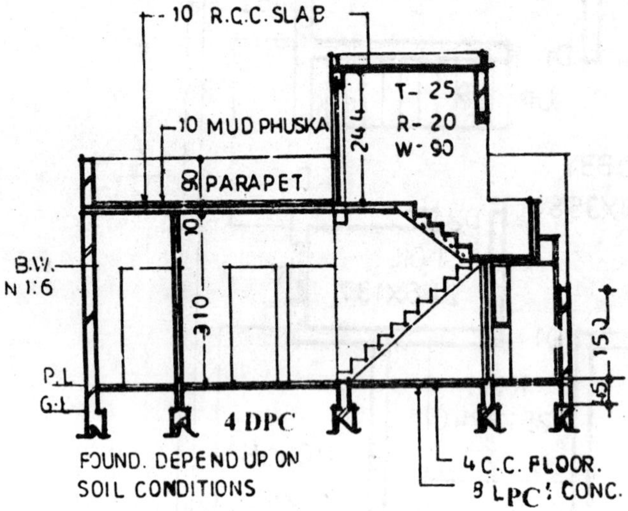


### AREA STATEMENT

| | SQ. M |
|---|---|
| PLOT AREA | 167·30 |
| COV. AREA AT G.F. | 96·00 |
| OPEN AREA AT G.F. | 71·30 |

ALL DIMENSIONS IN CM

**SEC-A—A**

**Fig. 6.30. B.**

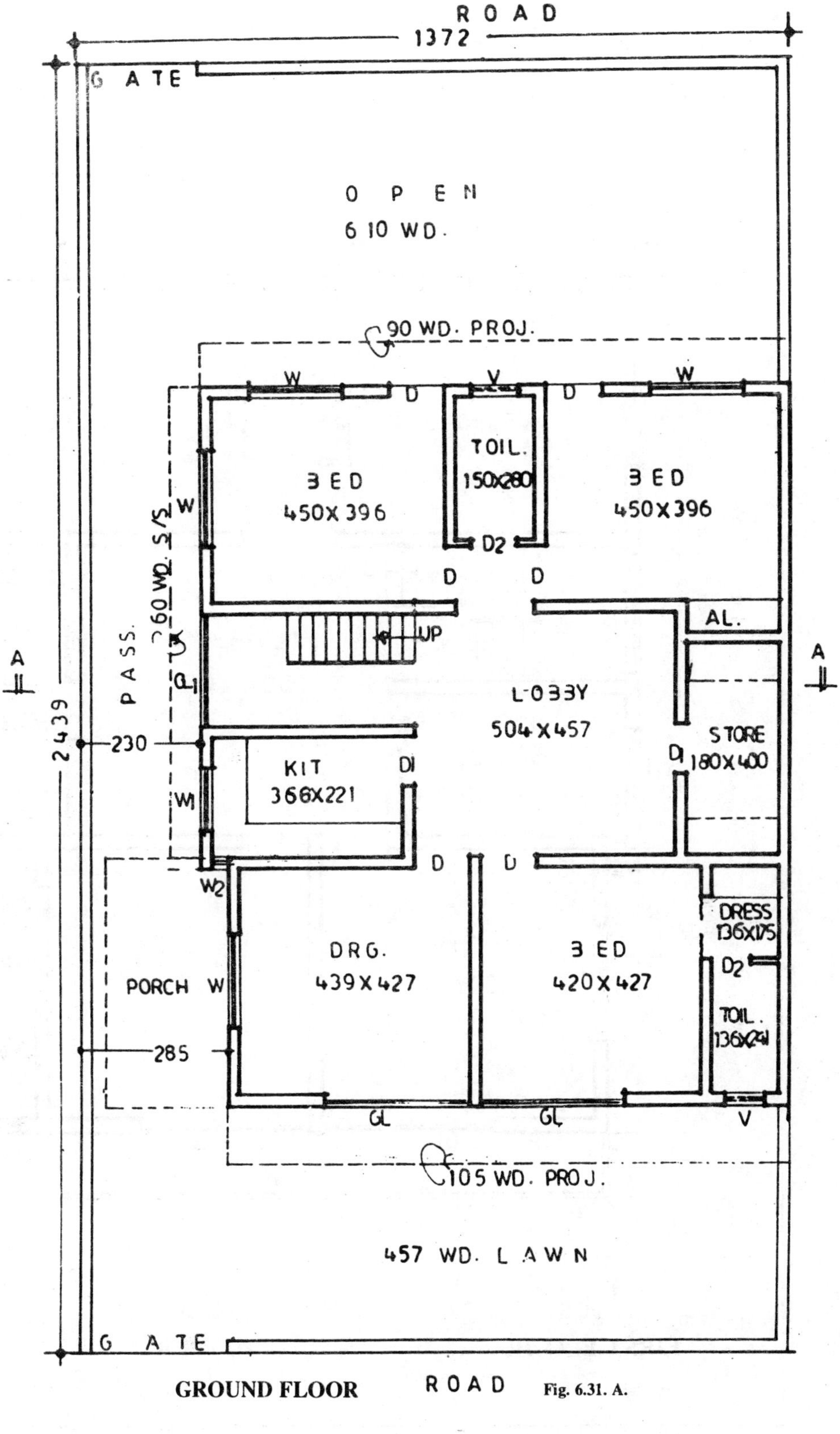


GROUND FLOOR

Fig. 6.31. A.

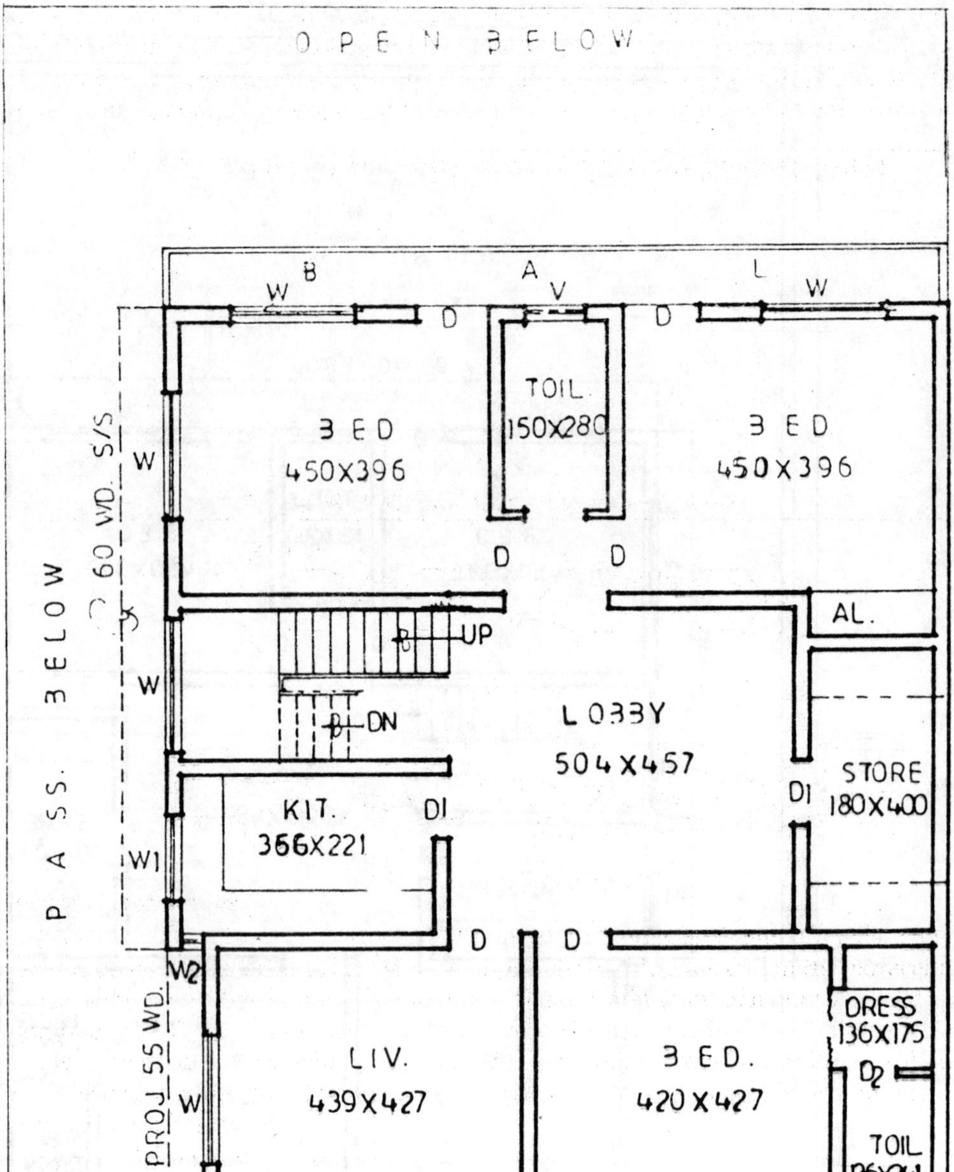


**FIRST FLOOR**

Fig. 6.31. B.

FIRST FLOOR

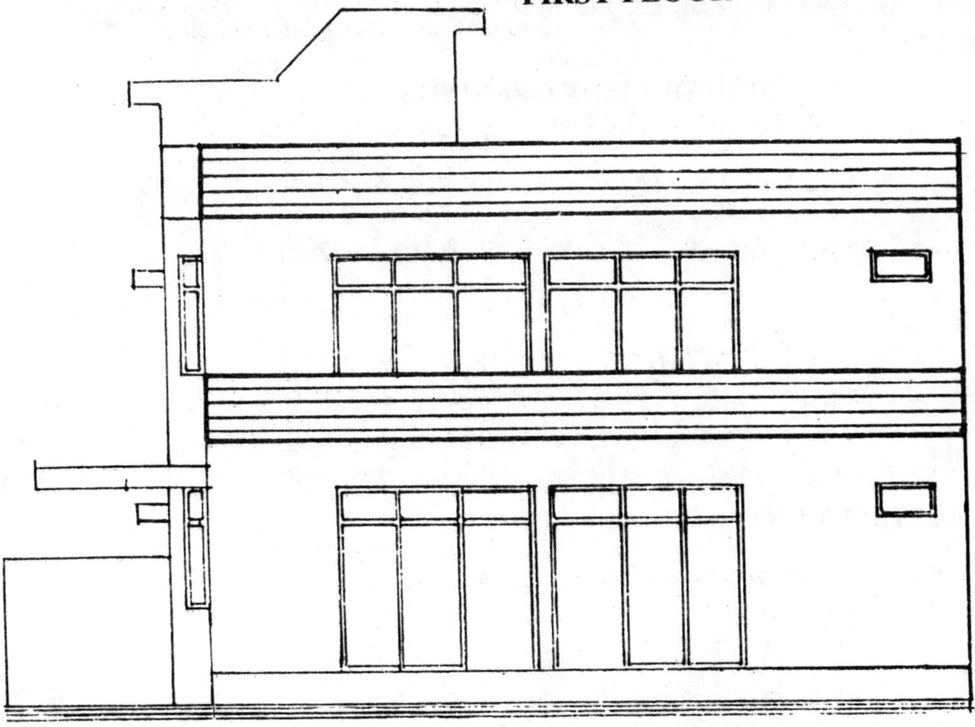

REAR ELEVATION

Fig. 6.31. C.

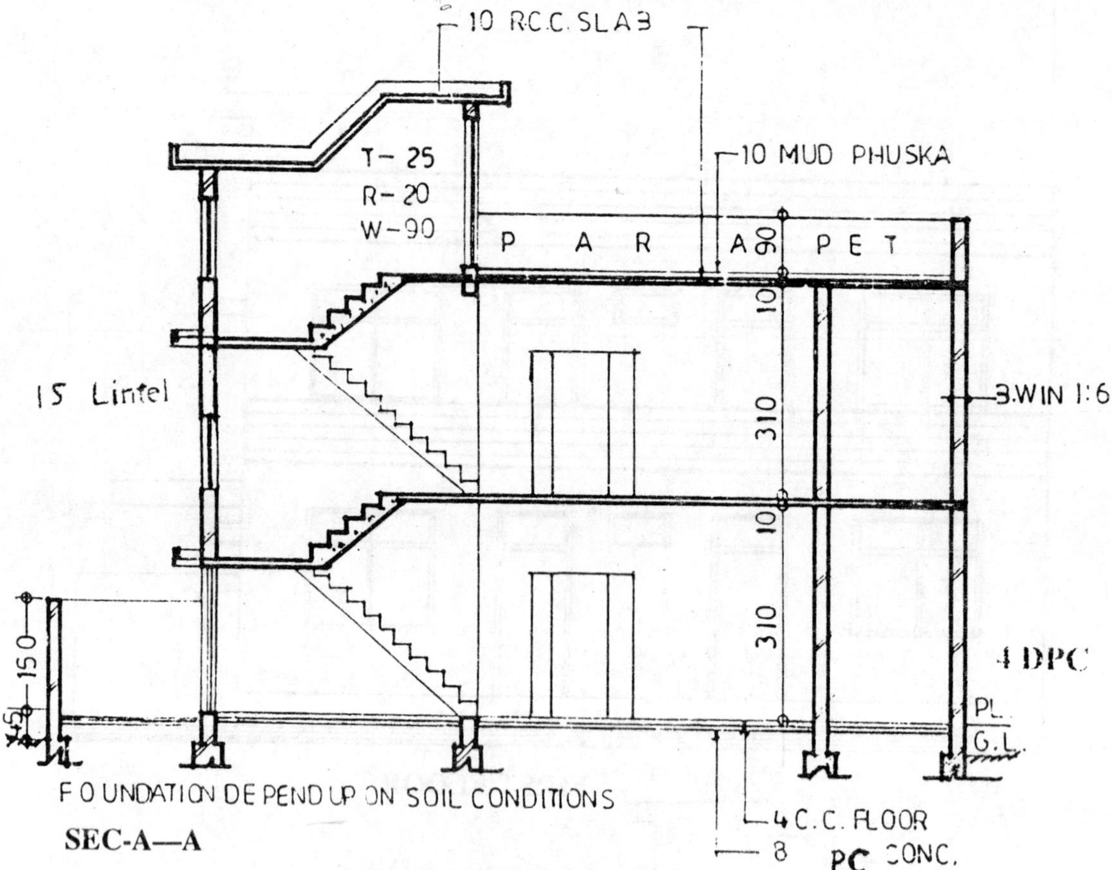


**SEC-A—A**

## SCHEDULE OF OPENINGS

| | | |
|---|---|---|
| D | DOOR | 105 X 210 |
| D1 | ″ | 90 X 210 |
| D2 | ″ | 75 X 210 |
| W | WINDOW | 180 X 120 |
| W1 | ″ | 120 X 120 |
| W2 | ″ | 32 X 120 |
| GL | GLAZING | 270 X 210 |
| GL1 | ″ | 213 X 210 |
| V | VENT | 75 X 45 |

## AREA STATEMENT

PLOT AREA ——— 334.6

COV. AREA AT G.F. ——— 154.2

OPEN AREA AT G.F. ——— 180.4

COV. AREA AT F.F. ——— 154.2

ALL DIMENSIONS IN CM

**Fig. 6.31. D.**

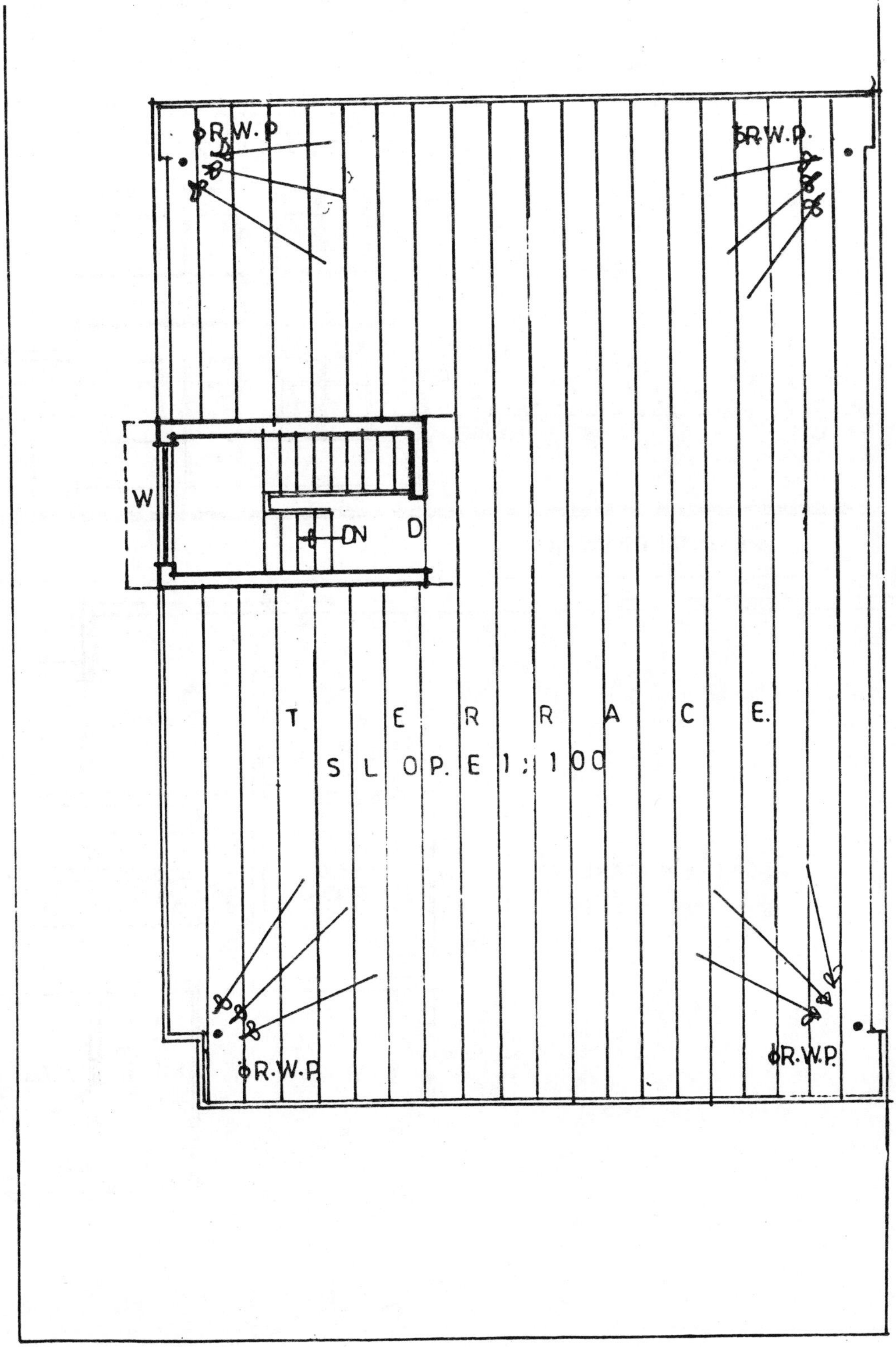


TERRACE PLAN

Fig. 6.31. E.

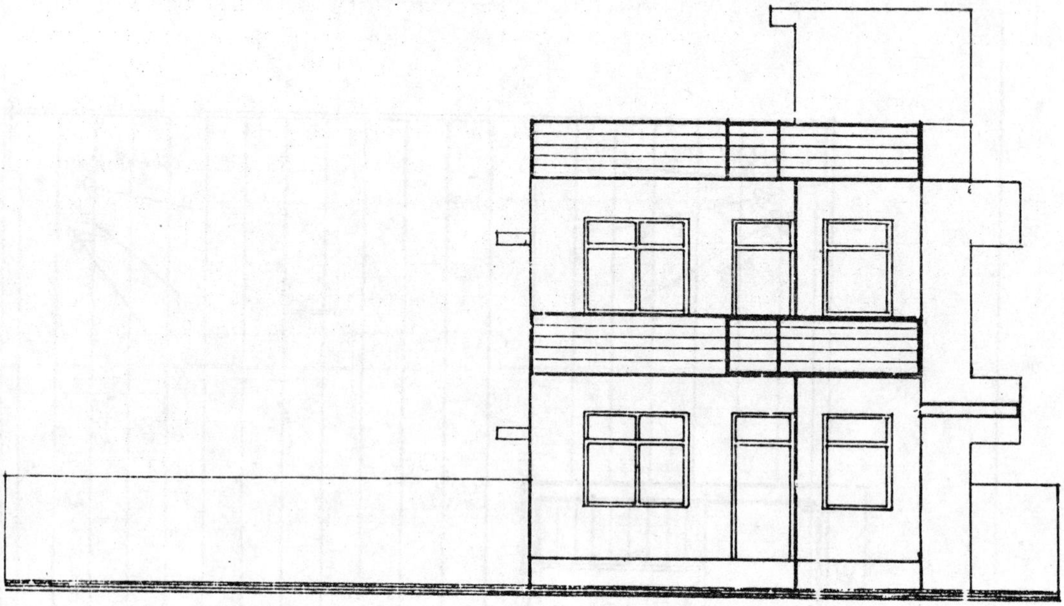

**FRONT ELEVATION**

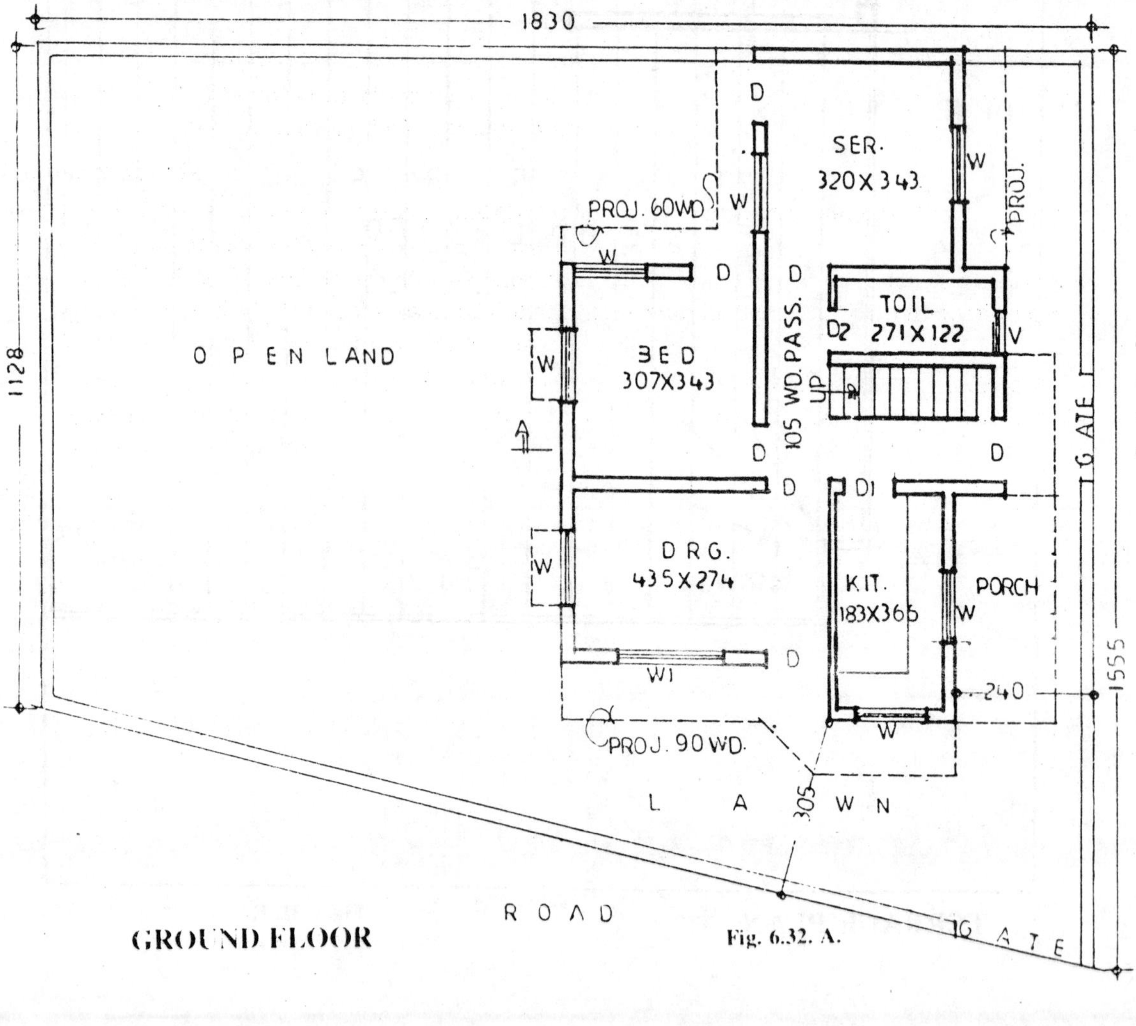


**GROUND FLOOR** **Fig. 6.32. A.**

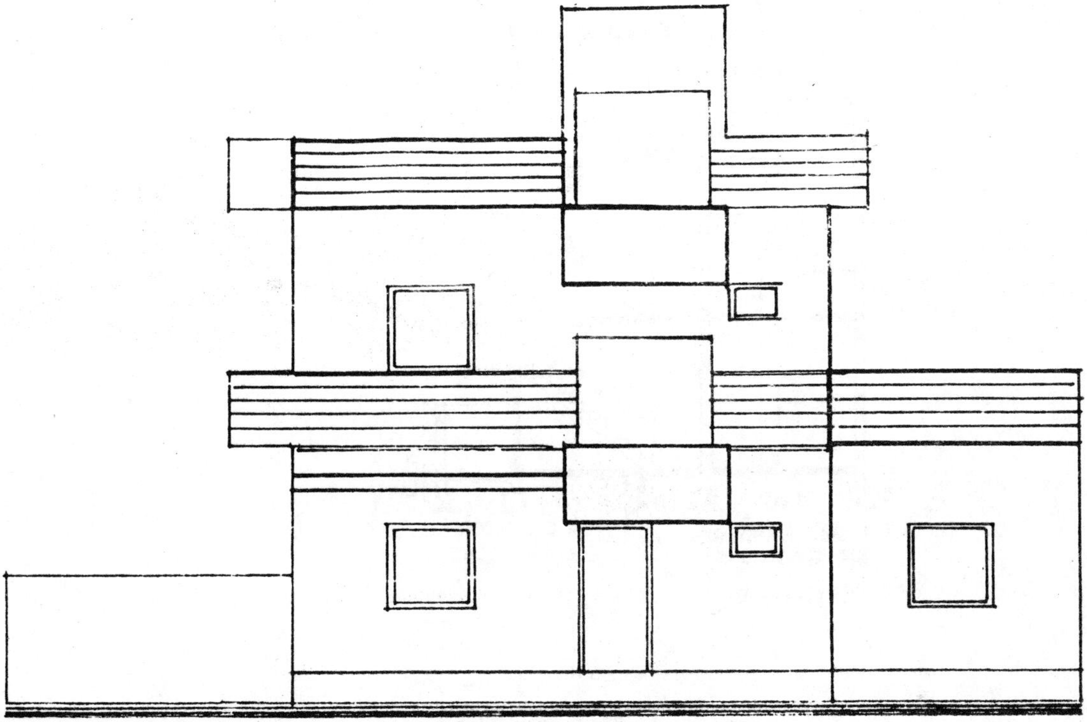

SIDE ELEVATION

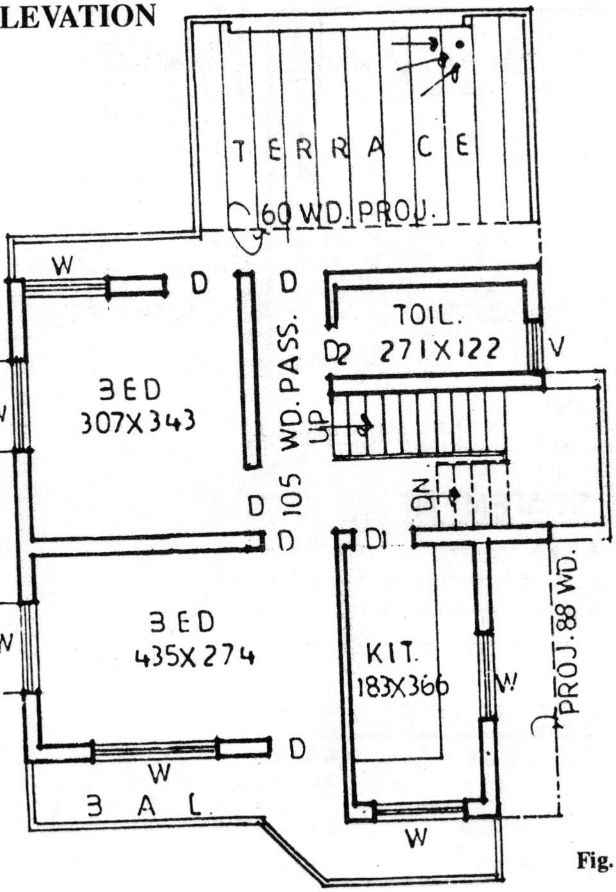


Fig. 6.32. B.

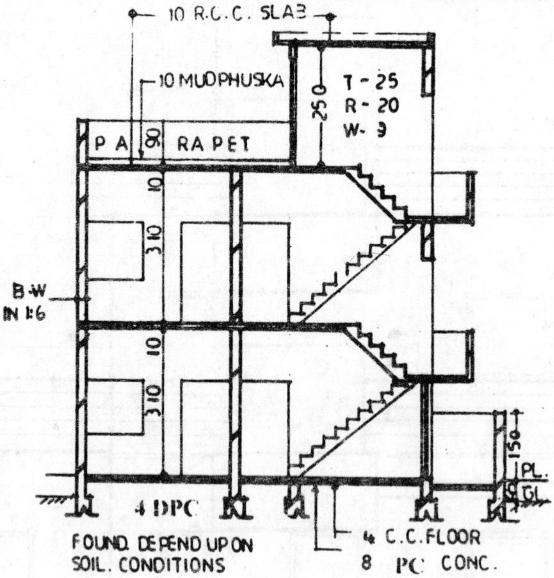


**SEC-A—A**

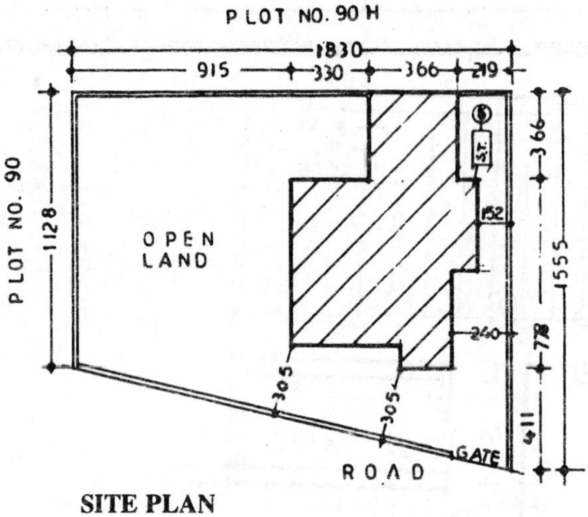


**SITE PLAN**

SCALE 1: 200

ALL DIMENSIONS IN

## AREA STATEMENT

| | SQ.M. |
|---|---|
| PLOT AREA | 245·50 |
| COV. AREA AT G.F. | 65·00 |
| OPEN AREA AT G.F. | 180·50 |
| COV. AREA AT F.F. | 51·60 |
| OPEN AREA AT F.F. | 13·40 |

## SCHEDULE OF OPENING

| | | |
|---|---|---|
| D | DOOR | 105 X 210 |
| D1 | " | 90 X 210 |
| D2 | " | 75 X 210 |
| W | WINDOW | 120 X 120 |
| W1 | " | 180 X 120 |
| V | VENT | 75 X 45 |

**Fig. 6.32. C.**

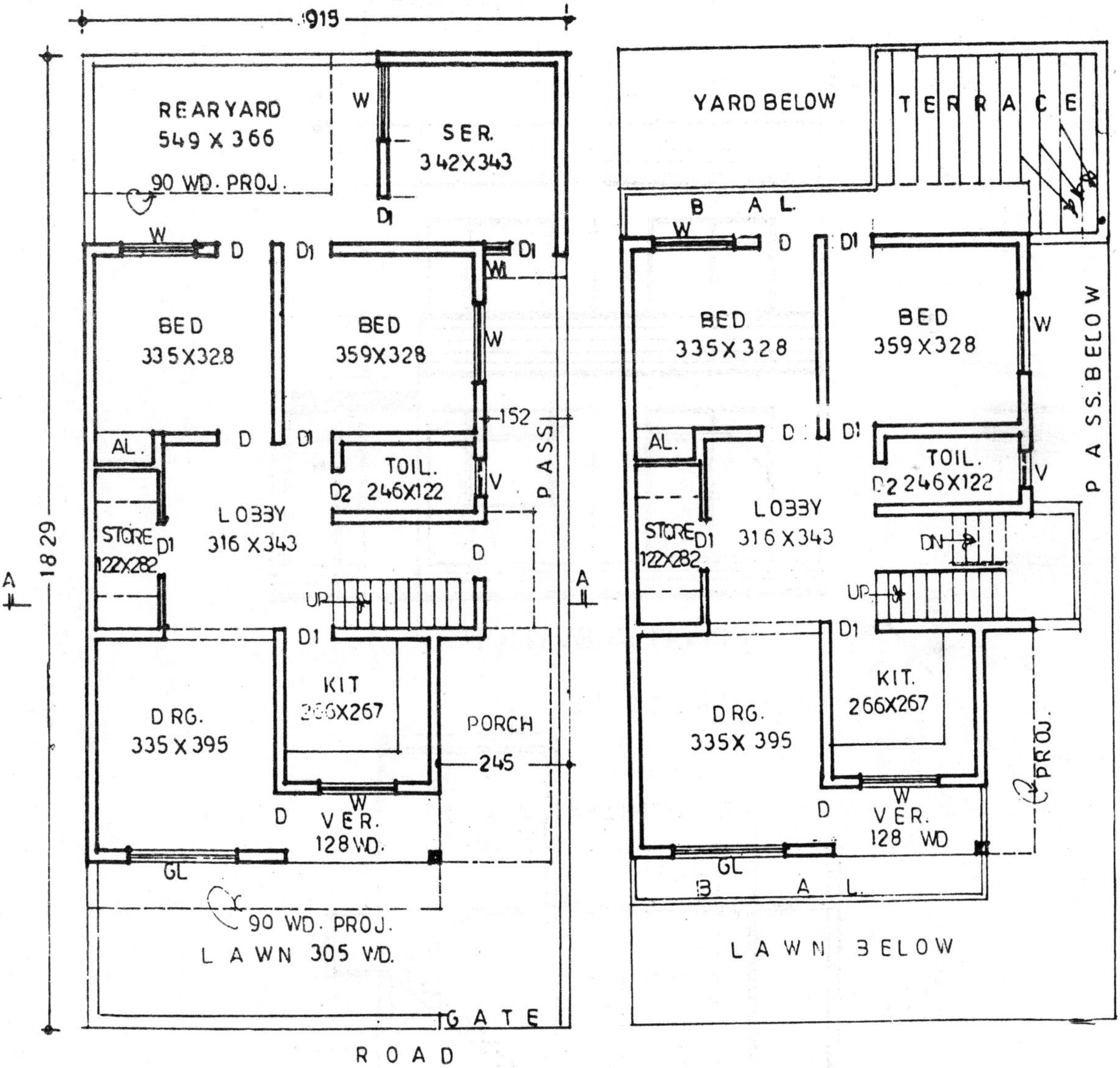


**GROUND FLOOR PLAN** **FIRST FLOOR PLAN**

Fig. 6.33. A.

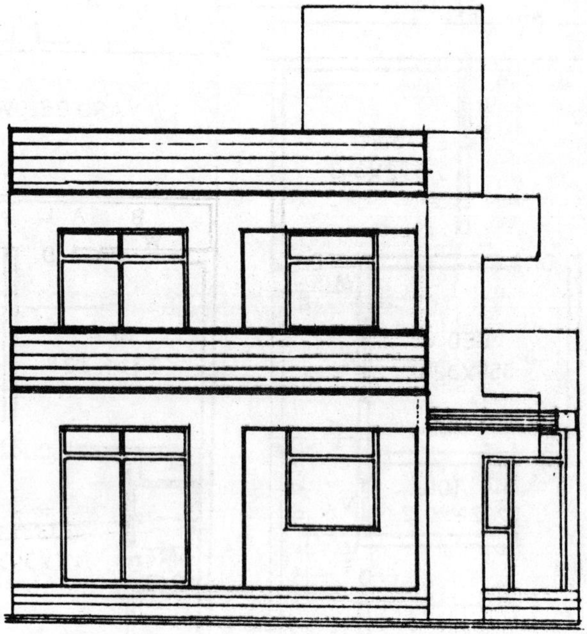

FRONT ELEVATION

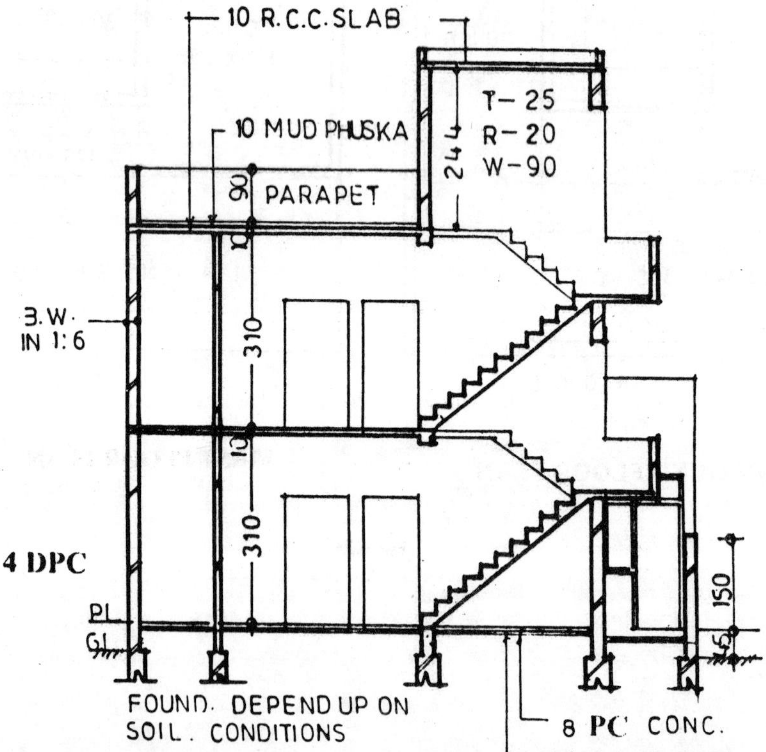


SEC-A—A

Fig. 6.33. B.

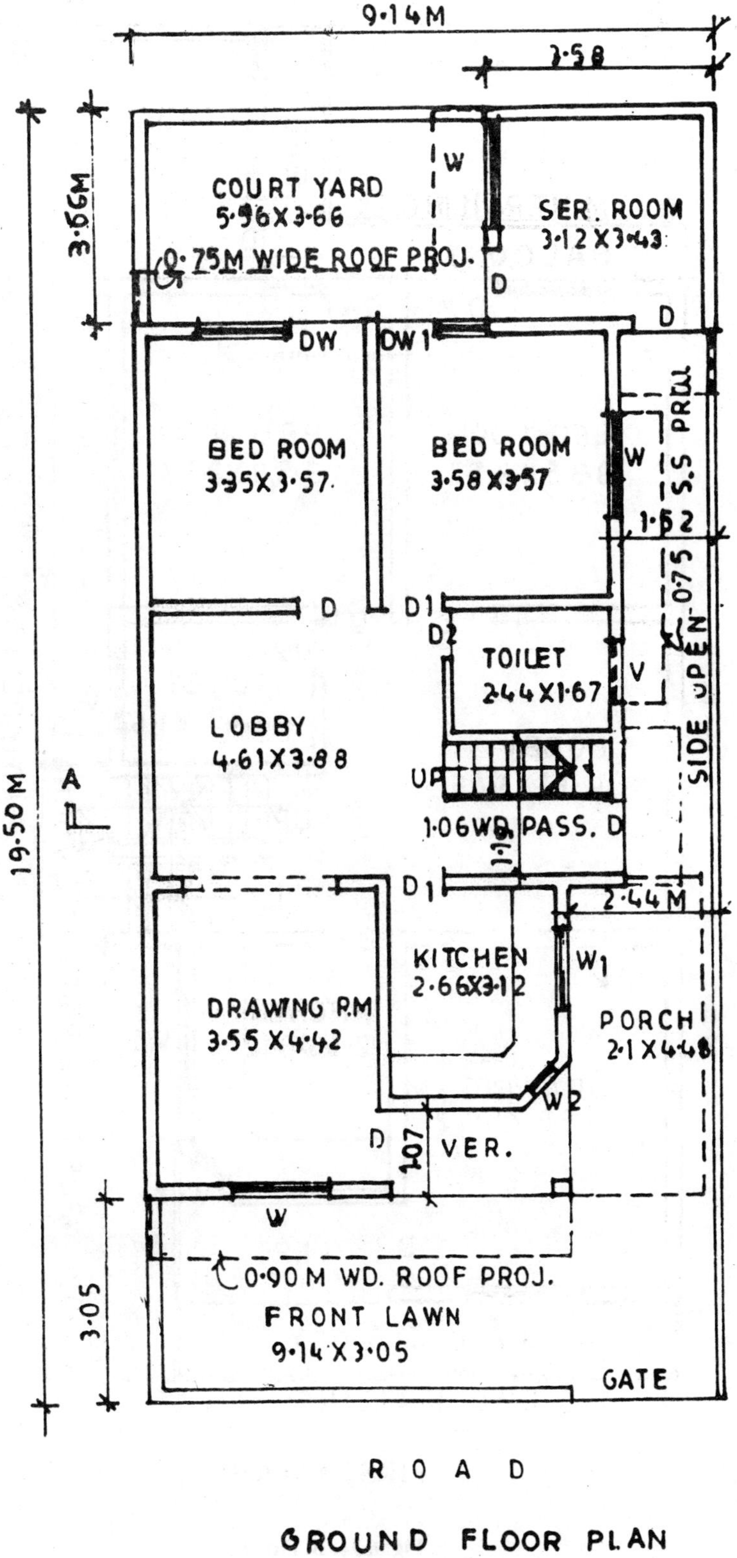


Fig. 6.34. A. Ground Floor Plan

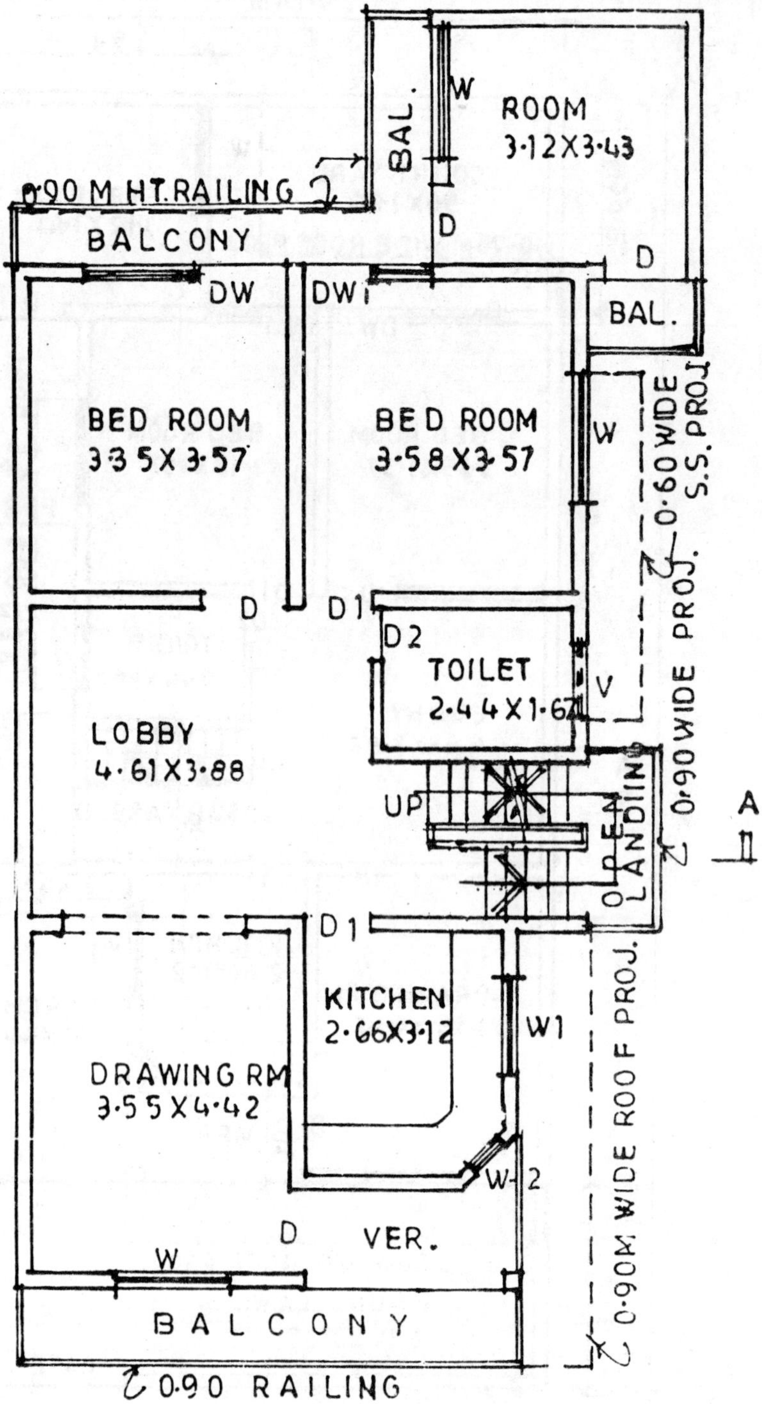


**FIRST FLOOR**

**Fig. 6.34. B.** First Floor Plan

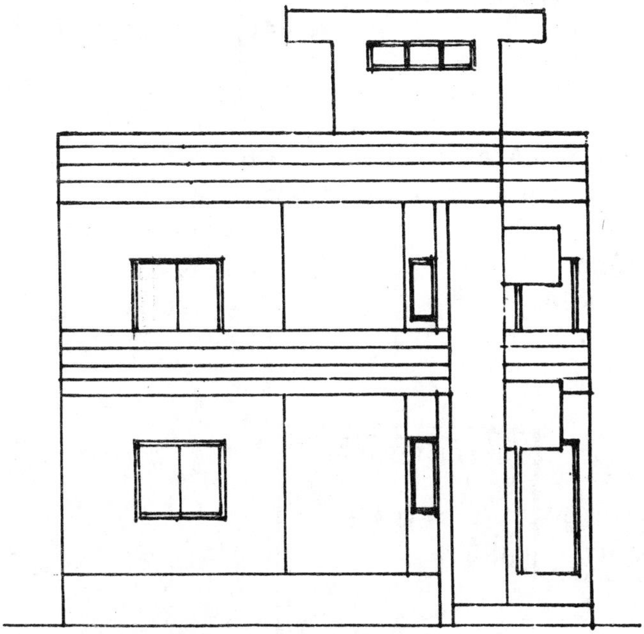

FRONT ELEVATION

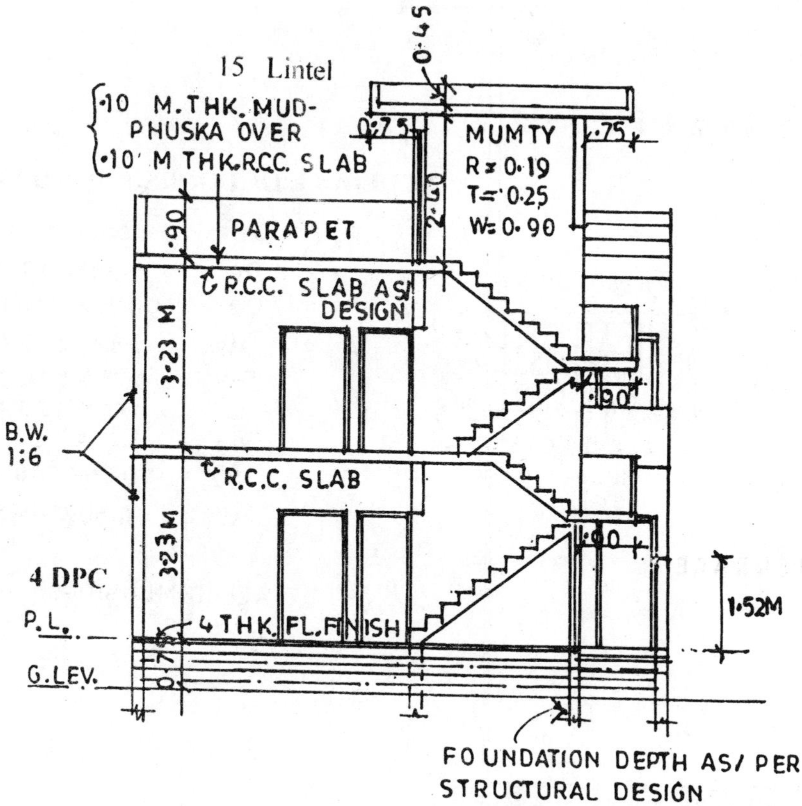


Fig. 6.34. C. **SEC-A—A**

**AREA CHART:**

| | SQ. MT. |
|---|---|
| PLOT AREA | = 178·23 |
| PROPOSED COVERED AREA AT GROUND FLOOR | = 106·63 |
| PROPOSED COVERED AREA AT FIRST FLOOR | = 106·63 |
| MUMTY AREA | = 6·78 |
| OPEN AREA OF PLOT | = 71·60 |
| TOTAL COVERED AREA | = 220·04 |

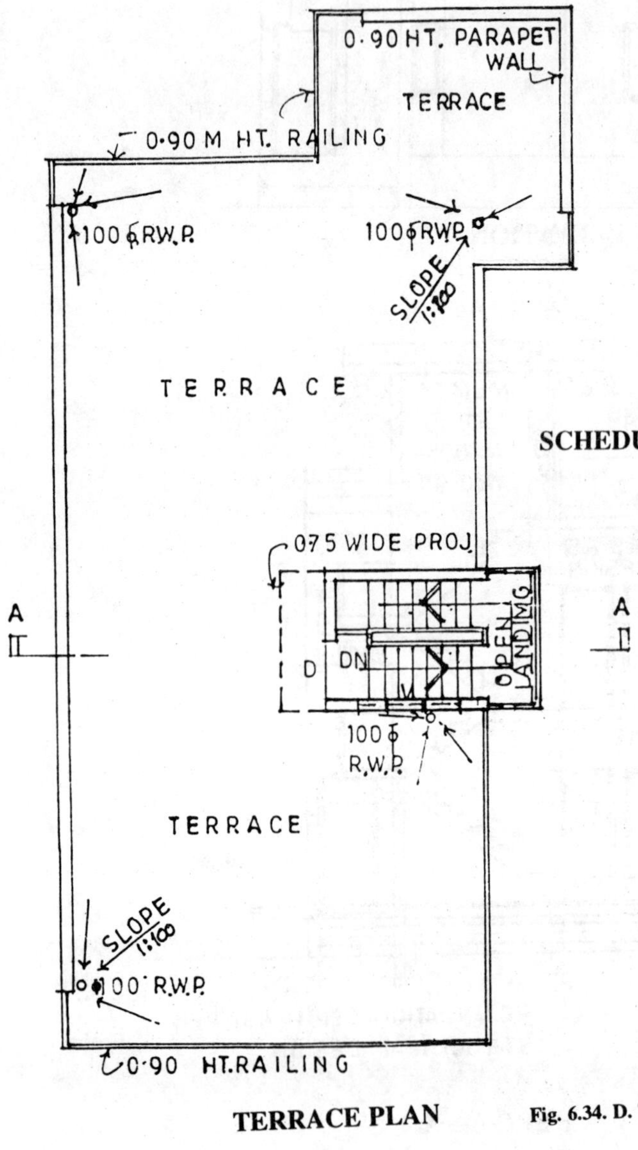


**SCHEDULE OF DOORS & WINDOWS:**

| | |
|---|---|
| D | 1·06 X 2·10 M |
| $D_1$ | 0·90 X 2·10 M |
| D2 | 0·75 X 2·10 M |
| DW | 2·59 X 2·10 M |
| DW1 | 1·75 X 2·10 M |
| W | 1·52 X 1·20 M |
| W1 | 1.20 X 1·06 M |
| W2 | 0·75 X 2·10 M |
| V | 0·60 X 0·45 |

ALL DIMENSIONS IN MTS.

**TERRACE PLAN** **Fig. 6.34. D.** Terrace Floor Plan

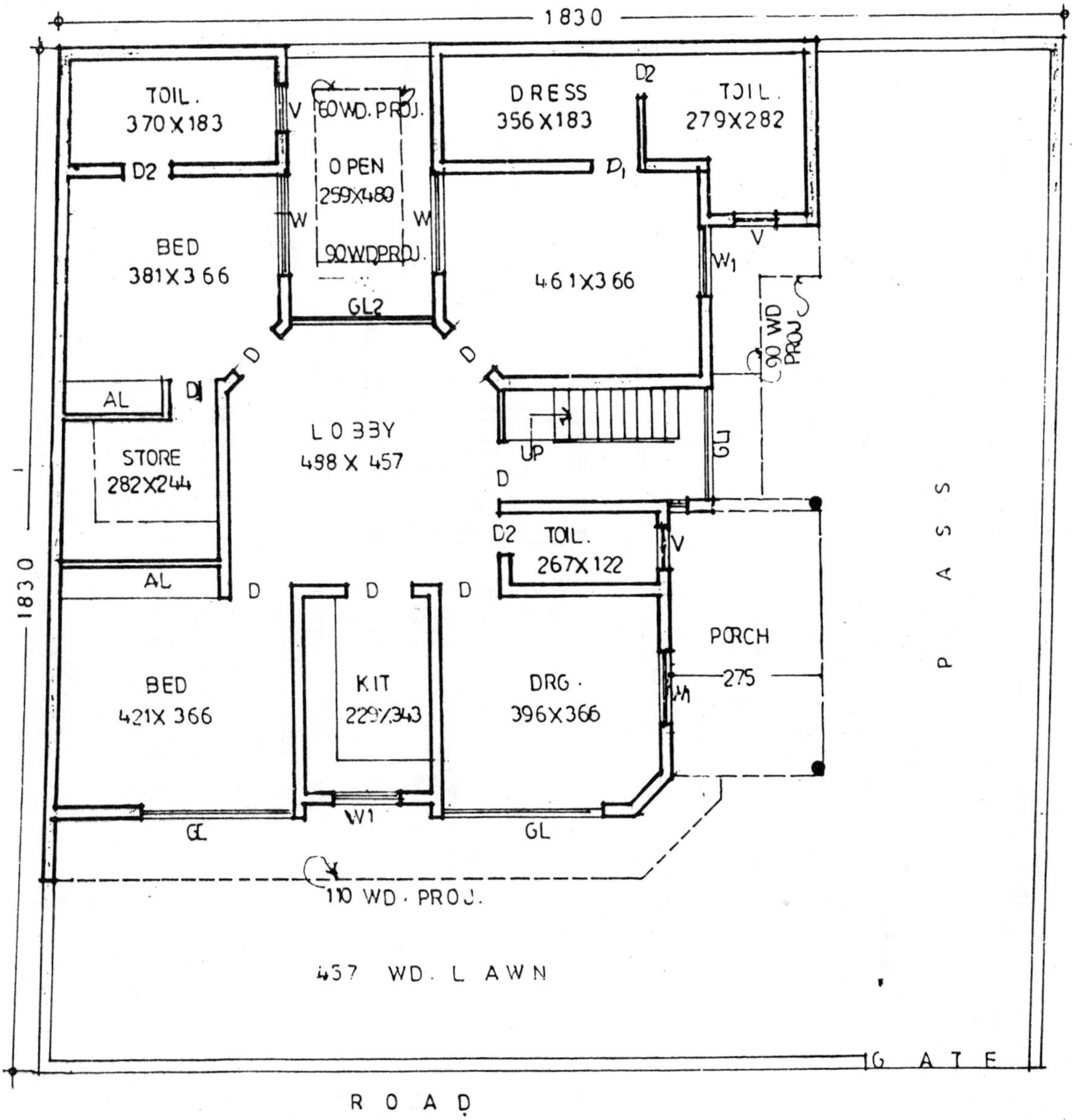


**GROUND FLOOR PLAN**

**Fig. 6.35. A.** Ground Floor Plan

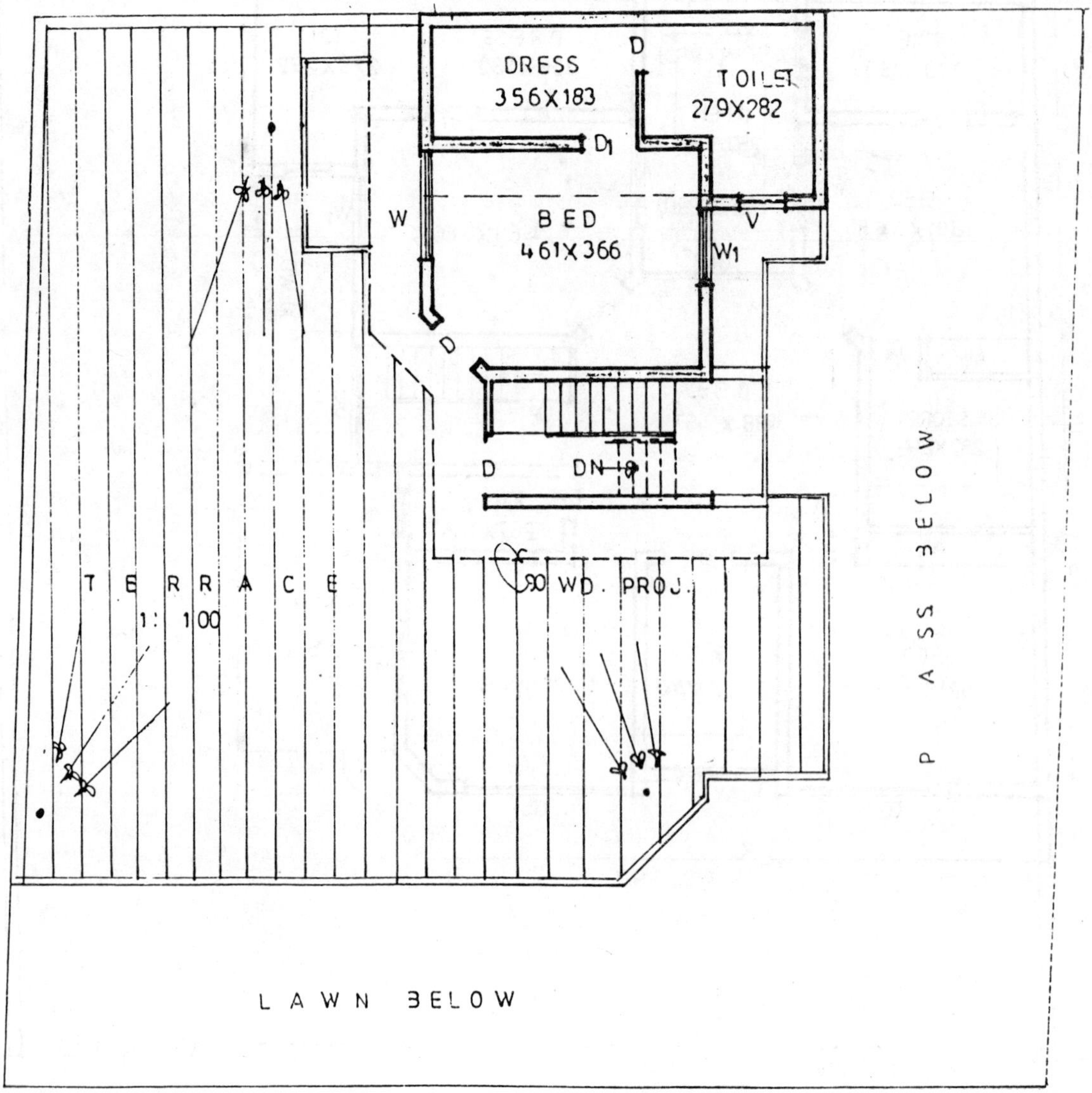


**FIRST FLOOR PLAN**

**Fig. 6.35. B.** First Floor Plan

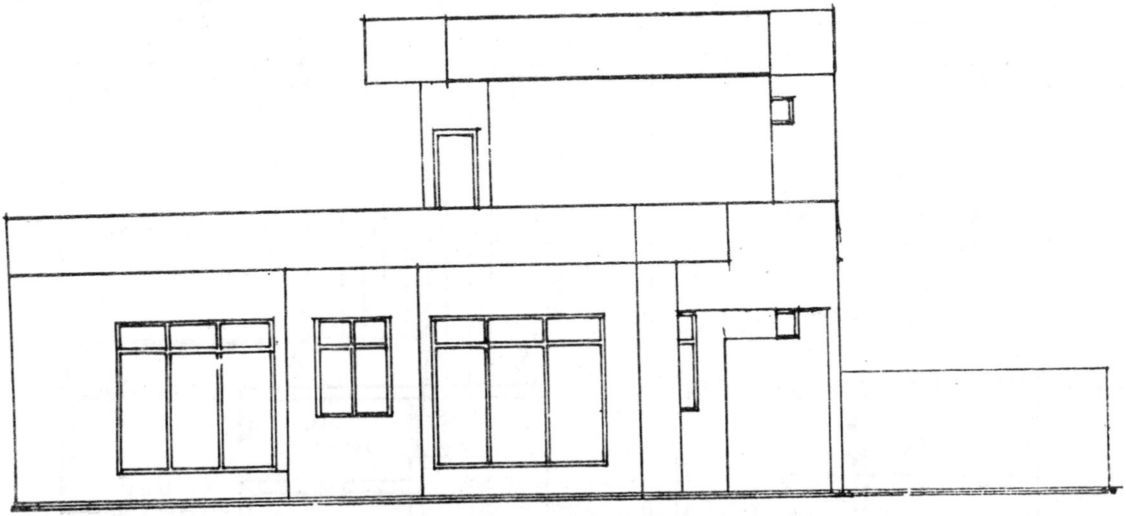

FRONT ELEVATION

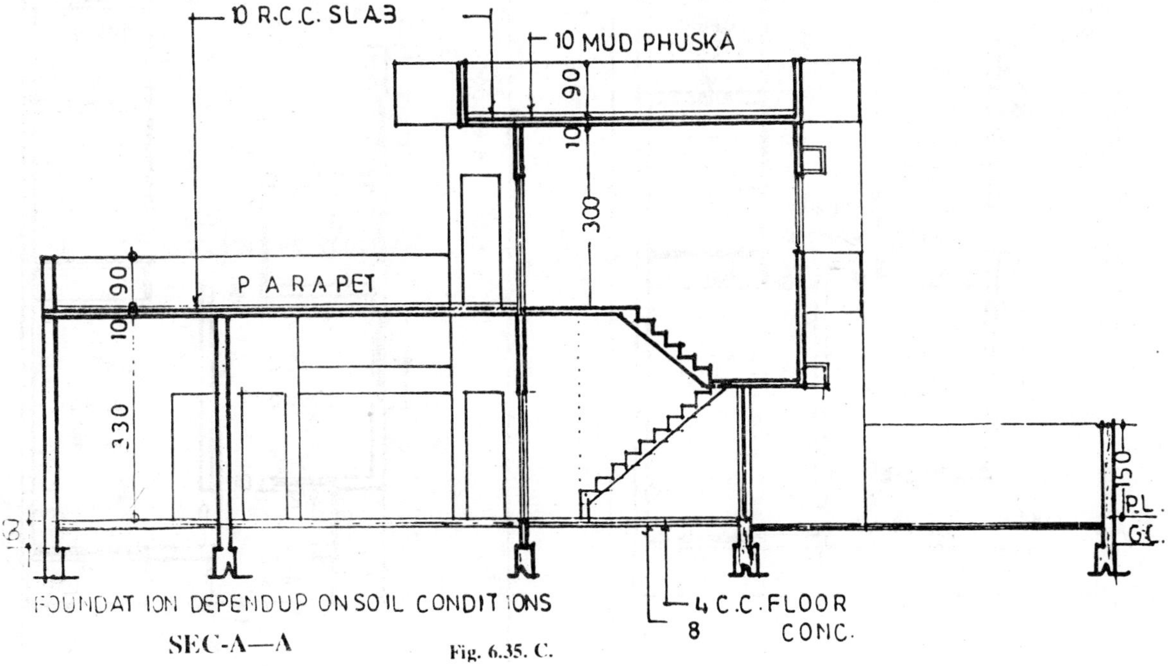


SEC-A—A

Fig. 6.35. C.

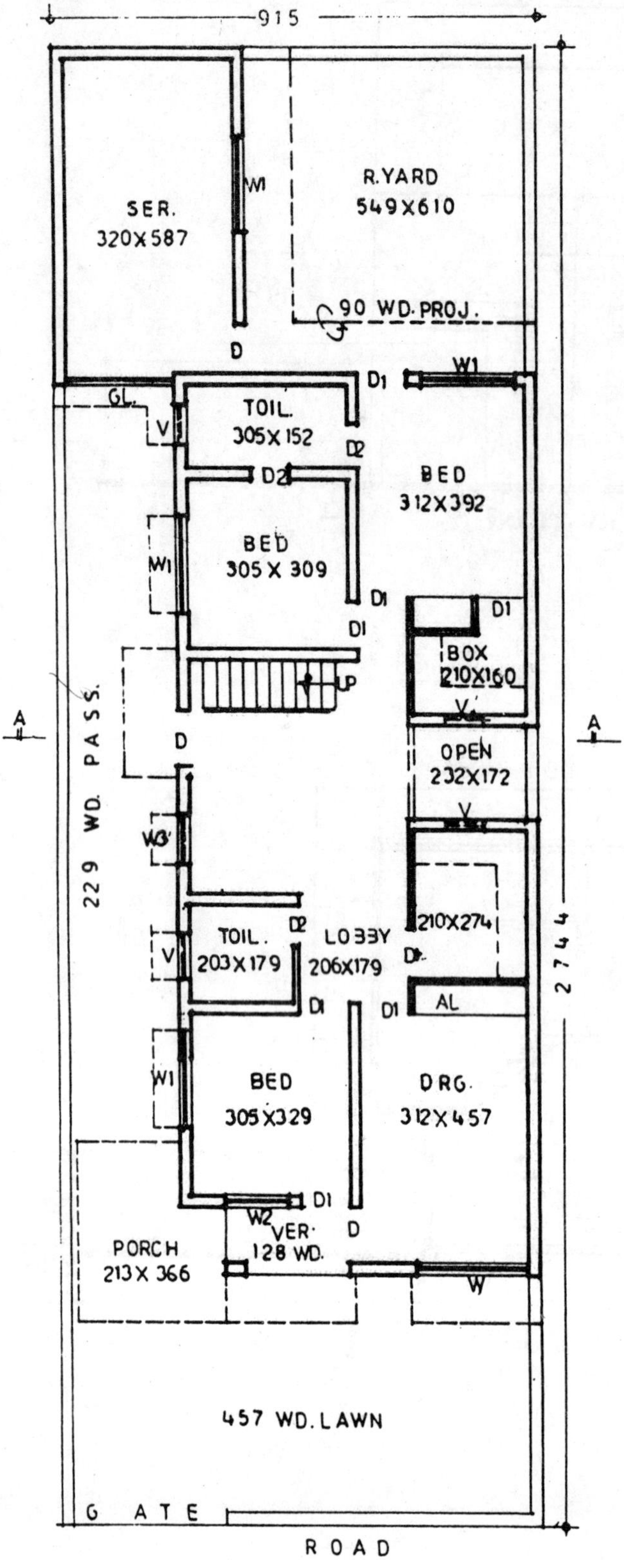


GROUND FLOOR PLAN

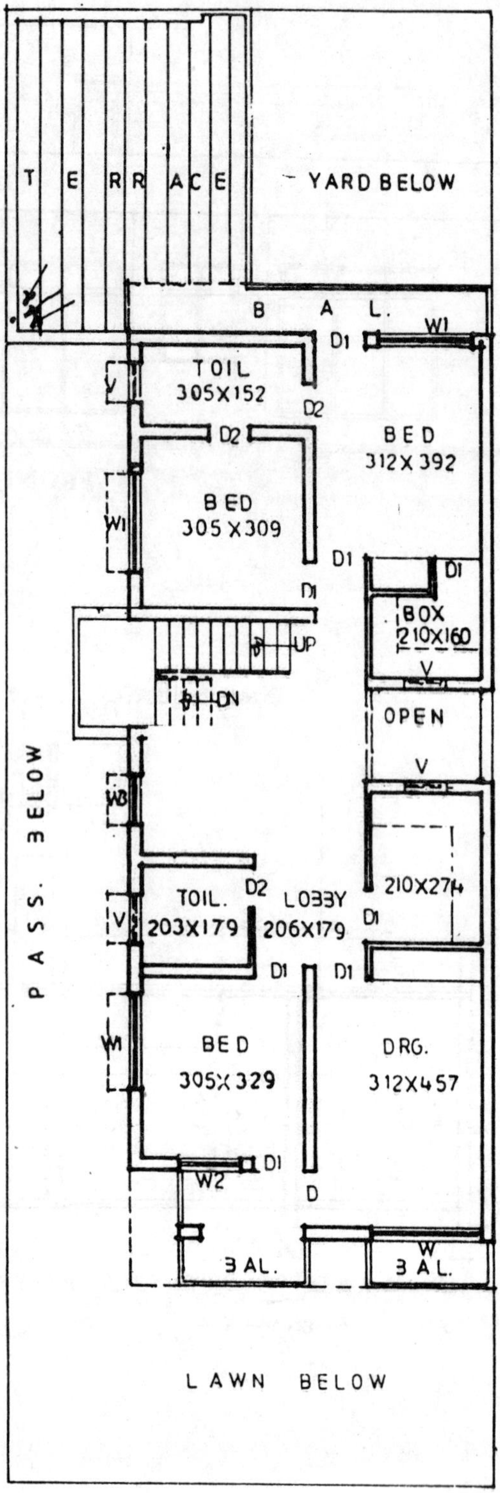


Fig. 6.36. A. FIRST FLOOR PLAN

FRONT ELEVATION

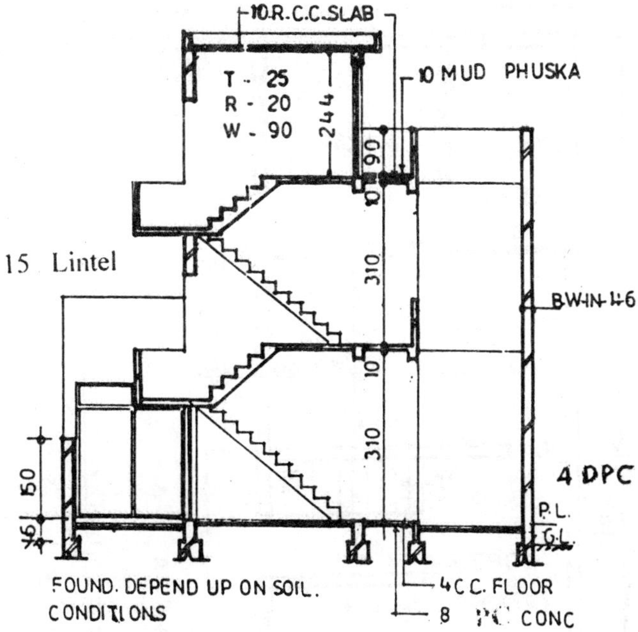


SEC-A—A

## SCHEDULE OF OPENINGS

| | | |
|---|---|---|
| D | DOOR | 105 X 210 |
| D1 | " | 90 X 210 |
| D2 | " | 75 X 210 |
| W | WINDOW | 210 X 210 |
| W1 | " | 180 X 120 |
| W2 | " | 120 X 210 |
| W3 | " | 90 X 210 |
| V | " | 90 X 45 |
| GL. | GLAZING | 205 X 210 |

## AREA STATEMENT SQ.M.

| | |
|---|---|
| PLOT AREA | 250·83 |
| EXIST. COV. AREA AT. G.F. | 109·80 |
| PROP. COV. AREA AT G.F. | 22·80 |
| OPEN AREA AT. G.F. | 118·23 |
| PROP. COV. AREA AT F.F. | 109·80 |

ALL DIMENSIONS IN CMS

**Fig. 6.36. B.**

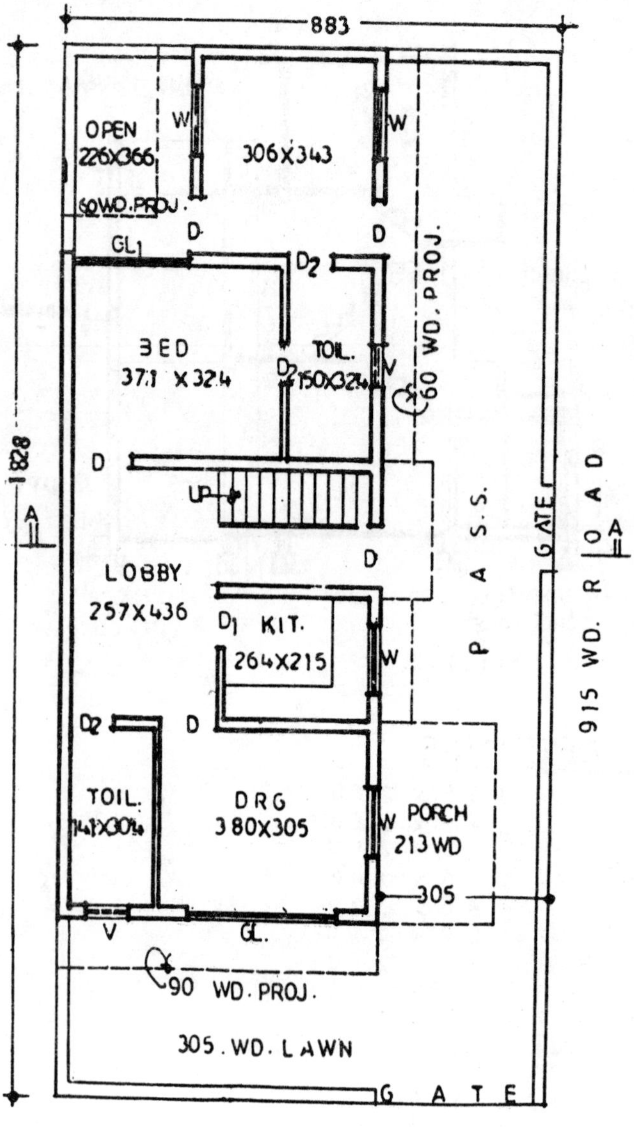


GROUND FLOOR PLAN

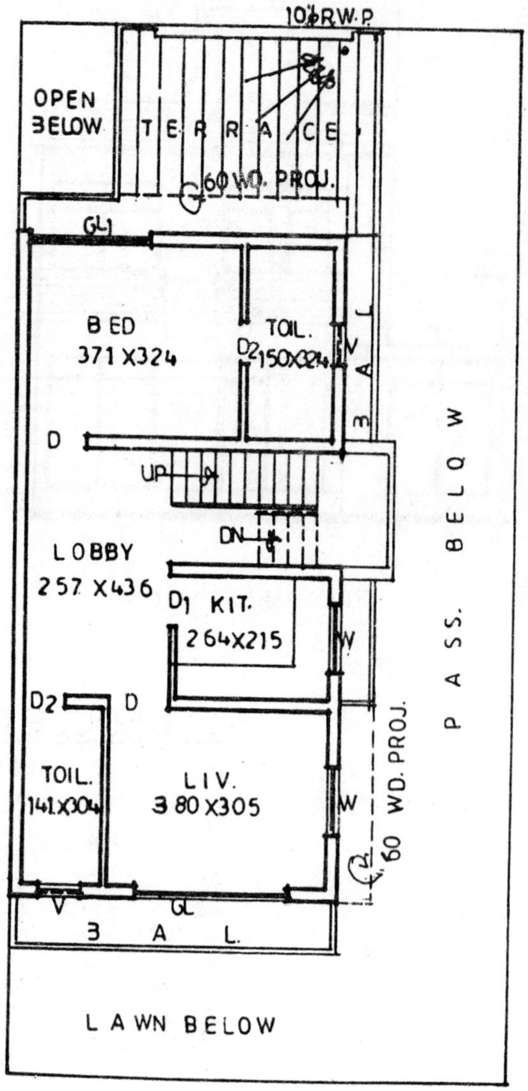


FIRST FLOOR PLAN

Fig. 6.37. A.

**FRONT ELEVATION**

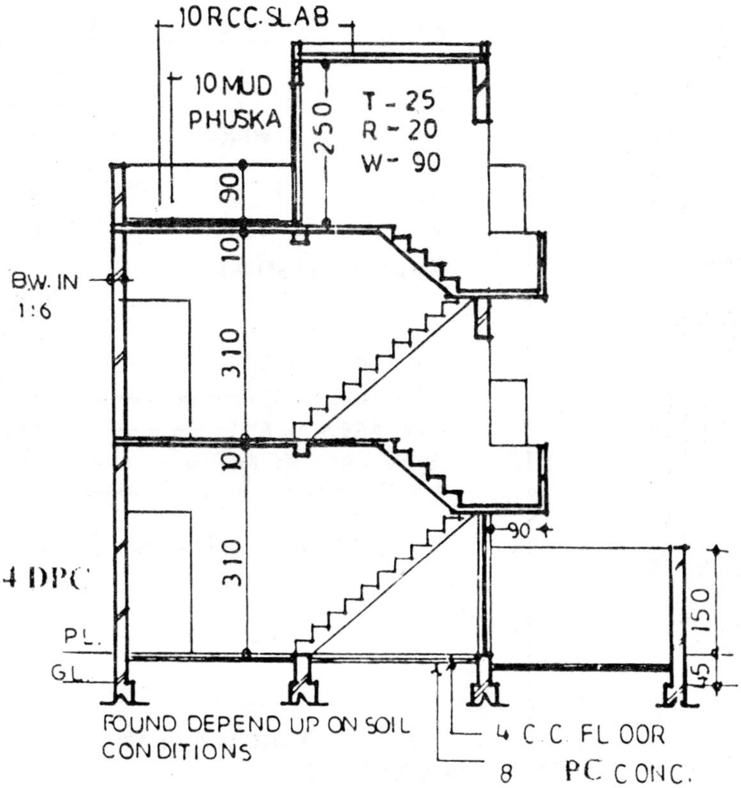


**SECTION AT A—A**

Fig. 6.37. B.

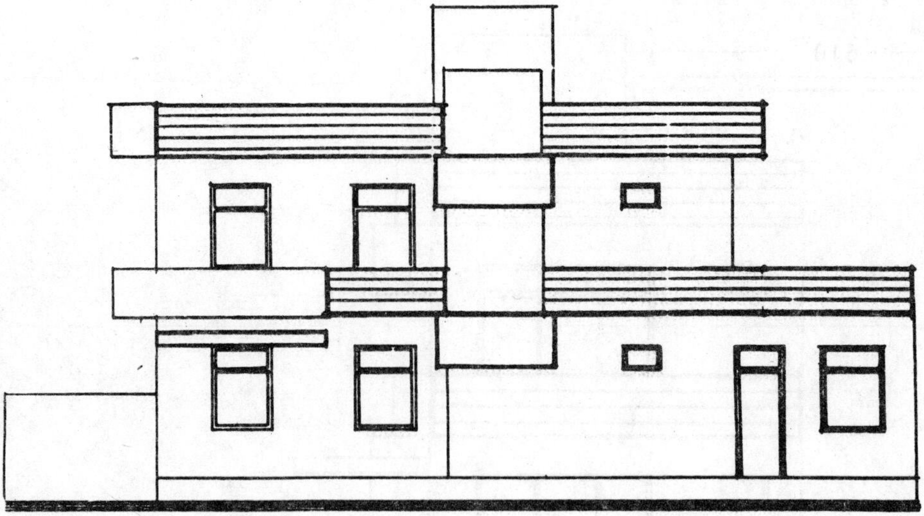

FRONT ELEVATION

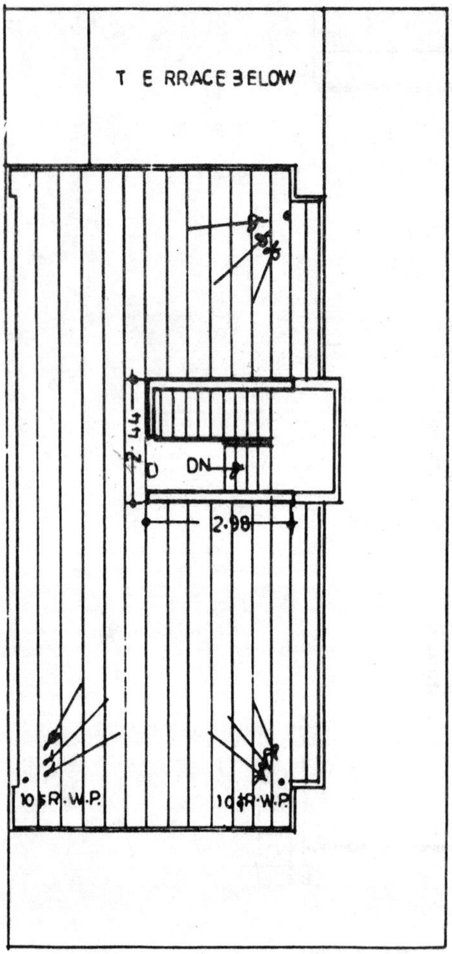


## SCHEDULE OF OPENINGS

| | | |
|---|---|---|
| D | DOOR | 105 X 210 |
| D1 | " | 90 X 210 |
| D2 | " | 75 X 210 |
| W | WINDOW | 120 X 120 |
| GL | GLAZING. | 270 X 210 |
| GL1 | " | 203 X 210 |
| V | VENTI | 75 X 45 |

## AREA STATEMENT

| | SQ.M. |
|---|---|
| PLOT AREA | 161·40 |
| COV. AREA AT G.F. | 79·80 |
| OPEN AREA AT G.F. | 81·60 |
| COV. AREA AT. F.F. | 66·90 |
| OPEN AREA AT. F.F. | 12·90 |
| MUMTY AREA | 7·30 |

ALL DIMENSIONS IN CM

TERRACE PLAN

Fig. 6.37. C.

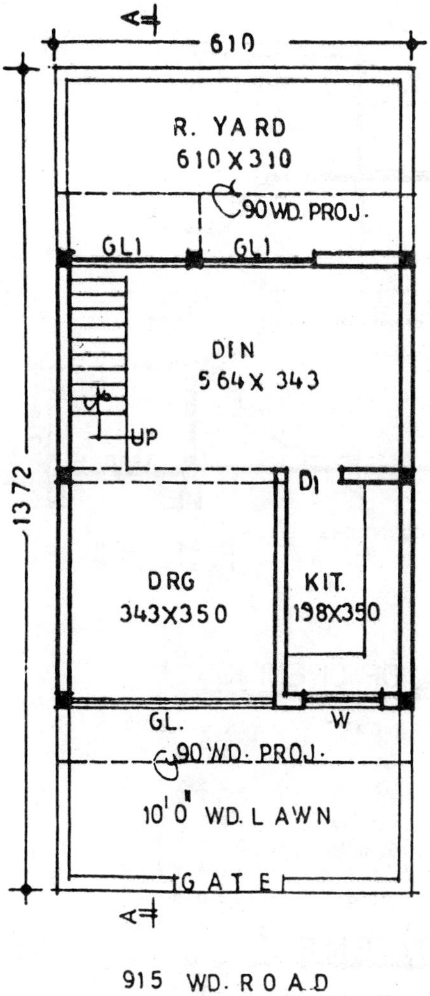


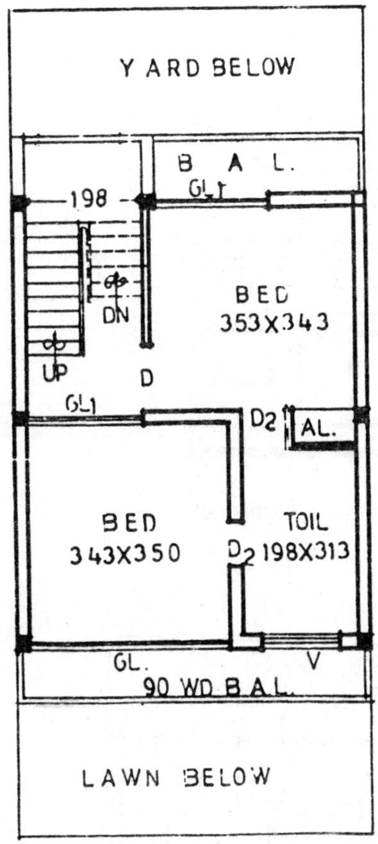


**GROUND FLOOR PLAN**

**FIRST FLOOR PLAN**

Fig. 6.38. A.

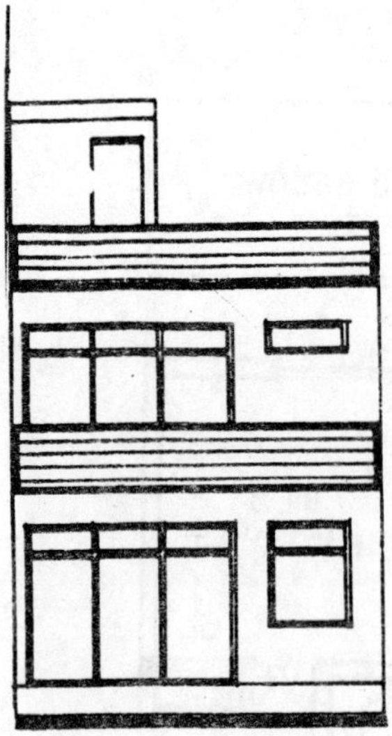

**FRONT ELEVATION**

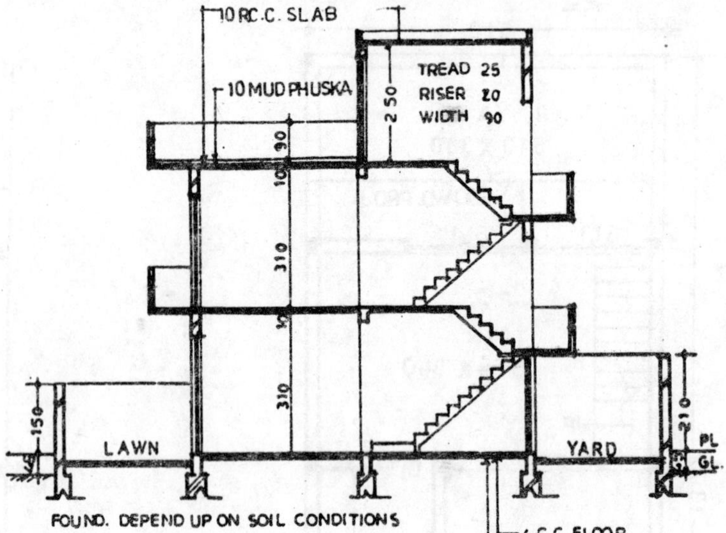


**SEC-A—A**

## SCHEDUL OF OPENINGS

| | | |
|---|---|---|
| D | DOOR | 105 X 210 |
| D1 | " | 90 X 210 |
| D2 | " | 75 X 210 |
| W | WINDOW | 138 X 120 |
| GL | GLAZING | 343 X 210 |
| GL1 | " | 198 X 210 |
| V | VENT | 138 X 75 |

## AREA STATEMENT

| | SQ.M |
|---|---|
| PLOT AREA | 83·7 |
| COV. AREA AT G.F | 46·5 |
| OPEN AREA AT G.F | 37 2 |
| COV. AREA AT F.F. | 46·5 |

ALL DIMENSIONS IN CM

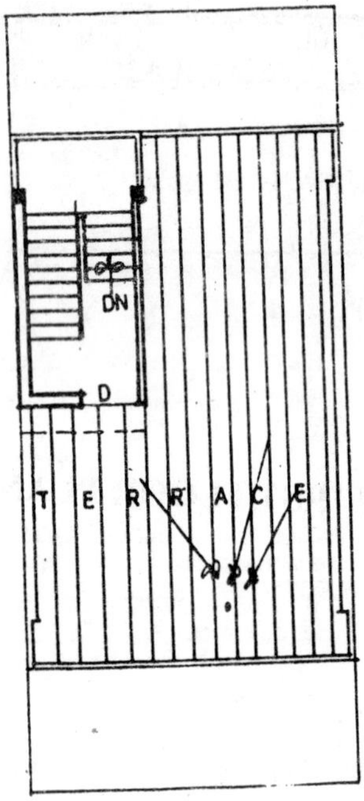


**TERRACE PLAN**

Fig. 6.38. B.

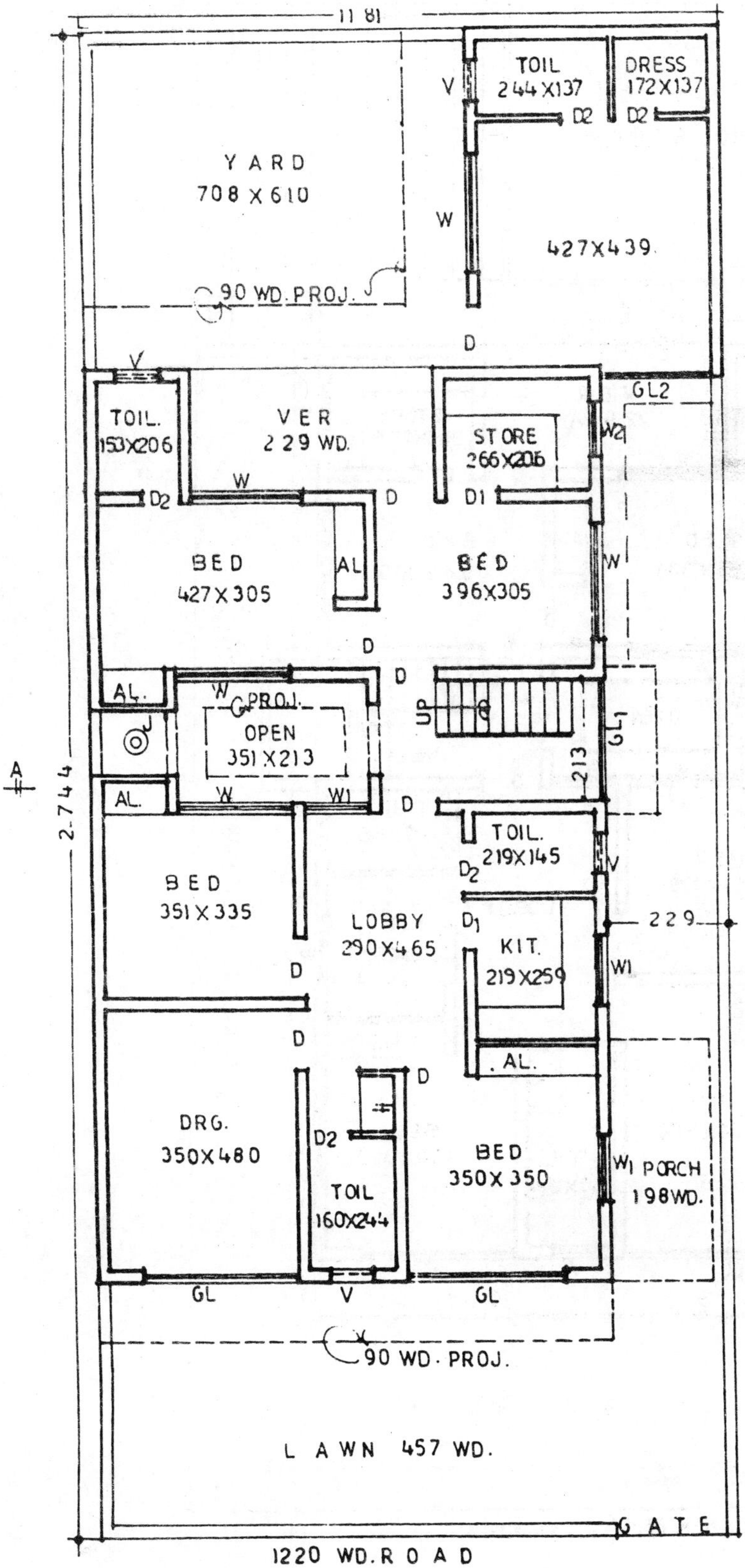


**GROUND FLOOR PLAN**

Fig. 6.39. A.

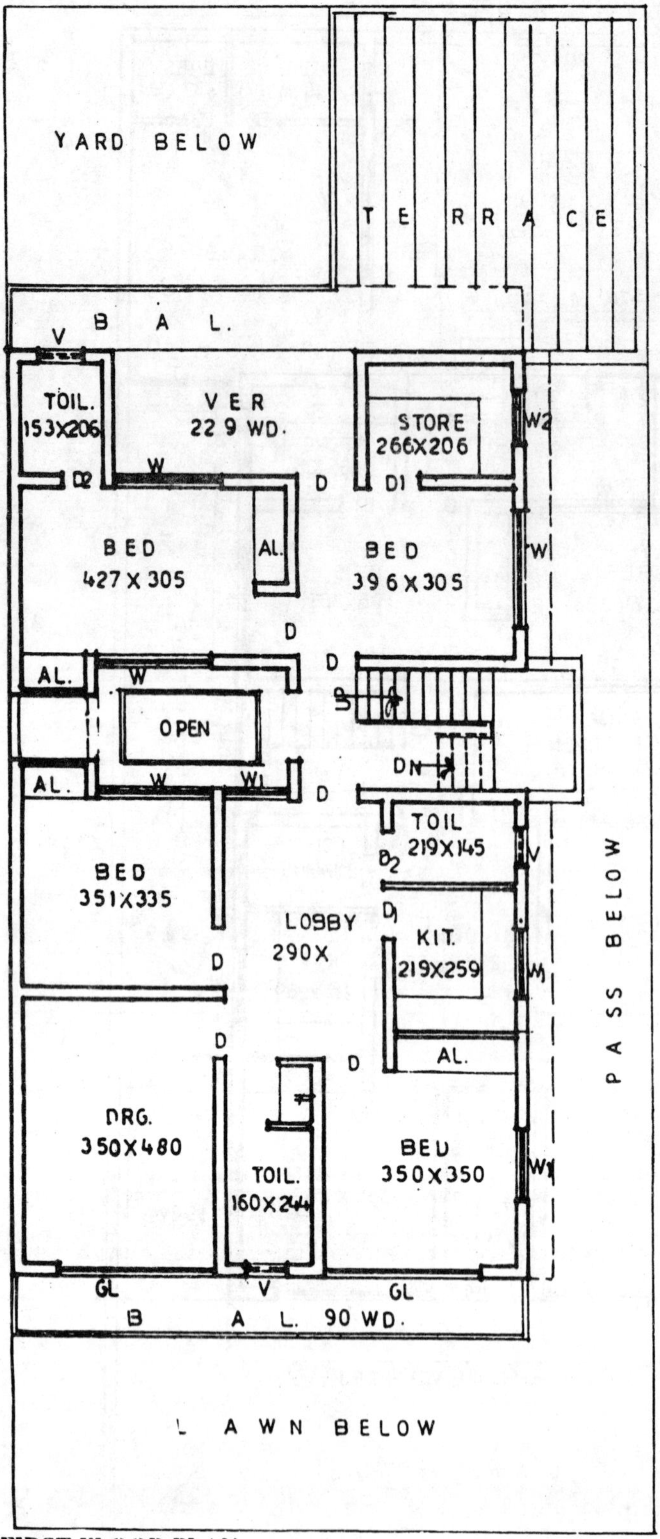


**FIRST FLOOR PLAN** Fig. 6.39. B.

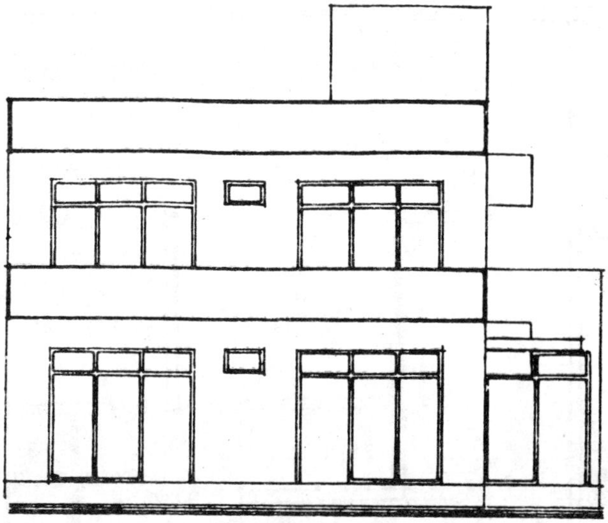

**FRONT ELEVATION**

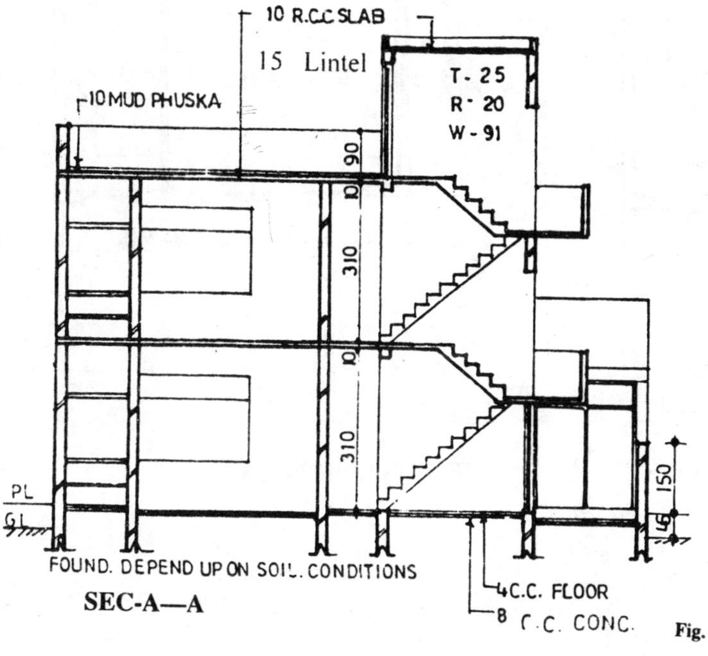


**SEC-A—A**

## SCHEDULE OF OPENINGS

| | | |
|---|---|---|
| D | DOOR | 107 X 210 |
| D1 | " | 90 X 210 |
| D2 | " | 75 X 210 |
| W | WINDOW | 206 X 120 |
| W1 | | 120 X 210 |
| W2 | " | 90 X 210 |
| V | VENT | 75 X 45 |
| GL. | GLAZING | 290 X 210 |
| GL1 | " | 213 X 210 |
| GL2 | | 206 X 210 |

## AREA STATEMENT

| | SQ.M |
|---|---|
| PLOT AREA | 324.0 |
| COV. AREA AT G.F. | 181.5 |
| OPEN AREA AT G.F. | 142.5 |
| COV. AREA AT F.F. | 152.1 |
| OPEN AREA AT F.F | 29.4 |

ALL DIMENSIONS IN CM

Fig. 6.39. C.

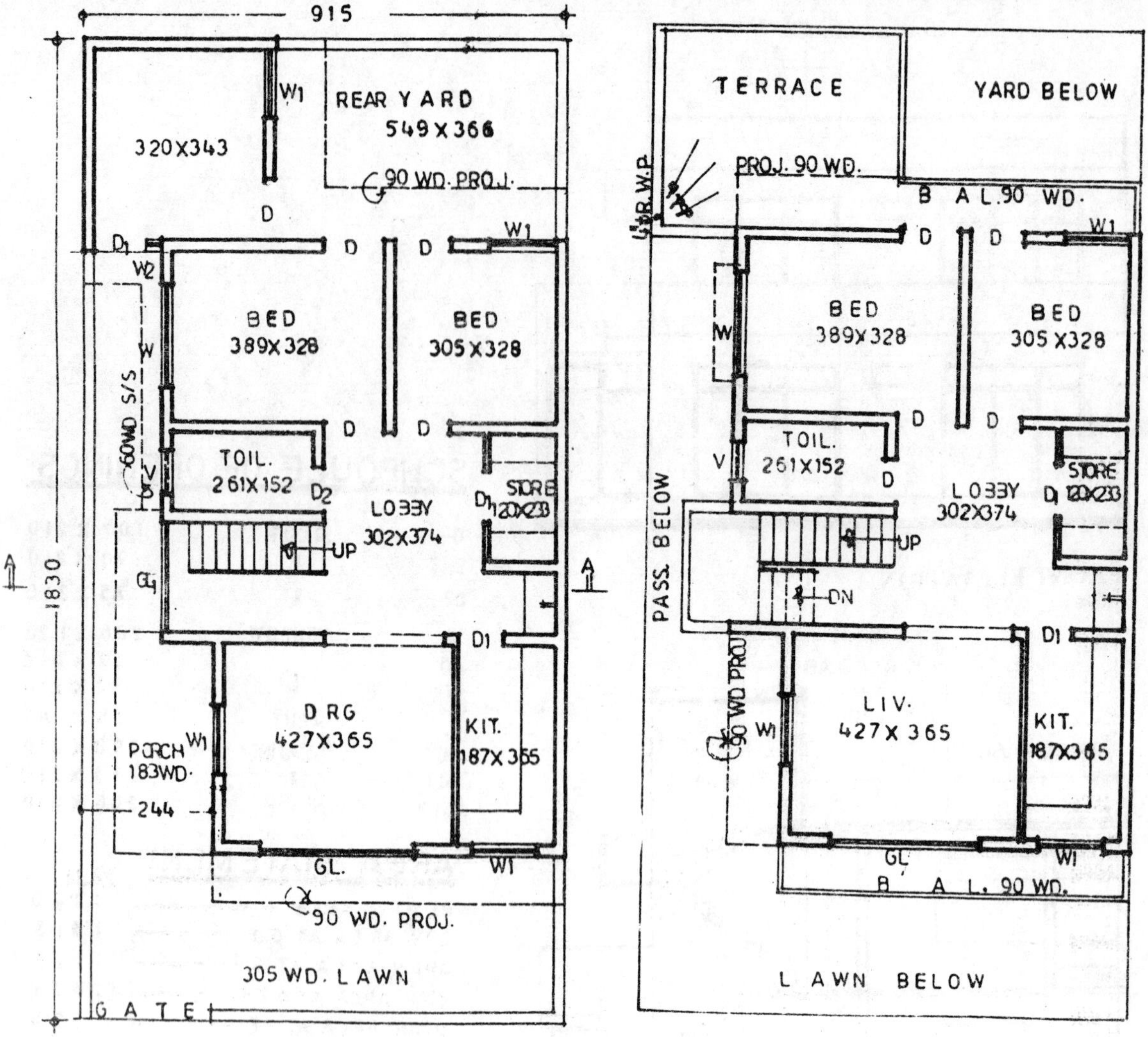


**GROUND FLOOR PLAN** **FIRST FLOOR PLAN**

Fig. 6.40. A.

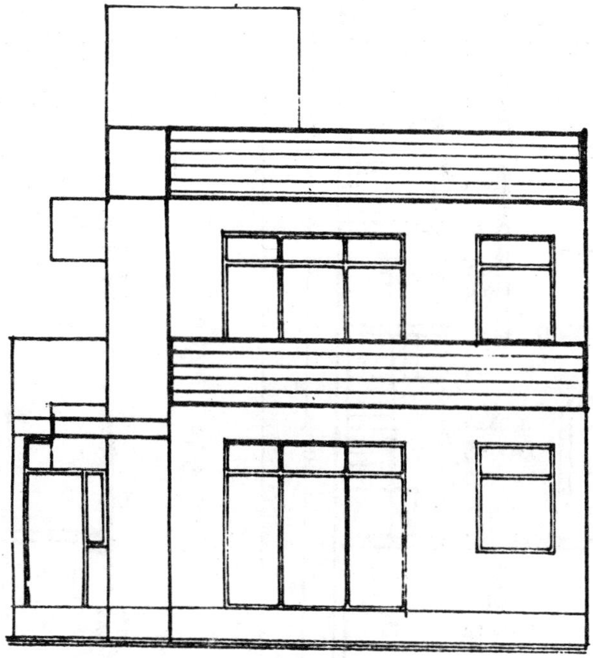

FRONT ELEVATION

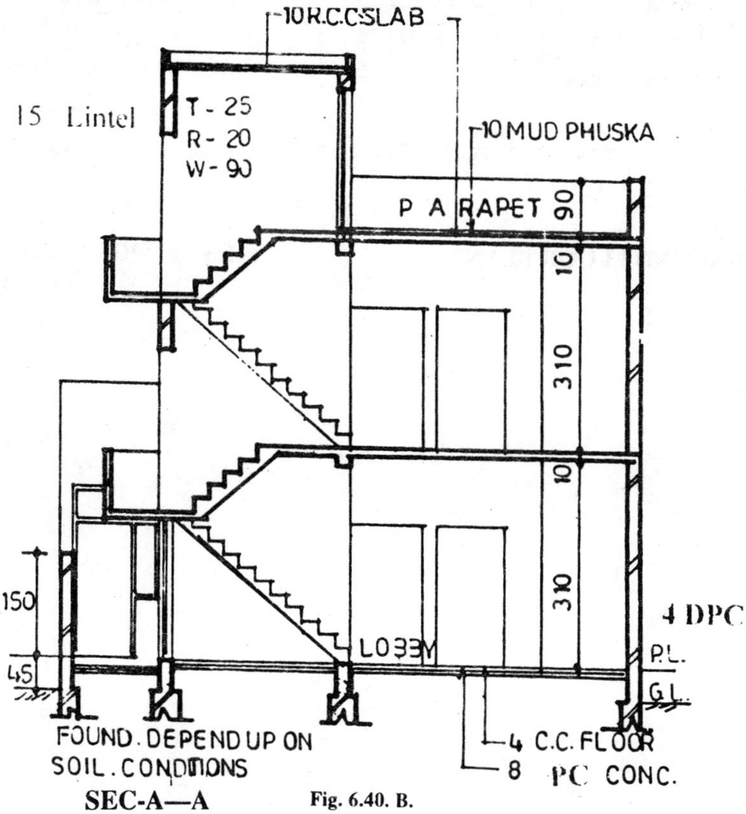


SEC-A—A Fig. 6.40. B.

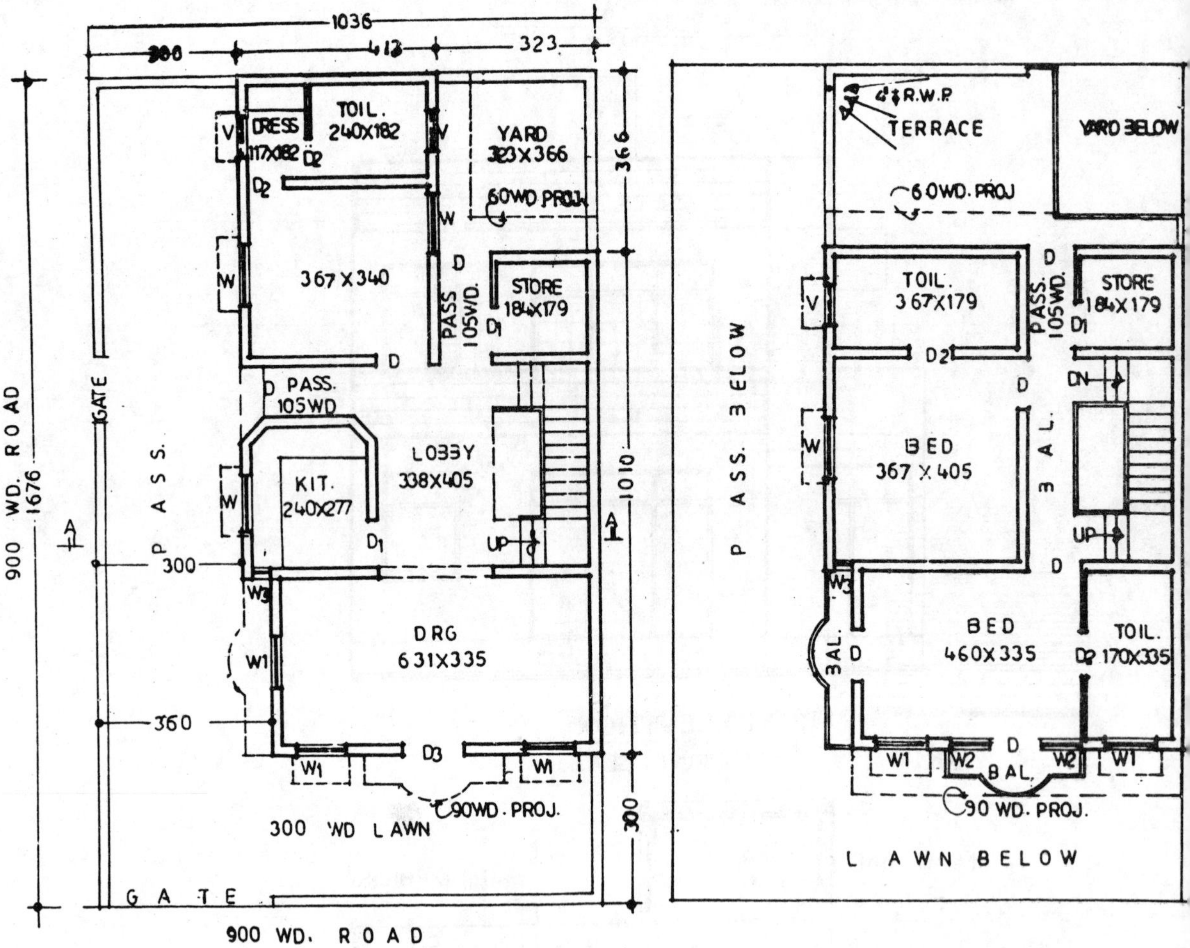


**GROUND FLOOR PLAN** **FIRST FLOOR PLAN**

Fig. 6.41. A.

FRONT ELEVATION

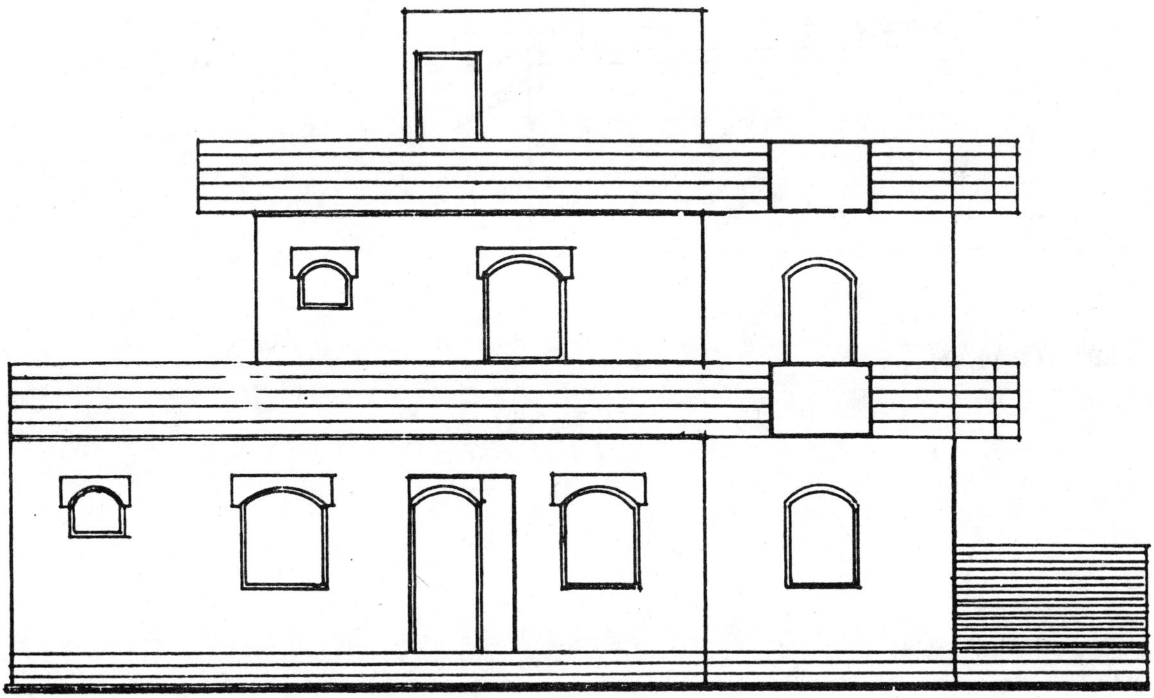

SITE ELEVATION

Fig. 6.41. B.

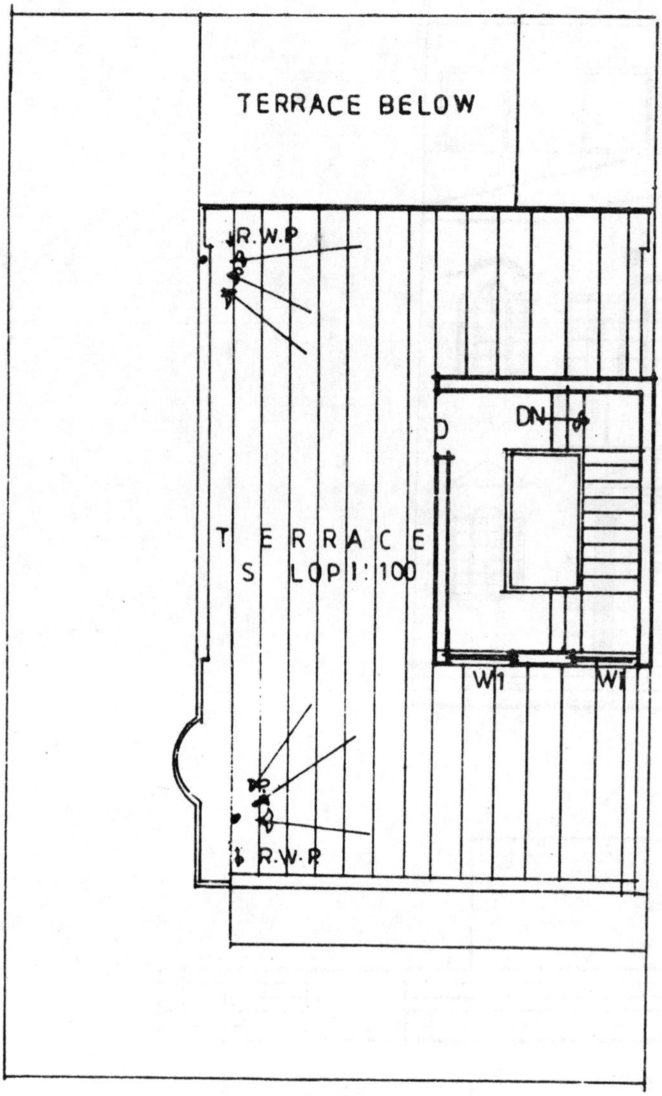


TERRACE PLAN

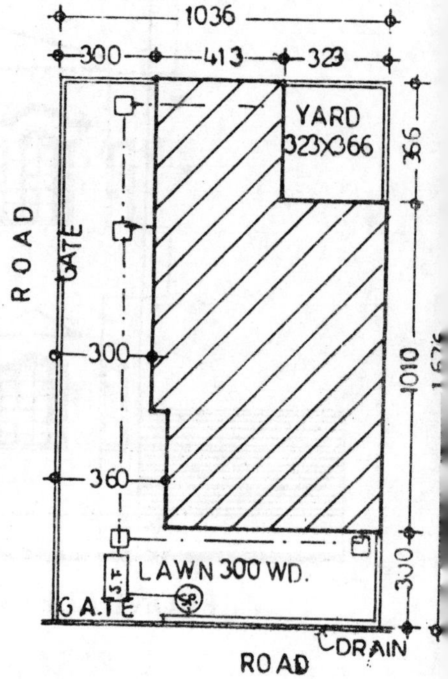


SITE PLAN

SCALE - 1:200

Fig. 6.41. C.

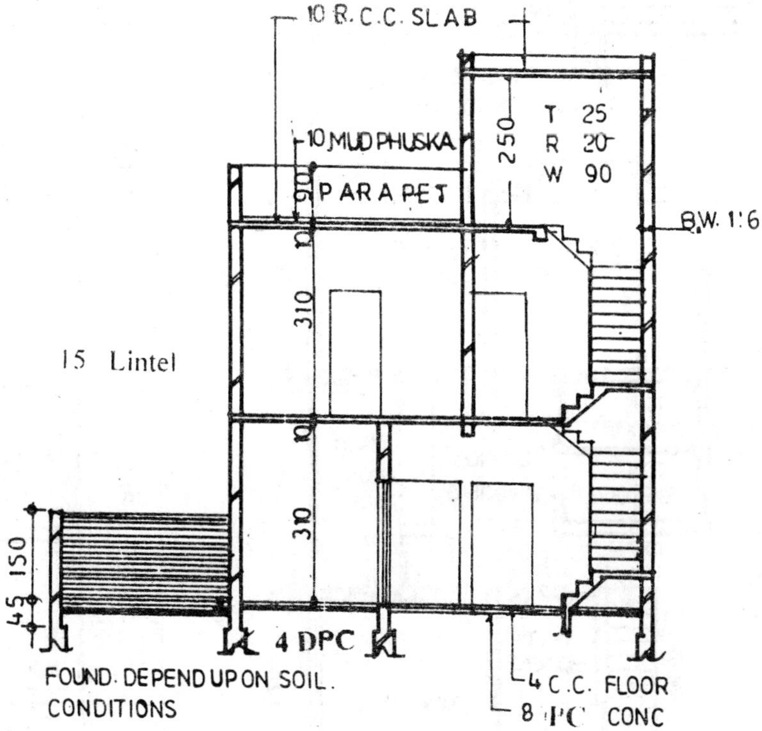


**SEC-A—A**

**AREA STATEMENT**

| | SQ.M. |
|---|---|
| PLOT AREA | 173·60 |
| COV. AREA AT G.F. | 87·30 |
| OPEN AREA AT G.F. | 86·30 |
| COV. AREA AT F.F. | 72·20 |
| OPEN AREA AT F.F. | 15·10 |
| MUMTY AREA | 15·60 |

**SCHEDULE OF OPENINGS**

| | | |
|---|---|---|
| D | DOOR. | 105 X 210 |
| D1 | ″ | 90 X 210 |
| D2 | ″ | 75 X 210 |
| D3 | ″ | 130 X 210 |
| W | WINDOW | 120 X 120 |
| W1 | ″ | 105 X 120 |
| W2 | ″ | 80 X 210 |
| W3 | ″ | 37 X 120 |
| V | VENT. | 75 X 45 |

ALL DIMENSIONS IN CMS.

**Fig. 6.41. D.**

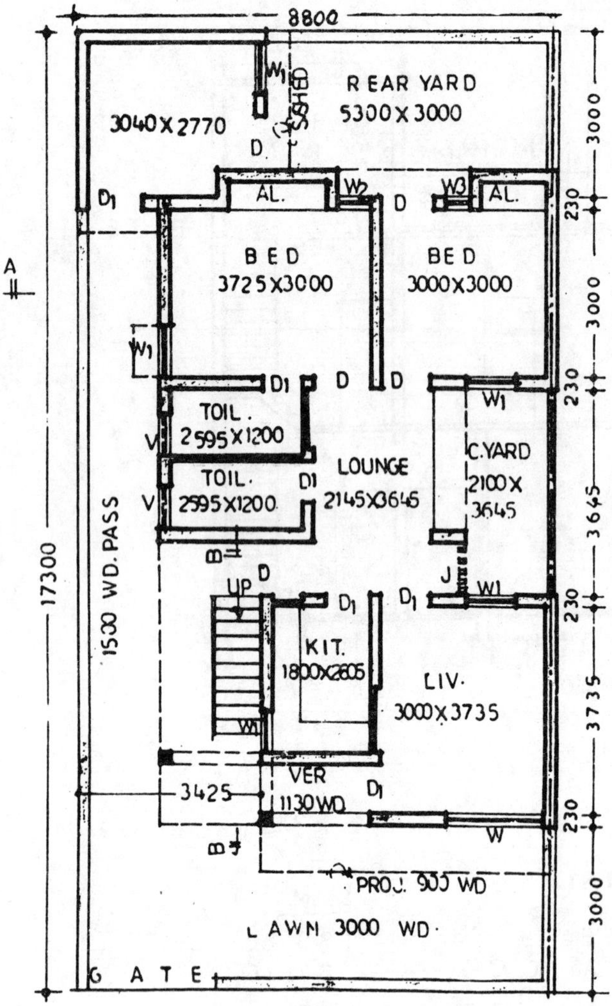


**GROUND FLOOR PLAN**

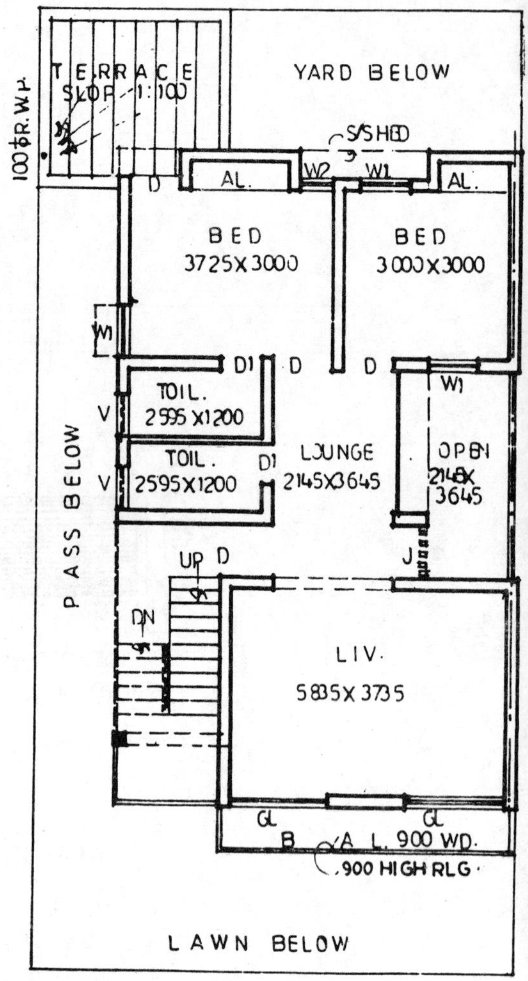


**FIRST FLOOR PLAN**

Fig. 6.42. A.

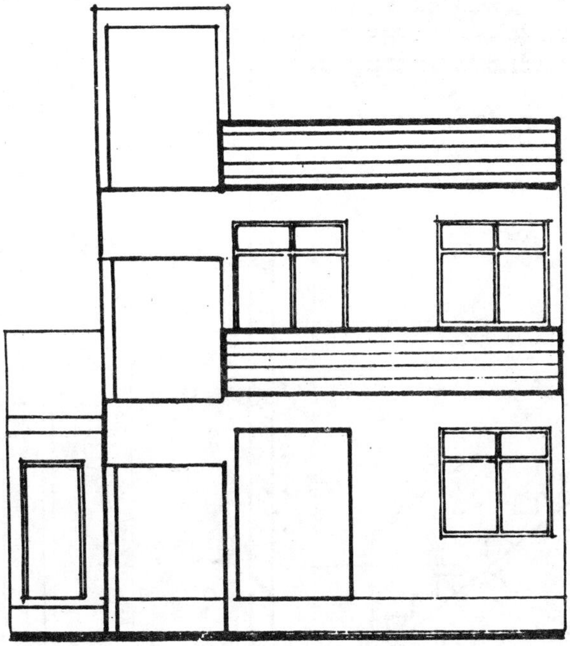

FRONT ELEVATION

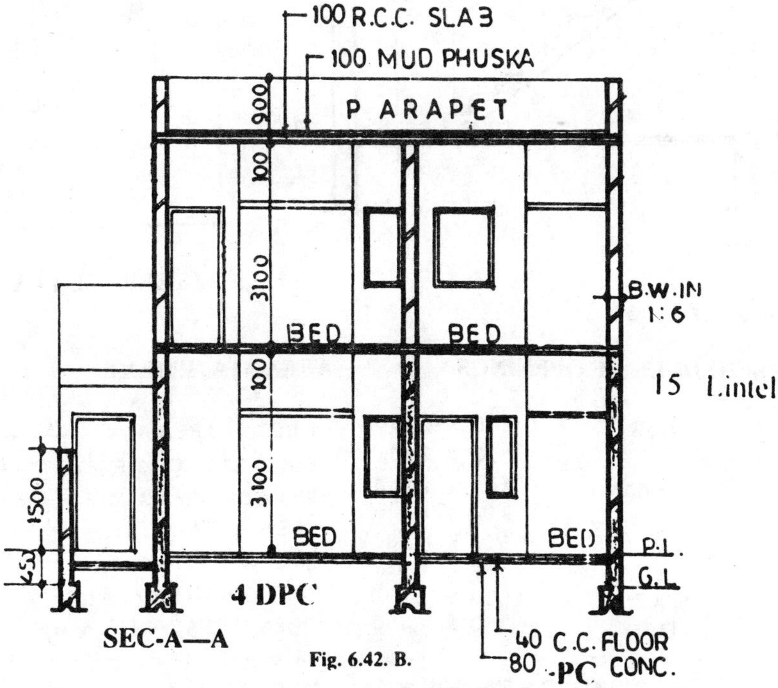


SEC-A—A

Fig. 6.42. B.

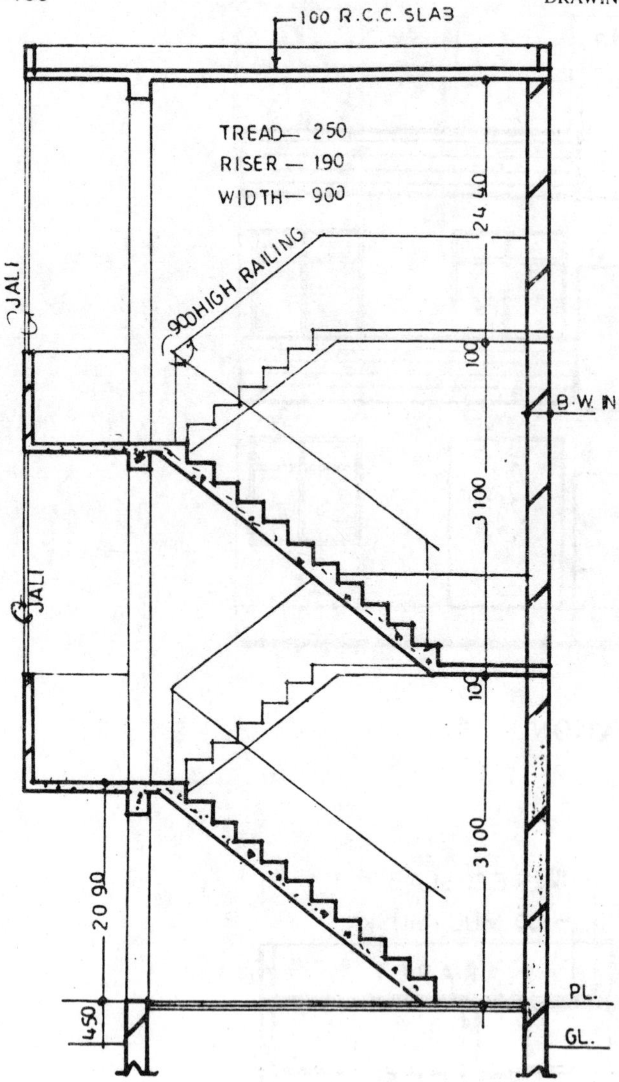


**SEC-A—A**

SCALE 1: 50

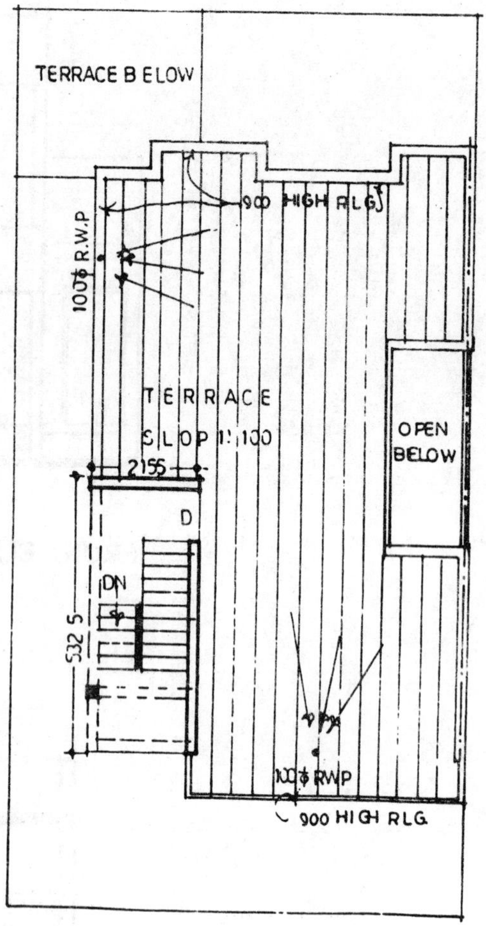


**TERRACE PLAN**

**SCHEDULE OF OPENINGS**

| | | |
|---|---|---|
| D | DOOR | 900 X 2100 |
| D1 | " | 750 X 2100 |
| W | WINDOW | 1800 X 1200 |
| W1 | " | 900 X 1200 |
| W2 | " | 600 X 1200 |
| W3 | " | 450 X 1200 |
| GL. | GLAZING | 1800 X 2100 |
| V | VENT | 750 X 450 |

ALL DIMENSIONS IN MM

**AREA STATEMENT**

| | SQ.M |
|---|---|
| PLOT AREA | 152·24 |
| COV. AREA AT G.F. (EXIST) | 67·35 |
| PROP. COV. AREA AT G.F. | 20·19 |
| OPEN AREA AT G.F. | 64·70 |
| PROJ. AREA AT G.F. 50% | 2·78 |
| PROP. COV. AREA AT F.F. | 76·70 |
| OPEN AREA AT F.F. | 10·84 |
| PROJ. AREA AT F.F. | 2·78 |
| MUMTY AREA | 11·47 |

Fig. 6.42. C.

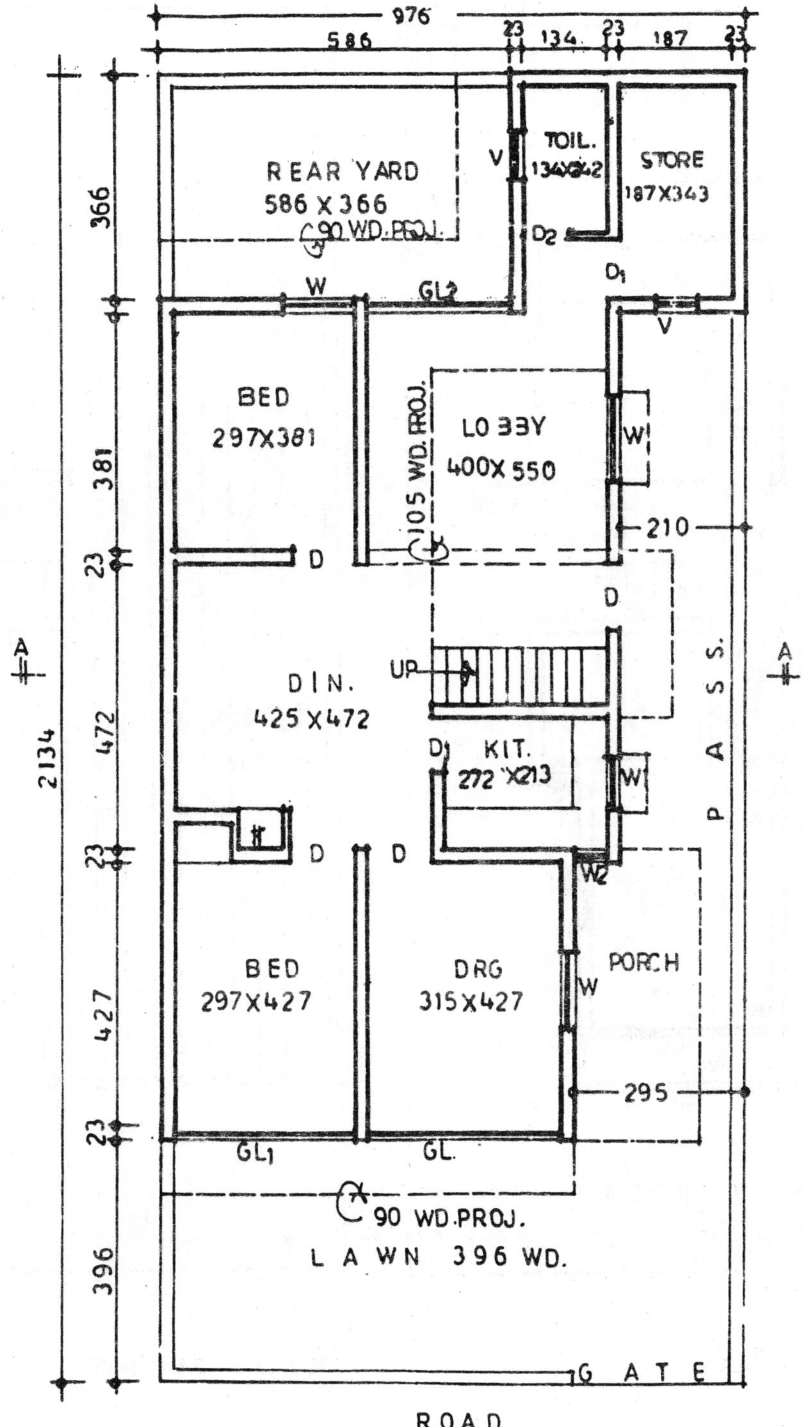


Fig. 6.43. A.

**GROUND FLOOR PLAN**

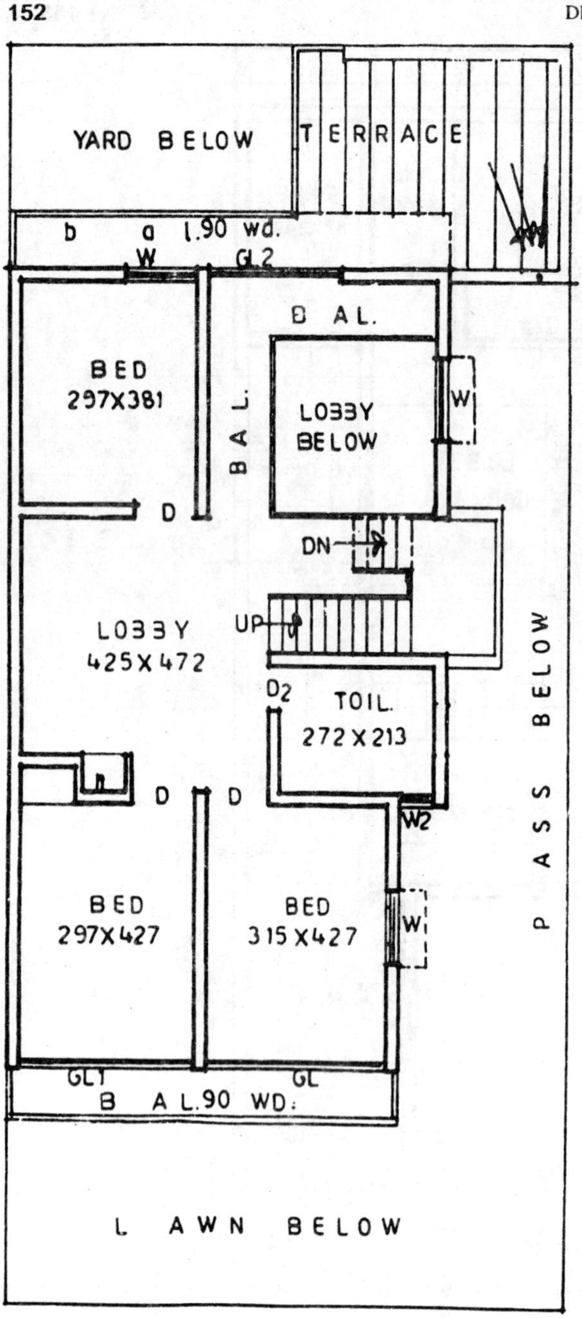


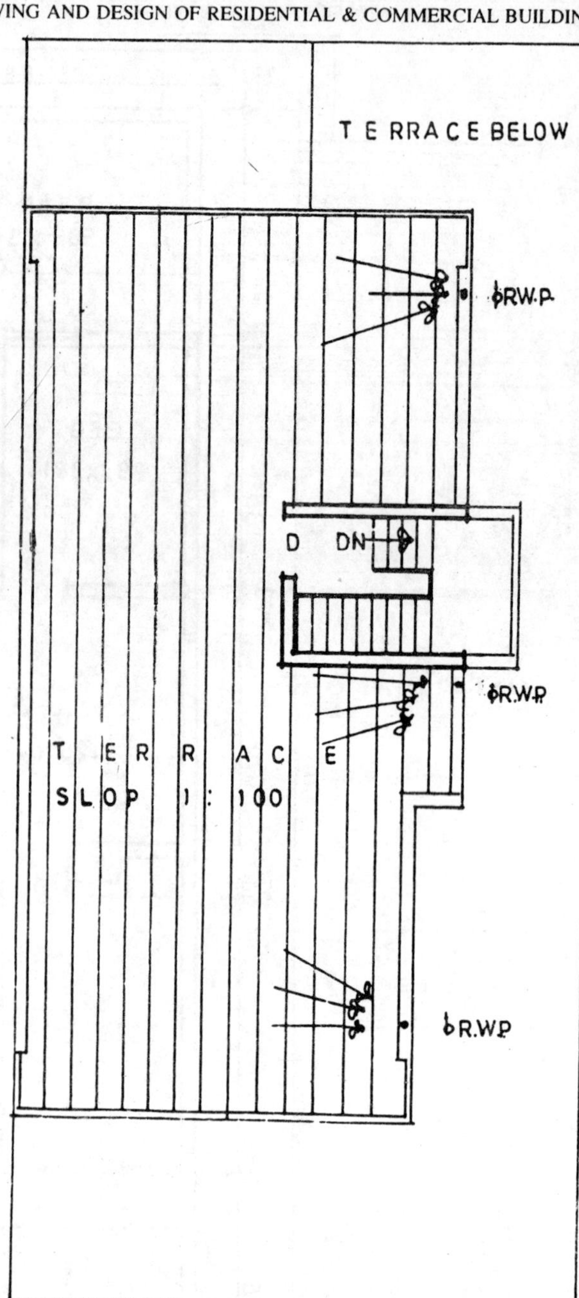


Fig. 6.43. B.

**FIRST FLOOR PLAN**

**FRONT ELEVATION**

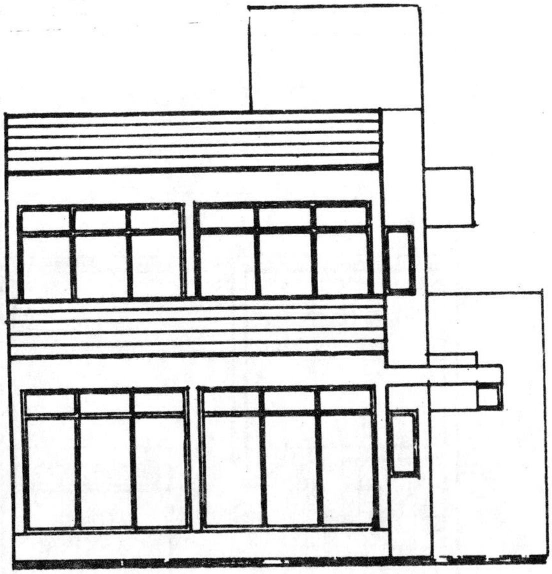

FRONT ELEVATION

## SCHEDULE OF OPENINGS

| | | |
|---|---|---|
| D | DOOR | 105 X 210 |
| D1 | " | 90 X 210 |
| D2 | " | 75 X 210 |
| W | WINDOW | 120 X 120 |
| W1 | " | 90 X 120 |
| W2 | | 62 X 120 |
| GL. | GLAZING | 315 X 210 |
| GL1 | " | 297 X 210 |
| GL2 | | 243 X 210 |
| V | VENT | 75 X 45 |

## AREA STATEMENT

| | SQ. M. |
|---|---|
| PLOT AREA | 208.20 |
| COV. AREA AT G.F. | 116.00 |
| OPEN AREA AT G.F. | 92.20 |
| COV. AREA AT F.F. | 101.20 |
| OPEN AREA AT F.F | 14.80 |

ALL DIMENSIONS IN CM

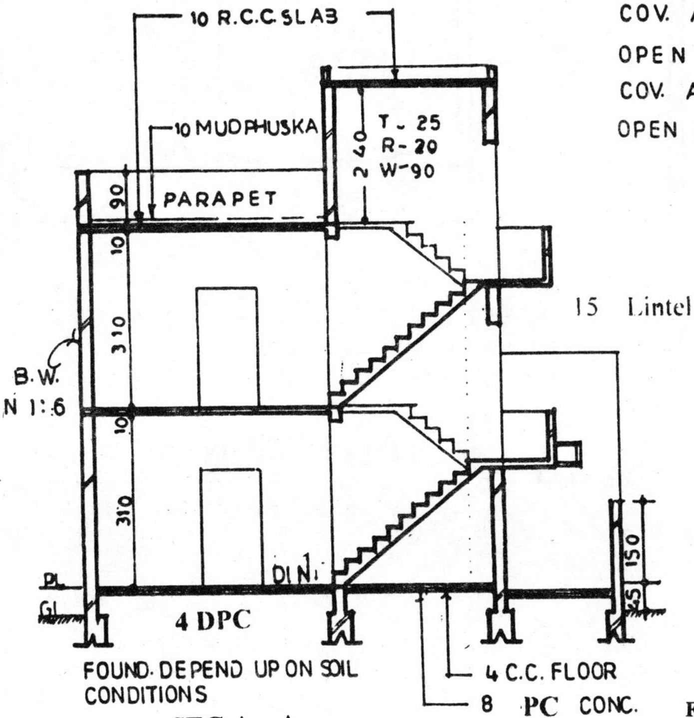


SEC-A—A

Fig. 6.43. C.

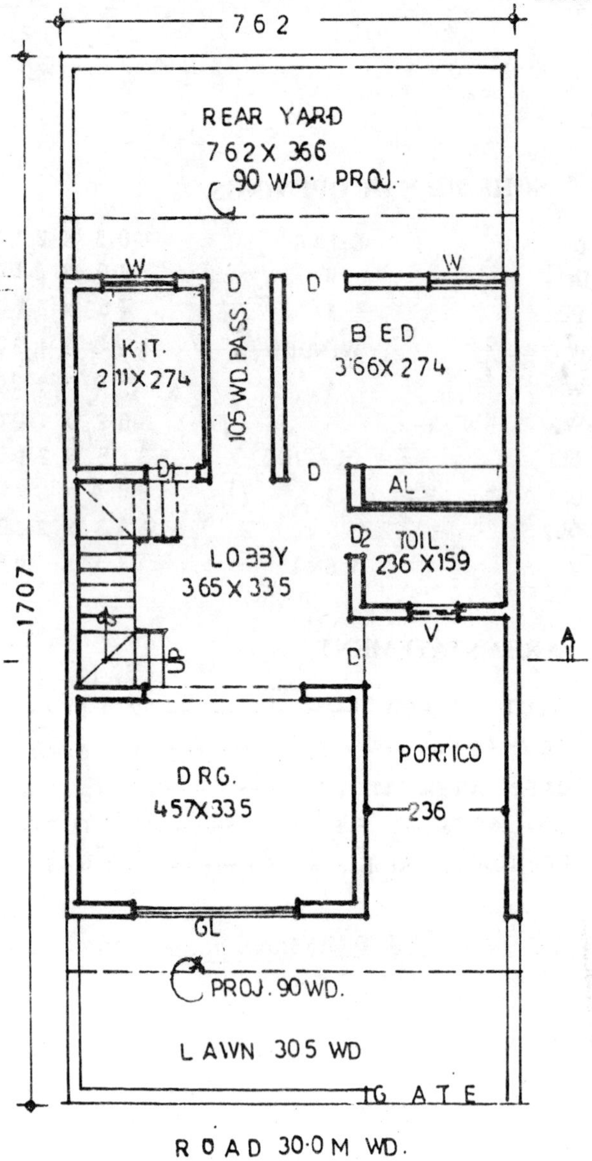


**GROUND FLOOR PLAN**

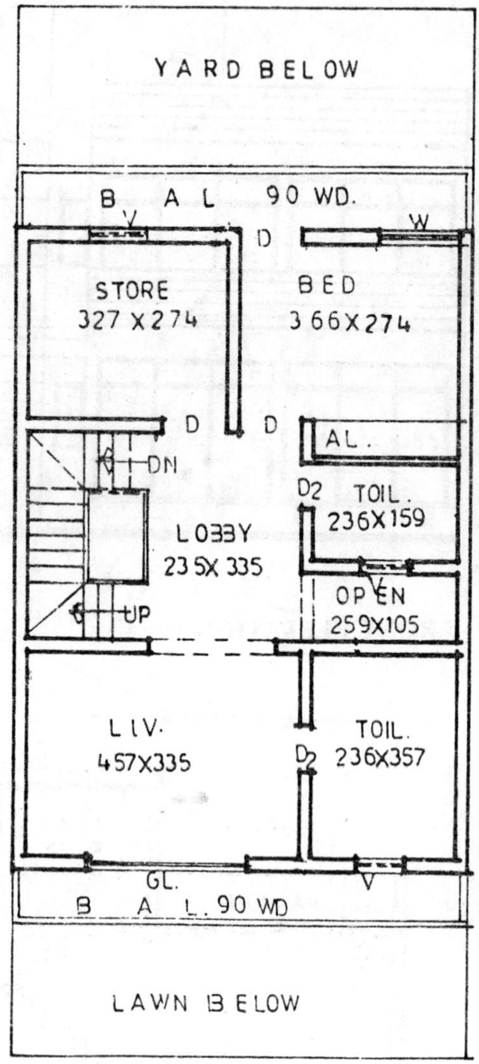


**FIRST FLOOR PLAN**

**Fig. 6.44. A.**

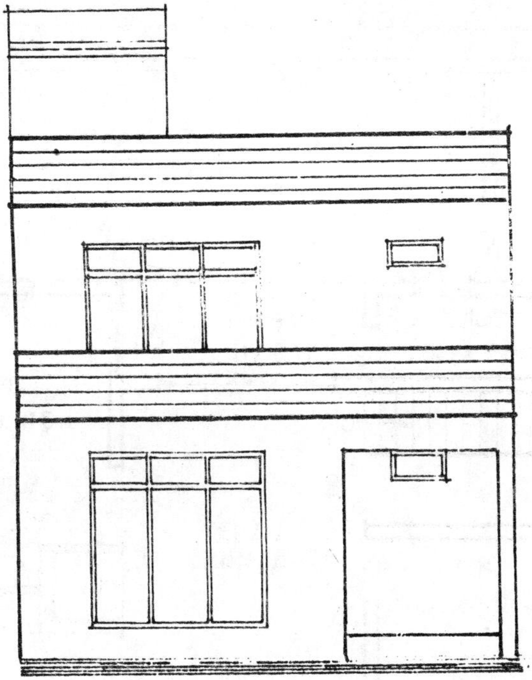

**FRONT ELEVATION**

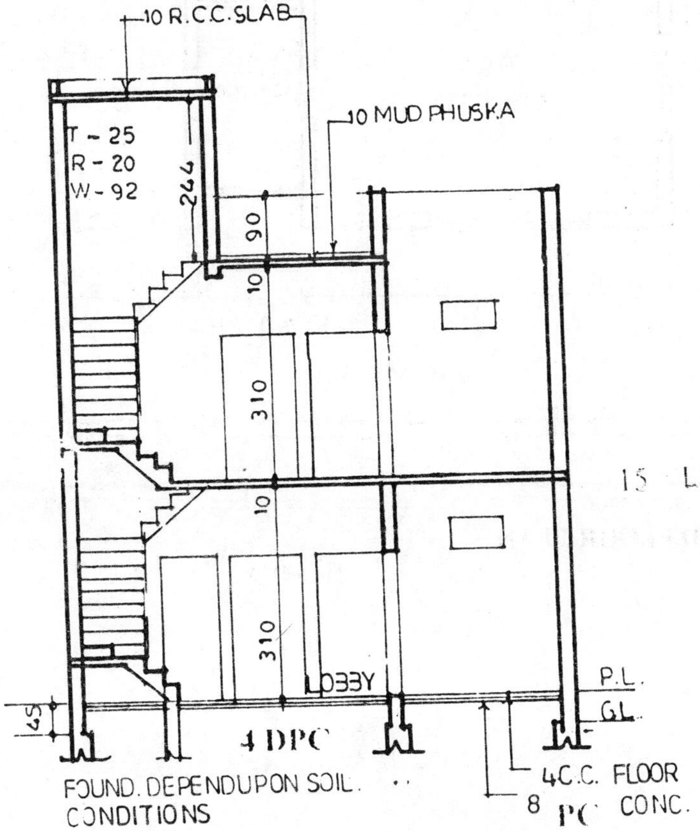


**SEC-A—A** Fig. 6.44. B.

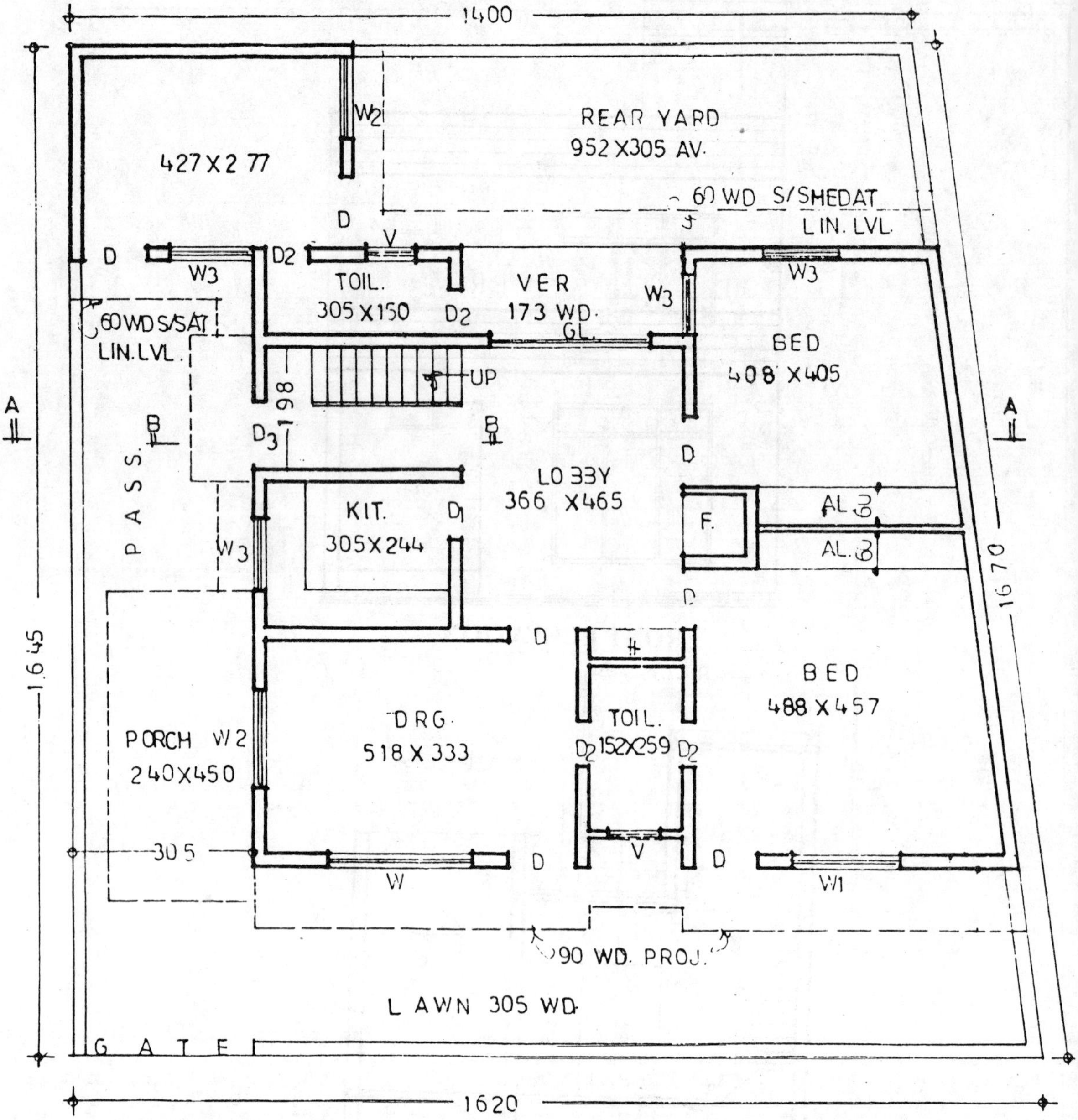


**GROUND FLOOR PLAN**

Fig. 6.45. A.

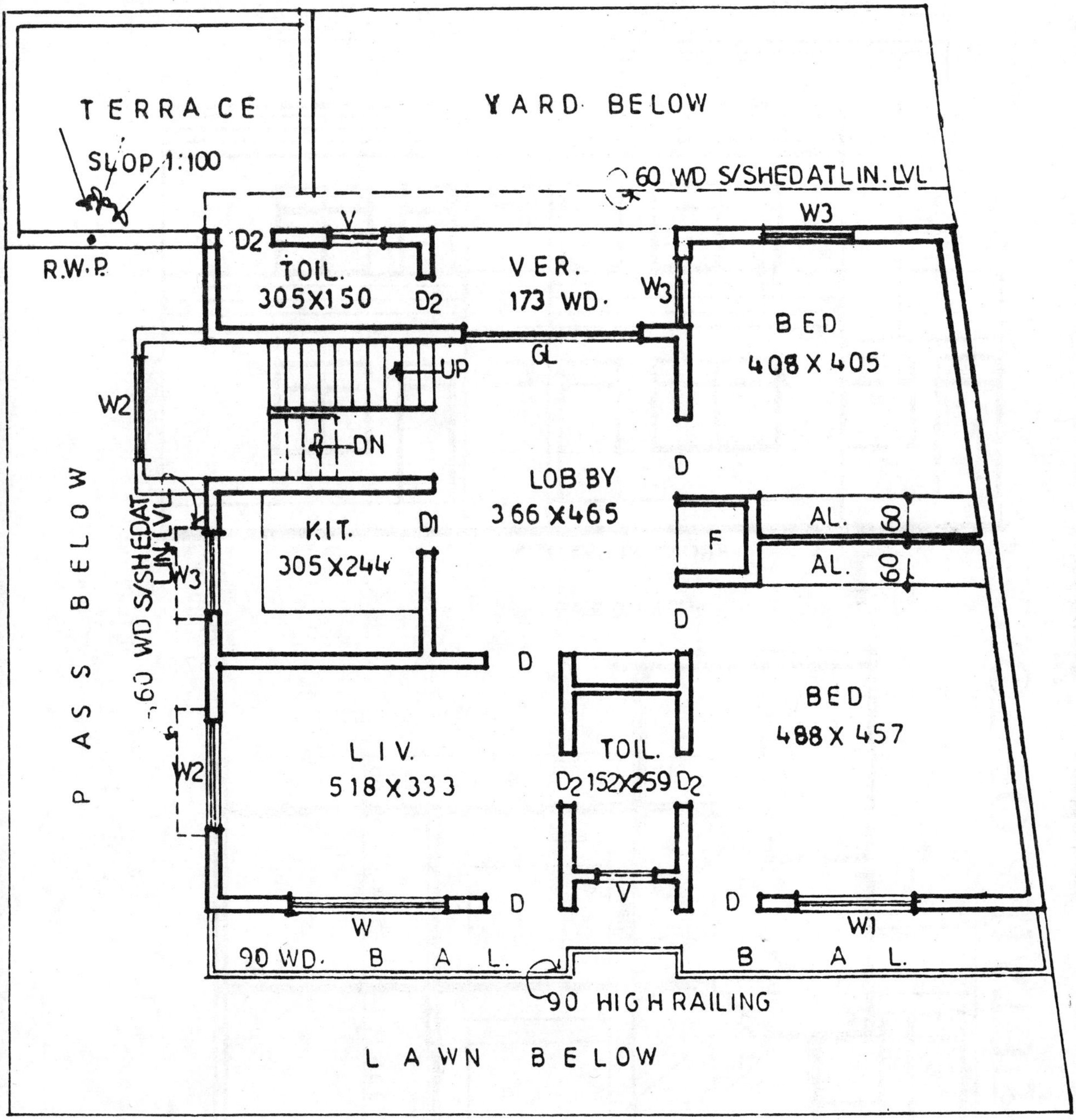


FIRST FLOOR PLAN

Fig. 6.45. B.

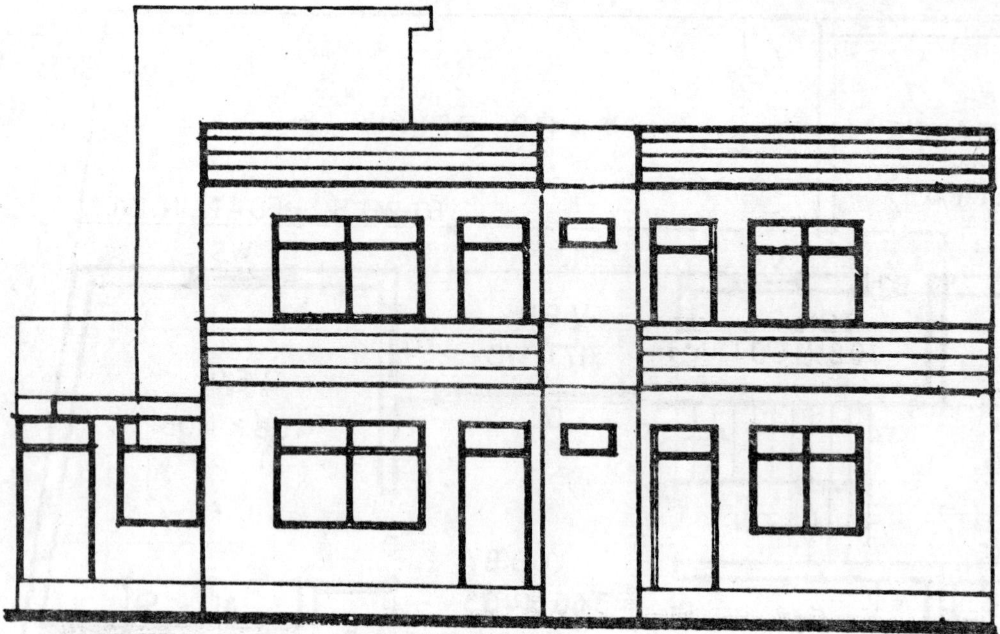

FRONT ELEVATION

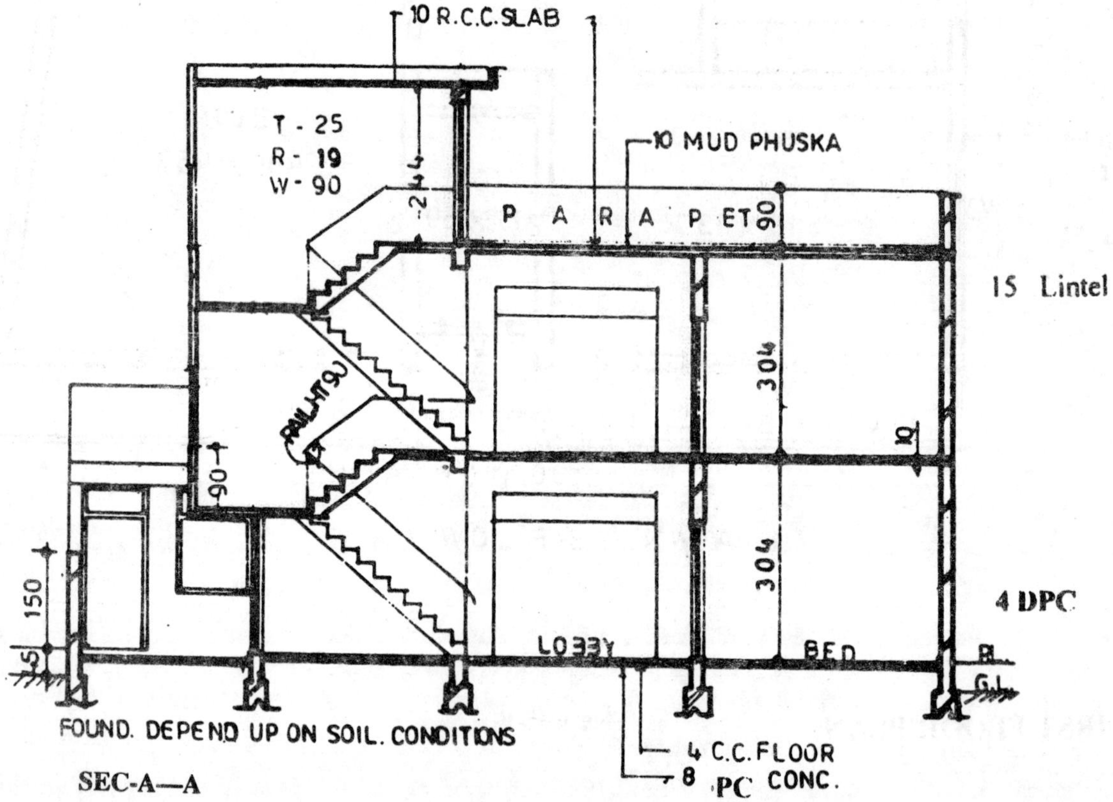


SEC-A—A

SCALE 1 : 100

Fig. 6.45. C.

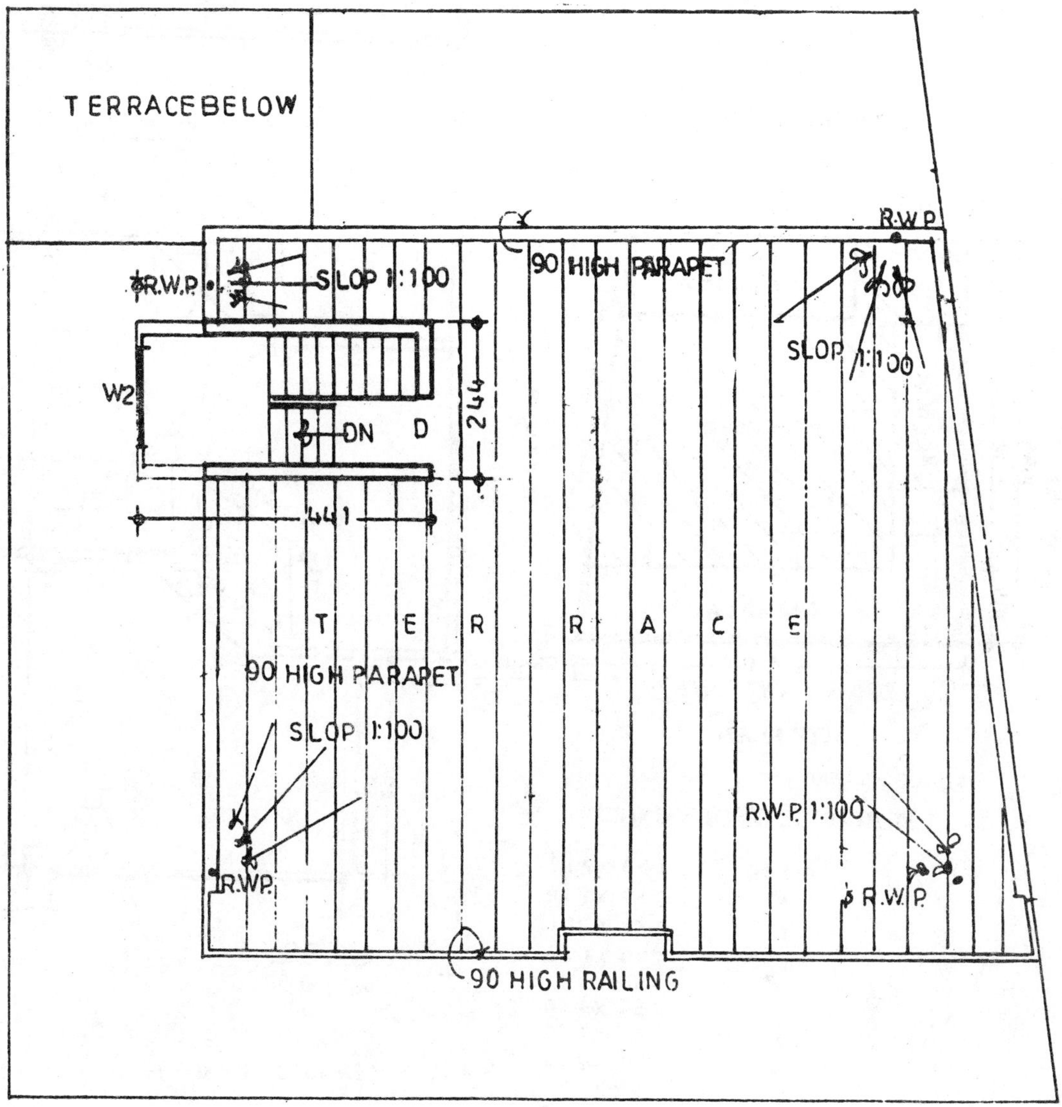


**TERRACE PLAN**

**Fig. 6.45. D.**

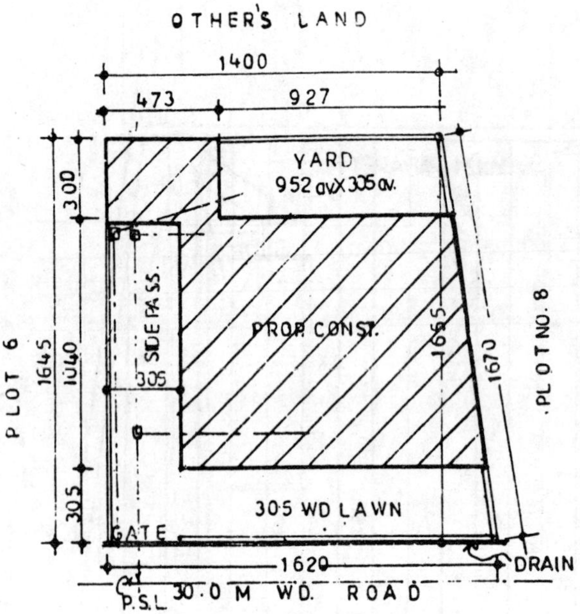


**SITE PLAN**

SCALE - 1:200

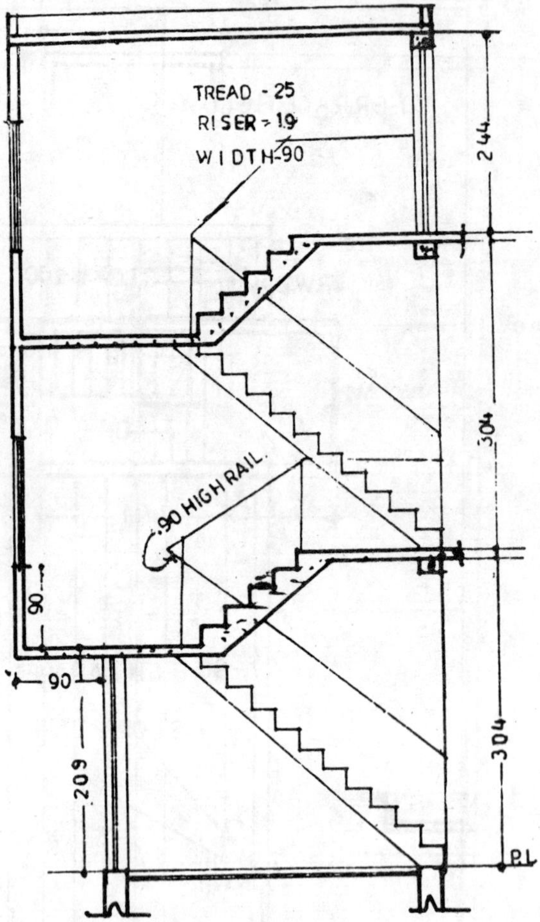


SEC-B-B

SCALE-1:50

## SCHEDULE OF OPENINGS

| | | |
|---|---|---|
| D | DOOR | 100 X 210 |
| D1 | " | 90 X 210 |
| D2 | " | 75 X 210 |
| W | WINDOW | 240 X 120 |
| W1 | " | 180 X 120 |
| W2 | " | 150 X 120 |
| W3 | " | 120 X 120 |
| GL. | GLAZING | 244 X 210 |
| V | VENT. | 75 X 45 |
| D3 | DOOR | 100 X 200 |

ALL DIMENSIONS IN CM.

## AREA STATEMENT

| | SQ.M. |
|---|---|
| PLOT AREA | 249.20 |
| COV. AREA AT G.F. | 140.70 |
| OPEN AREA AT G.F. | 108.50 |
| COV. AREA AT F.F. | 125.80 |
| OPEN AREA AT F.F. | 14.90 |
| MUMTY AREA | 10.80 |

| | SQ.M. (50%) |
|---|---|
| PROJ. AREA AT G.F. | 10.90 |
| PROJ. AREA AT F.F. | 5.50 |

Fig. 6.45. E.

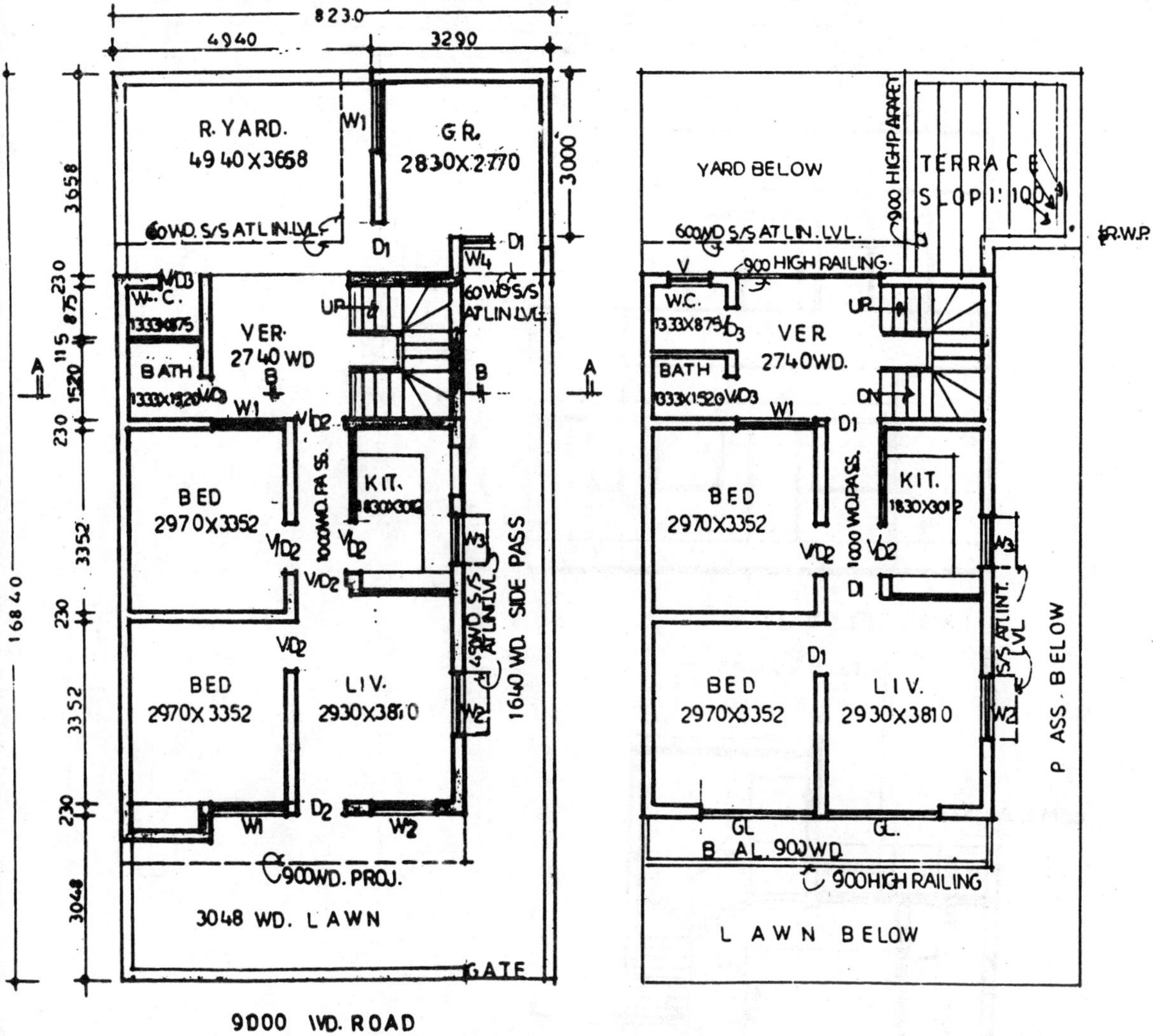


**GROUND FLOOR PLAN** **Fig. 6.46. A.** **FIRST FLOOR PLAN**

SCALE 1:100 SCALE 1:100

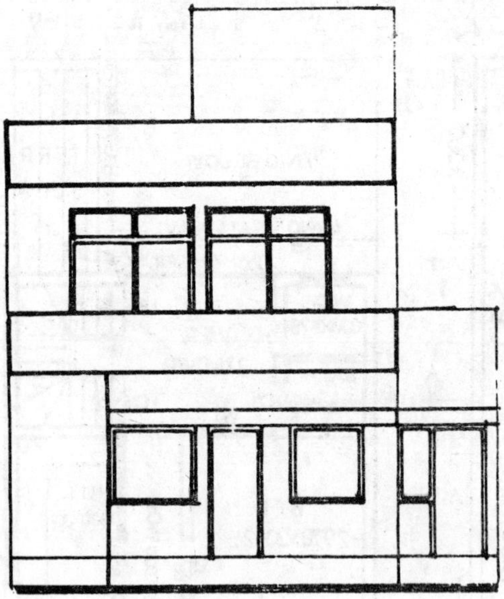

FRONT ELEVATION

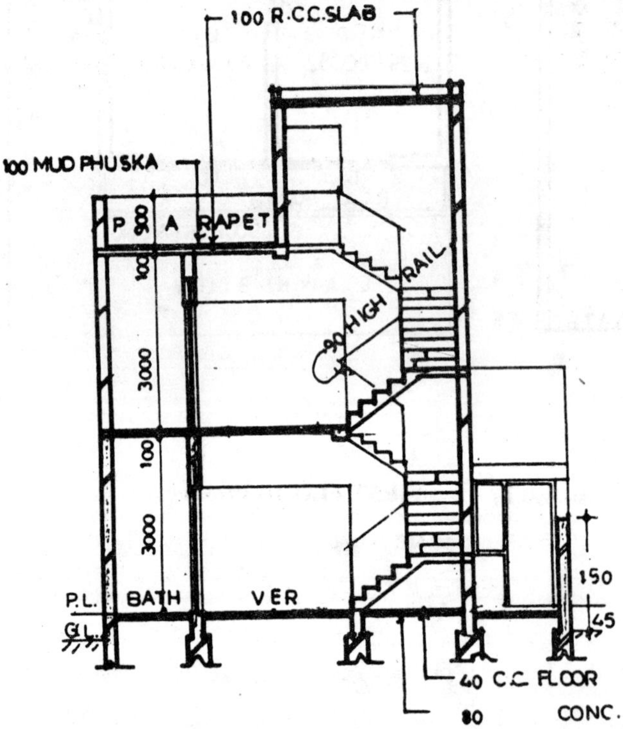


SEC-A—A Fig. 6.46. B.

SCALE 1:100

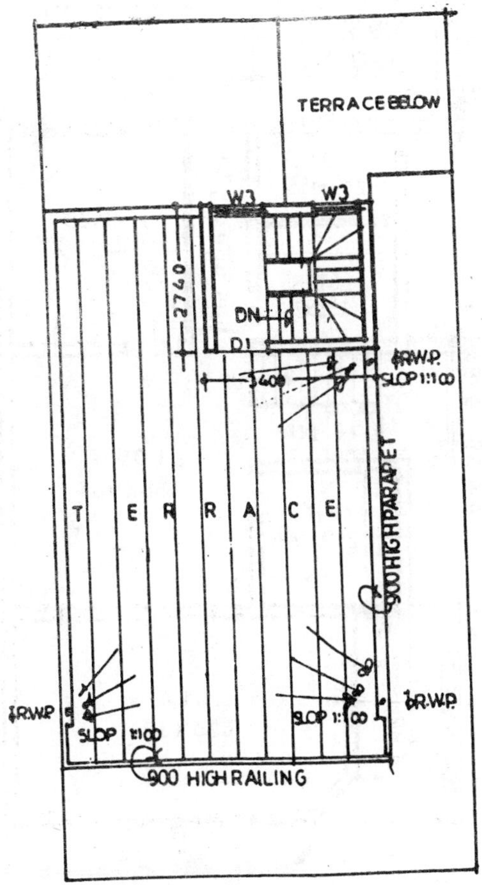


TERRACE PLAN

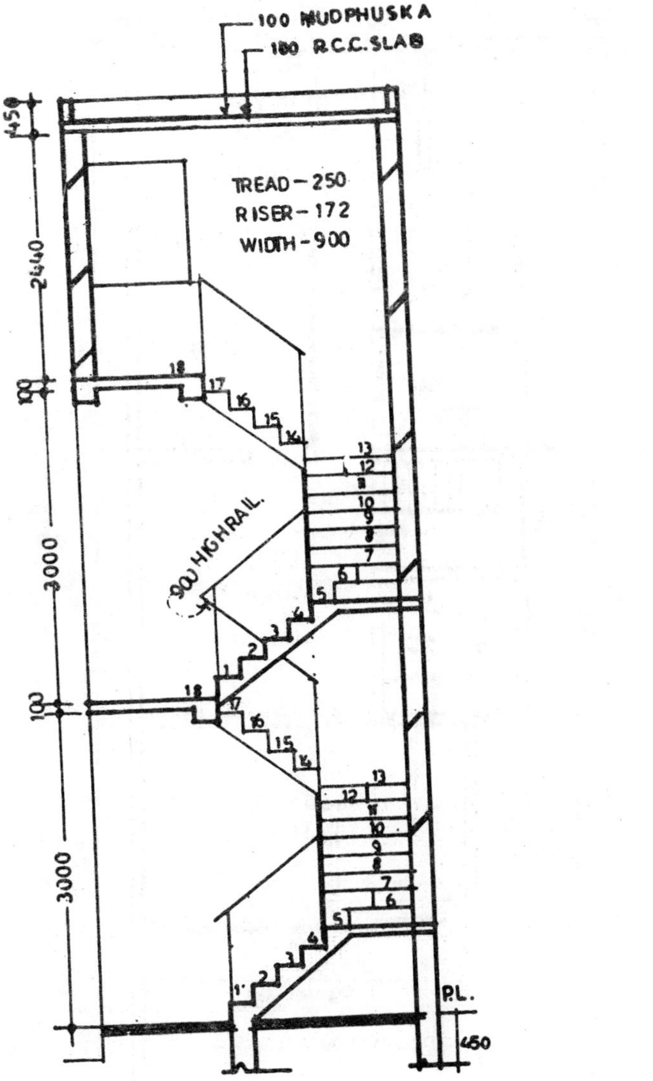


SEC-A—A

1 : 50

## SCHEDULE OF OPENINGS

| | | |
|---|---|---|
| D1 | DOOR | 1000 X 2100 |
| V/D2 | DOOR | 900 X 2550 |
| V/D3 | " | 750 X 2550 |
| W1 | WINDOW | 1400 X 1200 |
| W2 | " | 1200 X 1200 |
| W3 | " | 900 X 1200 |
| W4 | " | 400 X 1200 |
| GL. | GLAZING | 2100 X 2100 |
| V | VENT | 750 X 450 |

Fig. 6.46. C.

## AREA STATEMENT

| | SQ.M |
|---|---|
| PLOT AREA | 138.60 |
| EXIST COV. AREA AT G.F. | 69.00 |
| PROP. COV. AREA AT G.F. | 10.00 |
| PROJ. AREA AT G.F. 50% | 1.40 |
| OPEN AREA AT G.F. | 59.00 |
| PROP. COV. AREA AT F.F. | 69.00 |
| OPEN AREA AT F.F. | 10.00 |
| PROJ. AREA AT F.F. 50% | 3.00 |
| MUMTY AREA | 9.30 |
| PROP. COV. AREA, G.F. + F.F. + PROJ. + MUMTY | 92.70 |

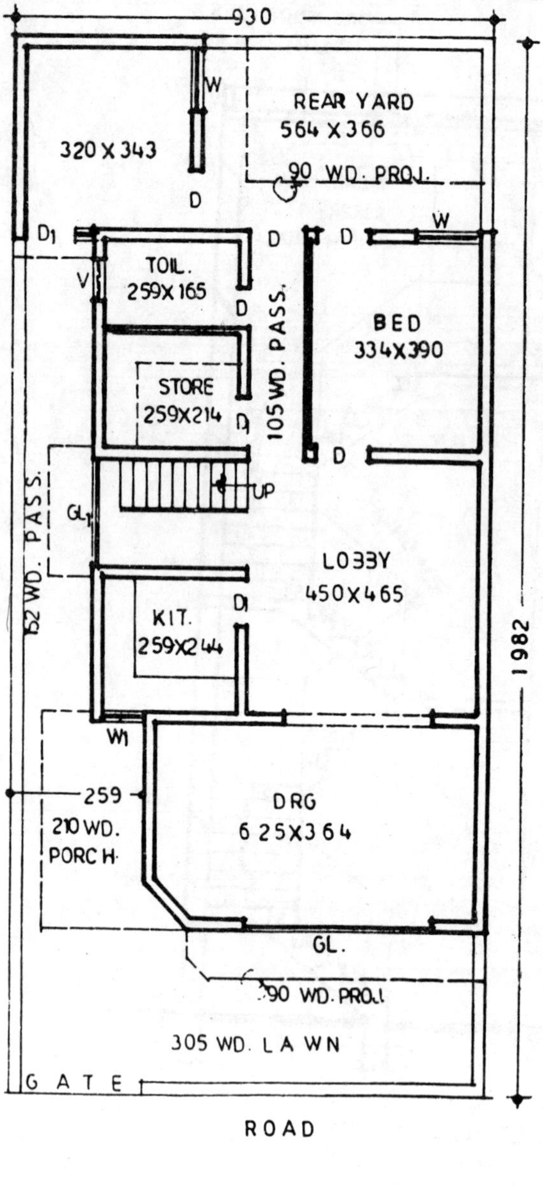


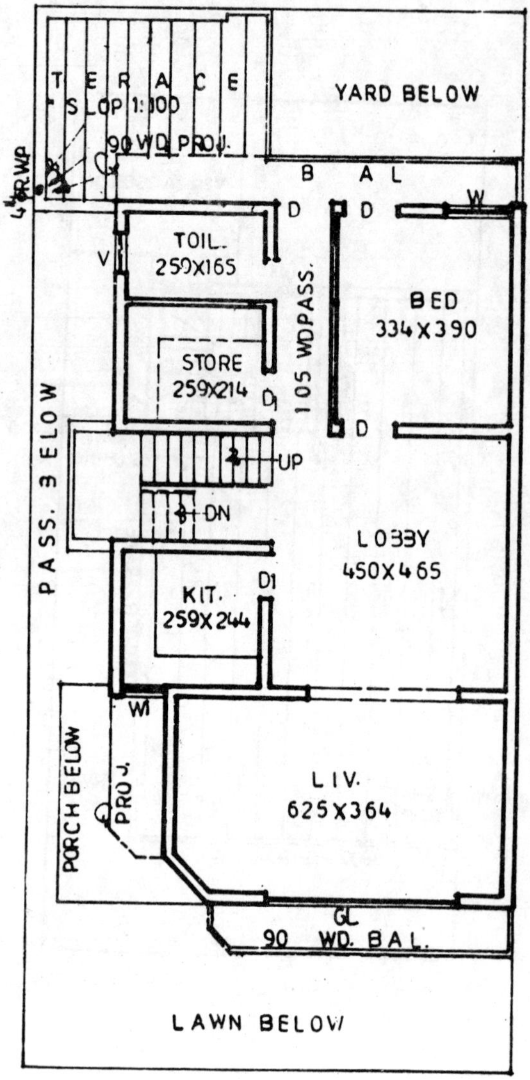


**GROUND FLOOR PLAN** Fig. 6.47. A. **FIRST FLOOR PLAN**

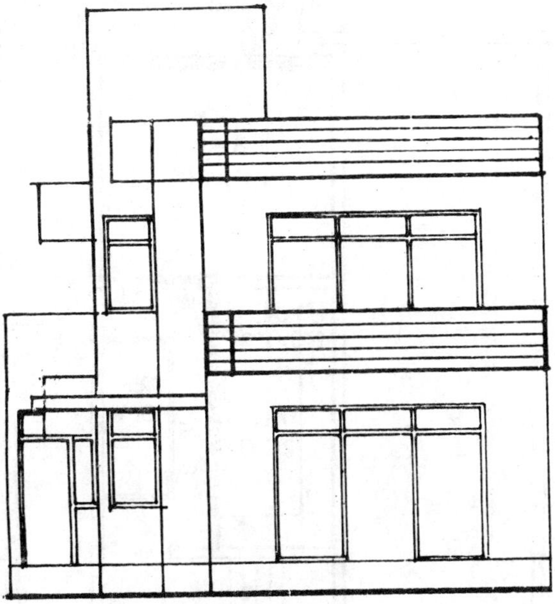

FRONT ELEVATION

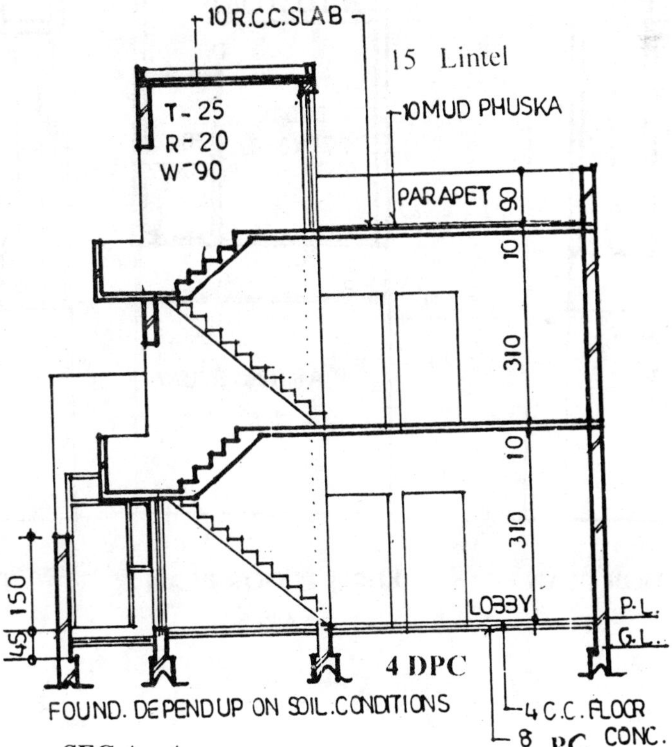


SEC-A—A

Fig. 6.47. B.

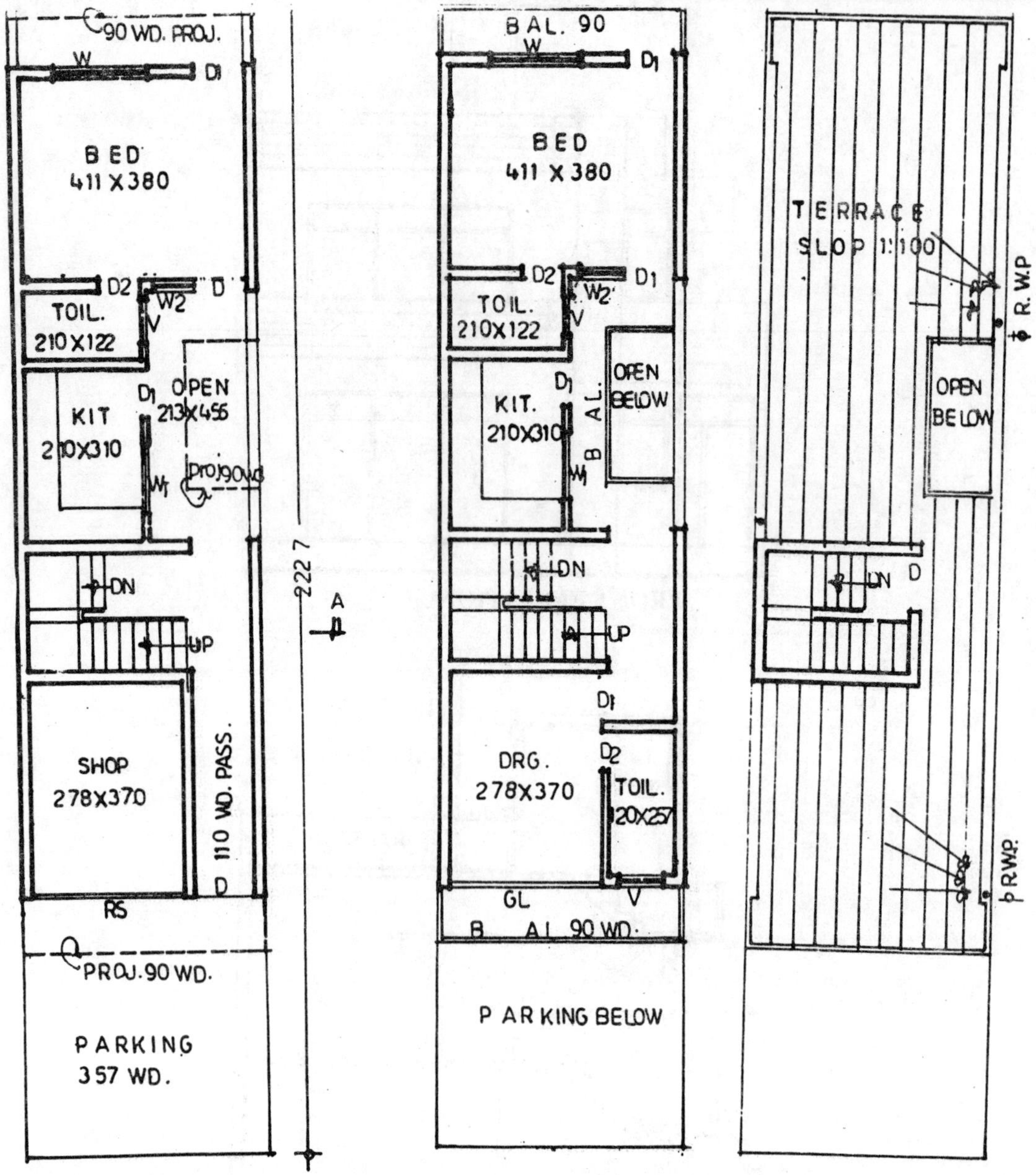


GROUND FLOOR PLAN FIRST FLOOR PLAN TERRACE PLAN

Fig. 6.48. A.

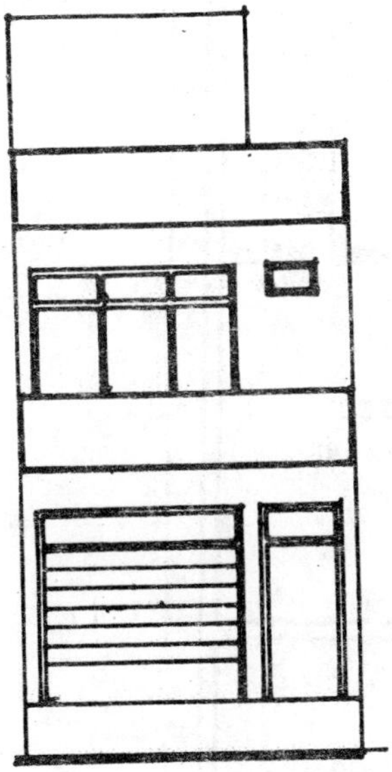

**FRONT ELEVATION**

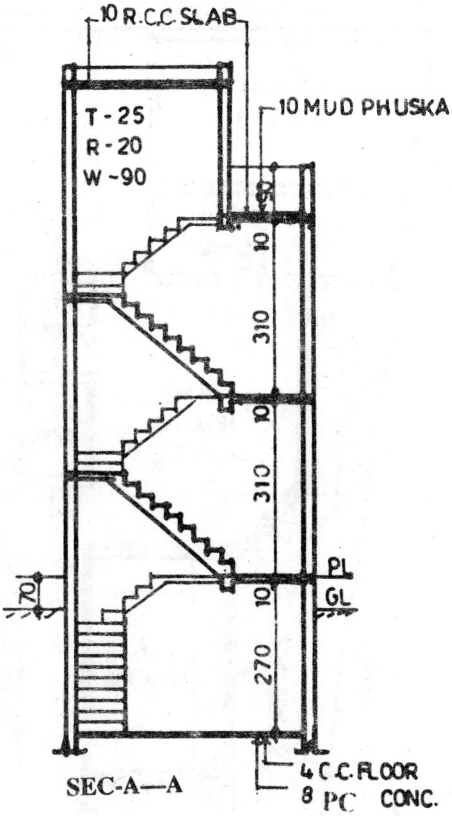


**SEC-A—A**

**AREA STATEMENT**

| | SQ. M |
|---|---|
| PLOT AREA | 104.50 |
| COV. AREA AT G.F. (COMMR.) | 13·50 |
| COV. AREA AT G.F. (RES.) | 46.50 |
| OPEN AREA AT G.F. | 44.50 |
| COV. AREA AT F.F. | 60·00 |
| COV. AREA AT BASEMENT | 19·80 |

**SCHEDULE OF OPENINGS**

| | | |
|---|---|---|
| D | DOOR | 105 X 210 |
| D1 | " | 90 X 210 |
| D2 | " | 75 X 210 |
| W | WINDOW | 180 X 120 |
| W1 | " | 120 X 120 |
| W2 | " | 90 X 120 |
| V | VENT | 75 X 45 |
| V1 | " | 90 X 45 |
| RS. | ROLL. SHUTT. | 278 X 260 |
| GL. | GLAZING. | 278 X 260 |

ALL DIMENSIONS IN CM. **Fig. 6.48. B.**

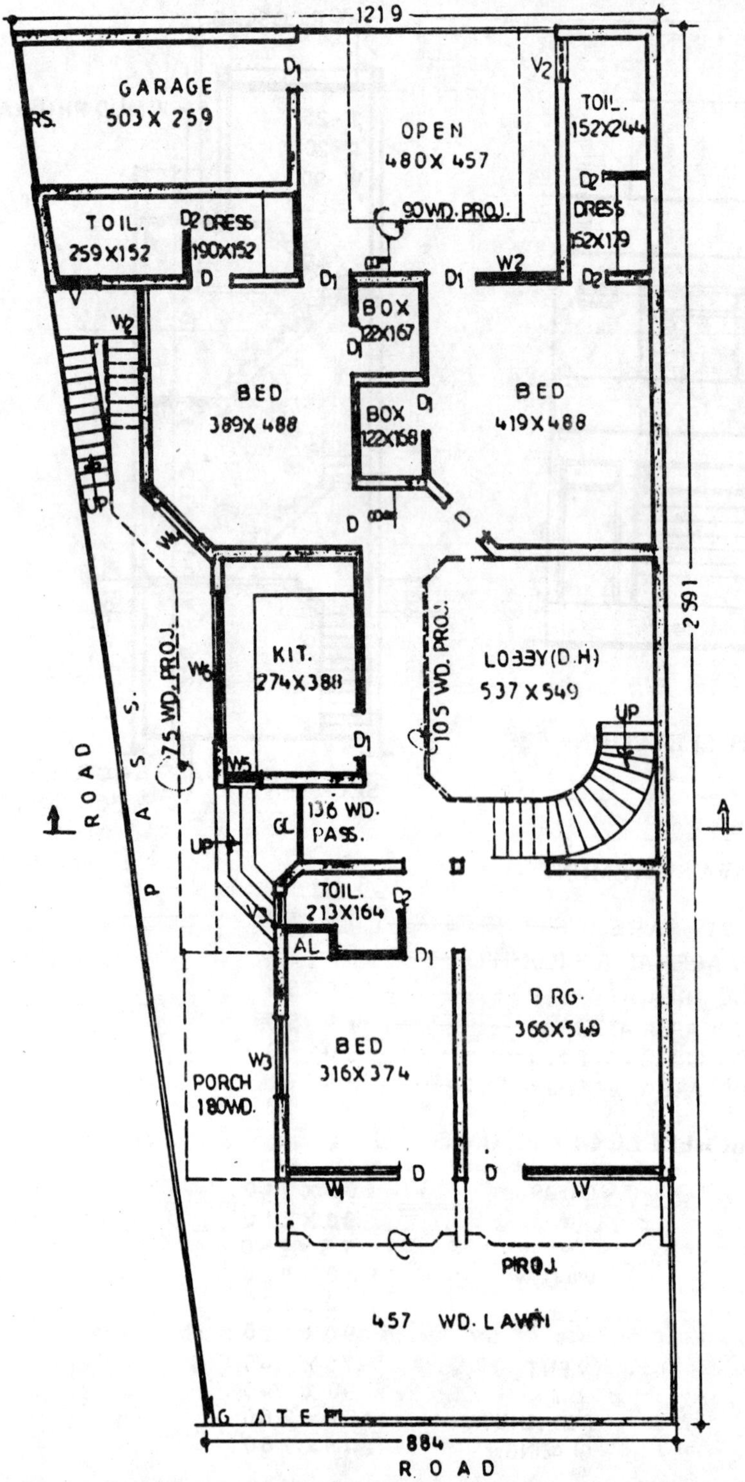


Fig. 6.49. A. **GROUND FLOOR PLAN**

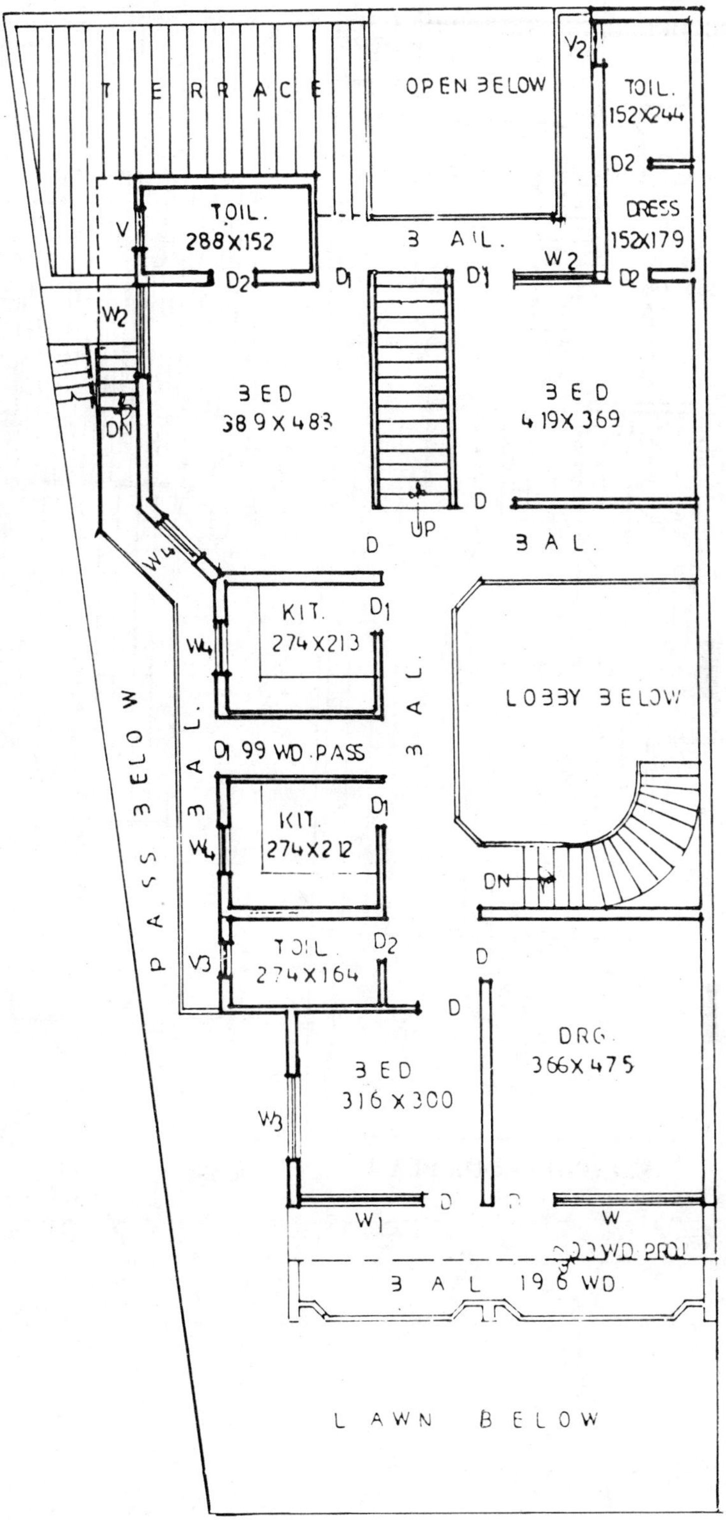


Fig. 6.49. B. **FIRST FLOOR PLAN**

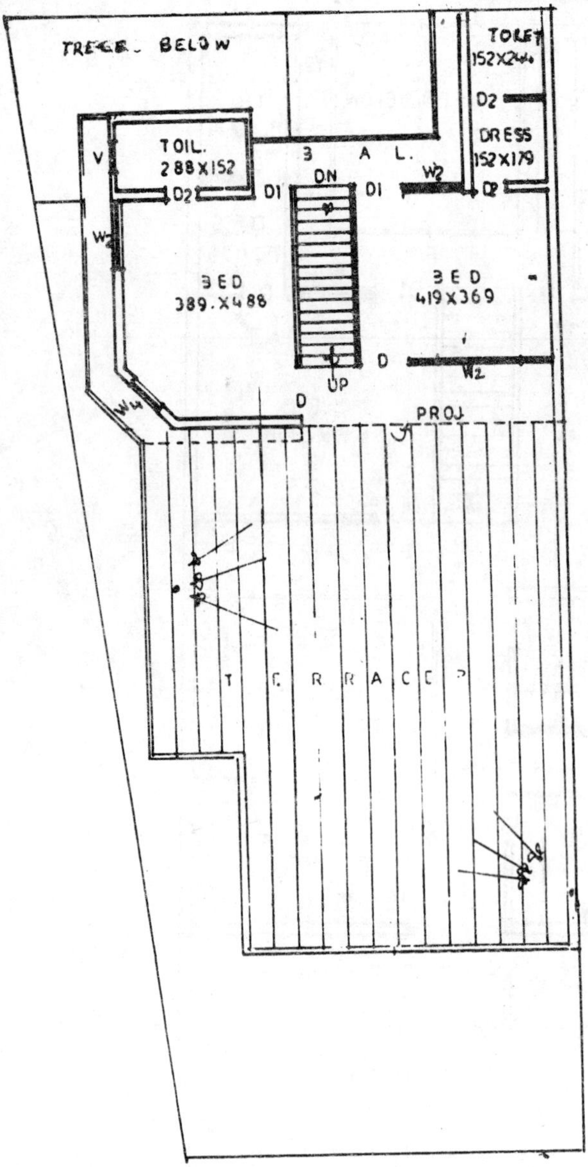


SECOND FLOOR PLAN

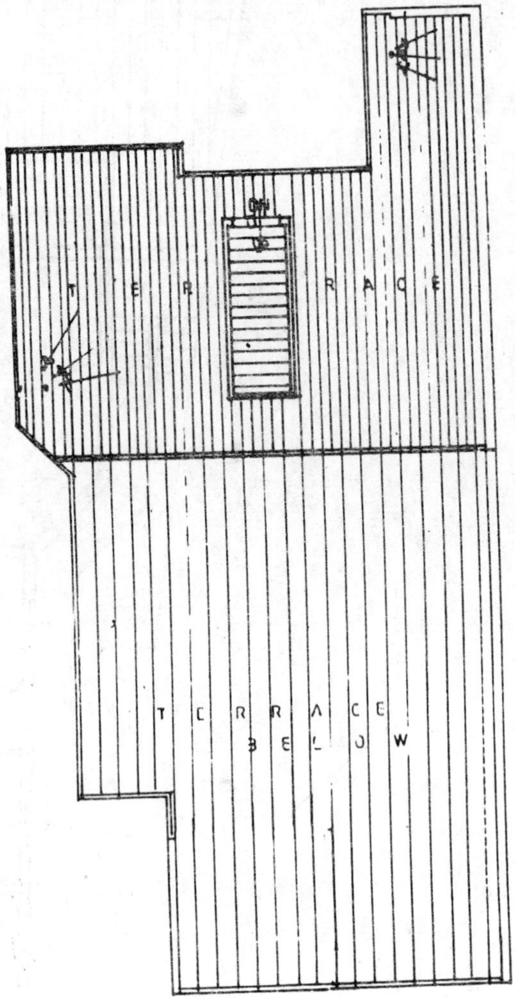


TERRACE PLAN

Fig. 6.49. C.

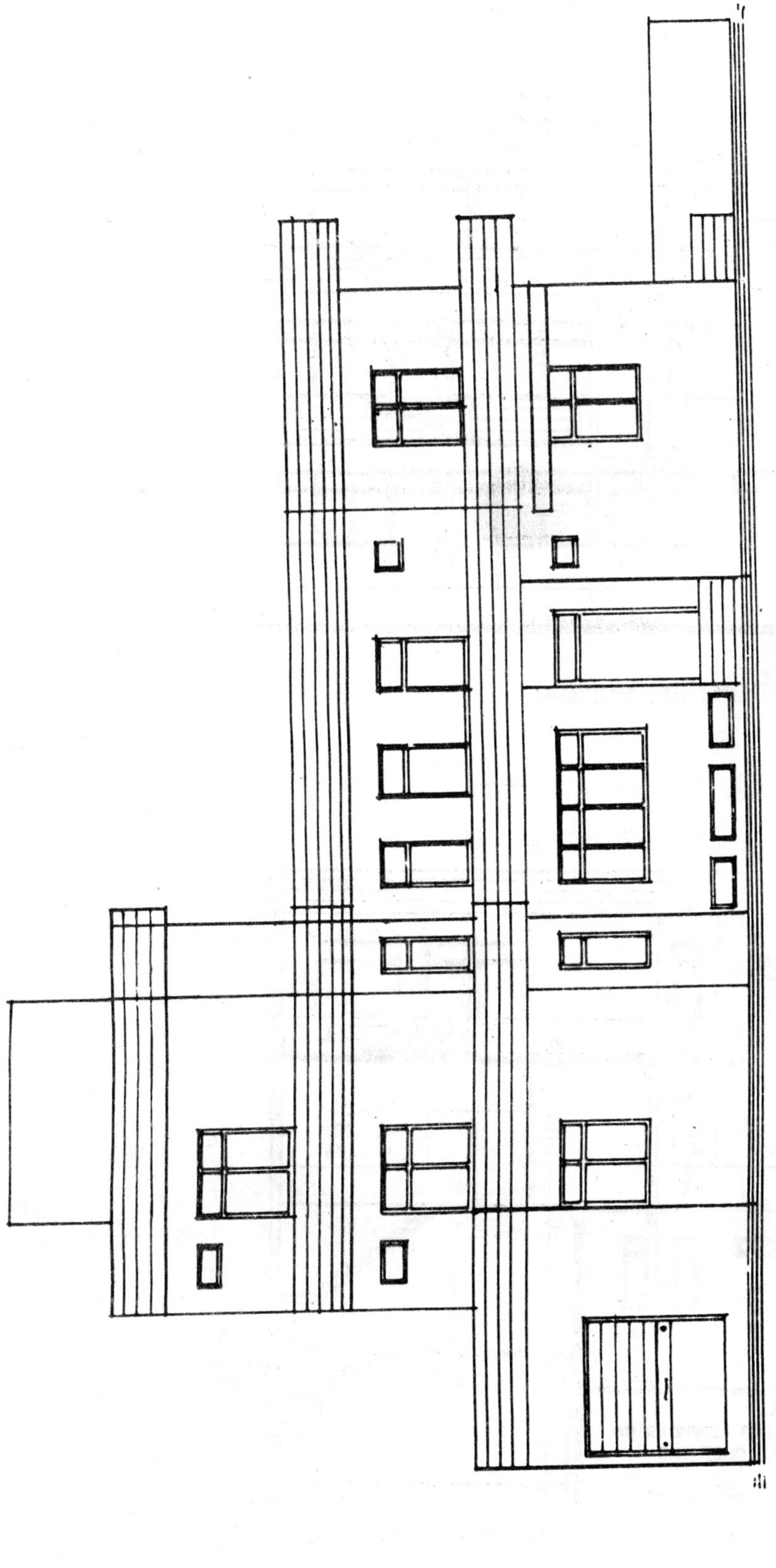

SIDE ELEVATION

Fig. 6.49. D.

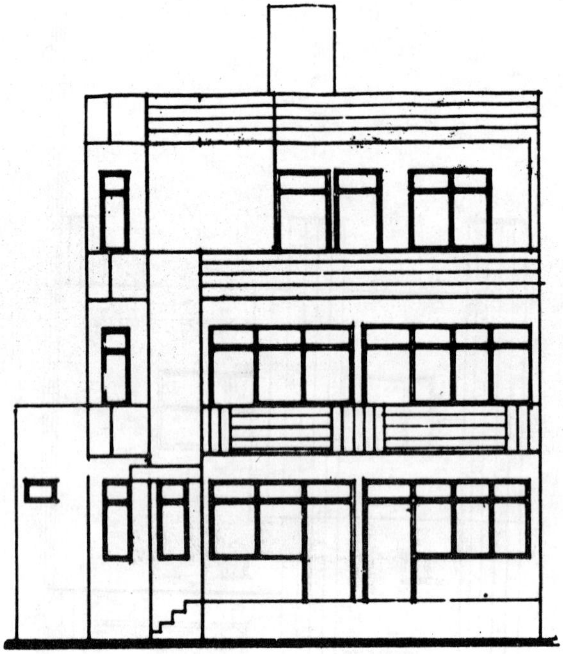

FRONT ELEVATION

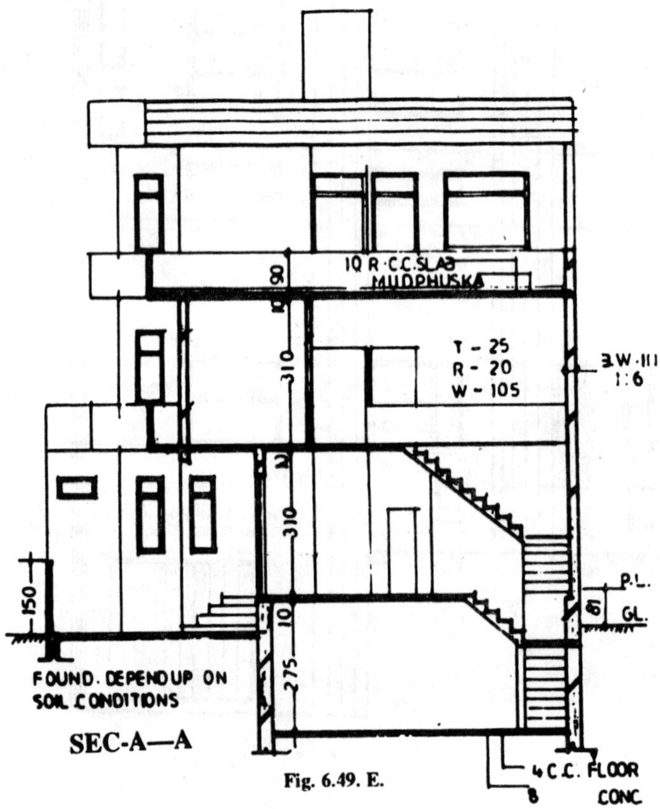


SEC-A—A

Fig. 6.49. E.

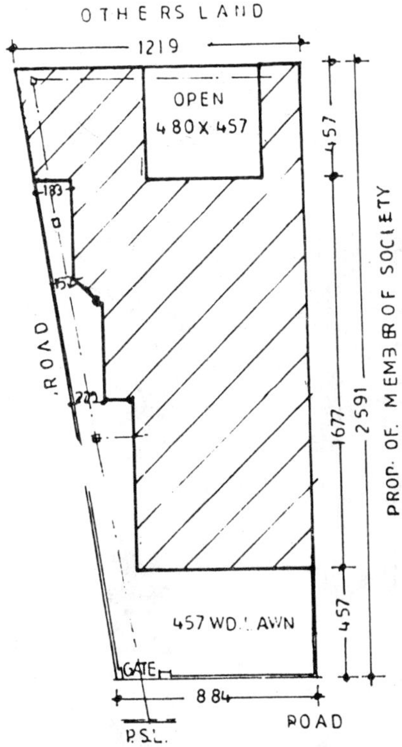


**SITE ELEVATION**

SCALE - 1:200

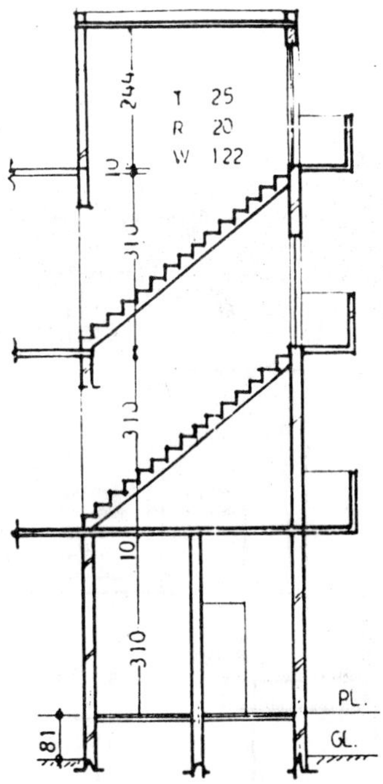


**SEC - B - B**

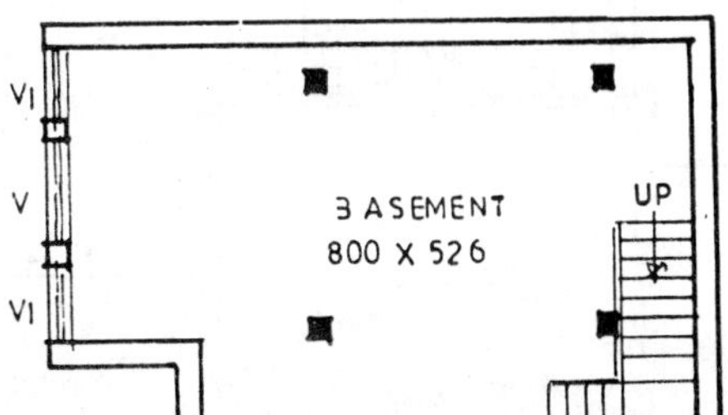


**BASEMENT**

ALL DIMENSINS IN CM

## SCHEDULE OF OPENINGS

| | | |
|---|---|---|
| D | DOOR | 105 X 210 |
| D1 | " | 90 X 210 |
| D2 | " | 75 X 210 |
| W | WINDOW | 259 X 120 |
| W1 | " | 209 X 120 |
| W2 | " | 150 X 120 |
| W3 | " | 137 X 120 |
| W4 | " | 90 X 120 |
| W5 | " | 60 X 120 |
| W6 | " | 275 X 120 |
| GL. | GLAZING. | 137 X 210 |
| V | VENT. | 120 X 145 |
| V1 | " | 90 X 45 |
| V2 | " | 75 X 45 |
| V3 | " | 60 X 45 |
| RS. | ROLL. SHUTT. | 259 X 255 |

## AREA STATEMENT

| | SQ. M |
|---|---|
| PLOT AREA | 272.40 |
| EXIST. COV. AREA AT. G.F. | 174.40 |
| OPEN AREA AT G.F. | 98.00 |
| PROP. COV. AREA AT F.F. | 134.95 |
| EXIST. COV. AREA AT F.F. | 18.32 |
| PROP. COV. AREA AT S.F. | 59.17 |
| EXIST. COV. AREA AT BASEMENT | 49.17 |

Fig. 6.49. F.

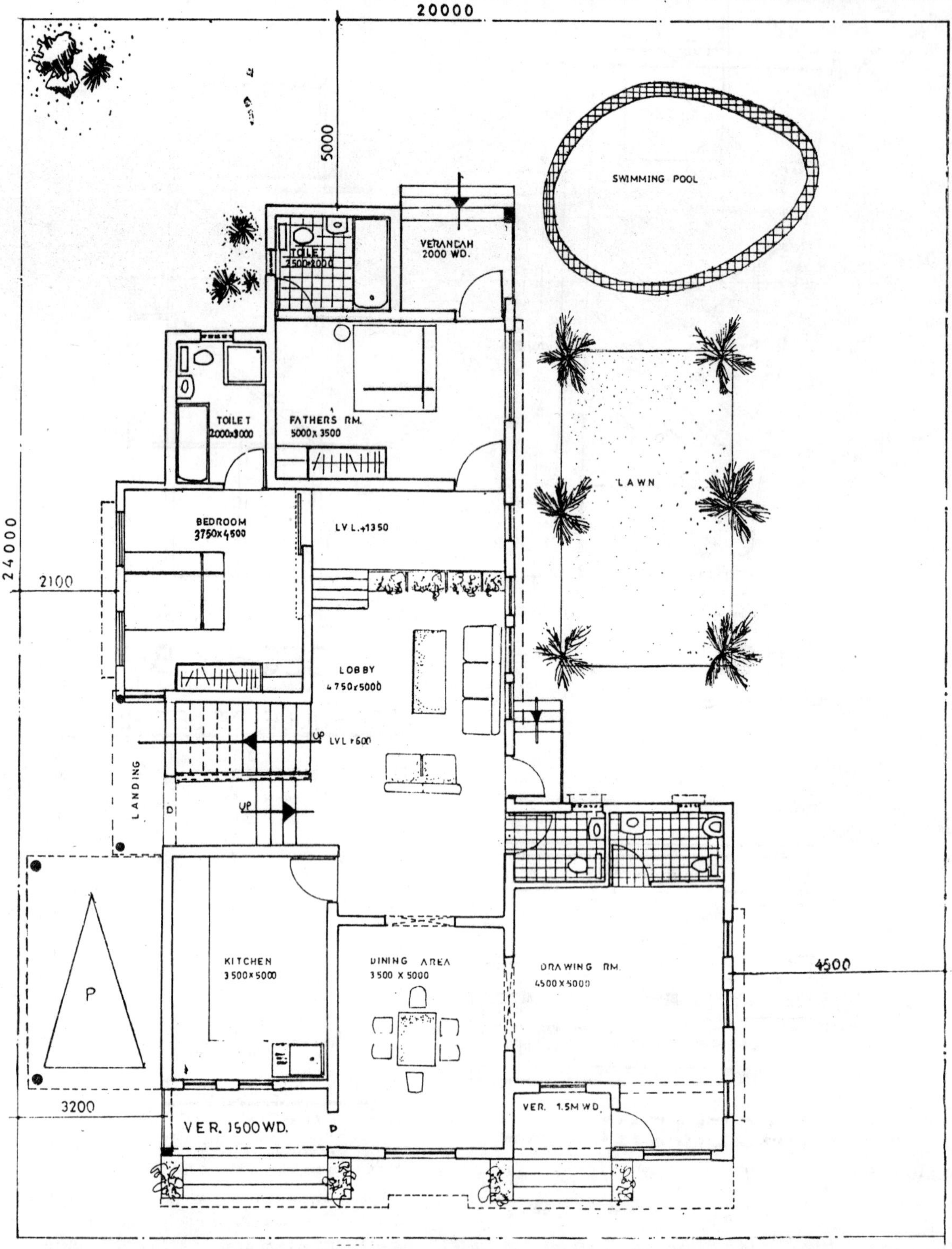


All dimensions in mm

Scale-1:75

**Fig. 6.50 A.** Ground floor plan

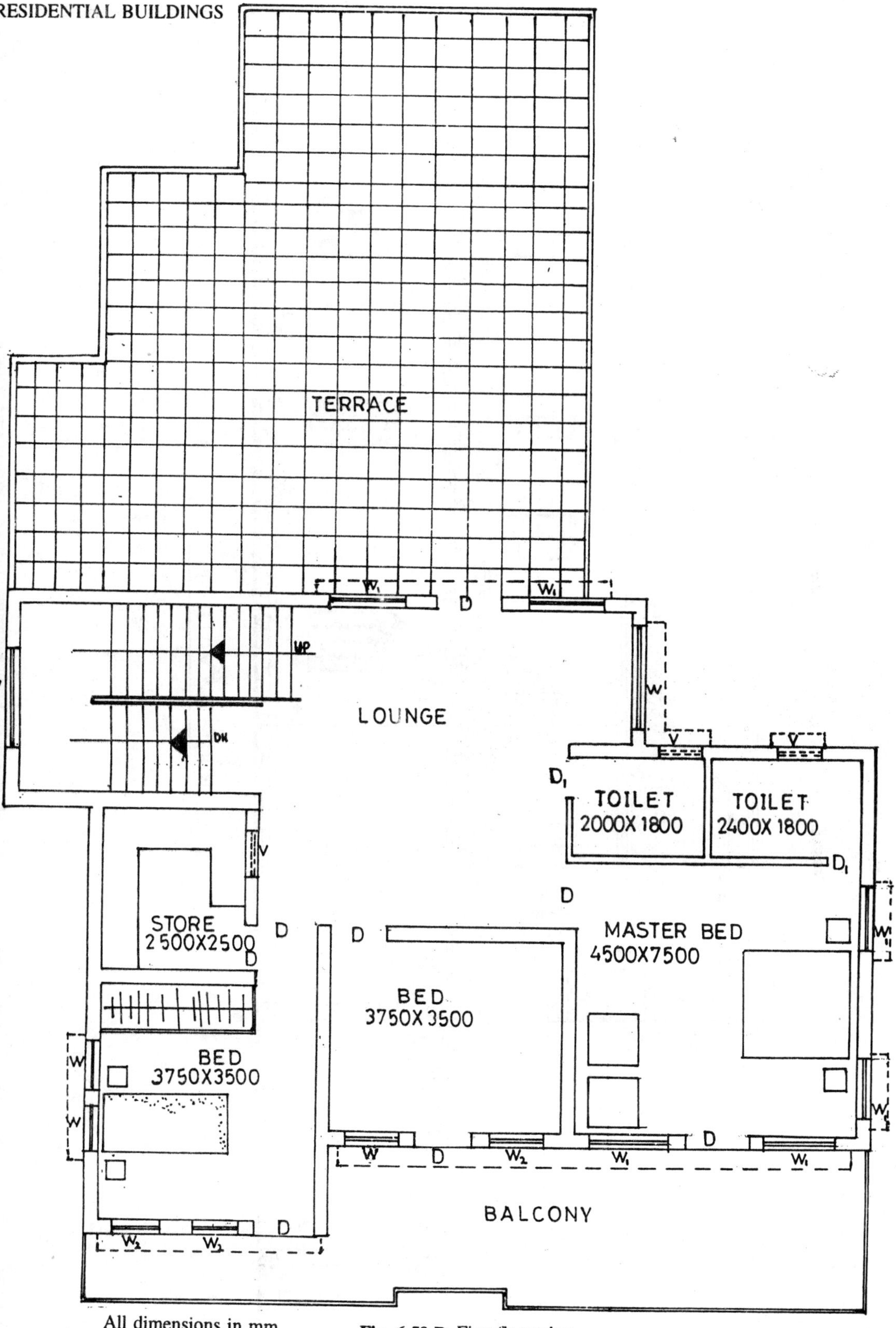


All dimensions in mm

**Fig. 6.50 B.** First floor plan

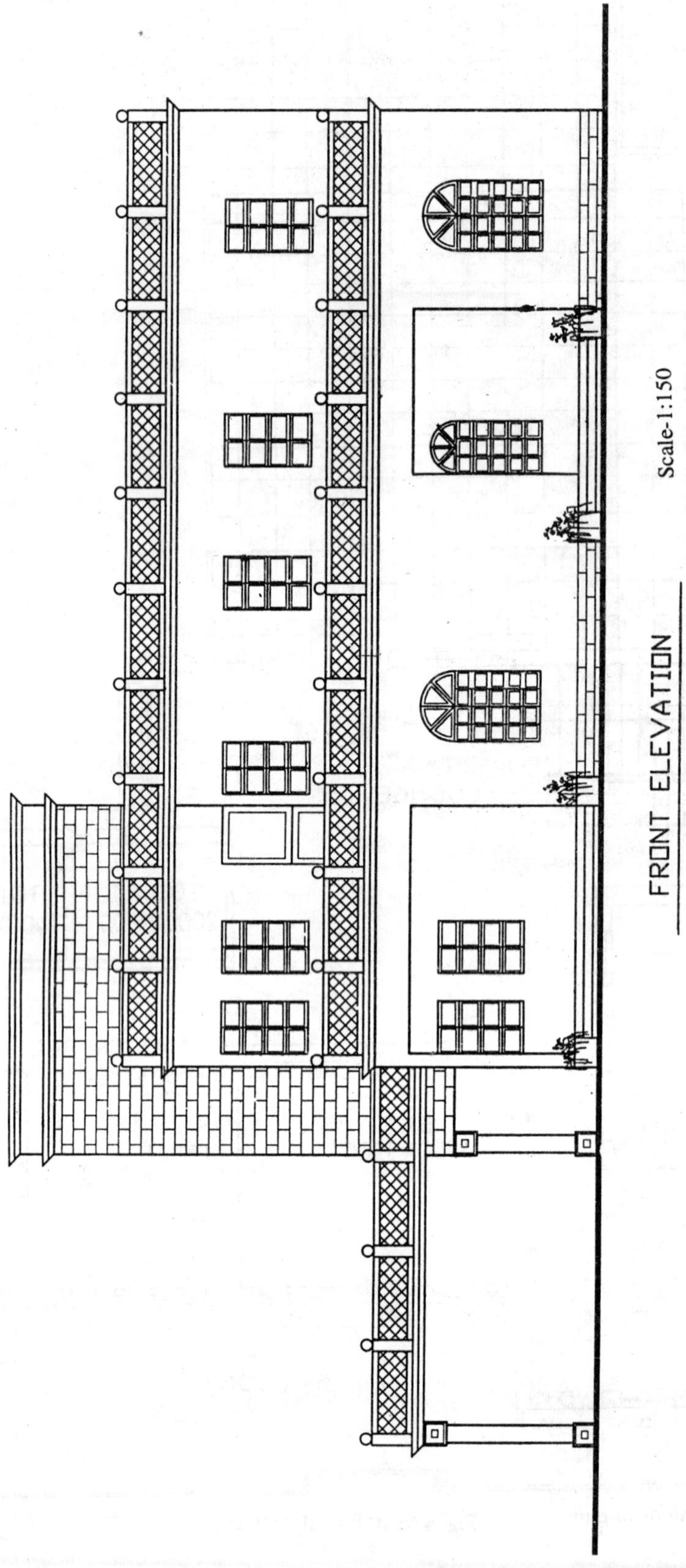


Fig. 6.50 C. Front Elevation

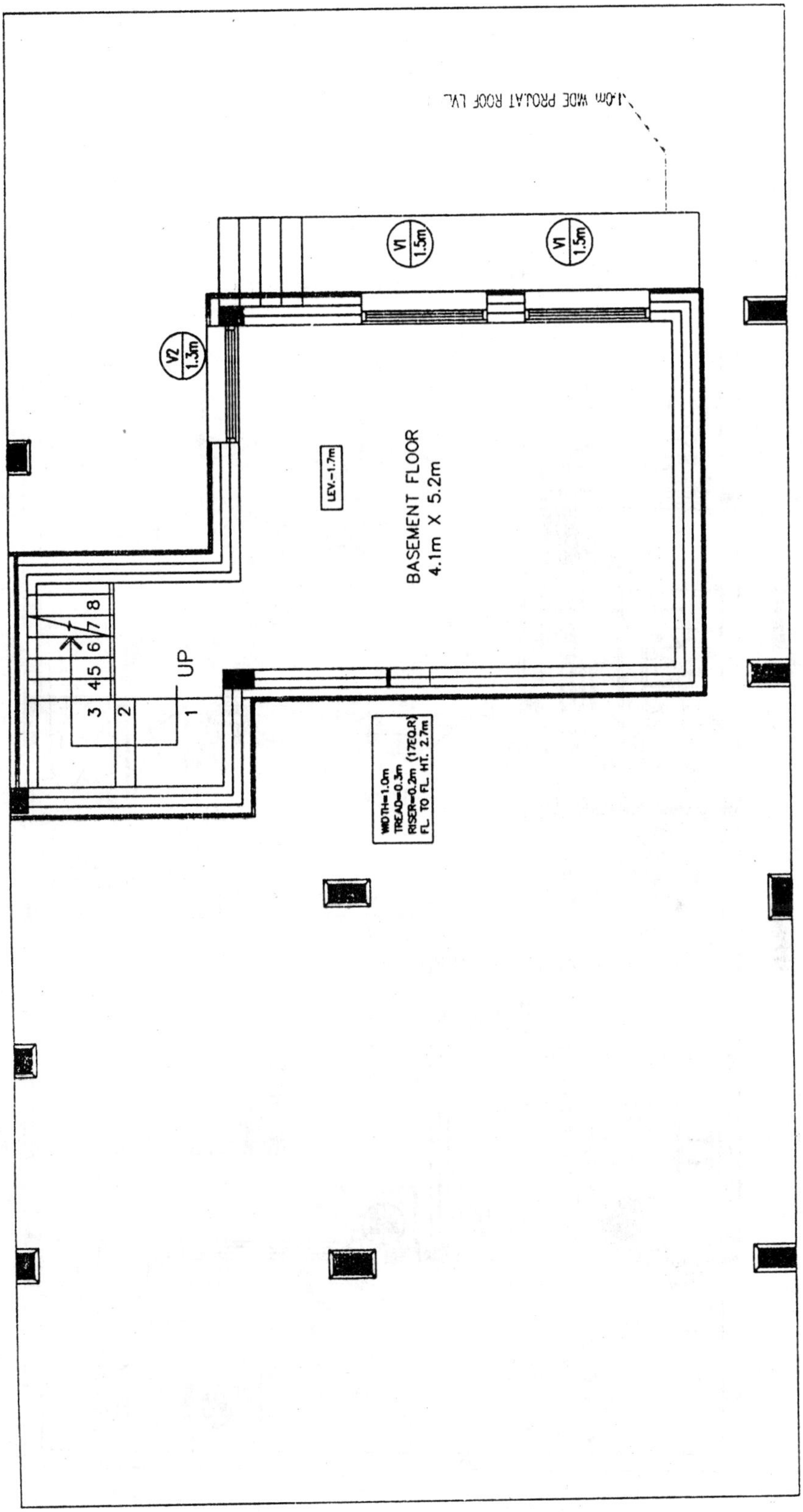


**Fig. 6.51 A.** Basement Floor Plan

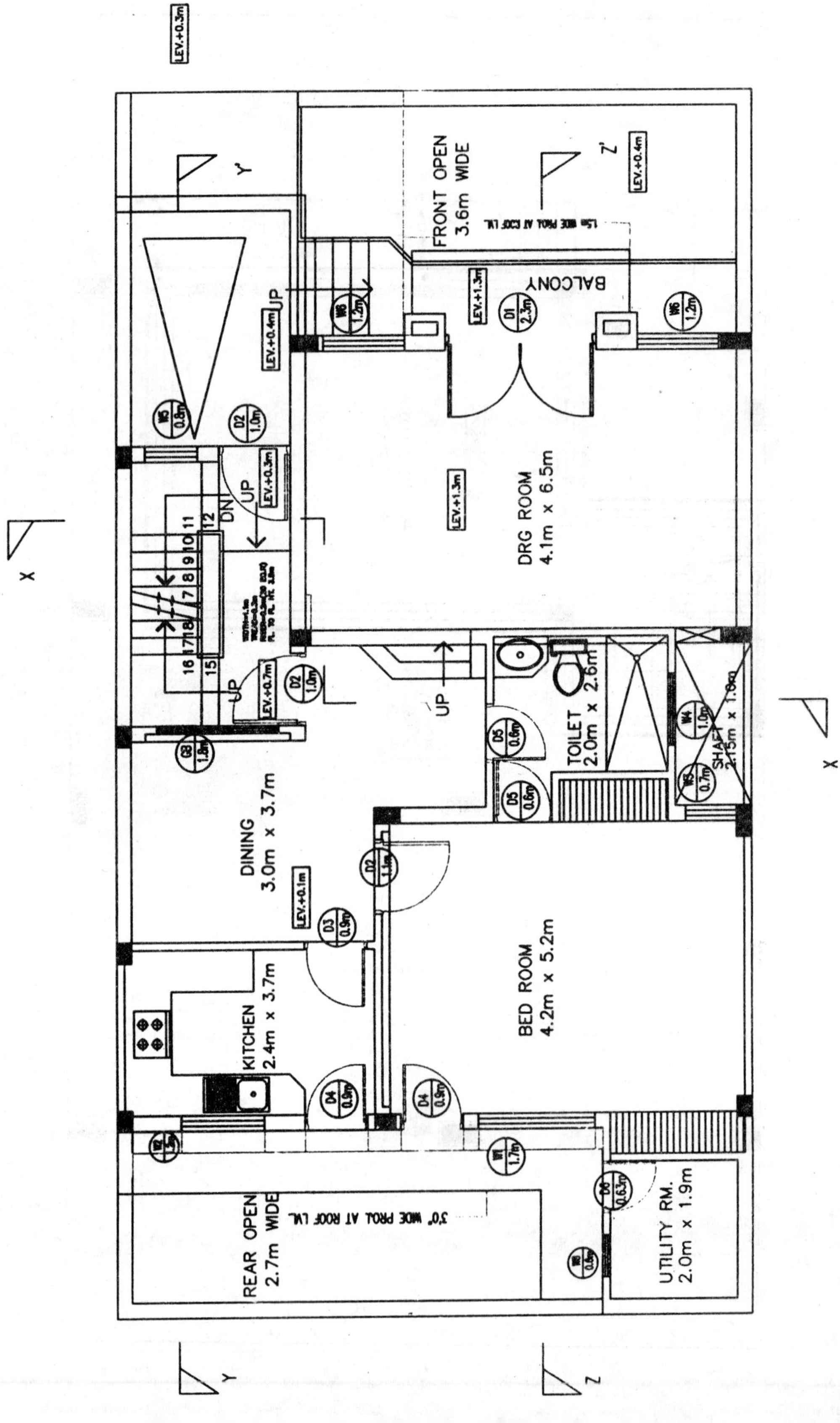


Fig. 6.51 B. Ground Floor Plan

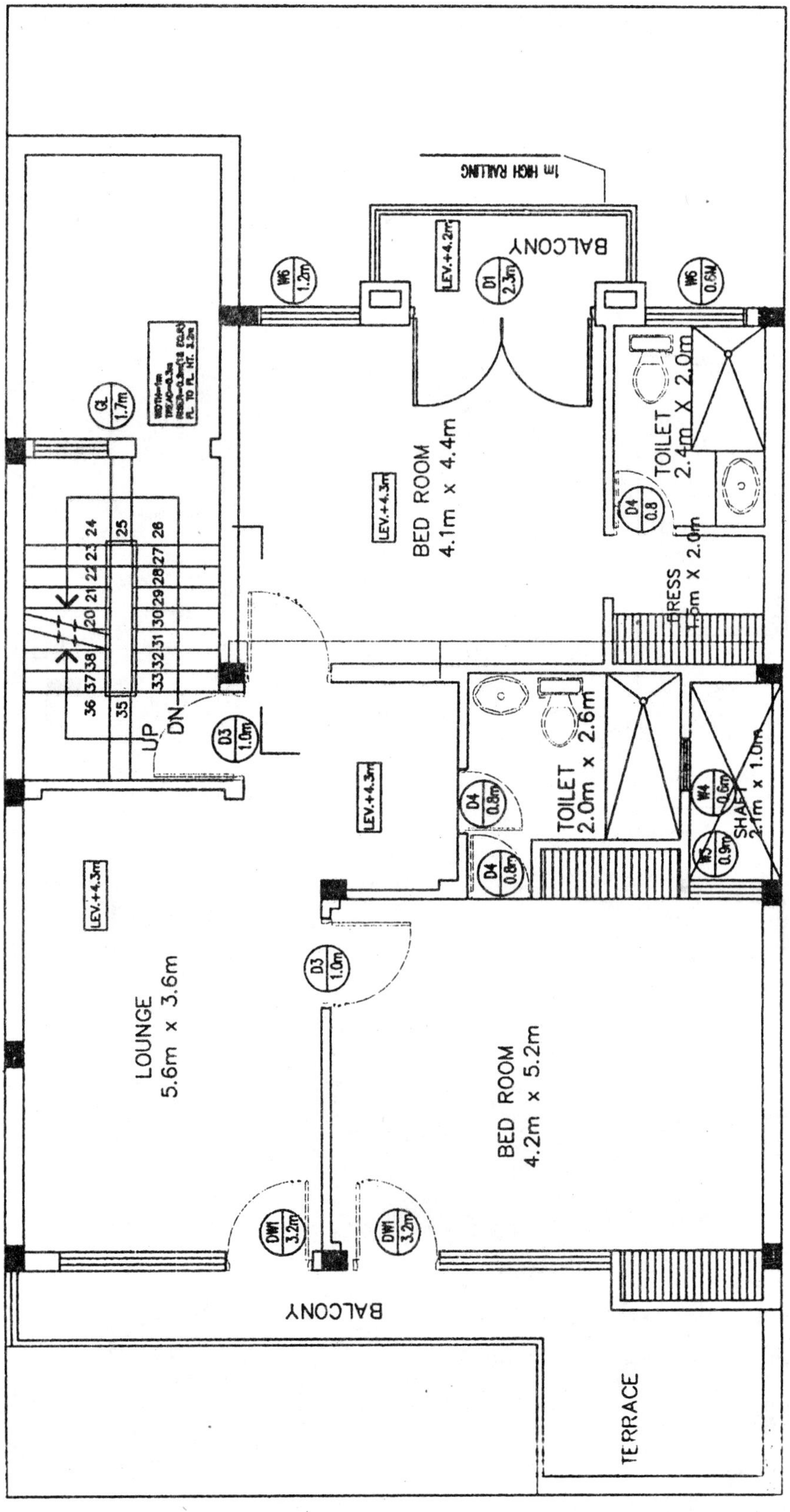


**Fig. 6.51 C.** First Floor Plan

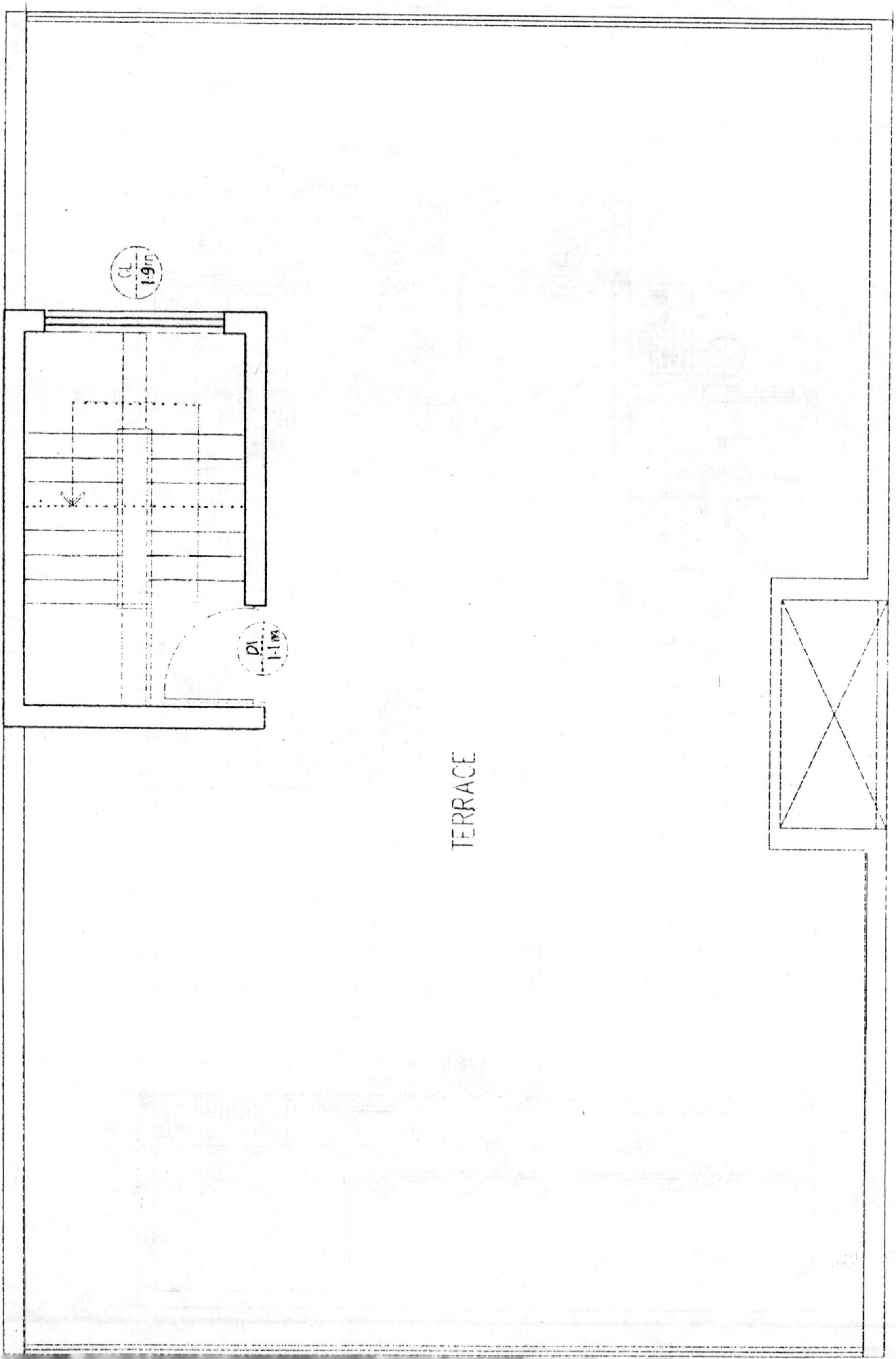


**Fig. 6.51 D.** Terrace Floor Plan

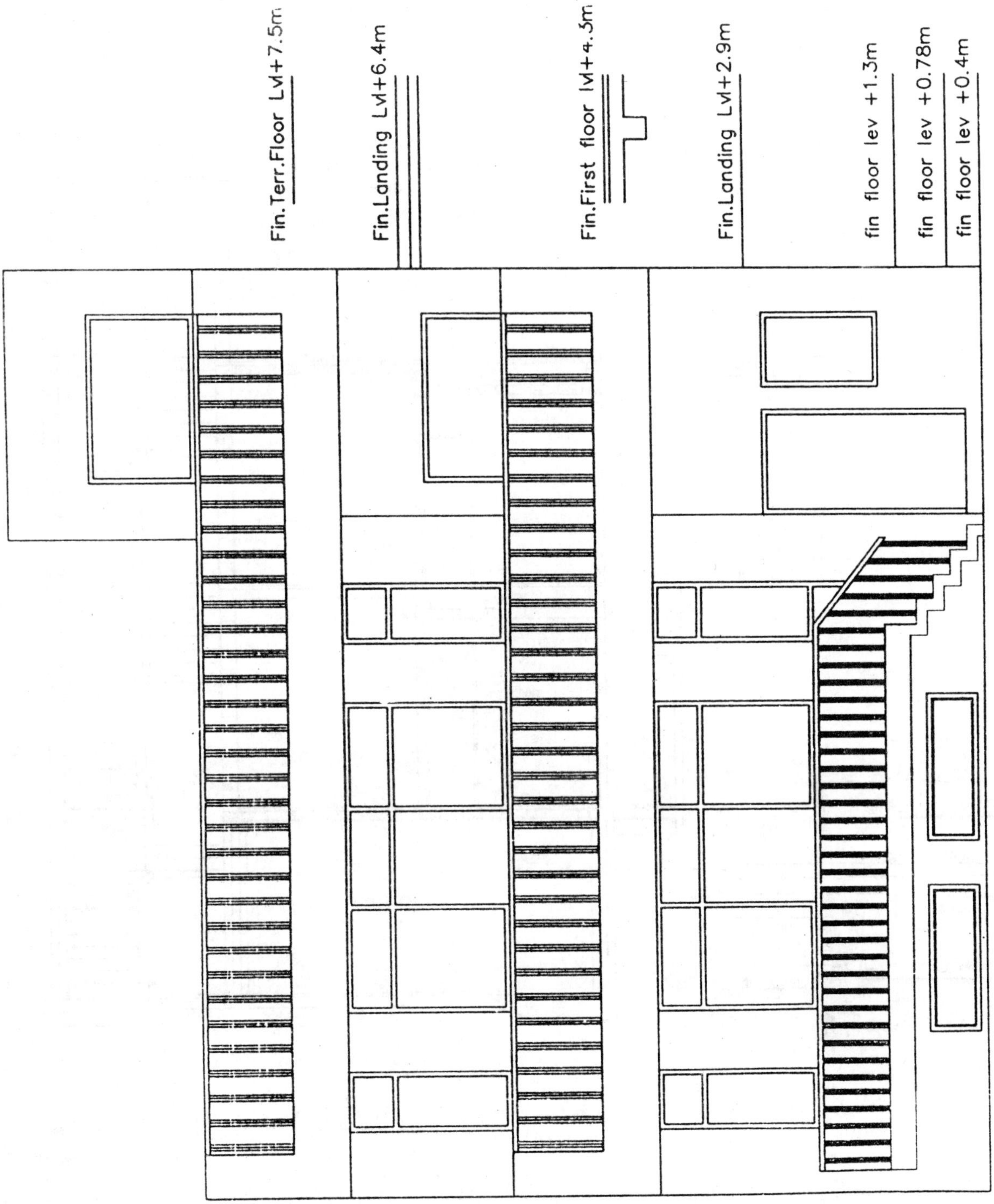


**Fig. 6.51 E.** Front Elevation

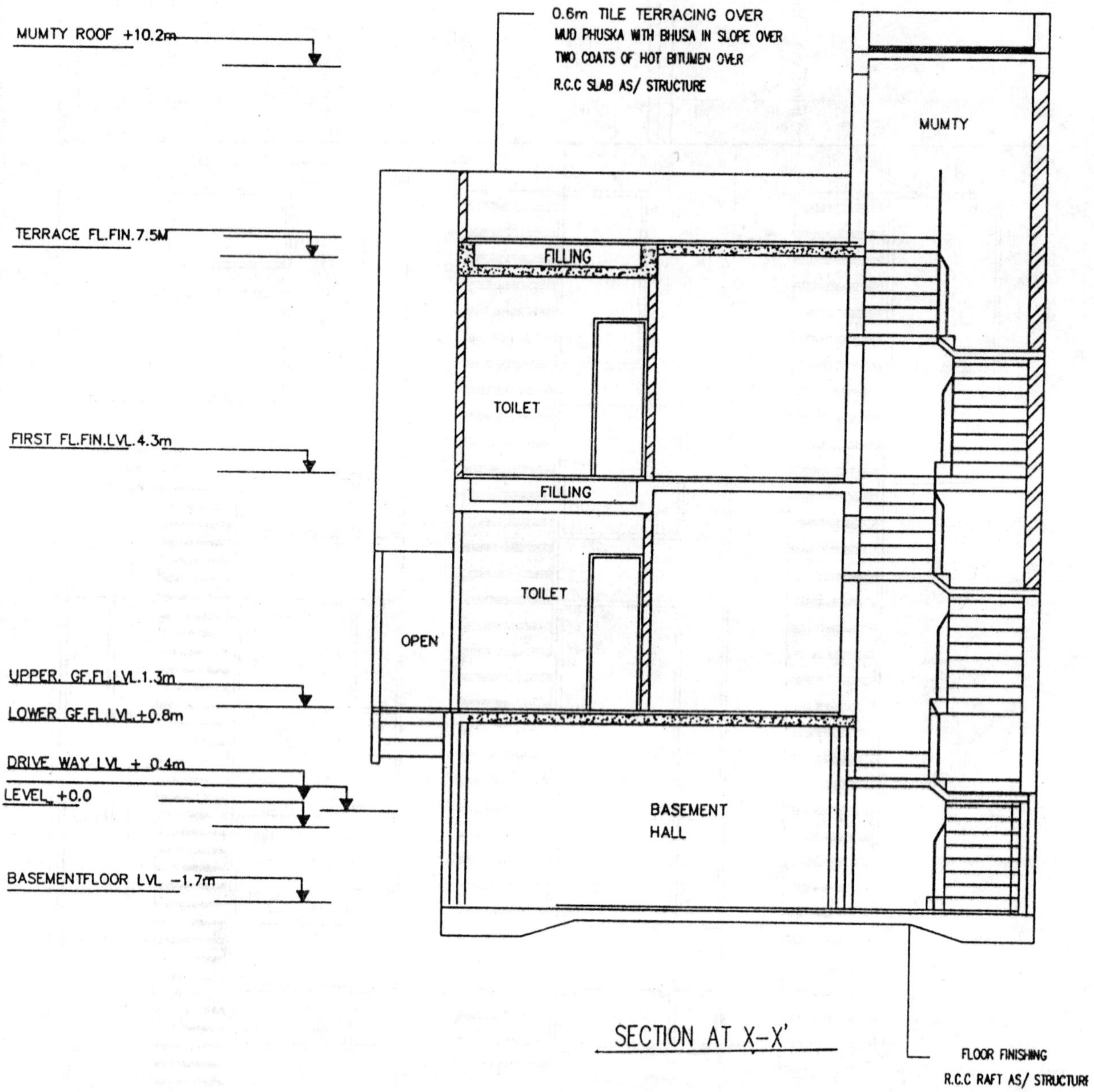
MUMTY ROOF +10.2m
TERRACE FL.FIN.7.5M
FIRST FL.FIN.LVL.4.3m
UPPER. GF.FL.LVL.1.3m
LOWER GF.FL.LVL.+0.8m
DRIVE WAY LVL + 0.4m
LEVEL +0.0
BASEMENTFLOOR LVL -1.7m
0.6m TILE TERRACING OVER
MUD PHUSKA WITH BHUSA IN SLOPE OVER
TWO COATS OF HOT BITUMEN OVER
R.C.C SLAB AS/ STRUCTURE
MUMTY
FILLING
TOILET
FILLING
TOILET
OPEN
BASEMENT
HALL
SECTION AT X-X'
FLOOR FINISHING
R.C.C RAFT AS/ STRUCTURE

Fig. 6.51 F.

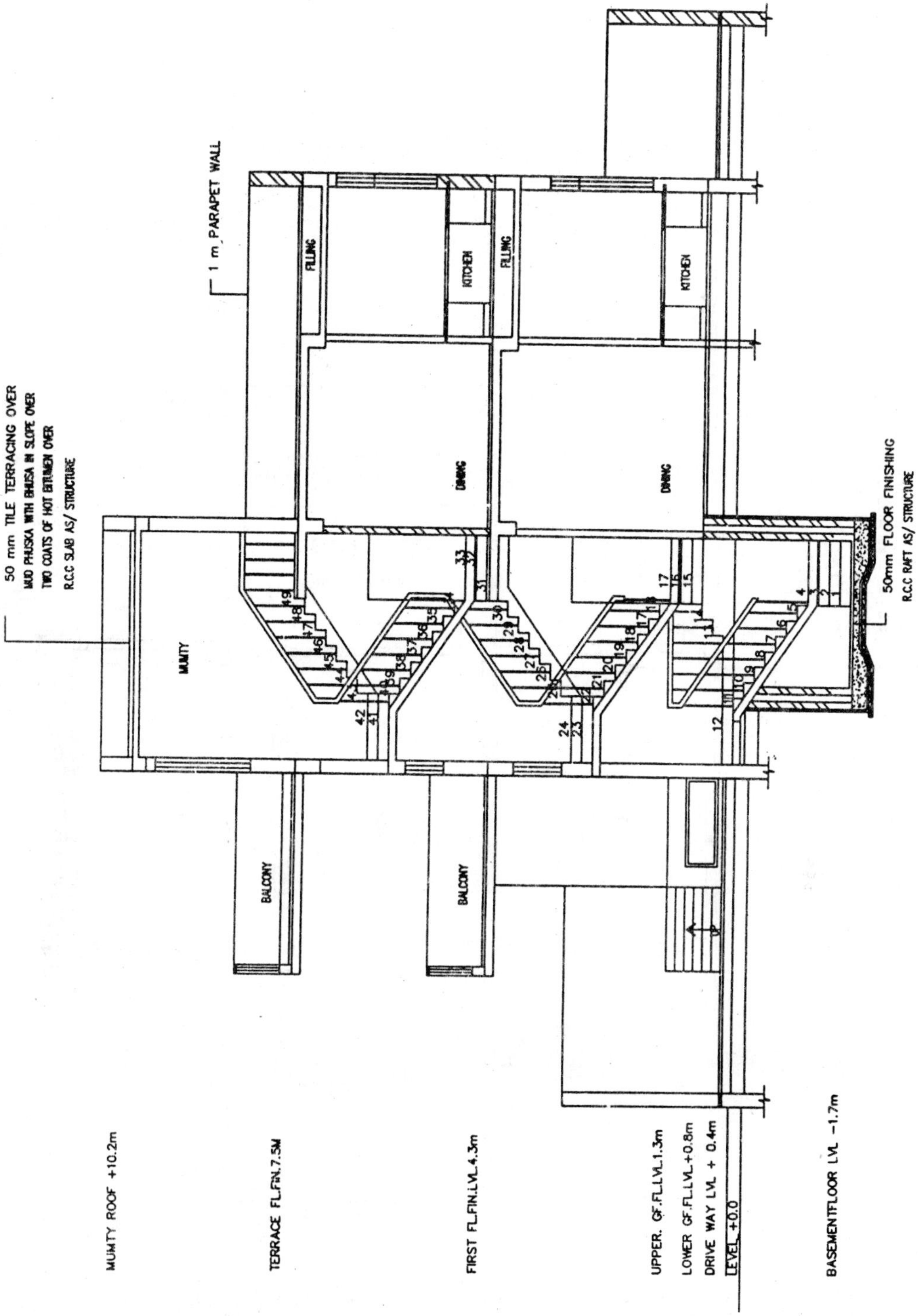


SECTION AT Y–Y'

**Fig. 6.51 G.**

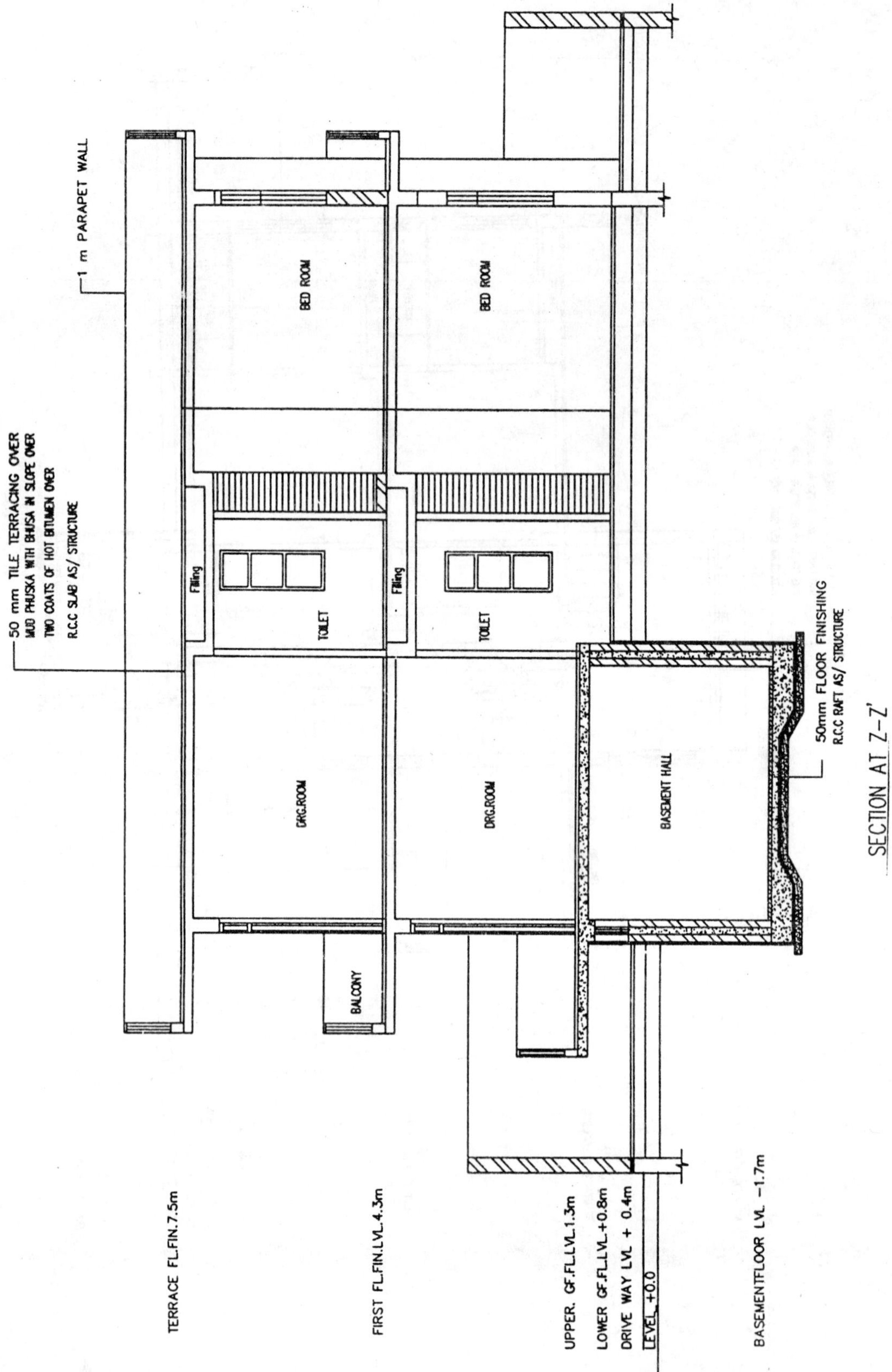
1 m PARAPET WALL
50 mm TILE TERRACING OVER
MUD PHUSKA WITH BHUSA IN SLOPE OVER
TWO COATS OF HOT BITUMEN OVER
R.C.C SLAB AS/ STRUCTURE
BED ROOM
BED ROOM
Filling
Filling
TOILET
TOILET
DRG.ROOM
DRG.ROOM
BASEMENT HALL
BALCONY
50mm FLOOR FINISHING
R.C.C RAFT AS/ STRUCTURE
TERRACE FL.FIN.7.5m
FIRST FL.FIN.LVL.4.3m
UPPER. GF.FL.LVL.1.3m
LOWER GF.FL.LVL.+0.8m
DRIVE WAY LVL + 0.4m
LEVEL +0.0
BASEMENTFLOOR LVL. -1.7m
SECTION AT Z-Z'

Fig. 6.51 H.

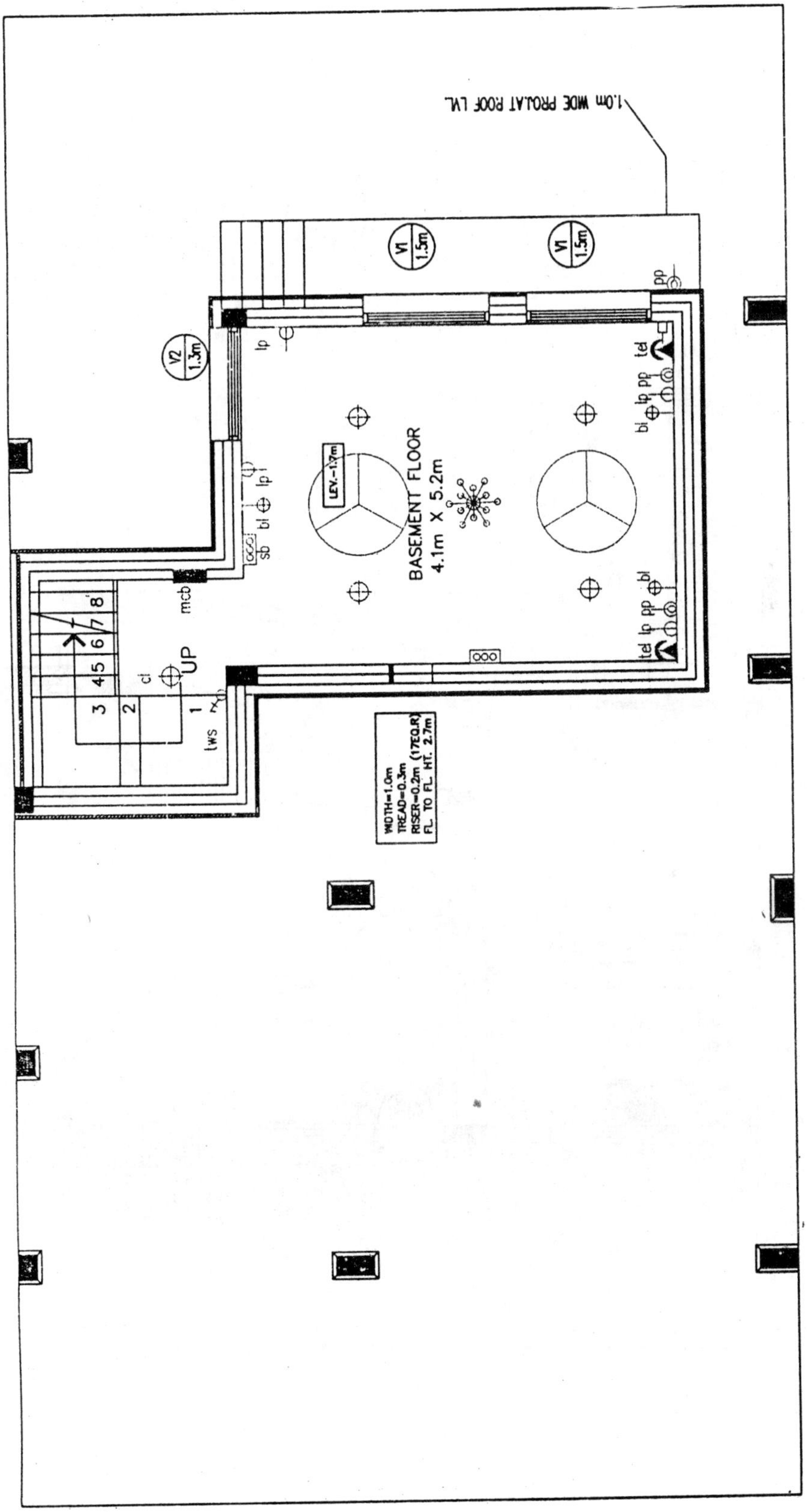


**Fig. 6.51 I.** Electrical plan of Basement floor plan

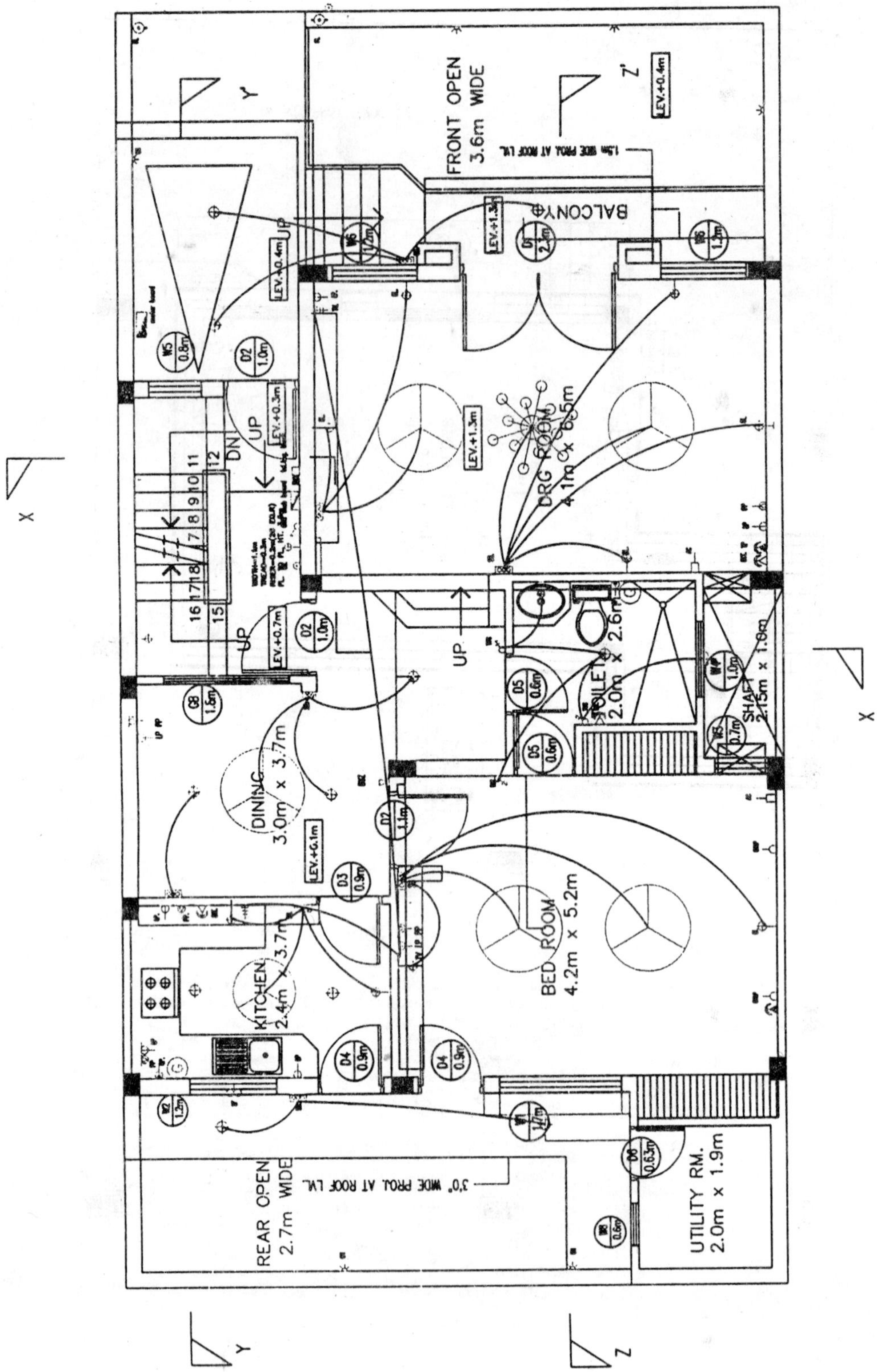


**Fig. 6.51 J.** Electrical plan of Ground floor plan

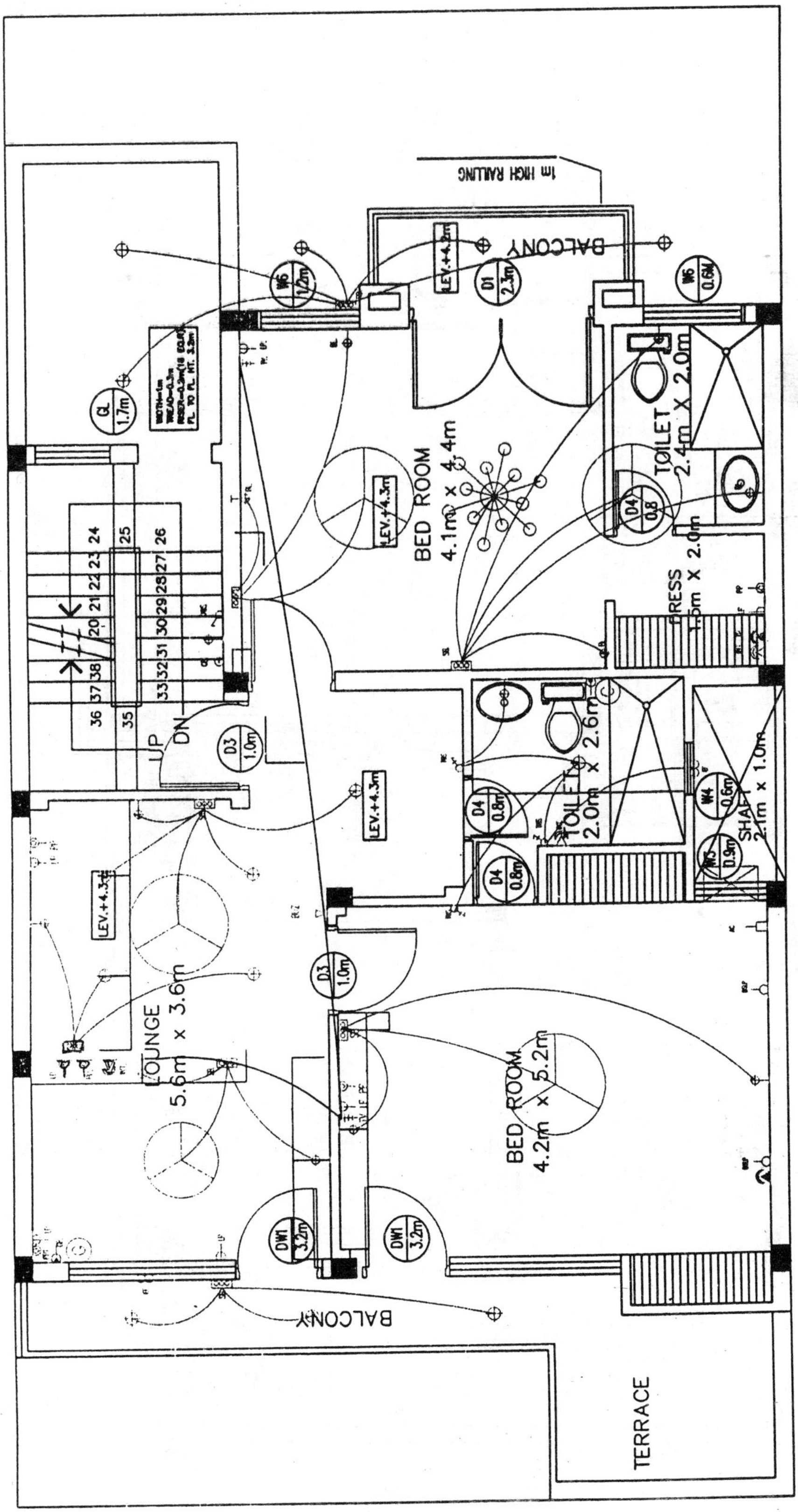


Fig. 6.51 K. Electrical plan of First floor plan

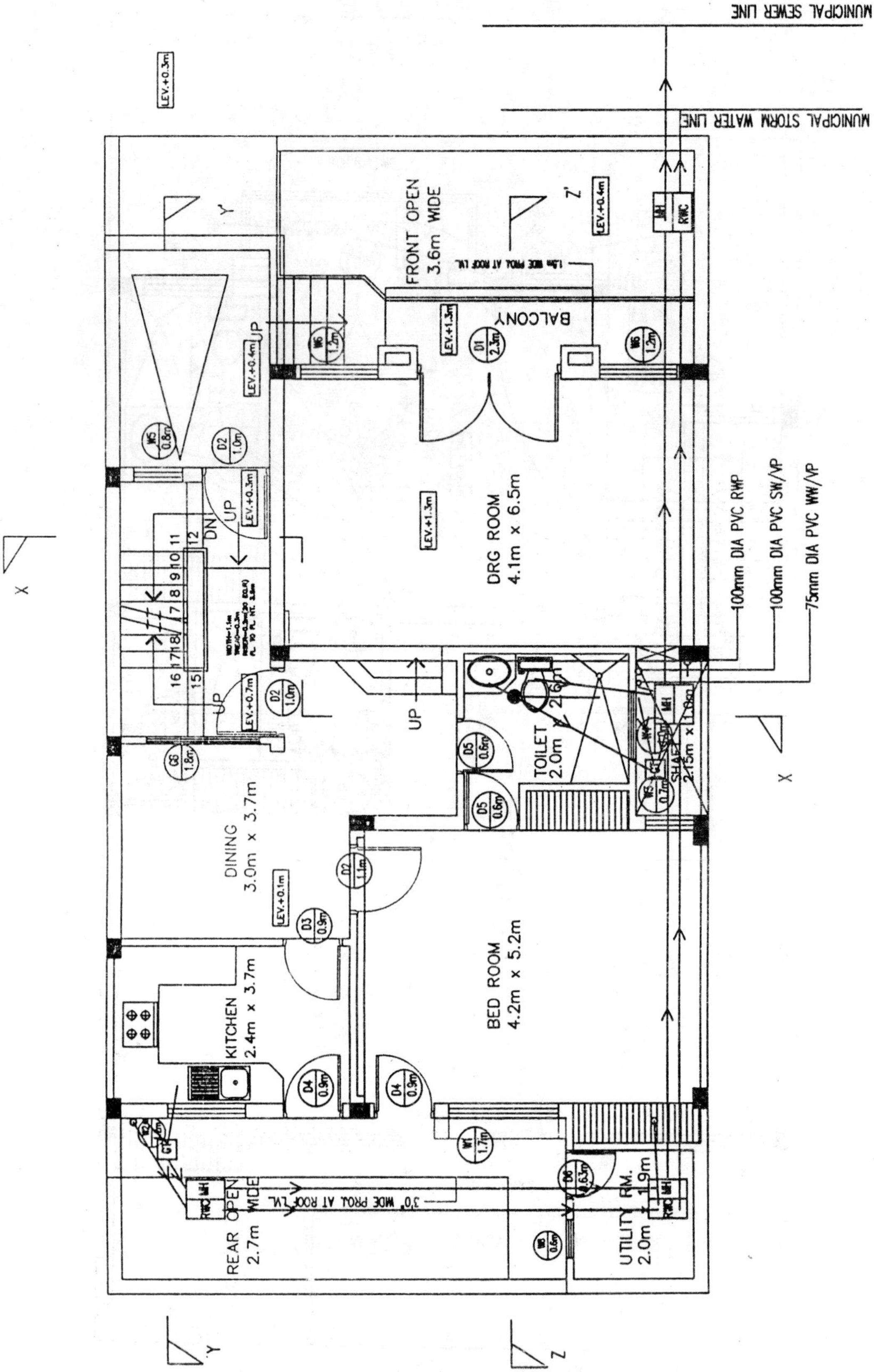


**Fig. 6.51 L.** Sanitary plan of First floor plan

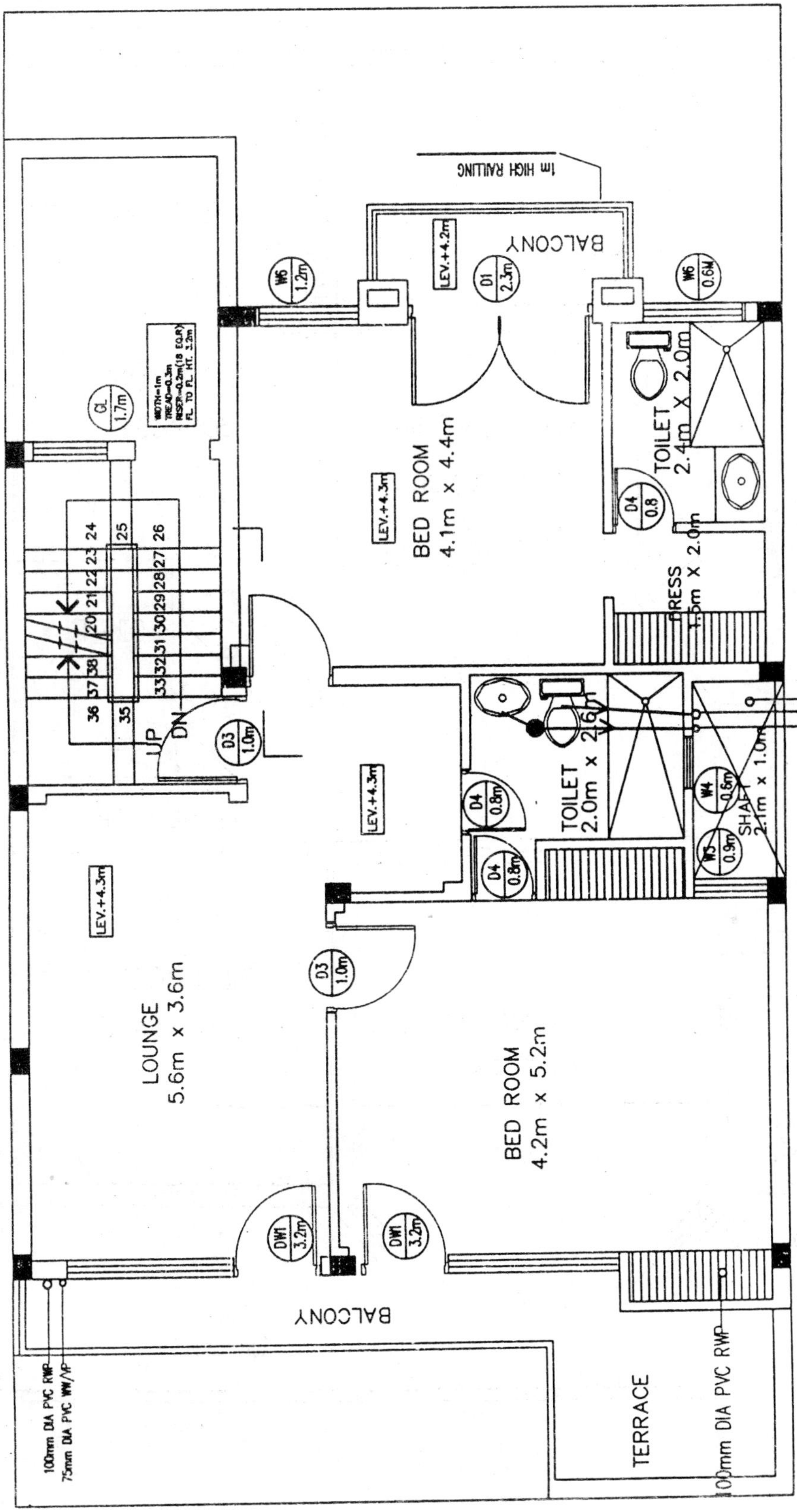


**Fig. 6.51 M.** Sanitary plan of First floor plan

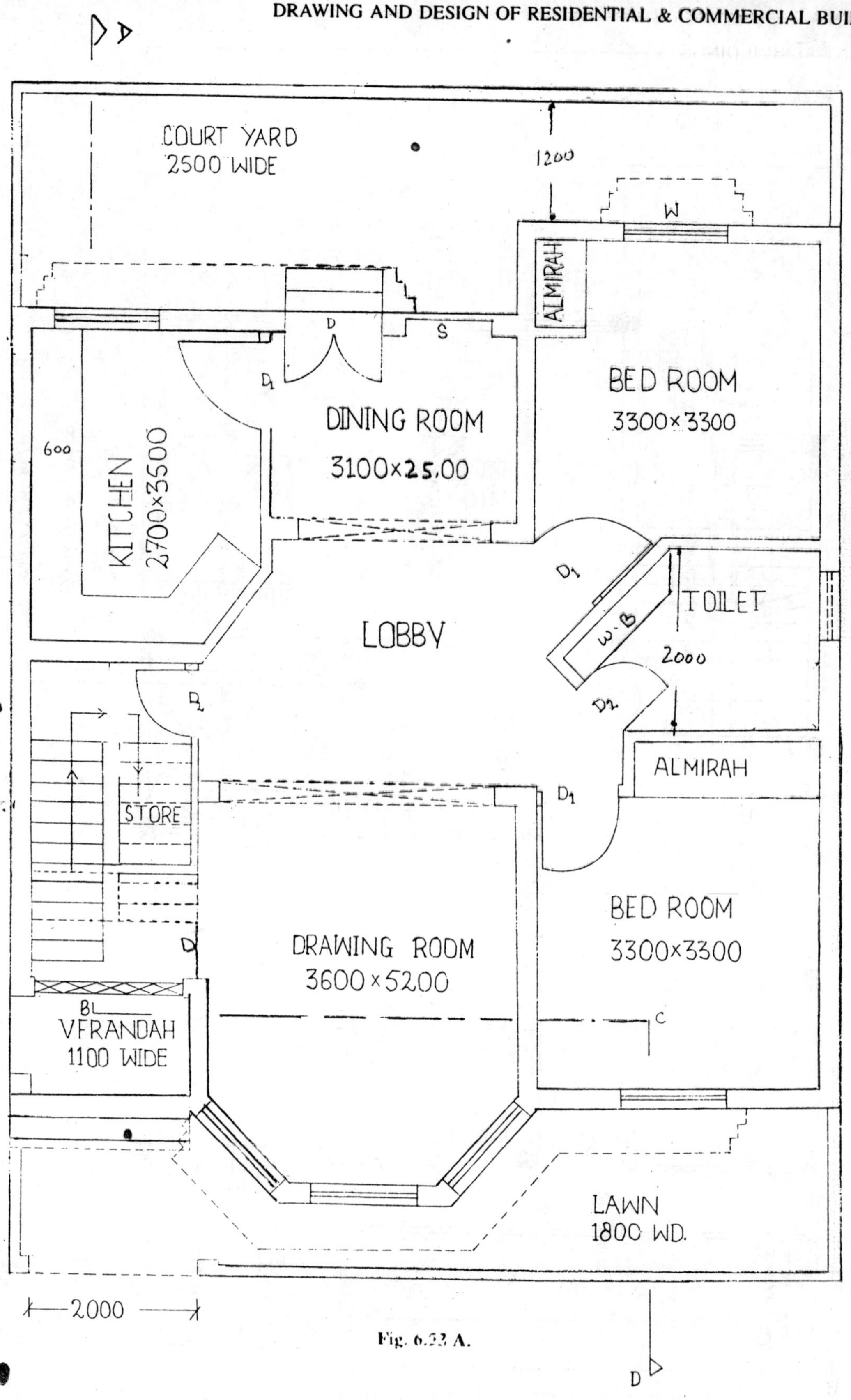
D
COURT YARD
2500 WIDE
1200
W
ALMIRAH
D
S
D1
BED ROOM
3300×3300
DINING ROOM
3100×25.00
600
KITCHEN
2700×3500
D1
TOILET
LOBBY
W.B
2000
D2
D2
ALMIRAH
D1
STORE
BED ROOM
3300×3300
D
DRAWING ROOM
3600×5200
B
VERANDAH
1100 WIDE
C
LAWN
1800 WD.
2000
D

Fig. 6.33 A.

**Fig. 6.52 B.** Front Elevation

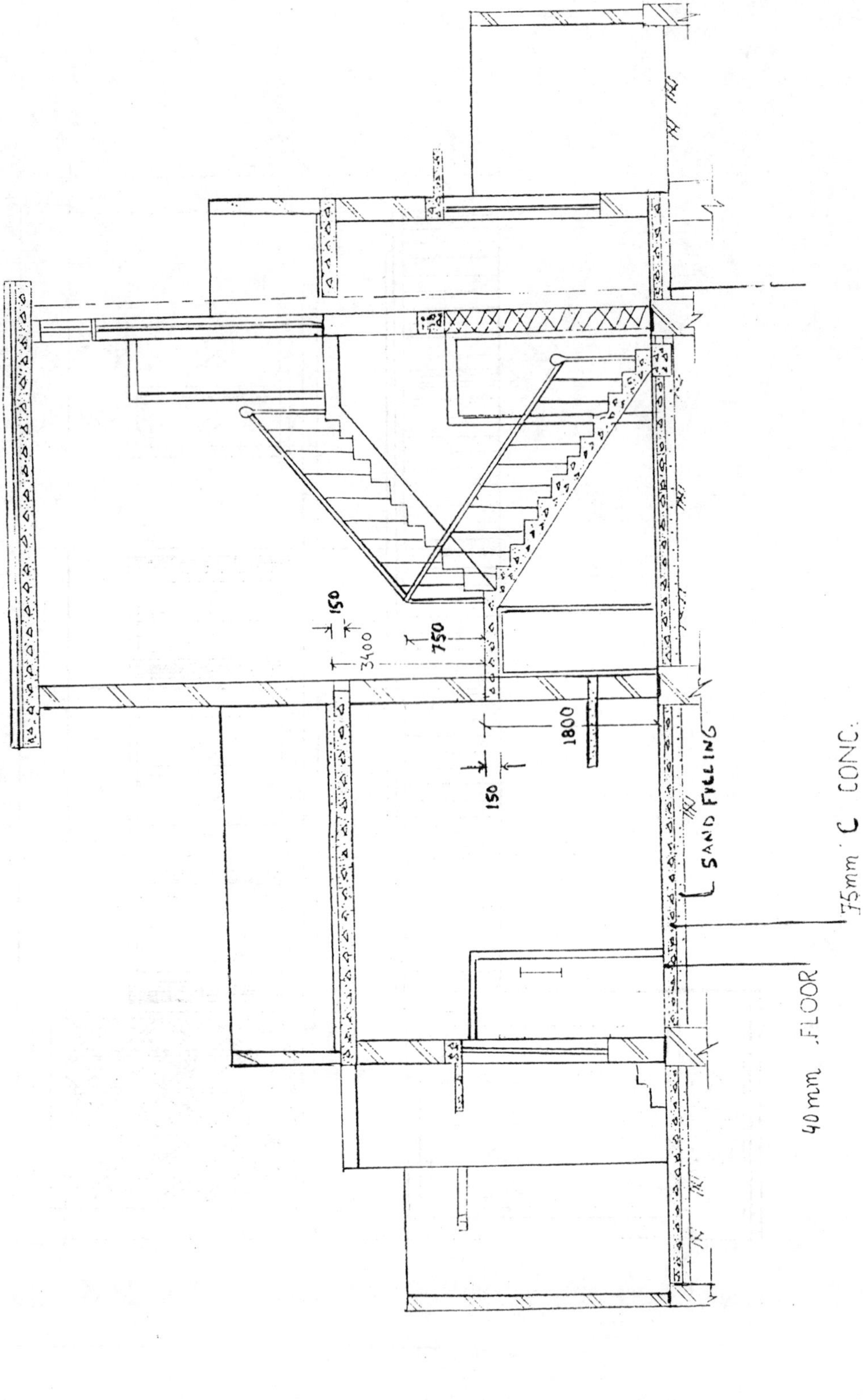


**Fig. 6.52 C.** Sec. Elevation-ABCD

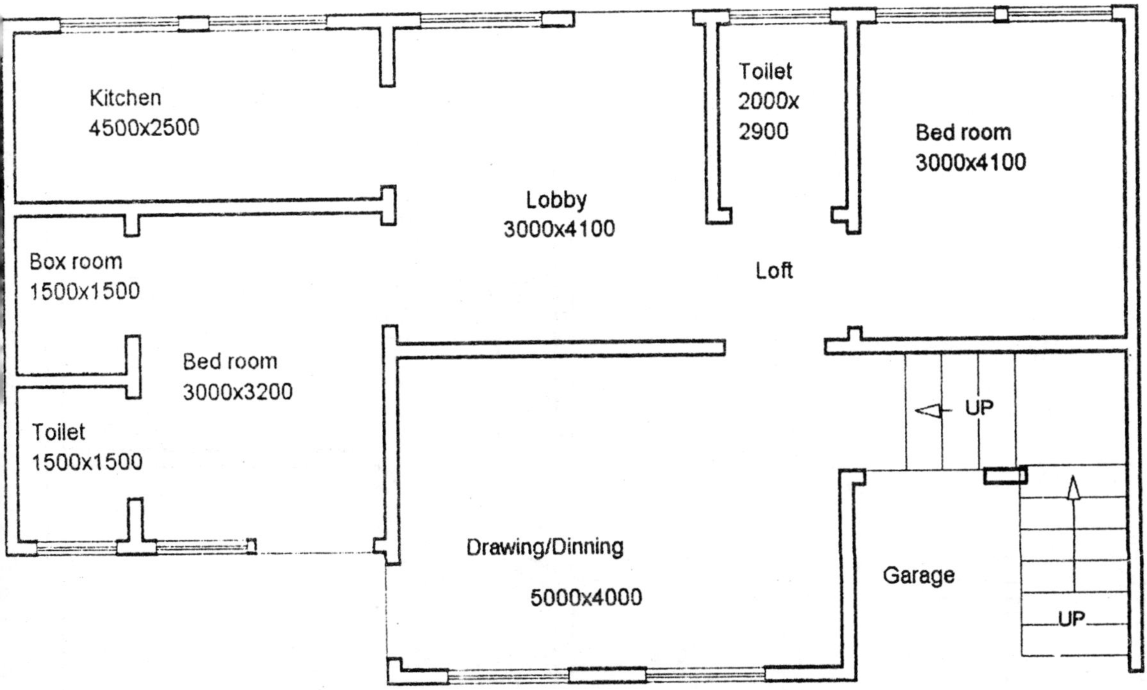


All dimensions in mm

**Fig. 6.53 A.** Two Bed rooms

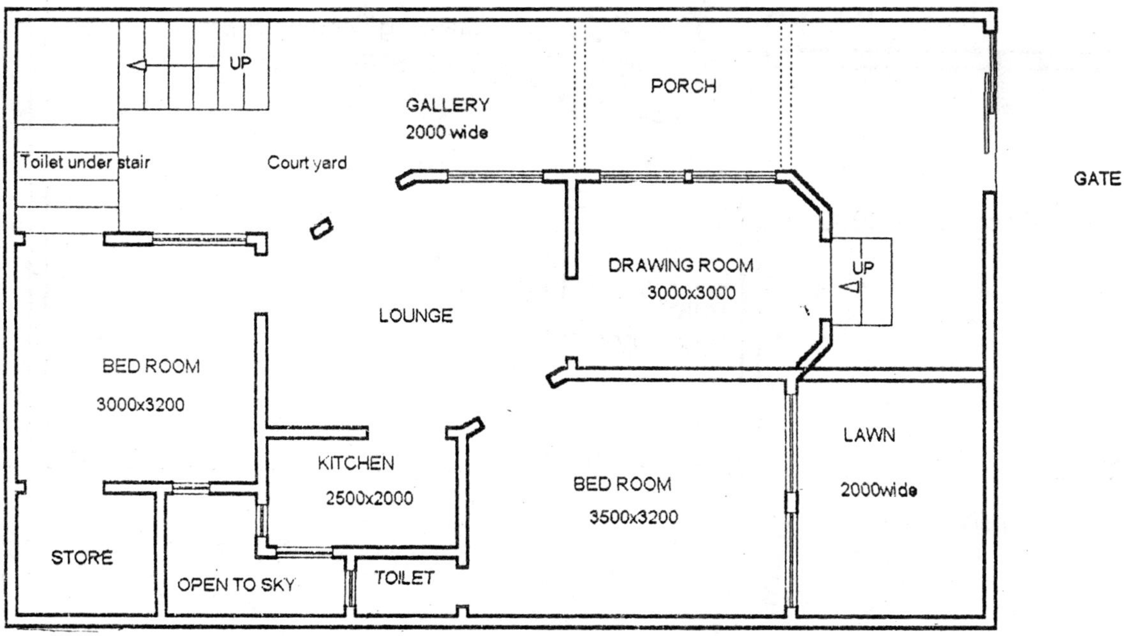


**Fig. 6.53 B.** Two rooms Building Plan

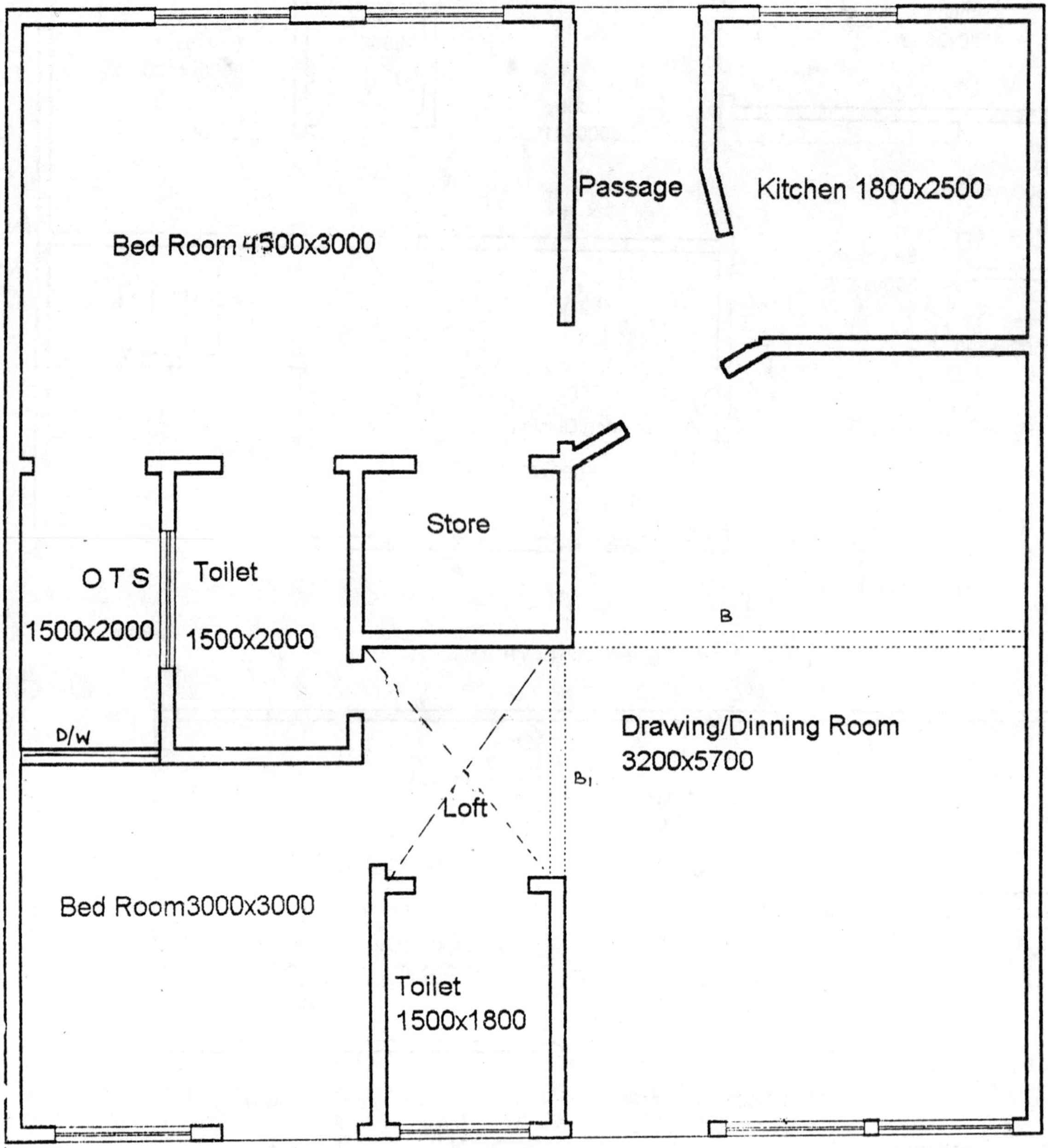


All dimensions in mm

**Fig. 6.53 C.** Two bed rooms

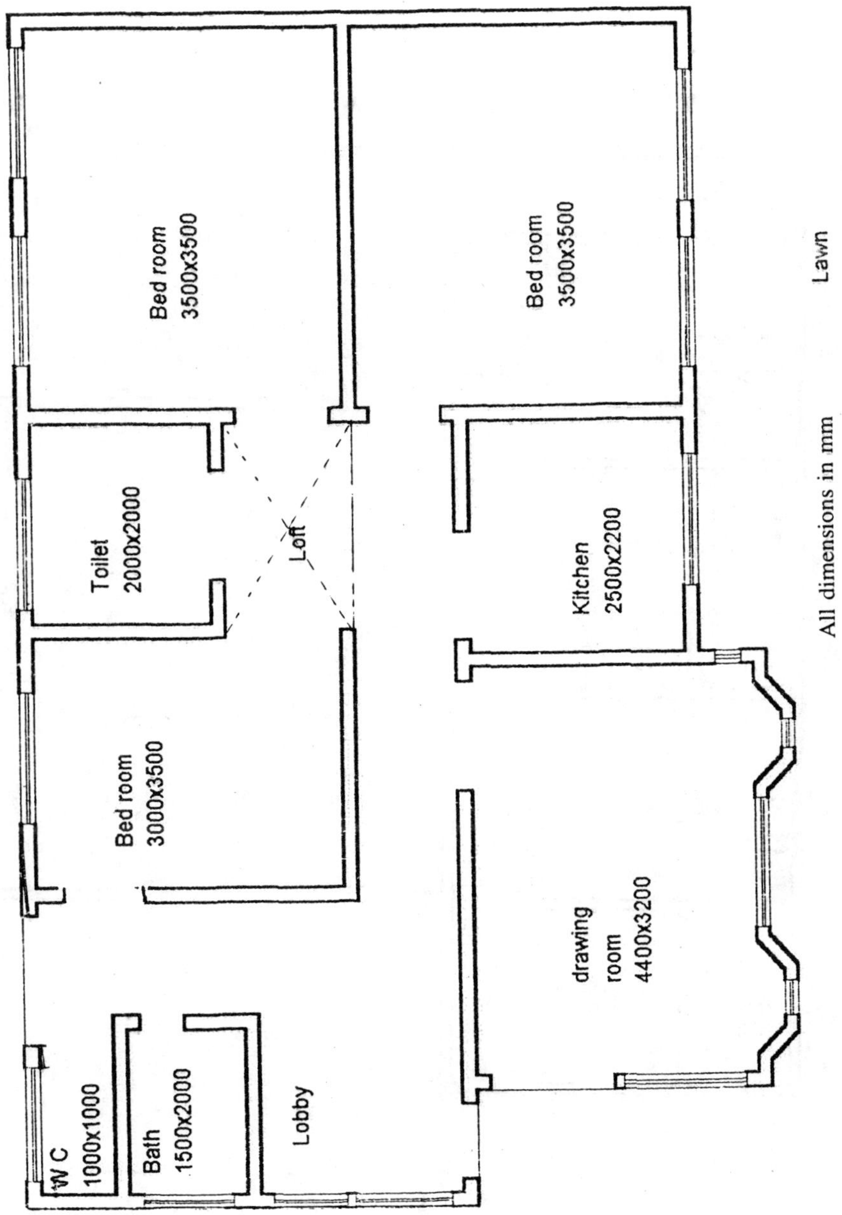


**Fig. 6.53 D.** Three bed rooms

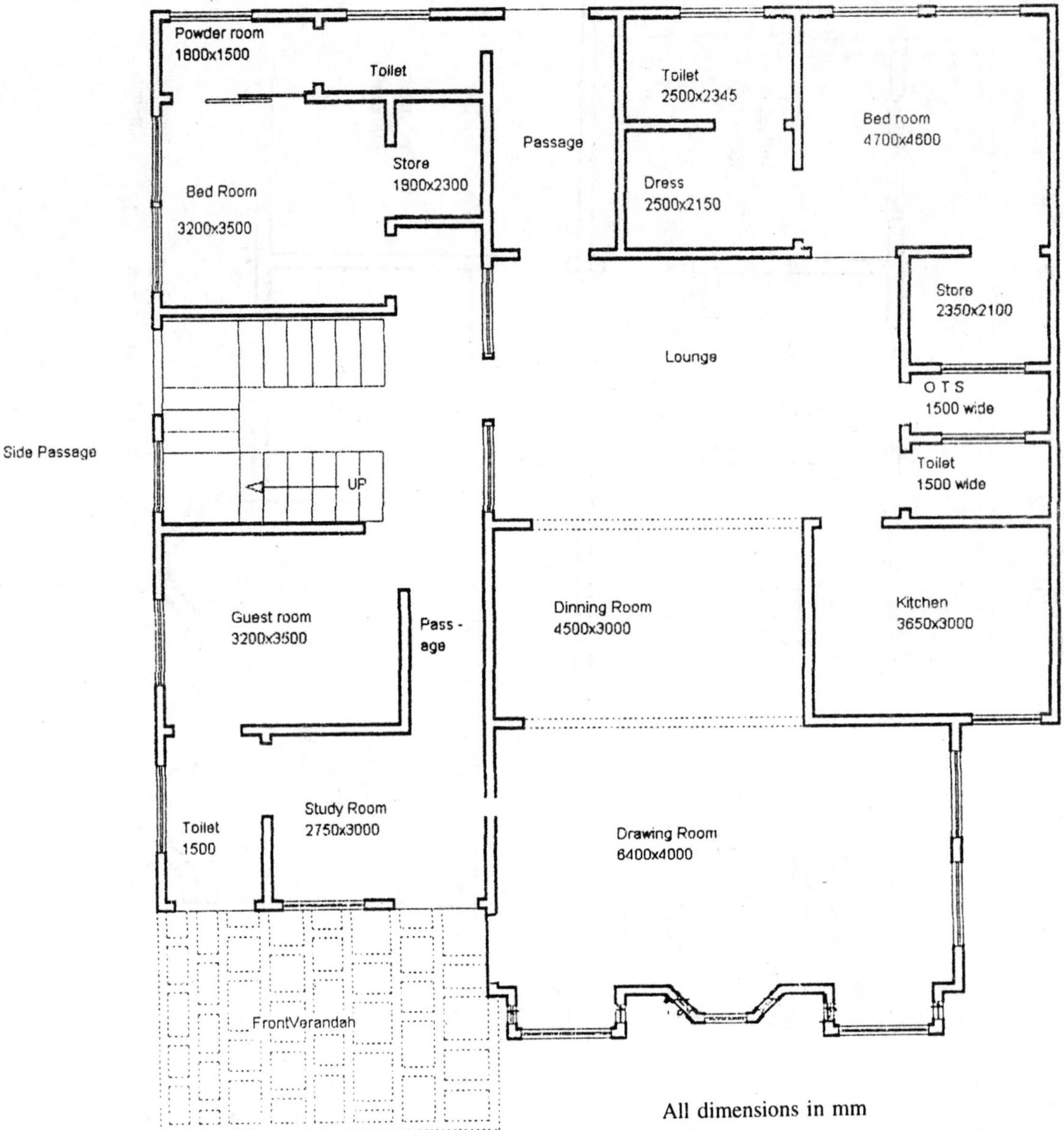


**Fig. 6.53 E.** Three rooms Set

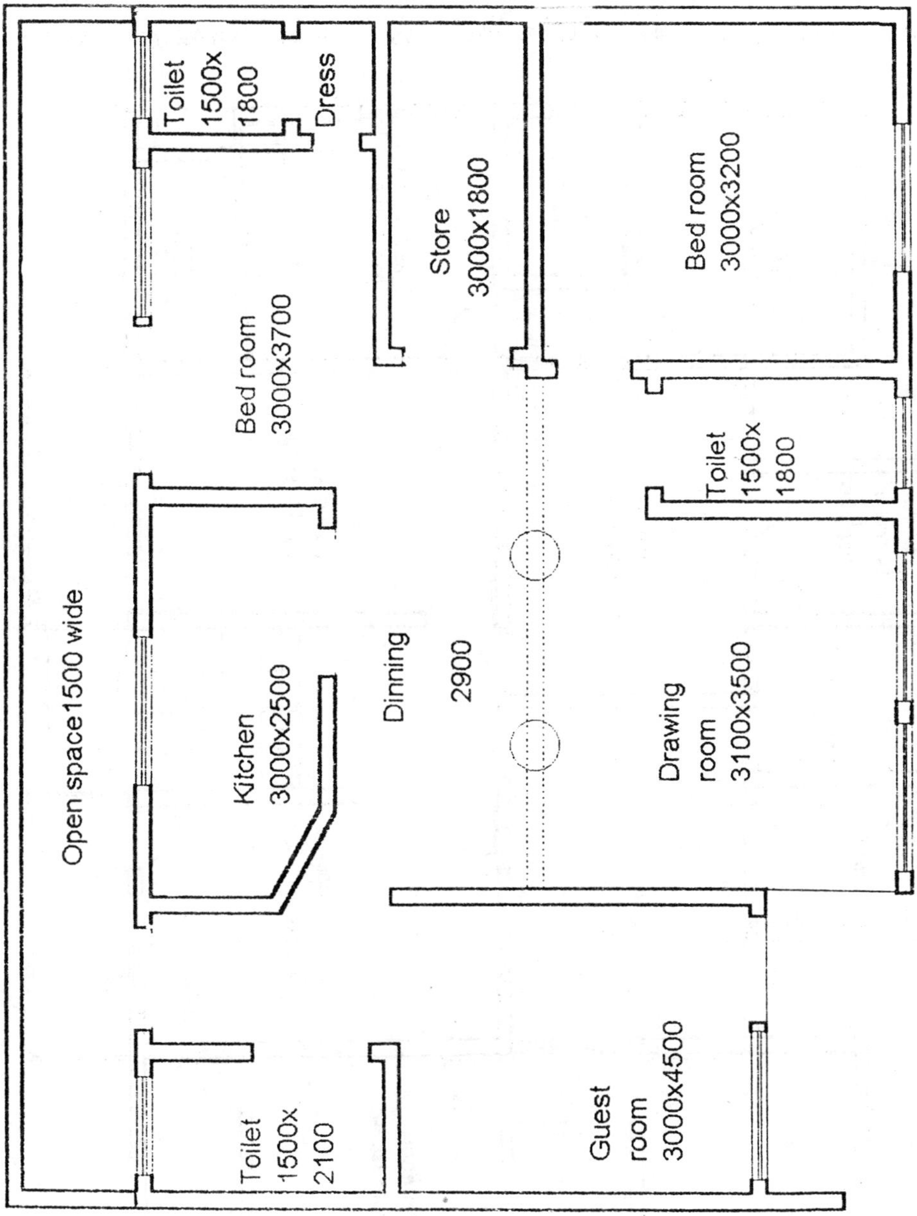


All dimensions in mm

**Fig. 6.53 F.** Three rooms Set

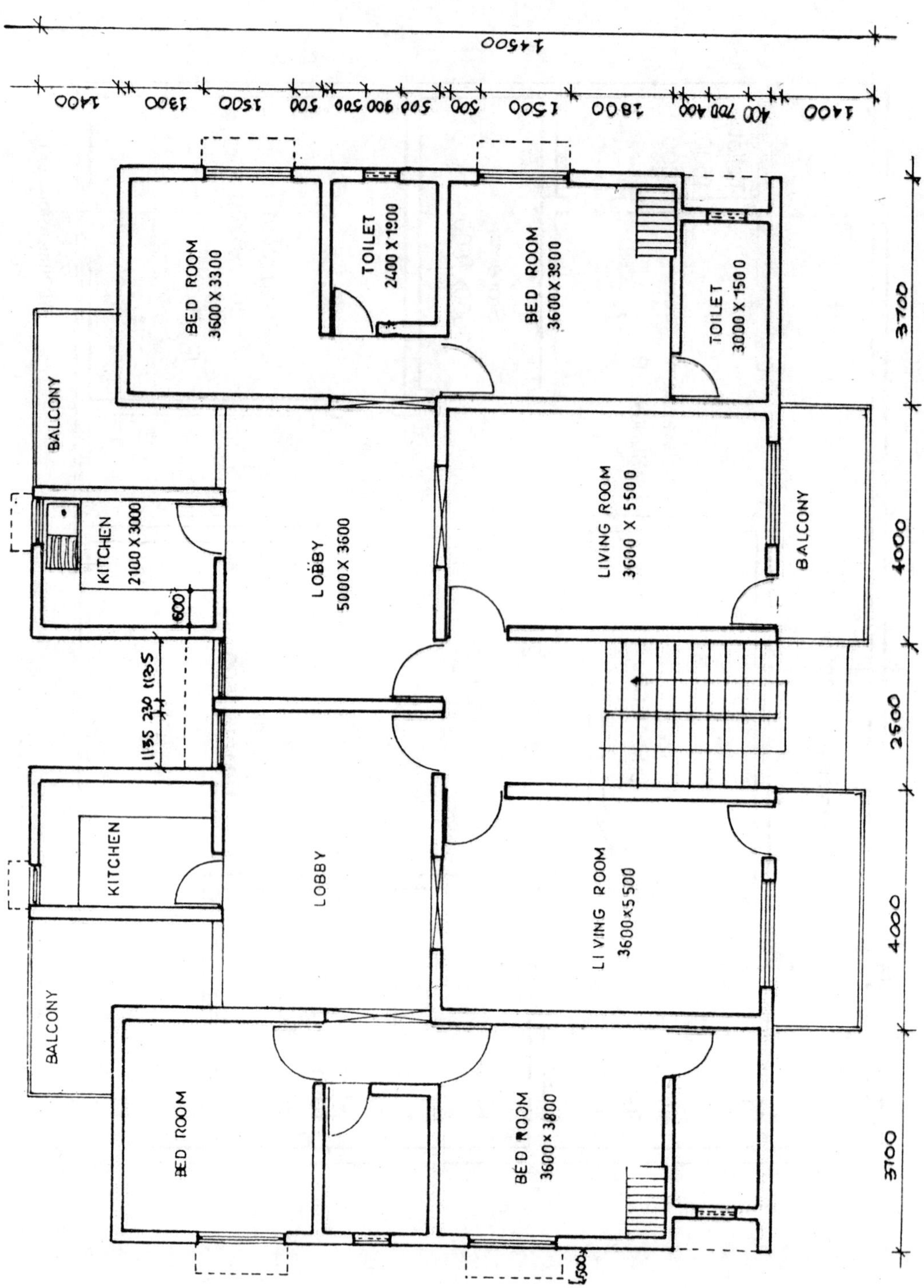


All dimensions in mm

**Fig. 6.53 G.** Typical Floor Plan

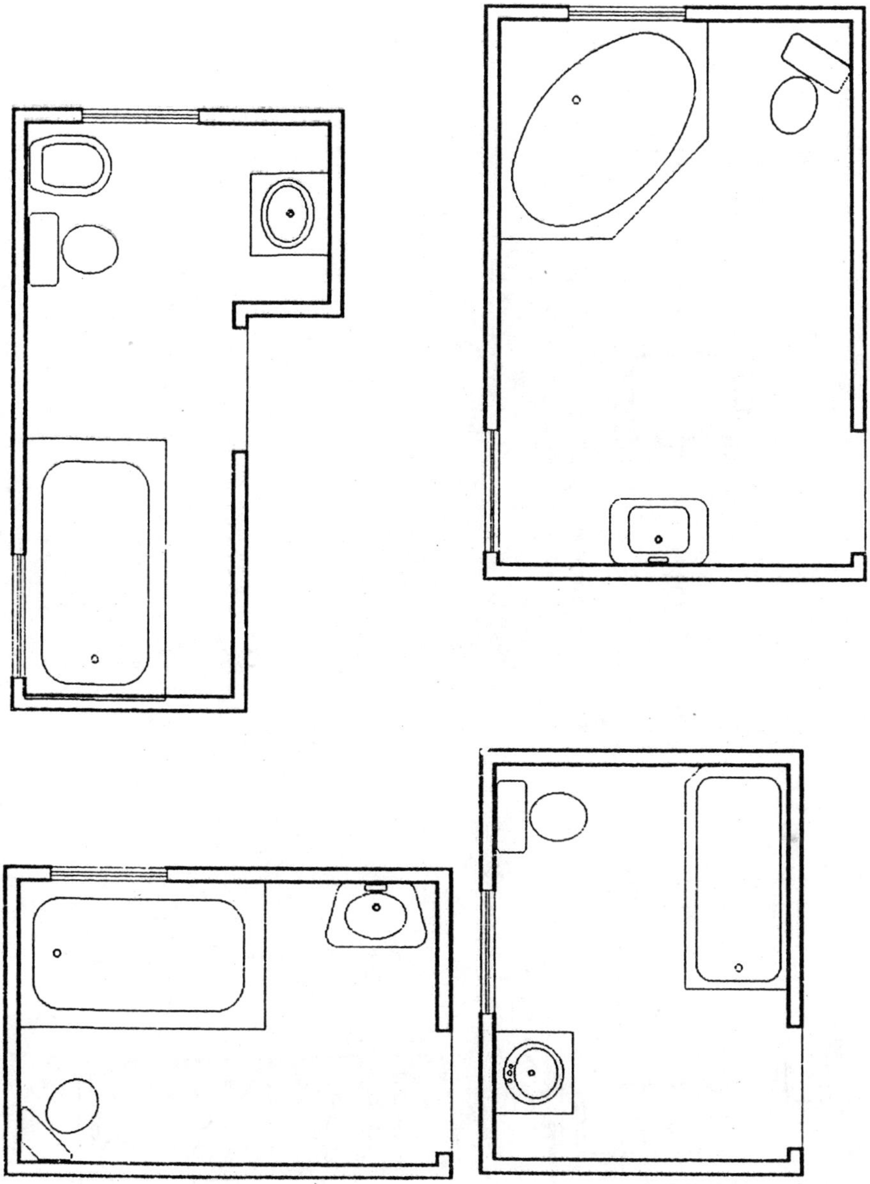

**Fig. 6.54 A.** Toilet Plans

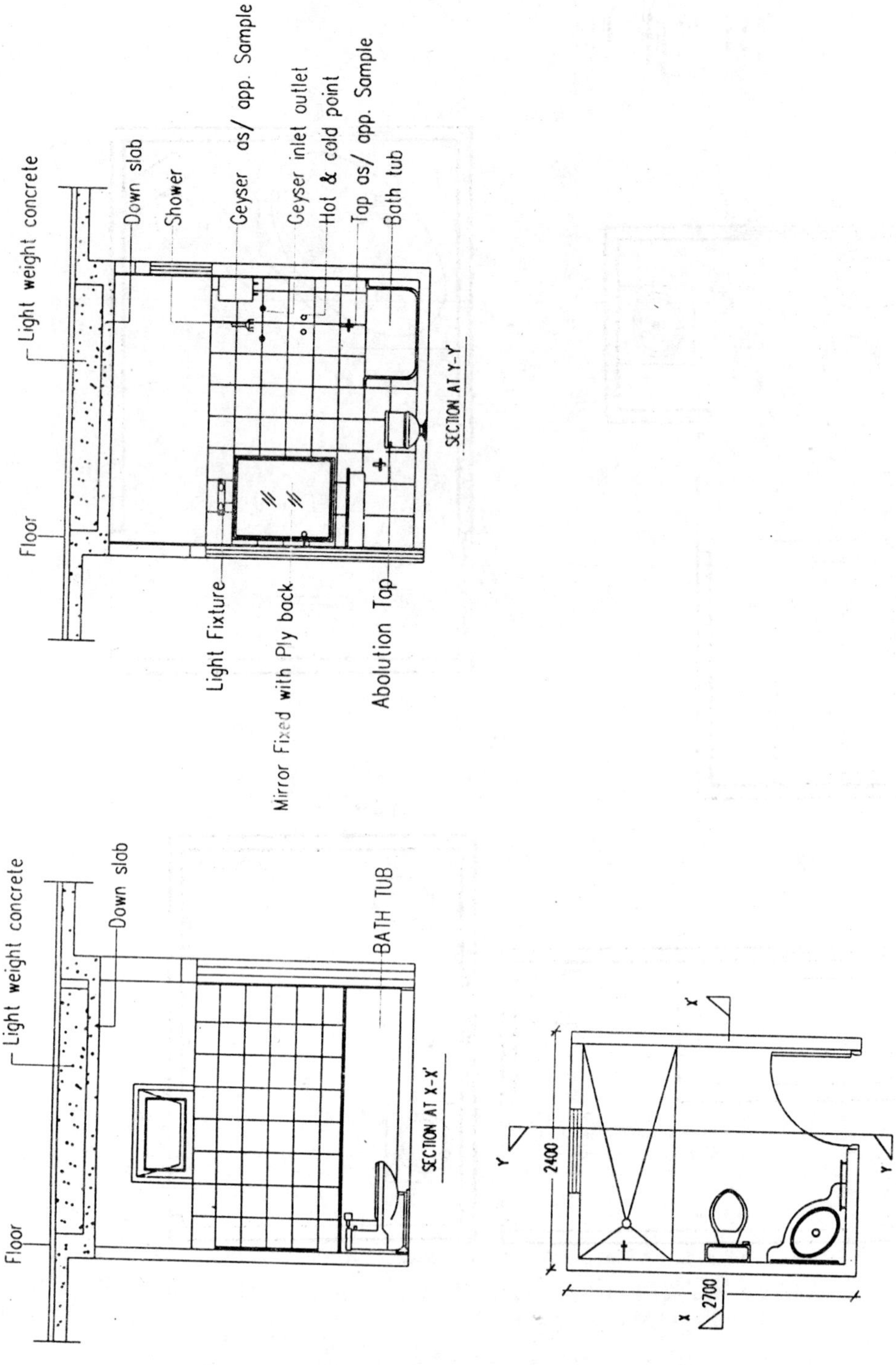


**Fig. 6.54 B.** Detail of Toilet Plan

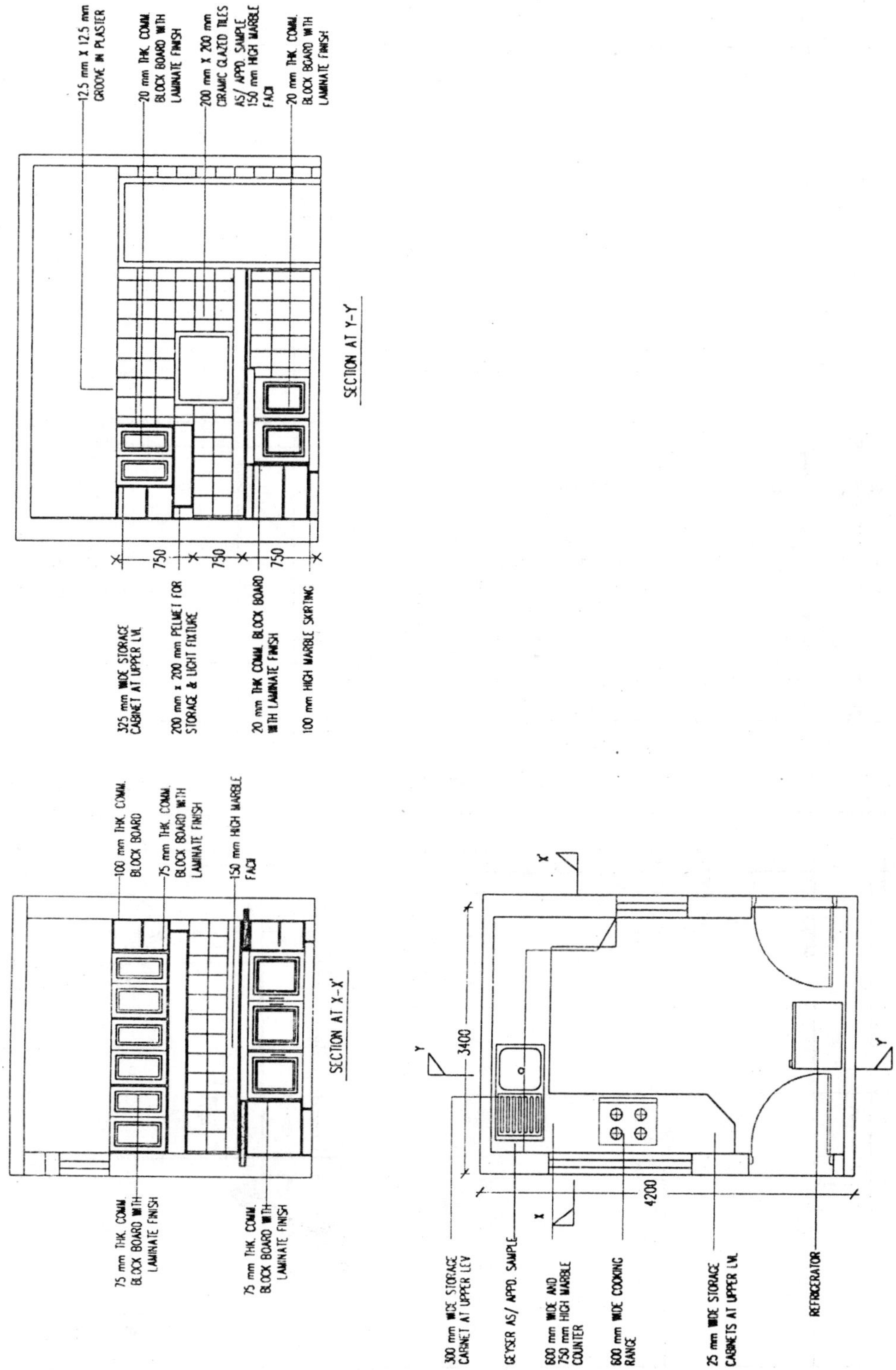


**Fig. 6.54 C.** Detail of Kitchen Plan

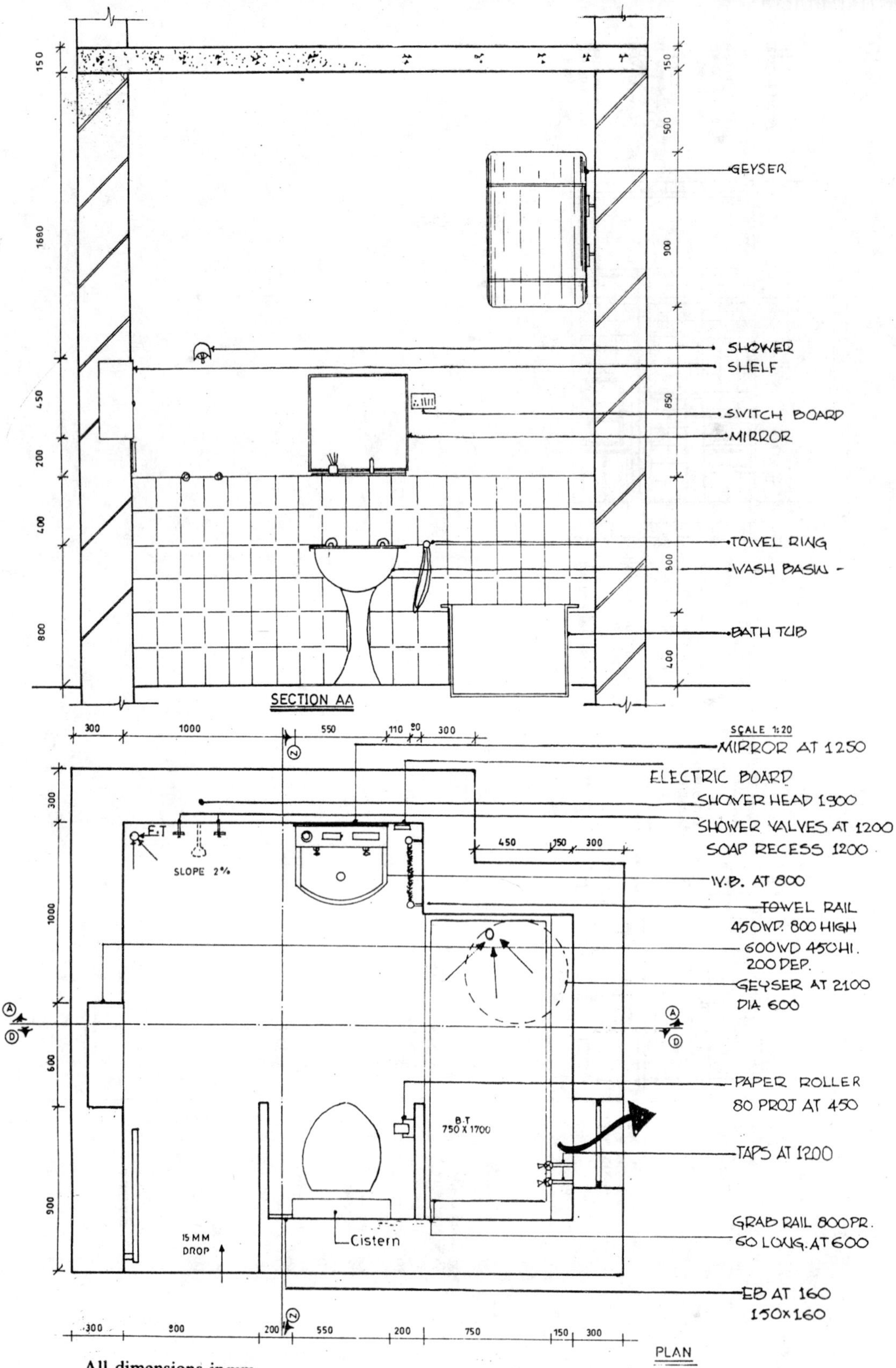


All dimensions in mm

**Fig. 6.55 A.** Detail Toilet Plan

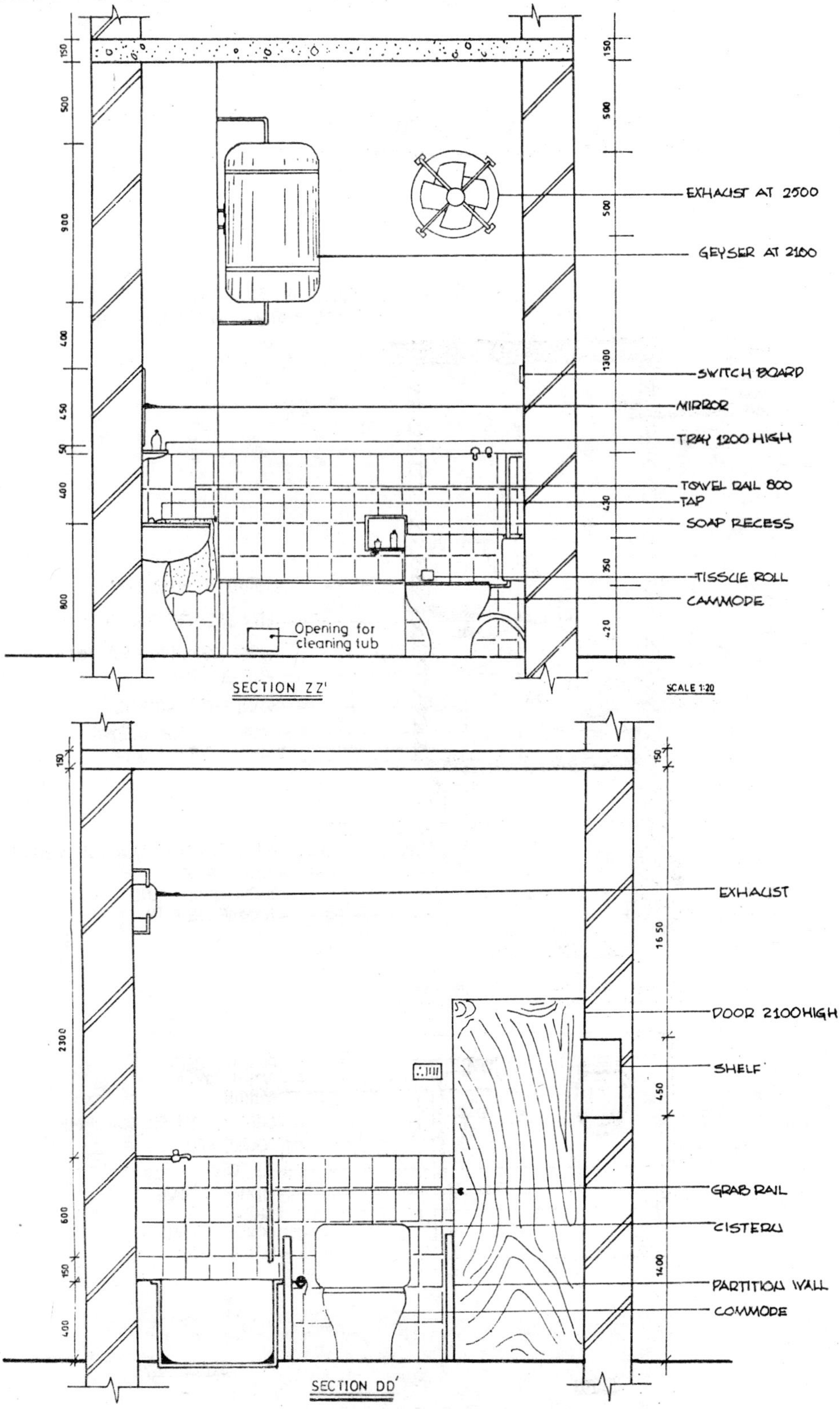


**Fig. 6.55 B.** All dimensions inmm

# DETAIL OF TOILET

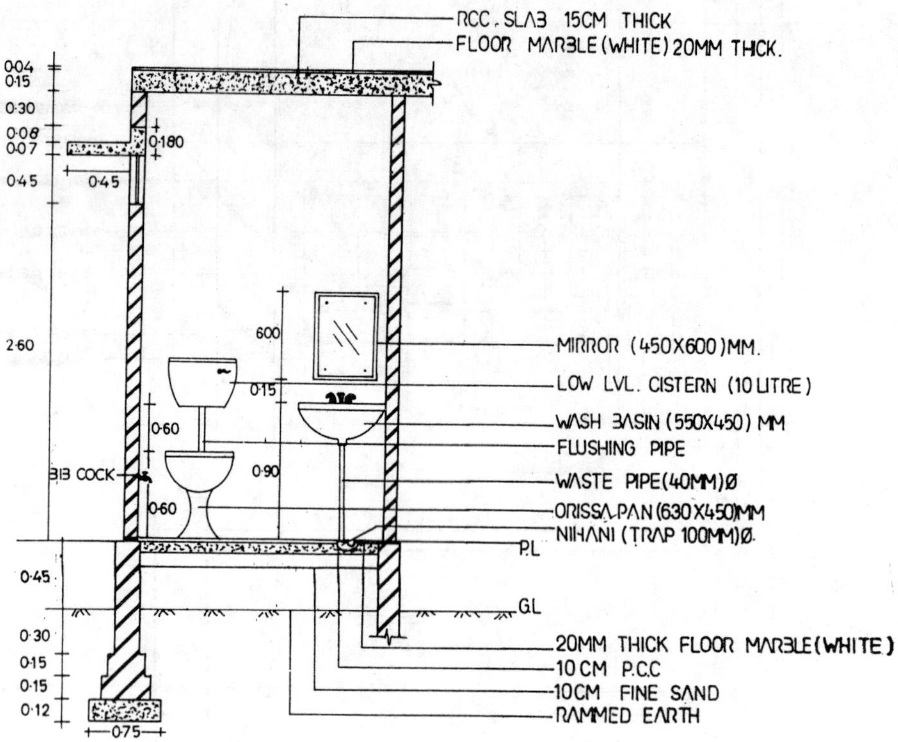


SECTION AT X-X

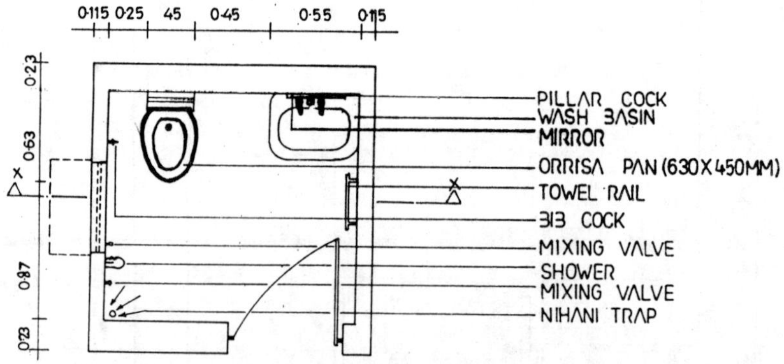


PLAN

SCALE – 1:25

Fig. 6. 56

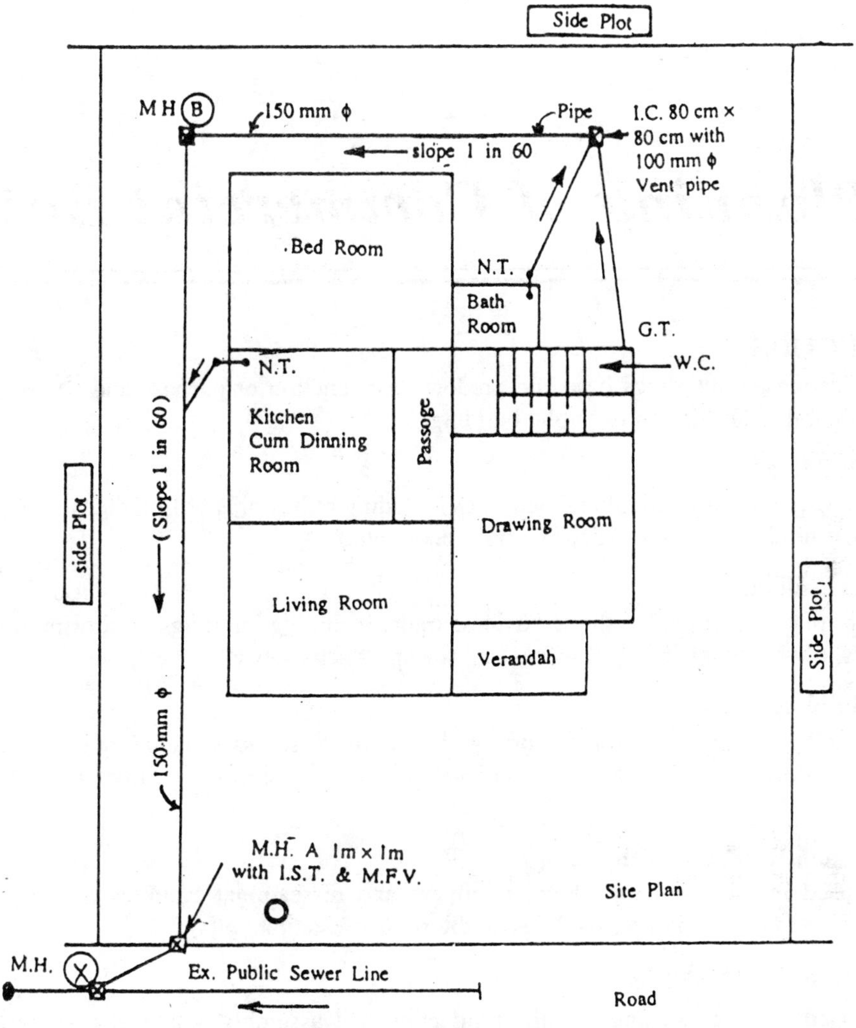


**Fig. 6.57.** General Sewerage Plan of a Building

# 7
# Planning of Commercial Building

## 7.1. INTRODUCTION

The classifications of buildings based on predominant function or purpose and correctors of its own. Following are the brief description of public buildings

**Agricultural Buildings**

Buildings associated with agricultural activities including bulk storage of products (*e.g.* shearing shed, grain silo, animal production units, dairy and milk booth etc.)

**Business Areas Buildings**

Buildings primarily occupied with the business tradė, including buildings used primarily in wholesale and retail trades, office, shops markets, plazas and transport activities etc.

**Educational Building**

Buildings used in the provision for supporting of educational services, including group accommodation buildings (*e.g.* hostels, classrooms, school, collage, university, library, institute, laboratories, canteen, dormitories etc).

**Entertainment and Recreational Buildings**

Buildings used in the provision of entertainment and recreational facilities or services (*e.g.* club, libraries, museums, casinos, sporting facilities, auditoriums, restaurant etc.).

**Factories and Industrial Building**

Buildings used for warehousing and the production and assembly activities of industrial establishments. It includes the factories and plants, production units and assembly processes of goods and end users.

**Hospitality Building**

Buildings used in the provision for medical services, and includes categories on Hospitals and other health care buildings (*e.g.* nursing homes, clinics, medicals and health centers and their respective laboratories).

**Offices Buildings**

Buildings primarily used in the provision of professional services or public administration (*e.g.* offices, banks, insurance or finance buildings, post office, police station, telephone departments and courts etc).

**Religious Buildings**

Buildings associated with worship, or in support of programs sponsored by religious bodies (*e.g.* mosque, church. temple, church hall etc).

**Short-term accommodation Buildings**

Buildings primarily providing short-term accommodation, includes the Hotels predominantly accommodation, motels, boatel, boarding houses, guesthouses, lodges etc.

**Transports Buildings**

Buildings primarily used in the provision of transport services, Passenger transport buildings (*e.g.* railway stations, bus stand, airports, garage, passenger terminals, car parking and docks etc.)

## 7.2. WATCH MAN\GUARD ROOM

This is a small room provided at the main entrance of the building and with a minimum size of 2.0 m × 2.0 m.

## 7.3. PUBLIC TELEPHONE

Public telephone in a building may be provided in the form of small booth measuring about 1.5 m × 1.5 m near the reception\ entrance of the building.

## 7.4. PARKING AREA

Parking space is an essential part of any public building. Its size may depend upon its function and no of user.

| *S. No.* | *Vehicle* | *Area required* |
|---|---|---|
| 1. | Car | 15 to 20 sqm |
| 2. | Two wheeler | 2.0 to 3.0 sqm |
| 3. | Bi-cycles | 1.0 to 1.25 sqn |

The passage between adjacent blocks for car should not less than 2.2 m.

## 7.5. RECEPTION

Entrance:-Every public building requires some space at the entrance, which is called reception lounges or lobby. The size of reception lounge may very slightly with the no of persons entering at one time. Following sizes may be adopted for entrance hall or reception lounges.

3.0 m × 6.0 m, 4.0 m × 5.0 m, 6.0 m× 7.0 m, 8.0 m × 10.0 m

## 7.6. CIRCULATION AREA; CIRCULATION IN A BUILDING IS OF TWO TYPES

(*a*) Horizontal circulation which includes passage, corridors, verandah and lobby etc,

(*b*) Vertical circulation includes Stair, Lifts, & elevators.

Following size may be adopted;

| | |
|---|---|
| Passage/corridor | 1.2 m to 1.5 m |
| Verandah/lobby | 2.0 m to 3.5 m |
| Stairs: | |
| Width | 1.2 m minimum |
| Riser | 150 mm to170 mm |
| Tread | 300 to 325 mm |
| Landing | 1.2 m to1.75 m |
| Headroom | 2.0 m |

## 7.7. LIFTS

For residential buildings the speed of lift should not be more than 0.5 m\s and in public building this speed of lift may very from 0.25 m/s to 2.5 m/s depending upon the function of the building.

## 7.8. SANITARY BLOCK

This includes bathroom, water closets, urinals, wash hand basins.

Following size may be adopted

| | |
|---|---|
| Bath room | 1.2 m × 2.0 m |
| Water closet (wc) | 0.9 m × 1.2 m |
| Urinals | 0.75 m × 0.9 m |
| Passage width | 1.0 m to 1.5 m |

## 7.9. OPEN SPACE (SET BACK) FOR SCHOOL BUILDING

| S. No. | *Size of plots (sqm)* | *Front (m)* | *Back (m)* | *Left side (m)* | *Right size (m)* |
|---|---|---|---|---|---|
| 1. | UP to 500 | 6.0 | 3.0 | 3.0 | — |
| 2. | 501 to 1000 | 9.0 | 3.0 | 3.0 | 3.0 |
| 3. | 1000 to 2000 | 9.0 | 4.0 | 3.0 | 3.0 |
| 4. | 2001 to 4000 | 9.0 | 4.5 | 3.0 | 3.0 |
| 5. | More than 4000 | 9.0 | 6.0 | 4.8 | 4.5 |

## 7.10. OPEN SPACE (SET BACK) FOR HOSPITAL BUILDING (UP TO 10 M HEIGHT)

| S. No. | *Size of plots (sqm)* | *Front (m)* | *Back (m)* | *Left size (m)* | *Right size (m)* |
|---|---|---|---|---|---|
| 1. | 500 to 1000 | 6.0 | 4.5 | 3.0 | — |
| 2. | 1000 and above | 9.0 | 9.0 | 3.0 | 3.0 |

Minimum width of plot 15 m.

## 7.11. OPEN SPACE (SET BACK) FOR HOTEL BUILDING (UP TO 10 M HEIGHT)

| S. No. | *Size of plots (sqm)* | *Front (m)* | *Back (m)* | *Left side (m)* | *Right size (m)* |
|---|---|---|---|---|---|
| 1. | UP to 500 | 4.5 | 3.0 | 3.0 | 3.0 |
| 2. | 501 to 1000 | 6.0 | 3.0 | 3.0 | 3.0 |
| 3. | More than 1000 | 9.0 | 3.0 | 3.0 | 3.0 |

## 7.12. OPEN SPACE(SET BACK)FOR OTHER PUBLIC BUILDING

| S. No. | *Size of plots (sqm)* | *Front (m)* | *Back (m)* | *Left side (m)* | *Right side (m)* |
|---|---|---|---|---|---|
| 1. | UP to 200 | 4.5 | 3.0 | — | — |
| 2. | 201 to 500 | 6.0 | 3.0 | 3.0 | 3.0 |
| 3. | More than 500 | 9.0 | 3.0 | 3.0 | 3.0 |

## 7.13. DATA FOR PUBLIC BUILDING

The data for various buildings is given below. The dimensions are given are for guidance and may be changed suitably according to the requirements.

## 7.14. EDUCATIONAL BUILDINGS

It include primary school, secondary school, colleges and institutes. (Fig. 7.3 to 7.5)

Classrooms:

| | |
|---|---|
| Students below 10 years | 1.0 to 1.25 sqm/student |
| Students above 10 years | 1.25 to 1.50 sqm/student |

General sizes for classroom may be taken as 4.3m × 6.0m, 5.0m × 6.5m, 6.0m × 8.0m, and 7.0m× 10.0m.

| | |
|---|---|
| Drawing studio/hall | 3.0 to 3.75 sqm/student |
| Laboratories | 3.0 to 4.0 sqm/student |

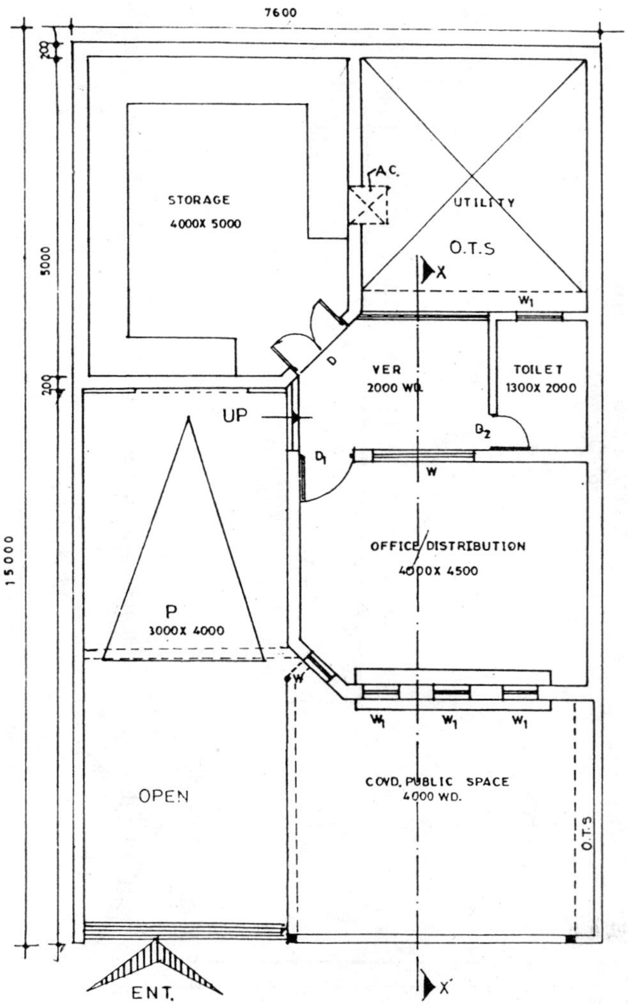


PLAN

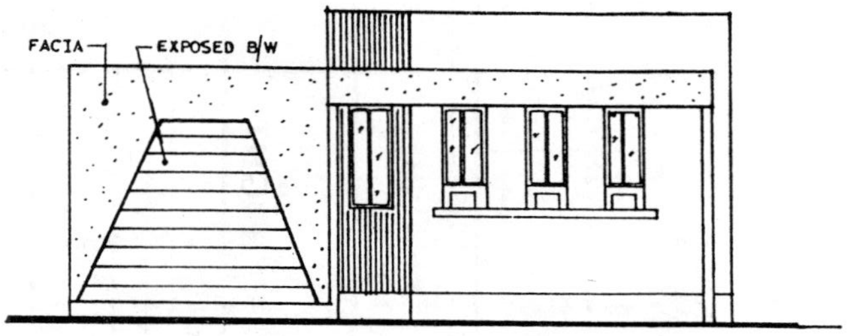


F. ELEVATION

| | OPENINGS | | CILL |
|---|---|---|---|
| D | 1200 | 2200 | - |
| $D_1$ | 1000 | 2200 | - |
| $D_2$ | 750 | 2200 | - |
| W | 1200 | 1200 | 1000 |
| $W_1$ | 750. | 1200 | 1000 |
| | SCALE — 1:50 | | |
| | DRG NO — | | |

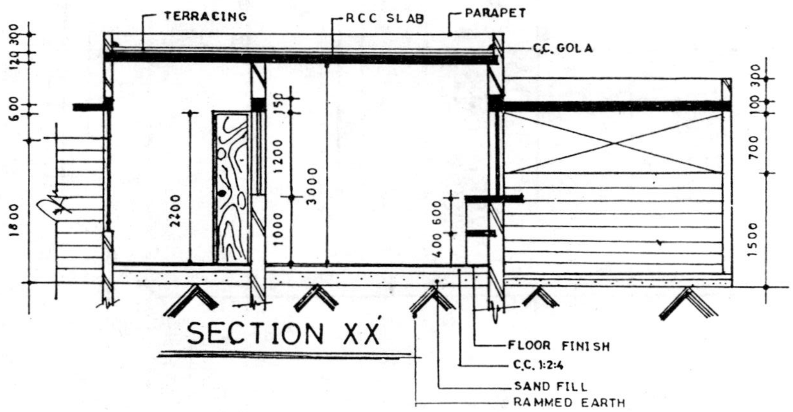


SECTION XX'

Scale-1:150

All dimensions in mm

**Fig. 7.1 A.** Milk Booth

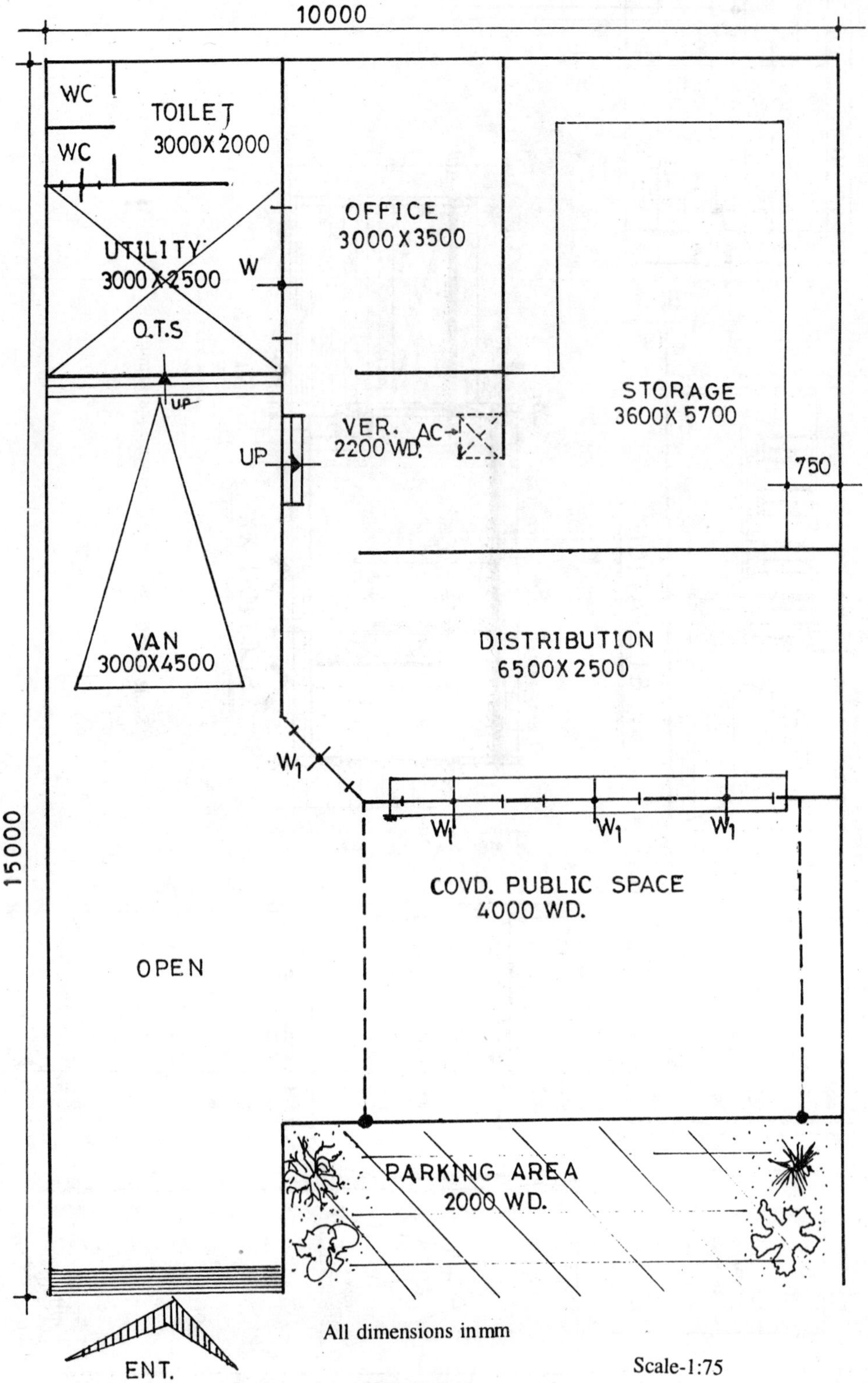


All dimensions in mm

Scale-1:75

LINE PLAN

**Fig. 7.1 B.**

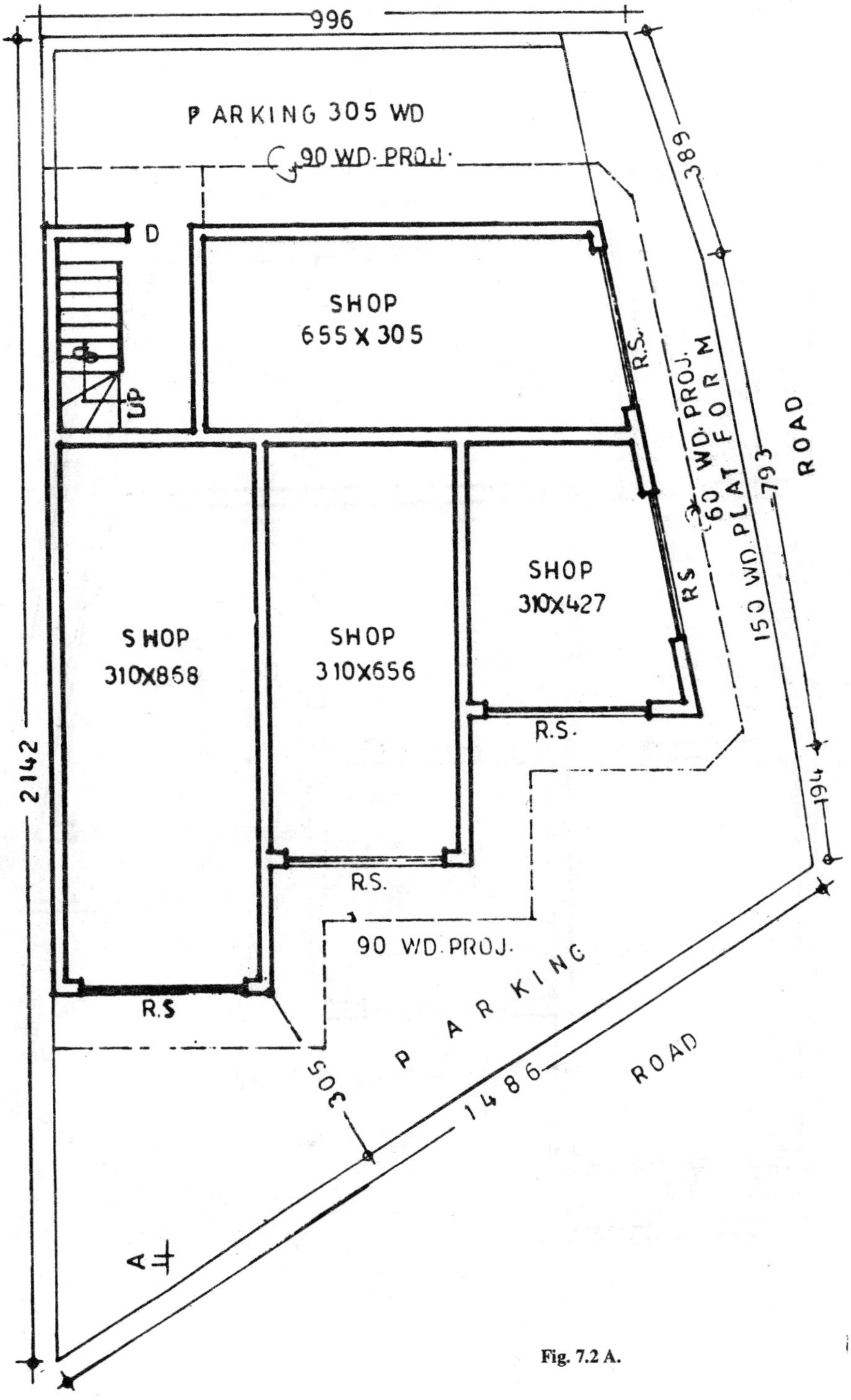


Fig. 7.2 A.

GROUND FLOOR

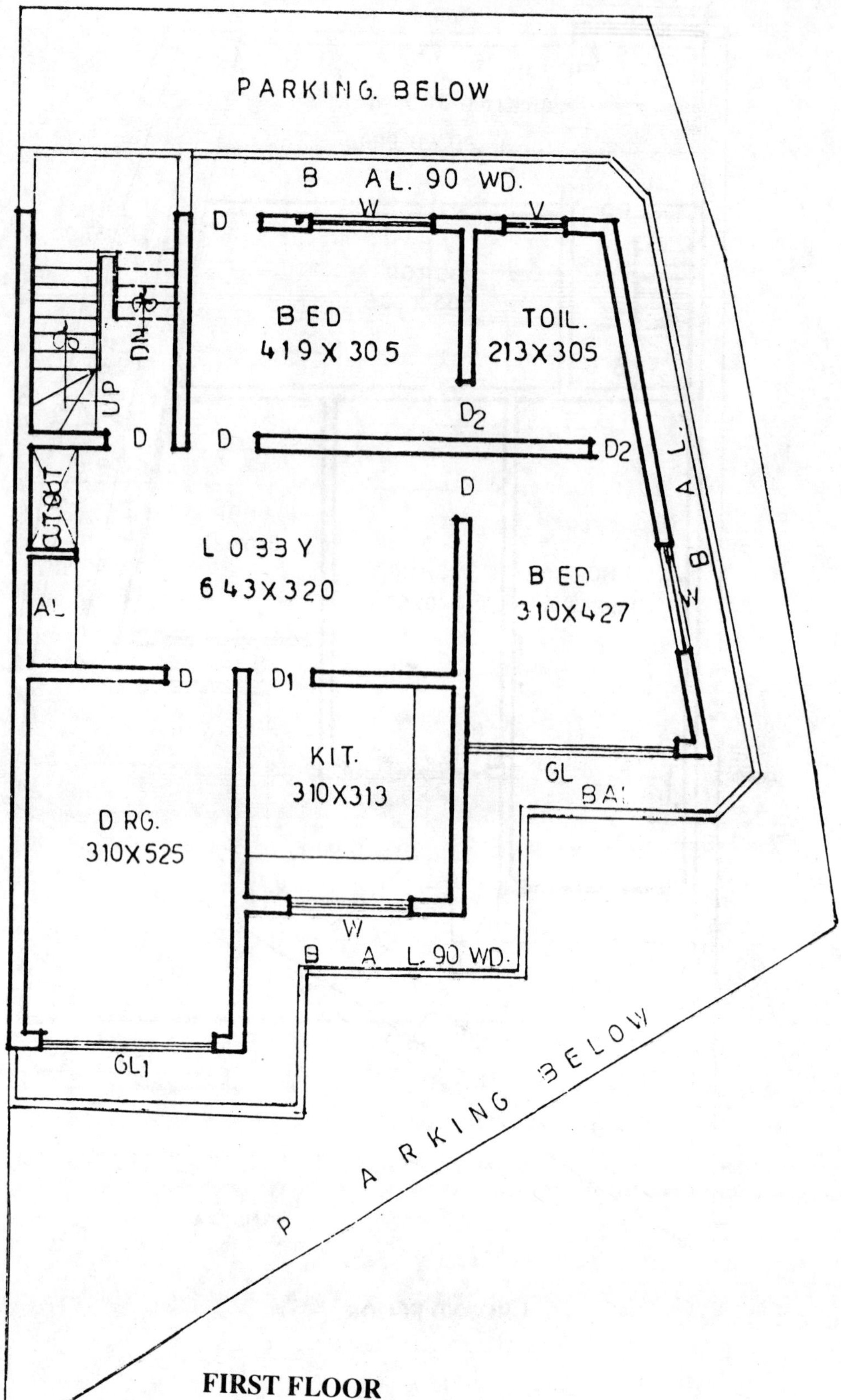


**FIRST FLOOR**

Fig. 7.2 B.

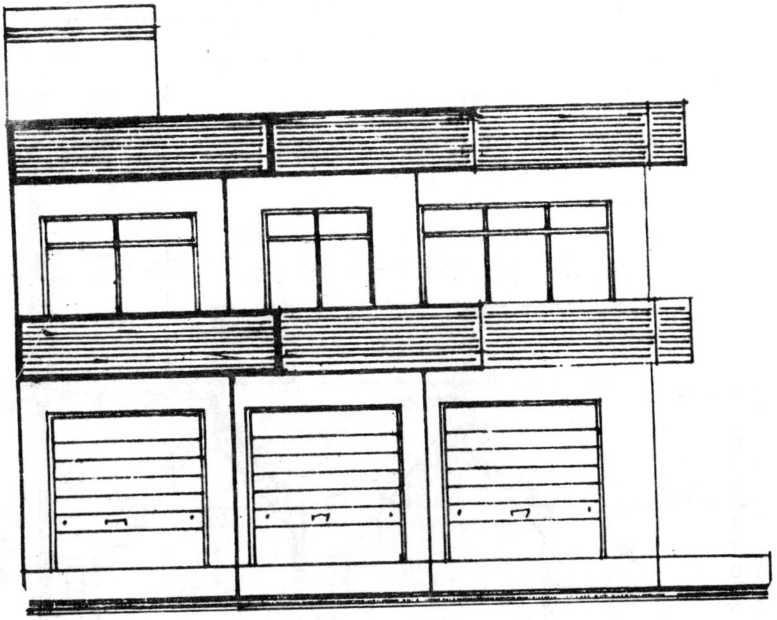

FRONT ELEVATION

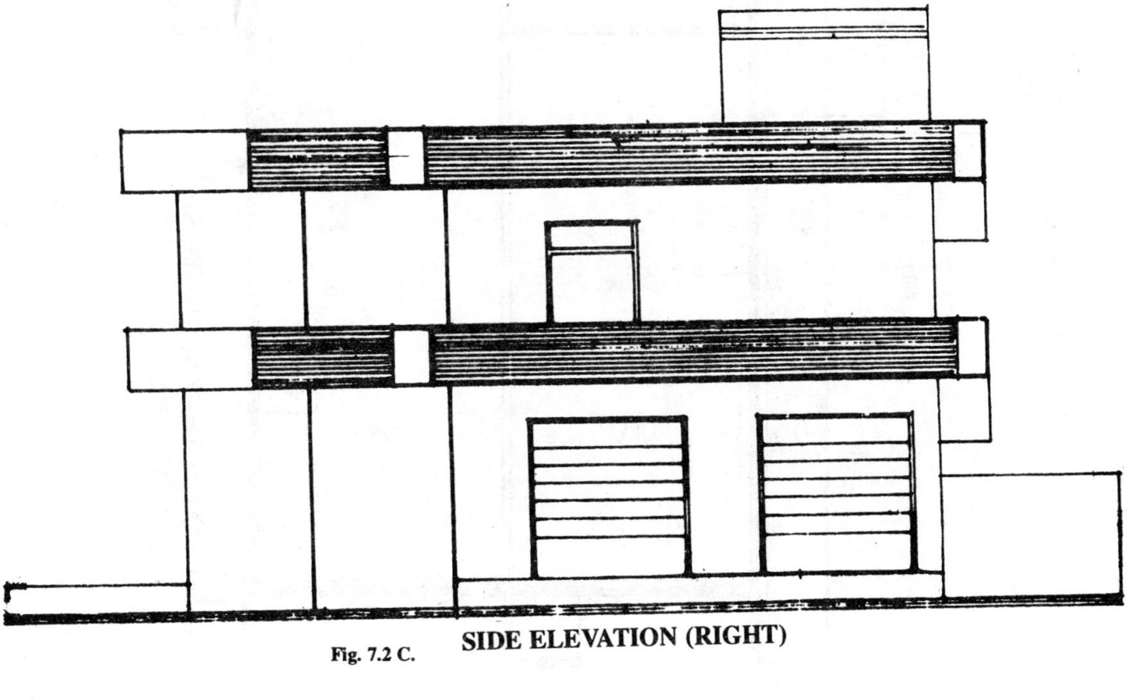

SIDE ELEVATION (RIGHT)

Fig. 7.2 C.

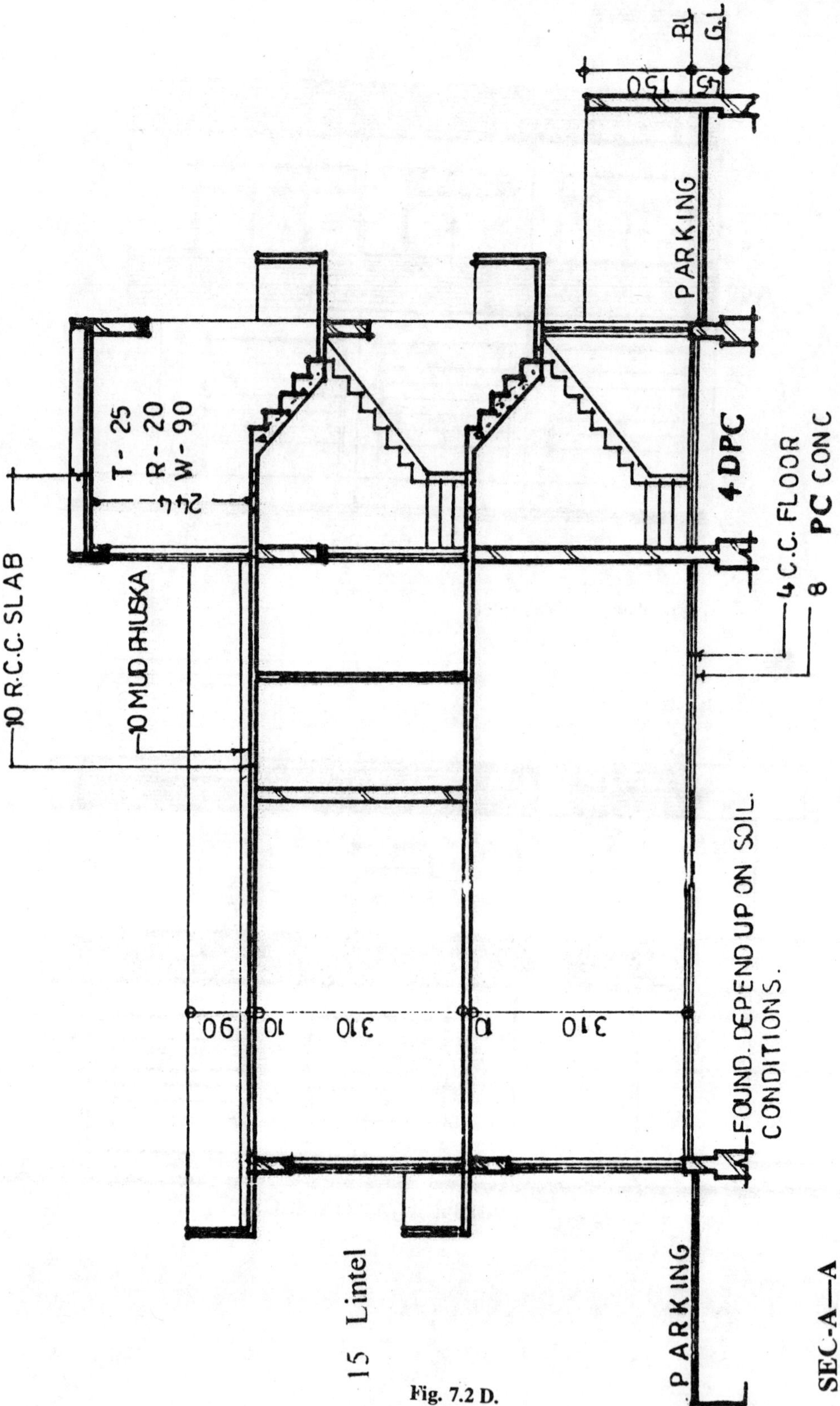

10 R.C.C. SLAB
10 MUD PHUSKA
T - 25
R - 20
W - 90
24
PARKING
150
45
RL
G.L
4 DPC
4 C.C. FLOOR
8
PC CONC
FOUND. DEPEND UP ON SOIL CONDITIONS.
90
10
310
10
310
15 Lintel
PARKING
SEC-A—A


Fig. 7.2 D.

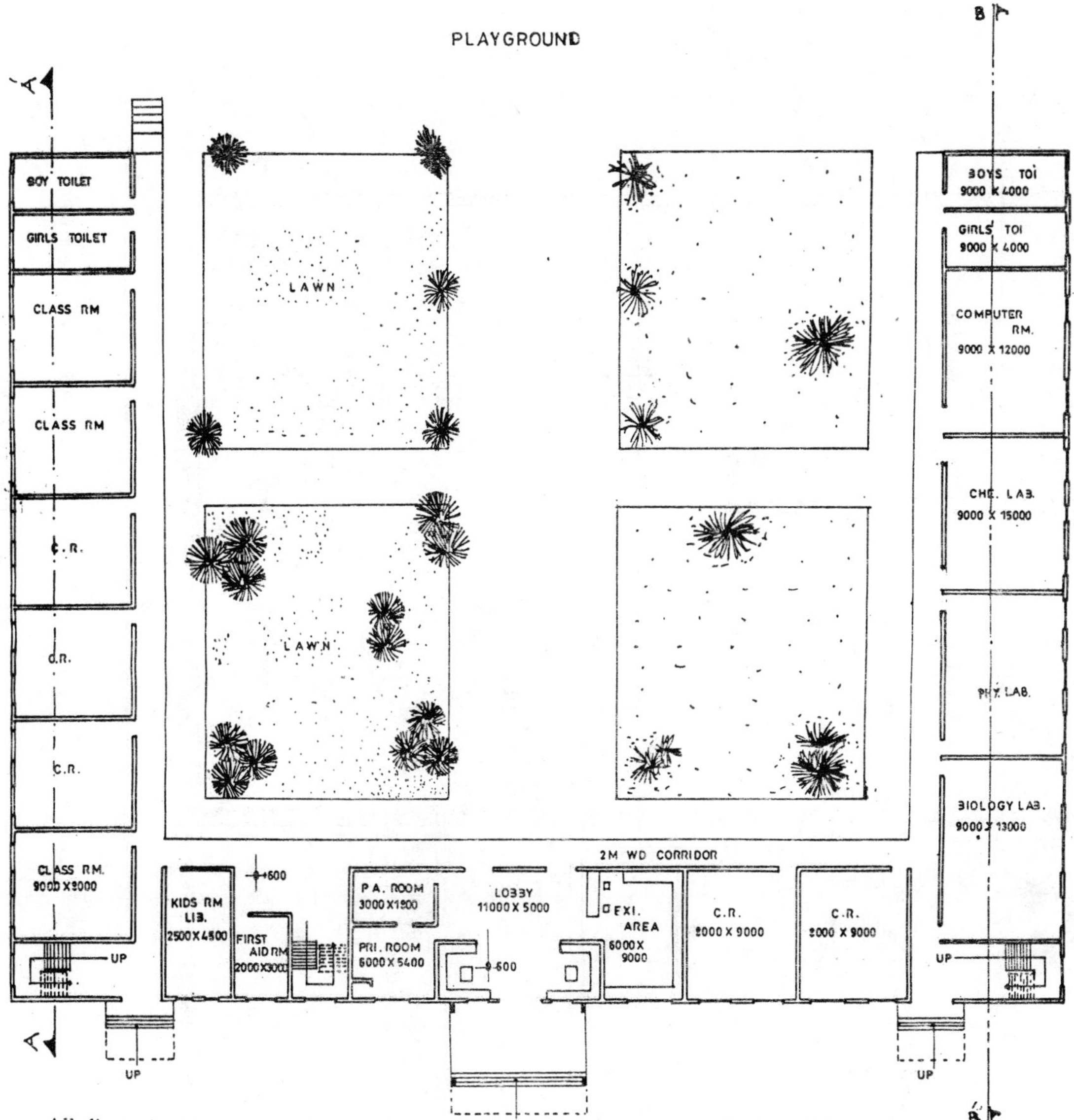


All dimensions in mm

Scale-1:200

GROUND FLOOR PLAN

**Fig. 7.3.** Secondary School

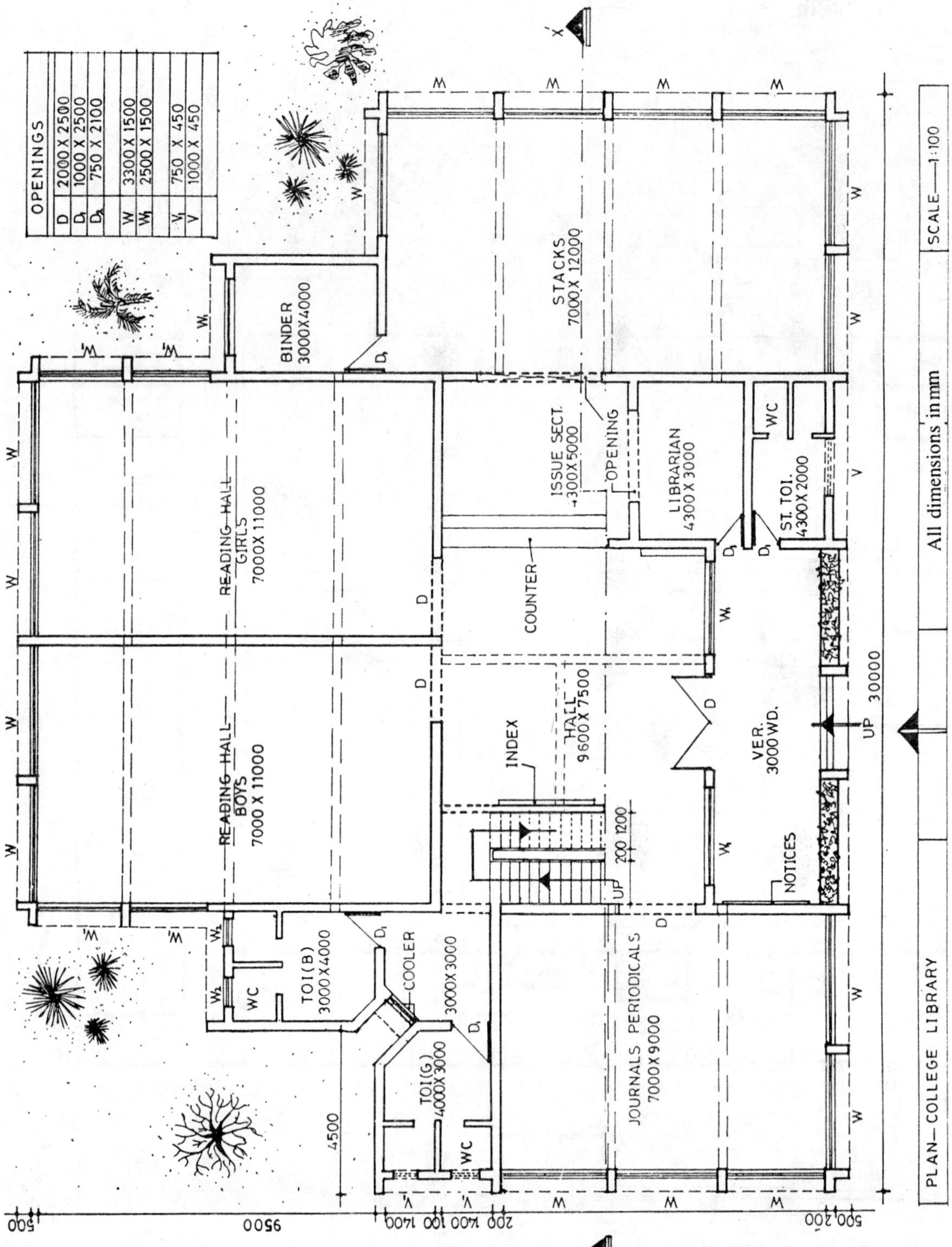


Fig. 7.4. College Library

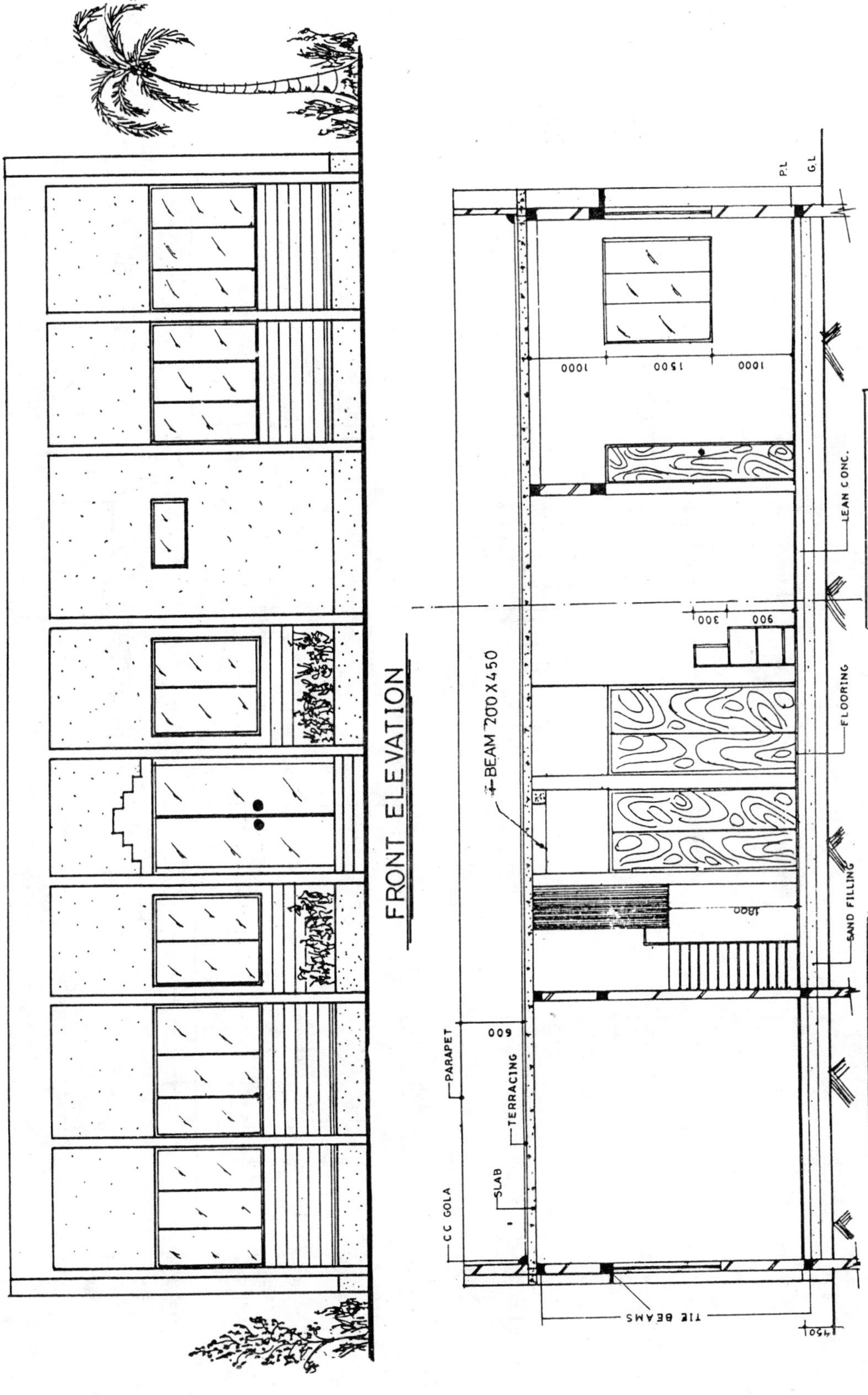


All dimensions inmm

Fig. 7.4 A.

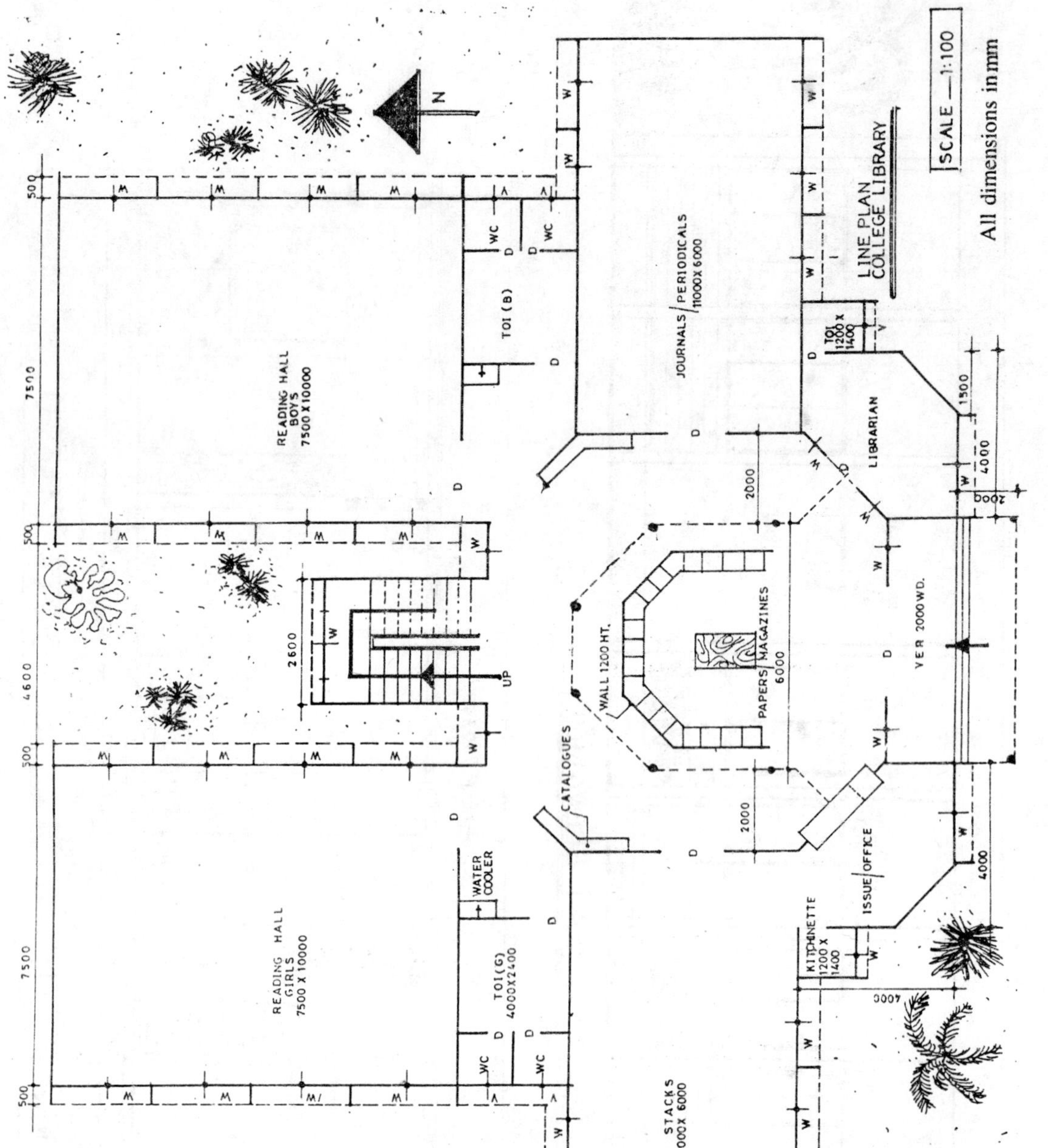


Fig. 7.5. College Library

| | |
|---|---|
| Wash basin | 1.0 for 35 student |
| Urinals | 1.0 for 35 student |
| Water closet | 1.0 for 35 students |

## 7.15. POST OFFICE (Fig 7.6)

Entrance and moving space around the counter 2.0 m wide

| | |
|---|---|
| Counter (height) | 1.4m to 1.6m |
| (Width) | 0 .6m to 0.8m |
| Working space behind the counter | 2.5m (min) |
| Postmasters room | 9.0sqm to 11.0sqm |
| Sorting space | 2.5sqm/postman |
| Telephone booth | 1.0m × 1.5m |

## 7.16. HOSTELS

| | |
|---|---|
| Entrance lobby/hall | 10.0sqm to 15.0sqm |
| Single seated room | 3.0m × 3.0m |
| Double seated room | 3.3m × 4.0m |
| Triple seated room | 4.25m × 5.0m |
| Recreation/ common room | 2.0 sqm/head |
| Dinning hall | 3.5 sqm/head |
| Kitchen | 15.0 sqm to 20.0 sqm |
| Pantry | 8.5 sqm to 12.0 sqm |
| Water closet | 1.0 for 15.0 students |
| Bath room | 1.0 for 15.0 student |
| Wash hand basin | 1.0 for 15.0 student |
| Urinals | 1.0 for 30.0 student |

## 7.17. AUDITORIUM/ CINEMA THEATRES (Fig. 7.7)

| | |
|---|---|
| Entrance lobby | Minimum 3.0m wide |
| Auditorium | 0.75 sqm to 1.0 sqm/chair |
| | 3.5 sqm to 4.25 sqm/chair |
| One door for every 150 people | |
| Distance between chairs | 0.45m |
| Stage height | 0.8mto 1.25m |
| Slope of floor | 1:20 to1: 10 |
| Office/booking window | 4.5 sqm |
| Projector room | 16.5 sqm to 20.0 sqm |
| Manager office | 10.0 sqm to 15.0 sqm |
| Snacks counter | 12.0 sqm |
| Screen stage | 30.0 sqm to 40.0 sqm |
| Costume room | 16.5 sqm to 25.0 sqm |
| Make up room | 35.0 sqm to 40.0 sqm |
| Stage manager | 10.0 sqm to 12.0 sqm |
| Dressing room | 18.0 sqm to 22.0 sqm |
| Water closet | 1.0 for 100.0 candidates |
| Wash hand basin | 1.0 for 150.0 candidate |
| Urinals | 1.0 for 50.0 candidate |

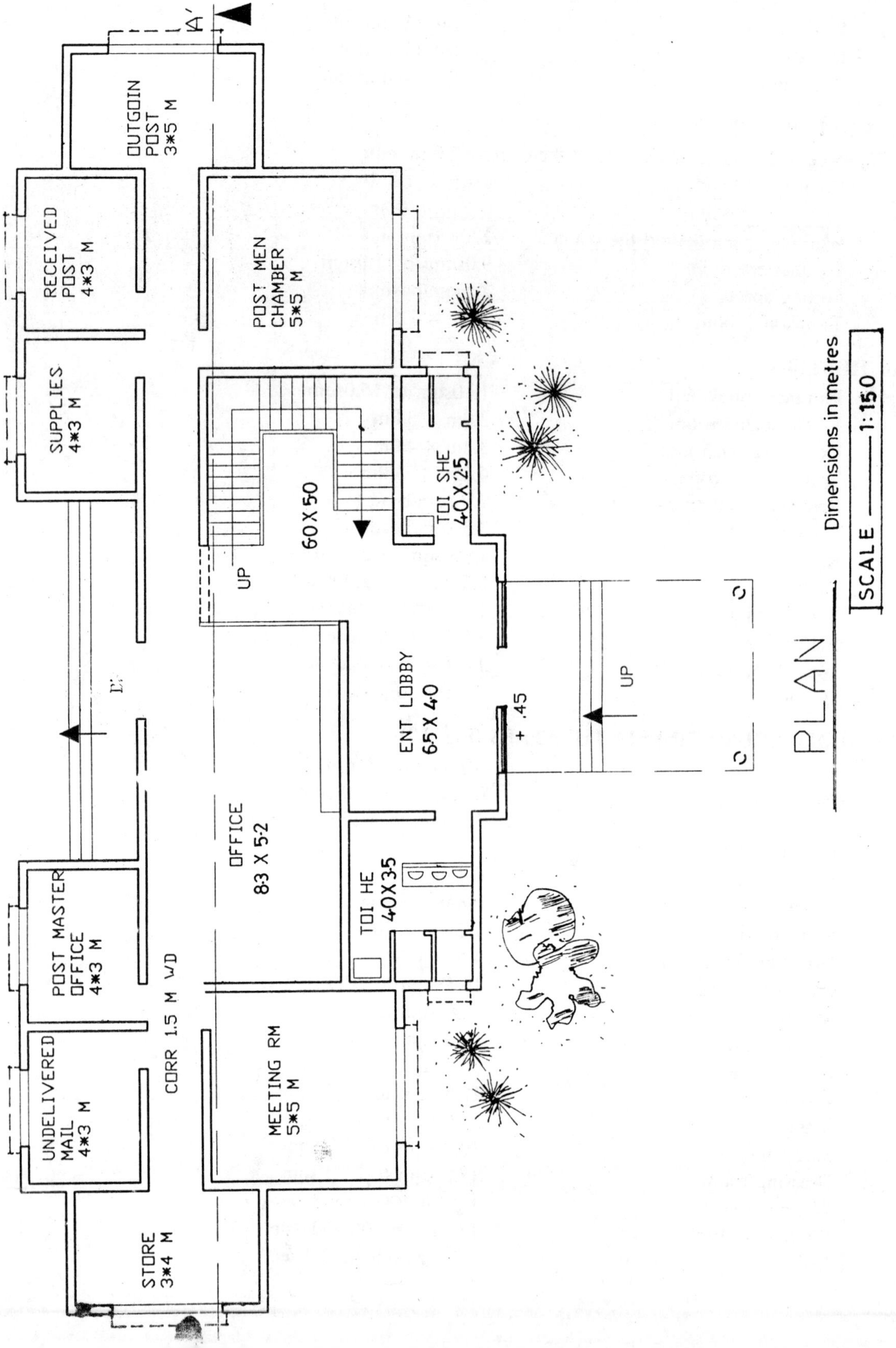


Fig. 7.6. Post Office

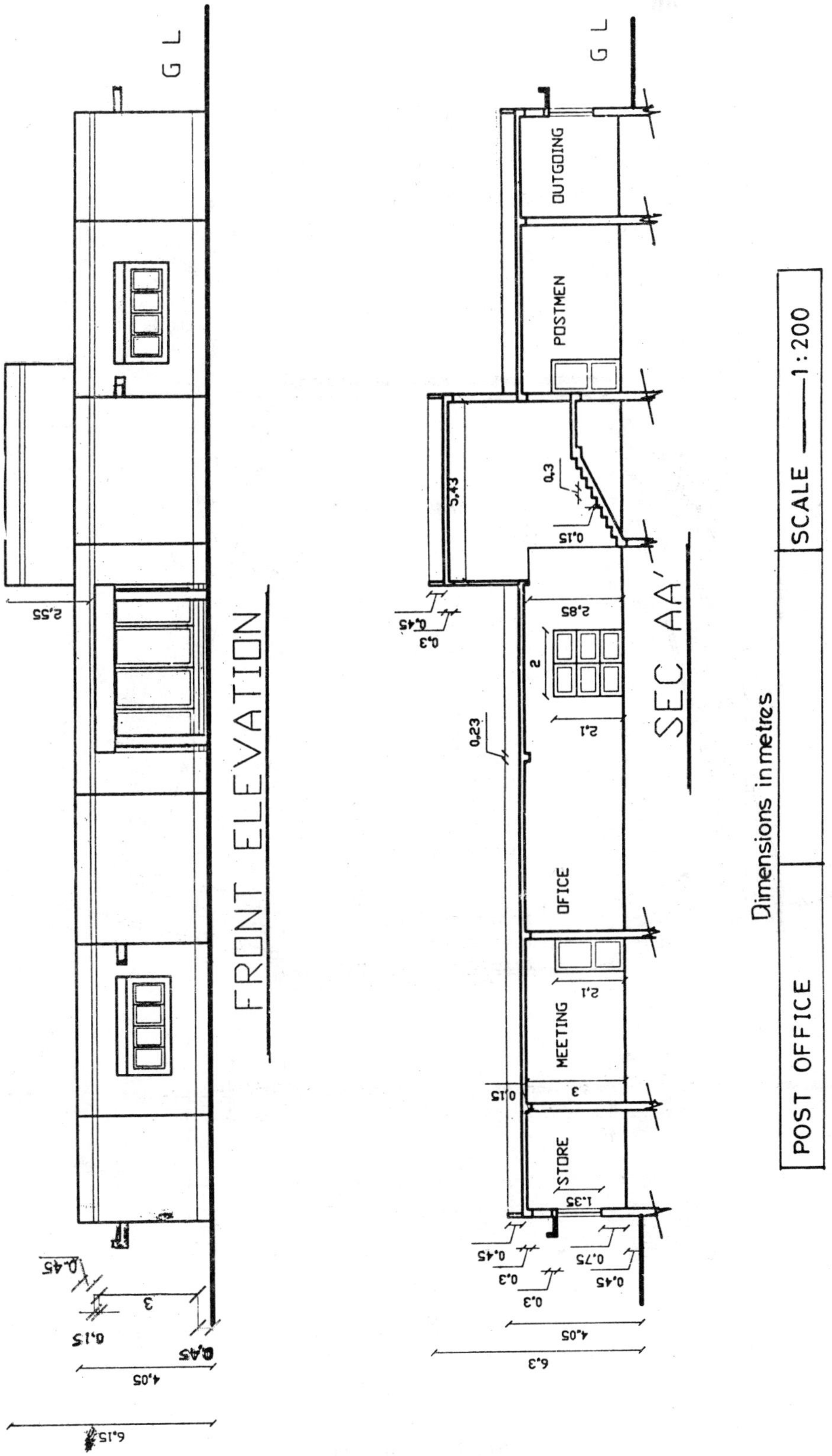


Fig. 7.6 A. Post Office

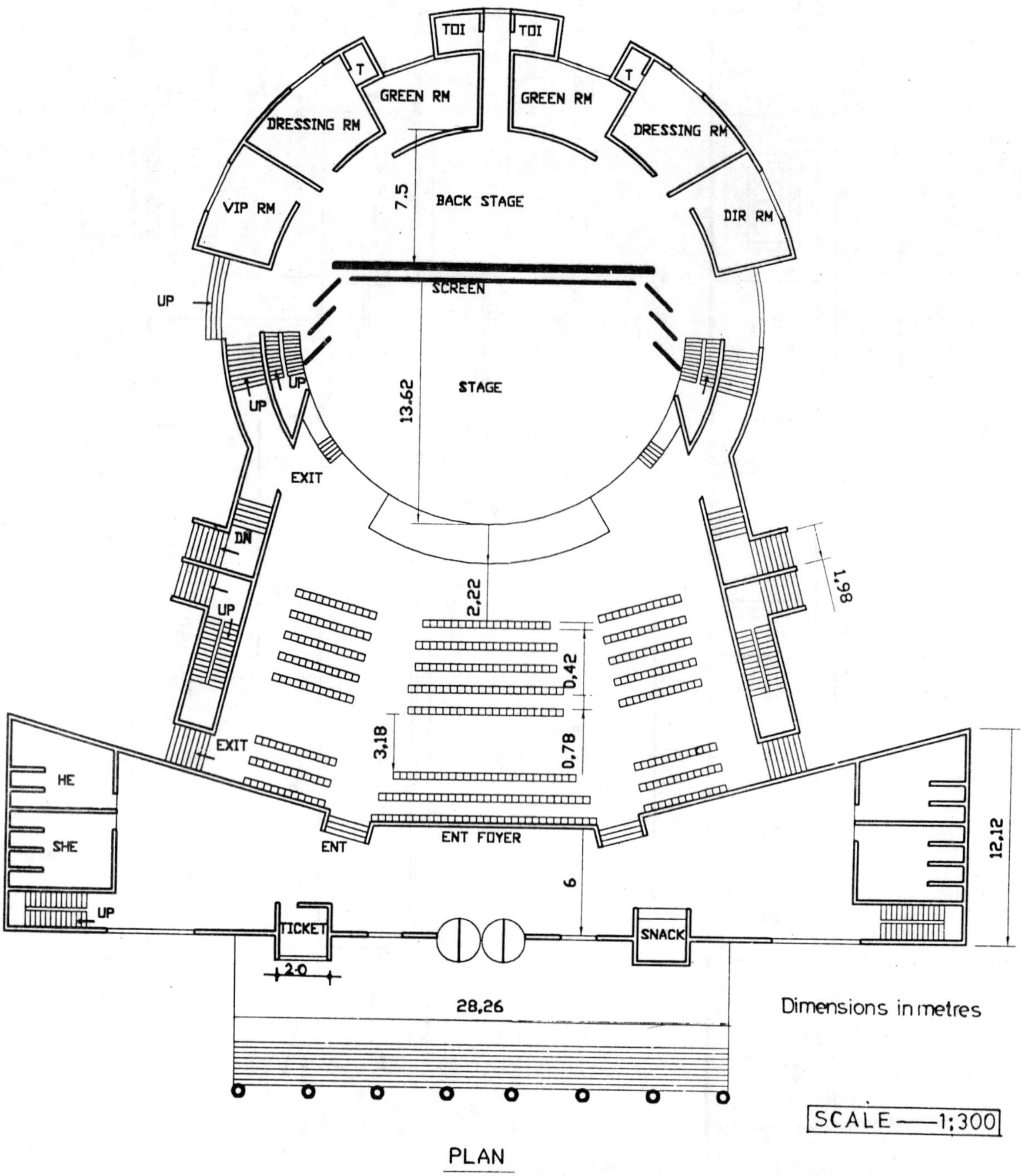


**Fig. 7.7.** Auditorium

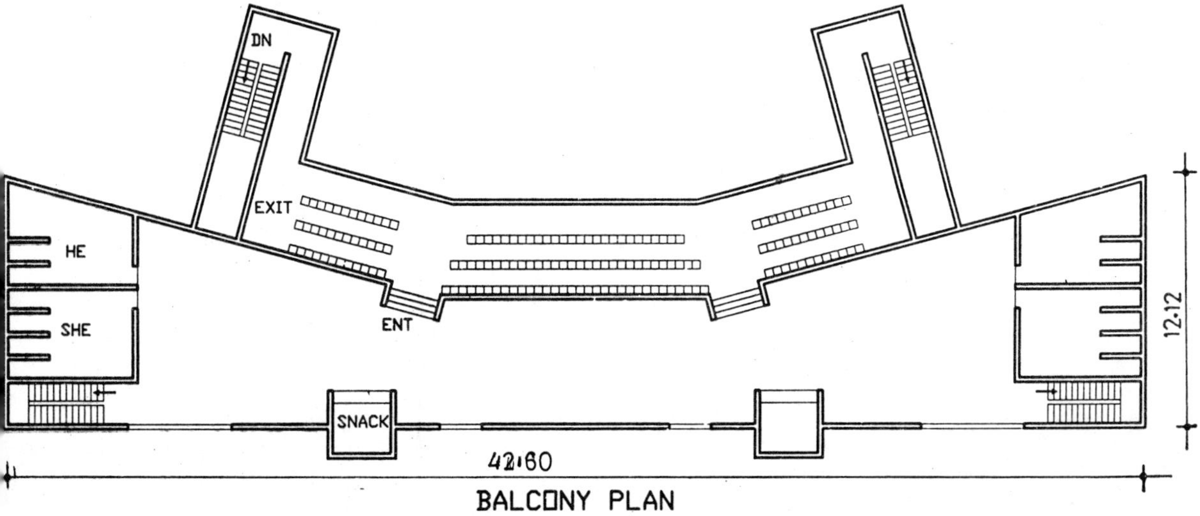


Scale-1:300

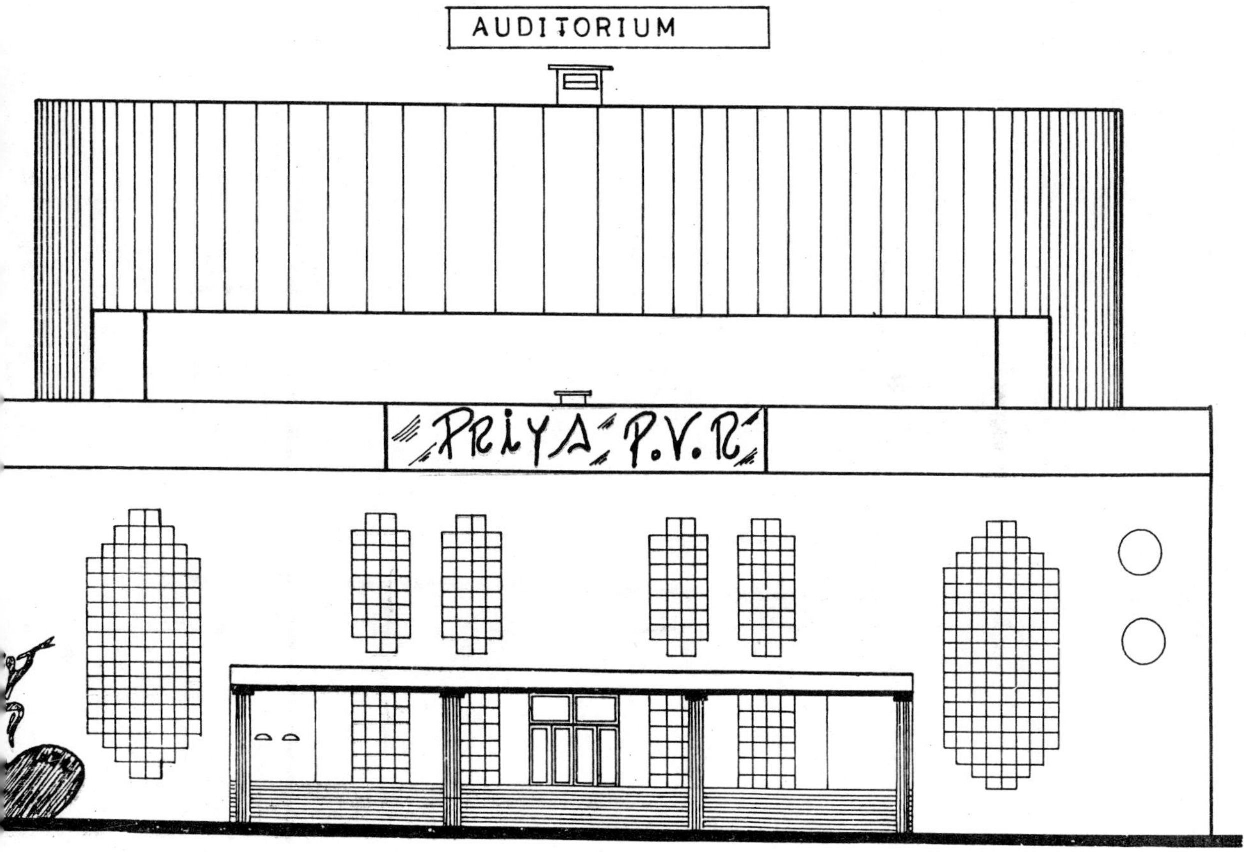


Scale-1:100

FRONT ELEVATION

**Fig. 7.7 A.**

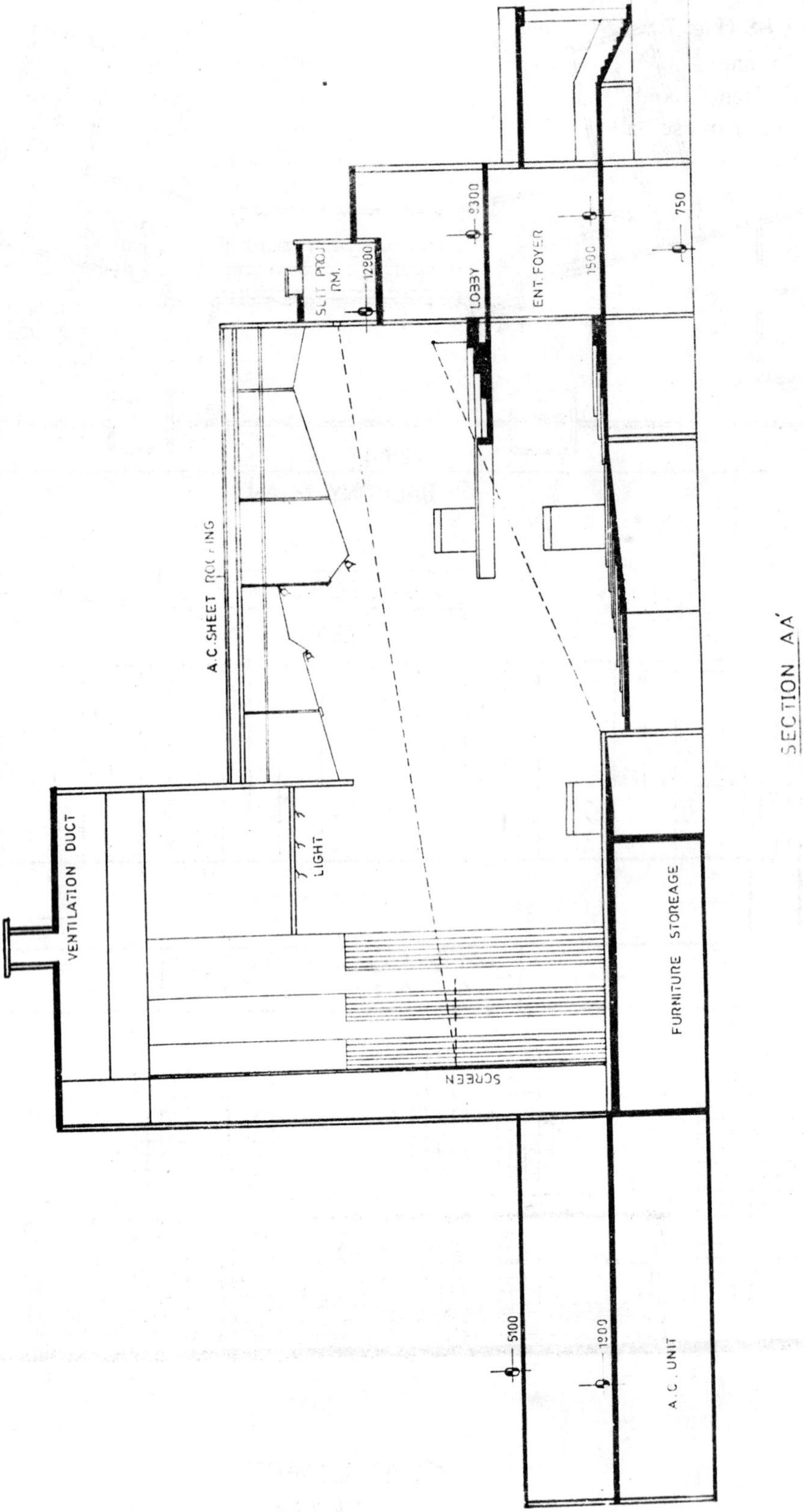
VENTILATION DUCT
LIGHT
SLIT PROJ RM.
12900
LOBBY
9300
ENT. FOYER
1500
750
SECTION AA'
FURNITURE STOREAGE
SCREEN
5100
A.C. UNIT

Fig. 7.7 B.

## 7.18. CLUBS (Fig. 7.8, 7.9)

| | |
|---|---|
| Entrance hall | 10.0 sqm to 16.0 sqm |
| Changing room | 9.0 sqm |
| Multipurpose hall | 30.0 sqm to 40.0 sqm |
| Billiards, T.T, Cards etc | 20.0 sqm each |
| Store | 7.0 sqm to 8.50 sqm |

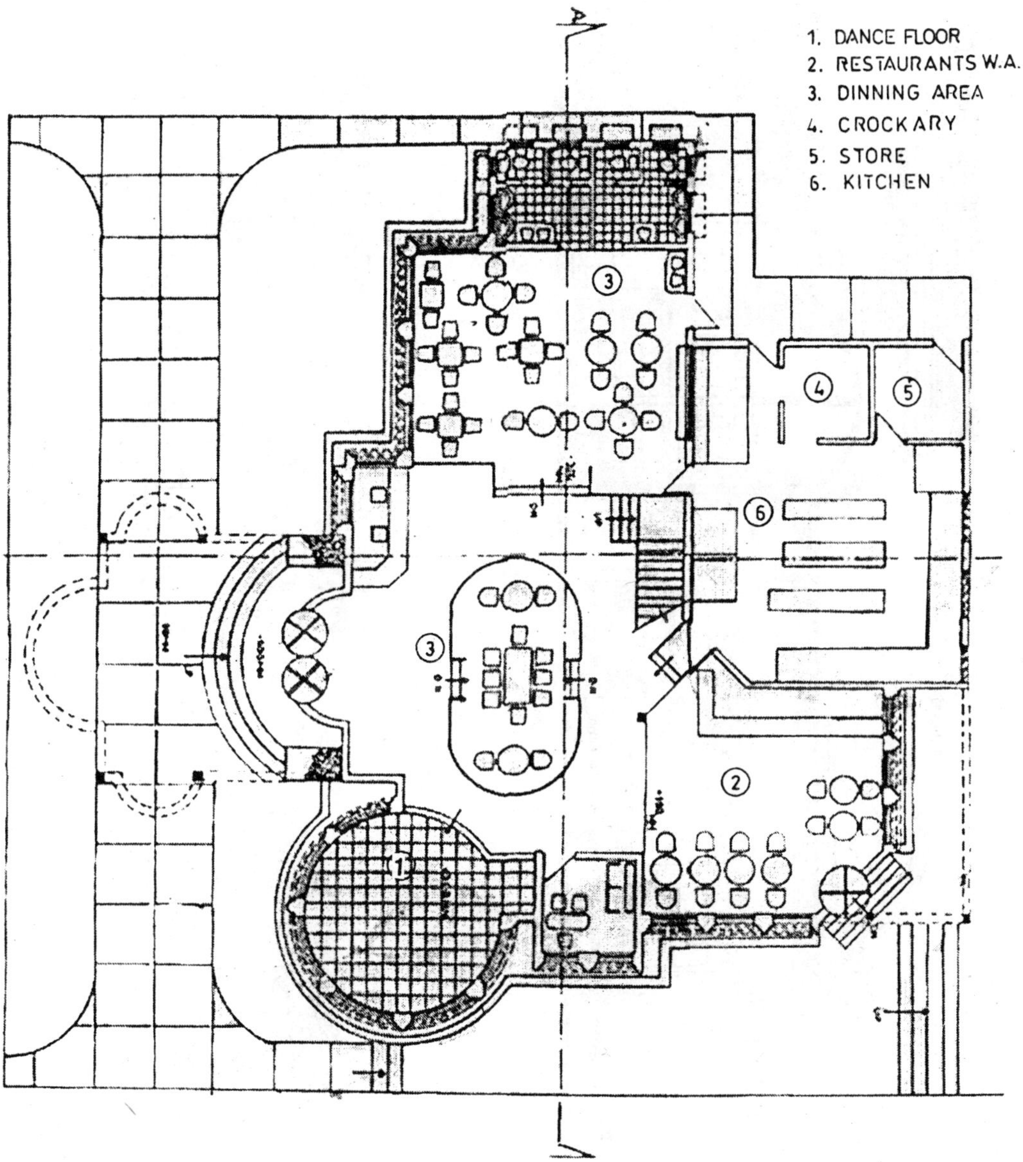


**Fig. 7.8.** Ground Floor Plan of Restaurant

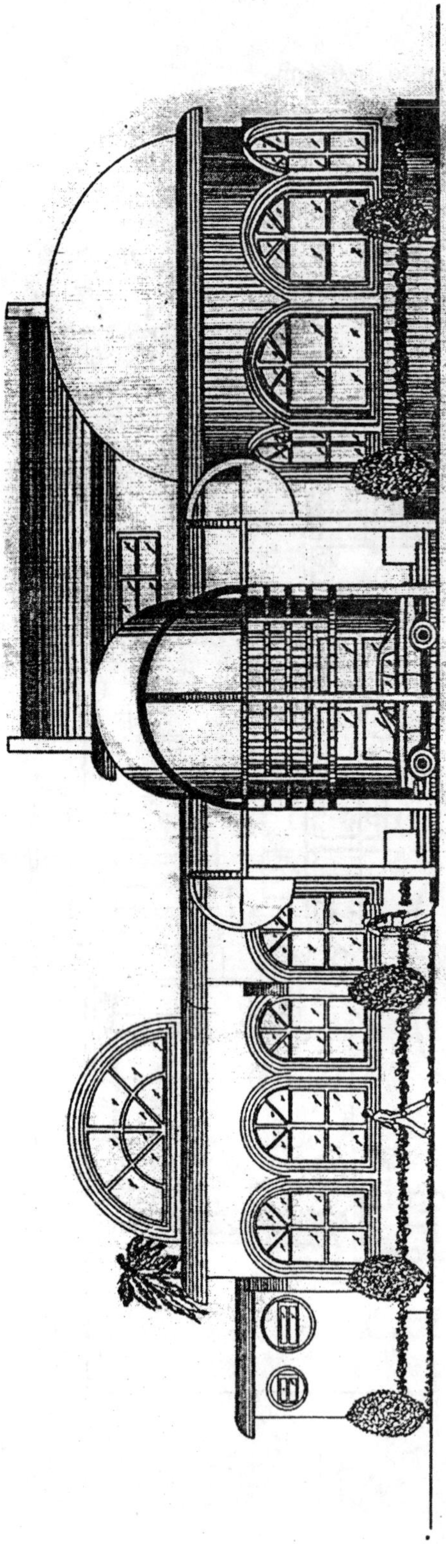

FRONT ELEVATION

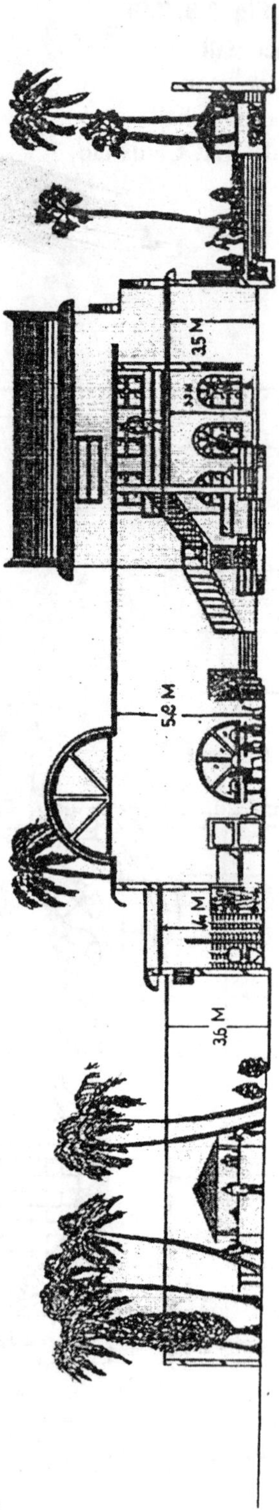


SECTION AB

**Fig. 7.8 A.**

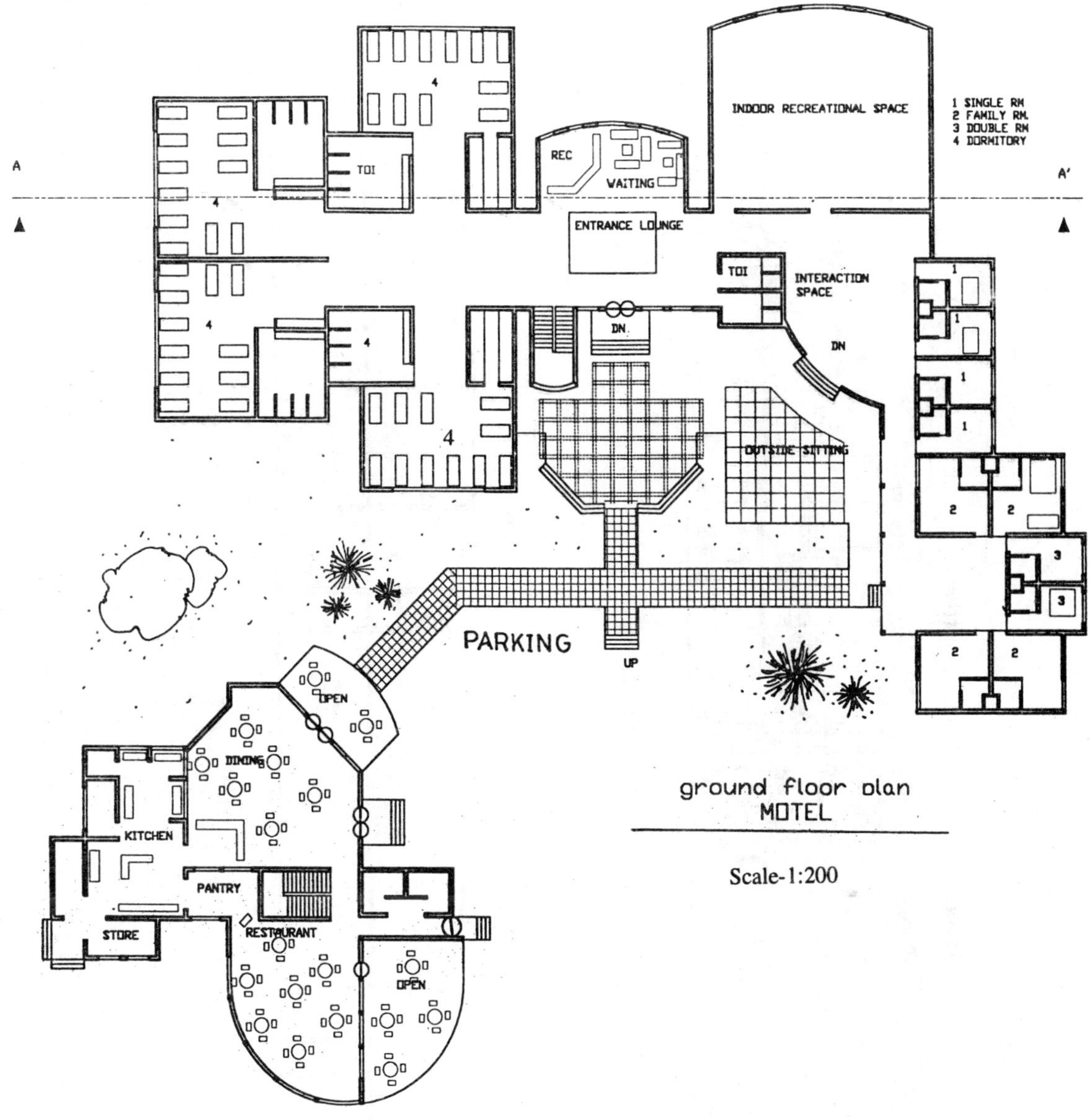


**Fig. 7.9.** Motel

## 7.19. GUEST HOUSE

| | |
|---|---|
| Bedrooms with attached toilet | 3.50m × 4.50m |
| Toilet | 1.5m × 2.4m |
| Verandah/ terrace | 2.0m wide (minimum) |
| Dinning hall | 15.0 sqm to 20.0 sqm |
| Kitchen | 8.50 sqm to 10.0 sqm |
| Office | 9.0 sqm to 11.0 sqm |
| Store | 6.0 sqm to 8.50 sqm |

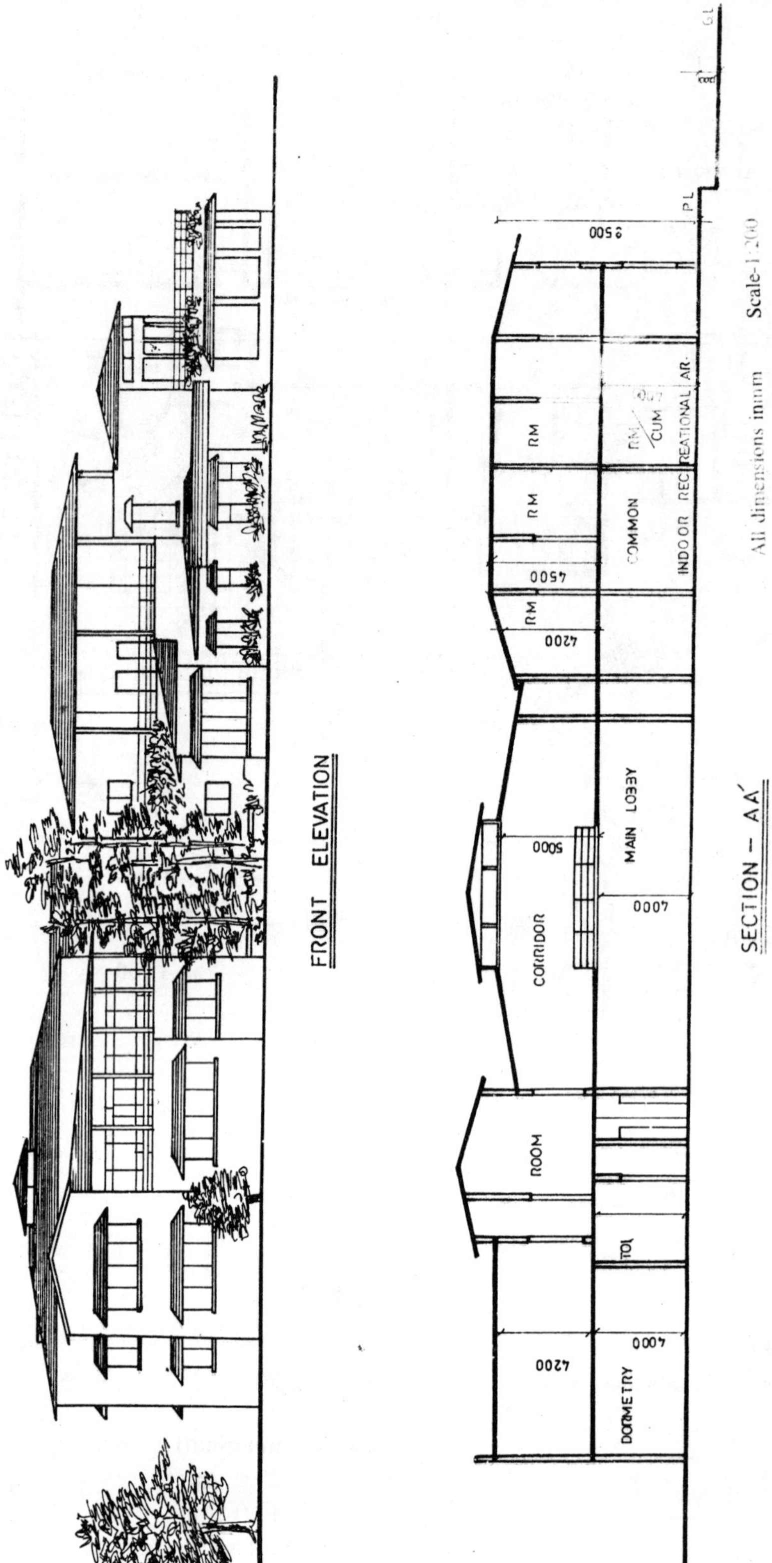


**Fig. 7.9 A. Motel**

**Building for health (Fig 7.10 to 7.13)**

Dispensaries

| | |
|---|---|
| Entrance/ Waiting space | Minimum 2.0 m wide |
| Doctor room | 3.0 m × 4.0 m |
| Dressing room | 10.0 sqm to12.0 sqm |
| Operation room/Dressing room | 12.0 sqm to 15.0 sqm |
| Componder room | 8.0 sqm to 10.0 sqm |

**Problem for practice**

1. Design a branch of State Bank of India in Aligarh having the following requirements and also draw the G.F plan, Front elevation, Section, Perspective view, site plan, and terrace plan.
   (*i*) Entrance hall = 50 sqm
   (*ii*) Asst.Manager's room with attached toilet = 15 sqm
   (*iii*) Accountant's room = 12 sqm
   (*iv*) N.R.I's room = 12 sqm
   (*v*) Computer's = 15 sqm
   (*vi*) Stationary room = 12 sqm
   (*vii*) Looker's room = 15 sqm
   (*viii*) Cash/strong room = 12 sqm
   (*ix*) Lunch room = 12 sqm
   (*x*) Pantry = 10 sqm
   (*xi*) Six counters with working space
   (*xii*) Stairs
   (*xiii*) Toilets (gents/ladies)
   (*xiv*) Parking
2. Design small clubs building for the society of elderly persons, where they can sit, talk, and walk. The size of plot is 26m × 32m facing east. The requirements of the building with sizes of room are as fallows.

   | **Particulars** | **size desired** |
   |---|---|
   | Common room having facilities- (Like magazine, paper, playing, chessboard, Carom etc.) | 10m × 12m |
   | Small kitchen with serving counter | 2.6 × 3.4m |
   | Toilets | 1.4 × 2.9m |

   Open space for walking and sitting as desired
   Draw the Plans, Front elevation, Section, Perspective, Site plan, and Terrace plan and Bird's eye view.
3. Design a post office building on a given site according to the necessary requirements. Draw the following.
   Plans (G +1 or 2)
   Front elevation
   Section through staircase
   Perspective view or Bird's eye view.
   Also draw site plans, showing gates, security Check, generator room and parking etc.

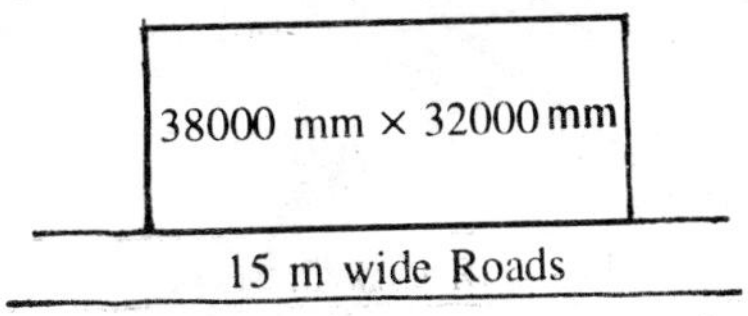


4. Plan a two storeyed collage Library for 100 students with the following requirements:
   At ground level: Staff room = 12 sqm
   Book bank section = 22 sqm
   Magazine section = 15 sqm
   Journal section = 30 sqm

| TYPE | SIZE | CILL | LNTL. | NOS |
|---|---|---|---|---|
| D1 | 1000X 2100 | | 2100 | 04 |
| D2 | 750X2100 | | 2100 | 04 |
| W1 | 1500X1200 | 900 | 2100 | 16 |
| W2 | 1000X1200 | 900 | 2100 | 16 |
| V | 600X450 | | | 06 |

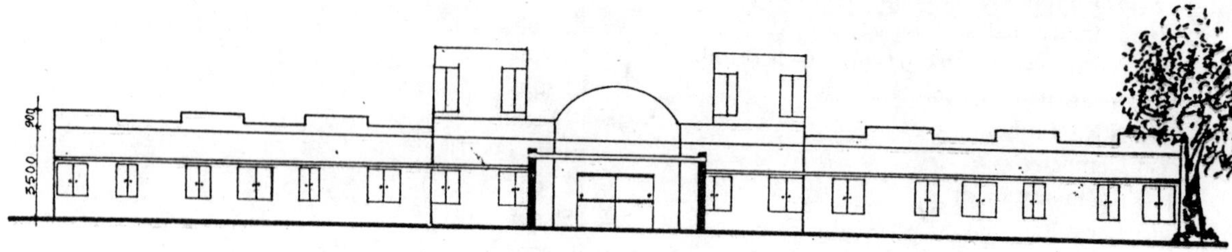


ELEVATION

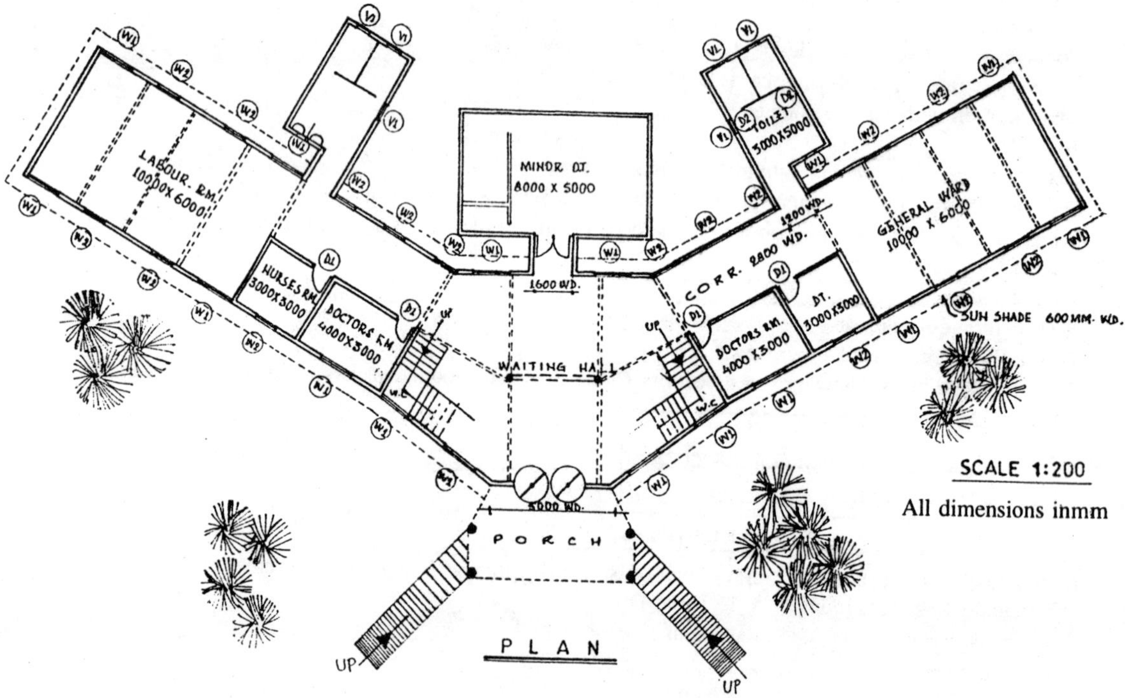


PLAN

SCALE 1:200

All dimensions inmm

**Fig. 7.10.** Primary Health Centre

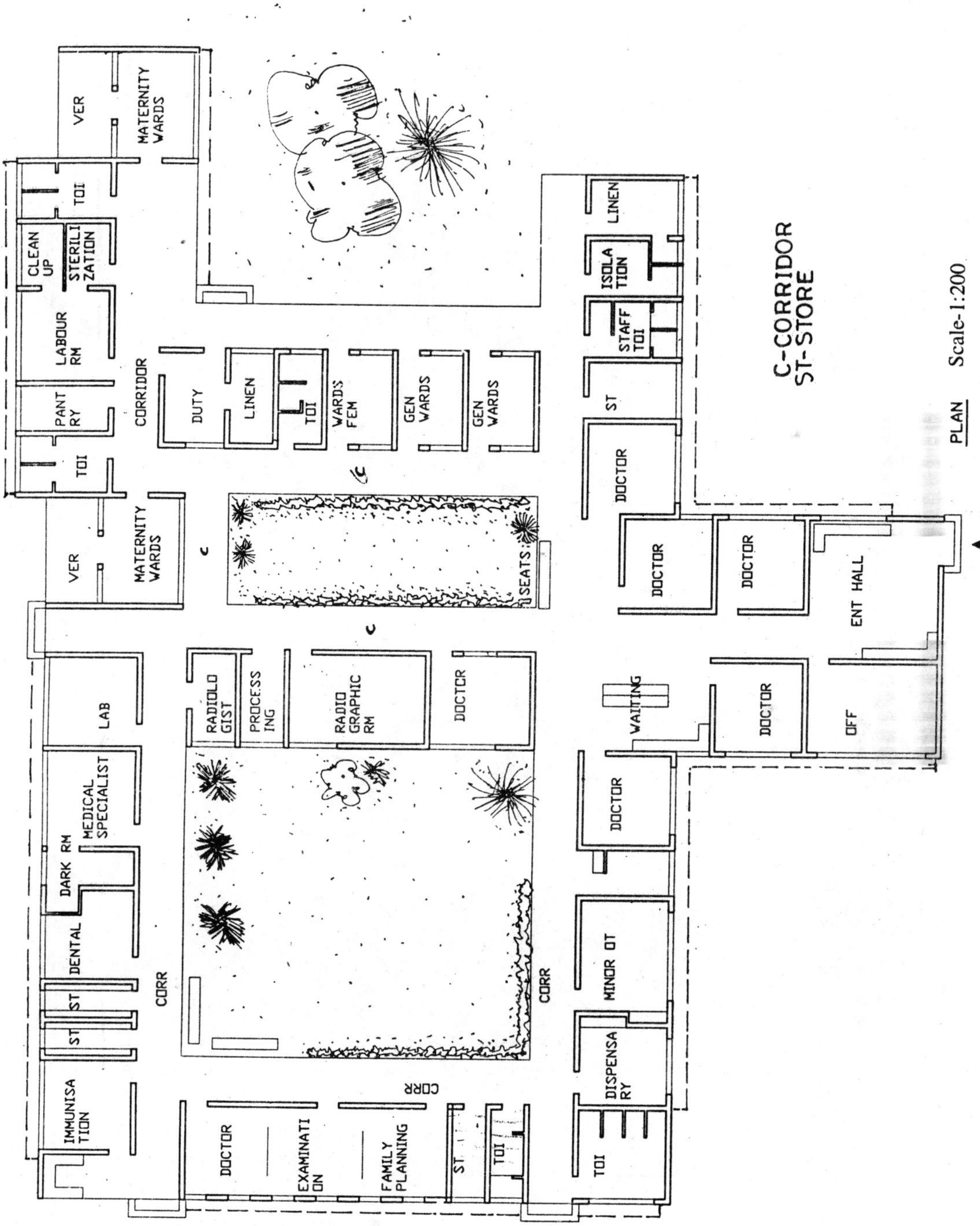


**Fig. 7.11.** Urban Health Centre

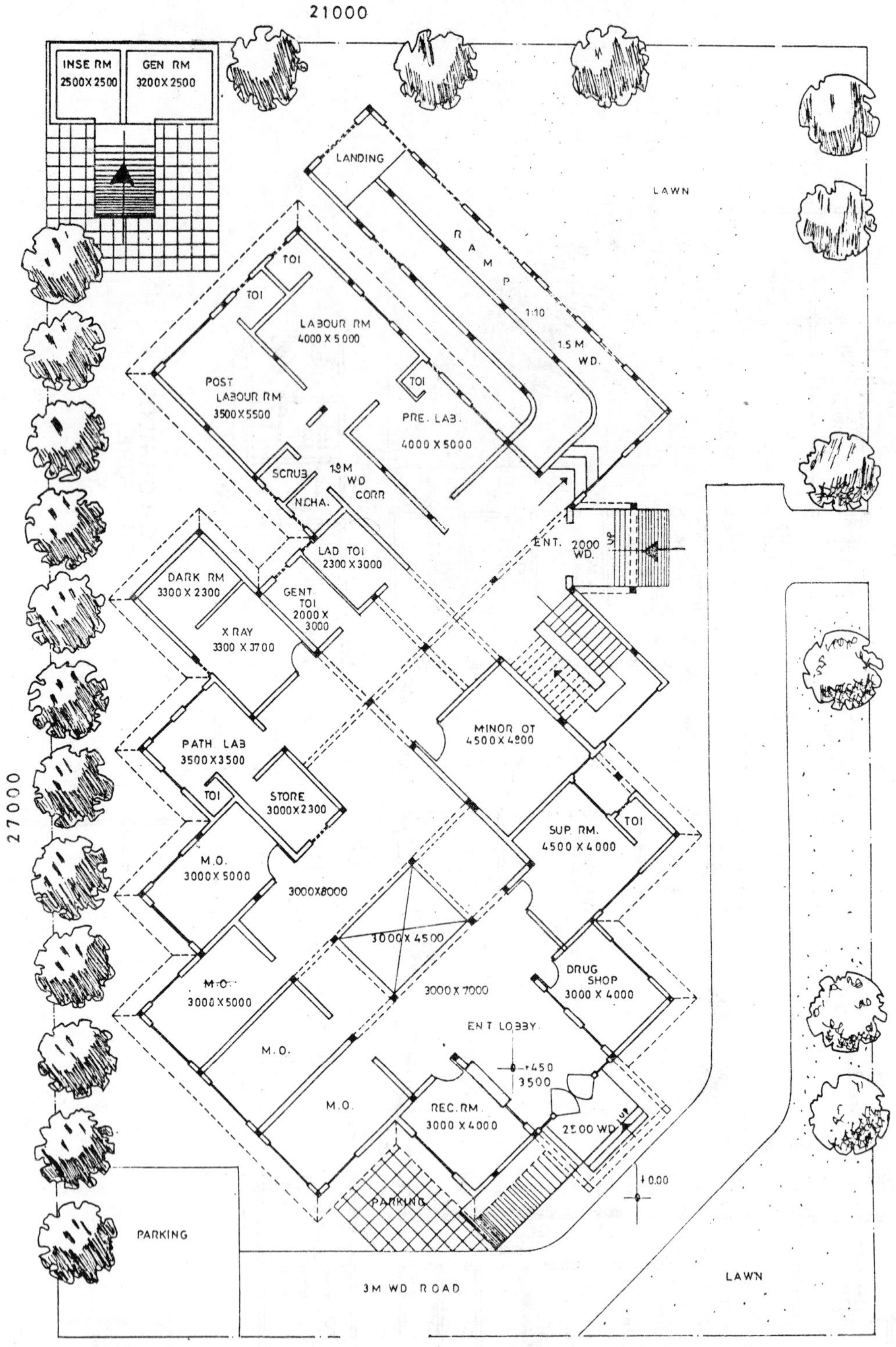


All dimensions inmm

Scale-1:100

**Fig. 7.12. Nursing Home**

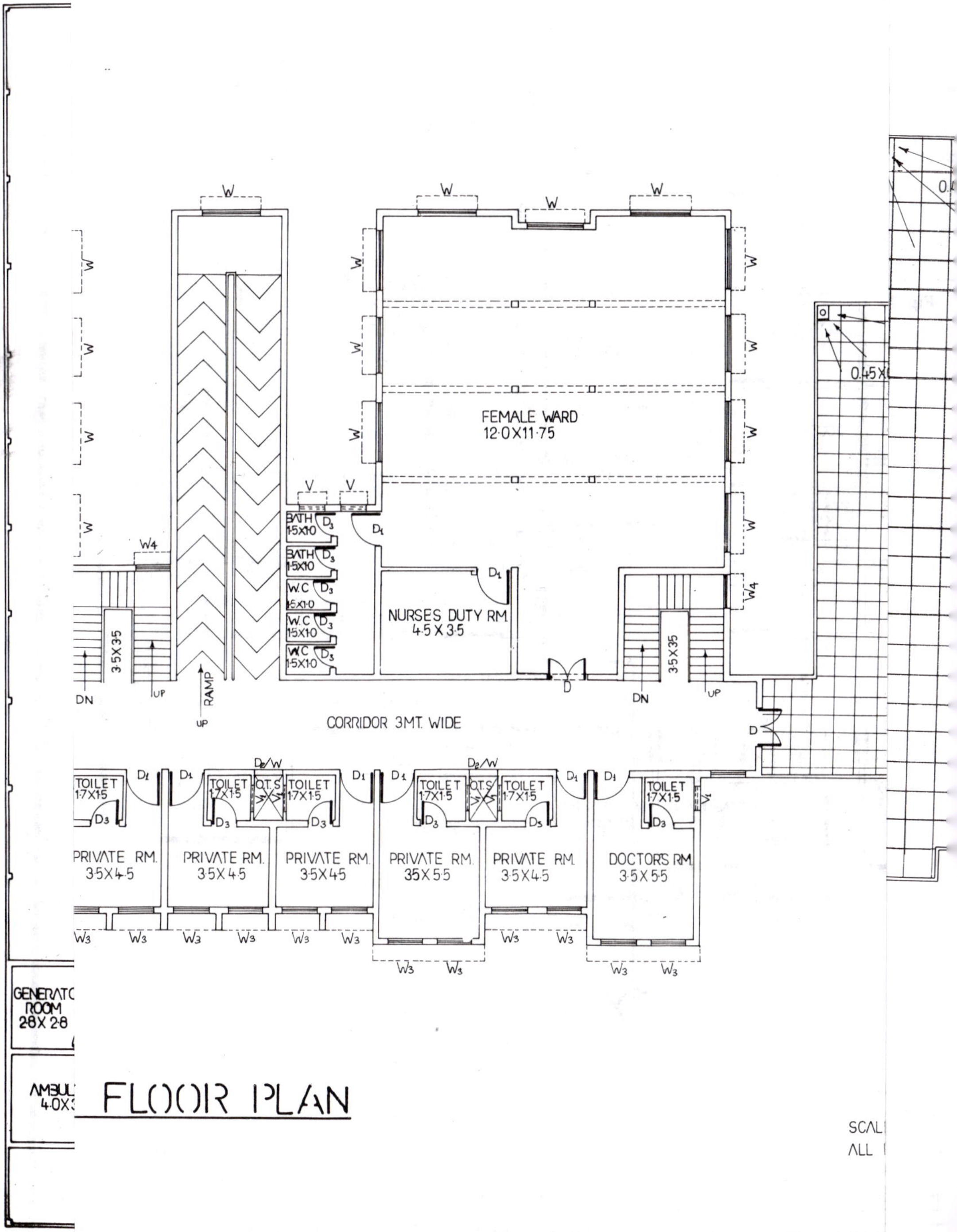
FEMALE WARD
12·0X11·75
NURSES DUTY RM.
4·5 X 3·5
BATH
1·5X1·0
W.C
1·5X1·0
RAMP
UP
DN
3·5X3·5
CORRIDOR 3MT. WIDE
TOILET
1·7X1·5
O.T.S
PRIVATE RM.
3·5X4·5
PRIVATE RM.
3·5X5·5
DOCTOR'S RM.
3·5X5·5
GENERATOR ROOM
2·8X 2·8
FLOOR PLAN

**Fig. 7.14. B.**

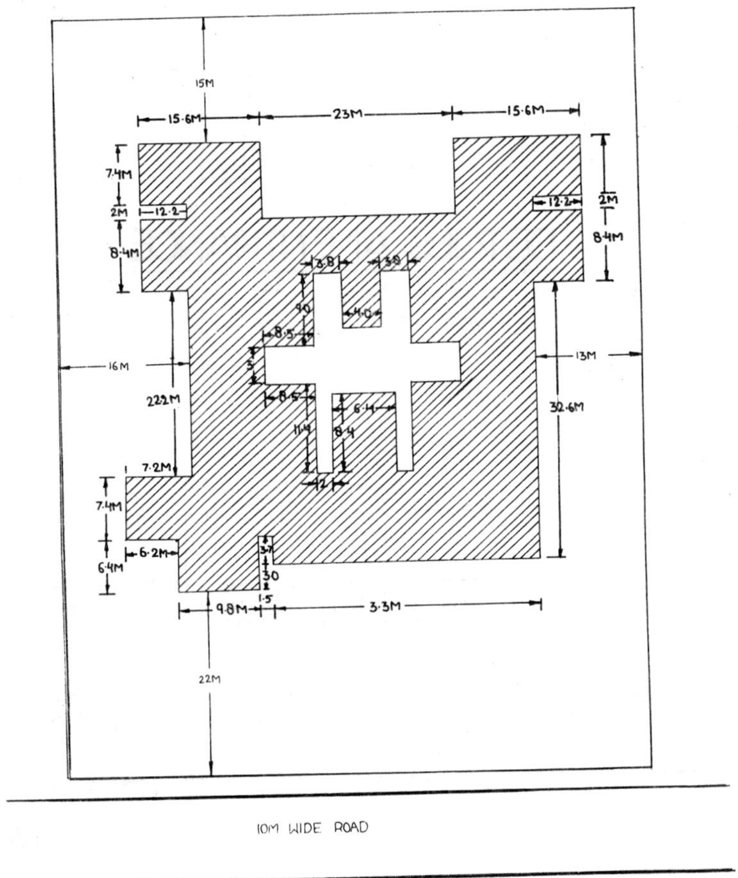


SITE PLAN

Fig. 7.15. D.

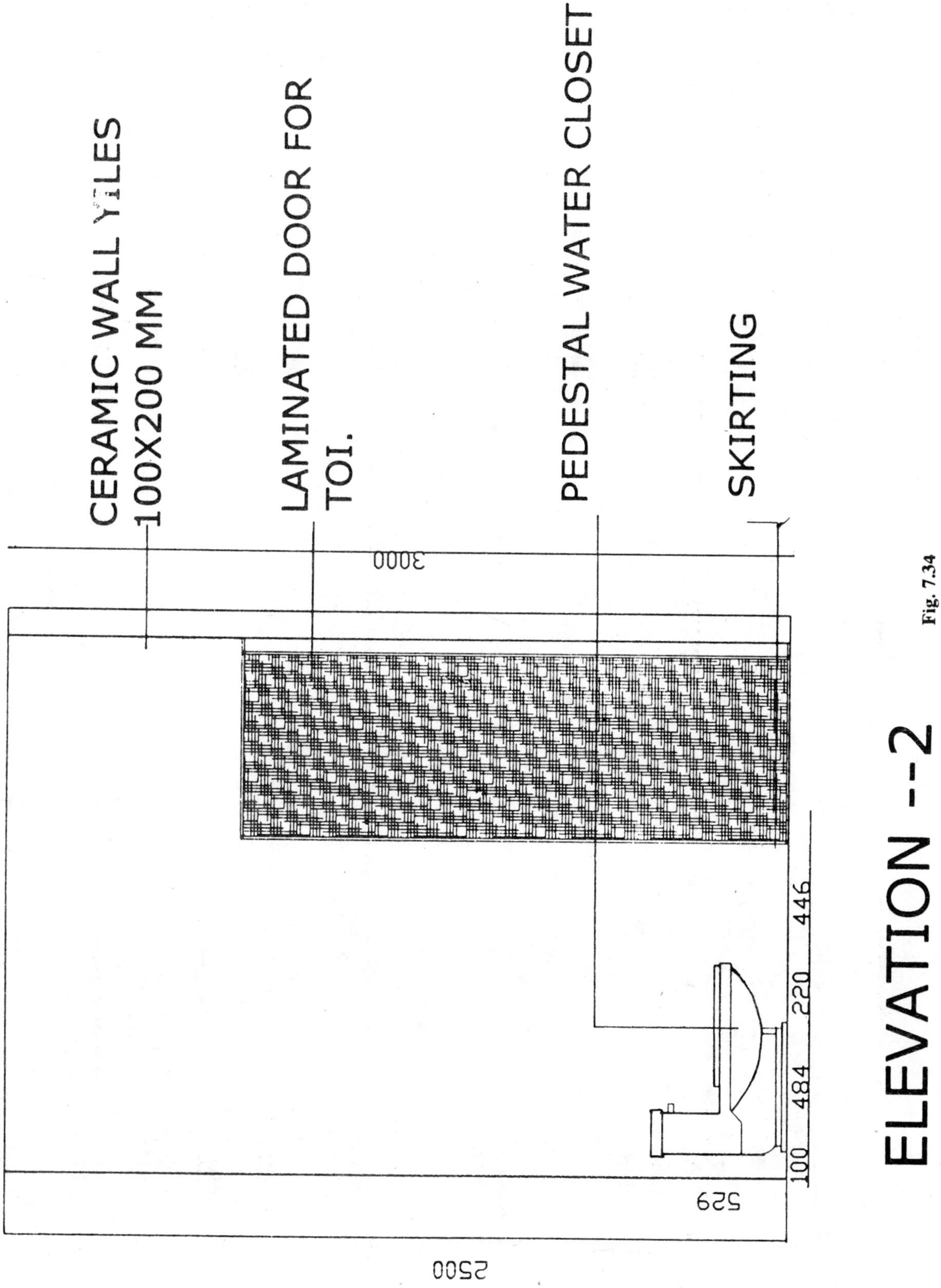
CERAMIC WALL TILES
100X200 MM
LAMINATED DOOR FOR
TOI.
PEDESTAL WATER CLOSET
SKIRTING
3000
446
220
484
100
529
2500
ELEVATION --2

Fig. 7.34

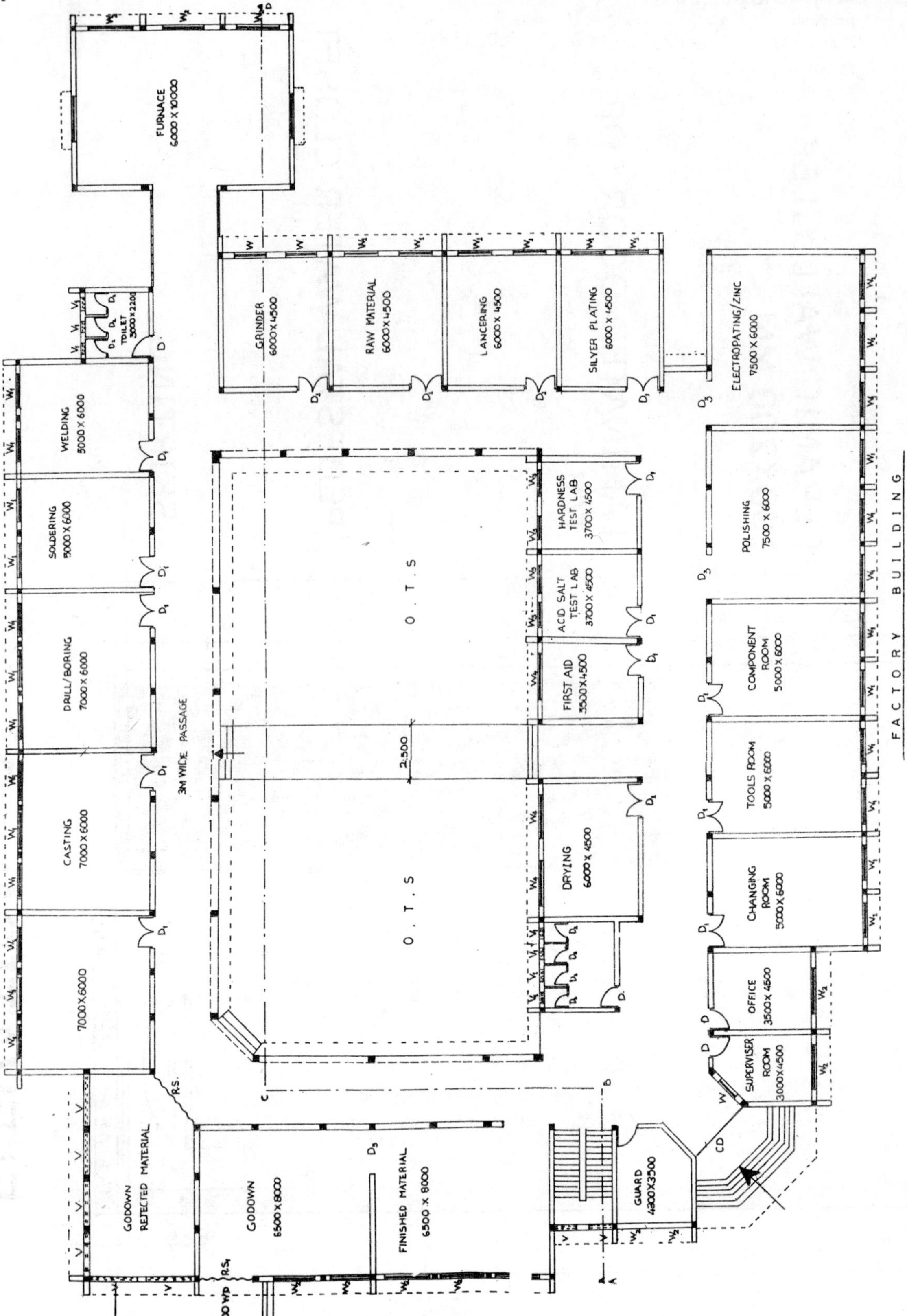
FURNACE
6000 X 10000
GRINDER
6000 X 4500
RAW MATERIAL
6000 X 4500
LANCERING
6000 X 4500
SILVER PLATING
6000 X 4500
ELECTROPATING/ZINC
7500 X 6000
TOILET
3000 X 2200
WELDING
5000 X 6000
SOLDERING
5000 X 6000
DRILL/BORING
7000 X 6000
CASTING
7000 X 6000
7000 X 6000
3M WIDE PASSAGE
O. T. S
O. T. S
2500
HARDNESS
TEST LAB
3700 X 4500
ACID SALT
TEST LAB
3700 X 4500
FIRST AID
3500 X 4500
DRYING
6000 X 4500
POLISHING
7500 X 6000
COMPONENT
ROOM
5000 X 6000
TOOLS ROOM
5000 X 6000
CHANGING
ROOM
5000 X 6000
OFFICE
3500 X 4500
SUPERVISER
ROOM
3000 X 4500
GUARD
4300 X 3500
GODOWN
REJECTED MATERIAL
GODOWN
6500 X 8000
FINISHED MATERIAL
6500 X 8000
PLATFORM
2500 WD
FACTORY BUILDING

**Fig. 7.36. F**

Librarian's room = 15 sqm
Entrance = 16 sqm
Counter space for receipt/issue of books = 28 sqm
Computer Lab = 25 sqm
Suitable Passage, staircase, lavatory, should also be provided
At First floor: Reading rooms = 30 sqm each
Books binding room = 15 sqm
Draw G.F & F.F Plans, sectional elevation and architectural elevation.

5. Draw the dimensional Plans and Elevation of a 3 story Nursing home for 25 beds with the following requirements.
   (*i*) Four numbers consulting room = 15 sqm each attached with w.c
   (*ii*) Waiting room = 20 sqm
   (*iii*) X-ray room = 17 sqm
   (*iv*) Pathology labs = 12 sqm
   (*v*) Two Operation Theatre = 25 sqm each
   (*vi*) Labor room = 12 sqm
   (*vii*) Instrument room = 10 sqm
   (*viii*) Nurses room = 14 sqm attached w.c
   (*ix*) Store = 10 sqm
   (*x*) Generator room = 6 sqm
   (*xi*) 4 Gernal ward for 5 beds each = 32 sqm
   (*xii*) 5 Special room with attached toilets = 15 sqm
   (*xiii*) Reception counter = 5 sqm
   (*xiv*) Medical Labirary = 15 sqm
   (*xv*) General toilets with 2 bath, 4 w.c, 2 urinals and 2 washbasins,
   (*xvi*) Medical store = 8 sqm
6. Design and Draw in double line plan of a canteen over the open land in university campus.. Also draw front elevation and detailed section. Assume all data at yours ends

# 8

# Structural detailing And Design

## 8.1. R C SLAB

**One way slab.** Slabs supported on two sides and bending take place in one direction only is said to span in one direction or one way slab. (Fig. 8.1, 8.2)

**Two way slab.** Slabs supported on all four sides and bending take place in two directions are said to span in two directions or two way slab.

**Continuous slab.** Slabs supported on three or more support in line are known as continuous slab. (Fig 8.5)

**Restrained slab.** The corners of slab is restrained by providing extra steel at corners, which require less depth and steel along their edges. (Fig. 8.3, 8.3A, 8.3B)

**Un restrained slab.** The corners of slab is not restrained by providing extra steel at the corners, in this slab more depth and steel is required as compared to held down slab. (Fig. 8.4, 8.4A, 8.4B)

**Effective span is the lesser of two specific spans.**

(*a*) Centre to centre distance between two supports

(*b*) Clear span + effective depth

**Thickness criteria**

Minimum thickness or depth span ratio of as fallows

| | |
|---|---|
| Simply supported Slabs. | Slab spanning in one direction (One way slab) 1/20 |
| | Slab spanning in two directions (two way slab) 1/26 of shorter direction. |
| Continuous Slabs. | Slab spanning in one direction 1/26 |
| Continuous Slabs. | Slab spanning in two directions 1/32 of shorter side |
| Cantilever Slab 1/7 | |

**Maximum spacing of bar (which ever is less)**

Main bars not more than 3 times effective depth or 300 mm

Distribution bars not more than 5 times effective depth or 450 mm

**Bar diameter (minimum)**

Main bars must not be smaller than 8 mm in diameter

Distribution bars must not be less 8 mm in diameter

Top bars can be supported by Z shape stools or chairs

Maximum bar diameter. The bar diameter used in slab shall not exceed 1/8 of the total thickness of slab.

**Embedded pipe in slab**

The maximum diameter of pipe must not exceed one third of slab thickness and

Should be placed in lower half of slab

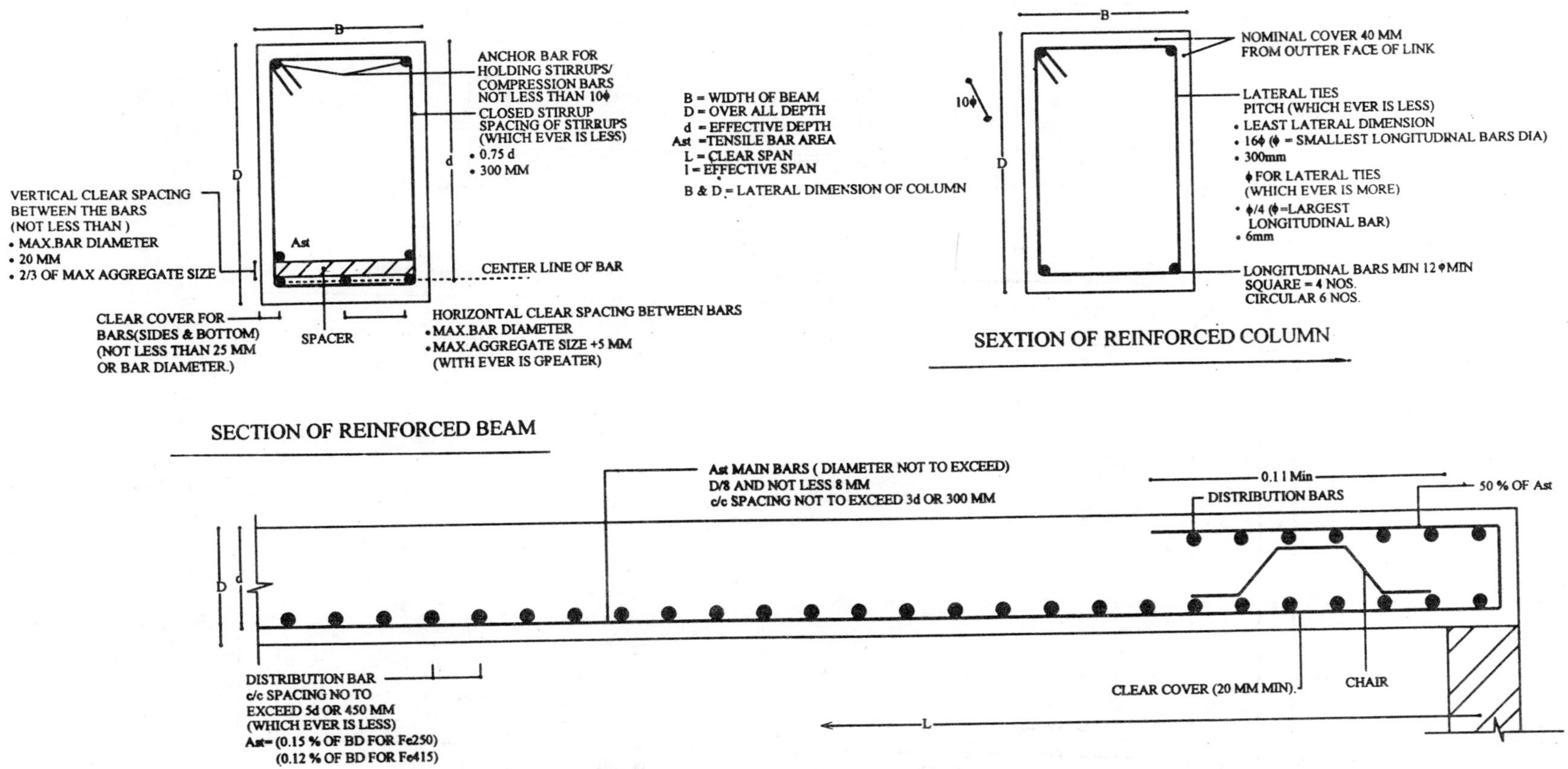


**Fig. 8.1.** Section of One-Way slab

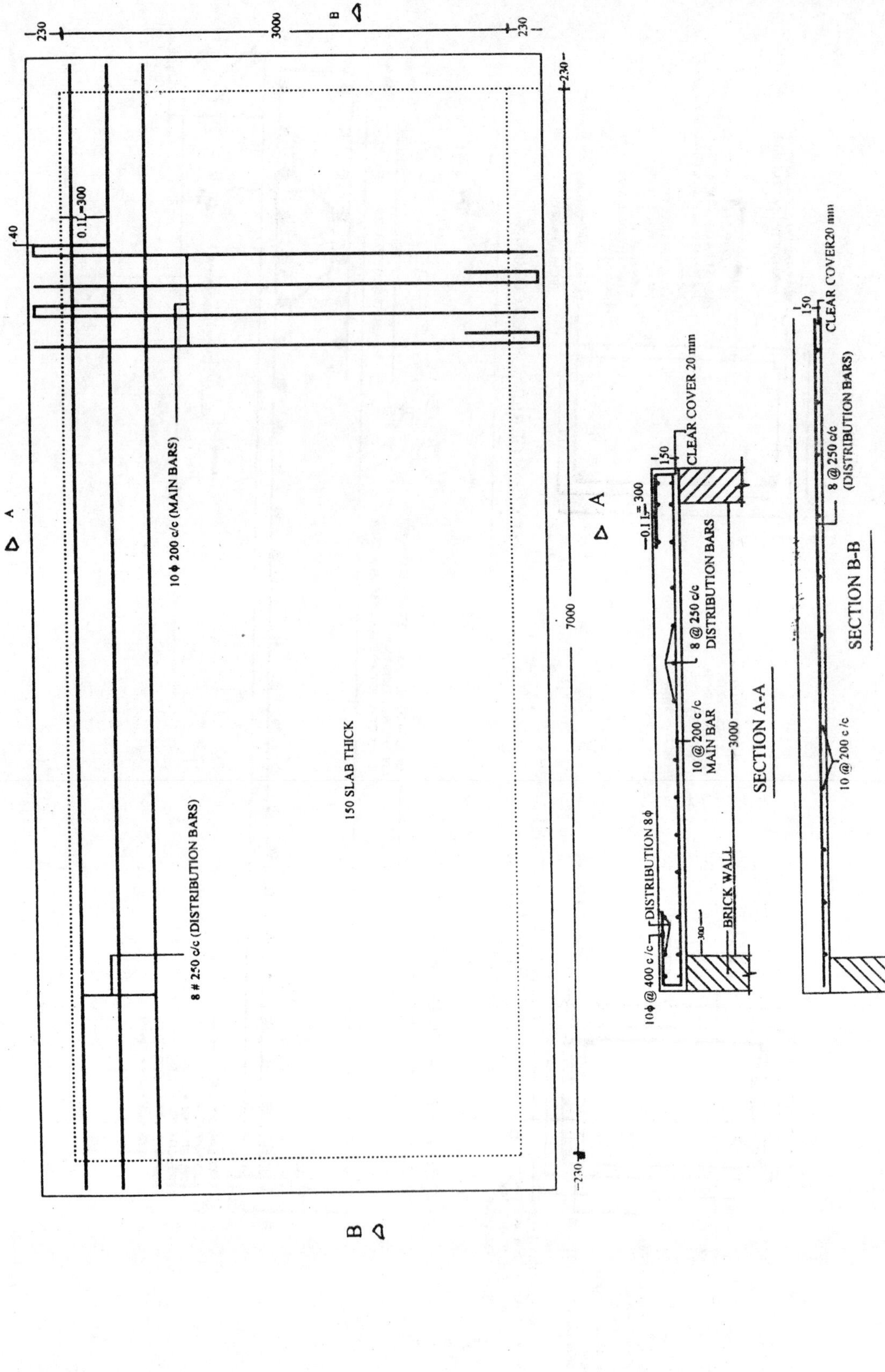


**Fig. 8.2 A.** Reinforcement Plan One Way slab

# ONE WAY SLAB

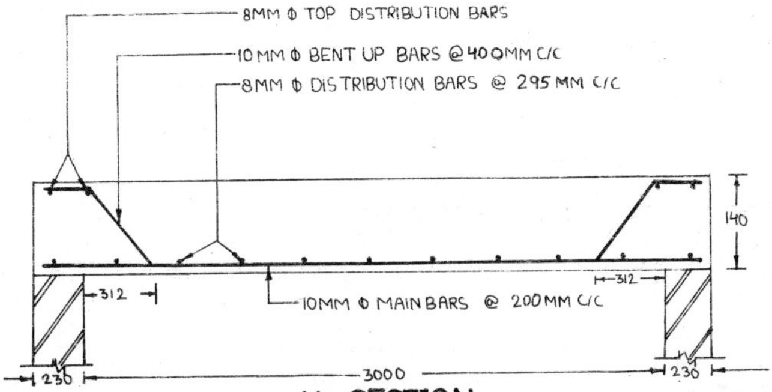


## X SECTION

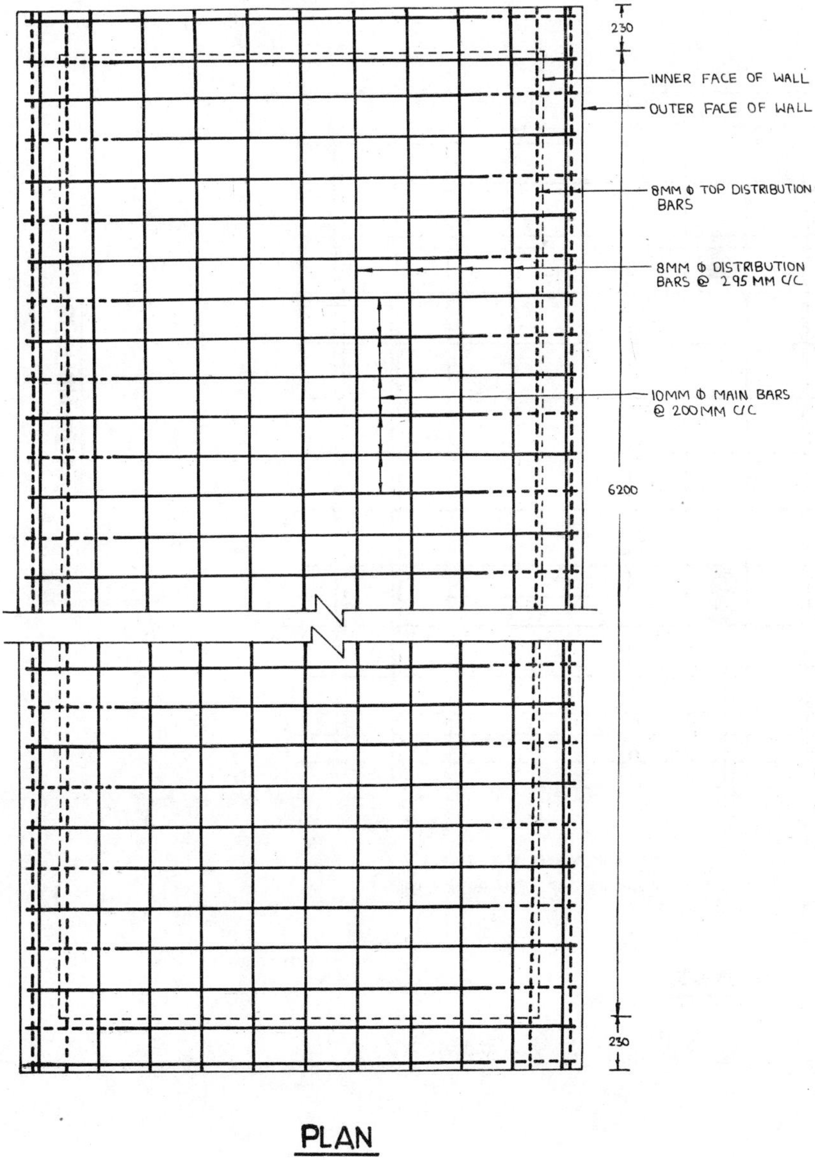


## PLAN

**Fig. 8.2 B.**

# TWO WAY SLAB

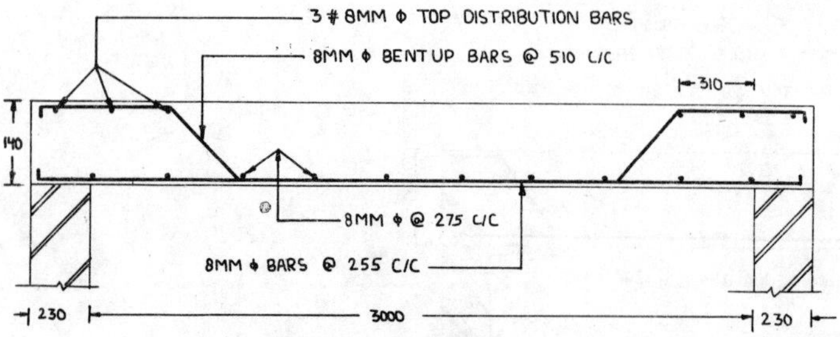


**SECTION AT XX**

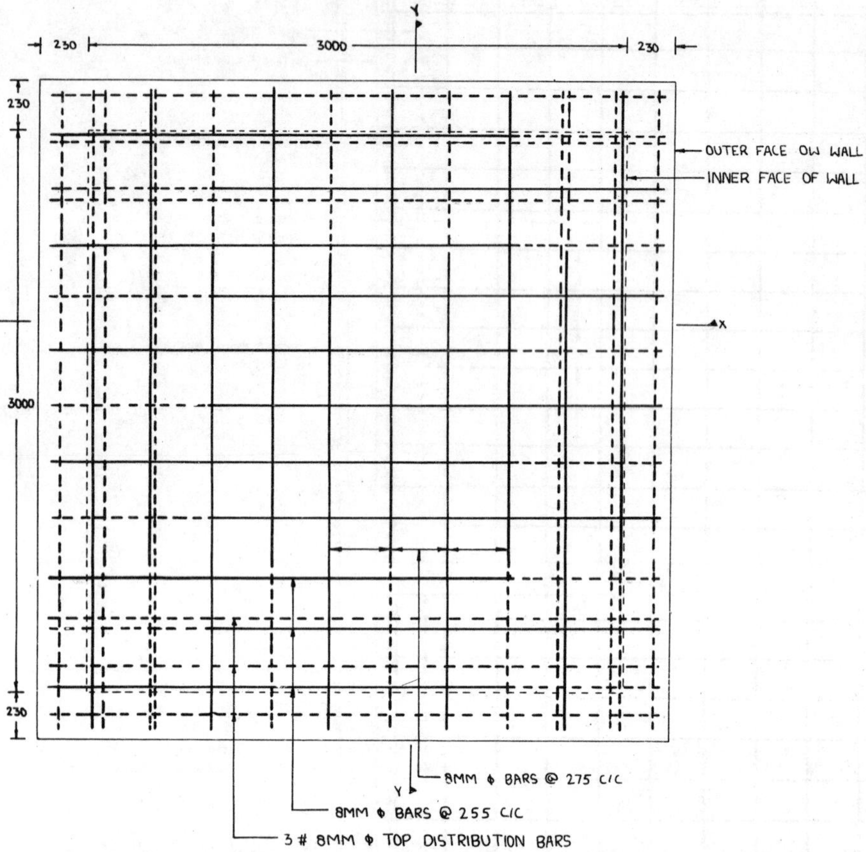


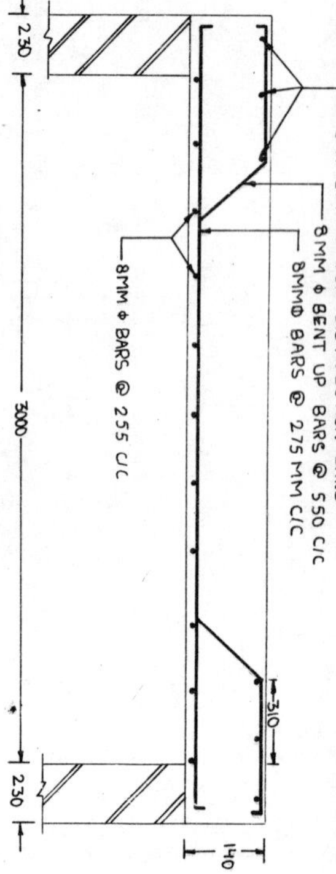


**SECTION AT YY**

**PLAN**

**8.3. A.**

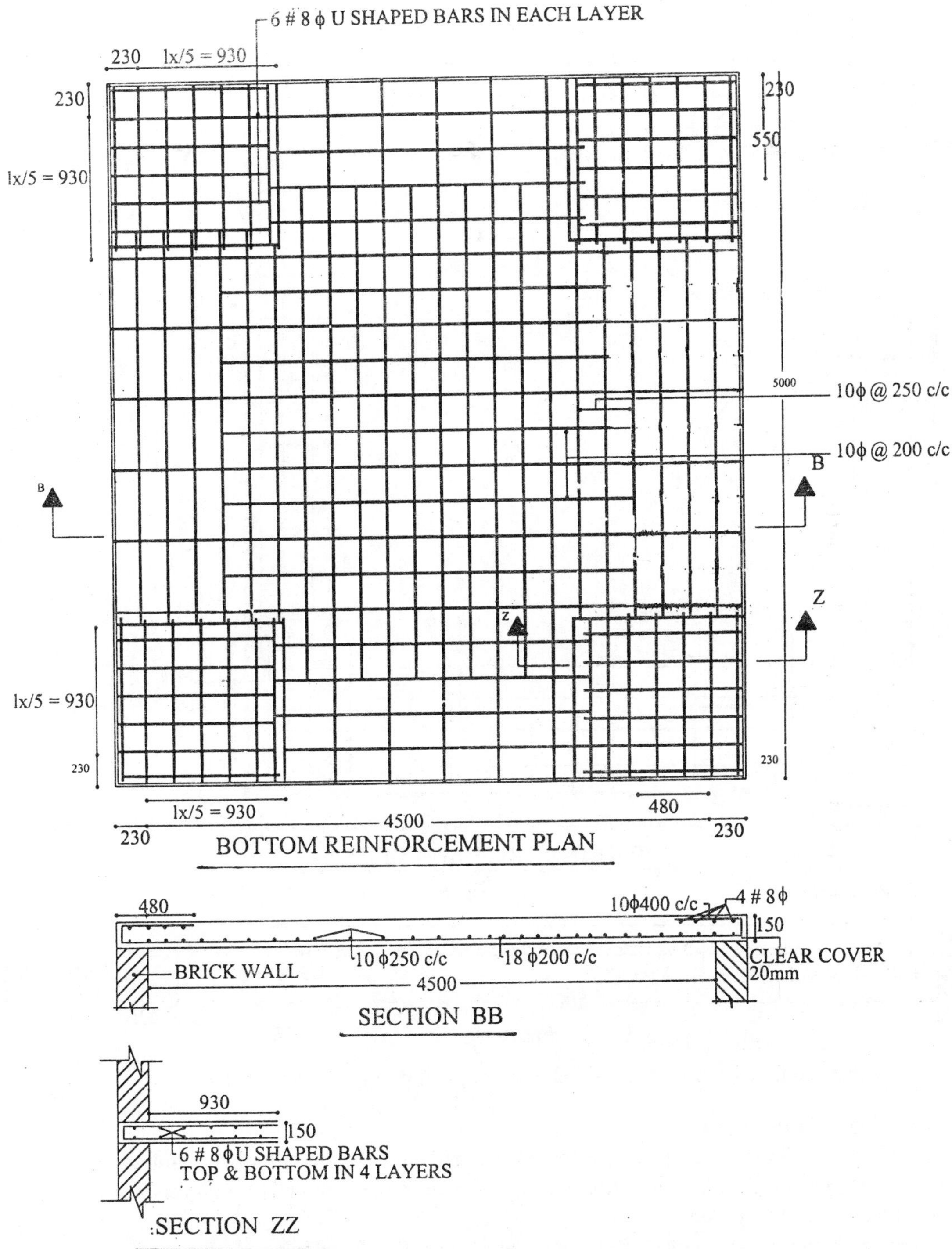


**Fig. 8.3 B. R.C.** Two-Way slab with corners Restrained

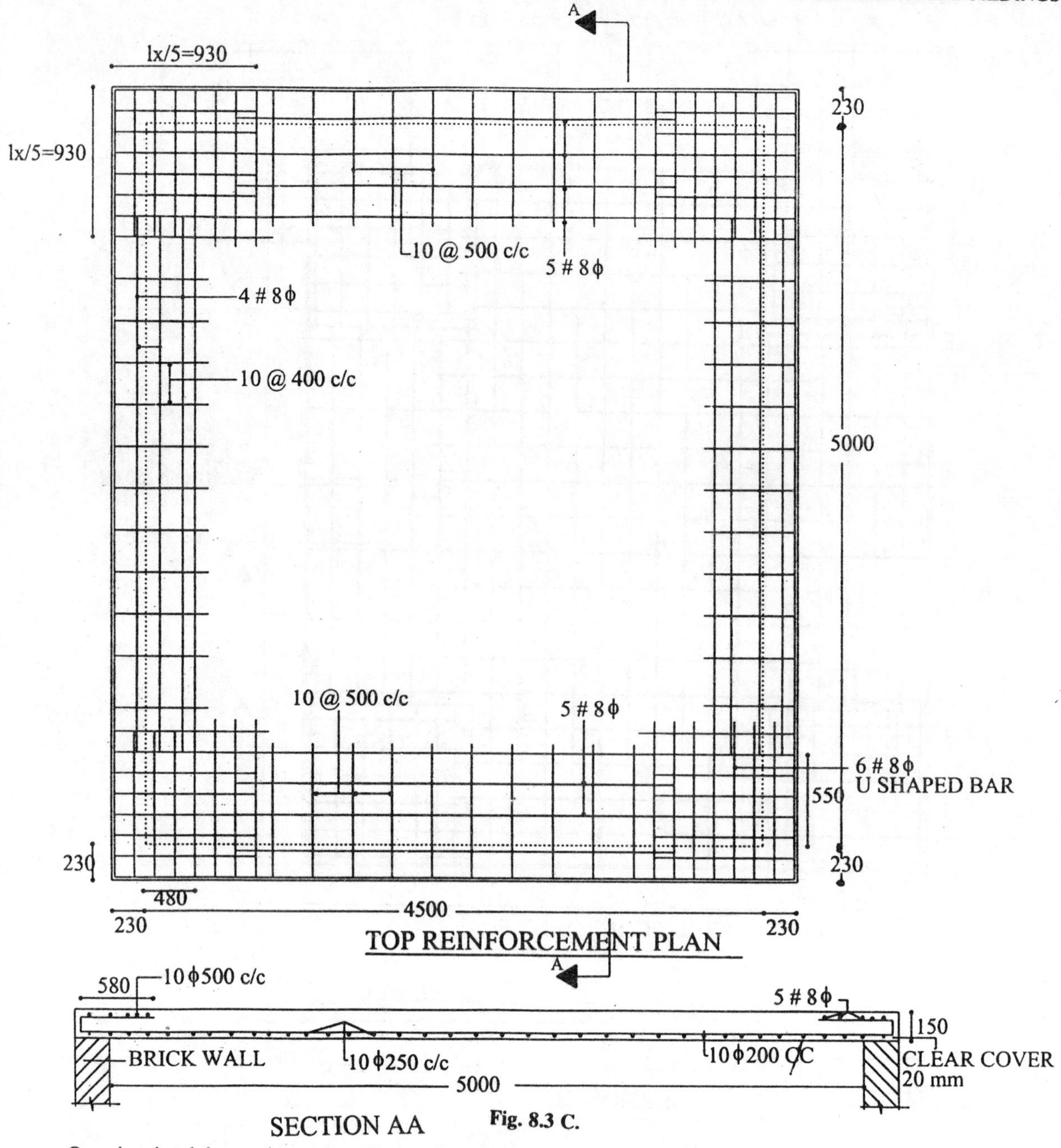


Fig. 8.3 C.

Opening in slab requires extra diagonal steel across opening to prevent cracking.

**Reinforcement and its placement**

Bars in the shorter direction are placed at the bottom and are called longitudinal main bars.

Bars in the longer direction are placed at the top of bottom bars are called transverse or distribution bars (or main bars in two way slab).

Minimum cross sectional area of steel in either direction is 0.12% of BD.

Showing number, size spacing and mark of bars

Clearly specify whether bars are in bottom or top of slab

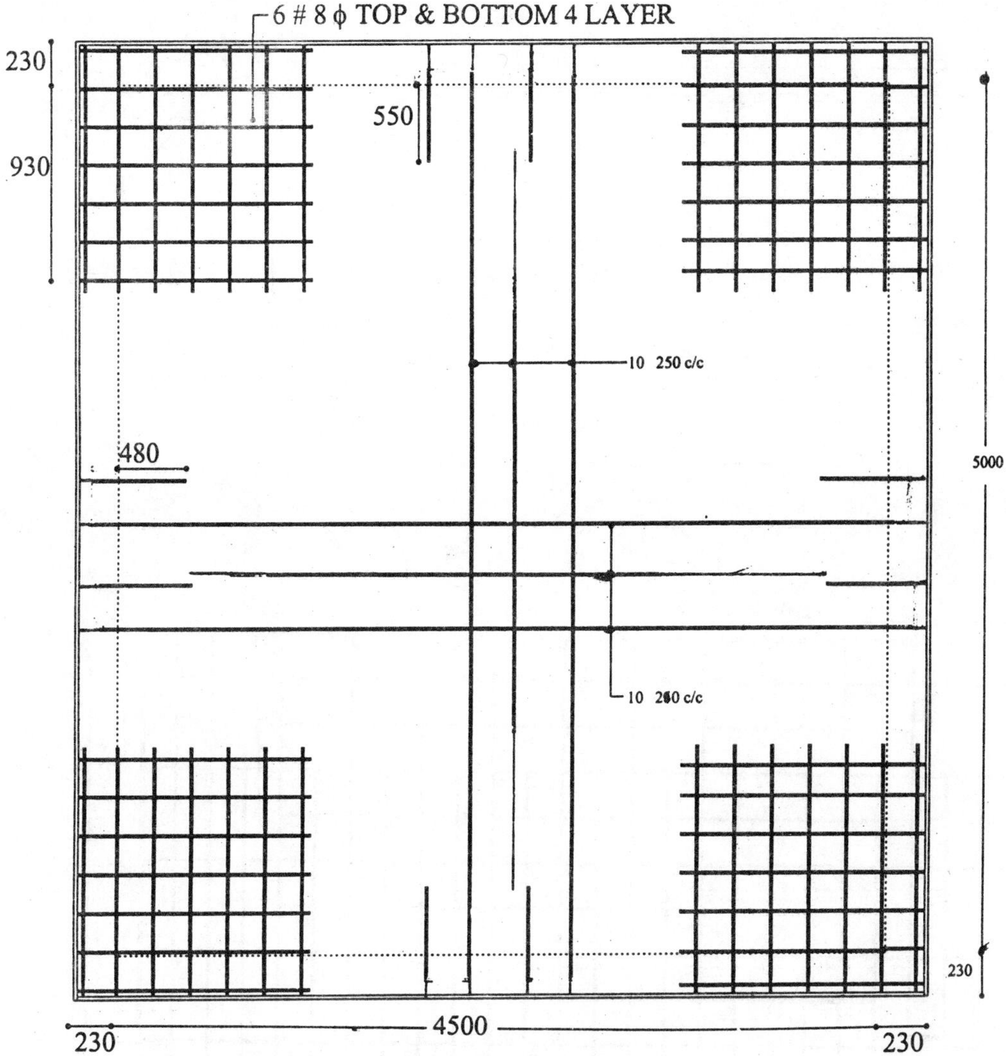


**Fig. 8.3 D.** Reinforcement Plan

Minimum two bars to full length should be draw in plan

**Sectional elevation**

*These should show*

Thickness of slab

Clear distance between face of supporting beams and width of such beams

Types and thickness of finish

Shape of each different bar

Shape and position of bends

Clear covers (side, bottom and top) *i.e.* 20 mm

Bars mark

Position of curtail points

**Economical Considerations**

This can be achieved by

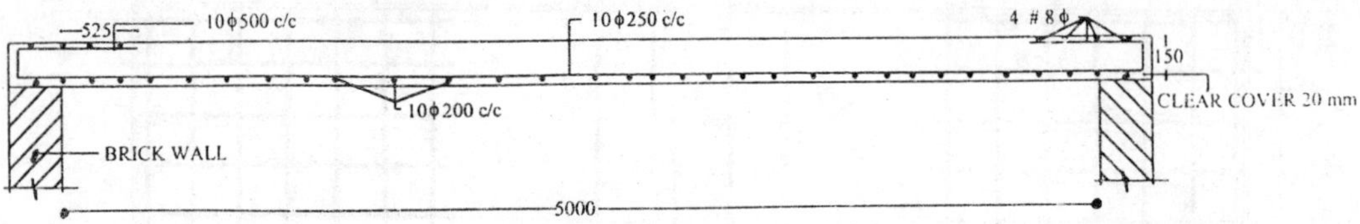


SECTION BB

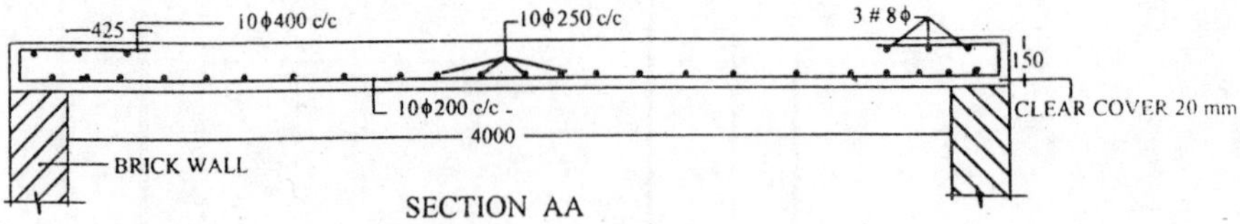


SECTION AA

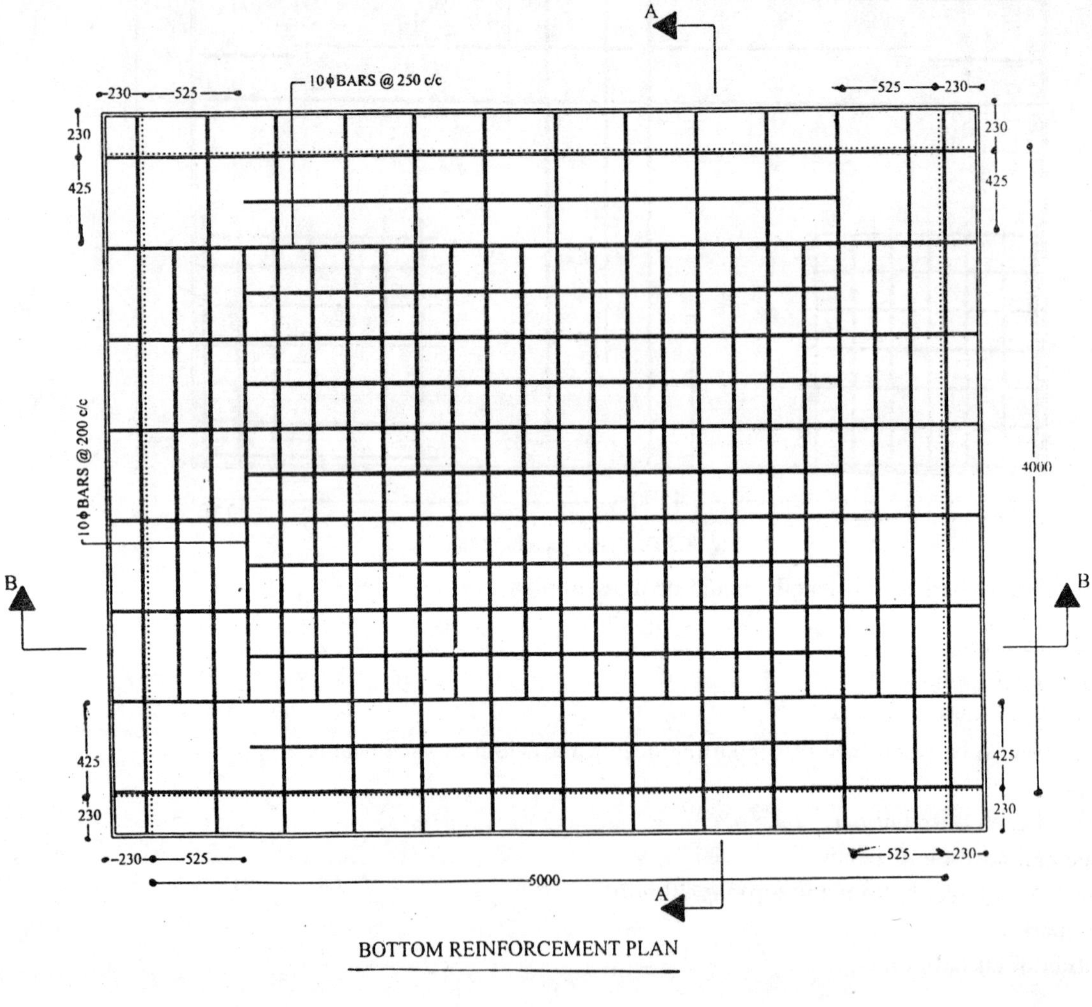


BOTTOM REINFORCEMENT PLAN

**Fig. 8.4 A.** R.C. Two way Slab with Corners Unrestrained

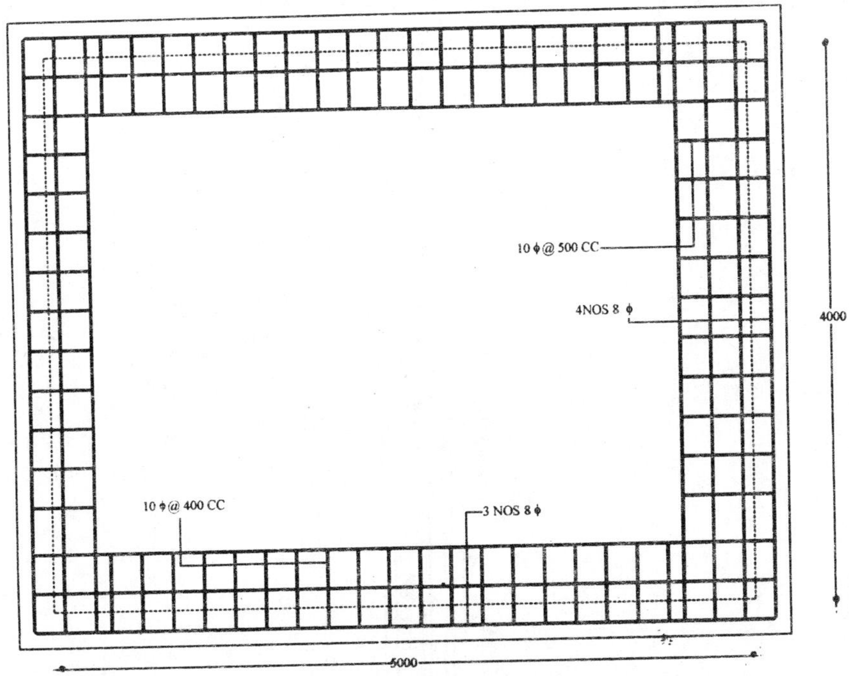


**Fig. 8.4 A.** Top Reinforcement Plan

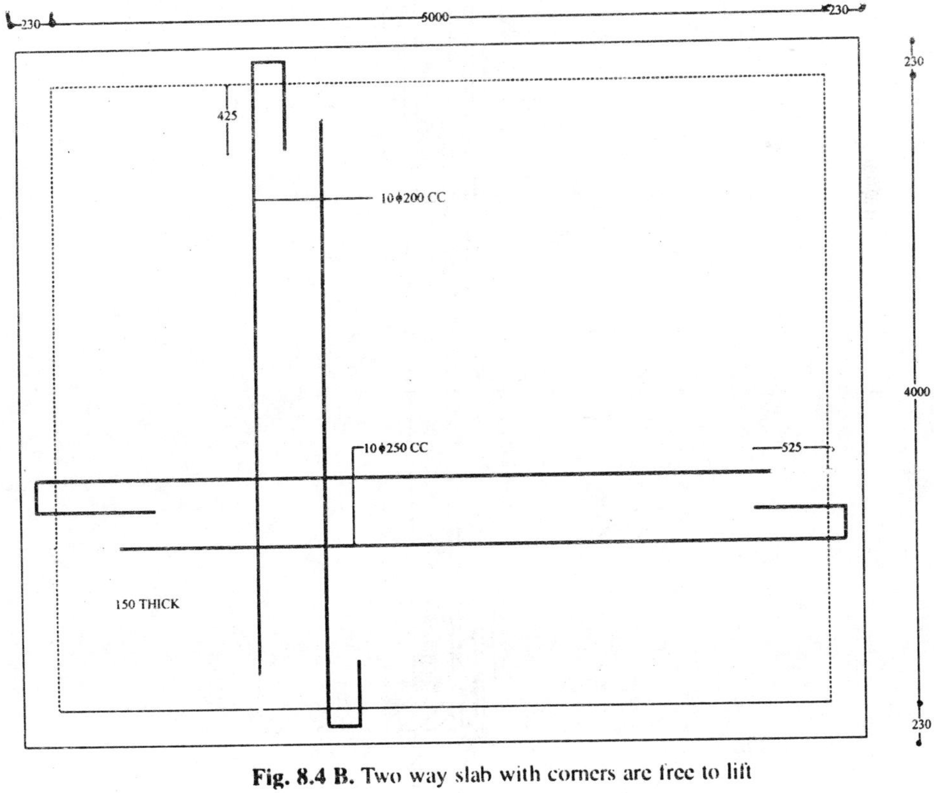


**Fig. 8.4 B.** Two way slab with corners are free to lift

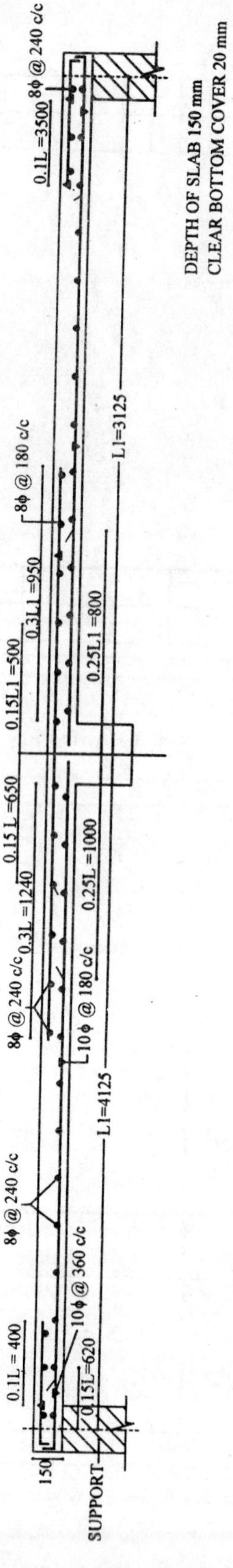


**Fig. 8.5.** L-Section of one way continous slab shorter direction (Using Straight Bars)

Reducing column or wall spacing
Spanning main beams in shorter direction
Making end spans shorter

## 8.2. BEAMS

Beams are generally used to transfer floor loads to columns and are carrying transverse loading.

### Types of beams

(*a*) According to shape. Rectangular, T and L, Haunches, cranked, circular etc

(*b*) According to supporting conditions. Simply supported, fixed, continuous and cantilever beams

(*c*) According to reinforcement. Singly reinforced and doubly reinforced

**Singly reinforced.** The beam is reinforced in tensile zone only. (Fig. 8.6, 8.6A)

**Doubly reinforced.** The beam cross section is limited and reinforced in both tension and compression zone. (Fig. 8.7, 8.8)

T &L beams-When beam and slab are cast monolithically, the effective part of the slab extends equally on both the sides of the beams its shape become like T and hence called T beam (Fig. 8.9, 8.10). If slab extends only on one side of the rib of the beam is known as L beam.They are detailed in the same manner as rectangular beams but some times special shape stirrups may be provided. (Fig. 8.11)

**Continuous beams.** This beams is supported at three or more supports. In this beam compression steel is also provided at supports as in doubly reinforced beam.

**Haunches beam.** The haunches beams are providing for heavy loads. The haunch to be between1/10 of beam length having slope approx 1:3. (Fig. 8.15)

### Size of beam

Satisfy certain depth/span ratio and depth and width ratio

Rough guide for thickness of beam-Span to overall depth ratio of 10 to 15 are generally found to be economical. The overall depth to width ratio in rectangular beam section should be in the range of 1.5 to 2.

### Arrangement of bars

Minimum cover must satisfy *i.e.* 25mm or shall not be less than the larger diameter of bar for all steel reinforcement including links.

Horizontal and vertical spacing must satisfy

If different bar diameters are used then the larger diameter bars must be placed in:

(*i*) single row-Placed on out side

(*ii*) For two or more row-Placed in lower row

### Reinforcement

**Longitudinal reinforcement.** At least two bars of 12mm diameter shall be provided at the support for resisting tensile stresses in the beam.

**Vertical reinforcement.** Can be achieved by providing vertical stirrups in two legged four legged or multiple legged systems and their spacing should be governed by shear force diagram. Maximum spacing must not exceed two-third the effective depth of beam or 300mm which ever is less and minimum spacing of stirrups shall be consider 100mm for practical purpose.

**Termination of bars.** Theoretical cut-off position determined from bending moment diagram and 50% of bottom bars to be carried through to the supports.

**Provision of holes.** Holes shall not be provided in high stress zones of beams and preferable placed in the middle depth of beam but up to 25mm diameter hole can be positioned any where in the beam.

**Side face reinforcement.** If the depth of the web in a beam exceeds 750 mm than side face reinforcement shall be provided along the two sided of the beam.

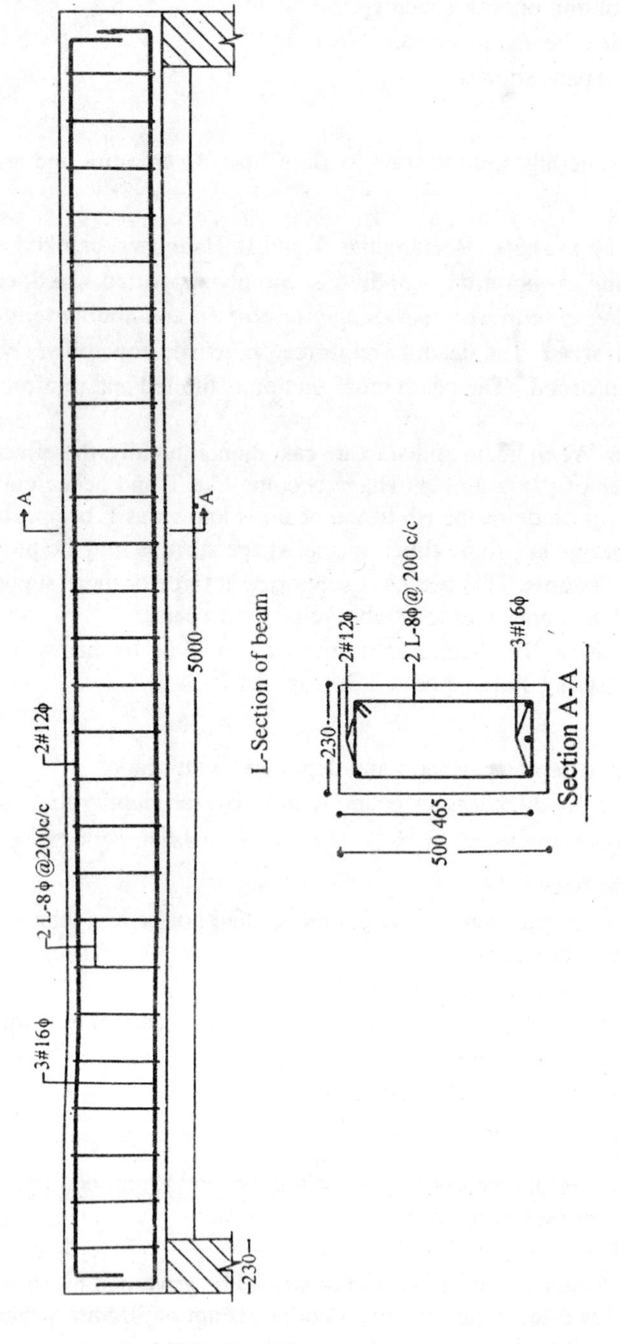


**Fig. 8.6.** Singly Reinforced beam

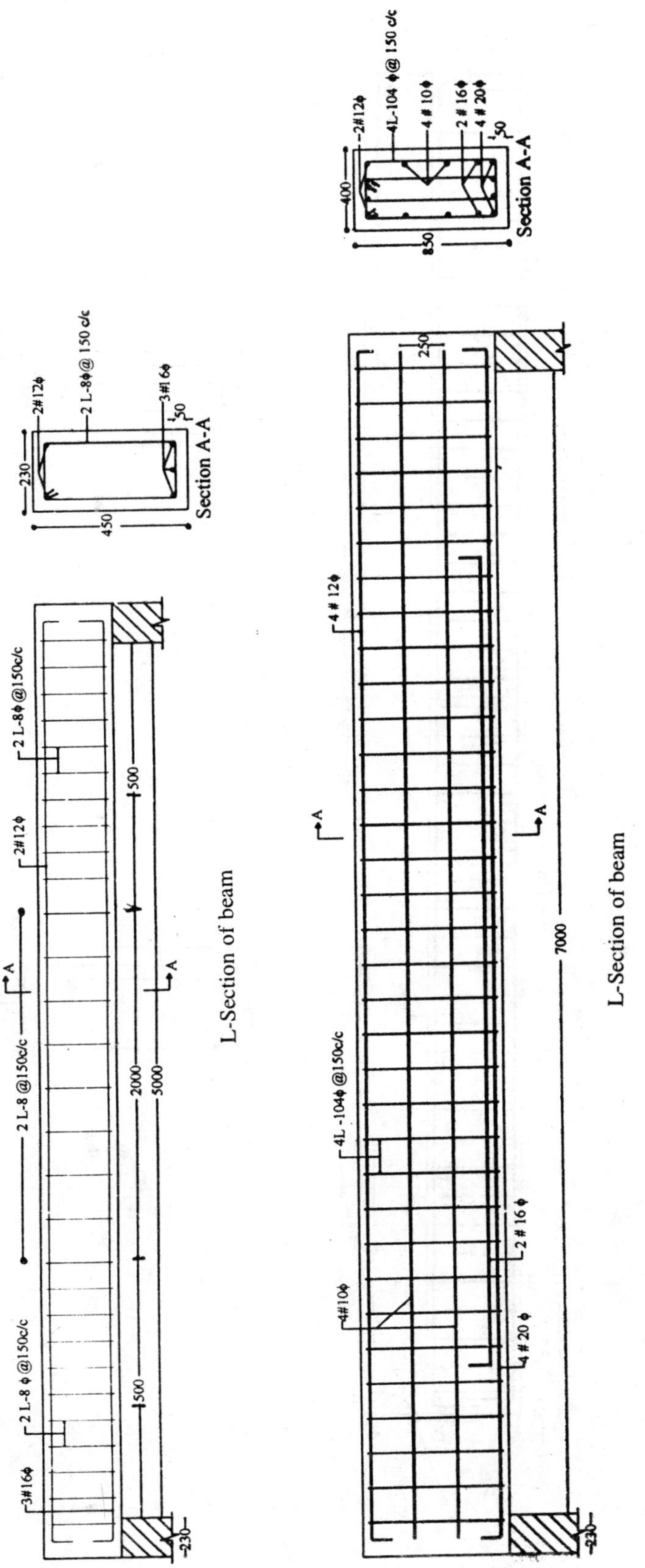


Fig. 8.6 A. Singly Reinforced beam

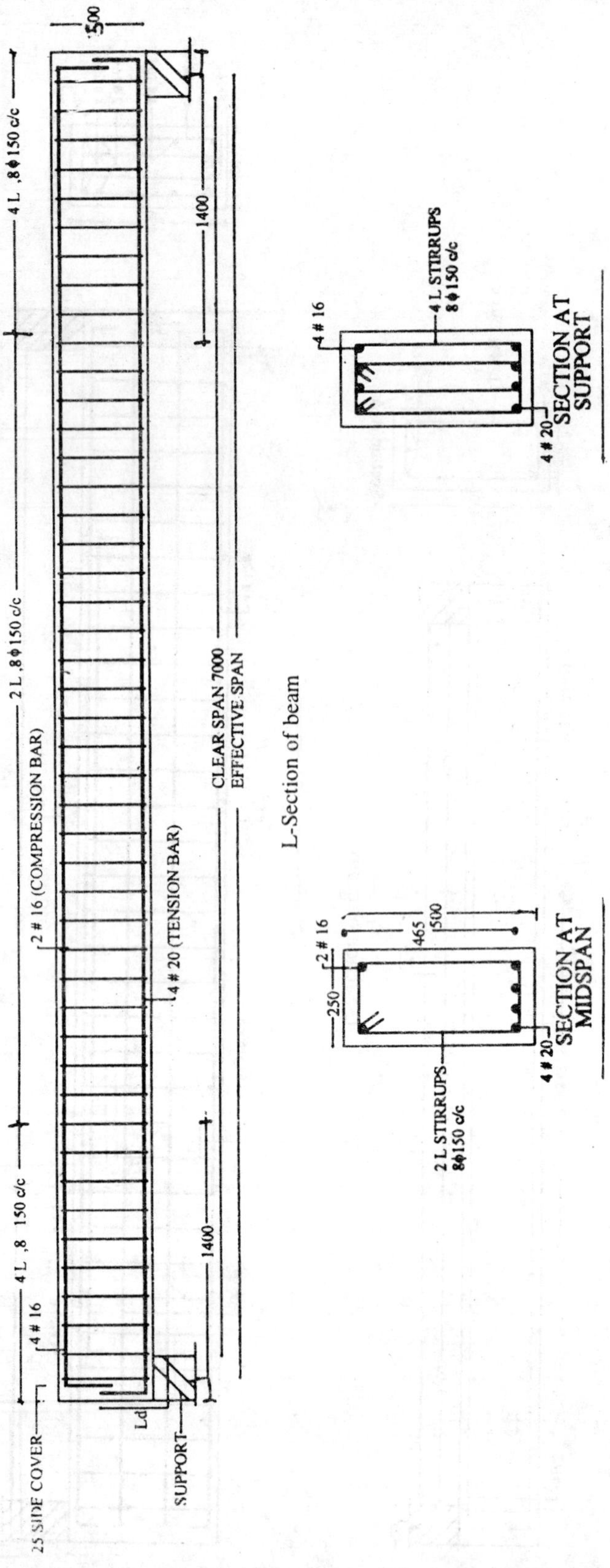


**Fig. 8.7**. Doubly Reinforcement beam

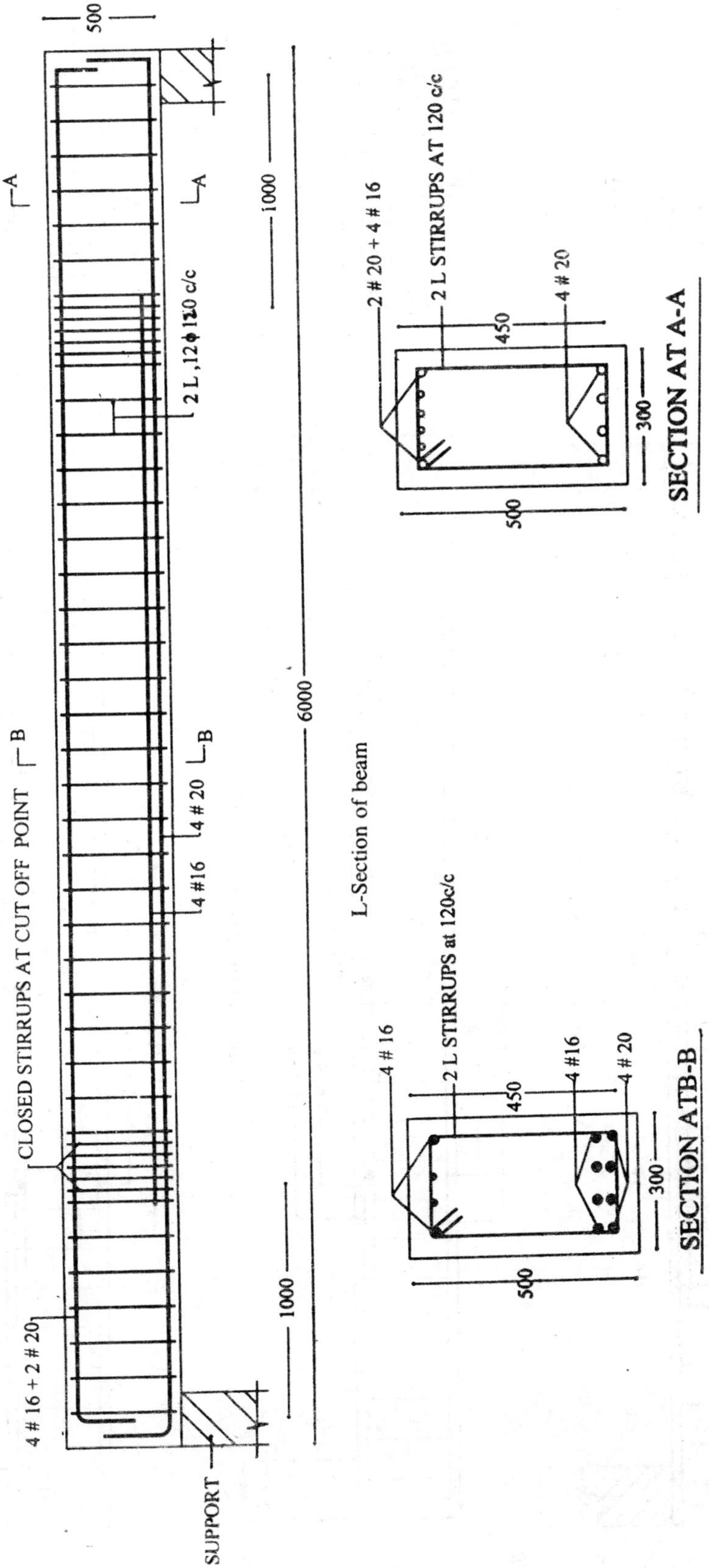


**Fig. 8.8.** Doubly Reinforced beam

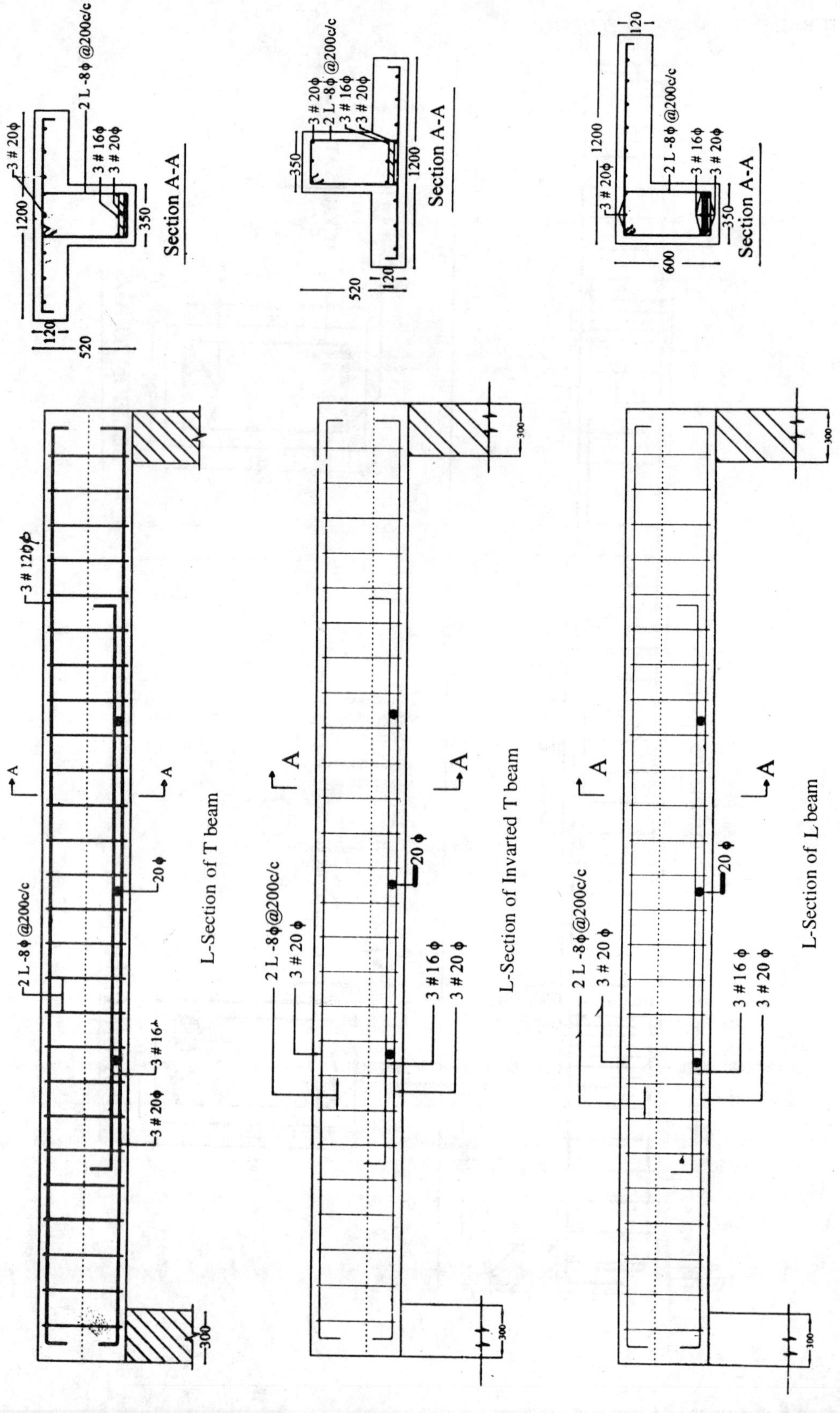


**Fig. 8.9.** T-Beam, **Fig. 8.10.** Inverted T-Beam, **Fig. 8.11.** L-Beam

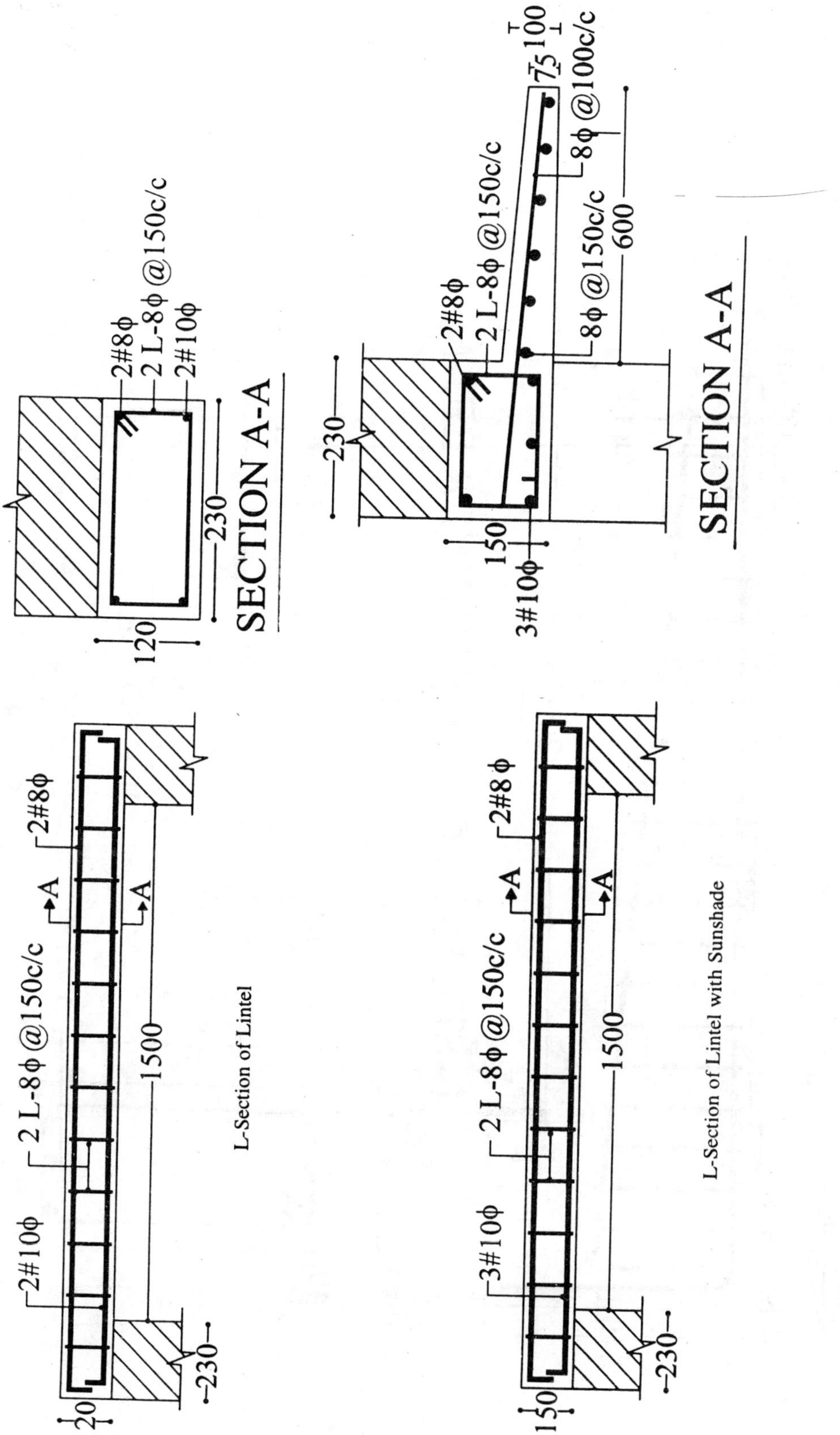
2#8ϕ
2 L-8ϕ @150c/c
2#10ϕ
120
230
SECTION A-A
230
150
3#10ϕ
2#8ϕ
2 L-8ϕ @150c/c
8ϕ @150c/c
8ϕ @100c/c
75
100
600
SECTION A-A
2#10ϕ
2 L-8ϕ @150c/c
2#8ϕ
A
A
1500
120
230
L-Section of Lintel
3#10ϕ
2 L-8ϕ @150c/c
2#8 ϕ
A
A
1500
150
230
L-Section of Lintel with Sunshade

Fig. 8.12

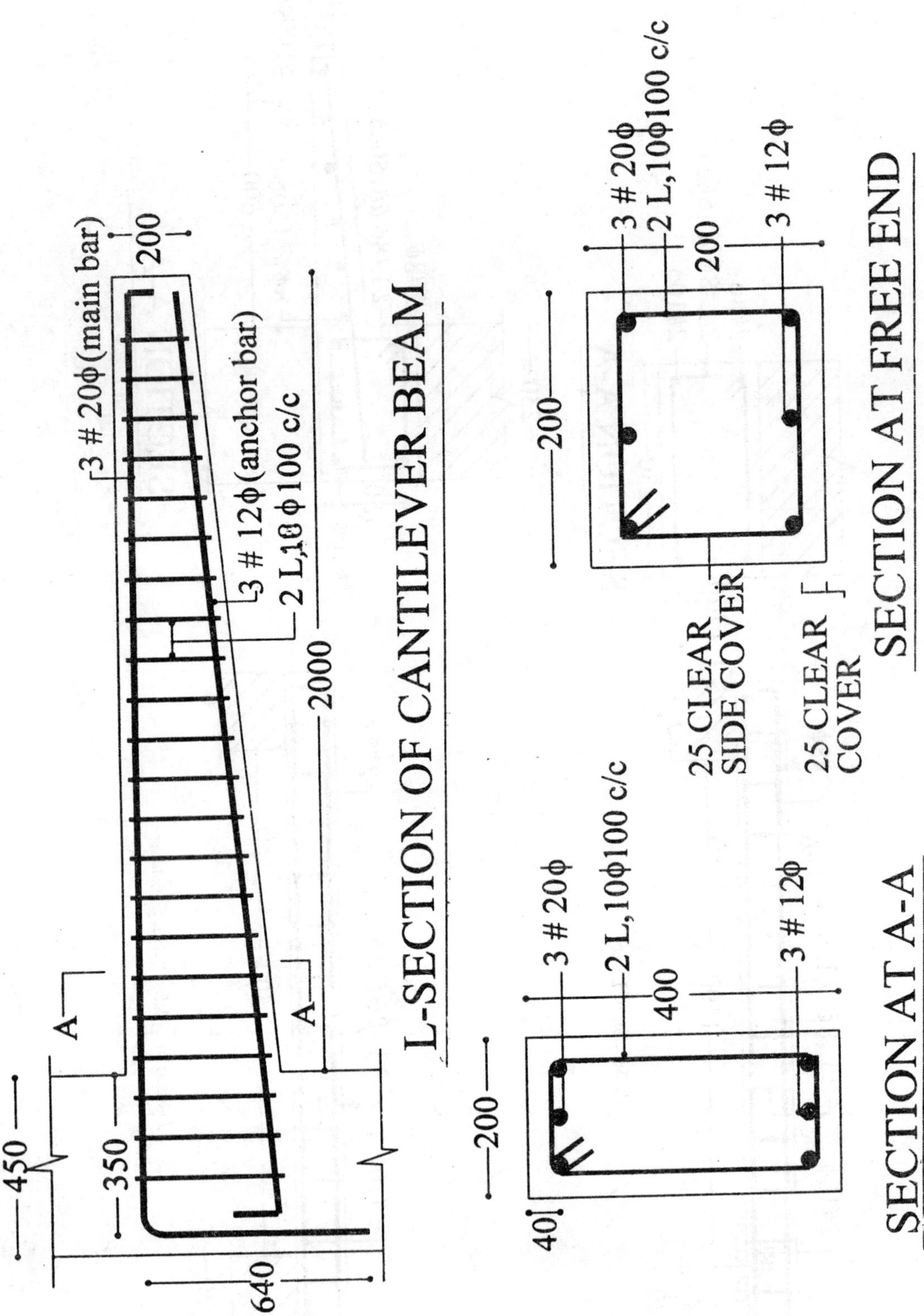
3 # 20ϕ (main bar)
200
3 # 12ϕ (anchor bar)
2 L,10 ϕ100 c/c
2000
450
350
640
A
A
L-SECTION OF CANTILEVER BEAM
200
40
400
3 # 20ϕ
2 L,10ϕ100 c/c
3 # 12ϕ
SECTION AT A-A
200
200
3 # 20ϕ
2 L,10ϕ100 c/c
3 # 12ϕ
25 CLEAR SIDE COVER
25 CLEAR COVER
SECTION AT FREE END

**Fig. 8.13.**

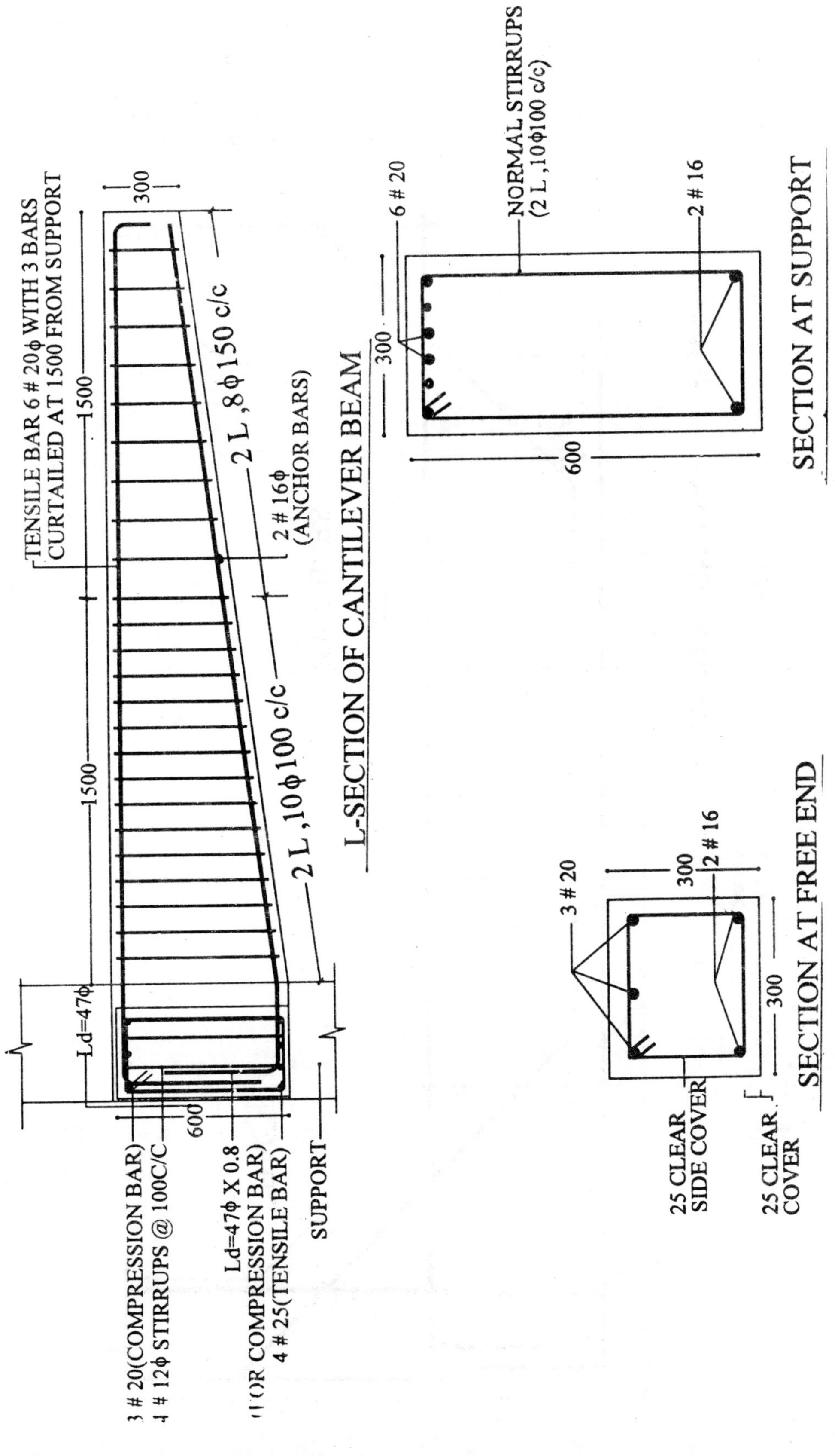
TENSILE BAR 6 # 20φ WITH 3 BARS CURTAILED AT 1500 FROM SUPPORT
300
1500
1500
Ld=47φ
2 L ,8φ150 c/c
2 # 16φ (ANCHOR BARS)
2 L ,10φ100 c/c
L-SECTION OF CANTILEVER BEAM
600
3 # 20(COMPRESSION BAR)
4 # 12φ STIRRUPS @ 100C/C
Ld=47φ X 0.8 FOR COMPRESSION BAR)
4 # 25(TENSILE BAR)
SUPPORT
NORMAL STIRRUPS (2 L ,10φ100 c/c)
6 # 20
2 # 16
300
600
SECTION AT SUPPORT
3 # 20
300
2 # 16
300
25 CLEAR SIDE COVER
25 CLEAR COVER
SECTION AT FREE END

Fig. 8.14.

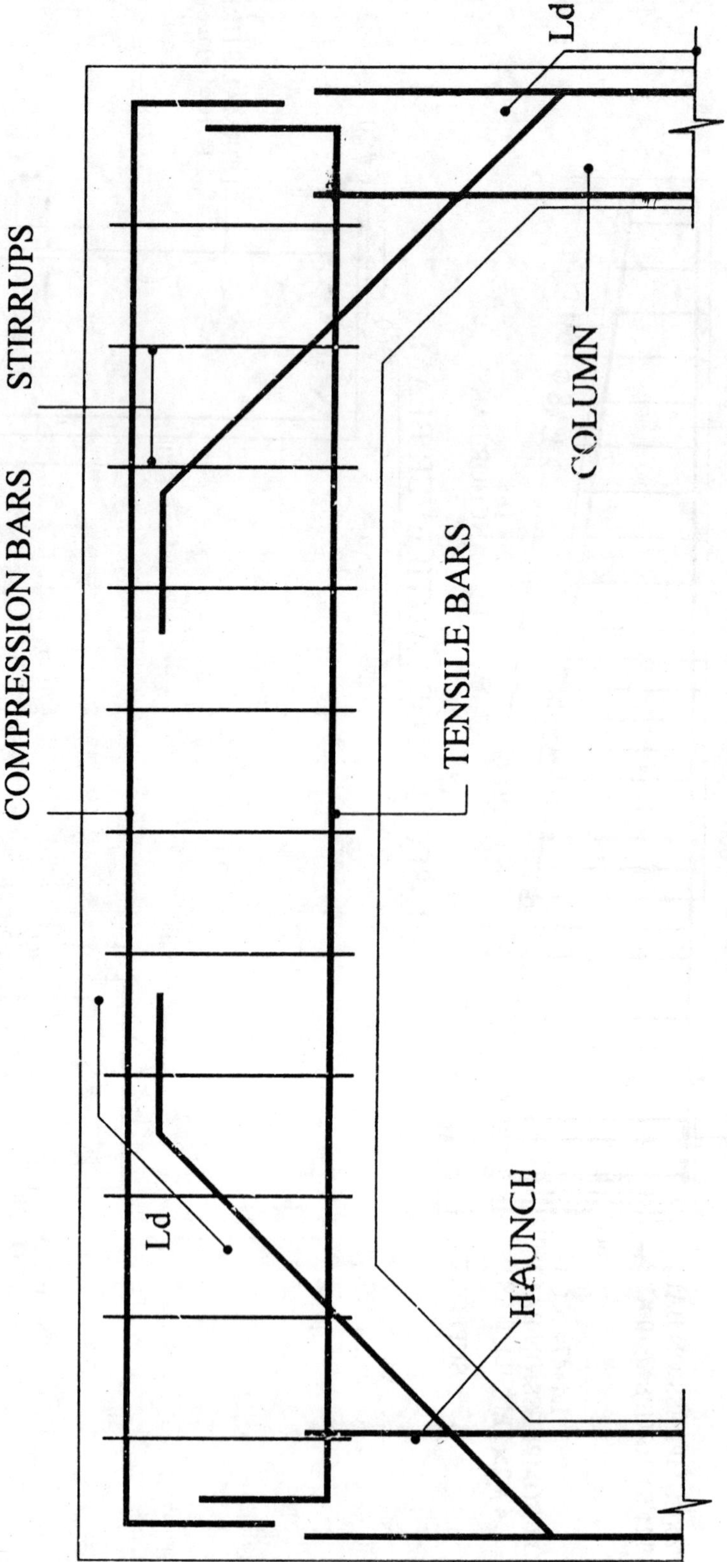


**Fig. 8.15.** L-Section of Haunch Beam

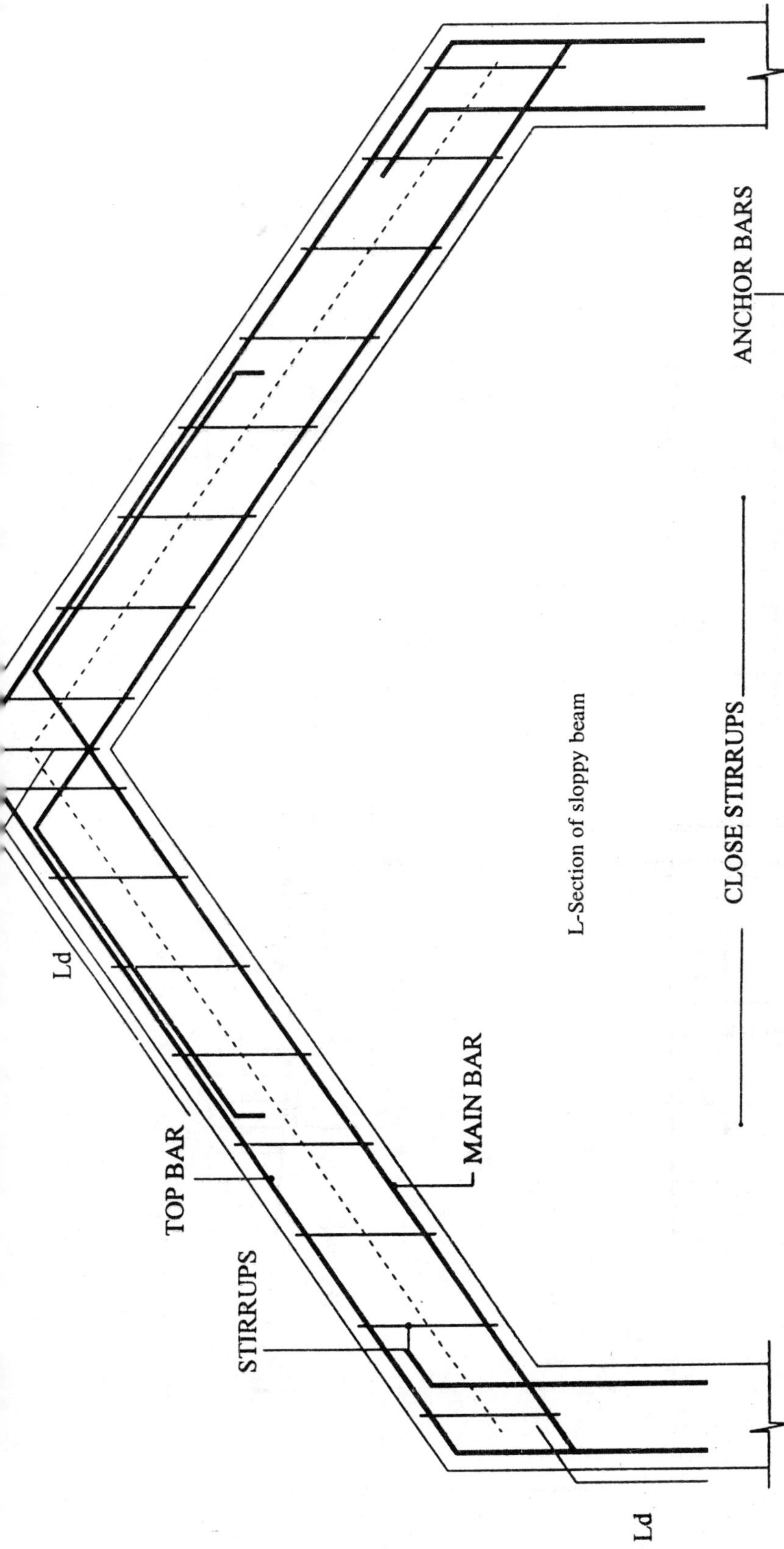


L-Section of sloppy beam

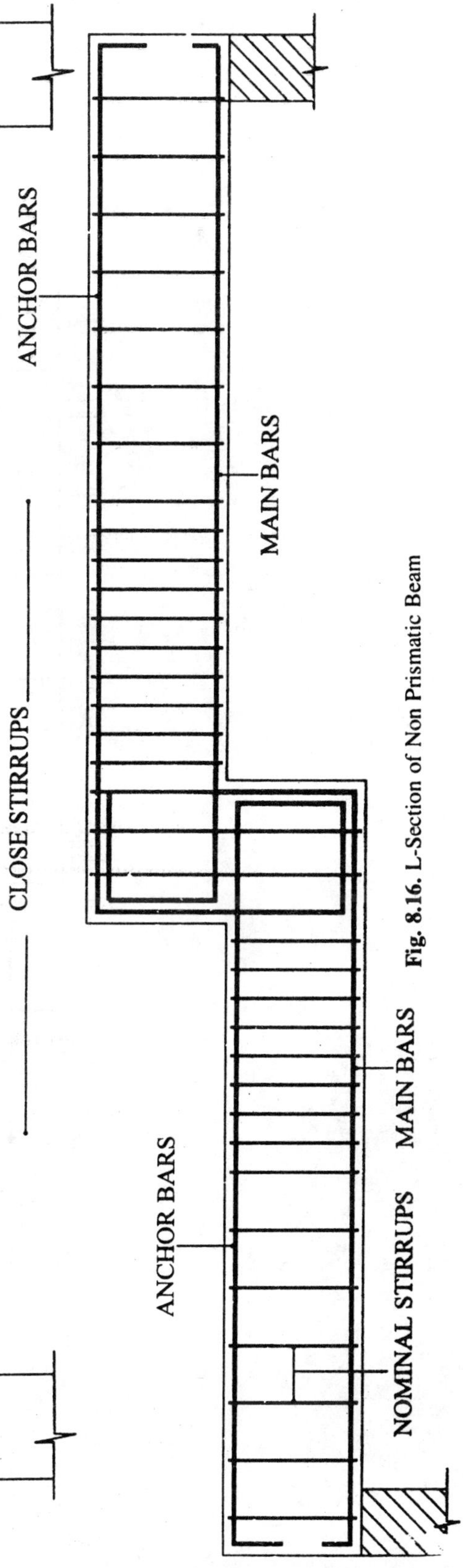


**Fig. 8.16.** L-Section of Non Prismatic Beam

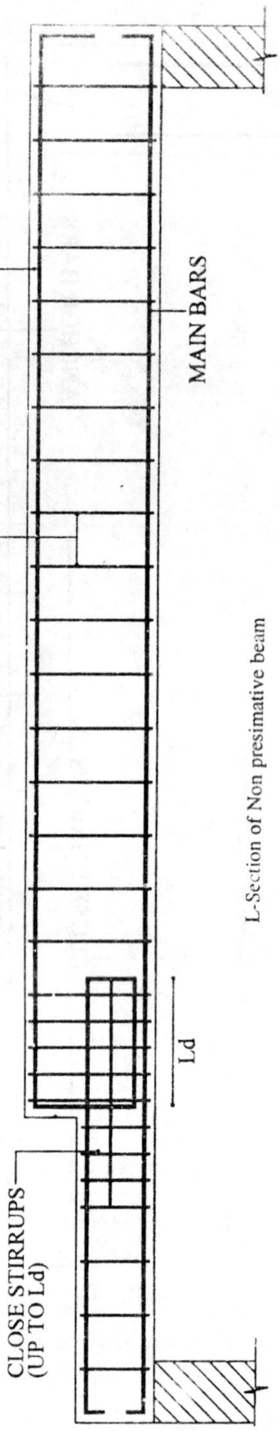


L-Section of Non presimative beam

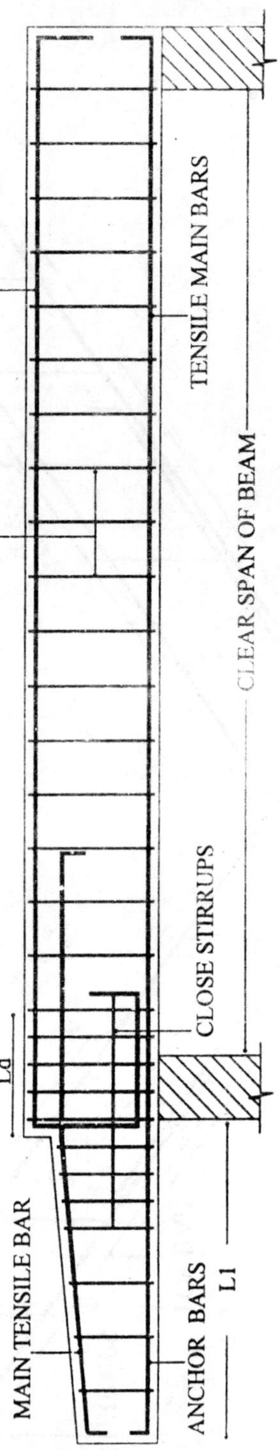


**Fig. 8.17.** Cantilever Beam Projected from a simply supported beam

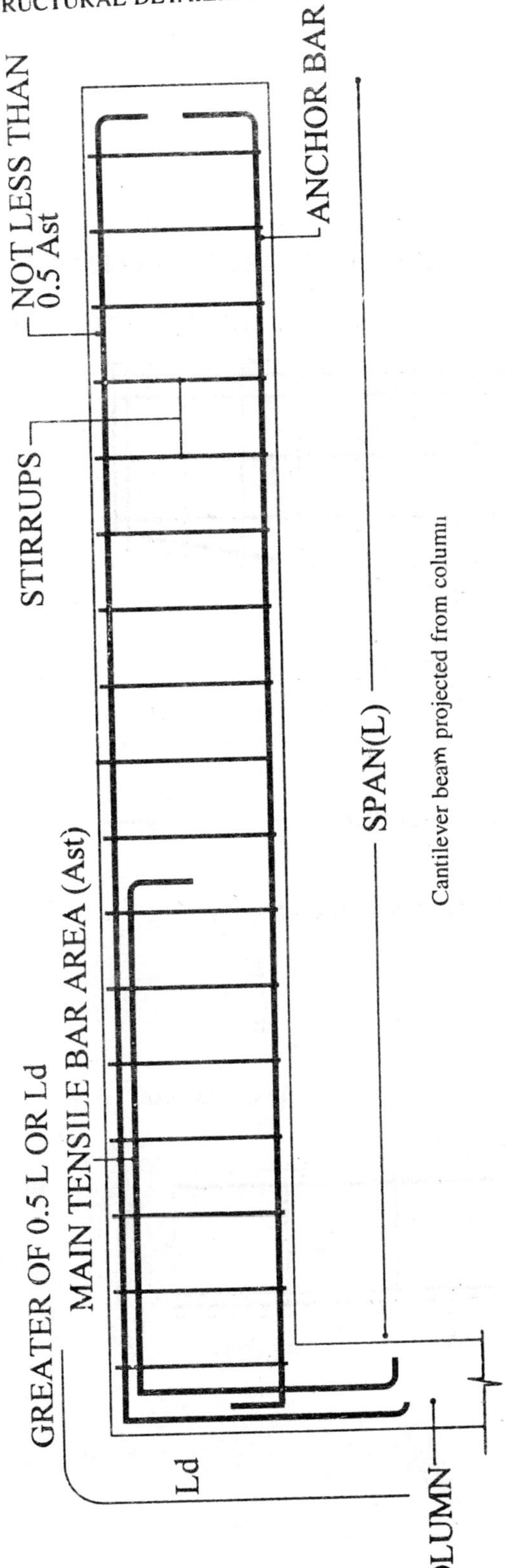


Cantilever beam projected from column

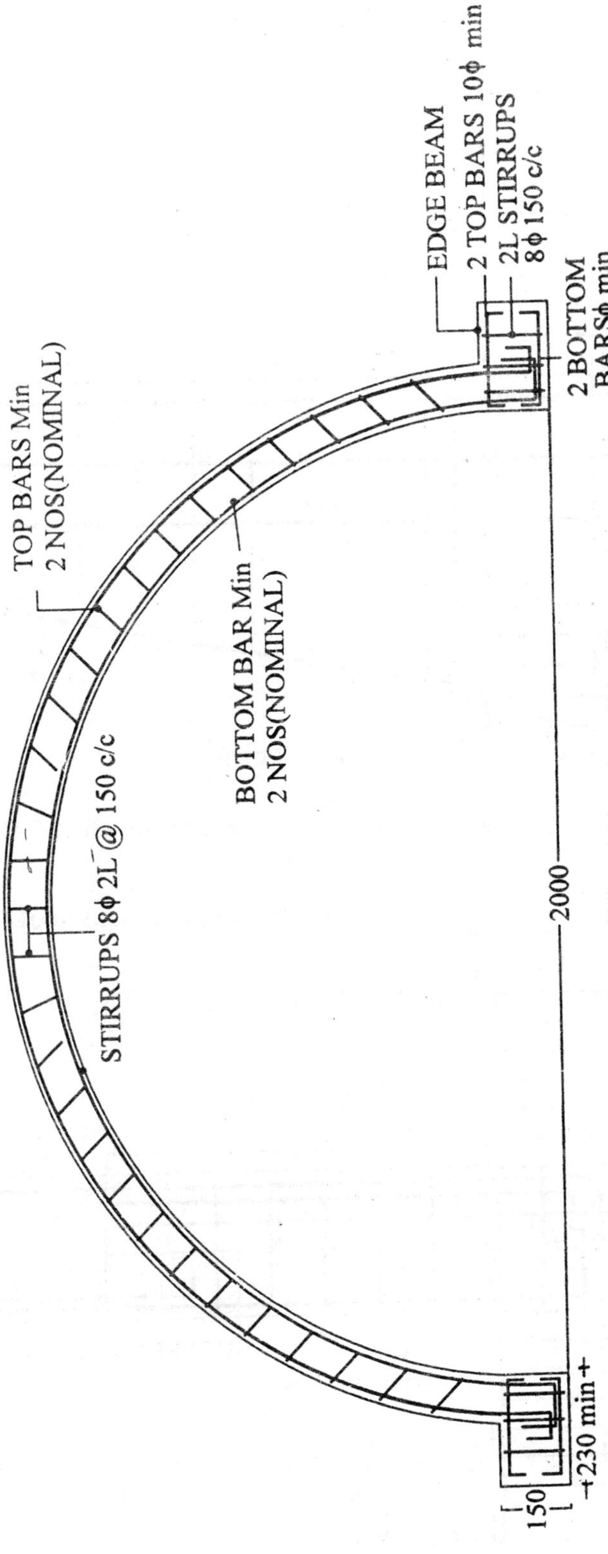


**Fig. 8.18.** Reinforcement in an arch

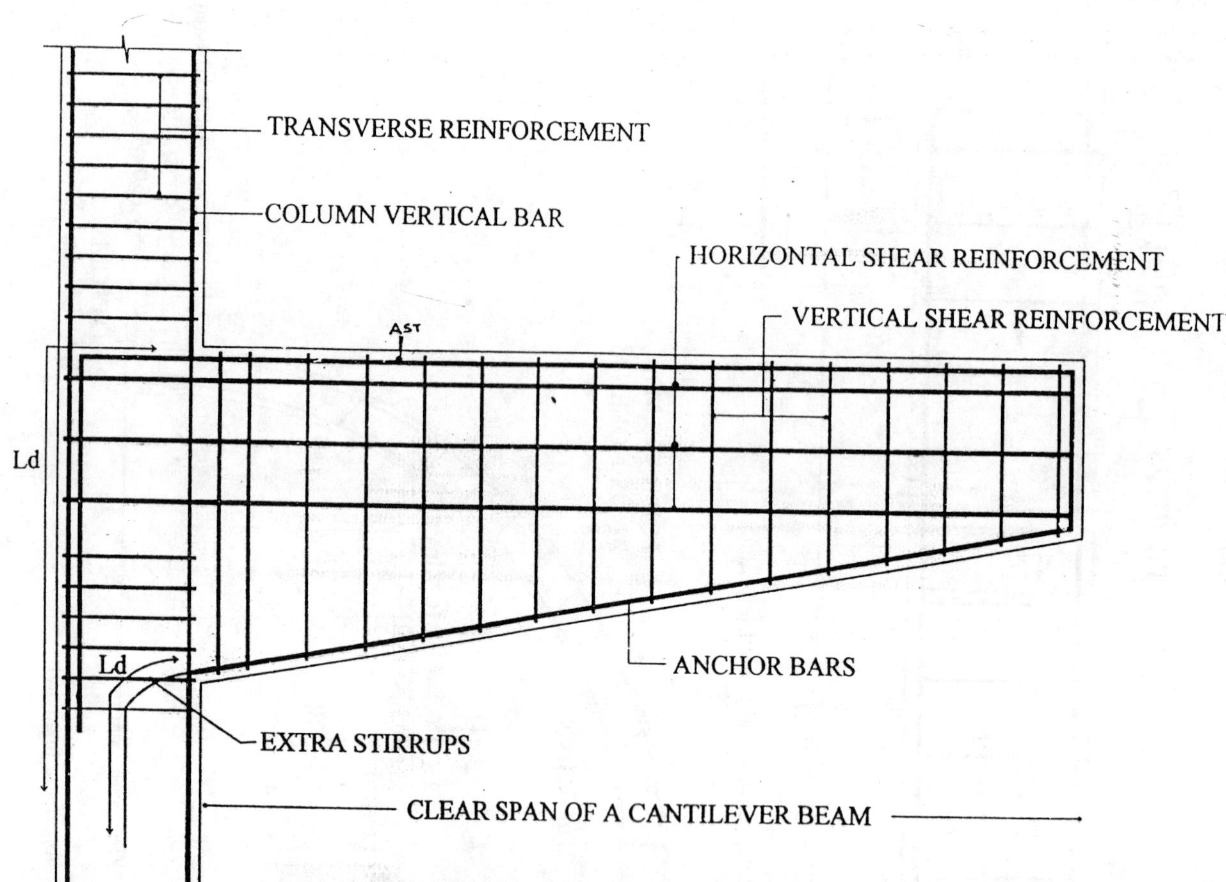


**CANTILEVER BEAM PROJECTED FROM COLUMN**

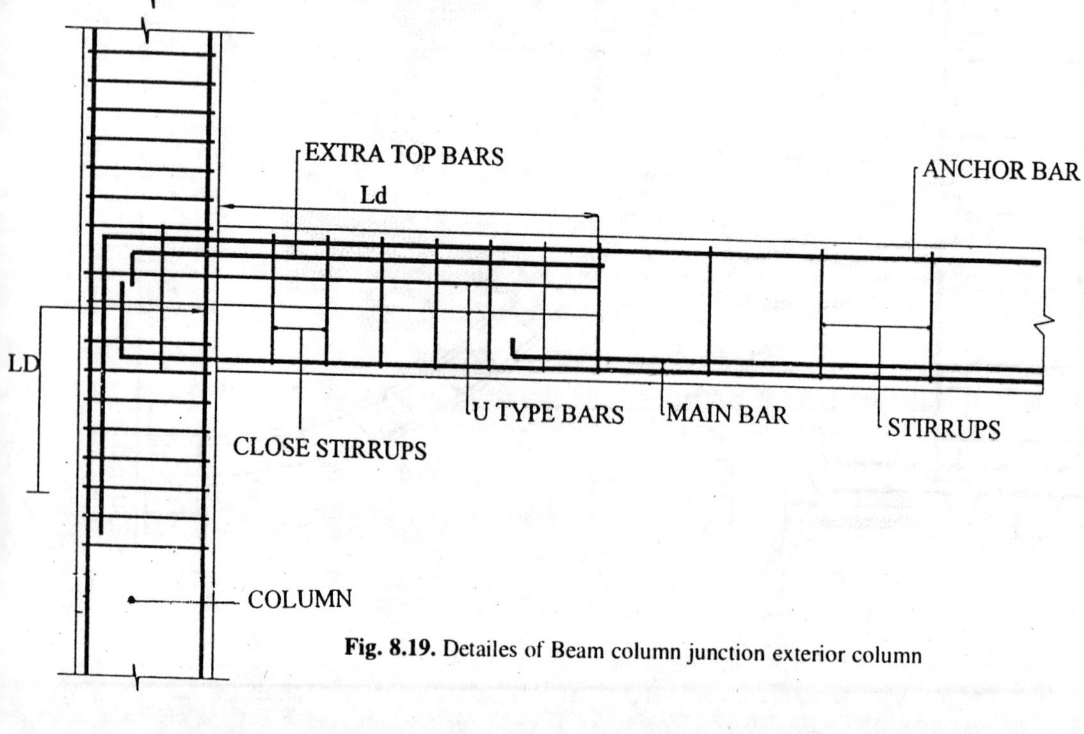


**Fig. 8.19.** Detailes of Beam column junction exterior column

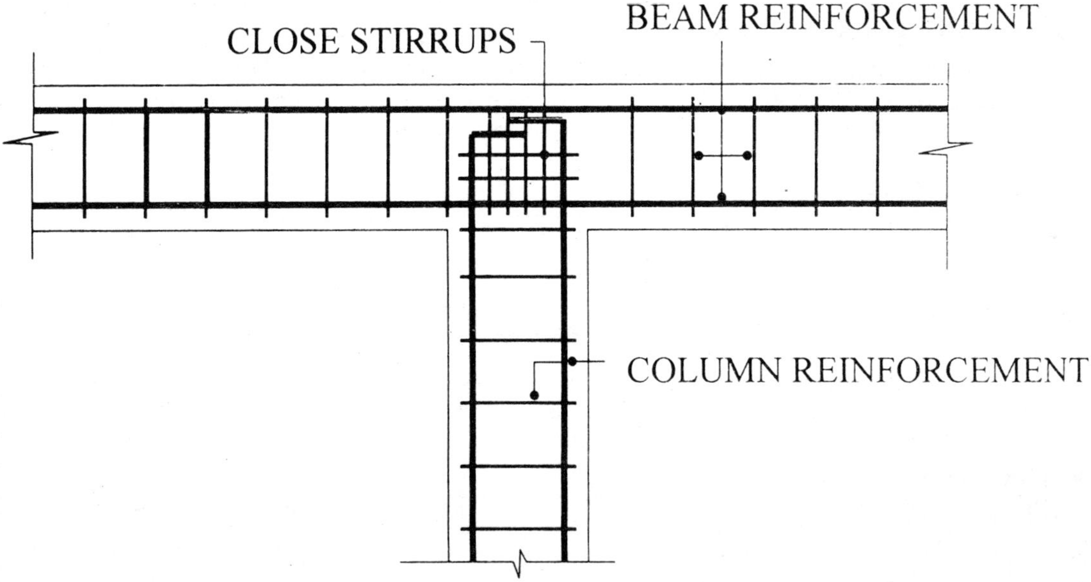


# TERMINATION OF COLUMN BARS INSIDE BEAM

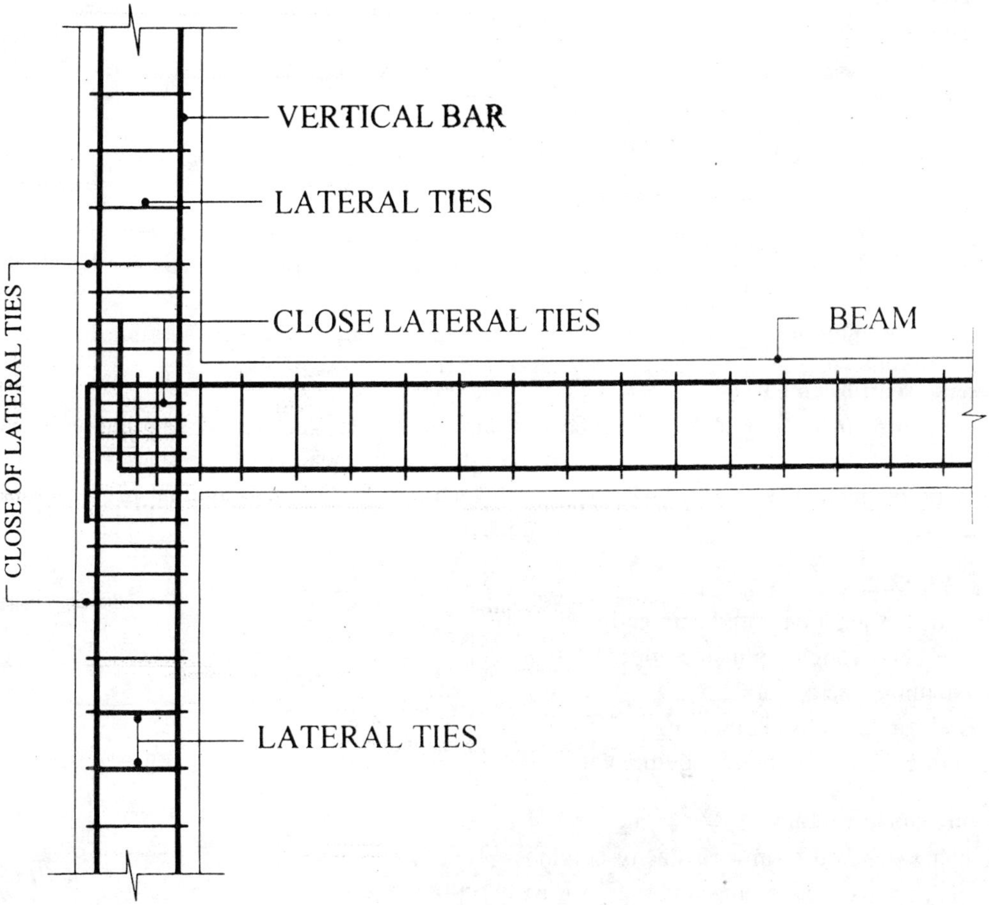


**Fig. 8.20.** Detailes of Beam column junction exterior column

## 8.3. RC COLUMN AND FOOTING

**Columns** are axial compression member whose length more than three times its least lateral dimension. Columns are reinforced with longitudinal bars to resist compression and bending, the horizontal reinforcement is provided in the form of ties or spirals to resist bursting of concrete.

### Shapes of column (Fig. 8.21)

Square, circular, Rectangular, Pentagonal, hexagonal, octagonal or any other shape as required for structural and architectural appearance.

### Classification of columns

*Based on dimensions*

(*i*) *Short column.* the slenderness ratio (L/d) is less than 12

(*ii*) *Long column.* the slenderness ratio (L/d) is more than 12

### Based on Reinforcement

(*i*) Tied column-the main longitudinal steel are enclosed with lateral ties or rings.

(*ii*) Spiral column-the main longitudinal steel are enclosed with closely spaced and continuous spiral ties.

### Based on type of loading

(*i*) Axial loading

(*ii*) Uniaxial eccentric loading

(*iii*) Biaxial eccentric loading

### Reinforcement. (Fig. 8.22)

*Longitudinal bars:*

Diameter of bar shall be minimum12 mm

Area of steel shall be 0.8 to 6% of concrete area of column but considers 0.8 to 4% for practical purpose.

Use even number of bars, ie.four bars in square and six bars in circular column.

### Transverse reinforcement

| | |
|---|---|
| Minimum diameter (which ever is more) | 6 mm or largest diameter of longitudinal bar/4<br>Least later dimension |
| Spacing or pitch (which ever is less) | 16 time the smallest longitudinal bar<br>300 mm |

### Splices (Fig. 8.23)

Provided at junction with beam and slab

Lower bars brought up inside upper bars

Maximum slope of bars 1:5

Dowel bars used as alternative

Length governed by bond requirement

### Economic consideration

Keeping standard formwork size of column

Keeping cross section constant over at least two floor levels

Using rich concrete mix *ie* M20 and above.

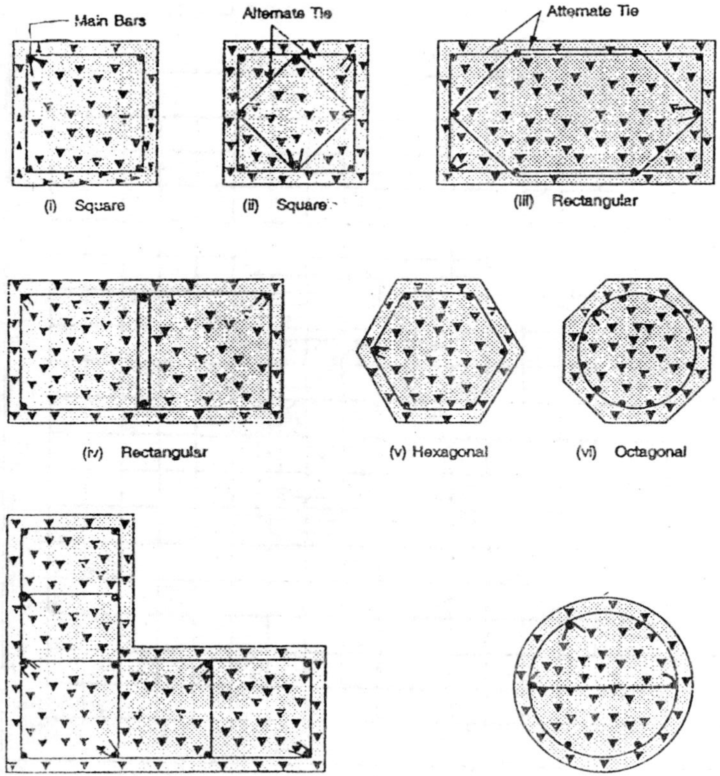


**SHAPES OF RCC COLUMNS**

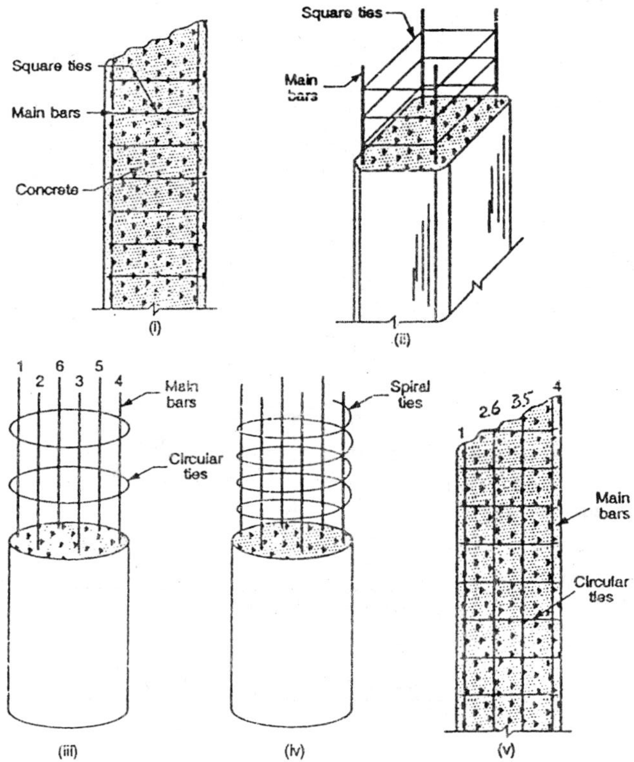


**DETAILS OF REINFORCEMENT IN R.C.C. COLUMNS**

**Fig. 8.21.** Details of Reinforcement in R.C.C. Columns

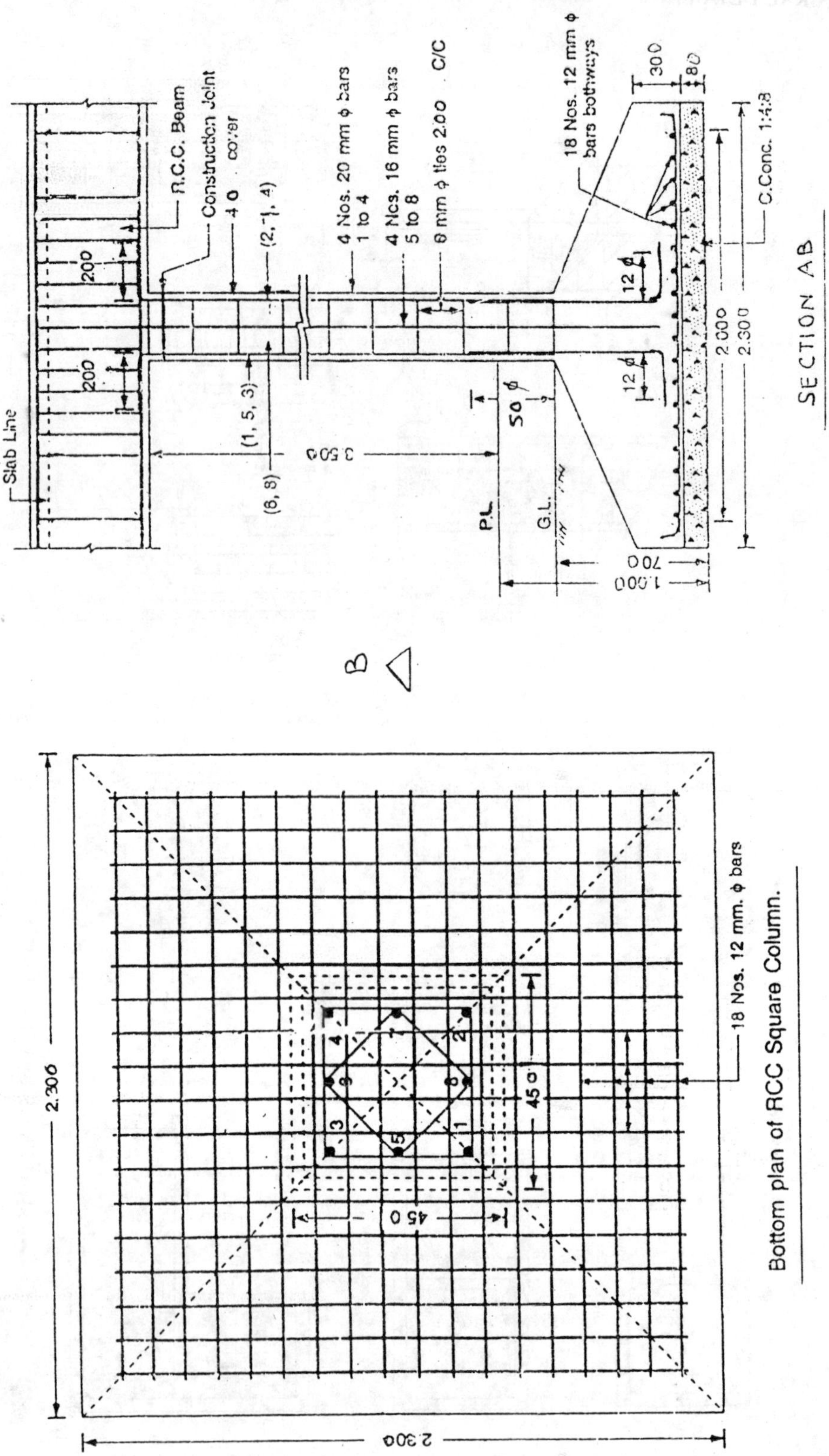


**Fig. 8.22.** Bottom plan of RCC Square Column

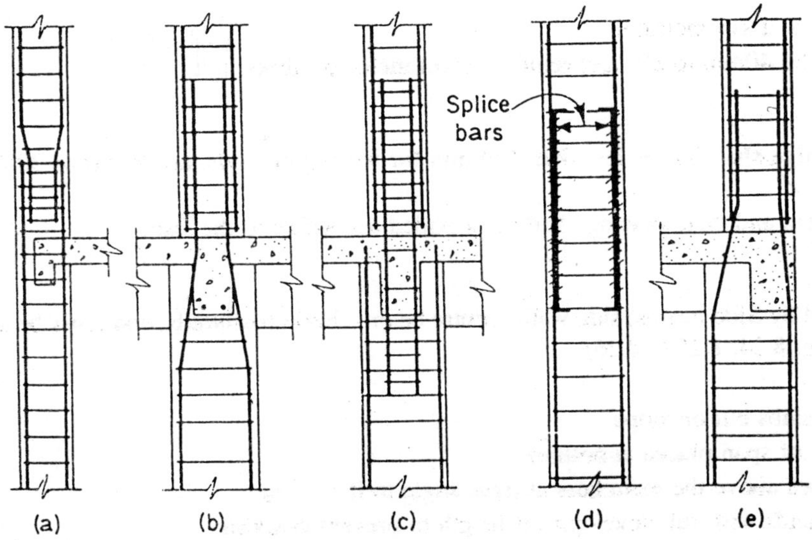


**Column splice details**

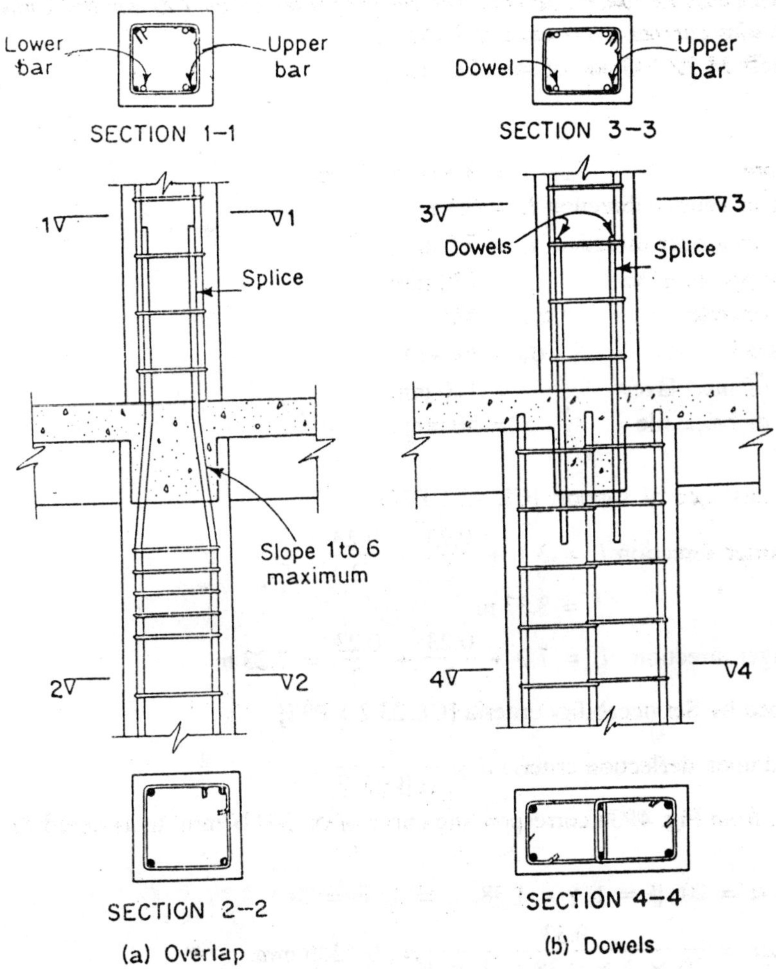


**Fig. 8.23.** Column splices

Keeping shape simple and symmetrical

Minimum cover shall be 40mm to all steel reinforcement including links.

**Footing**

The thickness at the edge shall not be less than 150 mm for footing on soils, nor less than 300 mm at the face of column.

Minimum reinforcement and their spacing shall be provided according to the slab.

## 8.4. STAIR CASE

They can be supported by Side beams, side walls, centre beams, End cross walls, end cross beams and combination of above. (Fig. 8.24, 8.25A, 8.26).

Reinforcement

Similar to beams and slabs but on slope

Main bars in direction of span placed at bottom

Distribution steel placed above the main bars at right angle to it.

Top steel provided at ends with full development length to prevent cracking.

**Problems 8.1.** *Design a simply supported RC slab of a room 3.1 m × 7.0 m in plan. The bearing of the slab on the supporting wall may be taken 230 mm. The roof is protected by 100 mm thick mud layer with 50 mm thick brick tile. It also carries a live load of 3 kN/m².*

Take Grade of concrete M 20 ^ Grade of steel Fe 415.

**Solution.**

Given data:

| | | |
|---|---|---|
| Size of room | | = 3.1 m × 7.0 m |
| Clear span in shorter direction | $l_x$ | = 3.1 m |
| Clear span in longer direction | $l_y$ | = 7.0 m |
| Width of supporting wall | | = 230 mm |
| Grade of concrete | $\sigma_{ck}$ | = *M*20 |
| Grade of steel | $\sigma_y$ | = *Fe* 415 |
| Thickness of mud layer | | = 100 mm |
| Thickness of brick tile | | = 50 mm |

DESIGN

Effective span = c/c distance of support [CL 22.2 P34]

Effective span in shorter direction $l_x = 3.1 + \frac{0.23}{2} + \frac{0.23}{2}$

$= 3.33$ m

Effective span in longer direction $l_y = 7.0 + \frac{0.23}{2} + \frac{0.23}{2} = 7.23$ m

Depth of slab governed by Serviceability criteria [CL 23.2.1 P37]

Effective depth based upon deflection criteria $d = \frac{1_x}{\alpha\,\beta\,\gamma\,\lambda\,\delta}$

Assuming $Pt = 0.4\%$, from Fig. 4P38 corresponding curve of $\sigma_y$ 240 N/mm² to assumed $Pt$ (Percentage of steel)

Modification factors $\alpha = 20, \beta = 1, \gamma = 1.38, \lambda = 1, \delta = 1$

$$dx = \frac{0.33}{20 \times 1 \times 1.38 \times 1 \times 1} = 0.1206 \text{ mm}$$

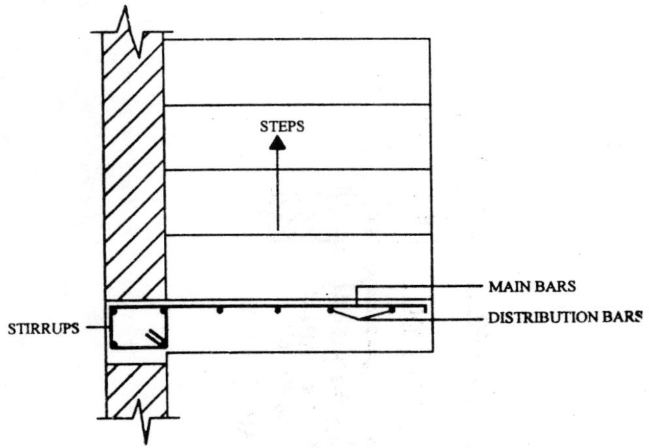


SLAB CANTILEVER FROM
A SPANDREI BEAM OR WALL

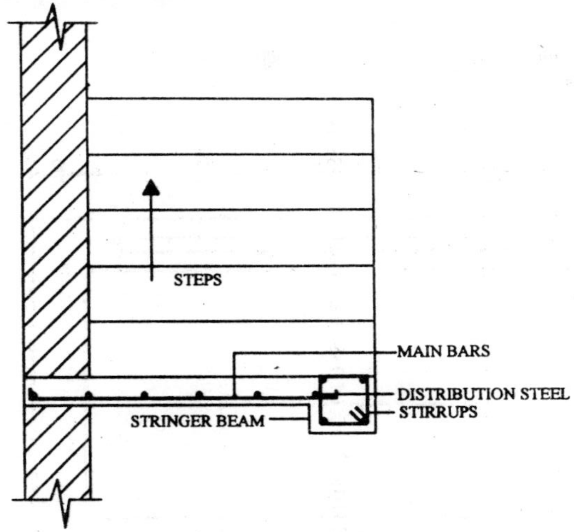


SLAB SUPPORTED BETWEEN
TWO STRINGER BEAM

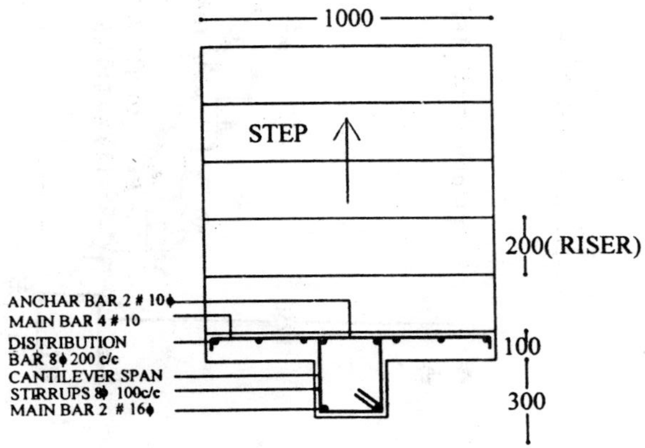


SLAB DOUBLY CANTILEVER
FROM A CENTRAL BEAM

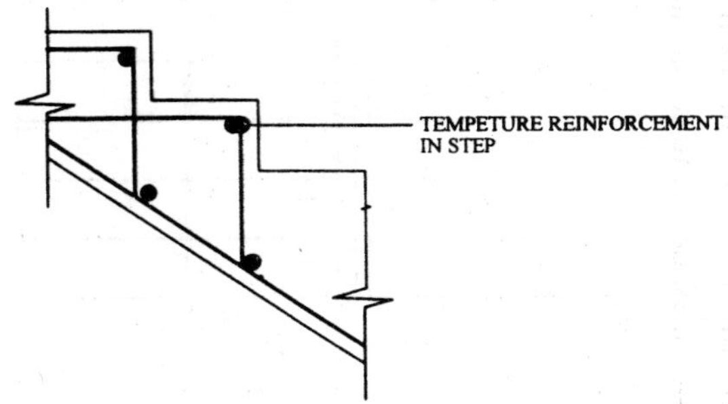


STAIRS SLABS SPANNING TRANSVERSELY

**Fig. 8.24.**Reinforcement in Stair case

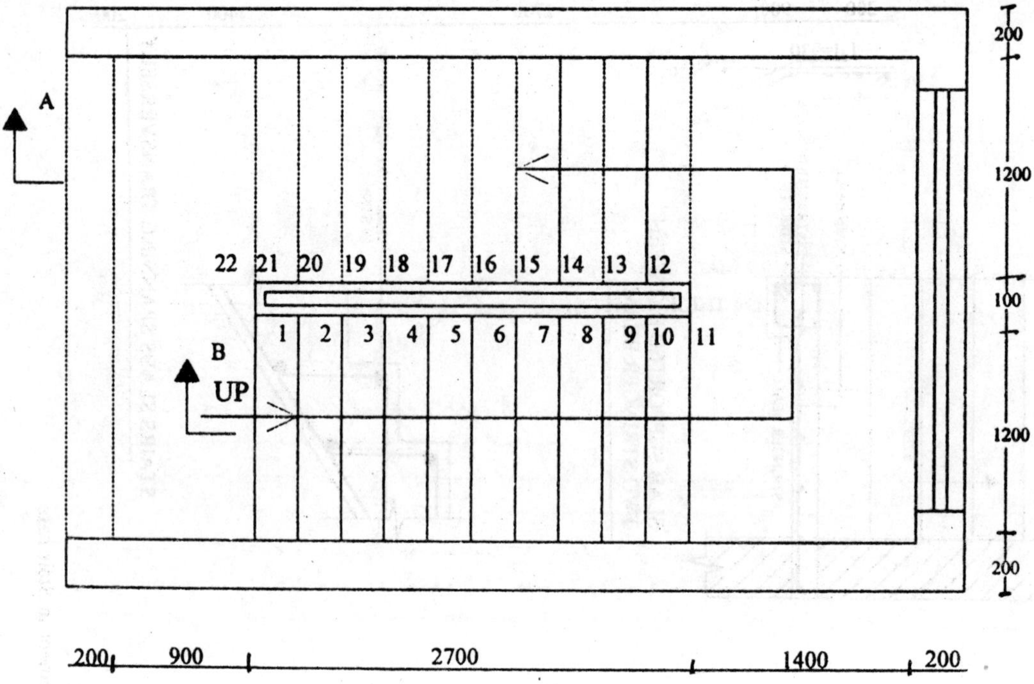


PLAN

DOGLEGGED STAIR CASE

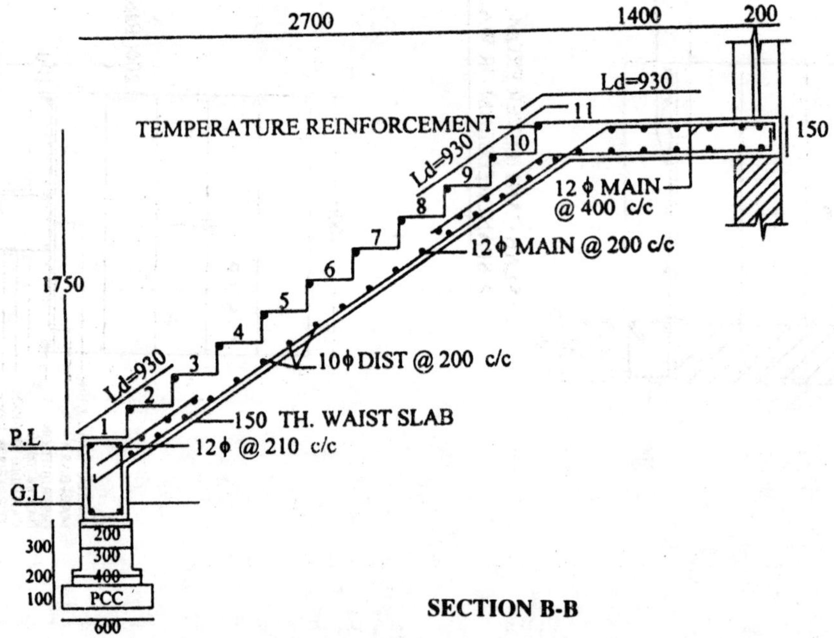


SECTION B-B

SHOWING DETAILS OF REINFORCEMENT

**Fig. 8.25.** Showing details of reinforcement

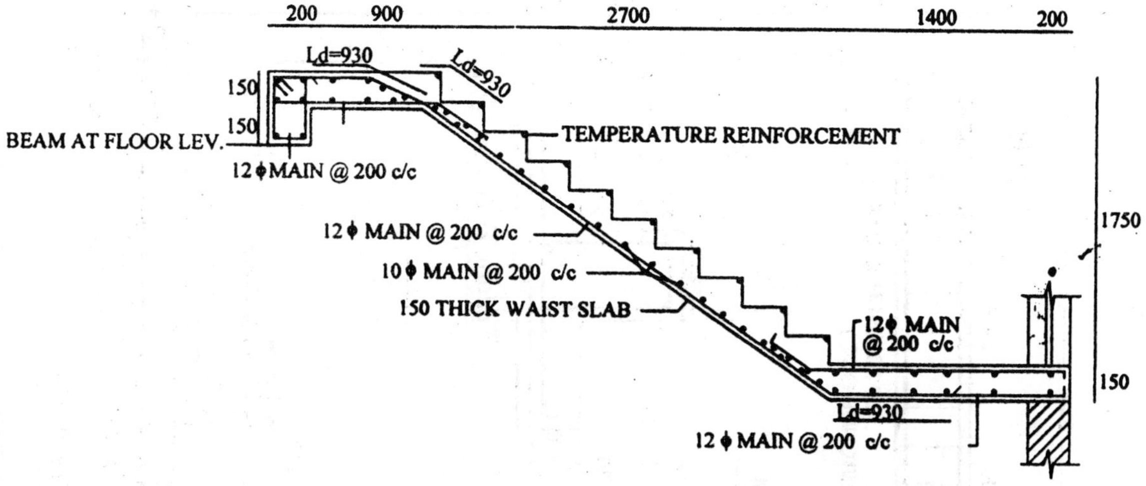


SECTION A-A

**Fig. 8.25 A.**

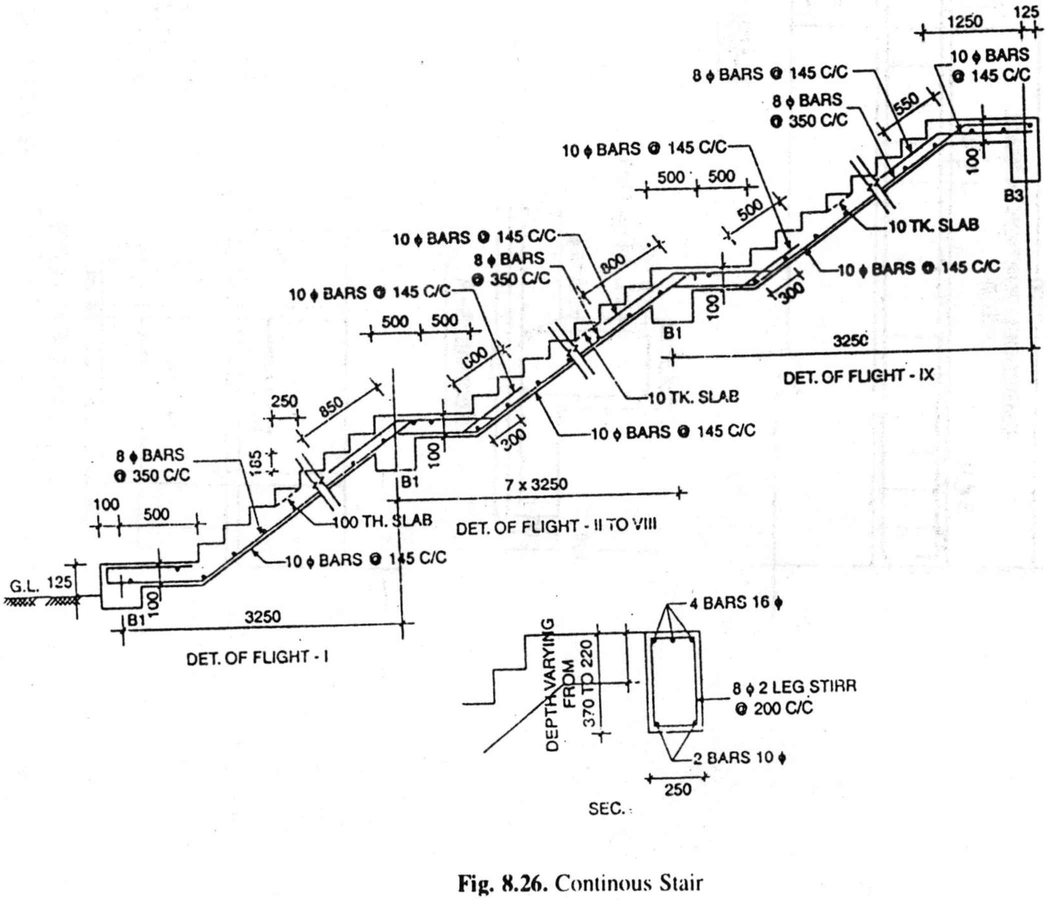


**Fig. 8.26.** Continous Stair

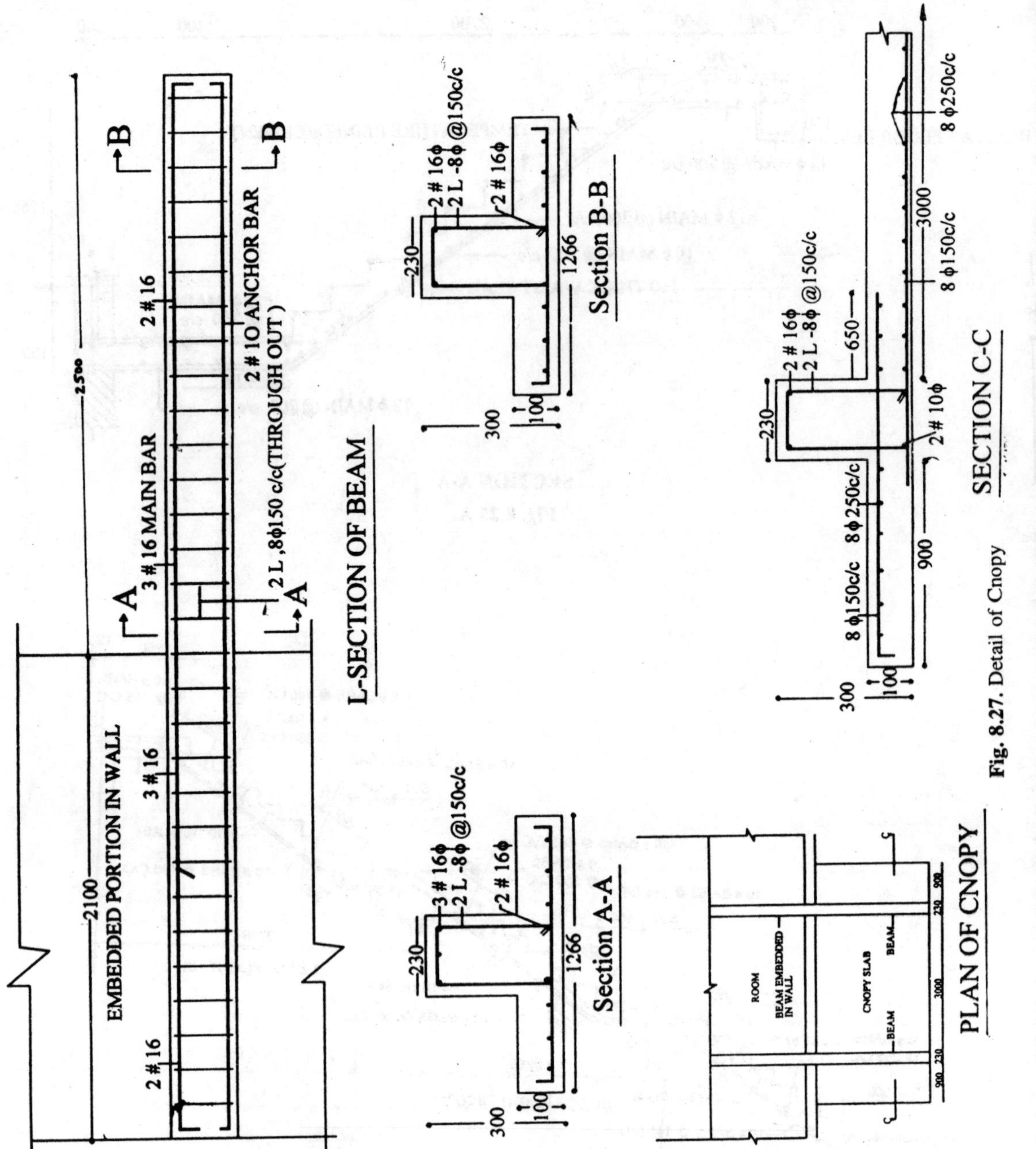


**Fig. 8.27.** Detail of Cnopy

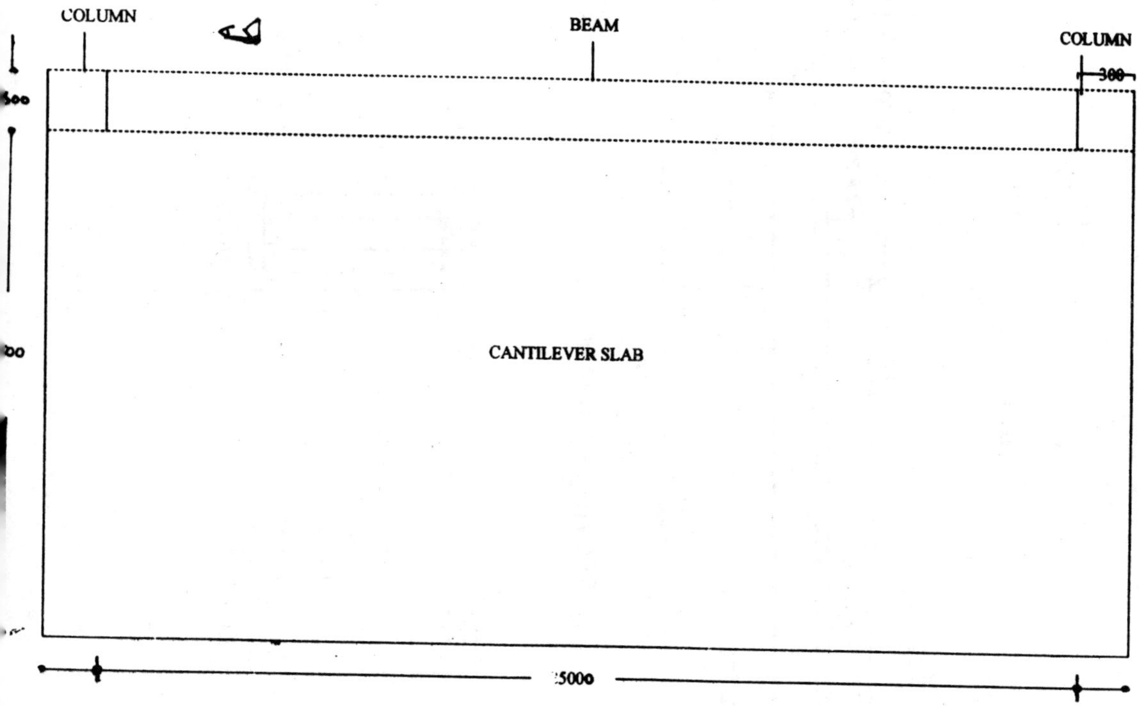


PLAN OF CANTILEVER PORCH

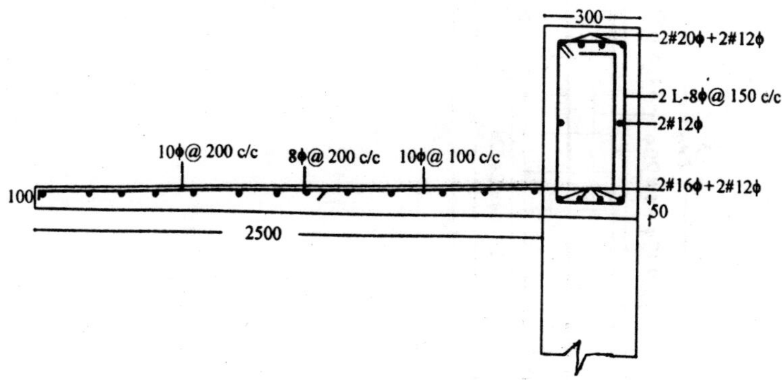


SECTION OF CANTILEVER SLAB

Fig. 8.28

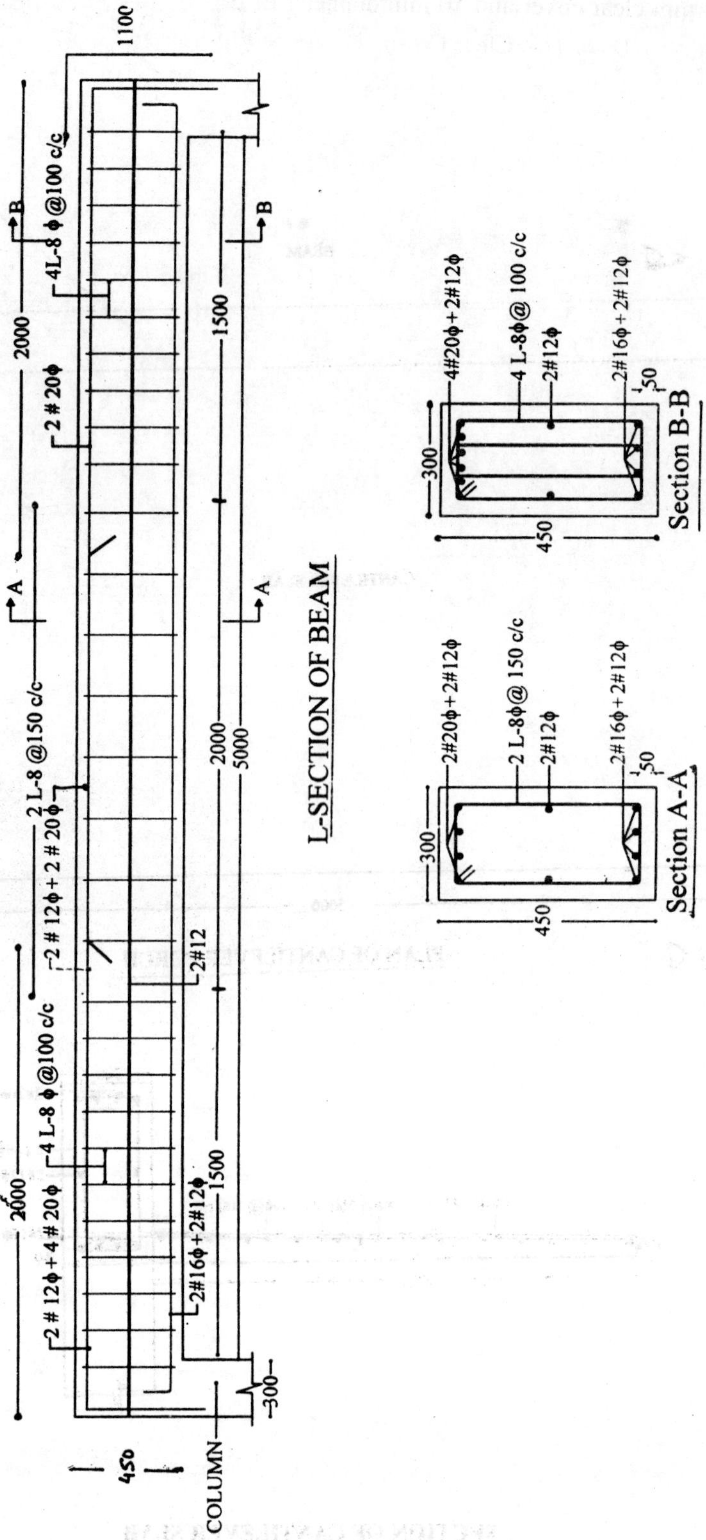
1100
4L-8 φ @100 c/c
B
B
2000
2 # 20φ
A
A
2 L-8 @150 c/c
2 # 12φ + 2 # 20φ
2#12
2000
4 L-8 φ @100 c/c
2 # 12φ + 4 # 20φ
2#16φ+2#12φ
1500
2000
5000
1500
450
COLUMN
300
L-SECTION OF BEAM
2#20φ+2#12φ
2 L-8φ@ 150 c/c
2#12φ
2#16φ+2#12φ
50
300
450
Section A-A
4#20φ+2#12φ
4 L-8φ@ 100 c/c
2#12φ
2#16φ+2#12φ
50
300
450
Section B-B

Fig. 8.29.

Consider 15 mm clear cover and 10 mm diameter of bar

Overall depth $D = d$ + Clear Cover + diameter of bar/2

$$= 120.6 + 15 + \frac{10}{2}$$

$$= 140.65 \text{ mm} \approx 150 \text{ mm}$$

According to IS-456-2000 [CL 23.0 P36]

Available effective depth in shorter span $dx = 150 - 15 - 5 = 130$ mm

Available effective depth in longer span $dy = dx$ – diameter of bar

$$= 130 - 10 = 120 \text{ mm}$$

Effective span in shorter span $l_x$ = Clear span + effective depth

$$= 3.1 + 0.130 = 3.23 \text{ m}$$

Effective span in longer span $l_y = 7.0 + 0.120 = 7.12$ m

According to [CL 22.2, P34] lesser effective span should be consider

$$\text{Aspect Ratior} = \frac{l_y}{l_x} = \frac{7.12}{3.22}$$

$$r = 2.20 > 2$$

Hence it is design as a one-way slab

**Calculation of loads and B.M**

Consider 1 metre wide strip ($b$) of slab

($i$) Self wt of slab $= D \times \rho = 0.150 \times 25 = 3.75 \text{ kN/m}^2$

($ii$) Mud layer $= D \times \rho = 0.1 \times 16 = 1.6 \text{ kN/m}^2$

($iii$) Brick tile $= D \times \rho = 0.05 \times 20 = 1.0 \text{ kN/m}^2$

($iv$) Live load on slab $= 3.0 \text{ kN/m}^2$

Total load $= 9.35 \text{ kN/m}^2$

Factored load $= 1.5 \times 0.35 = 14.025 \text{ kN/m}^2$

**Note.** Load ($i$) and ($iii$) are dead load

$$\text{Max.}^{\text{m}} \text{ B.M. on shorter direction } Mx = \frac{wl_x^2}{8}$$

$$= \frac{14.025 \times (3.23)^2}{8} = 18.17 \text{ kN–M}$$

$$\text{Design of Reinforcement, } R_x = \frac{Mx}{bdx^2}$$

$$= \frac{18.17 \times 10^6}{1000 \times (130)^2} = 1.075 \text{ N/mm}^2$$

$$\frac{\text{Astx required in shorter direction}}{bdx} = \frac{\sigma_{ck}}{2\,\sigma_y}\left[1 - \sqrt{1 - \frac{4.59\,Rx}{\sigma_{ck}}}\right]$$

$$\frac{\text{Required Ast x}}{1000 \times 130} = \frac{20}{2 \times 415}\left[1 - \sqrt{1 - \frac{4.59 \times 1.075}{20}}\right]$$

Required $Astx = 413.97 \text{ mm}^2$

Using 10 mm $\phi$ bar $A\phi = \frac{\pi}{4} 10^2 = 78.54 \text{ mm}^2$

Spacing $= \frac{A\phi}{Ast} \times 1000$

$= \frac{78.54}{413.97} \times 1000 = 189.72 \text{ mm}$

Check for Max$^m$ spacing [CL 26.3.3 P46]

$= 3dx = 3 \times 130 = 390 \text{ mm or } 300 \text{ mm}$

Provided 8 mm $\phi$ bar @ 180 mm c/c

Actual area of steel provided in shorter direction

$$Astx = \frac{A\phi}{\text{spacing}} \times 1000$$

$$= \frac{78.54}{180} \times 1000 = 436.33 \text{ mm}^2 > 413.97 \text{ mm}^2$$

Reinforcement in longer direction

Distribution reinforcement [CL26.5.2.1P48]

Area of distribution reinforcement = 0.12% of $bD$

$$= \frac{0.12}{100} \times 1000 \times 150 = 180 \text{ mm}^2$$

Using 8 mm diameter of bar

Spacing of bar $= \frac{50.24}{180} \times 1000 = 279 \text{ mm}$

Check for max spacing [CL 26.3.3.b2 P46] = $5d$ or 450 mm

$= 5 \times 130 = 650 \text{ mm}$

Provided 8 mm $\Phi$ 270 mm c/c

**Check for Serviceability criteria**

Check for deflection criteria

% of steel $= \frac{Astx \text{ provided}}{b \times dx} \times 100$

$= \frac{436.33}{1000 \times 130} \times 100 = 0.335\%$

Modification factors $\alpha = 20, \beta = 1, \gamma = 1.40, \lambda = 1, \delta = 1$

$$d = \frac{lx}{\alpha \beta \gamma \lambda \delta}$$

$$= \frac{3.23 \times 10^3}{20 \times 1 \times 1.40 \times 1 \times 1} = 115 \text{ mm} < 130 \text{ mm O.K}$$

$lx/dx$ max $= 20 \times 1.40 = 28$

$lx/dx$ provided $= \frac{3220}{120} = 26.8$

$lx/dx$ max > $lx/dx$ provided. Hence over all depth can be provided $120 + 15 + 5 = 140$ mm

Check for shear

$$\text{Max}^m \text{ shear force } Vu = \frac{wlx}{2}$$

$$= \frac{14.025 \times 10^3 \times 3.1}{2} = 21.73 \text{ kN}$$

$$\text{Nominal shear stress } \tau v = \frac{Vu}{bdx} \quad \text{[CL.B 5.1 P83]}$$

$$dx = 140 - 15 - 5 = 120 \text{ mm}$$

$$= \frac{21.73 \times 10^3}{1000 \times 120} = 0.181 \text{ N/mm}^2$$

For 0.335% of steel and M20 grade of concrete [Table 19, P73]

$$\tau_c = 0.36 + \frac{0.48 - 0.36}{0.50 - 0.25} \times (0.335 - 0.25) = 0.40 \text{ N/mm}^2$$

$\tau_c$ = 0.328 and thickness of slab up to 150 mm $K$ = 1.3 [CL 40.2.11, P73]

$$\tau_c' = k \times \tau_c = 1.3 \times 0.40$$

$$= 0.52 \text{ N/mm}^2$$

$$\tau_C' \; \tau V \text{ O.K.}$$

Check for development length: [CL26.2.1 P42]

$$L_d = \frac{0.87 \, \sigma y \, \phi}{4 \, \tau_{bd}} \quad [\tau_{bd} \text{ from CL 26.2.1.1, P43}]$$

$$= \frac{0.87 \times 415 \times 10}{4 \times 1.92} = 376.09 \text{ mm}$$

$$= 1.3 \frac{M1}{V} + Lo \geq Ld \quad \text{[CL26.2.3,P44]}$$

$$L_o = 12\phi \text{ OR } dx$$

$$= 12 \times 10 = 120 \text{ mm OR } 120 \text{ mm}$$

For partial fixity at support, 50% main reinforcement should be provided at top for a distance $0.1l_x$ from face of support

$$M1 = \frac{18.17 \times 10^6}{2} = 9.085 \times 10^6 \text{ N–mm}$$

$$Vu = 21.73 \text{ kN}$$

$$= \frac{1.3 \, M1}{Vu} + L_o$$

$$= \frac{1.3 \times 9.085 \times 10^6}{21.73 \times 10^3} + 120$$

$$= 663.5 \text{ mm} > 564.14 \text{ O.K.}$$

Distribution reinforcement for holding the top bars [CL 26.5.2.1 P48]

Area of distribution reinforcement = 0.12% of $bD$

$$= \frac{0.12}{100} \times 1000 \times 140 = 168 \text{ mm}^2$$

Using 8 mm diameter of bar

$$\text{Spacing of bar} = 1000 \times \frac{50.24}{168} = 299 \text{ mm}$$

Check for max spacing [CL 26.3.3.b2 P46] = $5d$ or 450 mm

$$= 5 \times 120 = 600 \text{ mm}$$

Provided 8 mm Φ @ 290 mm c/c

**Schedule of slab**

Grade of concrete M 20 and Grade of steel Fe 415

| *Thickness (mm)* | *Clear cover (mm)* | *Reinforcement parallel to* | | **Remark** |
|---|---|---|---|---|
| | | *Short side (mm)* | *Long side (mm)* | |
| 140 | 15 | 10 Φ @ 180 c/c | 8 Φ @ 260 c/c | Bottom bars |
| | | 10 Φ @ 360 c/c | — | Top bars |
| | | 8 Φ @ 270 c/c | — | Top Distribution |

**Problem 8.2.** *Design a RC floor slab over an isolated room of size 4.2 m × 4.6 m. The floor is simply supported on all four walls of thickness 230 mm, with a 40 mm thick mosaic flooring as a floor finished. The corners of the slab are free to lift and carrying a live load of 3 kN/m$^2$.*

*Take Grade of concrete M 20 and Grade of steel Fe 415.*

**Solution.**

Given data:

Size of room = 4.2 m × 4.6 m

Clear span in shorter direction $lx$ = 4.2 m

Clear span in longer direction $ly$ = 4.6 m

Width of supporting wall = 230 mm

Grade of concrete $\sigma_{ck}$ = *M* 20

Grade of steel $\sigma_y$ = *Fe* 415

Mosaic flooring 40 mm thick

Corners are free to lift or not held down

**DESIGN**

Effective span = c/c distance of support [CL 22.2 P34]

$$\text{Effective span in shorter direction } lx = 4.2 + \frac{0.23}{2} + \frac{0.23}{2} = 4.43 \text{ m}$$

$$\text{Effective span in longer direction } ly = 4.6 + \frac{0.23}{2} + \frac{0.23}{2} = 4.83 \text{ m}$$

Depth of slab governed by Serviceability criteria [CL 23.2.1 P37]

$$\text{Effective depth based upon deflection criteria } d = \frac{lx}{\alpha \beta \gamma \lambda \delta}$$

Assuming $Pt$ = 0.33%, from Fig. 4, P38 corresponding curve of $\sigma_y$ 240 N/mm$^2$ to assumed $Pt$.

Modification factors $\alpha = 20$, $\beta = 1$, $\gamma = 1.43$, $\lambda = 1$, $\delta = 1$

$$d = \frac{4.43}{20} \times 1 \times 1.43 \times 1 \times 1 = 0.154 \text{ mm}$$

Consider 20 mm clear cover and 8 mm diameter of bar

Overall depth $D = d$ + Clear Cover + diameter of bar/2

$$= 154 + 20 + \frac{8}{2} = 178 \text{ mm} \approx 180 \text{ mm}$$

According to [CL 23.0 P 36]

Available effective depth in shorter span $dx = 180 - 20 - 4 = 156$ mm

Available effective depth in longer span $dy = dx$ – diameter of bar

$$= 156 - 8 = 148 \text{ mm}$$

Effective span in shorter span $lx$ = Clear span + effective depth

$$= 4.2 + 0.156 = 4.356 \text{ m}$$

Effective span in longer span $ly = 4.6 + 0.148 = 4.748$ m

According to [CL 22.2 P34] lesser effective span should be consider

Aspect Ratio $r = \dfrac{ly}{lx} = \dfrac{4.748}{4.356}$

$r = 1.09 < 2$

Bending Moment coefficient [Table 27 P 91]

$$\alpha x = \frac{1}{8}\frac{r^4}{(1+r^4)} = \frac{1}{8} \times \frac{(1.09)^4}{(1+1.09^4)} = 0.074$$

$$\alpha y = \frac{1}{8}\frac{r^2}{(1+r^4)} = \frac{1}{8} \times \frac{(1.09)^2}{(1+1.09^4)} = 0.061$$

**Calculation of loads and B.M.**

Consider 1 metre wide strip ($b$) of slab

(*i*) Self *wt.* of slab $= D \times \rho = 0.180 \times 25 = 4.5 \text{ kN/m}^2$

(*ii*) Floor Finish $= D \times \rho = 0.040 \times 24 = 0.96 \text{ kN/m}^2$

(*iii*) Live load on slab $= 3.0 \text{ kN/m}^2$

Total load $= 8.46 \text{ kN/m}^2$

Factored load $= 1.5 \times 8.46 = 12.69 \text{ kN/m}^2$

Max$^m$ B.M. at shorter direction $Mx = \alpha x w lx^2$

$$= 0.074 \times 12.69 \times (4.356)^2$$
$$= 17.83 \text{ kN–M}$$

Max$^m$ B.M. on longer direction $My = \alpha y\, w lx^2$

$$= 0.061 \times 12.69 \times (4.356)^2$$
$$= 14.46 \text{ kN–M}$$

Design of Reinforcement, $Rx = \dfrac{Mx}{bdx^2}$

$$= \frac{17.83 \times 10^6}{1000 \times (156)^2} = 0.73 \text{ N/mm}^2$$

$$\frac{\text{Astx required in shorter direction}}{bdx} = \frac{\sigma_{ck}}{2\,\sigma_y}\left[1 - \sqrt{1 - \frac{4.59\,Rx}{\sigma_{ck}}}\right]$$

$$\frac{\text{Required Ast x}}{1000 \times 154} = \frac{20}{2 \times 415}\left[1 - \sqrt{1 - \frac{4.59 \times 0.72}{20}}\right]$$

Required $Astx$ $= 320.92 \text{ mm}^2$

Using 8 mm $\phi$ bar $A\phi = \frac{\pi}{4}(8)^2 = 50.24 \text{ mm}^2$

$$\text{Spacing} = \frac{A\phi}{Astx} \times 1000$$

$$= \frac{50.24}{320.92} \times 1000 = 156.53 \text{ mm}$$

Check for Max$^m$ spacing [CL. 26.3 P46] $= 3\,dx = 3 \times 156 = 468$ mm

or $= 300$ mm

Provided 8 mm $\phi$ bar @ 150 mm c/c

Actual area of steel provided in shorter direction

$$Astx = \frac{A\phi}{\text{spacing}} \times 1000$$

$$= \frac{50.24}{150} \times 1000 = 334.49 \text{ mm}^2 > 320.92 \text{ mm}^2$$

$$\text{Similarly, } Ry = \frac{My}{bdy^2} = \frac{14.46 \times 10^6}{1000 \times (148)^2} = 0.66 \text{ N/mm}^2$$

$$\text{Ast } y \text{ req. in longer direction} = \frac{bdy\,\sigma_{ck}}{2\times\sigma_y}\left[1 - \sqrt{1 - \frac{4.59\,Ry}{\sigma_{ck}}}\right]$$

$$= \frac{1000 \times 148 \times 20}{2 \times 415}\left[1 - \sqrt{1 - \frac{4.59 \times 0.67}{20}}\right] = 281.17 \text{ mm}^2$$

$$\text{Spacing} = \frac{A\phi}{Asty} \times 1000$$

$$= \frac{50.24}{281.17} \times 1000 = 178.67 \text{ mm}$$

Check for max$^m$ spacing $= 3\,dy$ or $300 = 3 \times 148 = 444$ mm

Provided 8 mm $\phi$ bar @ 175 mm c/c

**Check for Serviceability criteria**

Check for deflection criteria

$$\% \text{ of steel} = \frac{Astx \text{ provided}}{b \times dx} \times 100$$

$$= \frac{334.49}{1000 \times 156} \times 100 = 0.21\%$$

Modification factors $\alpha = 20,\ \beta = 1,\ \gamma = 1.62,\ \lambda = 1,\ \delta = 1$

$$d = \frac{1}{\alpha\,\beta\,\gamma\,\lambda\,\delta}$$

$$= \frac{4.356 \times 10^3}{20 \times 1 \times 1.62 \times 1 \times 1} = 134.4 \text{ mm} < 156 \text{ mm Hence O.K.}$$

$lx/dx$ max $= 20 \times 1.62 = 32.4$

$lx/dx$ provided $= \dfrac{4356}{156} = 27.92$

$lx/dx$ max > $lx/dx$ provided hence over all depth can be provided

$$134.4 + 20 + 4 = 158 \approx 160 \text{ mm} < 180 \text{ mm Hence O.K}$$

Check for shear

$$\text{Max}^{m} \text{ shear force } Vu = \frac{wlx}{2}$$

$$= \frac{12.69 \times 10^3 \times 4.2}{2} = 26.64 \text{ kN}$$

$$\text{Nominal shear stress } \tau v = \frac{Vu}{bdx} \text{ [CL.B5.1, P83]}$$

$$dx = 160 - 20 - 4 = 136$$

$$= \frac{25.64 \times 10^3}{1000 \times 136} = 0.195 \text{ N/mm}^2$$

For 0.25% of steel and M20 grade of concrete [Table 19 P73]

$$\tau c = 0.28 + \frac{0.36 - 0.28}{(0.25 - 0.15)} \times (0.21 - 0.15) = 0.328$$

$\tau c = 0.328$ and thickness of slab 180 mm $K = 1.21$ [CL 40.2.11, P73]

$$\tau c' = k \times \tau c$$

$$= 1.21 \times 0.328 = 0.426 \text{ N/mm}^2$$

$$\tau c' > \tau v = \text{O.K.}$$

Check for development length: [CL 26.2.1 P42]

$$L_d = \frac{0.87 \sigma y \phi}{4 \tau_{bd}} \text{ [}\tau_{bd} \text{ from CL26.2.1.1, P43]}$$

$$= \frac{0.87 \times 415 \times 8}{4 \times 1.92}$$

$$= 376.09 \text{ mm}$$

$$= 1.3 \frac{M1}{V} + L_o \geq L_d \text{ [CL26.2.3.3, P44]}$$

$$L_o = 12 \phi \text{ OR } dx$$

$$= 12 \times 8 = 96 \text{ mm or } 136 \text{ mm}$$

For partial fixity, 50% reinforcement should be provided at a distance $0.1 l_x$ from face of support

$$M1 = \frac{17.55 \times 10^6}{2} = 8.775 \times 10^6 \text{ N–mm}$$

$$V = 26.64 \text{ kN}$$

$$= \frac{1.3 \times 8.0 \times 10^6}{26.64 \times 10^3} + 136$$

$$= 563.95 \text{ mm} > 376.09 \text{ O.K}$$

Distribution reinforcement for holding the top bars [CL 26.5.2.1 P48]

Area of distribution reinforcement = 0.12% of $bD$

$$= \frac{0.12}{100} \times 1000 \times 155 = 186 \text{ mm}^2$$

Using 8 mm diameter of bar

$$\text{Spacing of bar} = \frac{1000 \times 50.24}{186} = 270 \text{ mm}$$

Check for max spacing [CL 26.3.3.b2 P46] = 5 *d* or 450 mm

$= 5 \times 136 = 680$ mm

Provided 8 mm Φ 270 mm c/c

**Schedule of Slab**

Grade of concrete M 20 and Grade of steel Fe 415

| *Thickness (mm)* | *Clear cover (mm)* | *Reinforcement parallel to* | | *Remark* |
|---|---|---|---|---|
| | | *Short side (mm)* | *Long side (mm)* | |
| 160 | 20 | 8 Φ @ 150 c/c<br>8 Φ @ 300 c/c<br>8 Φ @ 270 c/c | 8 Φ @ 175 c/c<br>8 Φ @ 350 c/c<br>8 Φ @ 270 c/c | Bottom bars<br>Top bars<br>Top Distribution |

**Problem 8.3.** *Design a two way RC floor slab over a room having internal dimension 4.6 m × 4.20 m. The floor is simply supported on all four wall of thickness 230 mm, with a 40 mm thick mosaic flooring as a floor finished. The corners of the slab are not free to lift and carrying a live load of 3 kN/m². Take Grade of concrete M 20 and Grade of steel Fe 415.*

**Solution.**

Given data

Size of room = 4.6 m × 4.2 m

Clear span in shorter direction $lx$ = 4.2 m

Clear span in longer direction $ly$ = 4.6 m

Width of supporting wall = 230 mm

Grade of concrete $\sigma_{ck} = M\ 20$

Grade of steel $\sigma_y = Fe\ 415$

Mosaic flooring 40 mm thick

Corners are not free to lift or held down or restrained.

**DESIGN**

Effective span = c/c distance of support [CL 22.2 P34]

$$\text{Effective span in shorter direction } lx = 4.2 + \frac{0.23}{2} + \frac{0.23}{2}$$

$$= 4.43 \text{ m}$$

$$\text{Effective span in longer direction } ly = 4.6 + \frac{0.23}{2} + \frac{0.23}{2}$$

$$= 4.83 \text{ m}$$

Depth of slab governed by Serviceability criteria [CL 23.2.1 P37]

$$\text{Effective depth based upon deflection criteria } d = \frac{lx}{\alpha \beta \gamma \lambda \delta}$$

Assuming $Pt = 0.2\%$, from Fig. 4 P 38 corresponding curve of $\sigma_y$ 240 N/mm² to assumed $Pt$.

Modification factors $\alpha = 20,\ \beta = 1,\ \gamma = 1.43,\ \lambda = 1,\ \delta = 1$

$$d = \frac{4.43}{20 \times 1 \times 1.60 \times 1 \times 1}$$

$= 0.138$ mm

Consider 15 mm clear cover [Table 16.CL 26.4.2 P47] and 8 mm diameter of bar

Overall depth $D = d$ + Clear Cover + diameter of bar/2

$= 138 + 20 + 8/2$

$= 157 \text{ mm} \approx 160 \text{ mm}$

According to [CL 23.0 P36]

Available effective depth in shorter span $dx = 160 - 15 - 4$

$= 141$ mm

Available effective depth in longer span $dy = dx$-diameter of bar

$= 141 - 8 = 133$ mm

Effective span in shorter span $lx$ = Clear span + effective depth

$= 4.2 + 0.141 + 4.341$ m

Effective span in longer span $ly = 4.6 + 0.133 = 4.733$ m

According to [CL 22.2 P34] lesser effective span should be consider

$$\text{Aspect Ratio } r = \frac{ly}{lx} = \frac{4.733}{4.341}$$

$r = 1.09 < 2$

Bending Moment coefficients [Table 26 P91] case 9. Four edge discontinuous

$$\alpha x = 0.056 + \frac{(0.064 - 0.056)}{(1.1 - 1.00)} (1.09 - 1.0)$$

$= 0.063$

$\alpha y = 0.056$

**Calculation of loads and B.M.**

Consider 1 metre wide strip ($b$) of slab

($i$) Self $wt.$ of slab $= D \times \rho = 0.160 \times 25 = 4.0 \text{ kN/m}^2$

($ii$) Floor Finish $= D \times \rho = 0.040 \times 24 = 0.96 \text{ kN/m}^2$

($iii$) Live load on slab $= 3.0 \text{ kN/m}^2$

Total load $= 7.96 \text{ kN/m}^2$

Factored load $= 1.5 \times 7.96 = 12.0 \text{ kN/m}^2$

Max$^m$ B.M. at shorter direction $Mx = \alpha x\, wlx^2$

$= 0.063 \times 12.0 \times (4.341)^2$

$= 14.25$ kN–M

Max$^m$ B.M. on longer direction $My = \alpha y\, wlx^2$

$= 0.056 \times 12.0 \times (4.341)^2$

$= 12.67$ kN–m

Design of Reinforcement for middle strips

$$Rx = \frac{Mx}{bdx^2}$$

$$= \frac{14.25 \times 10^6}{1000 \times (141)^2} = 0.72 \text{ N/m}^2$$

$$\frac{\text{Astx required in shorter direction}}{bdx} = \frac{\sigma_{ck}}{2\,\sigma_y}\left[1 - \sqrt{1 - \frac{4.59\,Rx}{\sigma_{ck}}}\right]$$

$$\frac{\text{Required Ast x}}{1000 \times 141} = \frac{20}{2 \times 415}\left[1 - \sqrt{1 - \frac{4.59 \times 0.72}{20}}\right]$$

Required Ast.x $= 293.8 \text{ mm}^2$

Using 8 mm $\phi$ bar $A\phi = \frac{\pi}{4} \times 8^2 = 50.24 \text{ mm}^2$

Spacing $= \frac{A\,\phi}{Ast} \times 1000$

$$= \frac{50.24 \times 1000}{293.8} = 170.98 \text{ mm say } 170 \text{ mm}$$

Check for Max$^m$ spacing [CL. 26.3.3 P46] $= 3dx = 3 \times 141 = 423$ mm

or $= 300$ mm

Provided 8 mm $\phi$ bar @ 170 mm c/c

Actual area of steel provided in shorter direction

Astx $= \frac{A\phi \times 1000}{\text{spacing}}$

$$= \frac{50.24 \times 1000}{170} = 295.52 \text{ mm}^2 > 293.8 \text{ mm}^2$$

Similarly, $Ry = \frac{My}{bdy^2}$

$$= \frac{12.67 \times 10^6}{1000 \times (133)^2} = 0.72 \text{ N/m}^2$$

Ast $y$ req. in longer direction $= \frac{bdy\,\sigma_{ck}}{2 \times \sigma y}\left[1 - \sqrt{1 - \frac{4.59\,Ry}{\sigma_{ck}}}\right]$

$$= \frac{1000 \times 133 \times 20}{2 \times 415}\left[1 - \sqrt{1 - \frac{4.59 \times 0.72}{20}}\right] = 275.84 \text{ mm}^2$$

Spacing $= \frac{A\phi \times 1000}{Asty}$

$$= \frac{50.24}{281.17} \times 1000 = 182 \text{ mm}$$

Check for max$^m$ spacing $= 3\,dy$ or $300 = 3 \times 133 = 399$ mm

Provided 8 mm $\phi$ bar @ 180 mm c/c

Reinforcement in edge strips [D.1.2 P90]

Length of the middle strips and edge strip along long side = 3550 mm and 300 mm each.

Length of the middle strips and edge strip along short side = 3255 mm and 270 mm each.

Minimum reinforcement [CL 26.5.2.1 P48]

Area of reinforcement = 0.12% of $bD$

$$= \frac{0.12}{100} \times 1000 \times 160 = 192 \text{ mm}^2$$

Using 8 mm dia of bar

$$\text{Spacing of bar} = \frac{1000 \times 50.24}{192} = 270 \text{ mm}$$

Provided 8 mm Φ @ 270 mm c/c both way

Corners reinforcement [D.1.8 P 90]

All the edges are discontinuous

$$\text{Size of corner mesh} = \frac{lx}{5} = \frac{4.34}{5} = 868 \text{ mm say } 870 \text{ mm}$$

$$\text{Area of steel in one layer} = 0.75\, Atsx = 0.75 \times 295.52 = 221.64 \text{ mm}^2$$

$$\text{Using 8 mm } \Phi \text{ spacing} = \frac{1000 \times 50.24}{221.64} = 226.67$$

Provide 8 mm Φ 225 mm c/c in four layers

Check for Serviceability criteria

Check for deflection criteria

$$\% \text{ of steel} = \frac{Astx \text{ provided}}{b \times dx} \times 100$$

$$= \frac{295.52 \times 100}{1000 \times 141} = 0.21\%$$

Modification factors $\alpha = 20, \beta = 1, \gamma = 1.62, \lambda = 1, \delta = 1$

$$d = \frac{1}{\alpha \beta \gamma \lambda \delta}$$

$$= \frac{4.341 \times 10^3}{20 \times 1 \times 1.62 \times 1 \times 1}$$

$$= 133.98 \text{ mm} < 141 \text{ mm Hence O.K}$$

$$lx/dx \text{ max} = 20 \times 1.62 = 32.4$$

$$lx/dx \text{ provided} = \frac{4341}{141} = 30.78$$

$lx/dx$ max > $lx/dx$ provided hence ok

Check for shear

$$\text{Max}^{m} \text{ shear force } Vu = \frac{wlx}{2}$$

$$= \frac{12.0 \times 10^3 \times 4.2}{2} = 25.2 \text{ kN}$$

$$\text{Nominal shear stress } \tau v = \frac{Vu}{bdx} \text{ [CL40.1, P72]}$$

$$= \frac{26.64 \times 10^3}{1000 \times 141} = 0.178 \text{ N/mm}^2$$

For 0.21% of steel and M20 grade of concrete [Table 19 P73]

$$\tau c = 0.28 + \frac{(0.36 - 0.28)}{(0.25 - 0.15)} \times (0.21 - 0.15) = 0.328$$

$$\tau c = 0.328 \text{ and thickness of slab 160 mm } K = 1.26 \text{ [CL40.2.11, P73]}$$

$$\tau c' = k \times \tau c = 1.26 \times 0.328 = 0.426 \text{ N/mm}^2$$

$\tau c' > \tau v$ O.K

Check for development length: [CL 26.2.1 P42]

$$Ld = \frac{0.87\, \sigma y\, \phi}{4\, \tau_{bd}} \quad [\tau_{bd} \text{ from CL 26.2.1.1, P43}]$$

$$= \frac{0.87 \times 415 \times 8}{4 \times 1.92} = 376.09 \text{ mm}$$

$$= \frac{1.3\, M1}{Vu} + Lo \geq Ld \text{ [CL26.2.3.3, P44]}$$

$$Lo = 12\, \phi \text{ OR } dx$$

$$= 12 \times 8 = 96 \text{ mm or 141 mm}$$

For partial fixity, 50% reinforcement should be provided at the top for a distance $0.1l_x$ from face of support.

$$M1 = \frac{14.25 \times 10^6}{2} = 7.125 \times 10^6 \text{ N–mm}$$

$$Vu = 25.20 \text{ kN}$$

$$= \frac{1.3\, M1}{Vu} + L_o = \frac{1.3 \times 7.125 \times 10^6}{26.64 \times 10^3} + 141$$

$$= 508.5 \text{ mm} > 376.09 \text{ O.K}$$

Distribution reinforcement for holding the top bars [CL 26.5.2.1 P48]

Area of distribution reinforcement = 0.12% of $bD$

$$= \frac{0.12}{100} \times 1000 \times 155 = 186 \text{ mm}^2$$

Using 8 mm diameter of bar

Spacing of bar $= \frac{1000 \times 50}{186} = 270$ mm

Check for max spacing [CL 26.3.3.b2 P46] = $5d$ or 450 mm

$= 5 \times 136 = 680$ mm

Provided 8 mm Φ @ 270 mm c/c

**Schedule of slab**

Grade of concrete M 20 and Grade of steel Fe 415

| *Thickness (mm)* | *Clear cover (mm)* | *Reinforcement parallel to* | | *Remark* |
|---|---|---|---|---|
| | | *Short side (mm)* | *Long side (mm)* | |
| 160 | 15 | 8 Φ @ 170 c/c | 8 Φ @ 180 c/c | Bottom bars middle strip |
| | | 8 Φ @ 225 c/c | 8 Φ @ 225 c/c | Edge strip |
| | | 8 Φ @ 340 c/c | 8 Φ @ 360 c/c | Top bars |
| | | 8 Φ @ 270 c/c | 8 Φ @ 270 c/c | Top Distribution |
| | | 8 Φ @ 225 c/c | 8 Φ @ 225 c/c | Corner mesh in four layer |

**Problem 8.4.** *Design a sunshade projecting 600 mm throughout the length of lintel flush with the bottom face 230 mm wide. Take M 20 concrete and Fe 415 steel. Assume a live load 0.75 kN/m² over the sunshade and a 12 mm thick plaster finishing.*

**Solution.**

Given:

$$\sigma_{ck} = 20 \text{ N/mm}^2$$

$$\sigma y = 415 \text{ N/mm}^2$$

Bearing = 230 mm

Width of sunshade = 600 mm

Live load = $0.75 \text{ kN/m}^2$

**DESIGN**

$$\text{Effective spans} \quad l = \text{Width of sun shade} + \frac{\text{bearing}}{2}$$

$$= 0.60 + \frac{0.23}{2} = 0.715 \text{ mm}$$

Assuming 0.2% of steel for M 20 and Fe 415

$$\text{Effective depth } (d) = \frac{l}{\alpha\,\beta\,\gamma\,\delta\,\lambda} \quad \text{[CL 23.2.1, P37]}$$

$(\alpha = 7, \beta = 1, \gamma = 1.55, \delta = 1, \lambda = 1)$

$$= 0.715/7 \times 1 \times 1.55 \times 1 \times 1 = 0.065 \text{ m}$$

Using 8 mm $\phi$ bar and 15 mm clear cover [Table 16 P47]

Required depth of sunshade $D$ = effective depth + clear cover + diameter of bar/2

$$= 65 + 15 + 8/2 = 82 \text{ mm}$$

Overall depth $(D) = 85$ mm

Available Effective depth $(d) = 85 - 15 - 4 = 66$ mm

Effective span $(l) = 600 + 66 = 660$ mm

*Calculation of load:*

Taking 1 m wide strip of cantilever slab/unit width

Self wt. of sunshade = depth of sunshade × density

$$= 0.085 \times 25 = 2.125 \text{ kN/m}$$

Plaster/floor load $= 0.012 \times 24 = 0.288$ kN/m

Live load @ 0.75 kN/m² = 0.75 = 0.75 kN/m

Total load = 3.16 kN/m

Factored load $= 1.5 \times 3.16 = 4.74$ kN/m

$$\text{Bending moment due to factored load} = \frac{wl^2}{2} = \frac{(4.74 \times 0.66)^2}{2}$$

$$= 1.03 \text{ kN–m} = 1.03 \times 10^6 \text{ N–mm}$$

*Calculation of steel:*

$$R = \frac{M}{bd^2} = \frac{1.03 \times 10^6}{1000 \times (66)^2} = 0.23 \text{ N/mm}^2$$

$$\frac{Ast\,(req.)}{bd} = \frac{\sigma_{ck}}{2\,\sigma y}\left[1 - \sqrt{1 - \frac{4.59\,R}{\sigma_{ck}}}\,\right]$$

$$= \frac{1000 \times 66 \times 20}{2 \times 415}\left[1 - \sqrt{1 - \frac{4.59 \times 0.23}{20}}\right]$$

$$= 43.89 \text{ mm}^2$$

Using 8 mm $\phi$ bar $A\phi = \frac{3.14}{4} \times 8^2 = 50.26 \text{ mm}^2$

Spacing $= \frac{A\phi}{Ast} \times 1000 = \frac{50.26 \times 1000}{43.89} = 1144$ mm c/c

Minimum reinforcement [CL 26.5.2.1 P48] = 0.12% $b \times D$

Using 8 mm $\phi$ bar of Fe 415 $A\phi = 50.24 \text{ mm}^2$

Area of reinforcement $= \frac{0.12}{100} \times 1000 \times 85 = 102 \text{ mm}^2$

Spacing $= \frac{A\phi \times 1000}{Ast} = \frac{50.26 \times 1000}{102} = 492.5$ mm c/c

Check for max$^m$ spacing [CL 26.3.3b.1 P46]

$= 3d = 3 \times 66 = 198$ mm

or $= 300$ mm

Provided 8 mm $\phi$ bar @ 200 mm c/c

Distribution/Temp. reinforcement [CL 26.6.5.2.1 P48]

$= 0.12\%\ b \times D$

Using 8 mm $\phi$ bar of Fe 415 $A\phi = 50.24 \text{ mm}^2$

Area of Distribution reinforcement = $102 \text{ mm}^2$

No. of bar $= \frac{102}{50.24} = 2.03 \approx 3$

Check for shear [CL 40.1 P72]

Factored Shear force $Vu = wL = 4.74 \times 0.60 = 4.74$ kN

Nominal shear stress $\tau v = \frac{Vu}{bd} = \frac{2.84 \times 10^3}{10^3 \times 66}$

$= 0.071 \text{ N/mm}^2$

Ast provided $= \frac{50.24 \times 1000}{200} = 251.2 \text{ mm}^2$

% of steel $= \frac{Ast}{bd} \times 100 = \frac{251.2}{1000 \times 66} \times 100 = 0.38\%$

[From table 19 P 73]

$$\tau c = 0.35 + \frac{0.35 + (0.46 - 0.35)(0.38 - 0.25)}{0.5 - 0.25}$$

$= 0.40 \text{ N/mm}^2$

According [CL 40.2.1 P72] $K = 1.3$ (depth < 150 mm)

$\tau c' = k \tau c$

$\tau c' = 1.3 \times 0.40 = 0.52 \text{ N/mm}^2$

$\tau c' > \tau v$ O.K

Check for deflection:

$l/d$ max $= 7 \times 1.28 = 8.96$ (M.F. at 0.38% = 1.28) [Fig. 4, P38]

$l/d$ provided $= \dfrac{660}{66} = 10$

$l/d$ provided > $l/d$ max

Check for development length $Ld = \dfrac{0.87\ \sigma y\Phi}{4\,\tau bd}$

[CL 26.2.1 P42]

$$\tau bd = 1.2 + \frac{60}{100} = 1.92 \text{ [CL 26.1.1, P43]}$$

$$= \frac{0.87 \times 415 \times 8}{4 \times 1.92} = 376.09 \text{ mm at the support}$$

**Schedule of Sunshade**

Grade of concrete M 20 and Grade of steel Fe 415

| *Thickness (mm)* | *Clear cover (mm)* | *Reinforcement parallel to* | | *Remark* |
|---|---|---|---|---|
| | | *Short side (mm)* | *Long side (mm)* | |
| 85 | 15 | 8 Φ @ 200 c/c<br>— | —<br>8 Φ 3 nos | Top bars<br>Top Distribution |
| 380 mm length of bar should be embedded at the support for lateral stability | | | | |

**Problem 8.5.** *Design a sunshade projecting 600 mm carries a fascia 100 mm × 200 mm in section at free end throughout the length of lintel flush with the bottom face 230 mm wide. Take M 20 concrete and Fe 415 steel. Assume a live load 5.0 kN/m² over the sunshade and a 10 mm thick c/c finishing.*

**Solution.**

Given:

$$\sigma_{ck} = 20 \text{ N/mm}^2$$

$$\sigma_y = 415 \text{ N/mm}^2$$

Bearing = 230 mm

Width of sunshade = 600 mm

Live load = $0.75 \text{ kN/m}^2$

**DESIGN**

Effective spans $l$ = Width of sun shade + bearing/2

$= 0.60 + 0.23/2 = 0.715$ m

Assuming 0.2% of steel for M 20 and Fe 415

Effective depth ($d$) $= \dfrac{1}{\alpha\beta\gamma\delta\lambda}$ [CL23.2.1, P37]

($\alpha = 7,\ \beta = 1,\ \gamma = 1.55,\ \delta = 1,\ \lambda = 1$)

$$= \frac{0.715}{7 \times 1 \times 1.55 \times 1 \times 1} = 0.065 \text{ m}$$

Using 8 mm $\phi$ bar and 15 mm clear cover [Table 16 P47]

Required depth of sunshade $D$ = effective depth + clear cover + diameter of bar/2

$= 65 + 15 + 8/2 = 82$ mm

Overall depth (D) = 85 mm

Available Effective depth ($d$) = $85 - 15 - 4 = 66$ mm

Effective span ($l$) = $600 + 66 = 660$ mm

**Calculation of Load**

Taking 1 m wide strip of cantilever slab/unit width

Self wt. of sunshade = depth of sunshade × density

$= 0.085 \times 25 = 2.125$ kN/m

Plaster/floor load $= 0.010 \times 24 = 0.24$

Live load @ 5.0 kN/m$^2$ = 5.0 = 5.0 kN/m

Total load = 7.36 kN/m

Factored load $= 1.5 \times 7.36 = 11.0$ kN/m

Bending moment due to uniformly distributed $= \dfrac{wl^2}{2}$

$$= \frac{(11 \times 0.66)^2}{2}$$

$= 2.4$ kN–m $= 2.4 \times 10^6$ N–mm

Load due to fasia $= 0.20 \times 0.10 \times 25 = 0.50$ kW

Factored Load $= 1.5 \times 0.50 = 0.75$ kW

Bending Moment due to fasia (Point load) $= wl = 0.75 \times 0.66 = 0.495$ kN–m

Total B.M. $= \dfrac{wl^2}{8} + wl$

$= 2.4 \times 10^6 + 0.495 \times 10^6$

$= 2.895 \times 10^6$ N–mm

Calculation of steel $R = \dfrac{M}{b \times d^2}$

$$= \frac{2.895 \times 10^6}{1000 \times (66)^2}$$

$= 0.66$ N/mm$^2$

$$\frac{Ast\,(req.)}{bd} = \frac{\sigma_{ck}}{2\,\sigma y}\left[1 - \sqrt{1 - \frac{4.59\,R}{\sigma_{ck}}}\right]$$

$$= \frac{1000 \times 66 \times 20}{2 \times 415}\left[1 - \sqrt{1 - \frac{4.59 \times 0.66}{20}}\right]$$

$= 126.31$ mm$^2$

Using 8 mm $\phi$ bar

$$A\,\phi = \frac{3.14}{4} \times 8^2 = 50.24 \text{ mm}^2$$

Spacing $= \dfrac{A\,\phi}{Ast} \times 1000 = \dfrac{50.24}{126.31} \times 1000 = 397.78$ mm

Minimum reinforcement [CL 26.5.2.1 P48] = 0.12% $b \times D$

Area of reinforcement $= \dfrac{0.12}{100} \times 1000 \times 85 = 102 \text{ mm}^2$

Spacing $= \dfrac{A\phi \times 1000}{Ast} = \dfrac{50.26 \times 1000}{102} = 492.5 \text{ mm c/c}$

Check for max$^m$ spacing [CL 26.3.3 b.1 P46]

$= 3d = 3 \times 66 = 198 \text{ mm}$

or $= 300 \text{ mm}$

Provide 8 mm Φ bar @ 200 mm c/c

Distribution/Temp. reinforcement [CL 26.5.2.1 P48]

$= 0.12\% \; b \times D$

Using 8 mm $\phi$ bar of Fe 415, $A\phi = 50.24 \text{ mm}^2$

Area of Distribution reinforcement $= \dfrac{0.12}{100} \times 1000 \times 85 = 102 \text{ mm}^2$

No. of bar $= \dfrac{102}{50.24} = 2.03 \approx 3$

Check for shear [CL 40.1 P 72]

Factored shear force due to u.d.l. $V = wL = 11.0 \times 0.60 = 6.6 \text{ kN}$

Factored shear force due to point load $= w = 0.75 \text{ kN}$

Total factored shear force 6.6 + 0.75

$Vu = 7.35 \text{ kN}$

Nominal shear stress $\tau V = \dfrac{Vu}{bd} = \dfrac{7.35 \times 10^3}{10^3 \times 66}$

$= 0.11 \text{ N/mm}^2$

Ast provided $= \dfrac{50.24 \times 1000}{200} = 251.2 \text{ mm}^2$

% of steel $= \dfrac{1000 \times Ast}{bd}$

$= \dfrac{251.2}{1000 \times 66} \times 100 = 0.38\%$

[From Table 19 P 73]

$$\tau c = 0.35 + \frac{(0.46 - 0.35)}{(0.5 - 0.25)} (0.38 - 0.25)$$

$= 0.40 \text{ N/mm}^2$

According [CL.40.2.1 P72] $K = 1.3$ depth $< 150$ mm

$\tau c' = k \tau c$

$\tau c' = 1.3 \times 0.40 = 0.52 \text{ N/mm}^2$

$\tau c' = \tau_v$ O.K

Check for deflection

$l/d$ max $= 7 \times 1.28 = 8.96$ (M.F at 0.38% = 1.28) [Fig. 4, P38]

$l/d$ provided $= \dfrac{660}{66} = 10$

$l/d$ provided > $l/d$ max

Check for development length $Ld = \dfrac{0.87\ \sigma\ y\ \Phi}{4\ \tau\ bd}$ [CL 26.2.1, P42]

$\tau\ bd = \dfrac{1.2 + 60}{100} = 1.92$ [CL26.1.1,P43]

$\dfrac{0.87 \times 415 \times 8}{4 \times 1.92} = 376.09$ mm at the support

**Schedule of sunshade**

Grade of concrete M20 and Grade of steel Fe 415

| *Thickness (mm)* | *Clear cover (mm)* | *Reinforcement parallel to* | | *Remark* |
|---|---|---|---|---|
| | | *Short side (mm)* | *Long side (mm)* | |
| 85 | 15 | 8 Φ @ 200 c/c<br>— | —<br>8 Φ 3 nos | Top bars<br>Top Distribution |
| 380 mm length of bar should be embedded at the support for lateral stability | | | | |

**Problem 8.6.** *A 1.5 m wide opening is located in a long wall 230 mm thick in such a way that one vertical edge of opening is just 600 mm, from the end of the wall while length of wall beyond second vertical edge is sufficiently large. The height of masonry wall above lintel is 1.9 m. Design suitable lintel adopts Fe 415 and M20.*

**Solution.**

Clean span (opening) $L = 1.5$ m

Width of support/wall $= 230$ m

Assume over all depth as 150 mm

Using 10 mm dia of bar and clear cover 25 mm

According to IS code 456; 2000 [CL 22.2 a P34]

Effective depth ($d$) $= \dfrac{150 - 25 - 10}{2} = 120$ m

Effective span ($l$) = clear span + one bearing

$= 1.50 + 0.230 = 1.730$ m

Effective span ($l$) = clear span + effective depth

$= 1.50 + 0.120 = 1.620$ m

Calculation of loads and bending moments

Since one vertical edge of the opening is at less than half the effective span of the lintel and distance on the other side is quite large the load on the lintel will have to be taken of rectangular masonry equal to the effective span of lintel.

Dead Load of lintel $= 0.23 \times 0.15 \times 25$

$= 0.86$ kN/m

Dead Load on masonry $= 0.23 \times 1.62 \times 1.92$

$= 7.15$ kN/m

Total load $= 8.013$ kN/m

Factored load $= 1.5 \times 8.01 = 12.02$ kN/m

Factored B.M. $= \dfrac{wl^2}{8} = \dfrac{12.01 \times (1.62)^2}{8} = 3.94$ kN.m

$$R = \frac{M}{b \times d^2} = \frac{3.94 \times 10^6}{230 \times (120)^2}$$

$$= 1.19 \text{ N/mm}^2$$

$$Ast = \frac{b \times d \times \sigma_{ck}}{2\,\sigma y}\left[1 - \sqrt{1 - \frac{4.59\,R}{\sigma_{ck}}}\right]$$

$$= \frac{230 \times 120 \times 20}{2 \times 415}\left[1 - \sqrt{1 - \frac{4.59 \times 1.19}{20}}\right]$$

$$= 98.10 \text{ mm}^2$$

Using 8 mm bars, No. of bar $= \dfrac{98.10}{50.24} = 1.95$

Hence provide 2 bar 8 mm $\phi$ bar

Check for shear

$$Vu = \frac{W}{2} = \frac{12.02}{2} = 6.01 \text{ kN}$$

Nominal shear [CL 40.1 P72]

$$\tau v = \frac{Vu}{bd} = \frac{6.01 \times 1000}{230 \times 120} = 0.21 \text{ N/mm}^2$$

% of steel $= \dfrac{100\,Ast}{bd}$

$$= \frac{100 \times 2 \times 50.24}{230 \times 120} = 0.36\%$$

$\tau_c$ for M20 grade of concrete and of % of steel = 0.36 [Table 19 P 73]

$$\tau c = 0.36 + \frac{(0.48 - 0.36)}{0.50 - 0.25} \times (0.5 - 0.36)$$

$$= 0.42 \text{ N/mm}^2$$

$= \tau c > \tau v$ Hence Safe

Provide shear reinforcement in the form of vertical stirrups *i.e.*
2 legged vertical stirrups 8 mm $\phi$ bar

$$A\,\phi = 2 \times (\pi/4)\,8^2 = 100.48 \text{ mm}^2$$

$$Ast = \frac{0.4\,Sv \times b}{0.87 \times \sigma y} \quad \text{[CL26.5.1.6, P48]}$$

$$Sv = \frac{100.48 \times 0.87 \times 415}{0.4 \times 230}$$

$$Sv = 394.32 \text{ mm}$$

Check for max$^m$ spacing 0.75 $d$ or 450 [CL 26.5.1.5 P47]

$$= 0.75 \times 120 = 90 \text{ mm}$$

Hence provide 8 mm $\phi$ 2 legged vertical stirrups @ 90 mm c/c.

Check for development length,

Ld required $= \dfrac{0.87\ \sigma y\ \phi}{4\ \tau\ bd}$ = [CL26.2.3.3, P44]

$= \dfrac{0.87 \times 415 \times 8}{4 \times 1.92} = 376.09$ mm

$M1 = BM = 3.94 \times 10^6$ N.mm

$Lo = 12\ \phi$ or $d$

$Lo = 12 \times 8 = 96$ mm or 120 mm

$= \dfrac{1.3\ M1}{Vu} + Lo$

$= \dfrac{1.3 \times 3.94 \times 10^6}{6.01 \times 10^3} + 120 = 972.1$ mm > 376.07 Hence O.K.

Hence it is safe in development length

Check for deflection

% of steel $= \dfrac{\text{Ast provided}}{\text{b} \times \text{d}} \times 100$

$= \dfrac{100.48}{230 \times 120} \times 100 = 0.36\%$

Now, $M.F. = 1.4$ [Fig.4, P38]

$l/d$ maximum $= 1.42 \times 20 = 28$

$l/d$ provided $= \dfrac{1.62}{0.120} = 13.5$

$l/d$ provided < $l/d$ max *i.e.* 28 > 13.5 Hence O.K.

**Schedule of lintel**

Grade of concrete M 20 and Grade of steel Fe 415

| *Thickness (mm)* | *Clear cover (mm)* | *Width (mm)* | *Reinforcement (mm)* | *Remark* |
|---|---|---|---|---|
| 150 | 25 | 230 | 8 Φ 2 nos<br>8 Φ 2 nos<br>8 Φ @ 90 c/c | Bottom bars<br>Top bars<br>2L stirrups throughout |

**Problem 8.7.** *Designs a lintel over 1.5 m wide windows, which is positioned in the central length of a long wall 230 mm thick. The height from floor to ceiling is 4 m and the sill level of window is 0.6 m. Consider grade of steel Fe 415 and grade of concrete M20.*

**Solution.**

Clean span (opening) $L = 1.5$ m

Width of supporting wall = 230 mm

Assume over all depth of lintel = 150 mm

Using 10 mm dia of bar and clear cover 25 mm

According to IS code 456; 2000 [CL 22.2 a P34]

Effective depth $d = 150 - 25 - 10/2 = 120$ mm

Effective span $l$ = clear span + one bearing

$= 1.50 + 0.230 = 1.730$ m

Effective span $l$ = clear span + effective depth

= 1.50 + 0.120 = 1.620 m

Calculation of loads and bending moments

Since the opening is centrally located

Required height above lintel ($h$) = $\tan 60 \times \frac{1.62}{2} = 1.40$ m

Load due to triangular loading $= \frac{1}{2} \times 1.62 \times 1.4 \times 0.23 \times 20$

= 5.21 kN

Factored load = 1.5 × 5.21 = 7.82 kN

Bending moment due to triangular loading

$$= \frac{wl}{6} = \frac{7.82 \times 1.62}{6}$$

= 2.11 kN–m

Self-weight of lintel = 0.23 × 0.15 × 25

= 0.86 kN/m

Factored load = 1.5 × 5.21 = 1.29 kN/m

$$\text{Factored B.M.} = \frac{wl^2}{8} = \frac{129 \times (1.62)^2}{8}$$

= 0.42 kN.m

$$\text{Total bending moment} = \frac{wl}{6} + \frac{wl^2}{8}$$

$$M = 2.11 + 0.42 = 2.53 \text{ kN–m}$$

$$R = \frac{M}{b \times d^2}$$

$$= \frac{2.53 \times 10^6}{230 \times (120)^2} = 0.76 \text{ N/mm}^2$$

$$Ast. = \frac{b \times d \times \sigma_{ck}}{2\sigma y}\left[1 - \sqrt{1 - \frac{4.59\,R}{\sigma_{ck}}}\right]$$

$$= \frac{230 \times 120 \times 20}{2 \times 415}\left[1 - \sqrt{1 - \frac{4.59 \times 0.76}{20}}\right]$$

$$= 61.10 \text{ mm}^2$$

Using 8 mm bars, No. of bar $= \frac{61.10}{50.24} = 1.21$

Hence provide 2 bar 8 mm $\phi$ bar

*Check for shear:*

$$Vu = \frac{W}{2} + \frac{wl}{2}$$

$$= \frac{7.82}{2} + \frac{1.29 \times 1.5}{2} = 4.88 \text{ kN}$$

Nominal shear [CL 40.1 P72]

$$\tau v = \frac{Vu}{bd} = \frac{4.88 \times 1000}{230 \times 120} = 0.17 \text{ N/mm}^2$$

$$\text{\% of steel} = \frac{1000\, Ast}{bd}$$

$$= \frac{100 \times 2 \times 50.24}{230 \times 120} = 0.36\%$$

$\tau_c$ for M 20 grade of concrete and of % of steel = 0.36 [Table 19, P73]

$$\tau c = 0.36 + \frac{(0.48 - 0.36)}{(0.50 - 0.25)} \times (0.5 - 0.36)$$

$$= 0.42 \text{ N/mm}^2$$

$$= \tau c > \tau v \text{ Hence Safe}$$

Provide shear reinforcement in the form of vertical stirrups *i.e.* 2 legged vertical stirrups 8 mm $\phi$ bar

$$A\phi = 2 \times \frac{\pi}{4} 8^2 = 100.48 \text{ mm}^2$$

$$Ast = \frac{0.4\, Sv \times b}{0.87 \times \sigma y} \quad \text{[CL26.5.1.6, P48]}$$

$$Sv = \frac{100.48 \times 0.87 \times 415}{0.4 \times 230}$$

$$Sv = 394.32 \text{ mm}$$

Check for max$^{m}$ spacing 0.75 *d* or 450 [CL 26.5.1.5 P47]

$$= 0.75 \times 120 = 90 \text{ mm}$$

Hence provide 8 mm $\phi$ 2 legged vertical stirrups @ 90 mm c/c.
Check for development length,

$$\text{Ld required} = \frac{0.87\, \sigma y\, \phi}{4\, \tau\, bd} \quad \text{[CL 26.2.3.3, P44]}$$

$$= 0.87 \times 415 \times 84 \times 1.92$$

$$= 376.09 \text{ mm}$$

$$M1 = M = 2.53 \times 10^6 \text{ N.mm}$$

$$Lo = 12\,\phi \text{ or } d$$

$$Lo = 12 \times 8 = 96 \text{ mm or } 120 \text{ mm}$$

$$= \frac{1.3\, M1}{Vu} + Lo$$

$$= \frac{1.3 \times 2.53 \times 10^6}{4.88 \times 10^3} + 120$$

$$= 793.9 \text{ mm} > 376.07 \text{ Hence O.K.}$$

Hence it is safe in development length

*Check for deflection:*

$$\text{\% of steel} = \frac{Ast \text{ provided}}{b \times d} \times 100$$

$$= \frac{100 \times 100.48}{230 \times 120}$$

$$= 0.36\%$$

Now, M.F. = 1.4 [Fig. 4·P38]

$l/d$ maximum $= 1.42 \times 20 = 28$

$l/d$ provided $= \frac{1.62}{0.120} = 13.5$

$l/d$ provided < $l/d$ max *i.e.* 28 > 13.5 Hence O.K.

**Schedule of lintel**

Grade of concrete M 20 and Grade of steel Fe 415

| *Thickness (mm)* | *Clear cover (mm)* | *Width (mm)* | *Reinforcement (mm)* | *Remark* |
|---|---|---|---|---|
| 150 | 25 | 230 | 8 Φ 2 nos<br>8 Φ 2 nos<br>8 Φ @ 90 c/c | Bottom bars<br>Top bars<br>2L stirrups throughout |

**Problem 8.8.** *A simply supported singly reinforced RC rectangular beam which is used over a clear span of 5000 mm. The entire length of the beam is loaded by a superimposed uniformly distributed load of 20kN/m in addition to its own weight. If $\sigma_{ck}$ = 20 MPa and $\sigma_y$ = 415 MPa, design suitable beam with wall thickness is 230 mm.*

**Solution.**

Clean span $L = 5$ m

Width of supporting wall = 230 mm

Effective span ($l$) = clear span + one bearing

= 5.0 + 0.230 = 5.230 m

Assume depth of beam 1/10 to 1/15

Effective depth $= \frac{5.230}{15} = 348.6$ mm

Using 25 mm dia of bar and clear cover 25 mm

According to IS code 456; 2000 [CL 22.2 a P34]

Overall depth ($D$) $= 348.6 + 25 + \frac{25}{2}$

= 386.16 mm say 400 mm

Available effective depth $= 400 - 25 - \frac{25}{2} = 362.5$ mm

Effective span ($l$) = clear span + one bearing

= 5.0 + 0.230 = 5.230 m

Effective span ($l$) = clear span + effective depth

= 5.0 + 0.362 = 5.362 m

Effective span $l = 5.230$ m

Calculation of loads and bending moments

Dead Load of beam $= 0.23 \times 0.40 \times 25$

= 2.3 kN/m

Superimposed load = 20 kN/m

Total load = 22.3 kN/m

Factored load = 1.5 × 22.3 = 33.45 kN/m

$$\text{Factored B.M.} = \frac{wl^2}{8} = \frac{33.45 \times (5.23)^2}{8}$$

= 114.36 kN.m

$$R = \frac{BM}{b \times d^2}$$

$$= \frac{114.36 \times 10^6}{230 \times (362.5)^2} = 3.78 \text{ N/mm}^2$$

$$Ast. = \frac{b \times d \times \sigma_{ck}}{2\,\sigma y}\left[1 - \sqrt{1 - \frac{4.59\,R}{\sigma_{ck}}}\right]$$

$$Ast. = \frac{230 \times 362.5 \times 20}{2\,415}\left[1 - \sqrt{1 - \frac{4.59 \times 3.78}{20}}\right]$$

= 1280.31 mm$^2$

$$\text{Area of 25 mm diameter bar} = \frac{3.14}{4} \times 25^2 = 490.87 \text{ mm}^2$$

$$\text{No. of bar} = \frac{1280.31}{490.87} = 2.6$$

Hence provide 2 bar 25 mm $\phi$ bar and 2 bar 16 mm $\phi$ bar

Area provided = 2 × 490.87 + 2 × 201.06 = 1383 mm$^2$ > 1280.31 mm$^2$

Check for required width of beam [CL 26.3.2. P45]

= 2 (side cover) + 2 (25 bar) + 2 (16 bar) + 3 (larger bar spacing)

= 2 × 25 + 2 × 25 + 2 × 16 + 3 × 25 = 207 mm < 230 mm O.K.

$$\text{Check for minimum steel Ast} = \frac{0.85\,b \times d}{\sigma y} \text{ [CL 26.5.1.1a P47]}$$

$$= \frac{0.85 \times 230 \times 362.5}{415} = 170 \text{ mm}^2$$

Check for maximum steel = 0.04 × $b$ × $D$ [CL 26.5.1.1a P47]

= 0.04 × 230 × 400 = 3680 mm$^2$

Hence 170 m$^2$ < 1383 mm$^2$ < 3680 mm$^2$

Provide 2 top bars of 12 mm diameter for holding the stirrups

*Check for shear:*

$$Vu = \frac{WL}{2}$$

$$= \frac{33.45 \times 5}{2} = 83.62 \text{ kN}$$

Nominal shear [CL 40.1 P72]

$$\tau v = \frac{Vu}{bd} = \frac{83.62 \times 1000}{230 \times 362.5} = 1.0 \text{ N/mm}^2$$

% of steel $= \dfrac{Ast}{b \times d} \times 100$

$= \dfrac{1383}{230 \times 362.5} \times 100 = 1.65\%$

$\tau_c$ for M20 grade of concrete and 1.65% of steel [Table 19 P73]

$$\tau c = 0.72 + \frac{(0.75 - 0.72)}{(1.75 - 1.50)}(1.65 - 1.5)$$

$$= 0.73 \text{ N/mm}^2$$

Design shear strength $Vus = Vu - \tau c \times b \times d$ [CL 40.4, P73]

$$= 83.62 \times 10^2 - 0.73 \times 230 \times 362.5$$

$$= 22089.25 \text{ kN}$$

Provide shear reinforcement in the form of vertical stirrups 2- legged vertical stirrups 8 mm $\phi$ bar

$$A\phi = 2 \times (\pi/4)\, 8^2 = 100.48 \text{ mm}^2$$

$$Sv = \frac{0.87 \times \sigma y \times d \times A\phi}{Vus}$$

$$= \frac{0.87 \times 415 \times 100.48 \times 362.5}{22089.25} = 595.3 \text{ mm}$$

Check for minimum shear steel [CL 26.5.1.6 P 48]

$$= \frac{0.87 \times \sigma y\, A\phi}{0.4\, b}$$

Spacing $Sv = \dfrac{100.48 \times 0.87 \times 415}{0.4 \times 230}$

$$Sv = 394.32 \text{ mm}$$

Check for max$^m$ spacing 0.75 $d$ or 450 [CL 26.5.1.5. P47]

$$= 0.75 \times 362.5 = 271.87 \text{ mm}$$

Hence provide 8 mm $\phi$ 2 legged vertical stirrups @ 250 mm c/c.

Check for development length,

Ld required $= \dfrac{0.87\, \sigma y \phi}{4\, \tau bd}$ [CL 26.2.3.3, P44]

$$= \frac{0.87 \times 415 \times 25}{4 \times 1.92}$$

$$= 1175.29 \text{ mm}$$

$M1 = BM = 114.36 \times 10^6$ N.mm [Neither bent up or curtailment of main bars at support]

$$Lo = 12\,\phi \text{ or } d$$

$$Lo = 12 \times 25 = 300 \text{ mm or } 362.5 \text{ mm}$$

$$= \frac{1.3\, M1}{Vu} + Lo$$

$$= \frac{1.3 \times 114.36 \times 10^6}{83.62 \times 10^3} + 362.5$$

$$= 2140 \text{ mm} > 1175.29 \text{ Hence O.K.}$$

Hence it is safe in development length

Check for deflection

% of steel $= \dfrac{\text{Ast. provided}}{\text{b} \times \text{d}} \times 100$

$= \dfrac{100 \times 1383}{230 \times 362.5} = 1.65\%$

Now, M.F = 0.88 [Fig. 4 P38]

*l/d* maximum $= 0.88 \times 20 = 17.6$

*l/d* provided $= \dfrac{5230}{362.5} = 14.42$

*l/d* provided < *l/d* max Hence O.K.

**Schedule of Beam**

Grade of concrete M 20 and Grade of steel Fe 415

| *Thickness (mm)* | *Clear cover (mm)* | *Width (mm)* | *Reinforcement (mm)* | *Remark* |
|---|---|---|---|---|
| 400 | 25 | 230 | 2 # 25 Φ + 2 # 16 Φ<br>2 # 25 Φ<br>8 Φ @ 250 c/c | Bottom bars<br>Top bars<br>2L stirrups throughout |

**Problem 8.9.** *Design a simply supported doubly reinforced RC rectangular beam which is used over a clear span of 5000 mm. The beam has to carry a superimposed uniformly distributed load of 20 kN/m in addition to its own weight. Consider $\sigma_{ck}$ = 20 MPa and $\sigma_y$ = 415 MPa, and bearing of wall is 230 mm.*

**Solution.**

Clean span = 5 m

Width of supporting wall = 230 mm

Effective span (*l*) = clear span + one bearing

= 5.0 + 0.230 = 5.230 m

Effective depth $d = \dfrac{l}{\alpha\,\beta\,\gamma\,\lambda\,\delta}$ [for 1.2% of tension steel]

Fig. 4 P38r = 0.95 and for 1% of compression steel Fig. 5 P39 = 1.25

$= \dfrac{5230}{20 \times 1 \times 0.95 \times 1.25 \times 1} = 220 \text{ mm}$

Using 20 mm dia of bar and clear cover 25 mm

According to IS code 456; 2000 [CL 22.2a P34]

Overall depth (D) $= 220 + 25 + \dfrac{20}{2}$

= 255 mm say 300 mm

Available effective depth $= 300 - 25 - \dfrac{20}{2} = 265 \text{ mm}$

Effective span (*l*) = clear span + one bearing

= 5.0 + 0.230 = 5.230 m

Effective span (*l*) = clear span + effective depth

= 5.0 + 0.265 = 5.265 m

Effective span $l$ = 5.230 m

Calculation of loads and bending moments

Dead Load of beam = $0.23 \times 0.30 \times 25$

$= 1.725$ kN/m

Superimposed load = 20 kN/m

Total load = 21.725 kN/m

Factored load = $1.5 \times 21.725 = 32.58$ kN/m

Factored B.M. $= \dfrac{wl^2}{8} = \dfrac{32.58 \times (5.23)^2}{8}$

$= 111.42$ kN.m

M (limited) [for single RC beam]

For Fe 415 $\dfrac{x}{d} = 0.48$

[CL G-1.1 c P 96]

M limited $= \dfrac{0.36\,xm}{d}\left[1 - \dfrac{0.42\,xm}{d}\right] \sigma_{ck}\, bd^2$

$= 0.36 \times 0.48\,[1 - 0.42 \times 0.48]\; 20 \times 230 \times 265^2 = 44.56 \times 10^6$

$$R = \frac{M \lim}{b \times d^2}$$

$$= \frac{44.56 \times 10^6}{230 \times (265)^2} = 2.75 \text{ N/mm}^2$$

$$Ast_1 = \frac{b \times d \times \sigma_{ck}}{2\,\sigma y}\left[1 - \sqrt{1 - \frac{4.59\,R}{\sigma_{ck}}}\right]$$

$$= \frac{230 \times 265 \times 20}{2 \times 415}\left[1 - \sqrt{1 - \frac{4.59 \times 2.75}{20}}\right]$$

$= 579.25$ mm$^2$

Strain in compression steel = $0.0035\,[1 - d'/xm]$ [CL.G 1.2P96]

$$d' = 25 + \frac{20}{2} = 35 \text{ mm}$$

and $xm = 0.48 \times 265 = 127.5$ mm

$= 0.0035\,[1 - 35/127.5] = 0.00253$

From table strain at 0.00241, stress = 342.8

Strain at 0.0076, stress = 351.8

Design stress in compression steel $\sigma_{sc} = 346.12$ N/mm$^2$

BM-Mlim $= \sigma\, sc\, Asc\, (d - d')$ [CLG-1.2, P96]

$Asc$ $= (111.42 - 44.56)\; 10^6/346.12\,(265 - 35)$

$= 839.86$ mm$^2$

$Ast_2$ $= Asc\; \sigma\, sc/0.87\, \sigma\, y$

$= 839.86 \times 346.12/0.87 \times 415$

$= 805$ mm$^2$

Total tension steel = 579.25 + 805 = 1610.13 $mm^2$

Area of 20 mm diameter bar = $\frac{3.14}{4} \times 20 \times 20 = 314\ mm^2$

No. of bar $= \frac{1610.13}{314} = 5.12$

Hence provide 5 bar 20 mm $\phi$ bar and 1 bar 12 mm $\phi$ bar

Area provided = $5 \times 314 + 1 \times 113 = 1683\ mm^2 > 1610.13\ mm^2$

Check for required width of beam [CL 26.3.2 P 45]

= 2 (side cover) + 5 (20 bar) + 1 (12 bar) + 5 (larger bar spacing)

$= 2 \times 25 + 5 \times 20 + 1 \times 12 + 5 \times 20 = 262\ mm > 230\ mm$

Hence provide tensile bars n two row

Check for minimum steel $Ast = \frac{0.85\, b \times d}{\sigma y}$ [CL 26.5.1.1. a P47]

$= \frac{0.85 \times 230 \times 362.5}{415} = 170\ mm^2$

Check for maximum steel $= 0.04 \times b \times D$ [CL 26.5.1.1b P47]

$= 0.04 \times 230 \times 400 = 3680\ mm^2$

Hence $170\ mm^2 < 1383\ mm^2 < 3680\ mm^2$

Total compression steel = 805 $mm^2$

Numbers of bars required $= \frac{805}{314} = 2.56$

Provide 2-bars of 20 mm diameters and 1 bar of 16 mm

Asc provided = $2 \times 314 + 1 \times 113 = 829\ mm^2 > 805\ mm^2$

% of compression steel $= \frac{829 \times 100}{230 \times 265} = 1.36$

*Check for shear:*

$$Vu = \frac{WL}{2}$$

$$= \frac{32.85 \times 5}{2} = 81.45\ kN$$

Nominal shear [CL 40.1 P72]

$$\tau v = \frac{Vu}{bd} = \frac{81.45 \times 1000}{230 \times 265}$$

$$= 1.33\ N/mm^2$$

% of steel $= \frac{100 \times Ast}{b \times d}$

$$= \frac{100 \times 1610.13}{230 \times 265} = 2.76\%$$

$\tau_c$ for M20 grade of concrete and 2.76% of steel [Table 19 P 73]

$$\tau c = 0.82\ N/mm^2$$

Design shear strength $Vus = Vu - \tau c \times b \times d$ [CL40.4, P73]

$= 81.45 \times 10^2 - 0.82 \times 230 \times 265$

$= 31.471$ kN

Provide shear reinforcement in the form of vertical stirrups *i.e.*

2-legged vertical stirrups 8 mm $\phi$ bar

$$A\phi = 2 \times (\pi/4)\, 8^2 = 100.48 \text{ mm}^2$$

$$Sv = 0.87 \times \sigma y \times d \times A\phi \big/ Vus$$

$$= \frac{0.87 \times 415 \times 100.48 \times 265}{31471}$$

$$= 304 \text{ mm}$$

Check for minimum shear steel [CL 26.5.1.6 P48]

$$= \frac{0.87 \times \sigma y\, A\phi}{0.4\, b}$$

$$Sv = \frac{100.48 \times 0.87 \times 415}{0.4 \times 230}$$

$$Sv = 394.32 \text{ mm}$$

Check for max$^{m}$ spacing 0.75 $d$ or 450 [CL 26.5.1.5 P47]

$$= 0.75 \times 265 = 198.75 \text{ mm}$$

Hence provide 8 mm $\phi$ 2 legged vertical stirrups @ 190 mm c/c.

Check for development length,

$$\text{Ld required} = \frac{0.87\ \sigma y \phi}{4\, \tau bd} \quad \text{[CL26.2.3.3P44]}$$

$$= \frac{0.87 \times 415 \times 20}{4 \times 1.92}$$

$$= 940.23 \text{ mm}$$

$M1 = BM = 114.36 \times 10^6$ N.mm [Neither bent up or curtailment of main bars at support]

$$Lo = 12\phi \text{ or } d$$

$$Lo = 12 \times 20 = 240 \text{ mm or } 265 \text{ mm}$$

$$= \frac{1.3\, M1}{Vu} + Lo$$

$$= \frac{1.3 \times 111.42 \times 10^6}{81.45 \times 10^3} + 265$$

$$= 2043 \text{ mm} > 940.23 \text{ Hence O.K.}$$

Hence it is safe in development length

Check for deflection

Now, M.F. $\gamma = 0.8$ [Fig. 4 P38]

$\lambda = 1.31$ [Fig. 5, P38]

$$l/d \text{ maximum} = 20 \times 1 \times 0.8 \times 1.31 \times 1$$

$$= 20.96$$

$$l/d \text{ provided} = \frac{5230}{265} = 19.73$$

$l/d$ provided < $l/d$ max Hence O.K.

**Schedule of beam**

Grade of concrete M20 and Grade of steel Fe 415

| *Thickness (mm)* | *Clear cover (mm)* | *Width (mm)* | *Reinforcement (mm)* | *Remark* |
|---|---|---|---|---|
| 300 | 25 (Top and bottom) | 230 | 5 # 20 Φ + 1 # 12 Φ<br>2 # 20 Φ + 1 # 16 Φ<br>8 Φ @ 190 mm c/c | Bottom bars (in two row)<br>Top bars<br>2L stirrups throughout |

**Problem 8.10.** *A 7.0 m × 21.0 m hall is to be roofed with RC T beams and slab. The beams ribs are spaced at 3 m c/c and thickness of the flange (slab) is 110 mm and a roof terracing 75 mm c.c over it with a live load of 3 kN/m² in addition to its weight. The thickness of wall is 230 mm all around and adopt* $\sigma_{ck}$ *= 20 MPa and* $\sigma_y$ *415 MPa, design suitable T beam.*

**Solution.**

Clean span $L = 7$ m

Width of supporting wall = 230 mm

Effective span ($l$) = (clear span + one bearing)

= 7.0 + 0.230 = 7.230 m

Assume depth of beam 1/10 to 1/15

$$\text{Effective depth} = \frac{7.230}{14} = 510 \text{ mm}$$

Using 20 mm dia of bar and clear cover 25 mm

According to IS code 456; 2000 [CL 22.2a P34]

$$\text{Overall depth } (D) = \frac{510 + 25 + 20}{2}$$

= 545 mm say 550 mm

$$\text{Available effective depth} = \frac{550 + 25 - 20}{2}$$

Effective span ($l$) = clear span + one bearing

= 7.0 + 0.230 = 5.230 m

Effective span ($l$) = clear span + effective depth

= 7.0 + 0.515 = 7.515 m

According to [CL 23.1.2a P37]

$$B_f = \frac{lo}{6} + bw + 6\,Df$$

$$B_f = \frac{7.23}{6} + 0.23 + 6 \times 0.11 = 2.095 \text{ m}$$

or $B_f < [0.5\,(L_1 \text{ left} + L_2 \text{ right}) + bw]$

Dimension of T beam,

Effective span = 7.23 m

$bw$ = 230 mm

$d$ = 515 mm (Available)

$D$ = 550 mm

$Df$ = 110 mm

$Bf$ = 2095 mm

Calculation of loads and bending moments

Consider 1 m wide strip

Self weight of Slab $= 0.11 \times 25 = 2.75\ \text{kN/m}^2$

Self weight of roof terracing $= 0.075 \times 24 = 1.8\ \text{kN/m}^2$

Live load on slab $= 3\ \text{kN/m}^2$

Total slab load $= 7.55\ \text{kN/m}^2$

Load transferred by slab on beam $= 7.55 \times 3 = 22.65\ \text{kN/m}$

Self weight of rib $= 0.23\ (0.550 - 0.11) \times 25 = 2.53\ \text{kN/m}$

Total load $= 22.65 + 2.53 = 25.18\ \text{kN/m}$

Factored load $= 1.5 \times 25.18 = 37.77\ \text{kN/m}$

$$\text{Factored B.M.} = \frac{wl^2}{8} = \frac{37.77 \times (7.23)^2}{8}$$

$$= 246.79\ \text{kN.m}$$

$Xm = 0.48\,d = 0.48 \times 515 = 247.2\ \text{mm}$

$Xm > Df$ [accordingly G.2.3P97]

Apply [G.2.2P96]

$$M\lim = 0.36\frac{xm}{d}\left[1 - \frac{0.42\,xm}{d}\right] bwd^2\,\sigma_{ck} + 0.45\,\sigma_{ck}\,(B_f - bw)\,Df\,\frac{(d - Df)}{2}$$

$$= 0.36 \times 0.48\ [1 - 0.42 \times 0.48]\ 230 \times 515^2 \times 20$$

$$+ 0.45 \times 20\,(2095 - 230)\ 110\left(515 - \frac{110}{2}\right)$$

$$= 1017.64\ \text{kN–m} > 246.79\ \text{kN–m}$$

Hence neutral-axis lies with in the flange.

$$R = \frac{BM}{B_f \times d^2}$$

$$= \frac{246.79 \times 10^6}{2095 \times (515)^2} = 0.445\ \text{N/mm}^2$$

$$Ast = \frac{Bf \times d \times \sigma_{ck}}{2\,\sigma y}\left[1 - \sqrt{1 - \frac{4.59\,R}{\sigma_{ck}}}\right]$$

$$= \frac{2095 \times 515 \times 20}{2 \times 415}\left[1 - \sqrt{1 - \frac{4.59 \times 0.445}{20}}\right]$$

$$= 1399.29\ \text{mm}^2$$

$$\text{Area of 20 mm diameter bar} = \frac{3.14 \times 20^2}{4} = 314.16\ \text{mm}^2$$

$$\text{No. of bar} = \frac{1366.29}{314.16} = 4.3$$

Hence provide 4 bar 20 mm $\phi$ bar and 1 bar 12 mm $\phi$ bar

Area provided $= 4 \times 314 + 1 \times 113 = 1369\ \text{mm}^2 > 1366.29\ \text{mm}^2$

Check for required width of beam [CL 26.3.2. P45]

$= 2$ (side cover) $+ 4$ (20 bar) $+ 4$ (12 bar) $+ 4$ (larger bar spacing)

$= 2 \times 25 + 4 \times 20 + 1 \times 12 + 4 \times 20$

$= 222$ mm $< 230$ mm O.K.

Check for minimum steel Ast $= \dfrac{0.85\, b \times d}{\sigma y}$

[CL 26.5.1.1a P47]

$$= \frac{0.85 \times 230 \times 515}{415} = 242 \text{ mm}^2$$

Check for maximum steel $= 0.04 \times bw \times D$
[CL 26.5.1.1.b P47]

$$= 0.04 \times 230 \times 550 = 5060 \text{ mm}^2$$

$242 \text{ mm}^2 < 1366.29 \text{ mm}^2 < 5060 \text{ mm}^2$
Provide 2 top bars of 12 mm diameter for holding the stirrups
*Check for shear:*

$$Vu = \frac{WL}{2}$$

$$= \frac{37.77 \times 7}{2} = 132.19 \text{ kN}$$

Nominal shear [CL 40.1 P72]

$$\tau v = \frac{Vu}{bw\, d}$$

$$= \frac{132.19 \times 1000}{230 \times 515} = 1.11 \text{ N/mm}^2$$

$$\% \text{ of steel} = \frac{100 \times Ast}{bw \times d}$$

$$= \frac{100 \times 1369}{230 \times 515} = 1.15\%$$

$\tau_c$ for M 20 grade of concrete and 1.15% of steel [Table 19 P73]

$$\tau c = \frac{0.62 + (0.67 - 0.62)\ (1.11 - 1.0)}{(1.25 - 1.00)}$$

$$= 0.642 \text{ N/mm}^2$$

Design shear strength $Vus = Vu - \tau c \times b \times d$ [CL 40.4, P73]

$$= 132.19 \times 10^3 - 0.642 \times 230 \times 515$$

$$= 56145.1 \text{ N}$$

Provide shear reinforcement in the form of vertical stirrups *i.e.*
2-legged vertical stirrups 8 mm $\phi$ bar

$$A\,\phi = 2 \times (\pi/4)\, 8^2 = 100.48 \text{ mm}^2$$

$$Sv = \frac{0.87 \times \sigma y \times d \times A\,\phi}{Vus}$$

$$= \frac{0.87 \times 415 \times 100.48 \times 515}{56145.1} = 332.95 \text{ mm}$$

Check for minimum shear steel [CL 26.5.1.6 P48]

$$= \frac{0.87 \times \sigma y \; A\,\phi}{0.4\, b}$$

$$Sv = \frac{100.48 \times 0.87 \times 415}{0.4 \times 230}$$

$$Sv = 394.32 \text{ mm}$$

Check for max$^{m}$ spacing 0.75 $d$ or 450 [CL 26.5.1.5 P47]

$$= 0.75 \times 515 = 386 \text{ mm}$$

Hence provide 8 mm $\phi$ 2 legged vertical stirrups @ 250 mm c/c.

Check for development length,

$$\text{Ld required} = \frac{0.87\, \sigma\, y\phi}{4\,\tau\, bd} \quad \text{[CL26.2.3.3, P44]}$$

$$= \frac{0.87 \times 415 \times 20}{4 \times 1.92} = 940.23 \text{ mm}$$

$M1 = BM = 132.19 \times 10^{6}$ N.mm [Neither bent up or curtailment of main bars at support]

$$Lo = 12\,\phi \text{ or } d$$

$$Lo = 12 \times 2 = 240 \text{ mm or } 515 \text{ mm}$$

$$= \frac{1.3\, M1}{Vu} + Lo$$

$$= \frac{1.3 \times 246.79 \times 10^{6}}{132.19 \times 10^{3}} + 515$$

$$= 2951.8 \text{ mm} > 940.23 \text{ mm Hence O.K.}$$

Hence it is safe in development length

Check for deflection

$$\% \text{ of steel} = \frac{\text{Ast provided}}{\text{bw} \times \text{d}} \times 100$$

$$= \frac{100 \times 1369}{230 \times 515} = 1.15\%$$

Now, M.F., $\gamma = 0.95$ [Fig.4, P38]

And bw/Bf, $\delta = \dfrac{230}{2095} = 1$ [Fig.6, P39]

$l/d$ maximum $= 0.95 \times 20 = 19$

$l/d$ provided $= \dfrac{7230}{515} = 14.02$

$l/d$ provide < $l/d$ max Hence O.K.

**Schedule of beam**

Grade of concrete M 20 and Grade of steel Fe 415

| *Thickness (mm)* | *Clear cover (mm)* | *Width (mm)* | *Reinforcement (mm)* | *Remark* |
|---|---|---|---|---|
| 550 | 25 | 230 | 4 # 20 Φ + 1 # 12 Φ<br>2 # 12 Φ<br>8 Φ @ 250 c/c | Bottom bars (in two row)<br>Top bars<br>2L stirrups throughout |

**Problem 8.11.** *A 7.0 m × 21.0 m hall is to be roofed with RC intermediate T beams and side L beams and slab. The beams ribs are spaced at 3 m c/c and thickness of the flange (slab) is 110 mm and a roof terracing 75 mm c.c over it with a live load of 3 kN/m² in addition to its own weight. The L beam is also carrying a 230 mm thick and 3.0 m high brick wall. The thickness of wall is 230 mm all around and adopt* $\sigma_{ck}$ *= 20 MPa and* $\sigma_y$ *= 415 MPa, design suitable L beam.*

**Solution.**

Clean span $L = 7$ m

Width of supporting wall = 230 mm

Effective span ($l$) = clear span + one bearing

$= 7.0 + 0.230 = 7.230$ m

Assume effective depth of beam 1/10 to 1/15

$$\text{Effective depth} = \frac{7.230}{14} = 510 \text{ mm}$$

Using 20 mm dia of bar and clear cover 25 mm

According to IS code 456; 2000 [CL 22.2a P34]

$$\text{Overall depth } (D) = 510 + 25 + \frac{20}{2}$$

$$= 545 \text{ mm say } 550 \text{ mm}$$

$$\text{Available effective depth} = \frac{550 - 25 - 20}{2} = 515 \text{ mm}$$

Effective span ($l$) = clear span + one bearing

$= 7.0 + 0.230 = 5.230$ m

Effective span ($l$) = clear span + effective depth

$= 7.0 + 0.515 = 7.515$ m

According to [CL 23.1.2a P37]

$$Bf = \frac{Lo}{12} + bw + 3\,Df$$

$$Bf = \frac{7.23}{12} + 0.23 + 3 \times 0.11 = 1.162 \text{ m}$$

or $bf < [0.5\,(L_{1)} + bw] = 1500$ mm

Dimension of L beam,

Effective span = 7.23 m

$bw$ = 230 mm

$d$ = 515 mm (Available)

$d$ = 550 mm

$Df$ = 110 mm

$Bf$ = 1162.5 mm

Calculation of loads and bending moments

Consider 1 m wide strip

Self weight of Slab $= 0.11 \times 25 = 2.75$ kN/m²

Self weight of roof terracing $= 0.75 \times 24 = 1.8$ kN/m²

Live load on slab = 3 kN/m²

Total slab load = 7.55 kN/m²

Load transferred by slab on beam = $7.55 \times \frac{3}{2} = 11.325$ kN/m

Self weight of rib = $0.23\ (0.550 - 0.11) \times 25 = 2.53$ kN/m

Load of brick wall = $0.23 \times 3 \times 19.20 = 13.24$ kN/m

Total load = $11.325 + 2.53 + 13.24 = 27.09$ kN/m

Factored load = $1.5 \times 27.09 = 40.64$ kN/m

Factored B.M. $= \frac{wl^2}{8} = \frac{40.64 \times (7.23)^2}{8} = 265.56$ kN–m

$Xm = 0.48\,d = 0.48 \times 515 = 247.2$ mm

$Xm > Df$ [accordingly G.2.3, P97]

Apply [G 2.2 P96]

$$M\lim = 0.36\frac{xm}{d}\left[1 - \frac{0.42\,xm}{d}\right] Bfd^2\,\sigma_{ck} + 0.45\ \sigma_{ck}\,(Bf - bw)\,Df\,\frac{(d - Df)}{2}$$

$$= 0.36 \times 0.48\,[1 - 0.42 \times 0.48]\ 1162.5 \times 515^2 \times 20 + 0.45 \times 20\,(1162.5 - 230)\ 110\,(515 - 110/2)$$

$$= 1367.72 \text{ kN–m} > 265.56 \text{ kN–m}$$

Hence natural axis lies is located with in flange.

$$R = \frac{BM}{B_f \times d^2}$$

$$= \frac{265.56 \times 10^6}{1162.5 \times (515)^2} = 0.86 \text{ N/mm}^2$$

$$Ast = \frac{Bf \times d \times \sigma_{ck}}{2\,\sigma y}\left[1 - \sqrt{1 - \frac{4.59\,R}{\sigma_{ck}}}\right]$$

$$= \frac{1162.5 \times 515 \times 20}{2 \times 415}\left[1 - \sqrt{1 - \frac{4.59 \times 0.86}{20}}\right]$$

$$= 1504.2 \text{ mm}^2$$

Area of 20mm diameter bar $= \frac{3.14 \times 20^2}{4} = 314.16$ mm$^2$

No. of bar $= \frac{1504.2}{314.16} = 4.78$

Hence provide 5 bar 20 mm $\phi$

Area provided = $5 \times 314.16 = 1570.8$ mm$^2$ $>$ 1504.2 mm$^2$

Check for required width of beam [CL 26.3.2 P45]

= 2 (side cover) + 5 (20 bar) + 4 (larger bar spacing)

= $2 \times 25 + 5 \times 20 + 4 \times 20 = > 230$ mm

Hence provide in two row

Check for minimum steel $Ast = \frac{0.85\,b \times d}{\sigma y}$

[CL 26.5.1.1a P47]

$$= \frac{0.85 \times 230 \times 515}{415} = 242 \text{ mm}^2$$

Check for maximum steel = $0.04 \times b \times D$
[CL 26.5.1.1 b P47]

$$= 0.04 \times 230 \times 550 = 5060 \text{ mm}^2$$

$242 \text{ mm}^2 < 1570.8 \text{ mm}^2 < 5060 \text{ mm}^2$

Provide 2 top bars of 12 mm diameter for holding the stirrups

*Check for shear:*

$$Vu = \frac{WL}{2}$$

$$= \frac{40.64 \times 7}{2} = 142.24 \text{ kN}$$

Nominal shear [CL 40.1 P72]

$$\tau v = \frac{Vu}{bw\, d} = \frac{142.24 \times 1000}{230 \times 515}$$

$$= 1.20 \text{ N/mm}^2$$

$$\% \text{ of steel} = \frac{100 \times Ast}{bw \times d}$$

$$= \frac{100 \times 1570.8}{230 \times 515} = 1.35\%$$

$\tau_c$ for M20 grade of concrete and 1.35% of steel [Table 19 P73]

$$\tau c = 0.67 + \frac{(0.72 - 0.67)}{(1.5 - 1.25)} (1.5 - 1.35)$$

$$= 0.7 \text{ N/mm}^2$$

Design shear strength $Vus = Vu - \tau c \times b \times d\}$ [CL40.4, P73]

$$= 142.24 \times 10^3 - 0.70 \times 230 \times 515 = 59325 \text{ N}$$

Provide shear reinforcement in the form of vertical stirrups *i.e.*
2-legged vertical stirrups 8 mm $\phi$ bar

$$A\phi = 2 \times (\pi/4)\, 8^2 = 100.48 \text{ mm}^2$$

$$Sv = \frac{0.87 \times \sigma y \times d \times A\phi}{Vus}$$

$$= \frac{0.87 \times 415 \times 100.48 \times 515}{59325} = 314 \text{ mm}$$

Check for minimum shear steel [CL 26.5.1.6 P48]

$$= \frac{0.87 \times \sigma y\, A\phi}{0.4\, b}$$

$$Sv = \frac{100.48 \times 0.87 \times 415}{0.4 \times 230}$$

$$Sv = 394.32 \text{ mm}$$

Check for max$^m$ spacing 0.75 $d$ or 450 [CL26.5.1.5 P47]

$$= 0.75 \times 515 = 386 \text{ mm}$$

Hence provide 8 mm $\phi$ 2 legged vertical stirrups @ 250 mm c/c.

Check for development length,

$$Ld \text{ required} = \frac{0.87\ \sigma y \phi}{4 \tau bd} \text{ [CL26.2.3, P44]}$$

$$= \frac{0.87 \times 415 \times 20}{4 \times 1.92} = 940.23 \text{ mm}$$

$M1 = BM = 265.56 \times 10^6$ N [Neither bent up or curtailment of main bars at support]

$$Lo = 12\,\phi \text{ or } d$$

$$Lo = 12 \times 2 = 240 \text{ mm or } 515 \text{ mm}$$

$$= \frac{1.3\ M1}{Vu} + Lo$$

$$= \frac{1.3 \times 265.56 \times 10^6}{142.24 \times 10^3} + 515$$

$= 2942$ mm $> 940.23$ mm Hence O.K.

Hence it is safe in development length

Check for deflection

% of steel $= 1.85\%$

Now, M.F., $\gamma = 0.90$ [Fig. 4, P38]

And bw/Bf, $\delta = \frac{230}{1162.5} = 1$ [Fig. 6, P39]

$$d = \frac{lx}{\alpha \beta \gamma \lambda \delta}$$

$$= \frac{7.23}{20 \times 1 \times 0.90 \times 1 \times 0.8} = 0.506 < 515 \text{ mm}$$

Hence O.K.

**Schedule of beam**

Grade of concrete M 20 and Grade of steel Fe 415

| *Depth (mm)* | *Clear cover (mm)* | *Width (mm)* | *Reinforcement (mm)* | *Remark* |
|---|---|---|---|---|
| 550 | 25 | 230 | 5 # 20 Φ<br>2 # 12 Φ<br>8 Φ @ 250 c/c | Bottom bars (in two row)<br>Top bars<br>2L stirrups throughout |

**Problem 8.12.** *The effective span of a T beam is 4.6 m carrying a uniformly distributed working load 59.25 kN/m. The height of building column from pedestal to soffit of beam equal to 3.85m. Take $\sigma_{ck}$ 20 MPa, $\sigma_y$ = 415 MPa, design the following:*

*(i) Square column with lateral ties*

*(ii) Circular ties with circular rings*

*(iii) Square footing for the above column*

**Solution.**

*(i) Design of square column:*

Given:

Height of each floor = 3.85 m

Take M20 for concrete and Fe 415 grade of steel

Assuming size of square column = 230 mm × 230 mm

*Calculation of load:*

Load coming from T-beam including DL + LL = $\frac{59.25 \times 4.6}{2}$ = 136.27 kN

Self wt. of column = $0.23 \times 0.23 \times 3.85 \times 25 = 5.09$ kN

Total load = 141.36 kN

Factored load = $1.5 \times 141.36 = 212.04$ kN

According [CL 39.3 P71] $Pu = 0.4\, \sigma_{ck} A_c + 0.67\, \sigma_y As_t$

Let %age of steel = 0.8% of Area of column

Side of the column = $a$

Area of square column = $a^2$

Net area of concrete $Ac$ = Area of column − Area of steel = $(a^2 - 0.8/100\, a^2)$

$$212.04 \times 10^3 = 0.4 \times 20 \times a^2 (1 - 0.008) + 0.67 \times 415 \times 0.008\, a^2$$

$$212.04 \times 10^3 = 10.1\, a^2$$

Required side of column $a$ = 144.46 mm < 230 OK

Provided size of column = 230 × 230 mm

Gross concrete required = $144.46 \times 144.46 = 20870.11$ mm$^2$

Check for Slenderness Ratio: [CL 25.1.2 P41]

$$= \frac{\text{effective span}}{\text{least lateral dimension}}$$

$$= \frac{(0.65 \times 3.85 \times 1000)}{230}$$

$$= 10.88 < 12$$

Column is a short column

Check for Minimum Eccentricity: [CL 25.4 P42]

$$\text{Minimum Eccentricity} = \frac{\text{unsupported length of column}}{500} + \frac{\text{lateral dimensions}}{30} \text{ OR } 20 \text{ mm}$$

$$= \frac{1}{500} + \frac{a}{30}$$

$$= \frac{0.65 \times 3.85 \times 10^3}{500} + \frac{230}{30}$$

$$= 12.67 \text{ mm}$$

$$E_{\min} = 0.05\, a = 0.05 \times 230 = 11.5 \text{ mm}$$

Consider the column is reinforced by lateral ties and $e_{\min}$ is less than 20 mm.

Hence the column is short.

Reinforcement calculation [CL 26:5.3.1b P48]

Longitudinal area of steel = $0.008 \times 20870.11 = 166.96$ mm$^2$

According to [CL 26.5.3.1 c and d, P48]

Using 12 mm $\phi$, area of one bar = $\frac{\pi}{4} \times 12^2 = 113.04$ mm$^2$

Provided 4 # 12 mm $\phi$ bar

Lateral Ties or rings [CL 26.5.3.2 c 2 P49]

$$\text{Diameter of ties} = 6 \text{ mm or} = \frac{\text{min}^{m} \text{ dia of bar}}{4}$$

$$= \frac{12}{4} = 3 \text{ mm}$$

Hence using 6 mm $\phi$ bar

Spacing [CL 26.5.3.2 c 1 P49]

(*i*) Least lateral dimension = 230 mm

(*ii*) 16 times the smallest diameter of bar = 16 × 12 = 192 mm

(*iii*) 300 mm

Hence adopt 6 mm $\phi$ bar @ 190 mm c/c

**Schedule of column**

Grade of concrete M 20 and Grade of steel Fe 415

| *Thickness (mm)* | *Clear cover (mm)* | *Width (mm)* | *Reinforcement (mm)* | *Remark* |
|---|---|---|---|---|
| 230 | 40 | 230 | 4 # 12 Φ<br>6 Φ @ 190 c/c | Longitudinal bars<br>Square ties throughout |

(*ii*) *Design of Circular Column:*

Given:

Height on each floor = 3.85 m

M 20 and Fe 415

Assuming size of diameter 230 mm

*Calculation of load:*

$$\text{Load coming from } 1^{st} \text{ floor T-beam} = \frac{(55.03 \times 5)}{2} = 137.57 \text{ kN}$$

$$\text{Self weight of } 1^{st} \text{ floor column} = \frac{\pi}{4} \times 0.23^2 \times 3.85 \times 25 = 3.99 \text{ kN}$$

$$\text{Total load from } 1^{st} \text{ floor column} = 142.66 \text{ kN}$$

$$\text{Load of T-beam (Ground floor)} = \frac{(55.03 \times 5)}{2} = 137.57 \text{ kN}$$

$$\text{Total load} = (37.57 + 3.99 + 137.57) = 279.13 \text{ kN}$$

$$\text{Factored load} = 1.5 \times 279.13 = 418.69 \text{ kN}$$

We know that

$$Pu = 0.4\,\sigma_{ck}\,AC + 0.67\,\sigma y\,Asc \text{ [CL 39.3, P71]}$$

Assuming % age of steel = 0.8% and diameter of the column = $d$

$$\therefore \quad \text{Area of column} = \frac{\pi}{4} \times d^2$$

$$418.67 \times 10^3 = 0.4 \times 20\,\pi/4(d)^2\,(1 - 0.008) + 0.67 \times 415 + 0.008 \times \pi/4\,(d)^2$$

$$418.69 \times 10^3 = 623\,d^2 + 1.74\,d^2$$

$$418.69 \times 10^3 = 7.97\,d^2 \quad d = 229.20 \text{ mm}$$

229.20 < 230 mm

Adopting the diameter of column = 230 mm

Gross area of concrete required = $\frac{\pi}{4} \times (229.20)^2 = 41259.51 \text{ mm}^2$

Slenderness ratio:

$$= \frac{\text{effective span}}{\text{diameter of column}}$$

$$= \frac{0.65 \times 3.85 \times 1000}{230}$$

$$= 10.88 < 12 \text{ Hence the column is short}$$

Eccentricity:

$$e_{min} = \frac{1}{500} + \frac{d}{30}$$

$$= \frac{2.50 \times 10^3}{5000} + \frac{230}{30} = 12.67 \text{ mm}$$

$$e_{min} = 0.05\, d = 0.05 \times 230 = 11.5 \text{ mm}$$

It is assuming that the column is laterally ties column and $e_{min}$ not more than 0.05 times of lateral dimension. Hence the column is short column.

Area of steel:

Longitudinal area of steel = $0.008 \times 41259.51 = 330.07 \text{ mm}^2$

Using 16 mm $\phi$ bar $A\,\phi = \frac{\pi}{4} \times 12^2 = 113.14 \text{ mm}^2$

Area of steel provide $= 6 \times \frac{\pi}{4\,(12)^2} = 678.24 \text{ mm}^2 > 330.01 \text{ mm}^1$

Hence provide 6 # 12 mm $\phi$ bar

Lateral Ties:

Diameter of ties = 6 mm

Or Min$^m$ diameter of bar/4 = 16/4 = 4 mm

Hence use 6 mm $\phi$ bar

Spacing:

(*i*) Latest lateral dimension = 230 mm

(*ii*) 16 times the small diameter bar = 16 × 6 = 256 mm

(*iii*) 300 mm

Hence provide 6 mm $\phi$ bar @ 230 mm c/c.

**Schedule of column**

Grade of concrete M 20 and Grade of steel Fe 415

| *Diameter (mm)* | *Clear cover (mm)* | *Reinforcement (mm)* | *Remark* |
|---|---|---|---|
| 230 | 40 | 6 # 12 Φ<br>6 Φ @ 230 c/c | Longitudinal bars<br>Circular rings throughout |

*Design of Square Column Footing:*

Given:

Size of the column = 230 × 230 mm

M20 grade of concrete and Fe 415 grade of steel

Safe bearing capacity of soil = 120 kN/m$^2$

*Calculation of load:*

Load transfer through T-beam on column $= \dfrac{(59.25 \times 4.6)}{2}$

$= 136.27$ kN

Self weight of the column $= 0.23 \times 0.23 \times 3.85 \times 25 = 5.09$ kN

Total load $= 136.27 + 5.09 = 141.36$ kN

Factored load transfer through column at bar $= 1.5 \times 141.36 = 212.04$ kN

Add self wt. of footing @ 10% $= 21.20$ kN

Total load $(p) = 233.24$ kN

Required area of footing $= \dfrac{p}{w} = \dfrac{233.24}{(120 \times 1.5)} = 1.29\ \text{m}^2$

Width of square footing $= \sqrt{1.29} = 1.13$ m

Provide size of footing $= 1.20\ \text{m} \times 1.20\ \text{m}$

Depth of the footing some times governed by bending moment consideration and found less. Hence increased depth is taking due to shear strength criteria. Depth of the footing must be decided on shear criteria.

Net soil pressure at factored load $w_u = \dfrac{233.24 \times 1.5}{1.2 \times 1.2}$

$= 161.93\ \text{kN/m}^2$

One-way shear action, the critical section at a distance '*d*' from the face of the column face [CL 34.2.4.1a P65]

Factored shear force $V_{u1} = 0.161 \times 1200 \times (485 - d)$

$= 93702 - 193.2\,d$ ...(1)

Assuming 0.25% of steel for M20 concrete

$\tau c = 0.36\ \text{N/mm}^2$ [Table 19 P73]

Shear resistance of concrete section $= 0.36 \times 1200 \times d = 432\,d$ ...(2)

Equate equation (*i*) and (*ii*) equation $432\,d = 93702 - 193.2\,d$

$d = 149.87\ \text{mm} \approx 150\ \text{mm}$

Two-way share action, the critical section is at *d*/2 from the periphery of the column [CL 34.24.1b, P65]

Factored shear force $V_{u2} = wux\ [B^2 - (b + d)^2]$

$= 0.161\ [1200)^2 - (230 + d)^2]$

$d = 150$ mm

$V_{u2} = 0.161\ [(1200)^2 - (230 + 150)^2]\ N$ ...(3)

$= 208.59 \times 10^3$

According to clause [31.6.3.1, P58] $\tau c = 0.25\sqrt{\sigma_{ck}} = 0.25 \times \sqrt{20} = 1.18$

$K = 1.3$ [CL 40.2.1, P72]

$K\tau c = 1.3 \times 1.18 = 1.45$

Two way shear resistant $Vc_2 = K\tau c\ [4\,(230 + d) \times d]$

$= 1.45\ [4\,(230\,d + d^2]$ ...(4)

From equation (3) and equation (4)

$$208.59 \times 10^3 = 1.45\,[4\,(230 + d) \times d^2]$$

$$5.8\,d^2 + 1334d - 208.59 \times 10^3 = 0 \qquad \ldots(5)$$

From equation (5) $d = 106$ mm

Consider effective depth of footing 150 mm and 10 mm diameter of bar with a clear cover of 75 mm [CL 26.4.2.23, P46]

$$\text{Over all depth of footing } D = 150 + 75 + \frac{10}{2}$$

$$= 230 \text{ mm} > 150 \text{ mm OK}$$

Check [CL 34.1.2, P 64]

*Design of flexural reinforcement:*

Factored B.M. at the face of column [CL 34.2.3.2a, P65]

$$M = 0.148 \times 1200\,\frac{(485)^2}{2} = 22.72 \times 10^6 \text{ N–mm}$$

$$d\,avg. = \frac{(225 + 150)}{2} = 187.5 \text{ mm}$$

$$R = \frac{M}{Bd^2\,(avg)} = \frac{22.72 \times 10^6}{1200\,(187.5)^2} = 0.538 \text{ N/mm}^2$$

$$\text{Required area of steel Ast } Ast = \frac{b \times dx \times \sigma_{ck}}{2\,\sigma y}\left[1 - \sqrt{1 - \frac{4.59\,R}{\sigma_{ck}}}\right]$$

$$= \frac{1200 \times 187.5 \times 20}{2 \times 415}\left[1 - \sqrt{1 - \frac{4.59 \times 0.538}{20}}\right]$$

$$= 354.71 \text{ mm}$$

$$\%\text{ of Steel} = [Ast/Bd\,(avg)] \times 100 = \frac{354.71}{1200 \times 187.5} \times 100 = 0.015$$

Since 0.15 < 0.25% of steel as assumed for one way shear

For one-way shear, required area of steel = 0.25 × 1200 × 178.5 = 535.5 mm$^2$

$$\text{Using 10 mm } \phi \text{ bar } A\,\phi = \frac{3.14}{4} \times 10^2 = 78.5 \text{ mm}^2$$

$$\text{No. of bars} = \frac{Ast}{A\,\phi} = \frac{535.5}{78.5} = 6.79 \approx 7$$

$$\text{Spacing} = \frac{A\,\phi \times 1000}{Ast} = \frac{78.5 \times 1000}{535.5} = 146 \text{ mm c/c}$$

Provide 10 mm $\phi$ 145 mm c/c in each direction

Transfer of load at the base of column [CL 34.4, P 65]

$$= 233.24 \times 1.5 = 349.86 \text{ kN}$$

Limiting Bearing stress $\sigma br$ (max) = $0.45\ \sigma_{ck}\sqrt{A_1/A_2}$

(*a*) For column face $A_1 = A_2 = 230 \times 230 = 52900$ mm$^2$

$$\sigma br\,(max) = 0.45 \times 20\,\sqrt{230/230} = 9 \text{ N/mm}^2$$

For footing face $A_1 = (1200)^2 = 144 \times 10^4$ mm$^2$

For column face $A_2 = (230)^2 = 529 \times 10^2$ mm$^2$

$\therefore \quad = \sqrt{A_1^2/A_2^2} = 5.21$ but limited to 2

Hence Limiting Bearing stress $\sigma_{br}$ (max) equal to 9N/mm$^2$ at the column face.

Bearing resistance by the column face = $9 \times 230^2 = 476 \times 10^1$ N < Factored Load

Excessive force subtends by the column face when $\sigma_{br}$ (max) equal to 9N/mm$^2$.

$$= 233.24 \times 10^3 - 476 \times 10^2 = 185.64 \times 10^3 \text{ N}$$

Required development of 4 # 12 mm $\phi$ provided in the column

$$Ld = \frac{0.87\, \sigma_{ck}\, \phi}{4\,(1.2 \times 1.6 \times 1.25)}$$

$$= \frac{0.84 \times 415 \times 12}{(1.2 \times 1.6 \times 1.25)} = 451 \text{ mm}$$

Depth of footing at the face of column is 300 mm and required development length is 451 mm hence provide 90 degree bend at a length equal to 115 mm rested on top of the footing reinforcement.

**Schedule of footing**

Grade of concrete M20 and Grade of steel Fe 415

| *Size of footing (mm)* | *Clear cover (mm)* | *Depth of footing* | *Reinforcement* | *Remark* |
|---|---|---|---|---|
| 1200 × 1200 | 75 | 300 mm at the face of column 230 mm at the free edge | 10 Φ @ 145 mm c/c | In Both directions |

**Problem 8.13.** *A stair case hall in residential building is 3.0 m × 4.4 m. The floor to floor height of the building is 3.75 m including the floor finish. Design a simply supported RC doglegged stair case slab. The bearing of the landing on the supporting wall may be taken 230 mm. The steps of stairs are finished 25 mm thick marble stones. Take Grade of concrete M 20 and Grade of steel Fe 415.*

**Solution.**

*Size of room:*

Geometrical design = 3.0 m × 4.4 m

Let the width of the stair = 1.4 m

Width of landing = 1.4 m

There are two flights in the stair case

Height of one flight $= \dfrac{3.75}{2} = 1.875$ m

Height of riser $(R) = 150$ mm

The numbers of riser in one flight $= \dfrac{1.875}{1.150} = 12.5$ say 13

Height of actual riser $= \dfrac{1.875}{12} = 0.142$ m

Numbers of steps in one flight $(T) = 13 - 1 = 12$

Width of step = 250 mm

Length covered by 12 treads = $12 \times 250 = 3000$ mm

*Structural design:*

Clear span in shorter direction $l = 3.0 + 1.4 = 4.4$ m

Width of supporting wall = 230 mm

Grade of concrete $\sigma_{ck}$ = M20

Grade of steel $\sigma_y$ = Fe 415

Thickness of stone finishing = 25 mm

**DESIGN**

Effective span = c/c distance of support [CL 22.2, P34]

$$\text{Effective span } lx = \frac{4.4 + 0.23}{2} = 4.515 \text{ m}$$

Depth of slab governed by Serviceability criteria [CL 23.2.1, P37]

$$\text{Effective depth based upon deflection criteria } d = \frac{lx}{\alpha\beta\gamma\lambda\delta}$$

Assuming $Pt = 0.4\%$, from Fig. 4, P38 corresponding curve of $\sigma_y$ 240 N/mm$^2$ to assumed *Pt*.

Modification factors $\alpha = 20,\ \beta = 1,\ \gamma = 1.38,\ \lambda = 1,\ \delta = 1$

$$dx = \frac{4.63}{20 \times 1 \times 1.38 \times 1 \times 1}$$

$$= 0.167 \text{ mm}$$

Consider 20 mm clear cover and 12 mm diameter of bar

$$\text{Overall depth } D = \frac{d \text{ clear cover} + \text{diameter of bar}}{2}$$

$$= \frac{167 + 20\ 12}{2} = 193 \text{ mm} \approx 200 \text{ mm}$$

According to [CL 23.0, P 36]

Available effective depth $dx = 200 - 20 - 6 = 174$ mm

Effective span in $lx$ = clear span + effective depth

$= 4.4 + 0.174 = 4.574$ m

According to [CL 33.1c, P63] lesser effective span should be consider [$l = 4.515$]

Stair is spanning longitudinally *i.e.* the first support under the first step and second support (landing) rest on wall.

*Calculation of loads and B.M.:*

Loads on inclined slab

(*i*) Self wt. of waist slab on projecting plan area

$$= D \times \rho \times \frac{(\sqrt{R^2 + T^2})}{T}$$

$$= 0.20 \times 25\ \frac{(\sqrt{0.142^2 + 0.250^2})}{0.250} = 5.75 \text{ kN/m}^2$$

(*ii*) Self weight of c/c steps $= \dfrac{\rho \times R}{2}$

$$= \frac{24 \times 0.142}{2} = 1.70 \text{ kN/m}^2$$

(*iii*) Stone finishing $= \rho \times t = 20 \times 0.025$

$= 0.5$ kN/m$^2$

(*iv*) Live load $= 3.0$ kN/m$^2$

Total load $= 10.95$ kN/m$^2$

Factored load $= 1.5 \times 12.95 = 16.42$ kN/m$^2$

Factored load/m length $= 16.42 \times 1.4 = 22.99$ kN/m

Loads on landing:

(i) Self wt. of landing $= D \times \rho = 0.20 \times 25 = 5.0\ kN/m^2$

(ii) Stone finishing $= \rho \times t = 20 \times 0.025 = 0.5\ kN/m^2$

(iii) Live load $= 3.0\ kN/m^2$

Total load $= 8.5\ kN/m^2$

Factored load $= 1.5 \times 8.5 = 12.75\ kN/m^2$

Factored load/m length $= 15.75 \times 1.4 = 17.85\ kN/m$

**Note:** Since difference in loading on waist slab and landing is not much and hence uniform loading is being consider for avoiding complication in the calculation.

Maximum B.M. $Mx = \dfrac{wlx^2}{8}$

$$= \frac{23 \times (4.515)^2}{8} = 58.60\ kN\text{–}m$$

Design of Reinforcement,

$$Rx = \frac{Mx}{bdx^2}$$

$$= \frac{58.60 \times 10^6}{1000 \times (174)^2} = 1.93\ N/m^2$$

Ast x required $= \dfrac{bdx \times \sigma_{ck}}{2\sigma y}\left[1 - \sqrt{1 - \dfrac{4.59\ Rx}{\sigma_{ck}}}\right]$

$$Ast\ x = \frac{1000 \times 174 \times 20}{2 \times 415}\left[1 - \sqrt{1 - \frac{4.59 \times 1.93}{20}}\right]$$

Required $Ast.x = 1063.4\ mm^2$

Using 12 mm $\phi$ bar $A\phi = \pi/4\ (12)^2 = 113\ mm^2$

Spacing $= \dfrac{A\phi \times 1000}{Ast}$

$$= \frac{113 \times 1000}{1063.4} = 106.26\ mm$$

Check for Max$^m$ spacing $= 3\,dx = 3 \times 174 = 522\ mm$
[CL 26.3.3, P46]

or $= 300\ mm$

Providing 12 mm $\phi$ bar @ 100 mm c/c

Actual area of steel provided

$$Astx = \frac{A\phi \times 1000}{spacing}$$

$$= \frac{113 \times 1000}{100}$$

$$= 1130\ mm^2 > 1063.4\ mm^2$$

Distribution reinforcement [CL 26.5.2.1, P48]

Area of distribution reinforcement = 0.12% of $bD$

$$= \frac{0.12 \times 1000 \times 200}{100} = 240 \text{ mm}^2$$

Using 8 mm diameter of bar

$$\text{Spacing of bar} = \frac{1000 \times 50.24}{240} = 209 \text{ mm}$$

Check for max spacing [CL 26.3.3b2, P46]

$$= 5 \times 174 = 870 \text{ mm}$$

Provided 8 mm Φ P @ 200 mm c/c

**Check for Serviceability Criteria**

Check for deflection criteria

$$\% \text{ of steel} = \frac{\text{Astx provided}}{\text{bxdx}} \times 100$$

$$= \frac{1130 \times 100}{1000 \times 174} = 0.64\%$$

Modification factors $\alpha = 20, \beta = 1, \gamma = 1.15, \lambda = 1, \delta = 1$

$$d = \frac{1}{\alpha \beta \gamma \lambda \delta}$$

$$= \frac{4.515 \times 10^3}{20 \times 1 \times 1.15 \times 1 \times 1}$$

$$= 115 \text{ mm} < 130 \text{ mm O.K.}$$

$$l/d \text{ maximum} = 20 \times 1.15 = 23$$

$$l/d \text{ provided} = \frac{4515}{174} = 25.9$$

$l/d$ provide < $l/d$ provided, hence increase the over all depth and revised the section

*Check for shear:*

$$\text{Max}^{m} \text{ shear force } Vu = \frac{wl}{2}$$

$$= \frac{23.10^3 \times 4.515}{2} = 51922.5 \text{ N}$$

$$\text{Nominal shear stress} \tau v = \frac{Vu}{bdx} \text{ [CL.B5.1, P83]}$$

$$= \frac{51922.5}{1000 \times 174} = 0.29 \text{ N/mm}^2$$

For 0.64% of steel and M20 grade of concrete [Table 19, P73]

$$\tau c = \frac{0.48 + (0.56 - 0.48) \times (0.64 - 0.50)}{(0.75 - 0.50)} = 0.52 \text{ N/mm}^2$$

$\tau_c = 0.328$ and thickness of slab up to 150 mm $K = 1.2$

[CL 40.2.11, P 73]

$$\tau c' = k \times \tau c$$

$$= 1.2 \times 0.52 = 0.69 \text{ N/mm}^2$$

$\tau c' > \tau v$ O.K.

Check for development length: [CL 26.2.1, P42]

$$Ld = \frac{0.87\ \sigma\ y\phi}{4\ \tau_{bd}} \quad [\tau_{bd} \text{ from CL 26.2.1.1, P43}]$$

$$= \frac{0.87 \times 415 \times 12}{4 \times 1.92} = 564.1 \text{ mm}$$

$$= \frac{1.3\ M1}{Vu} + Lo \geq Ld \quad [\text{CL26.2.3.3, P44}]$$

$$Lo = 12\ \phi \text{ OR } dx$$

$$= 12 \times 12 = 144 \text{ mm OR } 174 \text{ mm}$$

$$M1 = 58.60 \times 10^6$$

$$Vu = 51.92 \text{ kN}$$

$$= \frac{1.3\ M1}{Vu} + Lo$$

$$= \frac{1.3 \times 58.60 \times 10^6}{51.92 \times 10^3} + 174$$

$$= 1641.27 \text{ mm} > 564.14 \text{ O.K.}$$

**Note:** The main bars 12 Φ @ 200 c/c should be bent to fallow the bottom profile of the stair case. However if this pattern fallowed at the junction of waist slab and landing an angle will be formed in the bar. When the bars are stressed they may throw off the concrete cover. Hence at landing junction the main bars should be taken straight up and then bent in the landing as a top reinforcement. Its desirable to use the same bars diameter and spacing as above in the form of bottom reinforcement and extended up to the length of (Ld) in the waist slab.

**Schedule of stair**

Grade of Concrete M 20 and Grade of steel Fe 415

| *Thickness (mm)* | *Clear cover (mm)* | *Reinforcement* | | *Remark* |
|---|---|---|---|---|
| | | *Long side (mm)* | *Short side (mm)* | |
| 200 | 20 | 12 Φ @ 100 c/c | 8 Φ @ 200 c/c | Bottom bars<br>Distributions (in landing also) |

# 9

# Earth Quake Resistant Structure

## 9.1. INTRODUCTION

Earthquakes have been an integral component of the geological evolution of planet earth. An earthquake is a sudden transient motion or series of motion of the ground originating in a limited region and spreading from three in all direction. The motion occur an account of sudden release of elastics strain energy stored along active geology features. The greatest earthquake losses in terms of life and property are attributed to ground shaking. It is observed that the damage incurred to any one type of construction increases as the amount of displacement increases and the engineering building sustained less damage than non-engineering structures even when larger movement occur.

Before planning, designing and constructing any building following points should be kept in mind.

1. The structure is to resist minor earthquake without any damage.
2. The structure is to resist moderate and frequently occurring earthquakes with out any structural damage, but minor cracks may be appearing during earthquake.
3. The structure should not collapse under severe earthquake.

## 9.2. PLANNING ASPECT

## 9.3. SHAPE OF BUILDING

The building having plans with shapes likeL, T, E, U, H, I, + &Y shall preferably be separated into rectangular parts by providing separation section at appropriate place. In order to avoid torsion the plan of the building should having symmetry and simplicity as shown in Fig. 9.1. If the building having small lengths of projections in plan and elevation, there shapes need not be avoided into separation sections. In such cases the length of the projections may not exceed 15 to20% of the total dimensions of the building in the directions of the projections as indicate in Fig. 9.2. Pilasters are also provided at all corners and junctions of walls they also increase the seismic stability of the building as in Fig. 9.3. Simple symmetrical configurations such as square, rectangle and circular shapes are preferable be consider.

## 9.4. OPENING IN WALL

Openings weaken the walls, because doors, windows and ventilators etc reduces shear and bending strength of wall. There sizes should be small according to the standard requirements and they should be centrally located. If it is unavoidable the walls shall be reinforced with steel bars around opening. The openings in load bearing wall must satisfy the following dimensions.

| *Contents* | *Building Category A, B, & C* | *D* |
|---|---|---|
| Minimum distance $b_5$ from the inside corners of out side wall | 230 mm | 600 mm |
| Maximum ratio-Total width of openings to length of wall<br>1. $\frac{(b_1+b_2+b_3)}{l_1}$ or $\frac{(b_6+b_7)}{l_2}$ For single story building | 0.46 | 0.42 |

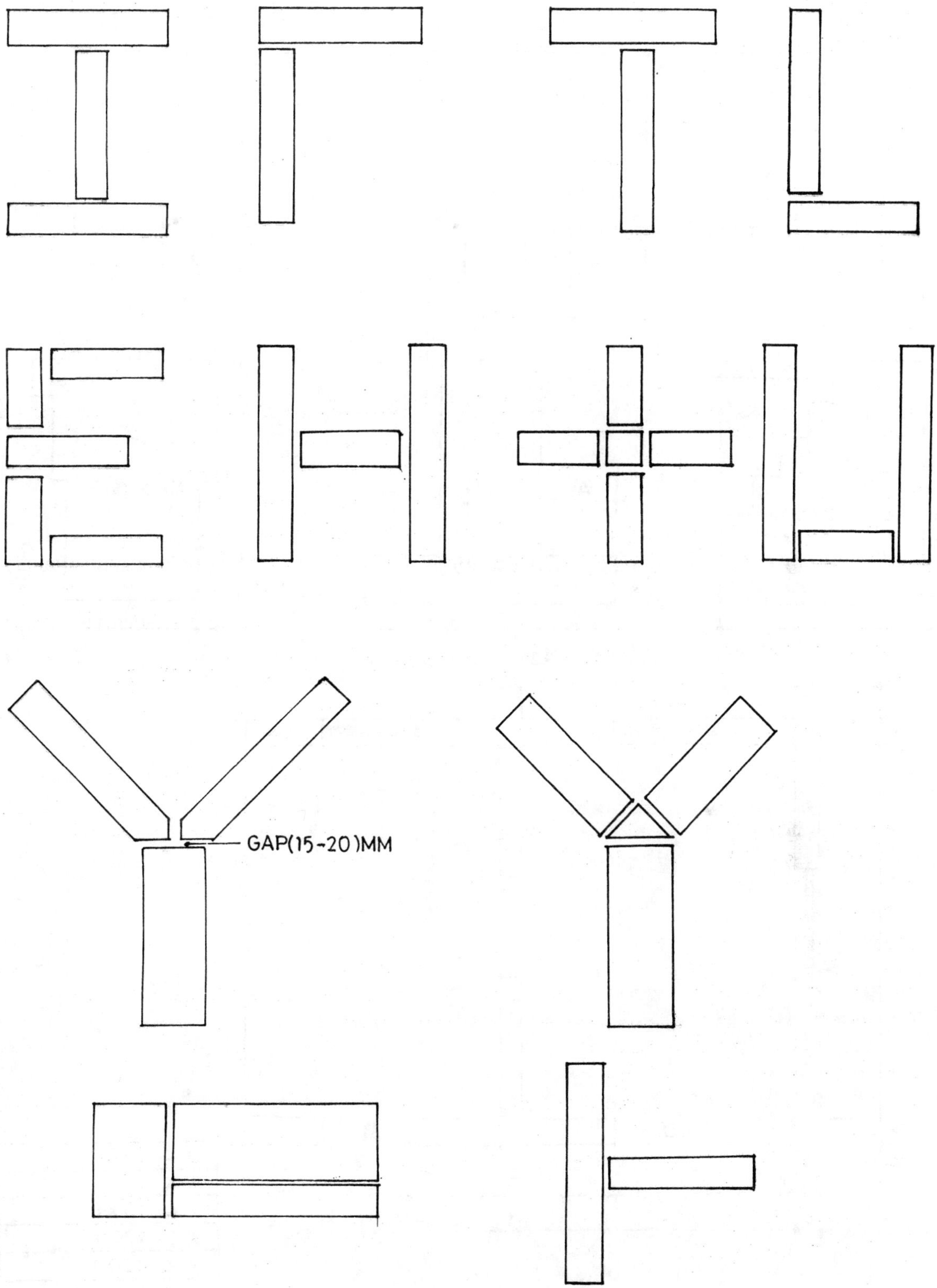


**Fig. 9.1.** Typical Shapes of Buildings with Separation Sections

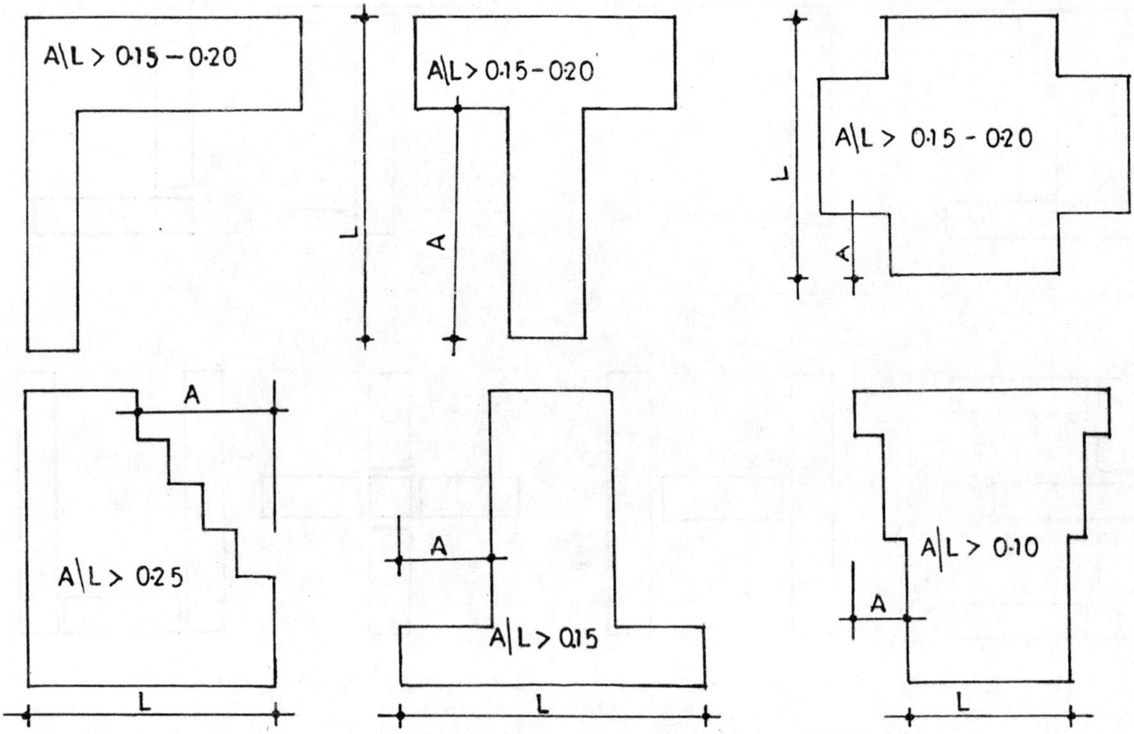


**Fig. 9.2.** Vertical Irregularities

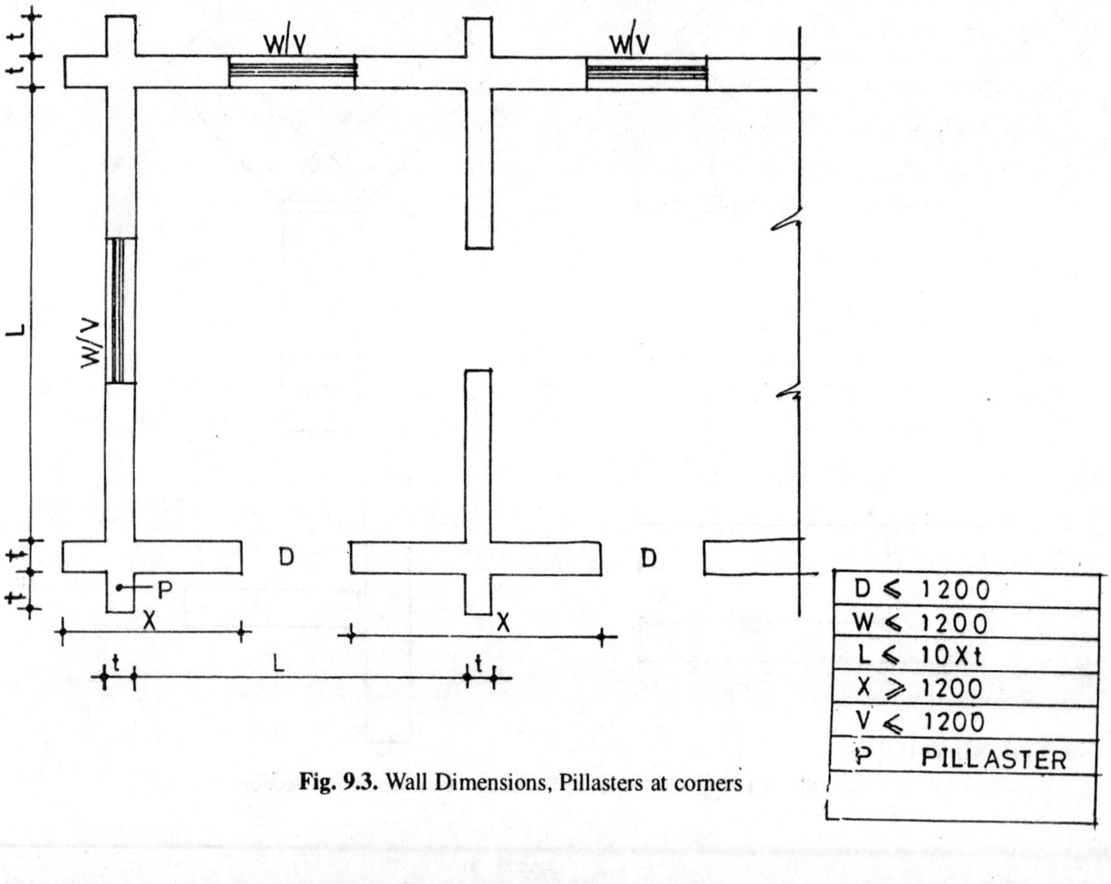


**Fig. 9.3.** Wall Dimensions, Pillasters at corners

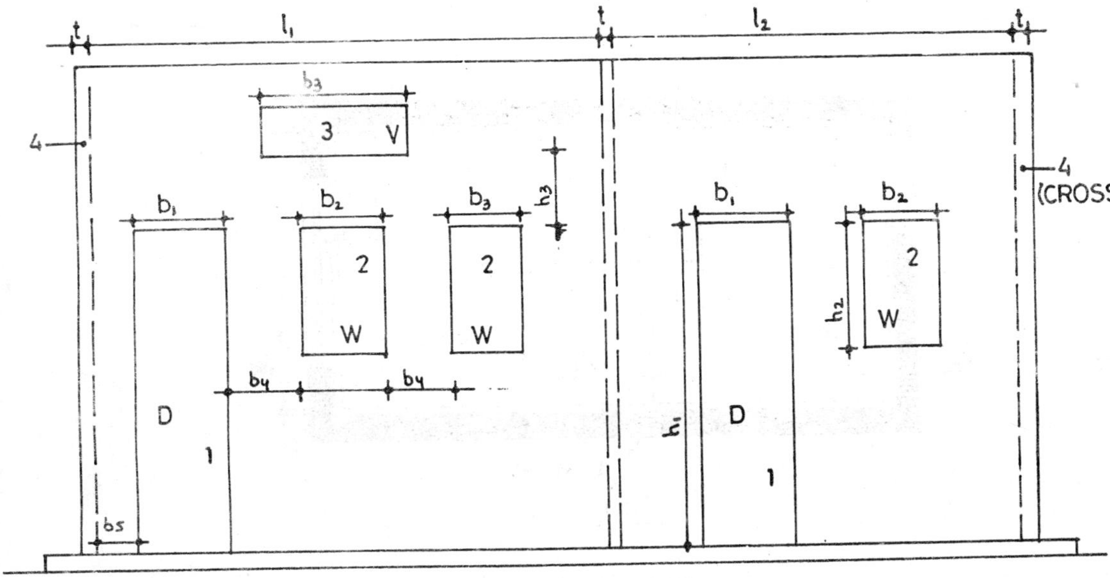


**Fig. 9.4.** Openings and Piers

| *Contents* | *Building Category A, B, & C* | *D* |
|---|---|---|
| 2. $\frac{(b_1+b_2+b_3)}{l_1}$ or $\frac{(b_6+b_7)}{l_2}$ For two and three story building | 0.37 | 0.33 |
| Minimum pier width between consecutive openings $b_4$ | 450 mm | 560 mm |
| Minimum vertical distance between opening one above others $h_3$ | 600 mm | 600 mm |

The respective symbols are prescribed in Fig. 9.4.

## 9.5. HEIGHT OF BUILDING AND SPAN OF WALLS

Each story height shall not be more than 3.5 m and span of wall between cross wall to be limited to 5.0 m. In case of wall longer than 5.0 m buttresses must be provided at intermediate points not more than 4.0 m apart. The size of buttresses shall be kept of uniform thickness with top width equal to width of wall and bottom width equal to1/6 of wall height.

## 9.6. STAIRS CASE

The staircase is also a week structure to resist the earthquake because its does not act as diagonal strut in earthquakes. This action can be prevented by providing sliding joints at adjacent floor. Large stair hall be separated from the rest of the building by means of separation or crumple joints as in Fig. 9.5.

## 9.7. PROJECTING PARTS

Avoid the projecting structural elements such as parapets, cornices, and canopies and cantilevers sunshade if unavoidable, adequate earth quake resistant measures must be provided. In this connection full development length of bars must be embedded in the supporting concrete member.

## 9.8. ROOFS

The roof and floor must be tied to the perimeter walls and they should be adequately connected by roof band or supporting beams. The construction material of roof must be light in weight.

## 9.9. FOUNDATIONS

Foundation must be provided on hard strata of ground and does not settle and liquefy. Liquefactions

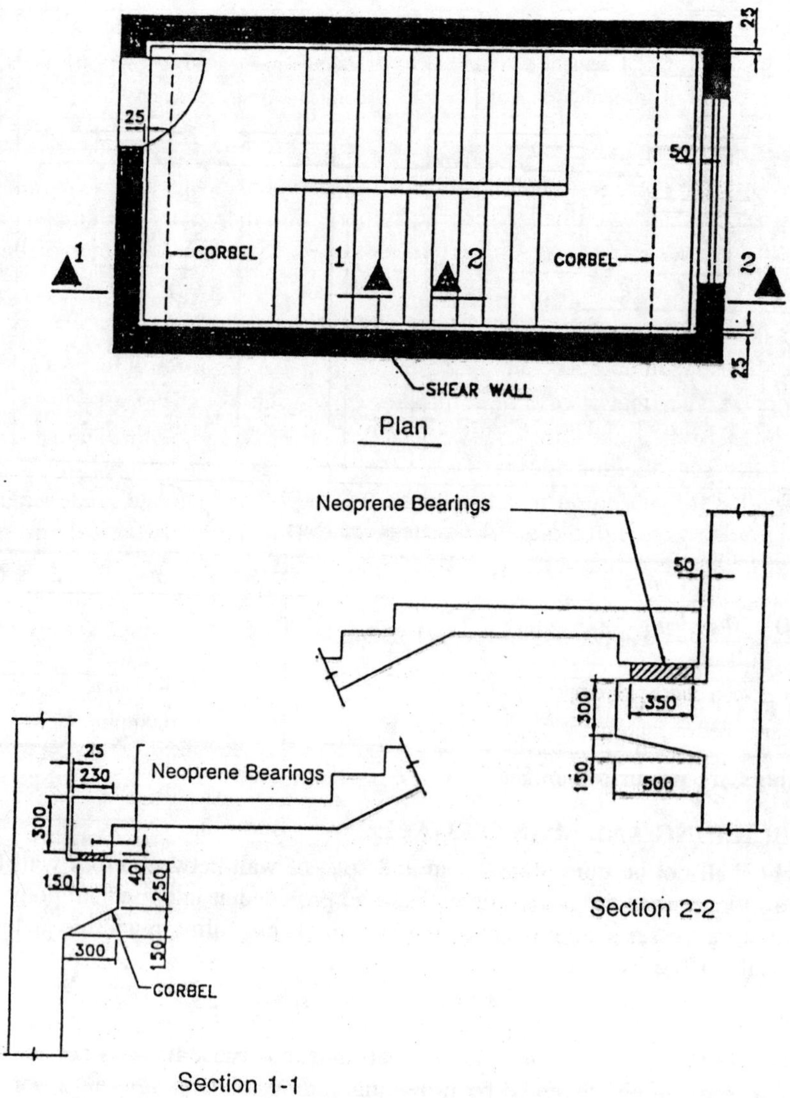


**Fig. 9.5.** Separation of Staircase from Building

may result tilting, overturning and sinking of structure. During the earth quake large differential settlement of foundations causing damage of structure. To avoid such failure all the individual footing or pile caps should be connected by ties the caps or columns to form a single unit.

## 9.10. CONSTRUCTION ASPECT

## 9.11. RECTANGULAR MASONRY UNITS

Building made of heavy material such as well-burnt brick, and solid concrete blocks fails during earthquake because it attracts inertia forces proportional to the mass of the structure, the rectangular masonry units should not have a crushing strength less than 75 MPa.

## 9.12. QUALITY OF MORTAR

| *Category of construction* | *Proportions of mortar* |
|---|---|
| A type | $M_3$ 1:6, 1 cement & 6 sand or1: 3,1 lime & 3 cinder |
| B or C types | $M_2$ 1:6, 1 cement & 6 sand (3 fine sand +3 coarse sand) or1:2:9, 1 cement, 2 lime &9 sand |
| D or E types | $M_1$ 1:61 cement & 4 and or 1:1:6 1 cement 1 lime &6 sand. |

## 9.13. REINFORCED BRICK MASONRY

Reinforced brick masonry proves batter result during earthquake. Steel bars (8 mm to 12 mm) are provided in masonry which shall be embedded in rich cement sand mortar 1:3 with a clear cover of 10 mm or in cement concrete of grade $M_{20}$ having minimum cover of 15 mm or diameter of bar which ever is greater.

## 9.14. STRENGTHENING THE BRICK MASONRY

The rectangular masonry units can be strengthening by considering the following:

— Masonry mortar. Richer mortar of cement sand or cement lime sand must be used.

— Bands or seismic bands. Bands are reinforced concrete or reinforced brick beams runner provided horizontally in the walls to tie them together and to impart horizontally bending strength to the wall. The band provided full structural integrity of the building. The concrete grade should not less than $M_{20}$ and steel grade should not more than Fe415 respectively. The longitudinal reinforcement should be of 2 bars of 8 mm (and transverse reinforcement of 6 mm $\phi$ @150 mm c/c in the form of stirrups through out the full width of wall for a minimum band depth of 75 mm.The depth of band should be increased150 mm over the openings. Following types of band are generally used in masonry construction (Fig. 9.6).

## 9.15. PLINTH OR FLOOR BAND (Fig. 9.7, 9.7 A)

This bend is provided at plinth level of all walls on top of foundation. This band is beneficial for sustaining differential settlement of foundation. While providing this band damp proof coarse does not required.

**Sill band.** This band is provided at sill level. This band reduces the effective length of masonry piers between openings and also reduces the extent of shear crack in piers. Some times U-Shape stirrups of 8 mm diameter bars in 1:3 cement sand mortar with a minimum cover of 10mm on all sides is being provided at corners and T-junction of wall at the sill level of window to a length of 900mm from inside corner to in each wall.

**Lintel band.** As the name indicates this band is provided at lintel level on all longitudinal wall and cross walls.

## 9.16. ROOF BAND

This type of band is provided immediately below roof or floor. Such a band need not be provided underneath R C slabs resting on bearing wall.

**Gable band.** This type of band is provided at the top of gable masonry below the purling in sloping roof. (Fig. 9.8)

## 9.17. LONGITUDINAL STEEL BARS OF HYSD IN R.C. BANDS

| *Span* | *Category B* | *Category C* | *Category D* | *Category E* |
|---|---|---|---|---|
| > 5.0 m | 2 # 8 mm$\phi$ | 2 # 8 mm$\phi$ | 2 # 8 mm$\phi$ | 2 # 10 mm$\phi$ |
| 6.0 m | 2 # 8 mm$\phi$ | 2 # 8 mm$\phi$ | 2 # 10 mm$\phi$ | 2 # 10 mm$\phi$ |
| 7.0 m | 2 # 8 mm$\phi$ | 2 # 10 mm$\phi$ | 2 # 12 mm$\phi$ | 4 # 10 mm$\phi$ |
| 8.0 m | 2 # 10 mm$\phi$ | 2 # 12 mm$\phi$ | 4 # 10 mm$\phi$ | 4 # 12 mm$\phi$ |

**Notes.**

Span. Distance between center lines of its cross walls.

Width of band. Minimum wall thickness 230 mm.

Depth of band. Minimum 75 mm if 2 no longitudinal bars are used.

Minimum 150 mm if 4 nos longitudinal bars are used

Stirrups 6 mm $\phi$ @150 mm c/c through out the wall.

Grade of concrete-$M_{20}$

## 9.18. VERTICAL REINFORCEMENT BAR PROVIDED AT CORNERS AND JUNCTIONS OF WALL

Consider the box action of walls-the steel bars should be used at corners and T-junctions of wall. The vertical bar shall be embedded in plinth masonry of foundation, lintel and roof band to increase the tensile strength of corners. (Fig. 9.9)

**Vertical reinforcement bar around jambs of doors and windows**

Further increase the box action of wall around opening the vertical steel bar shall be provided. It starts from foundation and terminate in lintel band so as to develop its tensile strength of wall. (Fig 9.10)

## 9.20. DIAMETERS OF VERTICAL STEEL BARS OF HYSD (FE415) GRADE IN RECTANGULAR MASONRY UNITS AT EACH CRITICAL SECTION.

| *No. of storeys* | *Storey* | *Category B* | *Category C* | *Category D* | *Category E* |
|---|---|---|---|---|---|
| One | — | Nil | Nil | 10 mm | 12 mm |
| Two | Top | Nil | Nil | 10 mm | 12 mm |
| Do | Bottom | Nil | Nil | 12 mm | 16 mm |
| Three | Top | Nil | 10 mm | 10 mm | 12 mm |
| Do | Middle | Nil | 10 mm | 12 mm | 16 mm |
| Do | Bottom | Nil | 12 mm | 12 mm | 16 mm |
| Four | Top | 10 mm | 10 mm | 10 mm | Not allowed |
| Do | Third | 10 mm | 10 mm | 12 mm | Not allowed |
| | Second | 10 mm | 12 mm | 16 mm | Not allowed |
| Do | Bottom | 12 mm | 12 mm | 20 mm | Not allowed |

**Note.** The vertical bars shall be embedded in $M_{20}$ concrete or mortar 1:3 in suitably created pockets around the bars as shown in Fig. 9.9.

## 9.21. STRENGTHENING ARRANGEMENTS RECOMMENDED FOR RECTANGULAR MASONRY UNITS

**For flat roof**

| *Building category* | *No of storey* | *Strengthen arrangement* |
|---|---|---|
| A | Up to 2<br>Up to 3 | Roof band only<br>Lintal, Roof, and Plinth band |
| B | Up to 2<br>Up to 3 | Lintel, Roof, and Plinth band<br>Lintel, Roof, Plinth band and vertical steel bar at corner and junction of wll |
| C | 1<br>2 and 3 | Lintel, Roof, and Plinth band<br>Lintel, Roof, Plinth band and vertical steel bar at corner and junction of wall |
| D | Up to 2 | Lintel, Roof, Plinth band and vertical steel bar at corner and junction of wall |

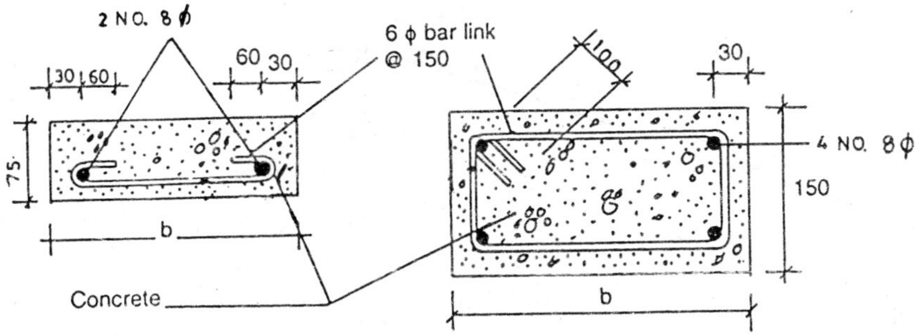


a) Cross section of R.C. band for two bars and four bars of dia. ϕ

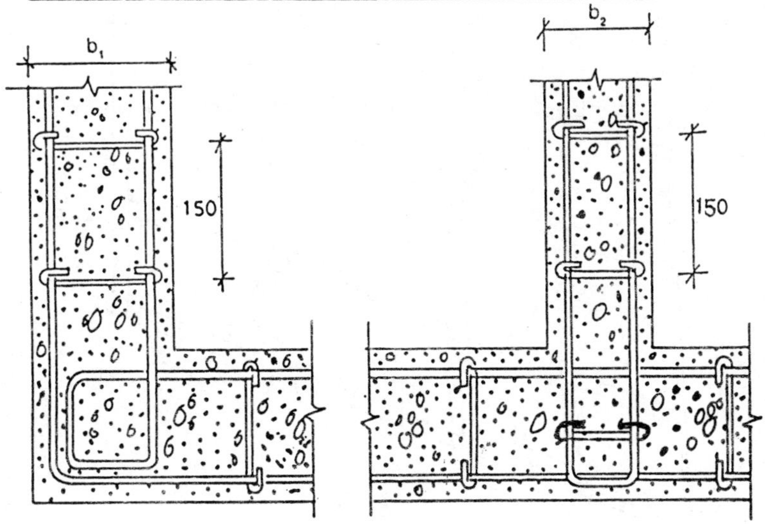


b) R.C. band reinforcement—details at corner and T junction

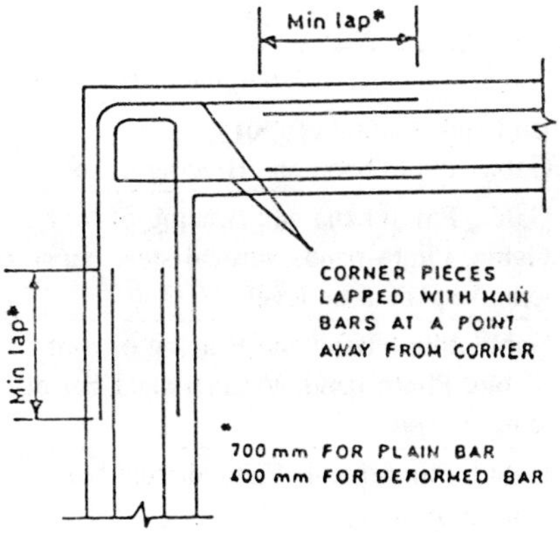


Typical Detail of Reinforcement
for Horizontal Bands

**Fig. 9.6.** Reinforcement Concrete Band Details

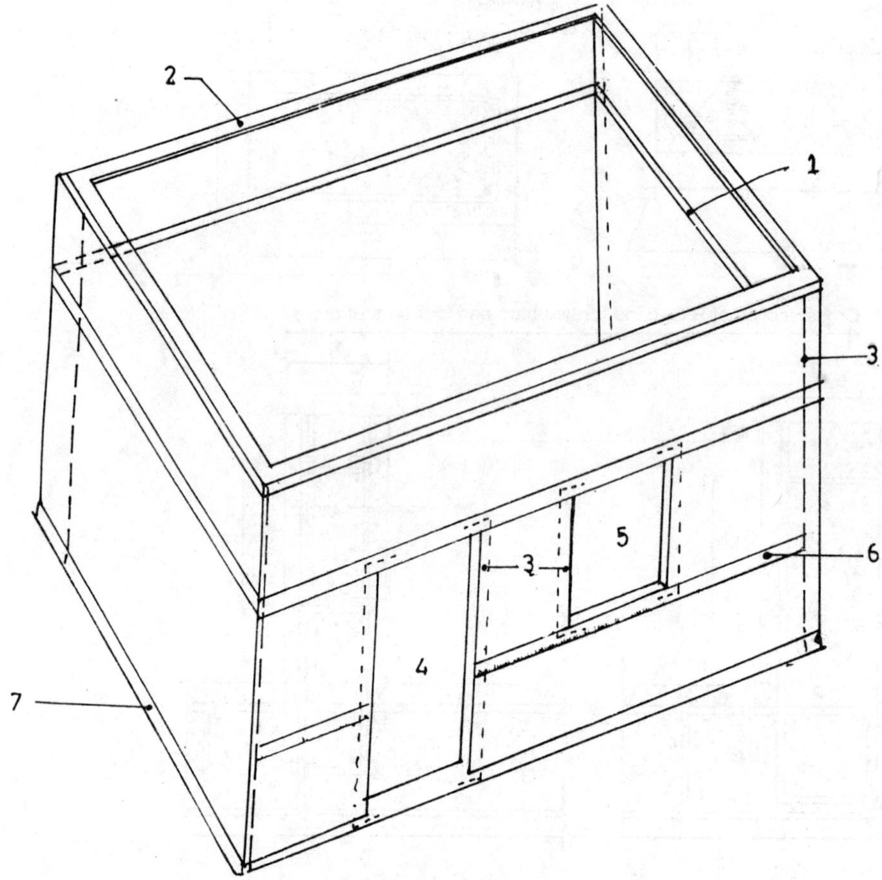


**Fig. 9.7.** Essential Requirement by Reinforcing low strength masonry building

## 9.22. STRENGTHENING ARRANGEMENTS RECOMMENDED FOR RECTANGULAR MASONRY

### (*a*) For Sloping roof

| *Building category* | *No. of storey* | *Strengthen arrangement* |
|---|---|---|
| A | UP to 2<br>Up to 3 | Gable band and Bracing of roof<br>Lintel, Gable, Plinth band and Bracing of roof |
| B | Up to 3<br>Up to 3 | Lintel, Gable, Plinth band and Bracing of roof<br>Lintel, Gable, Plinth band, Vertical steel bar at corner and junction of wall and Bracing in plan at tie level. |
| C | 1<br>2 and 3 | Lintel, Gable, Plinth band and Bracing of roof.<br>Lintel, Gable, Plinth band, Vertical steel bar at corner and junction of wall and Bracing of roof. |
| D | Up to 2 | Lintel, Gable, Plinth band, Vertical steel bar at corner and junction of wall, and Bracing of roof. |

(*b*) Bracing of roof. All the trusses and the gable end should be provided with diagonal bracing in plan so as to resist the lateral shear due to earthquake force to the gable walls acting as shear walls.

The rectangular masonry unit's construction is not earth quake resistant. Because masonry building are heavy in weight and suppose to be a non-engineer construction based on traditional manner with out formal

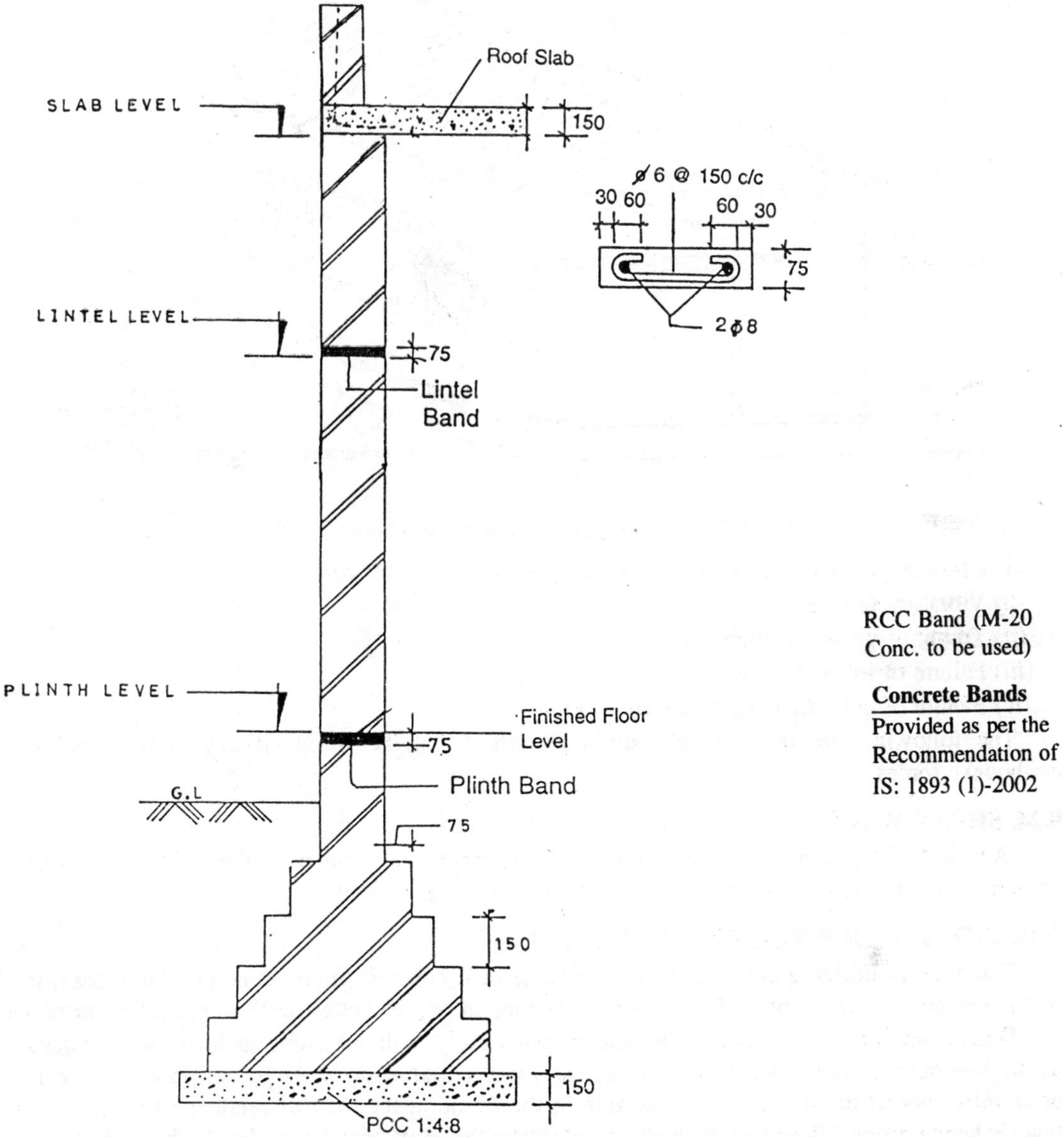


**Fig. 9.7 A.** Earthquake Resistant Detailing for Masonry Structure

engineering design. During earthquake the buildings suffer from minor cracks to collapse. The building becomes earth quake resistant using good quality of construction materials, workmen ship and necessary strengthening arrangements.

## 9.23. REINFORCED CONCRETE STRUCTURE

This type of building consists of Reinforced cement concrete frame structure and bricks or c.c. blocks etc are laid in cement sand mortar as infill. This type of construction is suitable for resisting earthquake forces because of its ductile behavior. The ductile capacity of R.C member may be increase with,

(*a*) Increasing the compression steel.

(*b*) Increasing the compressive strength of concrete.

(*c*) Increasing the ultimate concrete strain.

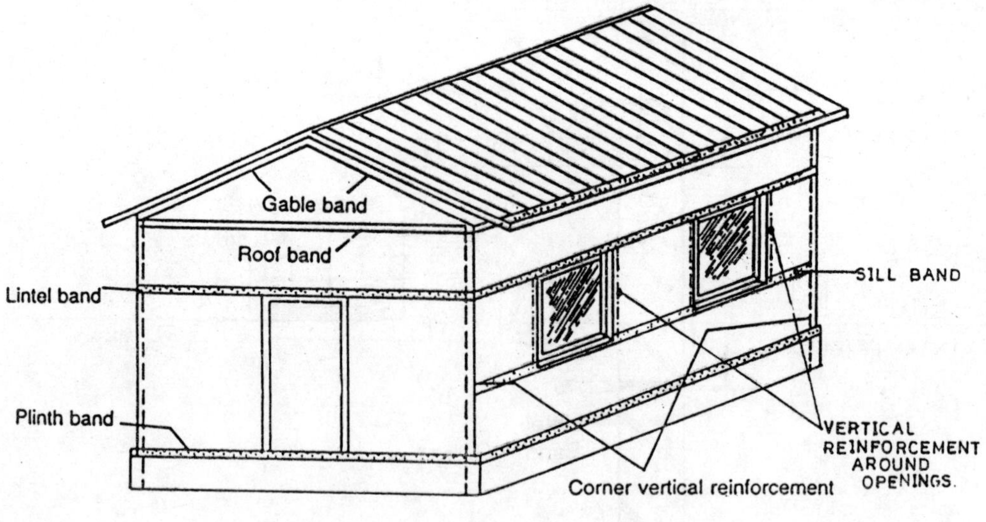


**Fig. 9.8.** Earthquake resistant features in a house (SLOPY ROOF)

The failure of R.C. building may be divided in to four categories.

(*i*) Vibratory failure.

(*ii*) Tilting or uneven settlement.

(*iii*) Failure of infill material.

(*iv*) Failure of column or beam and their joints.

The following are the concrete structure, which can be designed and constructed to resist the earthquake forces.

## 9.24. SHEAR WALL

A wall that is primarily designed to resist the lateral forces in its own plane. The shear walls are found to be effective to provide adequate strength to the buildings. (Fig. 9.5)

## 9.25. THE DUCTILE RCC FRAME BUILDING

This type of building consists of reinforced cement concrete frame structure and bricks or blocks are laid in cement mortar as infill. This type of construction proves better result to resist the earthquake forces.

Ductile detailing allow concrete to deform extensively with out losing its load carrying capacity, where as the non-ductile frame is relatively brittle and will collapse under large deformation The unreinforced brick infill (panel) do not allow deformation of the frame in the manner predicted by analysis. In the first few shake the ground floor panel's walls usually take the most beating, as that's where the forces are more. These panel walls are never intended to take in plane shear or out of plane bending. Once the panel walls have fallen off the building shakes in a manner of a very stiff upper part and a flexible lower part. This cause great distress to the ground floor columns and whole structure be come collapse. The in fill wall should be intended with the columns.

## 9.26. FLEXURAL MEMBERS

**1. Beam.** Beams are design to yield while the column remains elastic, so energy is dissipated through plastic moment hinges in the beam of frame structure. The beam failure is less damaging than the column failure. The following considerations are important for designing and detailing of flexural members. (Fig. 9.11)

**Size of beam**

B not less than 200 mm

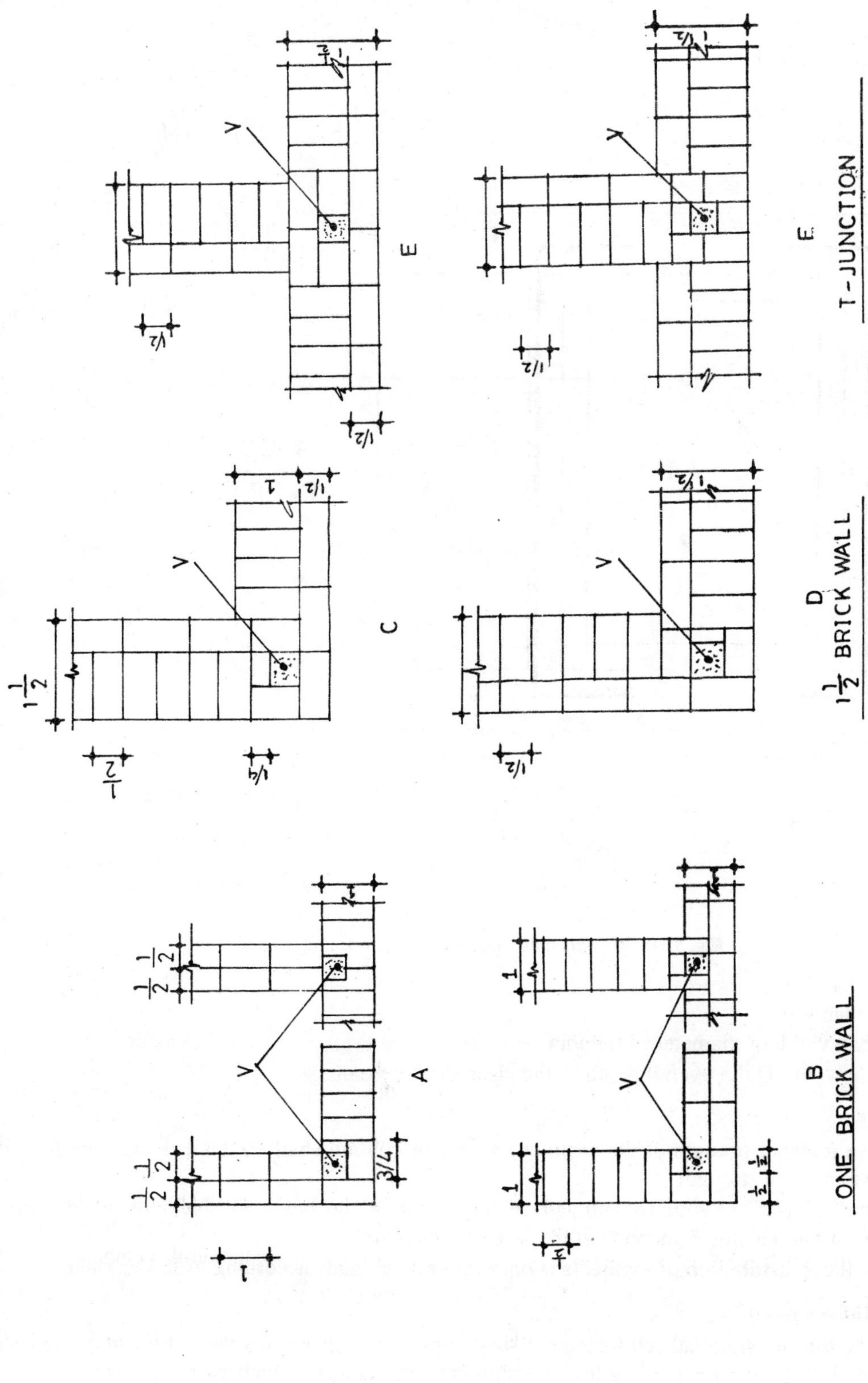


**Fig. 9.9.** Vertical Steel bars in Brick Masonry

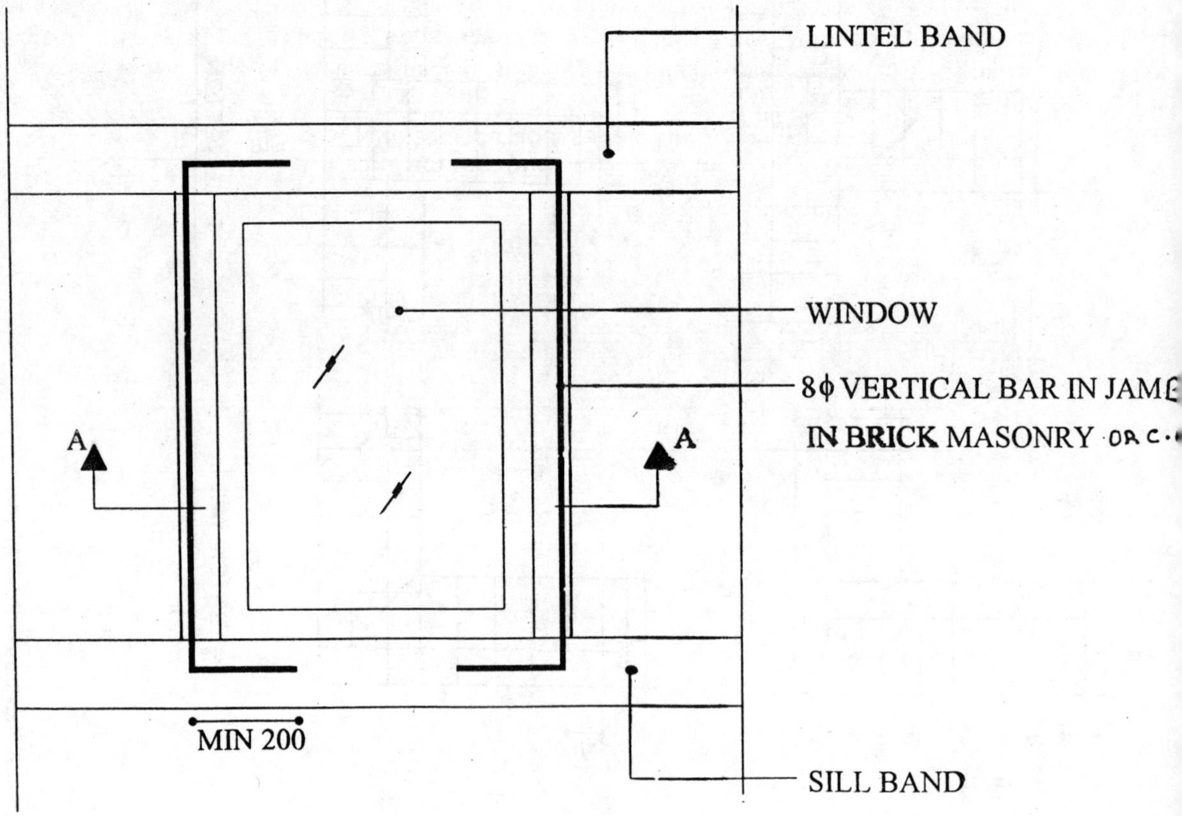


**Fig. 9.10.** Strengthening Masonry around opening

B/D not less than 0.3
L/D not less than 4.0
B not more than width or diameter of column.
Where *B* is the width, *D* the overall depth, *L* the clear span of beam

**Bending moment**

(*a*) The positive moment strength of the beam at the face of column shall not be less than one-half of the negative moment strength.

(*b*) The negative or positive moment strength at any point in the beam of shall not be less than one-quarter of the maximum moment at the face of the column.

It is clear that the redistribution of moments is only for vertical loads according to IS456:2000.

**Limitation of reinforcement**

The top and bottom longitudinal reinforcement shall consist of at least two bars of 12 mm diameter throughout the length of beam or according to the design bending moment which ever is greater.

The longitudinal tensile steel may be limited to 2.5%

Bent up bars and inclined stirrups as shear reinforcement are not provided.

In beams forming parts of a moment resisting framework, the large number of bars should not be curtailed at the same section.

Stirrups should be provided complying the minimum requirements. The diameter of stirrups should not be less than 8mmand their spacing over a length of 2d on either end of a beam (a) *d*/4 (*b*)8 $\phi$ the smallest longitudinal tensile bar (*c*) not less than100 mm and *d*/2 in the remaining length. In cantilever beam bottom steel should also be provided.

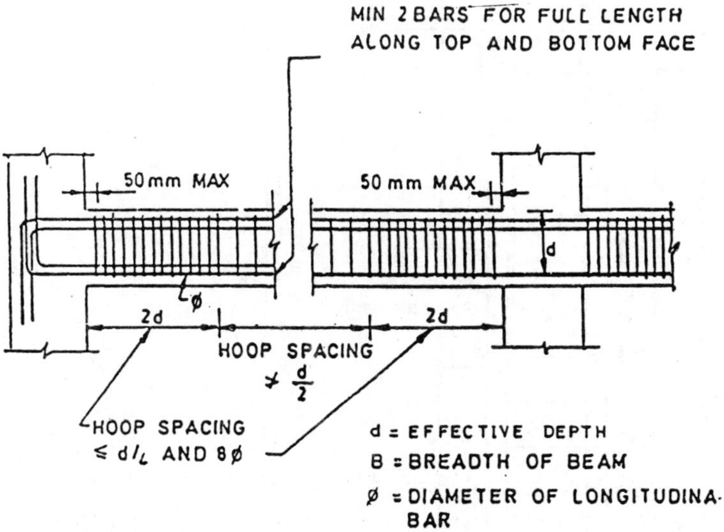


BEAM REINFORCEMENT

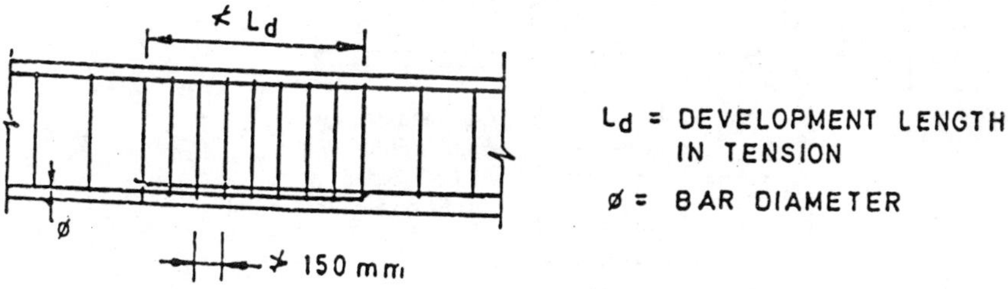


**Fig. 9.11.** Lap, Splice in Beam

**2. Slab.** The minimum diameter of bar shall be 10mm and the slab should be reinforced in both direction.

For cantilever slab bottom steel should be provided to counter act-bending tensions.

Corners must be adequately reinforced to take up the torsion and concentration of stress.

Opening in the slab/ floor should be located near the center of mass of the building and must be framed with extra steel bars.

## 9.27. COMPRESSION MEMBER

**1. Columns.** The ductility requirement is more difficult to achieve in the columns due to its buckling effect. The design should be based on strong column and weak beam frame. The size of column should be chosen so that it becomes a short column. (Fig. 9.12)

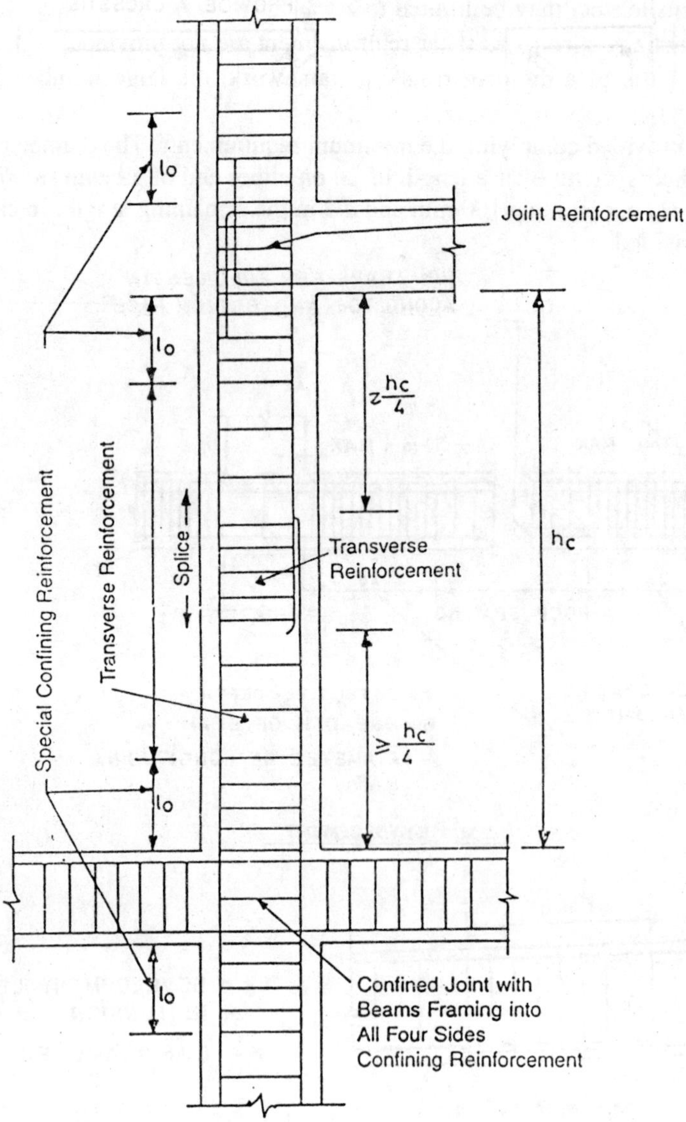


**Fig. 9.12.** Column and Joint Detailing

Its recommended that minimum shortest dimension of the column is 200mm up to an effective span of beam 5m.If the effective span of beam is greater than 5 m and unsupported length of column exceed 4 m, the shortest dimension shall not be less than 300 mm.

The diameter of longitudinal bar should not be less than 12 mm and should not spaced more than 200mm apart .The smallest diameter of bar should not be less than 2/3 of the largest bar diameter in any one row. The transverse reinforcement in the form of hoops or ties shall not be less than 8 m, and their spacing shall not exceed half the least lateral dimension of the column.

Splices must be placed in low stress area *i.e.* in the central half of the member.

Hoop shall be provided over the entire splice length not exceeding 150mm center to center. (Fig. 9.13)

## 9.28. BEAM AND COLUMN JOINTS

The design and detailing of beam- column joints requires much attention as the design of member them

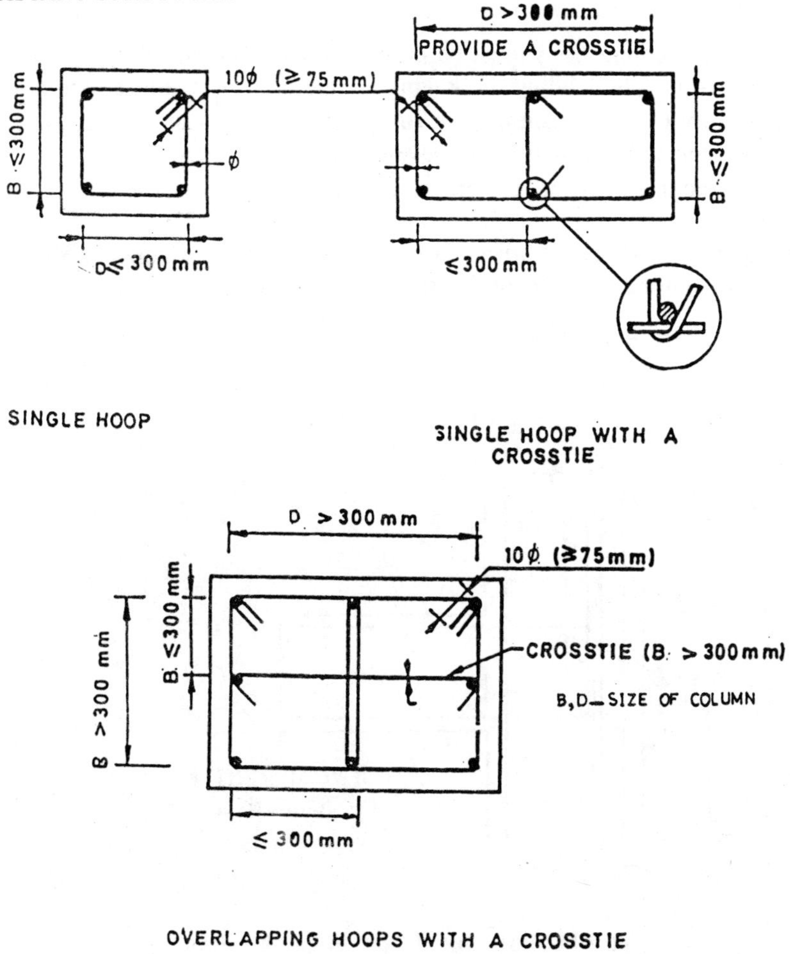


**TRANSVERSE REINFORCEMENT IN COLUMN**

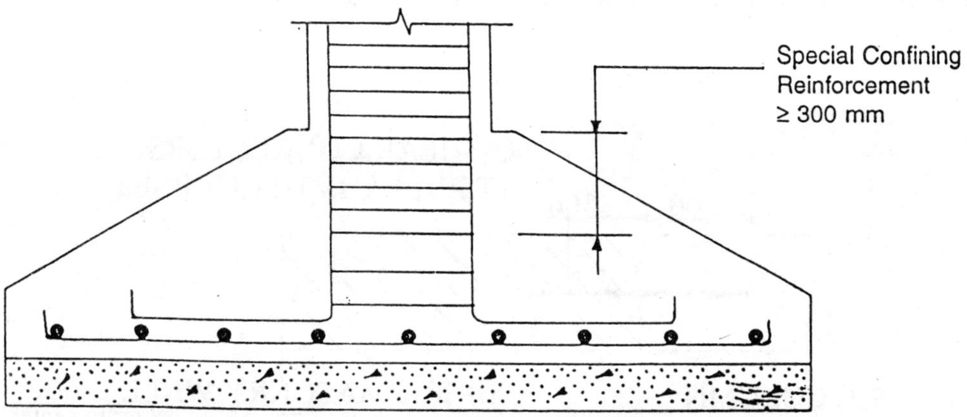


**Fig. 9.13.** Provision of Special Confining Reinforcement of Footing

selves. The strength of the connections must be more than the strength of member because the joint core strength may degrade with cyclic loading. Following are the modes of failure of a joint.

1. **Anchorage failure of bars anchored in the joints.** The provision of adequate anchorage for the flexural reinforcement to allow these to develop their yield strength.
2. **Shear failure.** The use of shear reinforcement to resist any shear force in excess of that carried by the concrete.
3. **Bond failure.** The provision of adequate lateral confinement of concrete to allow transmission of column load through the joints. (Fig. 9.14)

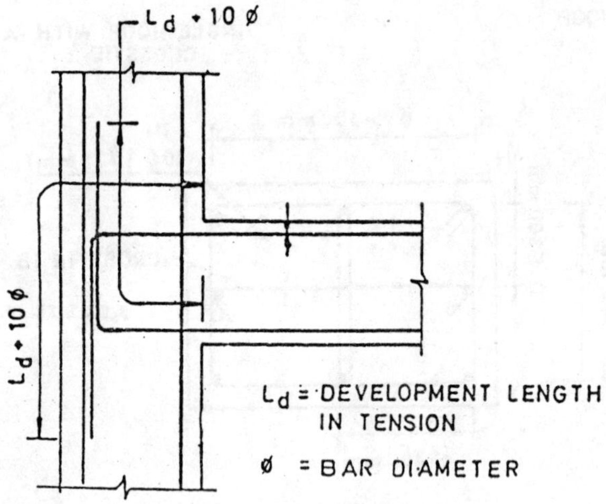


**Fig. 9.14.** Anchorage of Beam bars in an external joint

## 9.29. COLUMN AND BRICK MASONRY JOINTS

The 8mm diameter bar, 300mm in length shear connector to be bent inside the shuttering during casting of respective column. After removal of shuttering the shear connector shall be straightened and embedded with rich mortar in to the masonry wall during construction. (Fig. 9.15)

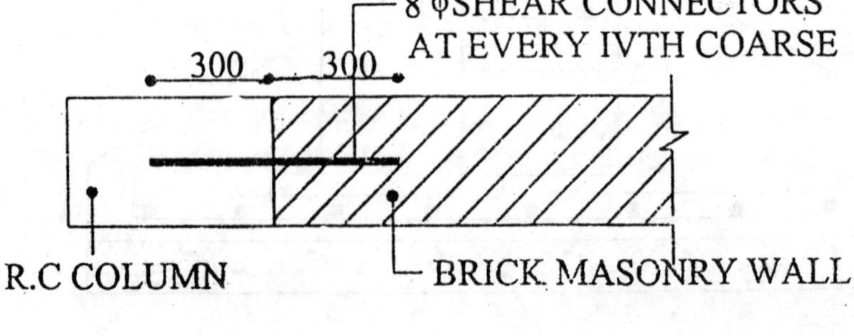


**Fig. 9.15.** Shear Connectors for External Masonry Walls

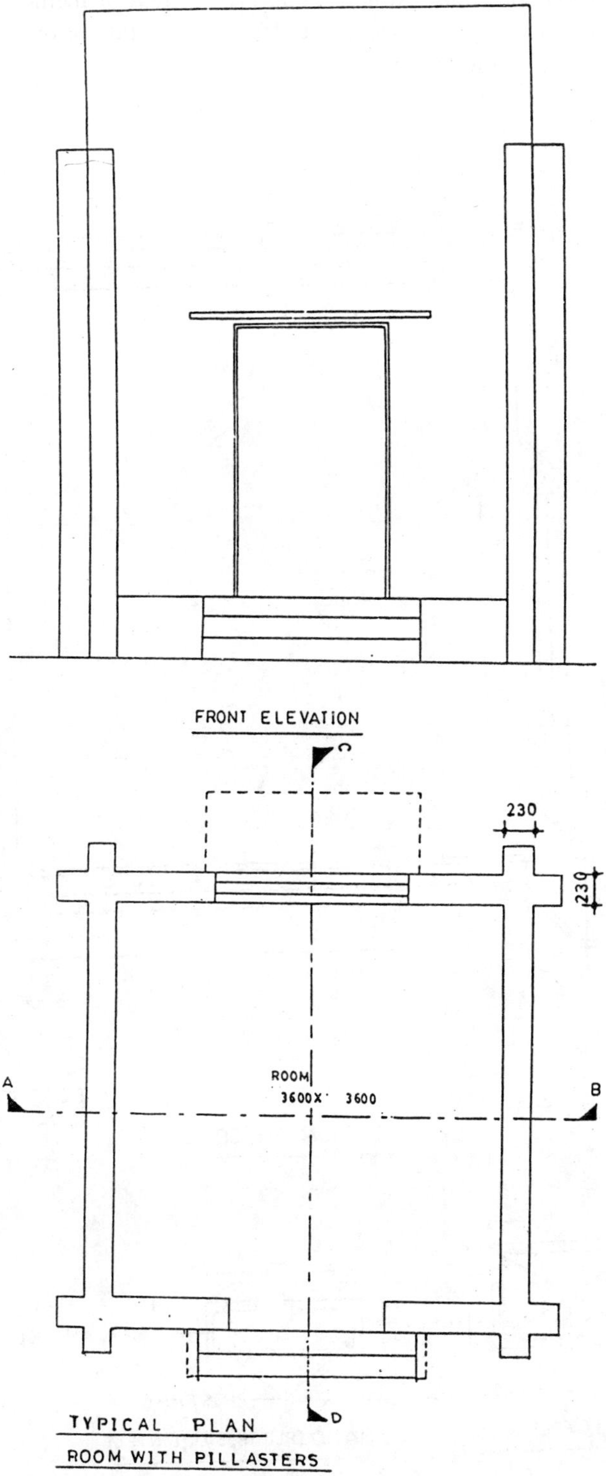


**Fig. 9.15 A.** Earth-quake resistant room

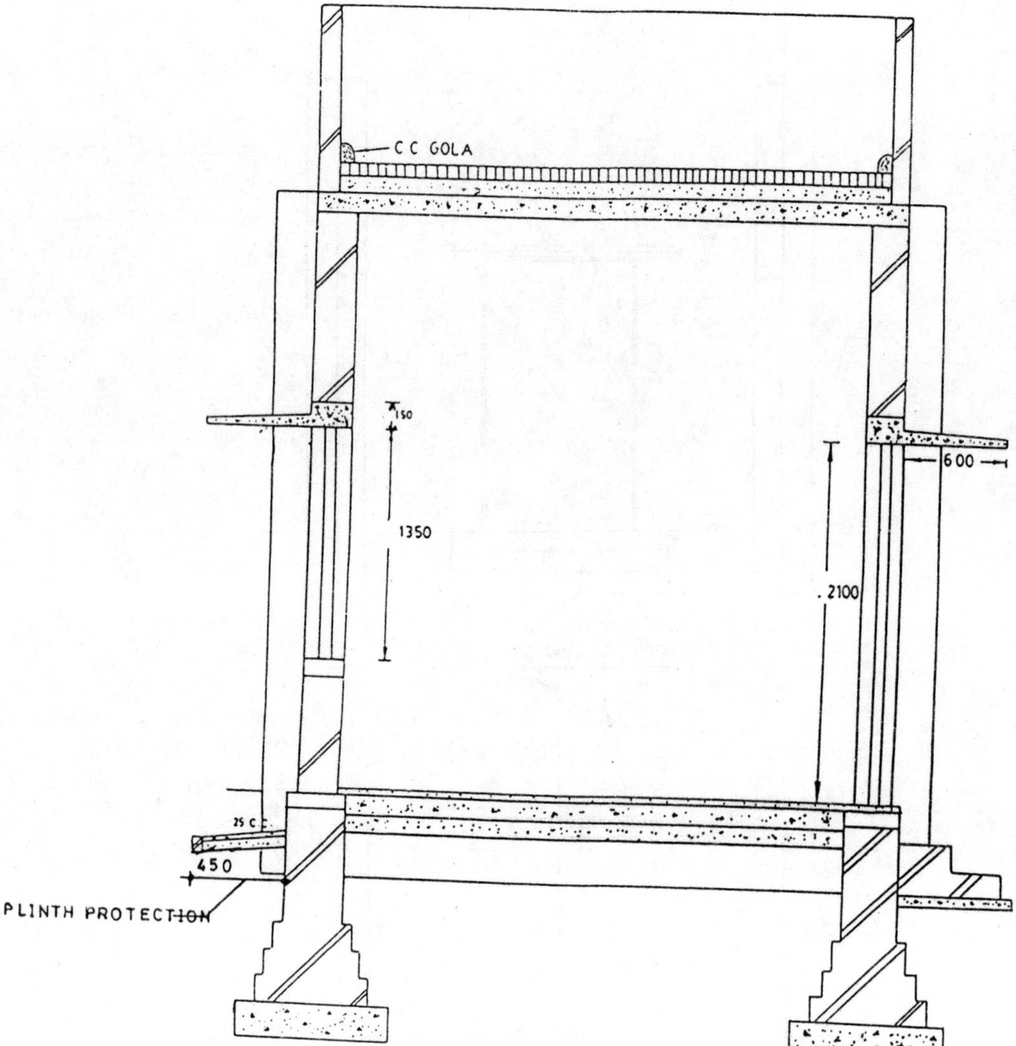


SECTION ON CD

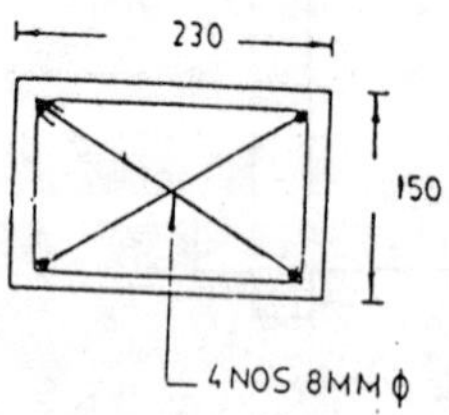


X-SEC OF LINTEL

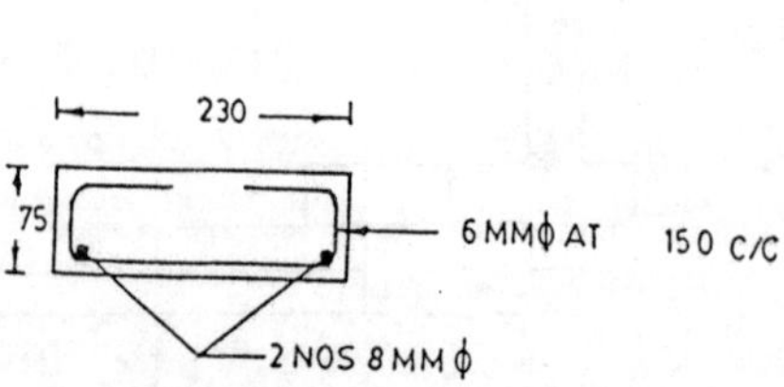


BAND (PLINTH, SILL, LINTEL)

**Fig. 9.15 B.**

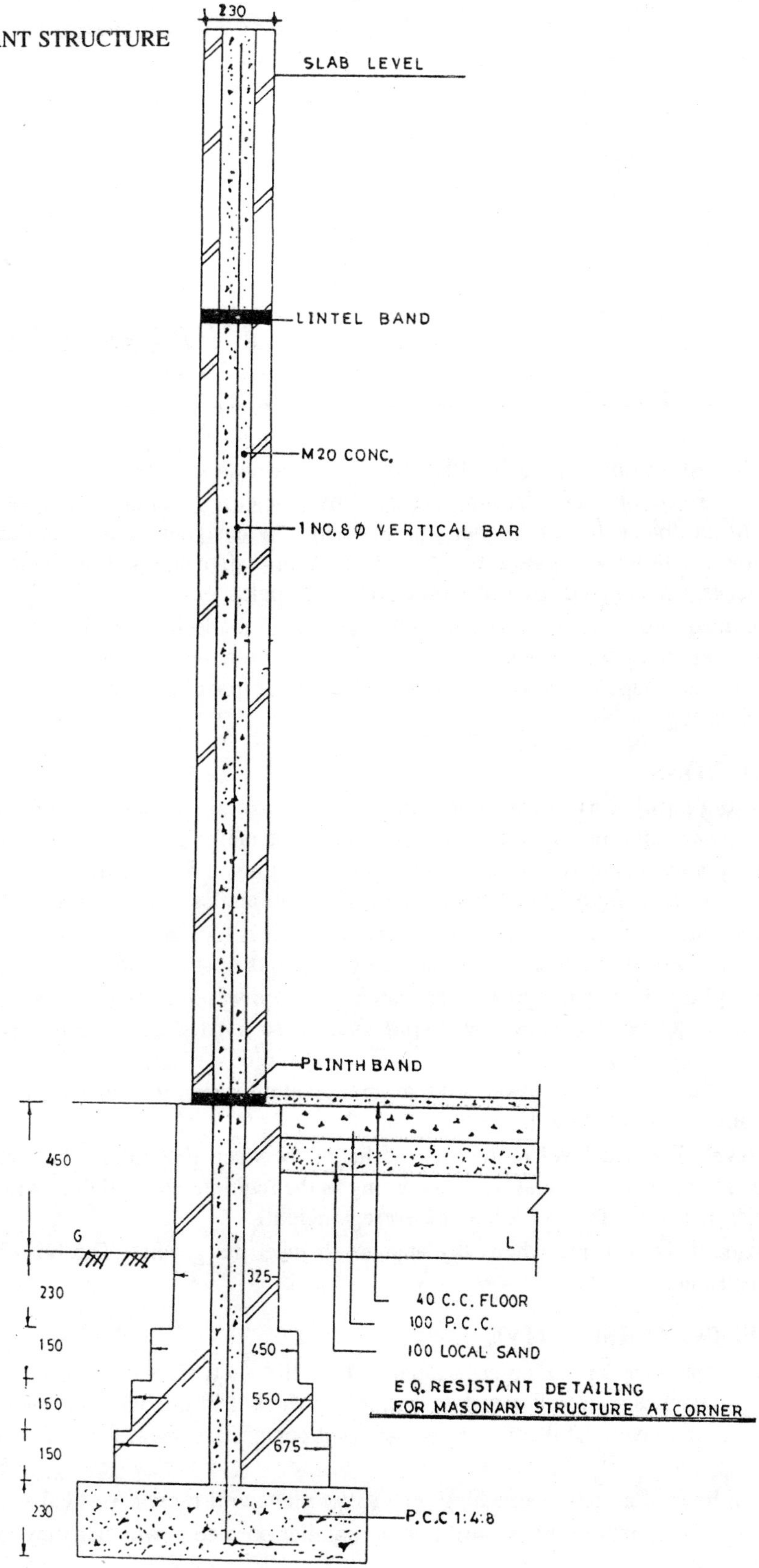
230
SLAB LEVEL
LINTEL BAND
M20 CONC.
1 NO. 8 ϕ VERTICAL BAR
PLINTH BAND
450
G
L
230
150
150
150
230
325
450
550
675
40 C.C. FLOOR
100 P.C.C.
100 LOCAL SAND
E Q. RESISTANT DETAILING
FOR MASONARY STRUCTURE AT CORNER
P.C.C 1:4:8

Fig. 9.15 C.

# 10
# *Perspective Views*

It is a view of an object perceived by the eye of an observer. The principle involved in perspective drawing is the Projections. The drawing prepared by isometric or oblique method does not represent the actual view of an object .In case of building drawing, the designer as well as the owner is interested to know that how the proposed building will really look like after completion. That is why the perspective drawing/sketches are prepared from different sides and angles.

As mentioned above the perspective drawing/view is made by the principle of conical projections. Rays coming from one point of observation (from eye to the object) and the view is formed on the picture plane .The size and shape of view always depend upon the position of plane, eye level, station point and vanishing points etc.

## 10.1. DEFINITIONS

**1. Vanishing point (v.p).** If someone stand between two rails on a railway track (straight), then it will be seen that the two rails appears to meet at one point but actually it is not so. The two rails are at a constant distance. The points above two rails appear to be meeting is known as the vanishing point. It is the tendency of our eyes to adjust simultaneously for different angles in horizontal and vertical planes.

**2. Station point.** It is a point from where the observer is looking at the object/building size and shape of the perspective vies of an object/building largely depends open the position of the station point.

**3. Picture plane.** It is an imaginary transparent plane on which the view of an object/building is drawn. While drawing a perspective view, the picture plan is so located that it touches at least one corner of building.

**4. Ground line.** The line represents the ground level on which the observer is standing. This line may be drawn at any position below the picture plane.

**5. Eye level.** The eye level represents the height between the ground line and the eye level of the observer. Though the eye level may very according to the requirement of the drawing but usually it is taken as 1.5m, which is the eye level of a man of average height.

**6. Horizon.** This is a line where sky appears to meet the ground .The horizon and the eye level is assumed to be same.

## 10.2. ONE-POINT PERSPECTIVE

When the one face of an object is parallel to the picture plane. Then it is find that all lines perpendicular to the observer will vanish to one point, which is in line with the station point and at a certain height above ground level. While drawing a one-point perspective view, following points should be kept in mind.

(*a*) Vertical lines of an object touching the picture plane will remain vertical.

(*b*) Line parallel to picture plane will remain parallel no matter whether they are touching the picture plane or not.

(*c*) Vertical lines that are away from the picture plane will vanish to the one vanishing point, which is also known as center of vision.

One-point perspective views are generally used for buildings, road views in case of row housing interior designing etc.

## 10.3. TWO POINT PERSPECTIVE

When the two sides of an object/building are inclined at a certain angle with the picture plane, the two vanishing points are required to show the entire view of an object/building. Detailed method of drawing a two-point perspective view is given below.

(*a*) Draw a line representing picture plane.

(*b*) Draw the plan inclined to the picture plane with convenient angles 300, 450, 600 degree, which are the most suitable angles.

(*c*) It is better to keep the corner of a building touching the picture plane so the same scale of measurement can be used for plan as well as perspective view.

(*d*) Mark the station point at a distance of three to four times the height of building.

(*e*) From station point, draw lines parallel to the two faces of the building to intersect the picture plane. From the point of intersection, draw perpendicular lines to cut the eye level to obtain vanishing points.

(*f*) Draw ground line any where between picture plane and station point.

(*g*) Mark the eye level above ground line.

(*h*) Draw rays from all the visible components (*i.e.* corners, door, window, steps, projections etc) from station point. Each ray will cut the picture plane and from that point draw perpendicular lines.

(*i*) Now mark all the height on a line that is touching the picture plane starting from ground level.

(*j*) The right face component will be governed by the right vanishing point and vice versa. The two point perspective views are suitable for buildings. If we change the height of eye level then we can obtain insect eye view or bird's eye view

## 10.4. 3-POINT PERSPECTIVE

This is used for drawing a view of a high rise building or sky scraper. In this case vertical lines also vanish to a 3rd vanishing point hence it is called 3-point perspective view.

**Problem 1.** *Draw one point perspective of the given block whose one face touches the picture plane. Station point is 70 mm away from P.P and eye level is 70 mm above ground level. (Fig. 10.1)*

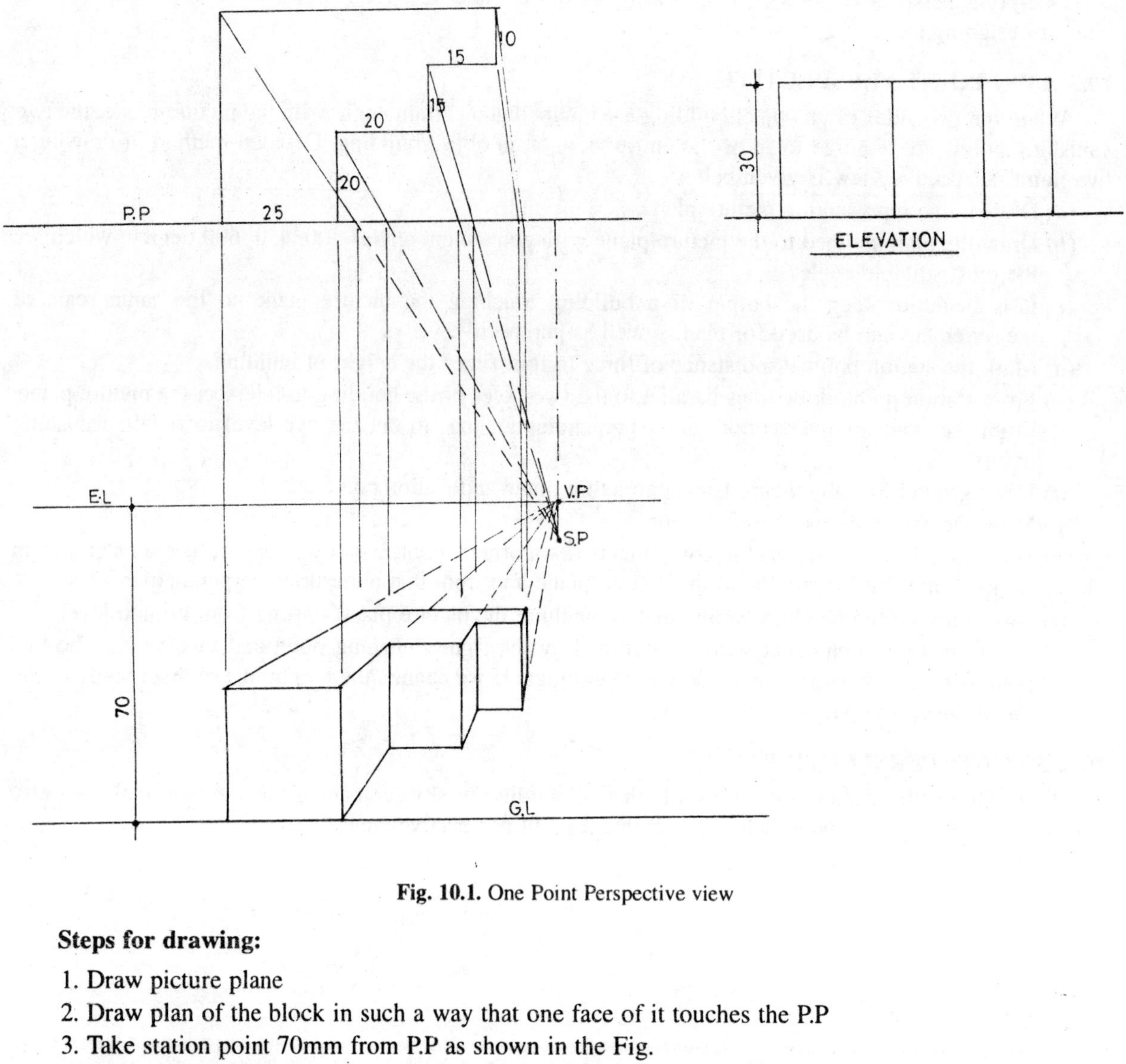


**Fig. 10.1.** One Point Perspective view

**Steps for drawing:**

1. Draw picture plane
2. Draw plan of the block in such a way that one face of it touches the P.P
3. Take station point 70mm from P.P as shown in the Fig.
4. Take ground level anywhere
5. Mark the height of eyelevel as 70mm above ground level
6. The line of station point and eye level will intersect each other to give vanishing point (v.p)
7. Now take the projections of each and every point of object except the point touching the picture plane.
8. Projection shall be taken with respect to station point up to picture plane. And from picture plan, the projections will be perpendicular.
9. The face touching the picture plane will remain vertical
10. Now, mark the height of block (30 mm) on the face touching the P.P and vanish it to the vanishing point.

**Problem 2.** *Draw a 2-point perspective of a given block. (40mm × 40mm × 50mm) station point is 80mm away from picture plane and the height of the eye level is 90mm from ground line. (Fig. 10.2)*

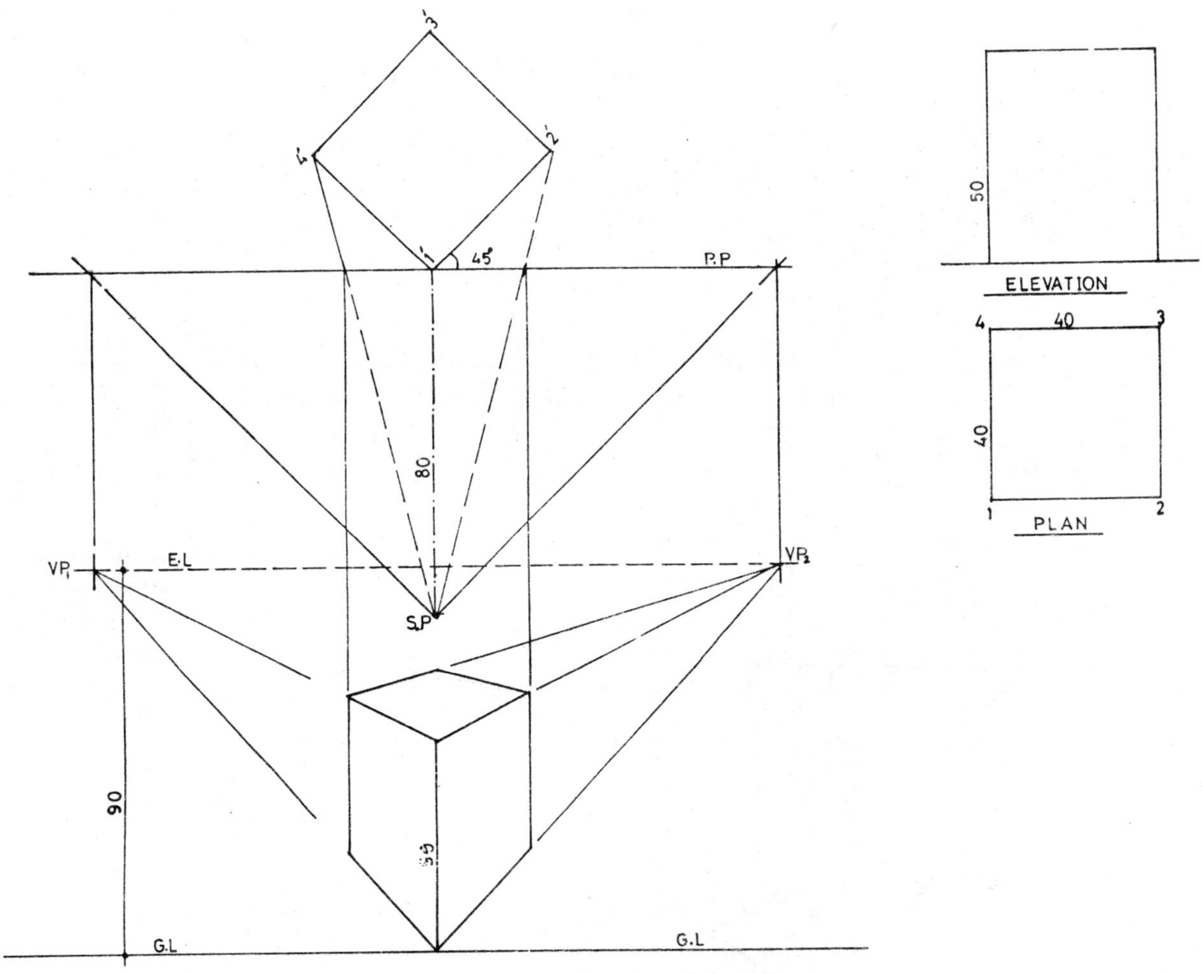


**Fig. 10.2.** Perspective view of a cuboid

**Steps for drawing:**

1. Draw the tilted plan at an angle of 45° to the picture plane at a point
2. From 1/draw a perpendicular line to mark station point that is 80mm
3. Mark ground level any where below the station point
4. Mark eye level that is 90 mm above ground level.
5. From station point draw a line parallel to the face (1′-2′) and face (1′-4′) to cut the P.P. from these points, draw perpendicular lines to cut the eye level that will give $V.P_1$ and $V.P_2$.
6. Now take the height of the block as 50mm from ground level and vanish the top and bottom from both the vanishing points.
7. Draw the projections of points 2′ and 4′ with respect to station point up to P.P and from P.P this projection shall be perpendicular downwards.
8. The right face and the line parallel to the right face will be govern by the right vanishing point ($V.P_2$) and the left face by the $V.P_1$.
9. Remember to mark the height on the line, which touches the perpendicular (in this case it is the point).

**Problem 3.** *Draw the perpendicular of the two block kept over each other when S.P is 85 mm away from P.P and height of eye level is 95mm from ground level (Fig. 10.3).*

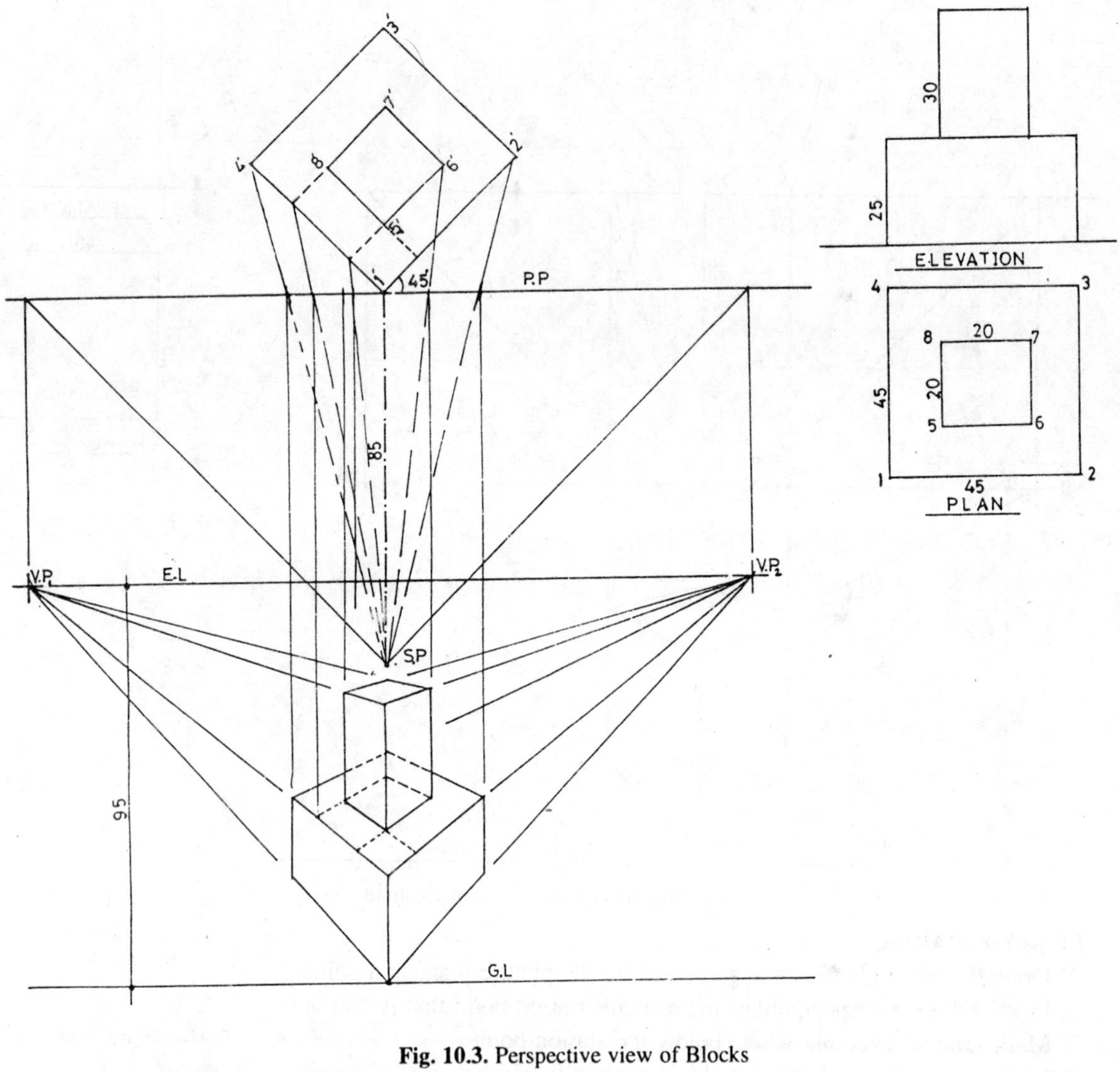


**Fig. 10.3.** Perspective view of Blocks

**Steps for drawing:**

1. The whole procedure is same as in problem number 2 when drawing the lower block.
2. To draw a upper block extend the line 7′-8′ up to the face 1′-4′ and also extend the face 6′-5′ up to the face 1′-4′.
3. Draw the projection of these above points to cut the face of lower block
4. Also extend the face 8′-5′ up to the face 1′-2′ and draw the projections.
5. Now we have, 3 points on the faces of lower block whose perspective has already been drawn.
6. Now we have these 3-points accordingly to get the base of the upper block.
7. Now mark the height of upper block and vanish its sides.

**Problem 4.** *Draw the perspective view of the composition of blocks when no point of the block touches the picture plane. Take station point any where below the P.P at 40mm and height of eye level is 30mm from G.L. (Fig. 10.4)*

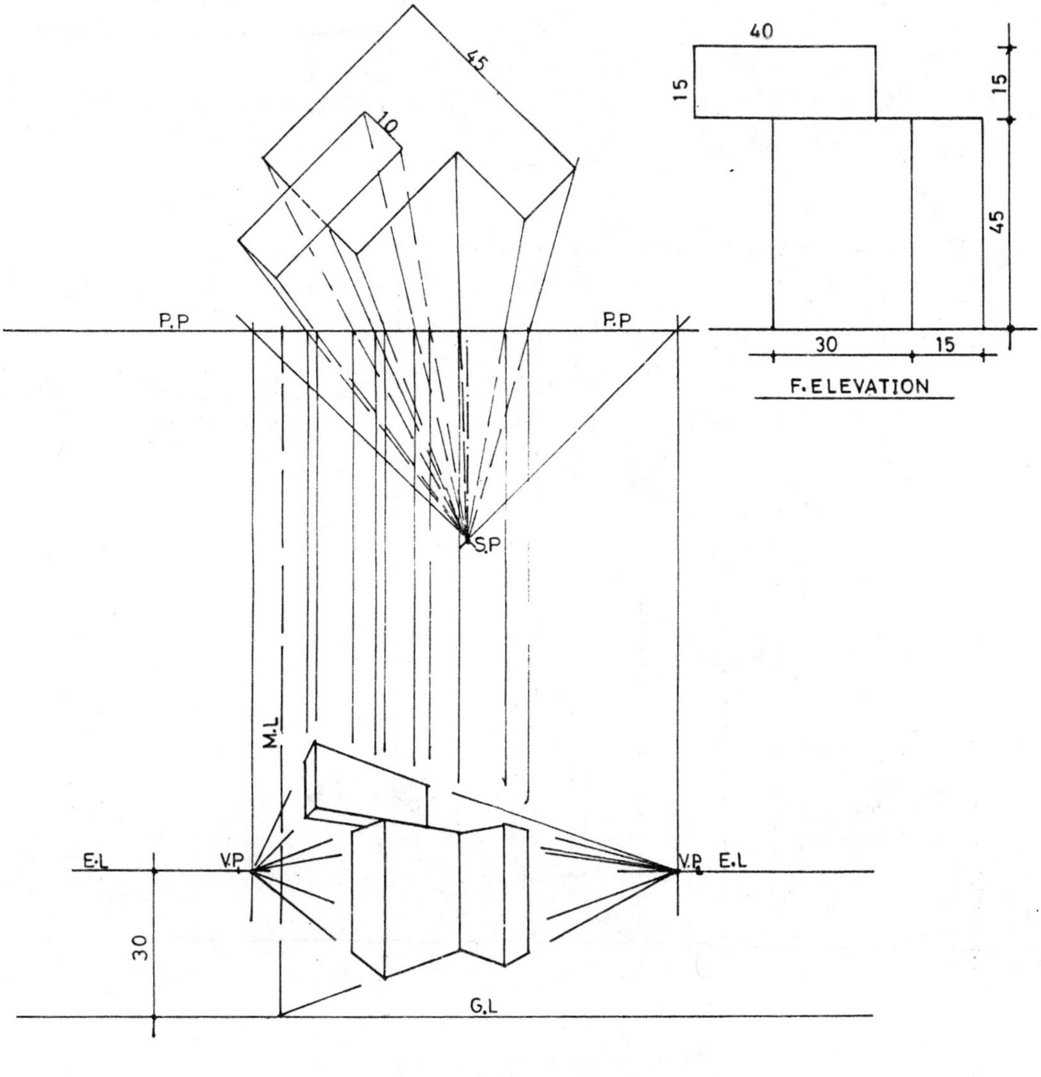


**Fig. 10.4.** Block Perspective

(Hint Take measurement line (M.L) by producing any face up to P.P)

**Problem 5.** *Draw the perspective view of blocks when S.P is 50mm away from P.P and height of ey level is 30 mm from Ground level. (Fig. 10.5).*

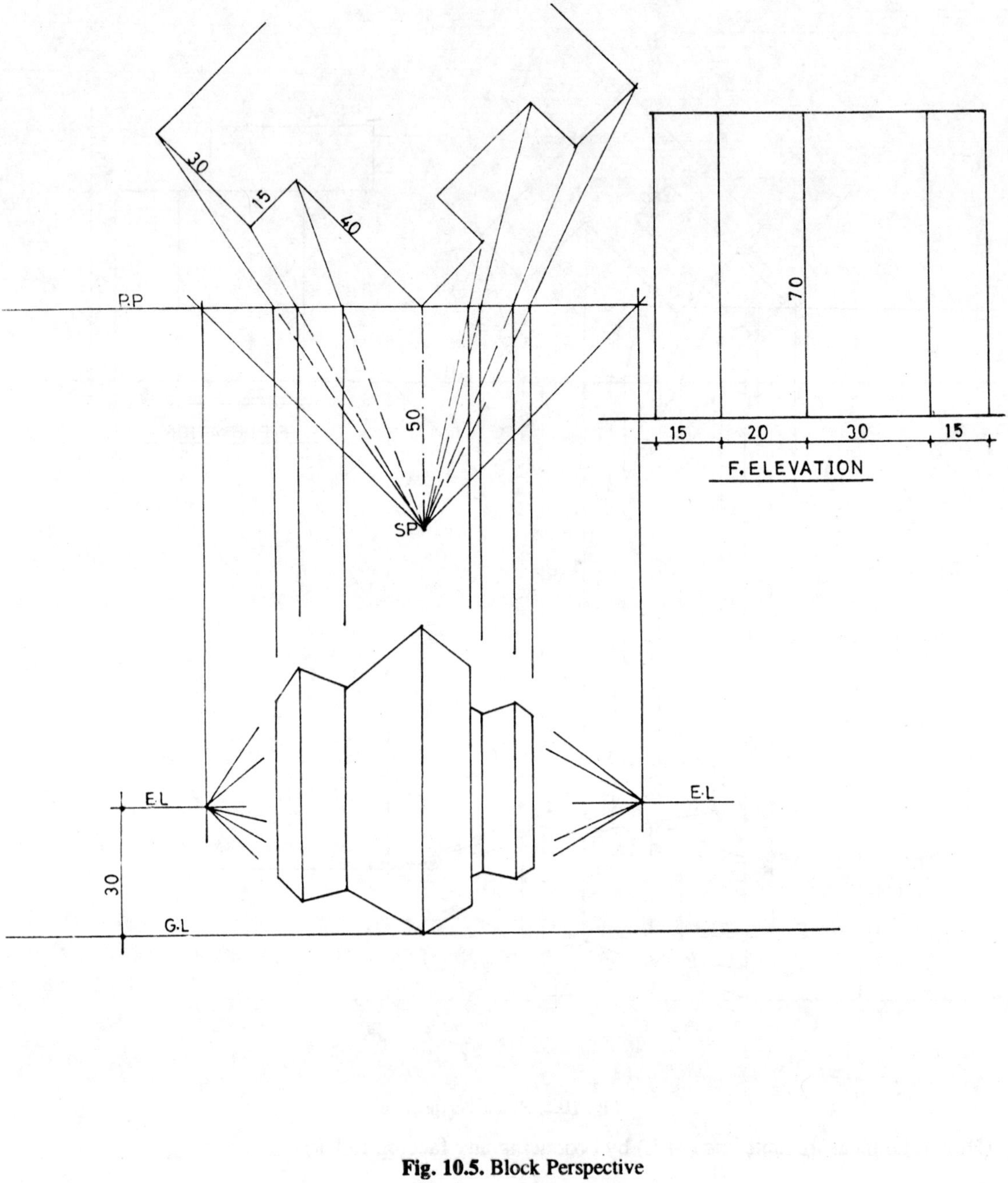


**Fig. 10.5.** Block Perspective

**Problem 6.** *Draw the perspective view of a single room building when S.P is 2500 mm from P.P, height of eye level is 1700 mm from G.L. Total height of room = 3500 mm (Fig. 10.6).*

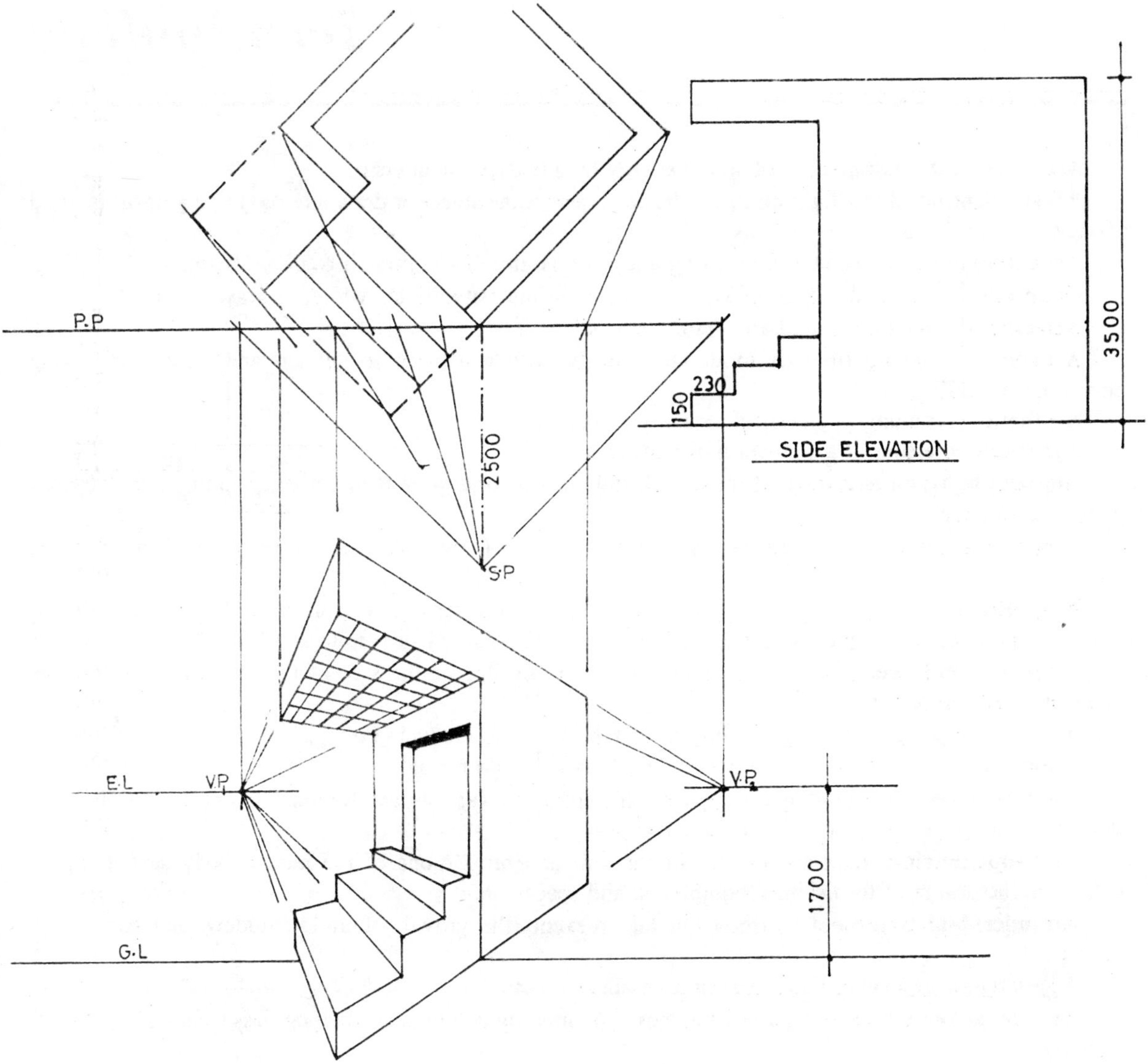


**Fig. 10.6.** Perspective view

# 11

# *Terminology*

**Absorption:** the assimilation of sound energy by a body without echo.

**Accent lighting:** direct lighting to emphasize a particular object or draw attention to a part of the field of view.

**Accent:** to enhance decoration by using a lesser quantity of a contrasting colour or finish.

**Achromatic:** a neutral colour, lacking in chroma or intensity: black, white, or gray.

**Acoustic tile:** modular sound absorption panels.

**Acrylic:** a synthetic fiber of moderate tenacity with resistance to scratch and light, and having dimensional stability.

**Aesthetic:** pertaining to an object's quality of beauty.

**Aggregate:** the sum of a collection of particulars.

**Ambient light:** measurement of the overall illumination of a room from reflected sunlight or Overhead lighting applications.

**Ampere:** a unit of electric current equal to the current of one Volt acting through a resistance of one Ohm.

**Amplification:** An increase in the volume of sound. The term is also used for the effect of colour intensification due to the inter-reflection of light from one coloured surface to another.

**Angle of incidence:** the angle (measured from the surface on the side of the approach) at which an element strikes an object.

**Anneal:** the process of strengthening through heating and gradual cooling.

**Anodize:** chemical process where a coating is etched onto metal

**Antique:** all items, including accessories, art, buildings, furnishings, lighting, sculpture, carvings and other personal possessions, which are over 100 years old.

**Anthropometrics:** the measurement of the size and proportions of the human body, and its applications to the design of furnishings, equipment, and spaces.

**Antimicrobial treatment:** a treatment that prevents the growth of mold, mildew, and bacteria on carpet.

**Appurtenance:** a subordinate part or accessory.

**Arcade:** an open or closed series of arches supported by columns used along passageways, courtyards or porches.

**Awing:** lightweight roof structure typically constructed of fabric or metal installed over an exterior opening such as a doorway, porch or balcony to provide shelter.

**Baluster:** small, heavily proportioned pillar used for vertical support in a railing, typically made of wood or stone.

**Balustrade:** railing composed of series of balusters, bottom rail and top handrail, also used in smaller scale to embellish furniture.

**Batik:** ancient hand-printing technique using wax as a resist, which is applied, removed and re-applied for each colour layer to create various patterns including a crackled appearance.

**Barrier-free design:** which presents no physical barriers to access and free movement within an environment.

**Bay window:** a window set in a frame projecting outward from a wall to create an interior recess, usually of fixed glass.

**Bay:** a volumetric or structural unit defined by columns or walls.

**Binder:** a substance, which brings cohesion to a collection of elements.

**Biodegradable:** capable of being broken down into innocuous products through biological processes.

**Bonded fabric:** a fabric formed by combining an outer face fabric with a backing fabric using an adhesive or laminate.

**Bow window:** a bay window in the form of an unbroken curve.

**Bubble diagram:** an initial planning sketch in which clustered circles represent activity zones placed in proximity relationships.

**Building byelaws:** rules and regulations imposed by local municipality or Municipal Corporation for the construction of buildings.

**Cantilever:** any part of a structural member (commonly a beam), that projects beyond its support.

**Carpet:** a soft-surface floor covering used to blanket a floor from wall to wall.

**Casement:** a loosely woven or knit sheer drapery fabric.

**Casement window:** a window hinged at the side, and which swings open like a door.

**Cathode:** the terminal from which electrons emanate in a fluorescent or other discharge-type lamp.

**Ceramic:** made from clay and heated (fired) in a kiln. A hard and durable material.

**Chandelier:** ceiling mounted light fixture with arms branching out from a central support.

**Chromaticity:** the aspect of a colour that describes its dominant wavelength and purity

**Clerestory** a window or bank of windows inserted between two roof levels to bring light into a room.

**Closed plan:** an architectural plan that divides the internal space of a structure into separate, discrete rooms.

**Coefficient of utilization (cu):** the ratio of light (lumens) from a luminaire received on a work plane to that emitted by the lamp.

**Coffered ceiling:** one with ornamental raised panels between closely spaced beams.

**Colour fastness:** the ability of a material to retain its colour when exposed to light or cleaning agents.

**Colour rendering index:** the general expression for the effect of a light source on the colour appearance of objects in comparison with their colour appearance under a referenced light source.

**Colour retention:** the ability of a material to retain its colour when exposed to light or cleaning agents.

**Colour spectrum:** the range of colour comprising visible light.

**Compact fluorescent:** an energy-saving replacement for incandescent sources, with greater efficiency and life.

**Concrete:** a material consisting of cement mixed in varying proportions with sand and gravel or other aggregates. With the addition of water, the mixture becomes mouldable, capable of assuming almost any shape. Concrete dries to a heavy, stone like mass of great strength.

**Concrete blocks:** large, generally hollow, bricklike blocks composed of concrete; widely used in building, especially for walls.

**Conduction:** the direct transfer of heat through a solid material, such as glass or metal.

**Conduit:** a tube used to protect electrical wires.

**Conservation area:** protection of an area with characteristic features typical to the area and defined in the local zoning regulations with historic and architectural importance.

**Construction documents:** the full volume of drawings, specifications and contracts, which comprise the complete description of a built project.

**Contract:** a legally binding, written agreement between two parties outlining services to be rendered, responsibilities, and compensation.

**Convection:** the transfer of heat through natural air circulation.

**Cotton:** a natural staple fiber harvested from the flower of the cotton plant.

**Couch:** upholstered furniture used for sitting or reclining.

**Courtyard:** space permanently open to sky enclosed fully or partially by buildings and may be at ground level or any other level within or adjacent to a building.

**Cove lighting:** provided by light sources shielded by a ledge and distributing light upward over the ceiling.

**Coved ceiling:** a ceiling that curves into the supporting walls rather than meeting them at an angle.

**Covered Area or Coverage:** the Ground area covered immediately above the plinth level covered by the building but does not include the space covered by:

**Critical path:** the time frame and overlapping order of steps in the building and finishing process which determines the minimum time or necessary progression required for an event.

**Decibel (dB, db):** a unit for expressing the relative intensity of sounds on a scale from zero for the least perceptible sound to about 130 for the average pain level.

**Delaminate:** to come apart in layers.

**Design concept:** In the present context, it means the idea for the solution to the process of planning a building, furnishings, or composite interiors; the organization of a work of interior design, architecture or art problem.

**Detail drawing:** a drawing on a scale greater than that of the general drawings, showing specific composition of an object to be built.

**Density:** Concentration of population expressed in terms of number of persons per hectare in a particular area. Density is often the most commonly accepted indicator and provides a reference for the amount of land needed for supporting facilities with regard to a given population and is also an indicator of the type of physical development.

**Diffusion:** the random dispersion or scattering of a sound or light wave when it strikes a surface that is irregular, concave, or convex in form; or when the wave form is not in line with, or not equal in size to, the object struck, the wavelength will tend to bend around the object and continue on its path.

**Dimensional stability:** the property of a material, which indicates its resistance to change in size due to climatic conditions like temperature or humidity.

**Dimmer:** a device used to control the intensity of light emitted by a luminaire through the control of the voltage or current available to it.

**Direct glare:** the result of areas of excessive contrast (such as insufficiently shielded light sources) in the direct field of view.

**Direct lighting:** Lighting provided on the work plane or object from a prominent and identifiable source.

**Double-glazing:** a process of providing windows with two sheets of glass sealed together trapping air or a vacuum between them to provide superior thermal insulation.

**Dowel:** round wooden or metal pin used to reinforce furniture construction.

**Down light:** a luminaire from which light emanates downward; may be recessed, surface or pendant mounted.

**Drapery:** a loosely hung, often heavy, fabric curtain.

**Drapery panel:** a drapery length made of one or more widths of fabric that travel together on a rod.

**Draw curtain:** a fabric panel that can be opened and closed by means of a draw cord on a traverse rod.

**Eave:** lower edge of a roof extending beyond the exterior wall.

**Ecletic:** utilizing elements from multiple sources and styles

**Ecology:** the study of the relationship between organisms and their environment.

**Efficacy:** the measure of the effectiveness of a solution; the ratio of light emitted by a lamp to the electrical power input, usually expressed in lumens per watt.

**Effluent:** something that flows out.

**Egress:** a means of exiting.

**Elevation:** a drawing, which represents a vertical image of one side of an object, room or building.

**Embellishment:** additional ornamentation.

**Emulsion:** a combination of two non-compatible liquids, such as oil and water.

**Engineered wood product:** any recombination of wood by-products to form a material of greater performance capacity than the original.

**Ergonomics:** the science that seeks to adapt the environment to its users.

**Etch:** to remove through corrosive action.

**Fabric:** cloth; more specifically, a construction of fibers, not necessarily woven.

**Faade:** the face or front view of a building or article.

**False ceiling:** that portion of a ceiling below the actual functional level or below other sections of the ceiling within the same space. Often, a false ceiling serves to articulate specific segments of a room such as a dining area, or to accommodate mechanical equipment.

**Fire retardant:** durable or non-durable applications to decrease flammability.

**Felting:** the joining of fibers into a fabric through the application of heat, agitation and moisture, or by mechanical treatment.

**Fenestration:** the arrangement and design of windows and other openings of a building.

**Fiber:** a material of natural or synthetic derivation capable of forming a continuous filament, such as yarn or thread.

**Fiberglass:** any number of plastic resins, such as polyesters, polypropylene, or nylon, reinforced with segments of glass fibers.

**Fiber optics:** the transmission of signals as pulses of light through an optical conductor, such as glass cord.

**Filament:** a single continuous strand of fiber.

**Finish floor:** the final visible flooring material or surface.

**Firebrick:** a very hard brick capable of withstanding the intense heat of a kiln or fireplace interior.

**Fire proof:** fire retardant barrier added to any object to inhibit the spread of fire

**Flame-resistant fabric:** a fabric whose fiber content or topical finish makes it difficult to ignite, slow to burn, and often self-extinguishing.

**Flame-retardant finish:** a chemical finish that renders a fabric made of a flammable fiber resistant to fire ignition and spread.

**Flat slice:** a method of cutting a log parallel to a plane through its center, which produces a vaulted, or cathedral like grain.

**Flood lamp:** a lamp providing a relatively wide light distribution pattern.

**Floor Area Ratio (FAR):** the quotient obtained by dividing the total covered area of all floors by the area of the plot. Floor area includes the mezzanine floor also.

F.A.R. = Total covered area of all floors / Plot area

The Floor Area Ratio can be used in zoning to limit the amount of construction in a certain area. A builder can plan for either a single-story building using the entire allowable area in one floor, or a multi-storey building that rises higher above the plane of the land.

**Floor plan:** a drawing that represents the horizontal arrangement of building parts and furnishings.

**Fluorescent lamp:** a low-pressure mercury electric discharge lamp in which a fluorescent coating (phosphor) transforms ultraviolet energy into visible light.

**Flue:** channel above a fireplace used to carry smoke and heat to the exterior of a structure.

**Flux:** the flow of light or the measure of the flow of electric charge in a wire.

**Foot-candle (fc):** a unit of illuminance on a surface equal to that produced by the light of one candle at a distance of one foot.

**Fresco:** painted mural or decoration done on a wet plaster wall or ceiling.

**Galvanized iron:** iron coated with zinc as a means of retarding rust.

**Gallery:** narrow exterior porch or balcony; succession of rooms to display art; rail with small wood or metal spindles attached to the outer edge of cabinetry.

**Glare:** any brightness that annoys, distracts or reduces visibility.

**Glass:** a mixture of silicates, alkalis, and lime that is extremely mouldable when heated to high temperatures, permitting blown, moulded, pressed, and stretched forms, and which cools to a rigid, nonabsorbent, transparent or translucent substance.

**Glass blocks:** brick-like forms of glass available in a variety of shapes and sizes. They can be set together or joined to other materials with mortar.

**Glaze:** protective or decorative glass-like coating formed on the surface of a ceramic piece by firing.

**Grout:** thin mortar used to fill in spaces between tiles, bricks or other surfaces

**Hammered:** a metal or stone finish produced by direct blows of a hammer on the material surface, or a finish giving the appearance.

**Hardboard:** a mat-formed flat panel consisting of particles of wood bonded together with a synthetic resin or other suitable binder.

**Hardware:** various materials, such as iron, brass, bronze, wood, chrome, plastic added to mechanise the operation of cabinetry drawers and doors, drapery, etc. For example, cremone bolt, doork-nocker, drapery rod, handle, hinge, kick plate, knob, lever, pull, etc.

**Header:** a horizontal structural member, which serves to tie vertical members together at the top of an element.

**Honed:** a medium to coarse stone finish produced by abrasion of a cut face.

**HVAC:** Heating, Ventilation and Air Conditioning.

**Hydrophobic fibers:** those, which resist water-borne soiling.

**Incandescent filament lamp (bulb):** a lamp in which light is produced by a filament heated to incandescence by an electric current.

**Indirect lighting:** luminaries, which distribute 90-100 percent of their emitted light first onto a reflective surface such as a ceiling or wall.

**Industrial board:** engineered wood products commonly used in the manufacturing of furniture and case goods.

**Ingress:** the way in or entrance.

**Insulation:** the prevention, by using certain materials, of an excessive transfer of electricity, heat, cold or sound between the inside and the outside of a structure or between portions of a structure.

**Jacquard weave:** a fabric of complex pattern, such as tapestry or brocade, produced on the Jacquard loom.

**Jamb:** interior sides of a door or window frame.

**Joist:** floor or ceiling beam support.

**Junction box:** a protective housing for the joining of electrical connections.

**Kelvin (K):** relating to the thermometric scale in which the unit of measurement equals the centigrade degree and according to which absolute zero, the temperature at which all atomic activity ceases, and the equivalent of '–273.16°' Celsius is '0' Kelvin.

**Kelvin temperature (K):** represents the relative whiteness of a light source; whether the source appears warm, cool, or neutral. The higher the temperature, the cooler the appearance of the source. The Kelvin temperature assigned is that of a unit black body radiator heated to the same whiteness.

**Lacquer:** a family of fast drying resin or synthetic finishes capable of being polished to high gloss sheen.

**Laminate:** the process of bonding together, thin sheets or small pieces of material to create a substance having properties the material would not otherwise possess, such as strength, durability or intricate form.

**Land use:** the purpose to which the site or part of the site or the building or part of the building is in use or permitted to be used by the Authority. Land use includes zoning of land use as stipulated in the development plan and the Zoning Regulations

**Latex:** milky, fluid, synthetic adhesive used to seal the back of carpet.

**Lath:** a framework of thin wood or metal ribs integral with a building skeleton for the support of tile, plaster, reinforced concrete, plastic forms etc.,

**Letter of agreement:** a legal contractual agreement between two parties that describes the obligations and responsibilities of each.

**Level loop:** a carpet style having all tufts in a loop form and of identical height; may be woven or tufted.

**Life-cycle cost:** the initial cost of a product (including installation) plus the cost of maintenance or operation over its useful life.

**Lumen:** a unit of light flow equal to the light emitted into a unit solid angle by a uniform point source of one candle.

**Luminance:** the density of light falling upon a surface, the units of which are the lux and footcandle.

**Luminaire:** a complete lighting unit consisting of a lamp, or lamps, together with parts designed to distribute the light, to position and protect the lamps, and to connect the lamps to the power supply; a ceiling or wall mounted light fixture, or a portable lamp.

**Luminance:** the luminous intensity of any surface in a given direction per unit area of that surface as viewed from that direction. All things visible have some luminance. Luminance is measured in candelas per square meter or candelas per square foot.

**Luminance ratio:** an expression of the relative brightness of any two areas in the visual field.

**Marquetry:** decorative wood veneer inlay.

**Masonry:** architectural construction of stone, brick, tile, concrete block, or glass block joined together with mortar; in broader usage, construction of plaster or concrete.

**Mastic:** originally a resin used in the production of adhesives, now commonly the generic term for flooring adhesives.

**Matte:** a flat, non-shiny finish, which thoroughly diffuses incident light.

**Medium Density Fiberboard (MDF):** a fine-grained smooth faced industrial board product, composed of wood fiber and adhesives. Easily cut, worked and finished.

**Medullary rays:** capillary-like structures within the body of a tree that run radially from the core to the bark and their expression in quarter-sawn lumber.

**Metamerism:** the shift in visual appearance of colours under varied illumination.

**Metamers:** lights of the same apparent colour but of different spectral energy.

**Mezzanine Floor:** an intermediate floor between the floor and ceiling of any storey.

**Microbial:** relating to micro-organisms such as bacteria.

**Microblind:** horizontal blinds with 13 mm (1/2") slats; also called micro-miniblinds.

**Miniblinds:** horizontal blinds with 25 mm (1") slats.

**Modacrylic:** synthetic fiber that is highly flame resistant and bulky. It has moderate resiliency, moderate dimensional stability, and high elastic recovery. It also has a low melting point and low abrasion resistance.

**Modular:** built of unit pieces or according to standardised sets of measurements.

**Module:** one of a series of units designed and scaled to integrate with others in different combinations to form, for example, a set of furnishings, a system of construction, or whole buildings. In current usage, the term is most often applied to mass-produced prefabricated units.

**Mohair:** a specialty wool fiber. The most resilient of all natural fibers, strong, and possessing a good affinity for dyes.

**Moulding:** an ornamental strip of wood or plaster that protrudes from a ceiling or wall surface.

**Monolithic construction:** a system in which the major part of a structure consists of a single, self-supporting mass, usually of reinforced concrete, plastic or fiberglass.

**Mortar:** cement, lime or plaster combined with sand and water. When wet, the substance is mouldable; it hardens to form the binding agent of masonry construction.

**Motif:** dominant or recurring theme throughout a project

**Mullion:** slender strips of wood or metal dividing panes of glass in door or window units.

**Mural:** scene or image painted or wallpapered onto a wall.

**Muslin:** plain woven cotton fabric

**NBC (National Building Code):** a set of specifications prepared to regulate materials and methods used in construction and establishing consistent standards to assure healthy, safe and sanitary conditions.

**Niche:** recessed opening, often arched at the top, set in a wall with a shelf, often lit from the top to display sculpture or objects of art.

**Nonwoven fabric:** a fabric which is either fibrous, but not made in a loom, or non-fibrous, made directly from a solution.

**Nylon:** the generic term (as well as trade name) for a family of plastics exhibiting high tensile strength in fiber or sheet form. It has excellent abrasion resistance, and resiliency, retains appearance well. Fiber modifications are antistatic, anti-soil, sunlight resistant, and flame retardant.

**Occupancy or use:** the main occupancy or use for which a building or a part of it is used or intended to be used i.e. contingent/subsidiary occupancies. Mixed occupancy buildings being those in which more than one occupancy is present in different portions of the buildings.

**Olefin:** a plastic used for fiber and container manufacturing. Advantages of olefin fibers include good abrasion resistance, tenacity, excellent resiliency, good dimensional stability, static resistant, and excellent resistance to most chemicals. It resists mildew and stains. Fiber modifications contribute to heat and light stabilization. Often referred to as polypropylene.

**Open plan:** an architectural plan organized with few fixed partitions; provides maximum flexibility in the use of interior space.

**Open space:** an area forming an integral part of a site left open to the sky.

**Orientation:** arrangement, alignment, or position in relation to other factors or elements.

**Oriented strand board:** an industrial board product composed of wood chips created and bound specifically to take advantage of their non-homogeneous nature to produce a product with specific structural properties.

**Oxidation:** a chemical process by which one material combines with oxygen to form a second (iron oxidizes to form rust).

**Padding:** fabric or materials used to provide additional cushioning.

**Paneling:** thin, flat wooden boards or other similarly rectangular pieces of construction material joined side by side to form an interior decorative surface for walls or ceilings.

**Parquetry:** inlay of wood that takes the form of geometric patterns; used primarily for floors and sometimes for tabletops.

**Particleboard:** a mat-formed flat panel consisting of particles of wood bonded together with a synthetic resin or other suitable binder.

**Partition:** a non-load-bearing subordinate wall between two piers or other supporting members.

**Passive solar heating system:** a technique of solar heating that uses parts of the building structure to collect, store and distribute solar heat without pumps or fans.

**Patina:** the sheen, colour and texture of an object, produced by age, use, waxing, or design. On metal, patina is the film that develops from long exposure to the atmosphere.

**Pelmet:** framework to conceal drapery hardware at the top of a window.

**Pendant:** hanging ornamentation or electrical fixture mounted from the ceiling.

**Perspective:** a system of realistic pictorial representation of objects and spaces in relative distance or depth. The optical effects perceived in viewing objects over a distance.

**Pigment:** substance imparting a colour to other materials.

**Pile:** the visible wear surface of carpet, consisting of yarn tufts in loop or cut configuration; also called face or nap.

**Pile weave:** a fabric construction in which cut or uncut loops protrude from the ground cloth.

**Pile yarn:** a yarn, which forms the tuft of carpet; also called face yarn.

**Pill:** the tendency of staple fibers to be shed from some fabrics and to form small tufts or balls on the face of the fabric.

**Pitch:** degree of roof slope; angle of inclination.

**Plain slice:** a method of cutting a log parallel to a plane through its center, which produces a vaulted or cathedral-like grain.

**Plan:** the configuration of spaces and rooms, walls and openings in an architectural structure; also, the graphic representation of such an arrangement.

**Plane:** a two-dimensional expanse; a flat surface.

**Plaster:** a paste, usually of lime, sand, and water, which hardens as it dries. Often used as a finish for interior wall and ceiling surfaces.

**Plastic:** a soft, ductile material, which is a member of any of the several families of synthetic polymer substances.

**Pleating:** to tuck and bind fabric for additional fullness.

**Plenum:** space between ceiling and structure where mechanical and electrical components are typically run. In some instances the plenum itself may serve as a sort of super duct for air returning to the mechanical system from the volume beneath the ceiling.

**Plinth Area:** the built up covered area measured at the floor level of the basement or of any storey.

**Plumbing:** the system of pipes, which carries water and sewage within a building.

**Plush carpet:** a smooth carpet surface texture in which individual tufts are minimally visible and the overall effect is that of a single level of fiber ends.

**Ply:** a single thickness, layer or strand.

**Plywood:** a composite sheet of laminated veneers, some or all of which are made of wood, with the grain of adjacent strata arranged at perpendicular angles for increased strength.

**Polished:** smooth and glossy.

**Polyester:** a synthetic fiber with excellent strength, good abrasion resistance, and which resists wrinkling. Characterized by permanent body. Fiber modifications contribute to pill resistance, antistatic, and flame retardancy.

**Polyethylene:** a group of lightweight, flexible plastics characterized by a waxy surface and resistance to chemicals and moisture but not high temperatures.

**Polypropylene:** a family of plastics which are resistant to water-borne but not oil-borne staining.

**Polystyrenes:** a family of rigid, transparent-to-opaque plastics that are durable, capable of accepting varied finishes, and possessed of good insulation properties.

**Porcelain:** high-grade, translucent white ceramic ware fixed at extremely high temperatures; most common in fine dishes and ornaments, but having many industrial applications, such as plumbing fixtures electrical insulators, and tiles.

**Portable luminaire:** table or floor lamp, or wall unit, which is not permanently connected to the electrical power supply.

**Prefabricate:** to mass-produce standardized construction parts or modules for later assembly and/or combination.

**Primary backing:** a component of tufted carpet consisting of woven or non-woven fabric into which pile weave tufts are inserted by the tufting needles.

**Primer:** a coating that is applied before any other finish treatment to seal the pores in or otherwise prepare a surface to be treated.

**Printing:** as applied to textiles (fabric, carpet, etc.), the application of dyes according to a selective pattern to create a design by such methods as woodcut, silk screen, tie-dye, or injection.

**Programming:** the research phase of design, which determines the objectives and requirements of a design project.

**Proportion:** the relation of parts to each other or to the whole in terms of magnitude, quantity, or degree.

**Proxemics:** the study of human interaction with space and of personal and cultural spatial needs.

**PVC (Poly Vinyl chloride):** a tough, mouldable thermoplastic used in the manufacture of plumbing pipes and furniture.

**Quality of lighting:** distribution of luminance in a visual environment with regard to visual performance, visual comfort, ease of seeing, safety and aesthetics for the specific visual tasks involved.

**Rag-rug:** a plain weave rug woven with strips of fabric, historically rags or recycled clothing remnants.

**Ravel:** to untwist or unweave.

**Rayon:** a natural fiber made from cellulose, which has been chemically prepared. Soft hand, high moisture regain, smooth and soft fibers, good conductor of heat and static. Accepts durable press and dimensional stability finishes. Disadvantages include poor resiliency, progressive shrinkage, and weakness, especially when wet.

**Recessed light:** lighting fixture installed within a ceiling.

**Rectilinear:** straight lined.

**Reflectance:** the ratio of the light reflected by a surface to the light falling on it.

**Reflected glare:** results from specular reflections of high contrast from polished or glossy surfaces in the field of view.

**Reflection:** the process by which light or sound leaves a surface from the incident side.

**Refraction:** the change in direction or propagation of a sound or light wave due to a change in the velocity occurring when a change in materials, a thermal gradient or a wind velocity gradient is encountered.

**Regain:** a measure of the recovery of moisture lost to the atmosphere through drying.

**Reinforced concrete:** concrete embedded before hardening with steel rods that lend the material a tensile strength far beyond its original capacity.

**Rendering:** a pictorial representation of a proposed design, usual in perspective and full color.

**Renovate:** to restore condition by rebuilding, repairing or cleaning.

**Restore:** to renew or return to an original state or condition.

**Retrofit:** to fit with new parts or equipment not available at the time of initial construction or production.

**Reverberation:** a sound effect similar to that of a continuous echo.

**Rheostat:** a device used to control the intensity of light emitted by a luminaire through control of the voltage or current available to it.

**Riser:** the individual vertical faces of a stair. The term is also used for the collection of ducts or pipes, which provide vertical transport of air or water through a building.

**Room Height:** the vertical distance measured from the finished floor surface to the finished ceiling.

**r-value:** the thermal resistance of a material. A higher r-value indicates greater resistance.

**Sandblast:** abrasive cleaning with sand moved by an air jet.

**Sash curtain:** a semi-sheer fabric gathered or shirred onto rods at top and bottom and hung onto a window sash.

**Schedule:** a table that indicates the finish material used on floors, walls, and ceilings, or lists types of doors and windows.

**Schematic design drawings:** quick initial drawings used to generate or show ideas.

**Seasoning:** to bring to the proper state for use, as in seasoning wood by drying.

**Set-back:** a line usually parallel to the plot boundaries or center line of a road and laid down in each case by the Authority or as per recommendations of Master/Zonal Plan, beyond which nothing can be constructed towards the plot boundaries excepting with the permission of the Authority.

**Shade:** a low-value or dark color produced by adding black to a hue. A cover for window or lamp to control light distribution.

**Shingles:** narrow, overlapping pieces of wood or slate installed as roofing or siding.

**Stucco:** fine plaster or cement made of Portland cement, sand and lime applied to a structure used as ornamentation.

**Silk:** the only natural continuous filament fiber. Silk fiber is harvested from the cocoon of the silk worm. Silk fabric is highly valued for its strength, hand and luster.

**Sisal:** a natural plant fiber; smooth, straight, and yellow. May be used by itself or in blends with wool and acrylic for a softer bond. Sisal is used in wall coverings, especially in heavyduty commercial applications because of its durability and ease of application to a variety of surfaces.

**Soffit:** a dropped or underside horizontal surface.

**Space plan:** a drawing, which shows the arrangement of functional elements within an area.

**Space planning:** the functional planning of interior space; a design specialty, which concentrates on establishing space needs and utilization in the early stages of design.

**Spall:** the breaking away of a surface due to mechanical action within the material itself such as thermal expansion.

**Specification:** the criteria of minimum durability, cost and safety requirements of finished materials; all of the information necessary for the construction of custom-made items.

**Specular angle:** that angle between the perpendicular surface and the reflected ray. It is numerically equal to the angle of incidence.

**Specular reflection:** that process by which incident flux is redirected without diffusion.

**Specular surface:** shiny or glossy surface (including mirror and polished metals) from which the reflection is predominantly specular.

**Spun-bonded:** fabric manufactured by a non-woven method in which fibers are deployed in a near-random fashion and bound by chemical or thermal means.

**Standpipe:** station pipe for use by a fire department to allow connection of a pumper truck to the outside of a building for delivery of water to hose stations on the interior of the building.

**Stipple:** to decorate by repeated touching as in dots.

**Structural plan:** a drawing, the primary purpose is to show the means of supporting a thing.

**Substrate:** the underlying or supporting layer.

**Surface-mounted unit:** a luminaire mounted directly on the ceiling.

**Temper:** to harden a material (metal or glass) through a specific process of heating and cooling, thereby releasing internal stresses created during the forming process.

**Tenacity:** resistance to tearing.

**Tensile strength:** the capacity to resist breaking or tearing apart under longitudinal stress.

**Terrazzo:** a polished concrete flooring traditionally made of crushed marble and cement.

**Textile:** a fiber construction; technically, a woven fabric.

**Texture:** tactile surface quality, perceived directly through touch or indirectly through vision.

**Thermoplastic:** a material that softens with application of heat and hardens again when cooled.

**Thermoset:** an irreversible property of a substance that is attained by application of heat to change the chemistry of the substance, thereby making it firm.

**Tile:** stone, concrete, or ceramic pieces, flattened or curved, used for roofing as well as wall, ceiling and floor covering. Also, thin modules of cork, vinyl, or other resilient material used primarily to protect and enhance interior walls, floors, and ceilings.

**Tip-shear carpet:** a carpet texture created by shearing either level loop or high-low loop carpet lightly so that only the higher filaments within the loops are sheared.

**Torchere:** an indirect floor lamp directing all, or nearly all, of the luminous flux upward.

**Track:** an electrical raceway permitting the flexible use and placement of various types of luminaries along its length.

**Transformer:** an electrical device for converting electrical potential.

**Translucent:** semi-opaque surface, which diffuses light while partially obscuring a view, i.e. privacy window, etched or frosted glass, window film

**Traverse rod:** a rod that uses carriers, pulleys, and cords to draw draperies open and closed.

**Tread:** the individual run, or horizontal distance from the face of one riser to the next, in a flight of stairs.

**Trevira:** polyester in which resistance to matting and crushing has been enhanced by autoclaving or heat setting the fibers.

**Tuft bind:** a measure of the effort required to remove a carpet tuft from its primary backing.

**Tufting:** a method of carpet construction which utilizes hundreds of needles to push pile yarns through a previously constructed primary backing sheet, forming loops or tufts of yarn which may be left uncut, cut, or selectively sheared to form a variety of surface textures, or by which high-low loops and sculptured effects can be created.

**Twisting:** the winding of two or more strands of fiber or yarn together to make a single multiple-ply yarn.

**Universal design:** appropriate to people of all ages, abilities, and sizes.

**Upholstery:** a soft covering of fabric on seating units, sometimes but not necessarily over padding, stuffing or springs.

**Urethane:** lightweight, cellular plastic capable of assuming nearly any density and thus any hardness from resilient to rigid. Urethane can be sprayed as surface coating, preformed as cushioning and insulation, or cast to form rigid components.

**Utility core:** a central space or unit, which contains all service elements, including bathrooms, heating, air conditioning etc.,

**Valance:** a decorative fabric heading at the top of a window.

**Value:** the attribute of perceived colour by which it seems to transmit or reflect a greater or lesser fraction of the light incident upon it.

**Vaulted ceiling:** a ceiling constructed as an extended arch, often semi-cylindrical in form (a barrel vault). Intersecting arches produce a groin vault; a ribbed vault reveals the framework of arched ribs.

**Veiling reflection:** partially or totally obscures the details to be seen by reducing the contrast.

**Velvet:** a fabric covered with a close, short, fine, dense nap or pile.

**Veneer:** paper-thin wood sheets applied to the outer surface of furniture, which are often inlaid or matched to create intricate, decorative patterns.

**Vinyl:** a versatile family of strong, lightweight plastics available in flexible, rigid, molded, film, foam, and cellular forms.

**Viscose:** a fiber manufactured from chemically treated cellulose.

**Visual comfort probability (VCP):** the rating of a lighting system expressed as a percentage of people who, when viewing from a specified location and in a specified direction, will be expected to find it acceptable in terms of discomfort glare.

**Visual field:** the sum of objects or points in space, which can be perceived when the head and eyes are kept fixed.

**Visual surround:** all portions of the visual field except the visual task.

**Visual task:** details and objects, which must be seen for the performance of a given activity, including the immediate background of details or objects.

**Visual weight:** the effect of visual impact regardless of actual weight, determined in part by color, texture and pattern.

**Vitrify:** to convert into glass by fusion; typically by heat.

**VOC (Volatile Organic Compounds):** a gaseous, sometimes harmful by-product of the curing process of some paints or adhesives.

**Wafer board:** a course-grained, rough-faced industrial board product, composed of wood flakes and adhesive; easily cut, but not intended for finish work.

**Warp:** the lengthwise yarns of a fabric, running through the loom, parallel to the edges of the run of fabric. The twist of an element away from its intended position caused by internal stresses due to changes in temperature or moisture.

**Wardrobe:** freestanding or built-in cabinet designed specifically to house clothing with hooks or rods.

**Weaving:** the process of interlacing two or more sets of yarns, usually at right angles to each other, to make textiles.

**Weft:** woven fabric. Also woof, the threads on a woven fabric which cross the warp.

**Wilton:** a specific weave of carpet in which yarns of different colors are raised in loops to form a pattern, after which the loops are cut to form a diverse plus pile.

**Woof:** the threads on a woven fabric, which cross the warp.

**Working drawings:** the final drawings that are used to obtain bids for and construct a design.

**Work plane:** the plane at which work is done and on which illuminance is specified and measured Unless otherwise indicated, this is assumed to be a horizontal plane 0.76 m (30 in.) above the floor.

**Wrought iron:** iron, which is heated, bent and hammered into shape by hand, *i.e.* handforged iron.

# References


1. M.P. Rao. Interior Design (Principles & Practice), Standard Publishers Distributors, Delhi.
2. Raj Rao. Planning and Designing of Residential Buildings, Standard Publishers Distributors, Delhi.
3. Civil Engg Drawing by Gurcharan Singh, Standard Publishers Distributors, Delhi.
4. Civil Engg Drawing Vol I & II by BB Gupta
5. Sushil Kumar. Building Construction, Standard Publishers Distributors, Delhi.
6. S.K. Thakkar. Earth-quake Resistance Measures in Masonry Building; short term course on Earthquake Resistance Design of Building May 22-26, 2001.
7. D.K. Paul. Ductility Provision for Better Seismic Performance; short-term course on Earthquake Resistance Design of Building May 22-26, 2001.
8. IS-4326 Earthquake Resistance Design and Construction of Building, BIS, New Delhi.
9. IS-13920 Ductility Detailing of Reinforced Concrete Structure Subjected to Seismic Force, BIS, New Delhi.
10. Arya, A.S. Efficient design of R.C. Multistoreyed Building for Earth-quake Resistant, Journal of Institution of Engineers (India), Civil Engineers.
11. IS-456-2000. Plain and Reinforced Concrete code of Practice.